WILEY PLUS

for *Accounting Principles,* Fourth Canadian Edition

Check with your instructor to find out if you have access to *WileyPLUS!*

Study More Effectively with a Multimedia Text

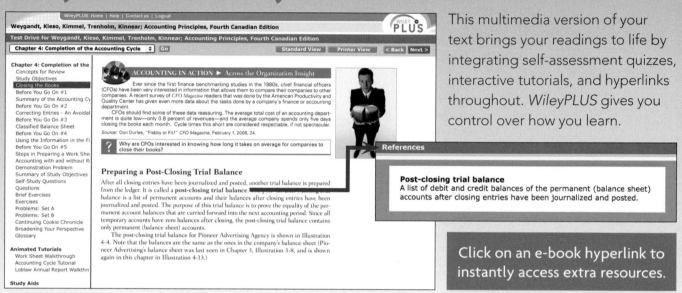

This multimedia version of your text brings your readings to life by integrating self-assessment quizzes, interactive tutorials, and hyperlinks throughout. *WileyPLUS* gives you control over how you learn.

Click on an e-book hyperlink to instantly access extra resources.

Grasp key concepts by exploring the various interactive tools in Read, Study & Practice.

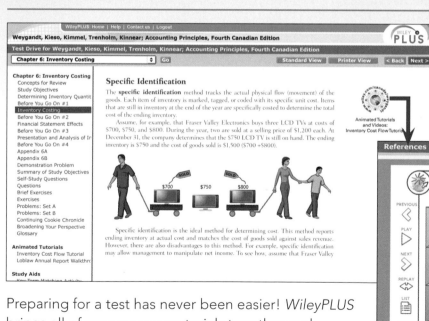

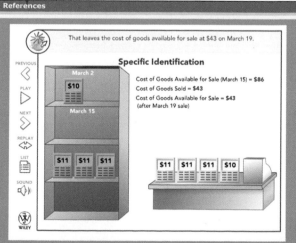

Preparing for a test has never been easier! *WileyPLUS* brings all of your course materials together and takes the stress out of organizing your study aids. A streamlined study routine saves you time and lets you focus on learning.

John Wiley & Sons Canada, Ltd.

WILEY PLUS

for *Accounting Principles,* Fourth Canadian Edition

Complete and Submit Assignments On-line Efficiently

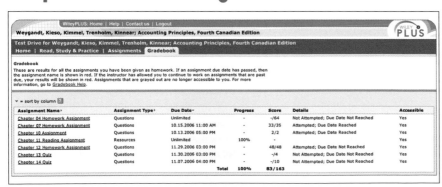

Your homework questions contain links to the relevant section of the multimedia text, so you know exactly where to go to get help solving each problem. In addition, use the Assignment area of *WileyPLUS* to monitor all of your assignments and their due dates.

Your instructor can assign homework online for automatic grading and you can keep up-to-date on your assignments with your assignment list.

Keep Track of Your Progress

Your personal Gradebook lets you review your answers and results from past assignments as well as any feedback your instructor may have for you.

Keep track of your progress and review your completed questions at any time.

Technical Support: http://higheredwiley.custhelp.com
Student Resource Centre: http://www.wileyplus.com

For further information regarding *WileyPLUS* and other Wiley products, please visit www.wiley.ca.

ACCOUNTING PRINCIPLES

FOURTH CANADIAN EDITION

ACCOUNTING
PRINCIPLES

▶ **Jerry J. Weygandt**   *Ph.D., C.P.A.*
Arthur Andersen Alumni Professor of Accounting
University of Wisconsin – Madison

▶ **Donald E. Kieso**   *Ph.D., C.P.A.*
KPMG Peat Marwick Emeritus Professor of Accounting
Northern Illinois University

▶ **Paul D. Kimmel**   *Ph.D., C.P.A.*
University of Wisconsin – Milwaukee

▶ **Barbara Trenholm**   *M.B.A., F.C.A.*
University of New Brunswick – Fredericton

▶ **Valerie A. Kinnear**   *M.Sc. (Bus. Admin.), C.A.*
Mount Royal College

John Wiley & Sons Canada, Ltd.

To our students — past, present, and future

Library and Archives Canada Cataloguing in Publication

Accounting principles / Jerry J. Weygandt ... [et al.].

4th Canadian ed.

Includes index.

ISBN 978-0-470-83858-7 (pt. 1)
ISBN 978-0-470-83860-0 (pt. 2)
ISBN 978-0-470-83861-7 (pt. 3)

1. Accounting--Textbooks. I. Weygandt, Jerry J.

HF5635.A3778 2006   657'.044   C2006-906471-7

Production Credits

Editorial Manager: Karen Staudinger
Publishing Services Director: Karen Bryan
Media Editor: Elsa Passera Berardi
Editorial Assistant: Sheri Coombs
Director of Marketing: Isabelle Moreau
Design & Typesetting: OrangeSprocket Communications
Cover Design: Interrobang Graphic Design
Wiley Bicentennial Logo: Richard J. Pacifico
Printing & Binding: Quebecor World Inc.

Printed and bound in the United States
1 2 3 4 5 QW 11 10 09 08 07

John Wiley & Sons Canada, Ltd.
6045 Freemont Blvd.
Mississauga, Ontario L5R 4J3
Visit our website at: www.wiley.ca

concepts for review >>

the navigator

Before studying this chapter, you should understand or, if necessary, review:

a. The external users of accounting information. (Ch. 1, p. 5)

b. How accounting standards are set in Canada and internationally. (Ch. 1, p. 7)

c. The going concern assumption, monetary unit assumption, economic entity assumption, and time period assumption. (Ch. 1, pp. 8–9 and Ch. 3, pp. 104–105)

d. The cost principle, revenue recognition principle, and matching principle. (Ch. 1, p. 8 and Ch. 3, pp. 105–106)

Nickel Mining Takes Time

VOISEY'S BAY, N.L.—In late 1993, a couple of prospectors looking for diamonds came across some rusty outcroppings in the Labrador wilderness, 350 kilometres north of Happy Valley-Goose Bay. These outcroppings turned out to be one of the biggest mineral discoveries in Canada in decades. A closer look revealed a bowl-shaped body of ore just below the surface, an "Ovoid" measuring 800 metres by 350 metres, and extending about 125 metres deep.

Toronto-based Inco Limited, owned by the Companhia Vale do Rio Doce (CVRD), is one of the world's leading nickel producers. Inco took up the challenge to develop the area after acquiring the rights to the Voisey's Bay property in 1996. Then, after a few years of negotiations with the provincial government and aboriginal organizations in Labrador, an agreement in principle to develop Voisey's Bay was signed in June 2002.

Voisey's Bay Nickel Company: www.vbnc.com

Inco's subsidiary, Voisey's Bay Nickel Company Limited (VBNC), is responsible for the development of the Voisey's Bay project, and expects to invest $3 billion over 30 years.

Resource estimates at Voisey's Bay include proven reserves of 32 million tonnes, indicated resources of 50 million tonnes, and inferred resources of 12 million tonnes. Because the "Ovoid" is located near the surface, it will be mined using open-pit mining methods. VBNC is currently doing advanced exploration to gather more information on the other resources below the surface, starting at about 500 metres and extending 1,000 metres deep. It will use this information to decide whether it can develop an underground mining plan.

VBNC has built a $950-million integrated mine and concentrator at Voisey's Bay, and in November 2005 it shipped its first nickel concentrate to Inco's operations in Manitoba and Ontario. The 2006 production estimate is about 120 million pounds of nickel concentrate annually from the operation.

Another $200 million has gone into a hydrometallurgical research and development program. This includes $100 million that was used to build a demonstration plant at Argentia, Newfoundland, which began operations in October 2005. The goal is to prove that hydromet technology can be used to process the Voisey's Bay nickel concentrate. If the technology works well, a commercial hydrometallurgical processing plant should be processing nickel concentrate and producing a finished product by the end of 2011. In the event hydromet technology cannot be used, VBNC will build a commercial nickel processing planing using proven technology.

Although the project life is estimated at 30 years, VBNC hopes that more exploration will lead to more mineral reserves and resources, and to operating the mine, concentrator, and commercial processing plant further still into the future.

the navigator ✔

- Understand *Concepts for Review*
- Read *Feature Story*
- Scan *Study Objectives*
- Read *Chapter Preview*
- Read text and answer *Before You Go On*
- Work *Demonstration Problem*
- Review *Summary of Study Objectives*
- Answer *Self-Study Questions*
- Complete assignments

chapter 11
Accounting Principles

study objectives >>

After studying this chapter, you should be able to:

1. Describe the conceptual framework of accounting.
2. Identify and apply the basic assumptions used by accountants.
3. Identify and apply the basic principles of accounting.
4. Identify and apply the constraints in accounting.

In the first ten chapters, you learned the process that leads to the preparation of a company's financial statements. You also learned that, to be useful, these statements must communicate financial information to users in an effective way. This means that generally accepted accounting principles must be respected. Otherwise, we would have to be familiar with each company's particular accounting and reporting practices in order to understand its financial statements. It would be difficult, if not impossible, to compare the financial results of different companies.

This chapter explores the conceptual framework that is used to develop generally accepted accounting principles. The chapter is organized as follows:

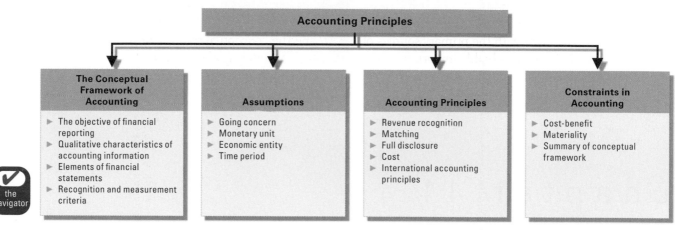

The Conceptual Framework of Accounting

study objective 1

Describe the conceptual framework of accounting.

According to standard-setters, the **conceptual framework of accounting** is "a coherent system of interrelated objectives and fundamentals that can lead to consistent standards and that prescribes the nature, function, and limits of financial accounting statements." In other words, the conceptual framework of accounting guides choices about what to present in financial statements, decisions about alternative ways of reporting economic events, and the selection of appropriate ways of communicating such information.

Why do we need a conceptual framework of accounting? As a foundation for accounting, the conceptual framework:

Alternative terminology
Recall that, as we saw in Chapter 1, the words *standards* and *principles* mean the same thing in accounting.

1. Ensures that existing standards and practices are clear and consistent
2. Makes it possible to respond quickly to new issues
3. Increases the understandability, relevance, reliability, and comparability of financial reporting results

In other words, new standards are easier to understand and are more consistent when they are built on the same foundation as existing standards. New issues can be more quickly resolved by considering the knowledge that already exists. And a framework increases users' understanding of, and confidence in, financial reporting. It also makes financial statements more relevant and reliable, and easier to compare.

The conceptual framework is published in the *CICA Handbook* in section 1000: "Financial Statements Concepts." This section presents the concepts that underlie the development and use of accounting principles. Section 1000 is followed by section 1100: "Generally Accepted Accounting Principles." This section sets standards for financial reporting that respect Canadian generally accepted accounting principles. It describes the generally accepted accounting principles and where they come from.

It is impossible to create accounting principles for all situations. Consequently, generally accepted accounting principles (GAAP) rank the sources to go to for help when the situation is unclear. In general, primary sources should be looked at first. These include the *CICA Handbook*, accounting guidelines, and abstracts of new issues discussed by the Emerging Issues Committee of the Accounting Standards Board.

If the primary sources of GAAP do not deal with a situation, the company should go to other sources—such as statements by other accounting standard-setting bodies, research studies, and information found in accounting textbooks and journals. However, it is important to remember that if an accounting principle from another source is going to be used, the principle must always be consistent with the primary sources of GAAP and the conceptual framework.

Professional judgement is highly important in deciding which accounting alternatives are consistent with GAAP and the conceptual framework. The Canadian philosophy on setting standards is that it is impractical and impossible to make a rule for every situation. Canadian standards—unlike standards in some other countries—are based on general principles rather than specific rules. Accountants can then use the professional judgement they develop through education and experience to apply the conceptual framework to any situation.

The conceptual framework has four major sections:

1. The objective of financial reporting
2. The qualitative characteristics of accounting information
3. The elements of financial statements
4. Recognition and measurement criteria (assumptions, principles, and constraints)

We will discuss these sections in the following pages.

Helpful hint Accounting principles are affected by economic and political conditions, which change over time. As a result, accounting principles can and do change.

The Objective of Financial Reporting

To decide what the objective of financial reporting should be, some basic questions need to be answered first: Who uses financial statements? Why? What information do the users need? How much do they know about business and accounting? How should financial information be reported so that it is best understood?

The main **objective of financial reporting** is to provide useful information for decision-making. More specifically, the conceptual framework states that the objective of financial statements is to communicate information that is useful to investors, creditors, and other users when they are making resource allocation decisions (deciding how resources should be used) and assessing management stewardship (evaluating how well a company is being managed).

To make resource allocation decisions (e.g., about investing or lending), users look for information in the financial statements about a company's ability to earn income and generate future cash flows. To assess management stewardship, users use the information in the financial statements to determine whether or not management acquired and used the company's resources in the best way possible. Consequently, financial statements must give information about the following:

1. Economic resources (assets), obligations (liabilities), and equity
2. Changes in economic resources, obligations, and equity
3. Economic performance

Qualitative Characteristics of Accounting Information

How does a company like The Forzani Group Ltd. decide how much financial information to disclose? In what format should its financial information be presented? How should assets, liabilities, revenues, and expenses be measured? According to the objective of financial reporting, the main criterion for judging these accounting choices is decision usefulness. In other words, the right choice is the accounting practice that generates the most useful financial information for making a decision. To be useful, information should have the following qualitative characteristics: understandability, relevance, reliability, and comparability.

Understandability

For the information in financial statements to be useful, it must be understandable to its users. However, financial statements cannot realistically satisfy the varied needs of all users. Consequently, the objective of financial statements is to focus mainly on the information needs of two types of external users: investors and creditors. Even in these two groups, though, users can be very different in the types of decisions they make and in their level of interest in the information. At one extreme is an unsophisticated investor who may only scan the text and not study the numbers. At the other extreme is a sophisticated creditor who carefully scrutinizes all aspects of the financial information.

It is therefore necessary to establish a base level of **understandability** that will help both the preparer of financial information and its user. The average user is assumed to have a reasonable understanding of accounting concepts and procedures, as well as of general business and economic conditions. If the potential user does not understand that much, then he or she is expected to rely on professionals. By taking this course, you are well on your way to becoming an average user!

Relevance

Accounting information has **relevance** if it makes a difference in a decision. Relevant information has either predictive value or feedback value, or both. Predictive value helps users forecast future events. For example, when Forzani issues financial statements, the information in them is considered relevant because it gives a basis for predicting future earnings. Feedback value confirms or corrects prior expectations. When Forzani issues financial statements, the company also confirms or corrects expectations about its financial health.

Accounting information also has relevance if it is timely. It must be available to decision-makers before it loses its ability to influence decisions. Many people believe that by the time annual financial statements are issued—sometimes up to six months after a company's year end—the information has limited usefulness for decision-making. Timely *interim* financial reporting is essential to decision-making.

Reliability

Accounting information has **reliability** if it has no errors and bias. In short, it can be depended on. To be reliable, accounting information must be verifiable: we must be able to prove that there are no errors and bias. It must also faithfully represent the economic substance of the transaction, not just its legal form. For example, external professional accountants audit financial statements to ensure that the financial statements reflect the financial reality of the company rather than the legal form of the transactions and events which underlie them.

Accounting information must also be neutral. It cannot be selected, prepared, or presented to favour one set of interested users over another. These three characteristics—verifiability, faithful representation, and neutrality—are often combined and called **objectivity**.

Objectivity means that two individuals, each working independently, can review the same information and reach the same results or similar conclusions. When a situation is uncertain, objectivity is affected by the use of conservatism.

Conservatism in accounting means that, when preparing financial statements, a company should choose the method that will be least likely to overstate assets and income. It does not mean, however, that assets or income should be understated on purpose.

Comparability

Accounting information about a company is most useful when it can be compared with accounting information about other companies. There is **comparability** when different companies use the same accounting principles.

At one level, accounting principles are fairly comparable because they are based on generally accepted accounting principles. These principles, however, do allow variations. For example, there are several acceptable cost flow assumptions for determining the cost of inventory. Often, these different cost flow assumptions result in different amounts of net income. As we will learn later in this chapter, the full disclosure principle makes it easier to compare companies, as each company must state which accounting principles it uses. Based on these disclosures, the external user can determine whether the financial information for two companies is comparable.

Comparability is easier when accounting policies are used consistently. **Consistency** means that a company uses the same accounting principles from year to year. If a company selects FIFO as its inventory cost flow assumption in the first year of operations, it is expected to use FIFO in subsequent years. When financial information has been reported on a consistent basis, the financial statements make it possible to do a meaningful analysis of trends in a company.

This does not mean, however, that a company can never change its accounting principles. Sometimes a change in an accounting principle is mandated by the CICA, such as the new requirement to report comprehensive income which we will learn about in Chapters 13 and 16. At other times, management may decide that it would be better to change to a new accounting principle. To do this, management must prove that the new principle will give a reliable and more relevant financial presentation in the statements.

In the year of a change in an accounting principle, the change (and its impact) must be disclosed in the notes to the financial statements. This disclosure makes users of the financial statements aware of the lack of consistency. In addition, the financial statements for past years must be restated as if the new accounting principle had been used in those years. We will learn more about accounting for, and reporting, changes in accounting principle in Chapter 14.

The qualitative characteristics of accounting information are summarized in Illustration 11-1.

Illustration 11-1 ◀

Qualitative characteristics of accounting information

Understandability	Relevance	Reliability	Comparability
1. Of accounting concepts and procedures.	1. Provides a basis for forecasts.	1. Is verifiable.	1. Different companies use similar accounting principles.
2. Of general business and economic conditions.	2. Confirms or corrects prior expectations.	2. Is a faithful representation.	2. A company uses the same accounting principles consistently from year to year.
	3. Is timely.	3. Is neutral.	
		4. Is conservative.	

Trade-Offs between Qualitative Characteristics

Many accounting choices require trade-offs between qualitative characteristics. For example, there is often a trade-off between relevance and reliability. That is, there may be a trade-off between ensuring that financial information is produced on a timely basis and verifying the accuracy of the information included. In order to produce financial statements annually, estimates are required. These estimates reduce the accuracy of the information provided. However, if we were to wait until estimates were no longer necessary for things like uncollectible accounts and the useful lives of property, plant, and equipment, the financial information would no longer be relevant. The conceptual framework does not always give obvious solutions to an accounting issue like this one. Rather, it enables professionals to judge the appropriate balance between these qualitative characteristics in a particular situation.

Elements of Financial Statements

An important part of the conceptual framework is a set of definitions that describe the basic terms that are used in accounting. This set of definitions is referred to as the **elements of financial statements**. They include such terms as assets, liabilities, equity, revenues, expenses, and other comprehensive income.

Because these elements are so important, they must be precisely defined and applied in the same way. Finding the appropriate definition for many of these elements is not easy. For example, should the value of a company's employees be reported as an asset on a balance sheet? Should the death of the company's president be reported as a loss? A good set of definitions should give answers to these types of questions. Because you have already read most of these definitions in earlier chapters, they are not repeated here.

Recognition and Measurement Criteria

The objective of financial reporting, the qualitative characteristics of accounting information, and the elements of financial statements are very broad. Because accountants must solve practical problems, they need more detailed criteria. Recognition criteria help determine when items should be included or recognized in the financial statements. Measurement criteria outline how to measure or assign an amount to those items. We classify these criteria as assumptions, principles, and constraints.

Assumptions create a foundation for the accounting process. Principles indicate how economic events should be reported in the accounting process. Constraints make it possible to relax the principles under certain circumstances.

Illustration 11-2 outlines these recognition and measurement criteria (you know some of them from earlier chapters). They will be discussed in more detail in the following sections.

Illustration 11-2 ▶

Recognition and measurement criteria

Assumptions	Generally Accepted Accounting Principles	Constraints
Going concern Monetary unit Economic entity Time period	Revenue recognition Matching Full disclosure Cost	Cost-benefit Materiality

BEFORE YOU GO ON . . .

▶**Review It**

1. Describe the conceptual framework of accounting.
2. Why do we need a conceptual framework of accounting?
3. What is the basic objective of financial information?
4. What are the qualitative characteristics that make accounting information useful? Give an example of a trade-off between qualitative characteristics.

Related exercise material: BE11–1, BE11–2, and BE11–3.

the
navigator

Assumptions

Assumptions create a foundation for the accounting process. You already know the major assumptions from earlier chapters—the going concern, monetary unit, economic entity, and time period assumptions. We will review them here briefly.

> **study objective 2**
> Identify and apply the basic assumptions used by accountants.

Going Concern Assumption

The **going concern assumption** assumes that the company will continue operating for the foreseeable future—that is, long enough to achieve its objectives and respect its commitments. Although there are many business failures, most companies continue operating for a long time.

This assumption has important implications for accounting. If a going concern assumption is not used, then assets such as buildings and equipment should be stated at their net realizable value (their selling price less the cost of disposal)—not at their historical cost. These assets would not need to be amortized. Also, without this assumption, the current/long-term classification of assets and liabilities would not matter. Labelling anything as long-term would be difficult to justify. By accepting the going concern assumption, the cost principle becomes more credible.

The only time the going concern assumption should not be used is when liquidation is likely. In that case, assets and liabilities should be revalued and stated at their net realizable value rather than at cost. Accounting for liquidations is discussed in advanced accounting courses.

ACCOUNTING IN ACTION ▶ Business Insight

On April 1, 2003, Air Canada filed for bankruptcy protection under the *Companies' Creditors Arrangement Act* (CCAA). Filing for protection under the CCAA gives companies time to reorganize their operations and hold talks with their major stakeholders—creditors, bondholders, unions, and suppliers. While CCAA protection is in place, creditors are prevented from taking any action against the airline.

While under CCAA, Air Canada issued its financial statements on a going concern basis, not a liquidation basis. Why was that? This was because, while under CCAA protection, Air Canada developed a plan to restructure its operations so that it could continue as a going concern. "Air Canada is determined to do all in its power to restructure itself through this process and emerge as a world-class competitive and profitable airline," an airline affidavit filed with the Ontario Superior Court of Justice said.

And indeed it did so. Air Canada emerged from CCAA protection on September 30, 2004, and continues today to exceed its profit targets.

Source: CBC News, "Air Canada Granted Bankruptcy Protection," April 2, 2003.

? How did Air Canada justify using the going concern assumption when it was so uncertain that the company would continue operating?

Monetary Unit Assumption

The **monetary unit assumption** states that only transaction data that can be expressed as an amount of money should be included in the accounting records. This assumption presumes that money is what is common to all economic activity and is therefore an appropriate basis for decision-making.

This assumption has important implications for financial reporting. It means that certain information that is needed for decision-making is *not* reported in the financial statements. For example, customer satisfaction is important for every business, but since it cannot be quantified, it is not reported in the financial statements. Similarly, the quality and integrity of management is not reported because it cannot be expressed in dollars.

The monetary unit assumption also assumes that the unit of measure remains stable over time. That is, any effects of inflation (or deflation) are assumed to be minor and are therefore ignored. As we learned in Chapter 1, Canada's inflation policy is to keep inflation between one and three percent. Consequently, inflation is considered a non-issue for accounting purposes in Canada.

Economic Entity Assumption

The **economic entity assumption** states that the economic activity can be identified with a particular accounting unit (e.g., a company) which is separate and distinct from the activities of the owner(s) and of all other economic entities. For example, it is assumed that the activities of Voisey's Bay Nickel Company in our feature story can be distinguished from those of its parent company, Inco, and that the activities of Inco can be distinguished from those of its parent company, CVRD.

For financial reporting, it is important to define the entity. It could be one company or a collection of companies consolidated under common ownership. We will learn more about consolidated companies in Chapter 16.

Time Period Assumption

The **time period assumption** states that the economic life of a business can be divided into artificial time periods. In other words, it is assumed that the activities of a company, such as Voisey's Bay Nickel Company, can be subdivided into months, quarters, or years for meaningful financial reporting even though the company's development operations are expected to go on for at least 30 years.

As discussed in Chapter 3, time periods of less than one year are called interim periods. Periods of one year are known as fiscal years or, if they extend from January through December, as calendar years. Public companies have to present both quarterly (interim) and annual financial statements.

The time period assumption results in a trade-off between reliability and relevance, as mentioned earlier in the chapter. The accuracy and reliability of the financial results would be much better if we could wait until an economic activity was complete before recording it. However, this would not result in timely financial information. Consequently, the time period assumption recognizes that estimates and accrual-based accounting are essential for producing information that is still relevant for decision-making.

▶Review It

1. What are the going concern assumption, monetary unit assumption, economic entity assumption, and time period assumption?
2. When might the going concern assumption not be appropriate to use?
3. Why does the time period assumption result in a trade-off between reliability and relevance?

Related exercise material: BE11–4 and E11–1.

Accounting Principles

From the fundamental assumptions of accounting described in the previous section, the accounting profession has developed principles that state how economic events should be recorded and reported. In Chapter 1, we discussed the process for setting Canadian generally accepted accounting principles and the cost principle. In Chapter 3, we introduced the revenue recognition and matching principles. We now examine some reporting issues related to these principles. And another principle, the full disclosure principle, will be discussed for the first time.

study objective 3

Identify and apply the basic principles of accounting.

Revenue Recognition Principle

The **revenue recognition principle** says that revenue should be recognized in the accounting period in which it is earned. Consequently, the sale of goods or services is recognized as revenue in the period in which the sale or service occurs, rather than in the period when the cash is received. And as we will discuss shortly, related expenses should be matched against these revenues.

This sounds pretty simple in theory, but doing it in practice can be difficult. What happens if the goods are sold on an instalment basis, rather than with payment due on delivery? What about publishing companies that ship university textbooks to bookstores that have the right to return any unsold books? What about long-term construction projects such as the integrated mine and concentrator, which took three years to build at Voisey's Bay? In these and many similar situations, when should revenues and related expenses be recorded?

In the opinion of many people, revenue recognition is the most difficult issue in accounting. And it is an issue that has been responsible for many of the accounting scandals of the past decade. There have been many high-profile cases that highlight improper use of the revenue recognition principle. These include the Livent, Bre-X, Nortel Networks, Enron, Lucent Technologies, Qwest Communications, Xerox, and AOL Time Warner cases, among others.

Why is revenue recognition such a difficult concept to apply? In a few cases, revenue recognition has been intentionally abused in order to manage earnings in a way that favours management or the shareholders. However, in most cases, revenue recognition is just a difficult concept because the activities that generate revenues have become a lot more innovative and complex than in the past. These include "swap" transactions, "bill and hold" sales arrangements, risk-sharing agreements, complex rights of return, price-protection guarantees, and post-sale maintenance contracts—all topics that go beyond an introductory accounting course.

In addition, until the early 2000s, there was not a lot of guidance about revenue recognition, so this made it easier to interpret this principle in ways that were never intended. Additional guidance was introduced in 2000 in the U.S. and in 2003 in Canada to stop abusive revenue recognition practices and to help accountants determine when to recognize revenue.

More specifically, revenue should be recognized when all of the guidelines below are met:

1. There is evidence that an arrangement exists between two parties.
2. Delivery has occurred or services have been provided.
3. The seller's price is fixed or can be determined.
4. It is reasonably certain that the cash will be collected.

The fourth guideline is not explicitly stated in Canada, but it is applied in practice.

Depending on the circumstances, the four guidelines for revenue recognition can be met at various points in time. These points range from at the point of sale to the later collection of cash. The most common points of revenue recognition are as follows:

1. At point of sale
2. During production
3. At completion of production
4. Upon collection of cash

ACCOUNTING IN ACTION ▶ Across the Organization Insight

Most managers would agree that bonus programs are a good way to motivate employees and make their interests match those of the company. In fact, 56 percent of respondents to a Human Resources Best Practices poll said that they give bonuses to their employees. Still, most respondents also admitted that it is hard to make such programs work well. Respondents noted that they have seen the negative consequences when employees expect bonuses but are told at the end of the year that the company did not reach its sales forecasts and revenues fell short. "Morale drops in a heartbeat."

Respondents said that bonuses should be based on a three-tier approach: with a low base for doing the basics, a second level for putting in the right effort (billable time, number of calls made, etc.), and a third level for revenue (or financial results). If you base bonuses only on revenue, employees are not always motivated to do what is best for the company.

Source: "Best Practices: Employee Bonuses," *Profitguide.com,* May 12, 2005.

? If bonuses are based only on revenue, how might this make employees less motivated to do what is best for the company?

Point of Sale

For sales in a retail establishment, revenue is usually recognized at the **point of sale**. Consider a sale by Forzani. At the point of sale, the customer pays the cash and takes the merchandise. The company records the sale by debiting Cash and crediting Sales Revenue. If the sale were on account rather than for cash (assuming the company accepts credit sales, and the customer has a good credit rating), the company would record the sale by debiting Accounts Receivable and crediting Sales Revenue. The cost of goods sold can be directly matched to the sales revenue at the point of sale.

Point of sale is the most common point of revenue recognition for goods and services. It is obvious that an arrangement to purchase and sell exists, the product or service has been delivered, the price has been agreed upon, and collection has occurred or is reasonably certain. At this point, revenue can be objectively measured and expenses can be matched to the revenue.

During Production

In certain cases, revenue can be recognized before delivery has occurred or the service has been fully provided. Consider a law or accounting firm that provides services for a client over several months. Companies that provide services like this are different from retail companies, as the client is identified and the work is agreed upon (usually with an engagement letter) before the services are performed. In such cases, the client is usually billed every month for the hours of service provided during the particular month. These situations result in a continuing earnings process where revenue can be recognized as chunks of services are provided at a predetermined price (as long as collectibility is assured).

Revenue recognition becomes even more difficult when the earnings process lasts years. This happens in the case of long-term construction contracts for large projects, such as building bridges, roads, and aircraft. For example, it took four years for Strait Crossing Development Inc. to build the 14-kilometre Confederation Bridge linking Prince Edward Island and New Brunswick.

In situations like this, revenue can be partially recognized before the contract is completed. All of the other guidelines must also be met and it must be completely certain that eventual delivery will take place.

Assume that Warrior Construction Co. has a contract to build a dam for the Province of British Columbia for $400 million. Construction is estimated to take three years (starting early in 2006) at a cost of $360 million. If Warrior recognizes revenue only at the point of sale, it will report no revenues and no profit in the first two years. When completion and sale take place, at the end of 2008, Warrior will report $400 million in revenues, costs of $360 million, and the entire profit of $40 million. Did Warrior really produce no revenues and earn no profit in 2006 and 2007? Obviously not. The earnings process can be considered completed at various stages. Therefore, revenue should be recognized as construction progresses. This is known as the percentage-of-completion method.

The **percentage-of-completion** method recognizes revenue on a long-term project based on reasonable estimates of the progress toward completion. Note that long-term construction contracts usually specify that the contractor (builder) may bill the purchaser at certain points of time throughout the contract period. However, revenue recognition should not be based on billings (this would be more similar to the cash basis of accounting). Rather, revenue should be recognized based on how much of the work has been performed to date.

There are three steps in the percentage-of-completion method. First, progress toward completion is measured by comparing the costs incurred in a period to the total estimated costs for the entire project. This results in a percentage that indicates the percentage of the work that is complete. Second, that percentage is multiplied by the total revenue for the current project, and the result is recognized as the revenue for the period. Third, the costs incurred are then subtracted from the revenue recognized to arrive at the gross profit for the current period. These three steps are presented in Illustration 11-3.

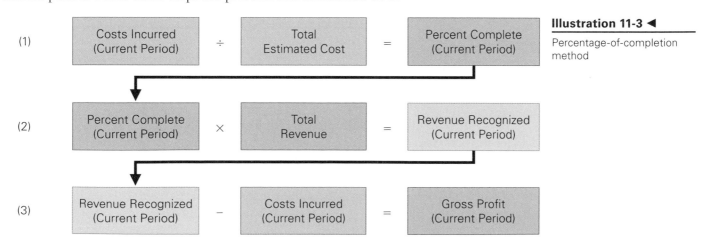

Illustration 11-3 ◄

Percentage-of-completion method

Let's look at an illustration of the percentage-of-completion method. Assume that Warrior Construction has costs of $54 million in 2006, $180 million in 2007, and $126 million in 2008 on the dam project mentioned earlier. The portion of the $400 million of revenue and gross profit that is recognized in each of the three years is shown below (all amounts are in millions):

Year	Costs Incurred (Current Period) ÷	Total Estimated Cost =	Percentage Complete (Current Period) ×	Total Revenue =	Revenue Recognized (Current Period) −	Costs Incurred (Current Period) =	Gross Profit (Current Period)
2006	$ 54	$360	15%	$400	$ 60	$ 54	$ 6
2007	180	360	50%	400	200	180	20
2008	126	360	35%	400	140	126	14
Totals	$360				$400	$360	$40

In this example, the company's cost estimates were completely accurate. The costs incurred in the third year brought the total cost to $360 million—exactly what had been estimated. In reality, this does not always happen. As additional information becomes available, it may be necessary to revise estimates for what remains to be done in a project.

When an estimate is revised, the amounts incurred for the current period are changed so they only include amounts incurred to date. In addition, an additional step is added to the formulas shown on the preceding page in Illustration 11-3 to adjust for the revenue that has already been recognized. Illustration 11-4 shows this new step (now step 3), and it also shows, in red, minor adjustments to the wording of the formula.

Illustration 11-4 ▶

Percentage-of-completion method—revision of estimate

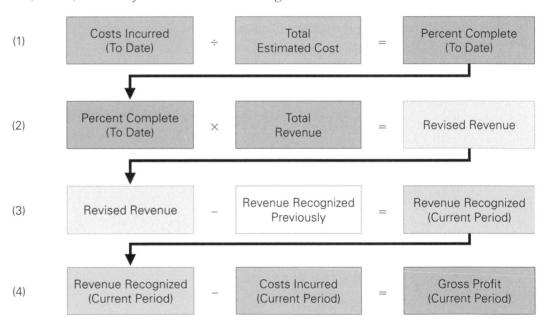

(1) Costs Incurred (To Date) ÷ Total Estimated Cost = Percent Complete (To Date)

(2) Percent Complete (To Date) × Total Revenue = Revised Revenue

(3) Revised Revenue − Revenue Recognized Previously = Revenue Recognized (Current Period)

(4) Revenue Recognized (Current Period) − Costs Incurred (Current Period) = Gross Profit (Current Period)

As when estimates are changed for useful lives or residual values for amortization, the data for the percentage-of-completion method are only changed for current and future years, rather than for past years also. The percentage that is complete is revised according to the new total estimated costs. A **cumulative percentage** is used. It is calculated by dividing the costs incurred to date by the revised total estimated cost. This formula is similar to the one shown in step 1 of Illustration 11-3, except that the costs incurred are cumulative (to date) rather than just for the current period.

Similar to step 2 of Illustration 11-3, this cumulative percentage is then multiplied by total revenue to determine the revised revenue amount. In a new step—which is not used when actual costs equal estimated costs—the revenue that was recognized previously is now deducted from the revised revenue. This has to be done in order to account for previously recorded amounts and to "catch up" the difference in the estimate.

The remaining step (now step 4) is the same as step 3 demonstrated in Illustration 11-3, where actual costs are deducted from revenue to determine the amount of gross profit to recognize, as shown below.

To apply this formula for a change in estimate, assume the costs estimated to complete the dam project change partway through the three-year contract period for Warrior Construction. In 2007, the estimated total cost rises to $390 million, from its earlier estimate of $360 million. Actual costs incurred are $200 million in 2007 and $136 million in 2008.

The revised calculations for revenue, cost, and gross profit are as follows (all amounts in millions):

Year	Costs Incurred (To Date) ÷	Total Estimated Cost	Percentage Complete = (To Date) ×	Total Revenue =	Revised Revenue −	Revenue Recognized (Previously) =	Revenue Recognized (Current Period) −	Costs Incurred (Current Period) =	Gross Profit (Current Period)
2006	$ 54	$360	15.0%	$400	$ 60.0	$ 0.0	$ 60.0	$ 54	$ 6.0
2007	254	390	65.1%	400	260.4	60.0	200.4	200	0.4
2008	390	390	100.0%	400	400.0	260.4	139.6	136	3.6
Totals							$400.0	$390	$10.0

The calculations for 2006 are unchanged from the ones on the previous page. However, because of the change in estimate in 2007, the revenue, cost, and gross profit change in 2007 and 2008. In 2007, the $254 million ($54 million in 2006 and $200 million in 2007) of actual costs incurred are shown on a cumulative basis. These costs are multiplied by the revised total estimated cost of $390 million in order to determine the percentage complete to date, 65.1%. This cumulative percentage is multiplied by total revenue to determine the revised revenue amount. This revenue amount, $260.4 million, includes the $60 million of revenue that was recognized in 2007. Therefore, the amount of revenue to be recognized in the current period is $200.4 million ($260.4 million − $60 million). The actual cost incurred for the period is then deducted from the revenue recognized in the same period to determine the gross profit.

In 2008, when the project is complete, costs incurred to date now total $390 million ($54 million in 2006, $200 million in 2007, and $136 million in 2008). One hundred percent of the contract revenue less any amounts recognized previously ($400 million − $260.4 million) is recognized in the current period. The actual cost incurred for the period is deducted from the revenue recognized in the same period to determine the gross profit.

The total contract revenue remains unchanged. However, the total cost rose from $360 million to $390 million after the change in estimate. This also means that total gross profit fell from $40 million to $10 million because of the increased costs.

Sometimes there are cost overruns in the last year of a contract. When that happens, the remaining amounts of revenue and costs are recognized in that year and the relevant percentage is ignored.

In the percentage-of-completion method, it is necessary to be subjective to some extent. As a result, errors are possible in determining the amount of revenue to be recognized and gross profit to be reported. But to wait until completion would seriously distort each period's financial statements. Naturally, if it is not possible to get dependable estimates of costs and progress, then the revenue should be recognized at the completion of production and not by the percentage-of-completion method.

Completion of Production

If Warrior Construction were not able to estimate its costs reliably, it would wait until the completion of the contract to recognize revenue, costs, and gross profit. This is known as the **completed-contract method**. Revenue of $400 million, revised costs of $390 million, and a gross profit of $10 million would be reported at the completion of production in the year 2008. This means that it really is not until production is complete that revenue, expenses, and gross profit can be reasonably determined.

If we compare the percentage-of-completion method and the completed-contract method for the same contract data, Warrior Construction would have recognized the following amounts for revenue and gross profit (all amounts in millions):

	Completed-Contract		Percentage-of-Completion	
	Revenue	Gross Profit	Revenue	Gross Profit
2006	$ 0	$ 0	$ 60.0	$ 6.0
2007	0	0	200.4	0.4
2008	400	10	139.6	3.6
Totals	$400	$10	$400.0	$10.0

The completed-contract method gives more reliable amounts than the percentage-of-completion method because revenue and gross profit are measured using actual results rather than estimates. However, the information is not as relevant nor as timely, because it is not reported until the contract is completed, and this results in distorted earnings for each year of the contract. Note that in total, over the three-year contract period, both methods result in the same total amounts.

Collection of Cash

When merchandise is sold on credit, or services are performed on credit, revenue is recognized at the point of sale as long as it is reasonably sure that the cash will be collected. Of course, not all accounts are, in actuality, collected. However, as we learned in Chapter 8, revenue can be recognized as long as an estimate can be made of any possible uncollectible accounts and bad debts matched against revenue in the appropriate period. Certain types of sales, especially sales collected over a long period of time, can be more difficult than others when it comes to estimating collectibility. These include instalment sales, where customers make periodic payments (known as instalments) over many months or years.

Many consumer products, such as cars, computers, home appliances, and furnishings, are sold on instalment payment plans. Companies that sell products on an instalment basis usually retain title to the merchandise (they still own it) until all payments have been made. This allows the company to repossess the merchandise if the customer does not pay. The repossessed merchandise is then resold for the highest price possible. This compensates the seller for the uncollected instalment payments and the cost of repossessing the merchandise.

If the company meets the revenue recognition guidelines (in particular, if it has a reasonable basis for estimating uncollectible accounts), it should recognize revenue from instalment sales at the point of sale. Sometimes, however, collection of the account is so uncertain that it cannot be reasonably estimated. In these cases, companies use the **instalment method**. It recognizes revenue when cash is collected rather than at the point of sale, and is justified as follows: if there is no reasonable basis for estimating collectibility, revenue should not be recognized until the cash is collected.

Under the instalment method, each cash collection from a customer consists of (1) a partial recovery of the cost of the goods sold, and (2) partial gross profit from the sale. For example, if the gross profit margin on the sale is 40%, each subsequent receipt of cash consists of 60% recovery of the cost of goods sold and 40% gross profit. The formula to recognize gross profit is shown in Illustration 11-5.

Cash Collections from Customers	×	Gross Profit Margin	=	Gross Profit

Illustration 11-5 ◀

Gross profit formula— instalment method

To illustrate, assume that in its first year of operations, a Saskatchewan farm machinery dealer has instalment sales of $600,000, and collection is uncertain. The dealer's cost of goods sold on these instalment sales is $420,000. Total gross profit is $180,000 ($600,000 – $420,000). The gross profit margin is 30% ($180,000 ÷ $600,000). The collections on the instalment sales are as follows: first year, $280,000 (down payment plus monthly payments); second year, $200,000; and third year, $120,000. The gross profit that is recognized is calculated as follows (interest charges are ignored in this illustration):

Helpful hint The gross profit margin is calculated by dividing gross profit by sales revenue.

Year	Cash Collections from Customers	×	Gross Profit Margin	=	Gross Profit
2006	$280,000		30%		$ 84,000
2007	200,000		30%		60,000
2008	120,000		30%		36,000
Totals	$600,000				$180,000

We have reviewed four common points of revenue recognition in this section: (1) at the point of sale, (2) during production, (3) at the completion of production, and (4) when cash is collected, as summarized in Illustration 11-6. Revenue recognition is a complex topic with many more dimensions that we have not explored here. You will learn more about revenue recognition in future accounting courses.

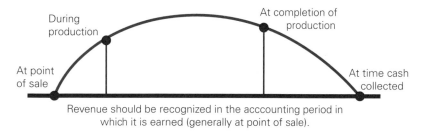

Illustration 11-6 ◀

Points of revenue recognition

Matching Principle (Expense Recognition)

The expression "Let the expense follow the revenue" shows that expense recognition is traditionally tied to revenue recognition. As you learned in Chapter 3, this is referred to as the **matching principle**. It says that costs must be matched with revenues in the period in which efforts are made to generate revenues. Costs are not necessarily recognized when cash is paid, when work is performed, or when the product is produced. They are recognized when the labour (service) or the product actually makes its contribution to revenue.

Matching expenses to the generation of revenue is not hard to do when there is a direct relationship, as there is between cost of goods sold and sales revenue. This direct relationship does not always exist, however. When it is hard to find a direct relationship, a rational and systematic allocation policy can sometimes be developed instead.

To develop an allocation policy, assumptions have to be made about the benefits that will be received. Assumptions must also be made about the costs associated with those benefits. For example, the cost of a long-lived asset can be allocated to amortization expense over the life of the asset because it can be determined that the asset contributes in some way to revenue generation during the asset's entire useful life—whether on a straight-line basis, on a declining-balance basis, on a units-of-activity basis, or some other basis.

In other cases, no direct relationship exists or can be assumed. For example, it is impossible to match administrative salaries or interest costs with the revenue they help earn. Consequently, these costs are expensed immediately in the period when they are incurred simply because there is no reasonable basis for allocating the cost. The transaction occurred in the current period and is assumed to benefit only the current period.

In our feature story, this is the case with the $200 million spent for hydrometallurgical research and development at Voisey's Bay. Because it has not yet been proven that hydromet technology can be successfully used to process Voisey's Bay nickel concentrate and because no product is expected until 2011, there is no relationship between the $200 million and future revenue. These research and development costs would therefore be expensed rather than capitalized at this point in time.

In summary, costs need to be analyzed to determine whether there is a direct relationship with revenue. If there is one, the costs are expensed and matched against the revenue in the period when the revenue is recognized. If it is hard to determine a direct relationship, the matching of expenses to revenue might be appropriate if a systematic and rational allocation method is used. If there is no direct relationship, costs should simply be expensed in the current period.

Full Disclosure Principle

The **full disclosure principle** requires companies to disclose circumstances and events which make a difference to financial statement users. It is important that investors be made aware of events that can affect the financial health of a company. In fact, five investors who lost money in Hollinger International have launched a class action lawsuit because of disclosure. They allege that money that belonged to Hollinger was pocketed by the former CEO, his wife, and associates without disclosure to the shareholders.

The full disclosure principle is respected through two elements in the financial statements: the data they contain and the accompanying notes. In most cases, the first note in the statements is a summary of significant accounting policies. The summary includes the methods used by the company when a choice is made between acceptable accounting principles. For example, it presents the methods used for inventory costing and amortization. The Forzani Group's note on its significant accounting policies (see Note 2 in Appendix A at the end of this textbook) discloses that the company has chosen the weighted average cost flow assumption and the declining-balance method to amortize its building.

The information that is disclosed in the notes to the financial statements generally falls into three additional categories. These categories:

1. Give supplementary detail or explanation (for example, a schedule of property, plant, and equipment)
2. Explain unrecorded transactions (for example, contingencies, commitments, and subsequent events)
3. Supply new information (for example, information about related party transactions)

Deciding how much disclosure is enough can be difficult. Accountants could disclose every financial event that occurs and every contingency that exists. But the benefits of giving this additional information may be less than the cost of making it available. Deciding how much disclosure is enough is not easy.

Cost Principle

As you know, the **cost principle** requires assets to be recorded at cost. Cost is used because it is both relevant and reliable. Cost is relevant because it represents the price paid, the assets sacrificed, or the commitment made at the date of acquisition. Cost is reliable because it is objectively measurable, factual, and verifiable. It is the result of an exchange transaction. Cost is also the basis used in preparing financial statements.

The cost principle has, however, been criticized. One criticism is that it is irrelevant, especially for predicting the value of an asset. After an asset is acquired, the argument goes, market value can move substantially away from the cost.

Recently, the CICA has moved to a modified cost model for some assets (and some liabilities, discussed in an intermediate accounting course). In this model, market values are used in certain cases, as summarized below:

Asset	Valuation
Trading securities	Market value
Available-for-sale securities	Market value
Merchandise inventory	Lower of cost and market
Long-lived assets	At cost, unless there is a permanent decline in market value, in which case market value is used

We will learn more about using market values to report trading securities and available-for-sale securities in Chapter 16.

International Accounting Principles

The discussion in the preceding sections focused on Canadian accounting principles. Canada, however, is only a small part of today's global marketplace where, to make their investment and credit decisions, foreigners may need to analyze Canadian financial statements and Canadians may need to analyze foreign financial statements. As an example, Bombardier is a global company headquartered in Canada. It operates on five continents, and more than 95 percent of its revenues are earned from markets outside of Canada. The Body Shop International is another example. Headquartered in the UK, it operates in 50 countries, including Canada. Unfortunately, many investors interested in investing in either company would find it difficult to read their financial statements because accounting principles differ between Canada and the UK, as well as among other countries.

Until recently, the Accounting Standards Board had been trying to harmonize Canadian GAAP with both U.S. GAAP and international GAAP. This was difficult to do, however, because international GAAP is principles-based, similar to Canadian GAAP, while U.S. GAAP is more rules-based. U.S. GAAP also presented another difficulty. Its rules are rigid, cumbersome, and costly to follow. They also leave loopholes that many critics believe make it easy to abuse the system.

Because international GAAP—known as international financial reporting standards (IFRS)—is based on principles, not rules, it is easier to apply to Canadian circumstances and Canadian companies. In addition, IFRS are simpler to understand than U.S. GAAP, and they are more flexible, which makes it easier to present a company's true financial condition. Consequently, the Accounting Standards Board has recommended that public companies adopt IFRS by 2010. Under this proposal, there will no longer be a unique set of Canadian GAAP for publicly traded companies. Instead, adoption of the IFRS will unify global standard-setting and improve the ability of investors, creditors, and others to make informed decisions about companies operating in today's global environment.

Publicly traded companies in Australia, Russia, and the European Union adopted IFRS in 2005 to harmonize their different accounting principles with one international standard. China is expected to adopt IFRS in 2007. IFRS are now used as the main basis for financial reporting in more than 100 industrialized companies, with the notable exception of the United States. And, the U.S. has agreed to converge a number of its existing standards with international standards by 2008.

 ACCOUNTING IN ACTION ▶ International Insight

Canadian GAAP is destined to disappear in 2010, to be replaced by International Financial Reporting Standards (IFRS). The Accounting Standards Board chair, Paul Cherry, said the decision came after a lot of consultation with Canadian companies and investors, who overwhelmingly indicated that they do not want Canada to copy "rules-oriented" U.S. GAAP. The movement to IFRS applies only to publicly traded companies, and not to private companies and not-for-profit organizations. "Our fundamental premise and experience is that one size does not necessarily fit all," Mr. Cherry said. "For example, developments in global capital markets are important for public companies and their investors, but not so important for private businesses and not-for-profit organizations."

Source: Janet McFarland, "Canadian Accounting Rules to Be Replaced," *The Globe and Mail*, January 11, 2006, B8.

? What benefits will result when publicly traded Canadian companies switch to international financial reporting standards?

BEFORE YOU GO ON . . .

▶Review It

1. What are the revenue recognition principle, matching principle, full disclosure principle, and cost principle?
2. Identify the four points of revenue recognition discussed in this chapter. Give an example of a company or product that would use each different point of revenue recognition.
3. What is stated about generally accepted accounting principles in the Auditors' Report found in the financial statements of The Forzani Group Ltd.? The answer to this question is at the end of the chapter.
4. Explain how Canadian and international accounting principles are similar.

▶Do It

In the current year, the Wacky Web Company has instalment sales of $900,000 for which collection is uncertain. The cost of goods sold is $600,000 and the company collected $330,000 cash on these instalment sales. How much gross profit should the company recognize, if any, in the current year?

Action Plan

- Use the instalment method when collection is uncertain.
- Calculate the gross profit margin: gross profit ÷ net sales.
- Recognize gross profit by multiplying the cash collected by the gross profit margin.

Solution

Gross profit margin = $900,000 − $600,000 = $300,000 ÷ $900,000 = 33⅓%
Gross profit recognized = $330,000 × 33⅓% = $110,000

Related exercise material: BE11–5, BE11–6, BE11–7, BE11–8, BE11–9, BE11–10, E11–2, E11–3, E11–4, E11–5, E11–6, E11–7, and E11–8.

Constraints in Accounting

Constraints allow a company to modify generally accepted accounting principles without reducing the usefulness of the information they report. There are two constraints: cost-benefit and materiality.

study objective 4

Identify and apply the constraints in accounting.

Cost-Benefit Constraint

The **cost-benefit constraint** exists so that the value of the information is more than the cost of providing it. As we discussed earlier in this chapter, when accountants apply the full disclosure principle they could disclose every financial event that occurs and every contingency. However, giving more information increases costs, and the benefits of giving this information may be less than the costs in some cases.

As there have been more and more changes to disclosure and reporting requirements, the costs of giving this information have increased. Because of these increasing costs, some critics have argued that the costs of applying GAAP to smaller or non–publicly traded companies are too high compared to the benefits. To respond to this problem, the CICA has developed a differential reporting model for smaller, private companies that allows them to use a simplified version of GAAP. As Paul Cherry, the chairman of the Accounting Standards Board recently concluded, "One size does not necessarily fit all." Accounting standard-setters continue to work to develop different financial reporting strategies for private companies "as a matter of urgency."

Materiality Constraint

The **materiality constraint** relates to an item's impact on a company's overall financial condition and operations. An item is material when it is likely to influence the decision of a reasonably careful investor or creditor. It is immaterial if including it or leaving it out has no impact on a decision-maker. In short, if the item does not make a difference in decision-making, GAAP does not have to be followed. To determine the materiality of an amount, the accountant usually compares it to such items as total assets, total liabilities, gross revenues, and cash and/or net income.

To illustrate how the materiality constraint works, assume that Yanik Co. purchases several inexpensive pieces of office equipment, such as wastepaper baskets. Although it would appear that the proper accounting is to amortize these wastepaper baskets over their useful lives, they would usually be expensed immediately instead. Doing this is justified because these costs are immaterial. Making amortization schedules for these assets is costly and time-consuming. It will not make a material difference to total assets and net income. The materiality constraint is also used in the nondisclosure of minor contingencies, and in the expensing of any long-lived assets under a certain dollar amount.

Summary of Conceptual Framework

As we have seen, the conceptual framework for developing sound reporting practices starts with the objective of financial reporting. It then describes the qualitative characteristics of accounting information and the elements of the financial statements. Finally, more detailed recognition and measurement criteria are provided. These criteria exist as assumptions, principles, and constraints. The conceptual framework is summarized in Illustration 11-7 on the following page.

Illustration 11-7 ▶

Conceptual framework

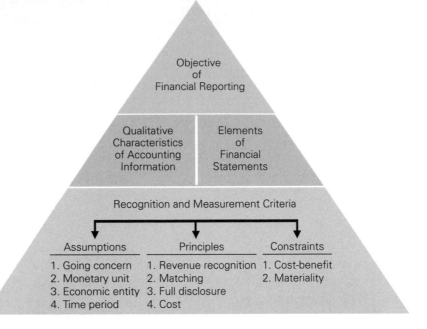

BEFORE YOU GO ON . . .

▶ **Review It**

1. What is the cost-benefit constraint?
2. Why is differential reporting necessary?
3. Describe the materiality constraint. Give an example.

Related exercise material: BE11–11, BE11–12, E11–9, E11–10, and E11–11.

Practice Tools:
Demonstration Problems

Demonstration Problem

The Wu Construction Company is under contract to build a condominium building at a contract price of $2 million. The building will take 18 months to complete, at an estimated cost of $1.4 million. Construction begins in November 2006 and is finished in April 2008. Actual construction costs incurred in each year are as follows: in 2006, $140,000; in 2007, $910,000; and in 2008, $350,000. The Wu Construction Company has a December year end.

Instructions

Calculate the gross profit to be recognized in each year using the percentage-of-completion method.

Solution to Demonstration Problem

($ in thousands)

Year	Costs Incurred (Current Period)	÷	Total Estimated Cost	=	Percentage Complete (Current Period)	×	Total Revenue	=	Revenue Recognized (Current Period)	−	Costs Incurred (Current Period)	=	Gross Profit (Current Period)
2006	$ 140		$1,400		10%		$2,000		$ 200		$ 140		$ 60
2007	910		1,400		65%		2,000		1,300		910		390
2008	350		1,400		25%		2,000		500		350		150
Totals	$1,400								$2,000		$1,400		$600

Action Plan

- The percentage-of-completion method recognizes revenue as construction occurs. The ongoing construction is viewed as a series of sales.
- Determine the percentage complete by dividing the costs incurred by total estimated costs.
- Multiply the percentage complete by the contract price to find the revenue to be recognized in the current period.
- Calculate gross profit: revenue recognized less actual costs incurred.

Summary of Study Objectives

1. **Describe the conceptual framework of accounting.** The key components of the conceptual framework are (1) the objective of financial reporting, (2) the qualitative characteristics of accounting information (understandability, relevance, reliability, and comparability), (3) the elements of financial statements, and (4) recognition and measurement criteria (assumptions, principles, and constraints).

2. **Identify and apply the basic assumptions used by accountants.** The major assumptions are the going concern assumption, monetary unit assumption, economic entity assumption, and time period assumption.

3. **Identify and apply the basic principles of accounting.** The major principles are the revenue recognition principle, matching principle, full disclosure principle, and cost principle. Four points of revenue recognition were described: at the point of sale, during production, at the completion of production, and when cash is collected.

4. **Identify and apply the constraints in accounting.** The major constraints are the cost-benefit and materiality constraints.

Glossary

Comparability A quality that information has if it can be compared to the accounting information of other companies because the companies all use the same accounting principles. (p. 571)

Completed-contract method A method in which revenue, expenses, and profit are recognized at the completion of production because revenues or costs cannot be reliably estimated. (p. 580)

Conceptual framework of accounting A coherent system of interrelated elements that guides the development and application of accounting principles: it includes the objective of financial reporting, qualitative characteristics of accounting information, elements of financial statements, and recognition and measurement criteria. (p. 568)

Conservatism The practice of choosing, when in doubt, an accounting method that is least likely to overstate assets and net income. Conservatism modifies the reliability of accounting information. (p. 571)

Consistency Use of the same accounting principles from year to year. Consistency is part of the comparability characteristic of accounting information. (p. 571)

Cost-benefit constraint The constraint that the costs of obtaining and providing information should not be more than the benefits that are gained. (p. 585)

Elements of financial statements Definitions of basic terms in accounting. (p. 572)

Full disclosure principle The accounting principle that requires circumstances and events which make a difference to financial statement users to be disclosed. (p. 582)

Instalment method A method of recognizing revenue using the cash basis. Each cash collection consists of a partial recovery of the cost of goods sold and partial gross profit from the sale. (p. 580)

Materiality constraint The constraint of determining whether an item is important enough to influence the decision of a reasonably careful investor or creditor. (p. 585)

Objective of financial reporting The objective of financial reporting is to provide useful information for decision-making. (p. 569)

Objectivity A quality that accounting information has if two individuals working independently can review the same information and reach the same results or similar conclusions. (p. 570)

Percentage-of-completion method A method of recognizing revenue on a long-term construction project. When costs can be reliably estimated, a portion of the total revenue can be recognized in each period by applying a percentage of completion. This percentage is determined by dividing the actual costs incurred during the period by the estimated costs for the entire project. (p. 577)

Point of sale The most common basis of revenue recognition, where revenue is recognized when goods or services are sold. Alternatives to this method are the percentage-of-completion, completed-contract, and instalment methods. (p. 576)

Relevance A quality that information has if it makes a difference in a decision. (p. 570)

Reliability A quality that information has if it can be verified as having no errors and bias. (p. 570)

Understandability A quality that information in the financial statements has if it is understandable to its users. (p. 570)

Self-Study Questions

Practice Tools: Self-Assessment Quizzes

Answers are at the end of the chapter.

(SO 1) K 1. Which of the following does the conceptual framework of accounting not guide?
(a) What to present in financial statements
(b) How to quantify non-financial information
(c) Decisions about alternative ways of reporting economic events
(d) The selection of appropriate ways of communicating financial information

(SO 1) K 2. Which of the following is not an objective of financial reporting?
(a) To provide information that is useful in making resource allocation decisions
(b) To provide information about economic resources, claims on those resources, and changes in them
(c) To provide information that is useful in assessing management stewardship
(d) To provide information about the market value of a business

(SO 1) K 3. The main criterion for judging accounting information is:
(a) consistency.
(b) objectivity.
(c) usefulness for decisions.
(d) comparability.

(SO 2) C 4. Valuing assets at their market value rather than at their cost is inconsistent with the:
(a) going concern assumption.
(b) monetary unit assumption.
(c) economic entity assumption.
(d) time period assumption.

(SO 2) C 5. The time period assumption results in a trade-off between which of the following qualitative characteristics of accounting information?

(a) Understandability and relevance
(b) Relevance and reliability
(c) Reliability and comparability
(d) Comparability and understandability

(SO 3) 6. The Rioux Construction Company began a long-term construction contract on January 1, 2007. The contract is expected to be completed in 2008 at a total cost of $20 million. Rioux's revenue for the project is $23 million. Rioux incurred contract costs of $4 million in 2007. What gross profit should be recognized in 2007?
(a) $0.6 million   (c) $4.6 million
(b) $3.0 million   (d) $19.0 million

(SO 3) 7. In its first year of operations, Glackin Company had instalment sales of $1 million with uncertain collectibility. The cost of goods sold on these instalment sales was $650,000. Glackin collected a total of $500,000 cash on the instalment sales. Using the instalment method, how much gross profit should be recognized in the first year?
(a) $175,000   (c) $350,000
(b) $325,000   (d) $500,000

(SO 3) 8. The full disclosure principle says that:
(a) financial statements should disclose all assets at their cost.
(b) financial statements should disclose only those events that can be measured in dollars.
(c) financial statements should disclose all events and circumstances that would matter to users of financial statements.
(d) financial statements should not be relied on unless an auditor has expressed an unqualified opinion on them.

SO 4) K 9. The accounting term that refers to the tendency of accountants to favour understating assets and revenues in situations of uncertainty is known as:
  (a) the matching principle.
  (b) materiality.
  (c) conservatism.
  (d) the monetary unit assumption.

10. International generally accepted accounting principles (SO 4) K are known as:
  (a) GAAP.
  (b) IGAAP.
  (c) IFRS.
  (d) IASB.

Questions

SO 1) C 1. Describe the conceptual framework of accounting and explain how it helps financial reporting.

SO 1) C 2. Why are principles-based standards better than rules-based standards?

SO 1) K 3. What is the basic objective of financial reporting?

SO 1) C 4. Identify and explain the four qualitative characteristics of accounting information.

SO 1) C 5. Raynard Company increased its net income substantially in 2008 while keeping its inventory mostly the same. The president is very pleased with this. The chief accountant cautions the president, however. She points out that since the company changed from the average cost to the FIFO cost flow assumption this year, there is a comparability problem. It will be difficult to determine whether the company's performance is better. Do you agree? Explain.

SO 1) C 6. Many accounting choices require trade-offs between the qualitative characteristics. Explain why and provide an example.

SO 1) C 7. How is the concept of objectivity related to the qualitative characteristic of reliability?

SO 2) K 8. Explain the following assumptions: (a) going concern, (b) monetary unit, (c) economic entity, and (d) time period.

SO 2) C 9. Why does the time period assumption result in a trade-off between the qualitative characteristics of reliability and relevance?

2, 3) C 10. (a) Why does it matter whether accountants assume an economic entity will remain a going concern? (b) How does the going concern assumption support the use of the cost principle?

1, 3) C 11. How does the concept of consistency relate to the full disclosure principle?

12. Why is the revenue recognition principle difficult to apply in practice? (SO 3) C

13. Describe the four guidelines for revenue recognition. (SO 3) K

14. (a) What are the four points at which revenue is often recognized? (b) Why is the point of sale usually chosen as the date when revenue is recognized? (SO 3) C

15. (a) What are the advantages of using the percentage-of-completion method to recognize revenue? (b) When should a company use the completed-contract method instead of percentage-of-completion? (SO 3) C

16. Explain how the percentage-of-completion method should be adjusted when a company's cost estimates change during the contract period. (SO 3) C

17. Under what circumstances is it correct to wait until cash is collected to recognize revenue? Refer to the revenue recognition guidelines in your explanation. (SO 3) AP

18. Explain why the CICA moved to a modified cost model of financial reporting that uses market values in addition to cost to report certain assets. (SO 3) C

19. How will the move to adopt international financial reporting standards benefit multinational corporations? (SO 3) C

20. Describe the two constraints in the presentation of accounting information and provide an example of each. (SO 4) C

21. The controller rounded all dollar figures in the company's financial statements to the nearest thousand dollars. "It's not important for our users to know how many pennies we spend," she said. Do you believe rounded financial figures can provide useful information for decision-making? Explain why or why not. (SO 4) C

22. Isabelle believes that the same GAAP should be used by every company, whether large or small and whether public or private. Do you agree? Explain your answer by referring to the appropriate accounting constraint. (SO 4) C

Brief Exercises

Identify items included in the conceptual framework.
(SO 1) K

BE11–1 Indicate which of the following items are included in the CICA's conceptual framework. (Write "Yes" or "No" beside each item.)

(a) The analysis of financial statement ratios
(b) The objective of financial reporting
(c) The qualitative characteristics of accounting information
(d) The elements of financial statements
(e) The rules for calculating taxable income
(f) The constraints on applying generally accepted accounting principles
(g) The measurement of the market value of a business

Identify qualitative characteristics.
(SO 1) K

BE11–2 Presented below is a set of qualitative characteristics of accounting information:

1. Predictive value
2. Neutrality
3. Verifiability
4. Timeliness
5. Faithful representation
6. Comparability
7. Feedback value
8. Consistency
9. Conservatism
10. Understandability

Instructions

Match these qualitative characteristics to the following statements, using numbers 1 to 10.

(a) ___ Accounting information must be available to decision-makers before it loses its ability to influence their decisions.
(b) ___ Accounting information provides a basis to evaluate decisions made in the past.
(c) ___ Accounting information cannot be selected, prepared, or presented to favour one set of interested users over another.
(d) ___ Accounting information reports the economic substance of a transaction, not its legal form.
(e) ___ Accounting information helps reduce uncertainty about the future.
(f) ___ Accounting information must have no errors or bias.
(g) ___ Accounting information about one company can be evaluated in relation to accounting information from another company.
(h) ___ Accounting information is prepared based on the assumption that users have a reasonable understanding of accounting concepts and procedures, and of general business and economic conditions.
(i) ___ When there is uncertainty, accounting information should be prepared using the method that is least likely to overstate assets and net income.
(j) ___ Accounting information in a company is prepared using the same principles and methods year after year.

Identify elements of financial statements.
(SO 1) K

BE11–3 Here are the basic elements of financial statements that we learned about in earlier chapters:

1. Assets
2. Liabilities
3. Owner's equity
4. Revenues
5. Expenses
6. Gains
7. Losses
8. Drawings

Instructions

Each statement that follows is an important aspect of an element's definition. Match the elements with the definitions. *Note:* More than one number can be placed in a blank. Each number may be used more than once or not at all.

(a) ___ Increases in assets or decreases in liabilities resulting from the main business activities of the organization
(b) ___ Existing debts and obligations from past transactions
(c) ___ Changes to owner's equity caused by the company's peripheral activities
(d) ___ Resources owned by a business

(e) ___ Goods or services used in the process of earning revenue
(f) ___ A residual claim on total assets after deducting liabilities
(g) ___ The capacity to provide future benefits to the organization

BE11–4 A list of basic accounting assumptions follows:

1. Going concern
2. Monetary unit
3. Economic entity
4. Time period

*Identify assumptions.
(SO 2) C*

Instructions

Match these assumptions to the following statements, using numbers 1 to 4.

(a) ___ The Plaza Company reports its activities quarterly, as well as annually.
(b) ___ The West Company reports its land at its cost of $100,000, even though it is worth $175,000.
(c) ___ The Zakuta Company does not report its high level of customer satisfaction in its financial statements.
(d) ___ The Trois Amis Company accounts for the activities of each of its three subsidiary companies separately.

BE11–5 A list of accounting principles follows:

1. Revenue recognition
2. Matching
3. Full disclosure
4. Cost

*Identify principles.
(SO 3) C*

Instructions

Match these principles to the following statements, using numbers 1 to 4.

(a) ___ The Hirjikaka Company reports information about pending lawsuits in the notes to its financial statements.
(b) ___ The Joss Company recognizes revenue at the point of sale, not when the cash is collected.
(c) ___ The Hilal Company reports its assets at the price it paid for them, not at what they are now worth.
(d) ___ The law firm Thériault, Lévesque, and Picard records interim billings and costs for its clients at the end of each month.

BE11–6 Howie, Price, and Whynot operate an accounting firm. In March, their staff worked a total of 1,000 hours at an average billing rate of $100 per hour. They sent bills to clients in the month of March that totalled $75,000. They expect to bill the balance of their time in April, when the work is complete. The firm's salary costs total $50,000 each month. How much revenue should the firm recognize in the month of March? How much salaries expense?

*Determine point of revenue and expense recognition.
(SO 3) AP*

BE11–7 Flin Flon Construction Company is under contract to build a commercial building at a price of $4.2 million. Construction begins in January 2006 and finishes in December 2008. Total estimated construction costs are $2.8 million. Actual construction costs incurred in each year are as follows: in 2006, $560,000; in 2007, $1,800,000; and in 2008, $440,000. Calculate the revenue and gross profit to be recognized in each year, using the percentage-of-completion method.

*Calculate revenue and gross profit—percentage-of-completion method.
(SO 3) AP*

BE11–8 Refer to the data presented in BE11–7. Assume that the estimated total costs rose from $2.8 million to $3.1 million in 2007. Actual costs incurred are $560,000 in 2006, $2 million in 2007, and $540,000 in 2008. Calculate the revenue and gross profit that should be recognized each year, using the percentage-of-completion method.

*Calculate revenue and gross profit with change in estimate—percentage-of-completion method.
(SO 3) AP*

BE11–9 Refer to the data presented in BE11–7. Calculate the revenue and gross profit to be recognized in each year, assuming that Flin Flon uses the completed-contract method instead of the percentage-of-completion method.

*Calculate revenue and gross profit—completed-contract method.
(SO 3) AP*

BE11–10 Brassard Co. uses the instalment method to account for certain instalment sales. In 2007, its first year of operations, it had sales of uncertain collectibility of $800,000 and a cost of

*Calculate gross profit—instalment method.
(SO 3) AP*

goods sold of $560,000. The collections on these sales were as follows: in 2007, $360,000; and in 2008, $440,000. (a) Calculate the gross profit to be recognized for 2007 and 2008. (b) Would your answer change if collectibility on these sales was certain?

Identify assumption, principle, or constraint.
(SO 2, 3, 4) C

BE11–11 Here are the accounting assumptions, principles, and constraints discussed in this chapter:

1. Going concern assumption
2. Monetary unit assumption
3. Economic entity assumption
4. Time period assumption
5. Revenue recognition principle
6. Matching principle
7. Full disclosure principle
8. Cost principle
9. Cost-benefit constraint
10. Materiality constraint

Instructions

Identify by number the accounting assumption, principle, or constraint that describes each situation below. Do not use a number more than once.

(a) ___ Is why land is not reported at its liquidation value. (Do not use the cost principle.)
(b) ___ Indicates that personal and business record-keeping should be kept separate.
(c) ___ Ensures that all relevant financial information is reported.
(d) ___ Assumes that the dollar is the "measuring stick" for reporting financial performance.
(e) ___ Requires that GAAP be followed for all significant items.
(f) ___ Separates financial information into time periods for reporting purposes.
(g) ___ Requires expenses to be recognized in the same period as related revenues.
(h) ___ Indicates that market value changes after an asset is purchased are not recorded in the accounts.

Identify violation of principle or constraint.
(SO 3, 4) AN

BE11–12 For each of the following, indicate the accounting principle or constraint that has been violated, if any:

(a) The company currently records its accounting transactions and prepares its financial reports manually. The cost of using a new computerized accounting system to do these tasks is estimated at $25,000. Annual savings are expected to be $10,000.
(b) Inventory is reported at cost when market value is higher.
(c) Revenue on instalment sales with uncertain collectibility is recognized at the time of sale.
(d) Paper clips expense appears on the income statement, at $10.
(e) Bad debt expense is recorded in the period when the account receivable is written off.
(f) Small tools are recorded as long-lived assets and amortized.

Exercises

Apply economic entity assumption.
(SO 2) AP

E11–1 The Skate Stop is owned by Marc Bélanger. It sells in-line skates and accessories. It shares space with another company, Ride Snowboards. Ride Snowboards is owned by Marc's wife, Dominique Maltais, who was an Olympic bronze medallist in snowboarding. Ride Snowboards sells snowboards and related accessories. The following transactions occurred during a recent year:

(a) In January, Dominique purchased fire and theft insurance for the year to cover the rented space and inventory. She paid for all the insurance since she had more cash than Marc.
(b) Marc paid the rent for the month of July since he had more cash that month than Dominique.
(c) Marc recorded skate sales for the month of September.
(d) Dominique purchased and paid for her winter inventory of snowboards in September.
(e) Marc and Dominique had such a successful year that they went out to a fancy restaurant to celebrate. They charged the bill to Dominique's company.
(f) Dominique paid her annual membership fee to the local ski hill from company funds.
(g) Marc paid his annual membership fee to the curling club from company funds.

Instructions

Identify which of the above transactions should be recorded by Skate Stop, and which should be recorded by Ride Snowboards. State also if the transaction cost is a personal one or if it relates to both companies and should be allocated to each of them.

E11–2   When they have to choose among generally accepted accounting principles, some managers may try to use principles that allow them to influence the company's net income.

Discuss accounting policy choices and objective of financial reporting.
(SO 1, 3) C

Instructions

(a) Explain why a manager might be motivated to try to influence net income.
(b) Give an example of an accounting principle choice that management could use to (1) improve the company's net income, and (2) reduce the company's net income.
(c) How would this type of behaviour meet, or not meet, the objective of financial reporting?
(d) Explain how likely it is that a manager would be able to change accounting principles to manage income as you describe in (b).

E11–3   The following situations require professional judgement to determine when to recognize revenue from the transactions:

Identify point of revenue recognition.
(SO 3) C

(a) Air Canada sells you a nonrefundable Tango fare airline ticket in September for your flight home at Christmas.
(b) Leon's Furniture sells you a home theatre on a "no money down, no interest, and no payments for one year" promotional deal.
(c) The Toronto Blue Jays sell season tickets to games in the Rogers Centre on-line. Fans can purchase the tickets at any time, although the season doesn't officially begin until April. It runs from April through October.
(d) Babineau Company sells merchandise with terms of 2/10, n/30, FOB destination.
(e) In September, Centennial College collects tuition revenue for the term from students. The term runs from September through December.
(f) The College Bookstore has the following return policy for textbook sales: "Textbooks (new and used) may be returned for seven calendar days from the start of classes. After that time, textbooks (new and used) may be returned within 48 hours of purchase."

Instructions

Identify when revenue should be recognized in each of the above situations.

E11–4   Over the winter months, the Green-Lawn Company pre-sells fertilizing and weed control lawn services to be performed from May through September, inclusive. If payment is made in full by April 1, a 10% discount is allowed. In March, 200 customers took advantage of the discount and purchased the summer lawn service package for $450 each. In June, 200 customers purchased the package for $500, and in July, 150 purchased it for the same price.

Identify point of revenue recognition.
(SO 3) C

Instructions

How much revenue should be recognized by the Green-Lawn Company in each of the months of March, April, May, June, July, August, and September? Explain.

E11–5   Consider the following transactions of the Mitrovica Company for the year ended December 31, 2007:

Determine amount of revenue to be recognized.
(SO 3) AP

(a) Leased office space for a one-year period beginning September 1. Two months of rent at $2,000 per month was received in advance.
(b) Received a sales order for merchandise that cost $9,000. It was sold for $14,000 on December 28 to Warfield Company. The goods were shipped FOB destination on December 31. Warfield received them on January 3, 2008.
(c) Signed a long-term contract to construct a building at a total price of $1.6 million. The total estimated cost of construction is $1.2 million. During 2007, the company incurred $300,000 of

costs and collected $400,000 in cash. The percentage-of-completion method is used to account for construction revenue.

(d) Had merchandise inventory on hand at year end that amounted to $160,000. Mitrovica expects to sell the inventory in 2008 for $180,000.

(e) Issued a $6,000, six-month, 5% note receivable on September 1, with interest payable at maturity.

(f) Sold merchandise in December for $50,000 on an instalment basis. The merchandise originally cost $30,000. The customers are expected to pay $25,000 in 2008 and $25,000 in 2009, but collectibility is uncertain.

Instructions

For each item above, indicate the amount of revenue Mitrovica should recognize in 2007. Explain.

Calculate gross profit—
percentage-of-completion
method.
(SO 3) AP

E11–6 Shen Construction Company had a long-term construction project that lasted three years. The project had a contract price of $140 million with total estimated costs of $100 million. Shen used the percentage-of-completion method. At the end of construction, the following actual costs had been incurred:

	2006	2007	2008
Actual cost	$30 million	$50 million	$20 million

Instructions

(a) Calculate the gross profit that was recognized for each year of the construction contract.

(b) Assume instead that at the beginning of 2007, Shen revised the total estimated cost remaining for the last year of the contract to $25 million instead of $20 million. Actual costs incurred in 2008 were later determined to be $25 million. Calculate the gross profit that was recognized for each year of the construction contract.

Calculate gross profit—
completed-contract method.
(SO 3) AP

E11–7 Refer to the data in E11–6 for Shen Construction Company. Assume that Shen used the completed-contract method instead of the percentage-of-completion method.

Instructions

(a) Calculate the gross profit that was recognized for each year of the construction contract.

(b) Does your answer in (a) change if Shen revises its total estimated cost at the beginning of 2007? Explain why or why not.

Calculate gross profit—point-
of-sale and instalment
methods.
(SO 3) AP

E11–8 Blairmore Company sold equipment for $300,000 in 2006. Collections on the sale were as follows: in 2006, $70,000; in 2007, $190,000; and in 2008, $40,000. Blairmore's cost of goods sold is 60% of sales.

Instructions

(a) Determine Blairmore's gross profit for 2006, 2007, and 2008, assuming that revenue is recognized at the point of sale.

(b) Determine Blairmore's gross profit for 2006, 2007, and 2008, assuming that revenue is recognized under the instalment method.

Identify assumption,
principle, or constraint.
(SO 2, 3, 4) C

E11–9 Here are the assumptions, principles, and constraints discussed in this chapter:

1. Going concern assumption
2. Monetary unit assumption
3. Economic entity assumption
4. Time period assumption
5. Revenue recognition principle
6. Matching principle
7. Full disclosure principle
8. Cost principle
9. Cost-benefit constraint
10. Materiality constraint

Instructions

Identify by number the accounting assumption, principle, or constraint that describes each situation below. Do not use a number more than once.

(a) ____ Barb Denton runs her accounting practice out of her home. She separates her business records from her household accounts.

(b) ____ Companies prepare quarterly reports.

(c) ____ Revenue is sometimes recognized at various points of production.

(d) ____ The cost should not be more than the benefits.

(e) ____ Significant accounting policies are reported in the notes to the financial statements.

(f) ____ Assets are not stated at their liquidation value.

(g) ____ The effect of inflation for the current year is ignored in determining net income.

(h) ____ Dollar amounts on financial statements are often rounded to the nearest thousand.

(i) ____ Bad debts expense is recorded using the allowance method of accounting.

(j) ____ Land is recorded at its cost of $100,000 rather than at its market value of $150,000.

E11–10 Several reporting situations follow:

1. Tercek Company recognizes revenue during the production cycle. The price of the product and how many items will be sold are not certain.

2. In preparing its financial statements, Seco Company left out information about its cost flow assumption for inventories.

3. Martinez Company amortizes patents over their legal life of 20 years instead of their economic life, which is usually about five years.

4. Ravine Hospital Supply Corporation reports only current assets and current liabilities on its balance sheet. Long-term assets and liabilities are reported as current. The company is unlikely to be liquidated.

5. Barton Company reports inventory on its balance sheet at its current market value of $100,000. The inventory has an original cost of $110,000.

6. Bonilla Company is in its third year of operations and has not yet issued financial statements.

7. Watts Company has inventory on hand that cost $400,000. Watts reports inventory on its balance sheet at its current market value of $425,000.

8. Steph Wolfson, president of the Download Music Company, bought a computer for her personal use. She paid for the computer with company funds and debited the computers account.

9. Smith Company does not use a security system to protect its inventory. It would cost $250,000 to install the security required to protect $100,000 of inventory.

10. The Valley Company sells merchandise on an instalment basis. It has a strong credit policy and is able to reasonably estimate uncollectible accounts. Because of the long-term collection period, it recognizes revenue when the cash is collected.

Identify assumption, principle, or constraint violated.
(SO 2, 3, 4) AN

Instructions

For each of the above, list the assumption, principle, or constraint that has been violated, if any.

E11–11 Business transactions for Ellis Co. follow:

1. Equipment worth $90,000 is acquired at a cost of $65,000 from a company going out of business. The following entry is made:

Equipment	90,000	
Cash		65,000
Gain		25,000

2. The president of Ellis Co., Evan Ellis, purchases a truck for personal use and charges it to his expense account. The following entry is made:

Travel Expense	29,000	
Cash		29,000

3. An account receivable becomes a bad debt. The following entry is made:

Bad Debts Expense	15,000	
Accounts Receivable		15,000

4. Merchandise inventory with a cost of $225,000 is reported at its market value of $260,000. The following entry is made:

Identify assumption, principle, or constraint violated and correct entries.
(SO 2, 3, 4) AN

Merchandise Inventory	35,000	
Gain		35,000

5. An electric pencil sharpener costing $50 is being amortized over five years. The following entry is made:

Amortization Expense	10	
Accumulated Amortization—Pencil Sharpener		10

Instructions

In each of the situations above, identify the assumption, principle, or constraint that has been violated, if any. If a journal entry is incorrect, give the correct entry.

Problems: Set A

Comment on relevance and reliability.
(SO 1) C

P11–1A Share prices rarely move in the same direction as reported income and losses. **Research in Motion Limited**, maker of wireless personal digital products, is an interesting example. Until 2004, the company had recorded bigger losses each year. Despite this, its share price reached a high of $107 in this period.

At the end of fiscal 2006, the company had reported three years of small net income amounts but its retained earnings was only U.S. $148 million—a pretty small proportion of its total assets of $2.3 billion. At the end of fiscal 2006, Research in Motion's shares were trading at a reduced price of $76.

Instructions

Explain why investors in Research in Motion were willing to pay such a high price (i.e., $107) for the shares when the company reported losses, and a lower price (i.e., $76) for the shares when the company reported net income. Include in your answer a discussion of the trade-off between relevance and reliability.

Identify assumption or principle violated and prepare entries.
(SO 2, 3) AN

P11–2A Jivraj and Juma are accountants at Desktop Computers. They disagree over the following transactions that occurred during the calendar year 2007:

1. Desktop purchased equipment for $35,000 at a going-out-of-business sale. The equipment was worth $45,000. Jivraj believes that the following entry should be made:

Equipment	45,000	
Cash		35,000
Gain		10,000

2. A patent costing $60,000 was appraised at $125,000. Jivraj suggests the following journal entry.

Patent	65,000	
Gain on Appreciation of Patent		65,000

3. Amortization for the year was $18,000. Since net income is expected to be lower this year, Jivraj suggests deferring amortization to a year when there is more net income.

4. Desktop bought a custom-made piece of equipment for $36,000. This equipment has a useful life of six years. Desktop amortizes equipment using the straight-line method. "Since the equipment is custom-made, it will have no resale value," Jivraj argues. "So, instead of amortizing it, it should be expensed immediately. Besides, it lowers our net income." Jivraj suggests the following entry:

Equipment Expense	36,000	
Cash		36,000

5. Jivraj suggests that the company building should be reported on the balance sheet at the lower of cost and market value. Market value is $15,000 less than cost, although it is expected to recover its value in the future.

6. On December 20, Desktop hired a marketing consultant to design and implement a marketing plan in 2008. The contract amount is $45,000 payable in three instalments in 2008. Jivraj argues

that the contract must be recorded in 2007 because the company is legally bound for the full amount. Jivraj suggest the following:

Marketing Expense	45,000	
Accounts Payable		45,000

7. In September, Desktop sold 100 computers to college students for $500 each. Each student signed an instalment contract in which the student agreed to pay $300 in July 2008 and another $200 in July 2009. Jivraj argues the merchandise has been delivered to the customers and that Desktop should record the following in 2007:

Accounts Receivable	50,000	
Sales		50,000

Juma disagrees with Jivraj on all of the above situations.

Instructions

(a) For each transaction, indicate why Juma disagrees. Identify the accounting principle or assumption that would be violated if Jivraj's suggestions were used.
(b) Prepare the correct journal entry to record each transaction.

P11–3A   Business transactions for SGI Company in the current year follow:

Identify assumption or principle and correct entries.
(SO 2, 3) AN

1. Materials were purchased on November 30 for $65,000. This amount was entered in the account Materials Inventory. On December 31, the materials would have cost $80,000, so the following entry was made:

Materials Inventory	15,000	
Gain on Inventory		15,000

2. An order for $30,000 was received from a customer for products on hand. This order is to be shipped on January 9 next year. The following entry was made:

Accounts Receivable	30,000	
Sales		30,000

3. The president of SGI Company, S. Ingram, used her expense account to purchase a pre-owned Saab for her personal use only. The following entry was made:

Miscellaneous Expense	44,000	
Cash		44,000

4. At a fire sale, equipment worth $250,000 was acquired at a cost of $225,000. It had soot and smoke damage, but was otherwise in good condition. The following entry was made:

Equipment	250,000	
Cash		225,000
Gain on Acquisition of Equipment		25,000

5. Because the general level of prices increased in the current year, SGI determined that its equipment and amortization were understated by $25,000. The following entry was made.

Equipment	25,000	
Accumulated Amortization		25,000

Instructions

(a) In each of the situations, identify the assumption or principle that has been violated, if any.
(b) Prepare the journal entry to correct each incorrect transaction identified in (a).

P11–4A   Superior Salmon Farm raises salmon that it sells to supermarket chains and restaurants. The average selling price for a mature salmon is $6. Many people believe that the selling price will increase in the future, because the demand for salmon is increasing as more people become aware of the health benefits of the omega-3 fatty acids in salmon.

Identify point of revenue and expense recognition.
(SO 3) C

It normally takes three years for the fish to grow to a saleable size. During that period, the fish must be fed and closely monitored to ensure they are healthy and free of disease. Their habitat must also be maintained. These costs average $4.50 per fish over the three-year growing period. The owner of Superior Salmon Farm believes the company should recognize revenue at a rate of $2 a year ($6 ÷ 3 years) for each fish that it harvests.

Instructions

(a) Do you agree with the proposed revenue recognition policy for Superior Salmon Farm? Explain why or why not. Use the revenue recognition guidelines to explain when you believe the revenue should be recognized for this salmon farming business.

(b) When should the cost of feeding, monitoring, and maintaining healthy fish and a proper habitat be recognized? Explain.

Calculate revenue at various points of recognition.
(SO 3) AP

P11–5A Devany Construction was awarded a $30-million contract for construction of a civic centre on June 19, 2008. Construction began on August 1 and estimated costs of completion at the contract date are $25 million over a two-year period. By November 30, 2008, Devany's year end, construction costs of $6.75 million have been incurred. Contract payments totalling $10 million have been collected so far.

Instructions

(a) Devany is considering using one of the following three points of revenue recognition. Define and describe each of the following:
  1. Point of sale
  2. Percentage-of-completion
  3. Completed-contract

(b) Calculate the amount of revenue that would be recognized in fiscal 2008 for Devany Construction under each of the above points of revenue recognition.

(c) Which method would you recommend that Devany Construction use? Explain why.

Calculate revenue, expense, and gross profit— percentage-of-completion and completed-contract methods.
(SO 3) AP

P11–6A MacNeil Construction Company has a long-term construction contract to build a shopping centre. The centre has a total estimated cost of $30 million, and a contract price of $38 million. Additional information follows:

Year	Cash Collections	Actual Costs Incurred
2005	$ 6,000,000	$ 4,500,000
2006	8,000,000	6,000,000
2007	12,500,000	12,000,000
2008	11,500,000	7,500,000
	$38,000,000	$30,000,000

The shopping centre is completed in 2008 as scheduled. All cash collections for the contract have been received.

Instructions

(a) Prepare a schedule to determine the revenue, expense, and gross profit for each year of the long-term construction contract, using the percentage-of-completion method.

(b) How would your answer in (a) change if MacNeil Construction used the completed-contract method rather than the percentage-of-completion method?

Revise revenue, expense, and gross profit—percentage-of-completion and completed-contract methods.
(SO 3) AP

P11–7A Refer to the data in P11–6A for MacNeil Construction. Assume instead that the actual costs were $14 million in 2007. Because costs were higher than expected, MacNeil revised its total estimated costs from $30 million to $34 million at the end of 2007. Actual costs incurred in 2008 were $9.5 million. All other data are unchanged.

Instructions

(a) Assuming MacNeil Construction uses the percentage-of-completion method, prepare a revised schedule to determine the revenue, expense, and gross profit for each year of the long-term construction contract.

(b) Assuming MacNeil Construction uses the completed-contract method, prepare a revised schedule to determine the revenue, expense, and gross profit for each year of the long-term construction contract.

(c) Which method would you recommend MacNeil Construction use? Explain why.

P11–8A Hamilton Construction Company has a contract for the construction of a new recreation centre. It accounts for this project using the percentage-of-completion method. The contract amount is $3 million and the cost of construction is expected to total $2.2 million. The actual costs incurred are shown below for the three-year life of the project:

Calculate revenue, expense, and gross profit—percentage-of-completion method.
(SO 3) AP

Year	Actual Costs Incurred
2006	$ 660,000
2007	990,000
2008	550,000
	$2,200,000

Instructions

(a) Calculate the amount of revenue, expense, and gross profit to be recognized in each year.
(b) What if Hamilton Construction receives less cash in each of the first two years than the amount it has recognized as revenue? Is it still appropriate to recognize the amount of revenue calculated in (a)? Explain.

P11–9A The Scotia Trawler Shipyard builds custom trawlers. During its first year of operations, it signed a two-year contract to build a 42-foot trawler for Jim McLeod. The sale price was $500,000. Scotia's cost to construct the boat was estimated at $400,000. Additional information follows:

Calculate gross profit—percentage-of-completion and instalment methods.
(SO 3) AP

Year	Cash Collections	Actual Costs Incurred
2007	$200,000	$250,000
2008	300,000	150,000
	$500,000	$400,000

Instructions

(a) Prepare a schedule to determine the gross profit for each year, using the percentage-of-completion method.
(b) Prepare a schedule to determine the gross profit for each year, using the instalment method.
(c) Which method is more appropriate for the Scotia Trawler Shipyard to use? Explain your reasoning.

P11–10A Vanderkooy Company reported the following instalment sales information:

Calculate gross profit—instalment sales.
(SO 3) AP

	2007	2008
Instalment sales	$1,900,000	$1,500,000
Cost of instalment sales	1,235,000	975,000
Cash collections on 2007 sales	650,000	475,000
Cash collections on 2008 sales	0	600,000

Instructions

(a) Prepare a schedule to determine the gross profit to be recognized for each year, assuming that collectibility is expected and any uncollectible amounts can be reasonably estimated.
(b) Prepare a schedule to determine the gross profit to be recognized for each year, assuming that collectibility is uncertain.

P11–11A Fran's Furniture Warehouse makes many of its sales on long-term instalment contracts. It accounts for these using the instalment method because collectibility is uncertain. During 2004, Fran's had $950,000 of instalment sales. The related cost of goods sold was $570,000. The required payments for the instalment contracts and the actual payments received are as follows:

Calculate gross profit—instalment method.
(SO 3) AP

Year	Contract Payments	Actual Payments
2004	$125,000	$125,000
2005	200,000	200,000
2006	200,000	200,000
2007	200,000	175,000
2008	225,000	250,000
	$950,000	$950,000

Instructions

(a) Calculate the amount of gross profit to be recognized for each year.
(b) What do you think would happen for accounting purposes if the actual payments didn't equal the contract payments? That is, assume that the company collected only $200,000 in 2008 rather than the $250,000 given in the problem.

P11–12A Under GAAP, no separate disclosure is required on the income statement for the cost of goods sold. Because this disclosure is not specifically required, less than half of Canadian companies that produce reports disclose their cost of goods sold separately on their income statement. Most companies include it with other expenses, as **Sears Canada Inc.** did in its income statement for the year ended December 31, 2005:

Cost of merchandise sold, operating, administrative, and selling expenses $6.2 billion

Instructions

(a) In your opinion, why does Sears not report its cost of merchandise sold separately on its income statement? Comment on how this disclosure does, or does not, meet the objective of financial reporting.
(b) What are the two constraints in accounting? Does either of these constraints likely have an impact on Sears' reporting policy for its cost of merchandise sold?

Margin note: Comment on objective of financial reporting and accounting constraints. (SO 1, 4) C

Problems: Set B

Margin note: Comment on qualitative characteristics of accounting information. (SO 1) C

P11–1B Nortel Networks Corporation, Canada's telecommunications giant with operations in more than 150 countries, has an inconsistent history. After reporting losses for six consecutive years, Nortel finally reported net income in 2003. However, shortly after that, in March 2004, it was revealed that significant accounting irregularities had occurred, and in January 2005 Nortel released revised financial statements for 2003, 2002, and 2001. In March 2006, it announced that it had discovered that revenue had been recognized in the wrong periods and that the company would have to once again restate its financial statements.

Instructions

Explain how the revision of financial statements for prior periods affects the qualitative characteristics of accounting information.

Margin note: Identify principle or assumption violated and prepare entries. (SO 2, 3) AN

P11–2B Czyz and Ng are accountants at Kwick Kopy Printers. They are having disagreements over the following transactions from the calendar year 2007:

1. Kwick Kopy bought equipment for $60,000, including installation costs. The equipment has a useful life of five years. Kwick Kopy amortizes equipment using the double declining-balance method. "Since the equipment as installed in our system cannot be removed without considerable damage, it will have no resale value. It should not be amortized but, instead, expensed immediately," Czyz argues.
2. Amortization for the year was $38,000. Since net income is expected to be low this year, Czyz suggests deferring amortization to a year when there is more net income.
3. Kwick Kopy purchased equipment at a fire sale for $18,000. The equipment would normally have cost $25,000. Czyz believes that the following entry should be made:

Equipment	25,000	
Cash		18,000
Gain		7,000

4. Czyz says that Kwick Kopy should carry its furnishings on the balance sheet at their liquidation value, which is $20,000 less than cost.

5. Kwick Kopy rented office space for one year, effective October 1, 2007. Six months of rent at $2,000 per month was paid in advance. Czyz believes that the following entry should be made on October 1:

Rent Expense	12,000	
Cash		12,000

6. Land that cost $41,000 was appraised at $49,000. Czyz suggests the following journal entry:

Land	8,000	
Gain on Appreciation of Land		8,000

7. On December 15, Kwick Kopy signed a contract with a customer to provide copying services for a six-month period at a rate of $1,000 per month starting January 1, 2008. The customer will pay on a monthly basis. Czyz argues that the contract should be recorded in December because the customer has always paid its bills on time in the past. The customer is legally obligated to pay the monthly amount because a contract has been signed. Czyz believes the following entry should be recorded:

Accounts Receivable	6,000	
Service Revenue		6,000

Ng disagrees with Czyz on each of the situations.

Instructions

(a) For each transaction, indicate why Ng disagrees. Identify the accounting principle or assumption that would be violated if Czyz's suggestions were used.
(b) Prepare the correct journal entry to record each transaction.

P11–3B Business transactions for Durkovitch Company from the current year follow:

1. An order for $70,000 was received from a customer for products on hand. This order is to be shipped on January 9 next year. The following entry was made:

Identify assumption or principle and correct entries. (SO 2, 3) AN

Accounts Receivable	70,000	
Sales		70,000

2. Because of a "flood sale," equipment worth $300,000 was acquired at a cost of $250,000. The following entry was made:

Equipment	300,000	
Cash		250,000
Gain on Acquisition of Equipment		50,000

3. Because the general level of prices decreased during the current year, Durkovitch determined that there was a $40,000 overstatement of amortization expense on its equipment. The following entry was made:

Accumulated Amortization	40,000	
Amortization Expense		40,000

4. The president of Durkovitch Company, B. Durkovitch, used his expense account to purchase a pre-owned Mercedes-Benz for his personal use only. The following entry was made:

Automobiles	68,000	
Cash		68,000

5. Land was purchased on April 30 for $200,000. On December 31, the land would have cost $220,000, so the following entry was made:

Land	20,000	
Gain on Appreciation of Land		20,000

Instructions

(a) In each of the situations above, identify the assumption or principle that has been violated, if any.
(b) Prepare the journal entry to correct each incorrect transaction identified in (a).

Identify point of revenue and expense recognition.
(SO 3) C

P11–4B Santa's Christmas Tree Farm grows pine, fir, and spruce trees. The company cuts and sells the trees for cash during the Christmas season. Most of the trees are exported to the U.S. The remaining trees are sold to local tree lot operators.

It normally takes about 12 years for a tree to grow to a good size. The average selling price for a mature tree is $24. The owner of Santa's Christmas Tree Farm believes that the company should recognize revenue at the rate of $2 a year ($24 ÷ 12 years) for each tree that it cuts. The biggest cost of this business is the cost of fertilizing, pruning, and maintaining the trees over the 12-year period. These costs average $22 a tree and the owner believes they should also be spread over the 12-year period.

Instructions

(a) Do you agree with the proposed revenue recognition policy for Santa's Christmas Tree Farms? Explain why or why not. Use the revenue recognition guidelines to explain your argument for when the revenue should be recognized for this tree-farming business.

(b) When should the cost of fertilizing, pruning, and maintaining the trees be recognized? Explain.

Calculate revenue at various points of recognition.
(SO 3) AP

P11–5B On February 11, 2008, Security Equipment was awarded a $3-million contract for the development of a new security system for a nuclear plant. Work began on April 1 and estimated costs of completion at the contract date are $2.25 million over a two-year period. By December 31, 2008, Security Equipment's year end, costs of $900,000 have been incurred. Contract payments totalling $1 million have been collected so far.

Instructions

(a) Security Equipment is considering using one of the following three points of revenue recognition. Define and describe each of the following:
  1. Point of sale
  2. Percentage-of-completion
  3. Completed-contract

(b) Calculate the amount of revenue that would be recognized in fiscal 2008 for Security Equipment under each of the above points of revenue recognition.

(c) Which method would you recommend that Security Equipment use? Explain why.

Calculate revenue, expense, and gross profit—percentage-of-completion and completed-contract methods.
(SO 3) AP

P11–6B Cosky Construction Company is involved in a long-term construction contract to build an office building. The estimated cost is $20 million and the contract price is $28 million. Additional information follows:

Year	Cash Collections	Actual Costs Incurred
2005	$ 4,500,000	$ 3,000,000
2006	10,000,000	9,000,000
2007	7,000,000	5,000,000
2008	6,500,000	3,000,000
	$28,000,000	$20,000,000

The project is completed in 2008 and all cash collections related to the contract have been received.

Instructions

(a) Prepare a schedule to determine the revenue, expense, and gross profit for each year of the contract, using the percentage-of-completion method.

(b) How would your answer in (a) change if Cosky Construction used the completed-contract method rather than the percentage-of-completion method?

Revise revenue, expense, and gross profit—percentage-of-completion and completed-contract methods.
(SO 3) AP

P11–7B Refer to the data in P11–6B for Cosky Construction. Assume instead that the actual costs were $7 million in 2007. Because costs were higher than expected, Cosky revised its total estimated costs from $20 million to $24 million at the end of 2007. Actual costs incurred in 2008 were $5 million. All other data are unchanged.

Instructions

(a) Assuming Cosky Construction uses the percentage-of-completion method, prepare a revised schedule to determine the revenue, expense, and gross profit for each year of the long-term construction contract.

(b) Assuming Cosky Construction uses the completed-contract method, prepare a revised schedule to determine the revenue, expense, and gross profit for each year of the long-term construction contract.

(c) Which method would you recommend Cosky Construction use? Explain why.

P11–8B Kamloops Construction Company has a contract for the construction of a new health and fitness centre. It is accounting for this project using the percentage-of-completion method. The contract amount is $2.5 million and the cost of construction is expected to total $1.4 million. The actual costs incurred are as follows for the three-year life of the project:

Calculate revenue, expense, and gross profit—percentage-of-completion method.
(SO 3) AP

Year	Actual Costs Incurred
2006	$ 560,000
2007	490,000
2008	350,000
	$1,400,000

Instructions

(a) Calculate the amount of revenue, expense, and gross profit to be recognized in each year.

(b) What if Kamloops Construction receives more cash in each of the first two years than the amount it has recognized as revenue? Is it still appropriate to recognize the amount of revenue calculated in (a)? Explain.

P11–9B Aasen Construction was hired to build an apartment building for Mattson Management Company for $2.5 million. Aasen's cost to construct the apartment building was $1.6 million. Additional information follows:

Calculate gross profit—percentage-of-completion and instalment methods.
(SO 3) AP

Year	Cash Collections	Actual Costs Incurred
2007	$1,000,000	$ 650,000
2008	1,500,000	950,000
	$2,500,000	$1,600,000

Instructions

(a) Prepare a schedule to determine the gross profit for each year, using the percentage-of-completion method.

(b) Prepare a schedule to determine the gross profit for each year, using the instalment method.

(c) Which method is more appropriate for Aasen Construction to use? Explain your reasoning.

P11–10B Turin Company reported the following instalment sales information:

Calculate gross profit—instalment sales.
(SO 3) AP

	2007	2008
Instalment sales	$950,000	$750,000
Cost of instalment sales	570,000	450,000
Cash collections on 2007 sales	285,000	285,000
Cash collections on 2008 sales	0	300,000

Instructions

(a) Prepare a schedule to determine the gross profit to be recognized for each year, assuming that collectibility is expected and any uncollectible amounts can be reasonably estimated.

(b) Prepare a schedule to determine the gross profit to be recognized for each year, assuming that collectibility is uncertain.

Calculate gross profit and comment—instalment method.
(SO 3) AP

P11–11B   Dave's Deep Discount Furniture Store makes many of its sales on long-term instalment contracts. It accounts for these using the instalment method because collectibility is uncertain. During 2004, Dave's had $850,000 of instalment sales. The related cost of goods sold was $527,000. The required payments on the instalment contracts and the actual payments received are as follows:

Year	Contract Payments	Actual Payments
2004	$170,000	$170,000
2005	200,000	200,000
2006	200,000	210,000
2007	200,000	170,000
2008	80,000	100,000
	$850,000	$850,000

Instructions

(a) Calculate the amount of gross profit to be recognized in each year.
(b) What do you think would happen for accounting purposes if the actual payments didn't equal the contract payments? That is, assume that the company collected $80,000 in 2008 rather than the $100,000 given in the problem.

Comment on objective of financial reporting and accounting constraints.
(SO 1, 4) C

P11–12B   A friend of yours, Ryan Konotopsky, has come to you for some answers about financial statements. Ryan tells you that he is thinking about opening a movie theatre in his home town. Before doing so, he wants to find out how much he could expect to make from food concessions and ticket sales. He wants to know what portion of ticket sales he could expect for children, youths, and seniors, who pay less, versus adults, who pay the highest admission rate. He also wants to know how much profit he would make on ticket sales versus sales at the concession stands, and the average wage per employee.

Ryan knows that **Empire Theatres Limited** operates in Atlantic Canada and is owned by **Empire Company Limited**. He couldn't find any financial information about Empire Theatres on the Internet but was able to download Empire Company Limited's annual report. He read through the entire report and learned that the financial results for Empire Theatres are reported as "other operations" on Empire Company's financial statements. The only information separately reported for Empire Theatres is revenue of $74.4 million and operating income of $9.5 million for the year ended May 7, 2005. Ryan is disillusioned because he cannot find any other details about Empire Theatres. He has come to you for explanations.

Instructions

(a) In your opinion, why does Empire Company not report any additional information about Empire Theatres separately in its financial statements? Comment on how this disclosure does, or does not, meet the objective of financial reporting.
(b) What are the two major constraints in accounting? What impact do these constraints appear to have on the financial reporting of Empire Company?

Continuing Cookie Chronicle

(*Note:* This is a continuation of the Cookie Chronicle from Chapters 1 through 10.)

Natalie's biggest competitor is Trial Appliances. Trial Appliances sells a fine European mixer that is similar to the one that customers can buy from Cookie Creations. Natalie estimates that Trial Appliances sells twice as many mixers as she does. Trial Appliances also sells microwaves, dishwashers, washing machines, and refrigerators. Natalie believes that Trial Appliances sells so many mixers because it sells all of its appliances on an extended payment plan.

Natalie knows that Trial Appliances sells its mixers for $1,100. She also knows that under the extended payment plan approximately $275 (25%) is collected in the year the mixer is sold, $550 (50%) is collected the year after the appliance is sold, and the remaining $275 (25%) is collected in the third year. Trial Appliances sells approximately 65 mixers a year and has an average gross profit margin of 50%.

Natalie comes to you to find out how to account for revenues when mixers are sold on an extended payment plan. She would really like to generate more sales revenues and cash flow. Based on her discussions with the sales manager at Trial Appliances, she believes that she could sell more mixers if she offered her customers the option of paying over an extended period of time.

Natalie asks you the following questions:

1. I currently sell 32 mixers a year at $1,050 apiece. My cost of goods sold averages $566 per mixer. What is my gross profit margin?
2. What are some of the advantages and disadvantages of giving my customers the option of paying through an extended payment plan?

Instructions

(a) Answer Natalie's questions.
(b) Calculate the amount of gross profit to be recorded in years 1, 2, and 3 if Cookie Creations decides to use an extended payment plan that is similar to what Trial Appliances offers. Assume that 32 mixers are sold in year 1 and that all the customers use the extended payment plan.

Cumulative Coverage—Chapters 6 to 11

Johan Company and Nordlund Company are competing businesses. Both began operations six years ago and they are quite similar. The current balance sheet data for the two companies are as follows:

	Johan Company	Nordlund Company
Cash	$ 70,300	$ 48,400
Accounts receivable	309,700	312,500
Allowance for doubtful accounts	(13,600)	0
Merchandise inventory	463,900	520,200
Property, plant, and equipment	255,300	257,300
Accumulated amortization	(112,650)	(189,850)
Total assets	$972,950	$948,550
Current liabilities	$440,200	$436,500
Long-term liabilities	78,000	80,000
Total liabilities	518,200	516,500
Owner's equity	454,750	432,050
Total liabilities and owner's equity	$972,950	$948,550

You have been hired as a consultant to do a review of the two companies. Your goal is to determine which one is in a stronger financial position. Your review of their financial statements quickly reveals that the two companies have not followed the same accounting principles. The differences, and your conclusions, are summarized below:

1. Johan Company has had good experience in estimating its uncollectible accounts. A review shows that the amount of its write-offs each year has been quite close to the allowances the company provided.

Nordlund Company has been somewhat slow to recognize its uncollectible accounts. Based on an aging analysis and review of its accounts receivable, it is estimated that $20,000 of its existing accounts will become uncollectible.

2. Johan Company has determined the cost of its merchandise inventory using the LIFO cost flow assumption. The result is that its inventory appears on the balance sheet at an amount that is slightly below its current replacement cost. Based on a detailed physical examination of its merchandise on hand, the current replacement cost of its inventory is estimated at $477,000.

Nordlund Company has used the FIFO cost flow assumption of valuing its merchandise inventory. The result is that its ending inventory appears on the balance sheet at an amount that is close to its current replacement cost.

3. Johan Company estimated a useful life of 12 years and a residual value of $30,000 for its property, plant, and equipment, and has been amortizing them on a straight-line basis.

Nordlund Company has the same type of property, plant, and equipment. However, it estimated a useful life of 10 years and a residual value of $10,000. It has been amortizing its property, plant, and equipment using the double declining-balance method.

Based on engineering studies of these types of property, plant, and equipment, you conclude that Nordlund's estimates and method for calculating amortization are more appropriate.

Instructions

(a) Where would you find the above information on the two companies' accounting principles? Be specific about what information would be available and where you would find it.
(b) Using similar accounting principles for both companies, revise the balance sheets presented above.
(c) Has preparing revised statements in (b) improved the quality of the accounting information for the two companies?
(d) Write a report for your client on which company is in a stronger financial position.

BROADENING YOUR PERSPECTIVE

Financial Reporting and Analysis

Financial Reporting Problem

BYP11–1 Refer to the Notes to Consolidated Financial Statements for **The Forzani Group Ltd.**, in Appendix A.

Instructions

(a) Subsection (h) of Note 2, Significant Accounting Policies, describes Forzani's revenue recognition policy. Does this policy sound reasonable to you, given the types of goods Forzani sells?
(b) Subsection (i) of Note 2, Significant Accounting Policies, describes Forzani's treatment of its store opening expenses. Explain how the company's treatment of these expenses relates, or does not relate, to the matching principle. Can you think of an alternative treatment for these expenses?
(c) Note 13, Contingencies and Guarantees, discloses several commitments by the company that are not recorded in the financial statements. Do you think this additional disclosure was necessary? Explain why or why not, referring to the appropriate generally accepted accounting principle(s) in your answer.

Interpreting Financial Statements

BYP11–2 Today, companies must compete in a global economy. For example, Canada's oldest candy company, **Ganong Bros., Limited**, which has been making chocolates since 1873, must compete with **Nestlé S.A.**, among others. Although Nestlé is best known for its chocolates and confections, this Swiss company is also the largest food company in the world.

Comparing companies such as Ganong and Nestlé can be challenging not only because of their size differences, but also because Ganong uses Canadian accounting principles and Nestlé uses international accounting principles. Consider the following excerpt from the notes to Nestlé's financial statements:

> **NESTLÉ S.A.**
> Notes to the Financial Statements (partial)
> December 31, 2005
>
> **Accounting policies**
> **Accounting convention and accounting standards**
> The Consolidated Financial Statements comply with International Financial Reporting Standards (IFRS) issued by the International Accounting Standards Board (IASB) and with the Interpretations issued by the International Financial Reporting Interpretations Committee (IFRIC).
> The accounts have been prepared on an accruals basis and under the historical cost convention, unless stated otherwise.

Instructions

Discuss the implications that Nestlé's (a) larger size with a more diversified product line, and (b) use of international financial reporting standards might have (positively or negatively) on your ability to compare Ganong to Nestlé.

Critical Thinking

Collaborative Learning Activity

Note to instructor: Additional instructions and material for this group activity can be found on the Instructor Resource Site.

BYP11–3 Recognition and measurement criteria are major components of the conceptual framework of accounting. In this group activity, you will apply your knowledge by choosing the assumption, principle, or constraint that applies in a situation and then explaining your choice to your classmates.

Instructions

(a) Look around the classroom at the signs taped on the wall by your instructor. After reviewing the accounting situation presented by your instructor, move to the sign that applies. Once all students have chosen a place, discuss with those in your group why you believe your choice is correct. The instructor will randomly select a student in each group to explain to everyone in the class why the members of the group selected their position. You may change groups if you are convinced by another group's explanation.

(b) Repeat the above activity for each situation presented by the instructor.

Study Aids:
Working in Groups

Communication Activity

BYP11–4 The **Algonquin College of Applied Arts and Technology** received $8.5 million from the Province of Ontario in the year ended March 31, 2003, to construct a new Transportation Technology Centre. The new building was completed in October 2004 at a cost of $6.8 million.

One of the difficulties in receiving provincial grants is to match expenses against revenues in the right fiscal year. For example, the funding for the new building was received in fiscal 2003 but was not all spent until fiscal 2004. Tuition fees from the increased capacity in the School of Transportation and Building Trades did not start to be collected until 2005.

Study Aids:
Writing Handbook

Instructions

Write a letter that answers the following questions:

(a) Why is the matching principle important in accounting for Algonquin College's revenues and expenses?

(b) How should the college account for the $8.5 million it received to build the new Transportation Technology Centre? In what period(s) should the college match the revenues and expenses related to this project?

(c) Does it matter that the college received $8.5 million but only spent $6.8 million? What do you think it will use the excess funding for?

(d) Give some examples of a situation in which the matching principle might be difficult to apply at your own college or university.

Ethics Case

Study Aids:
Ethics in Accounting

BYP11–5   When the CICA issues new accounting recommendations, the required implementation date (the date when a company has to start using the recommendations) is usually 12 months or more after the date of publication. Nevertheless, early implementation is encouraged.

Carol DesChenes, an accountant at Grocery Online, discusses with her vice-president of finance the need for early implementation of a recently issued recommendation. She says it will result in a much fairer presentation of the company's financial position. When the vice-president of finance determines that early implementation will have a negative impact on reported net income for the year, he strongly discourages Carol from implementing the recommendation until it is required.

Instructions

(a) Who are the stakeholders in this situation?

(b) What, if any, are the ethical considerations in this situation?

(c) What could Carol gain by supporting early implementation? Who might be affected by the decision against early implementation?

ANSWERS TO CHAPTER QUESTIONS

Answers to Accounting in Action Insight Questions

Business Insight, p. 573

Q: How did Air Canada justify using the going concern assumption when it was so uncertain that the company would continue operating?

A: Air Canada used the going concern assumption because it was in the process of developing a plan to restructure its operations. It expected that the company would continue to operate in the foreseeable future.

Across the Organization Insight, p. 576

Q: If bonuses are based only on revenue, how might this make employees less motivated to do what is best for the company?

A: Employees might do everything they can to manipulate income when revenue is recognized so that the company records and reports higher revenues and the employees get larger bonuses. A more balanced bonus structure will help eliminate any motivation to act against the best interests of the company.

International Insight, p. 584

Q: What benefits will result when publicly-traded Canadian companies switch to international financial reporting standards?

A: Using international financial reporting standards will make it easier for foreigners to read and understand Canadian financial statements, and ultimately be more confident in investing in Canadian companies.

Answer to Forzani Review It Question 3, p. 584

Ernst & Young, Forzani's auditors, state that the financial statements are presented fairly, in all material respects, in accordance with Canadian generally accepted accounting principles.

Answers to Self-Study Questions

1. b   2. d   3. c   4. a   5. b   6. d   7. b   8. c   9. c   10. c

Remember to go back to the Navigator Box at the beginning of the chapter to check off your completed work.

Before studying this chapter, you should understand or, if necessary, review:

a. The cost principle of accounting. (Ch. 1, p. 8)

b. The different forms of business organization. (Ch. 1, p. 9–11)

c. The statement of owner's equity. (Ch. 1, p. 23)

d. How to make closing entries. (Ch. 4, pp. 164–169)

e. The steps in the accounting cycle. (Ch. 4, pp. 171–172)

f. The classified balance sheet. (Ch. 4, pp. 175–180)

Partners Work Together for Success

SASKATOON, Sask.—When chartered accountants Glen Bailey and Clare Heagy started their partnership back in 1983, they knew that working together would be good for both them and their clients. Mr. Heagy had been a partner in a national firm and had clients who stayed loyal to him; Mr. Bailey was just starting out but had specialized training in taxation. By combining their talents and resources, they soon built a strong practice that served a wide range of Saskatchewan businesses.

Today there are five partners and a staff of 17. Mr. Bailey says the firm is successful because there is a clear understanding of what a partnership requires and everyone pulls their weight.

"When we got started, we drew up an agreement that basically covered how the business would be operated, splitting of income, draws of money, and provisions around death, disability, or withdrawal of partners," he recalls. The agreement also noted that Mr. Heagy had brought in the initial client base: as compensation for this, a provision stated that he would be paid a fee in addition to the value of his assets if he left the partnership.

A few years later, in 1988, Richard Altrogge joined the partnership as an associate. "After a while, we admitted him as a junior partner under a system that allowed him to become an equal partner by paying a specified amount of cash when his billings reached a certain percentage of total revenues," says Mr. Bailey.

The firm was a three-way partnership for several years. When Mr. Heagy retired in 1998, Richard Matchett became a junior partner. He had begun working for the firm as an employee, and as recently as 2006 achieved equal status with Mr. Bailey and Mr. Altrogge.

The firm brought in another partner in 2001 in Alan Ashdown and added James Schemenauer more recently. Each new partner's interest was determined by his client billings compared to the firm's total. When they were first admitted as partners, they were guaranteed a minimum share of the firm's income. This was to recognize that while they were each growing their own practice, they were also working on the firm's other client files.

In 2002, the province of Saskatchewan passed legislation that allows professionals to incorporate. The partnership structure changed in response. "We each set up our own professional corporation and rolled our interests in the partnership into those," explains Mr. Bailey. "We're still a partnership, but technically we're a partnership of corporations." The firm is now called Heagy Bailey Altrogge Matchett LLP.

"A partnership is much like a marriage," concludes Mr. Bailey. "You're going to have problems, but if all the partners do their part and work together, you have the best chance of success."

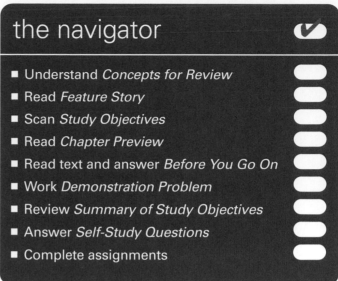

the navigator

- Understand *Concepts for Review*
- Read *Feature Story*
- Scan *Study Objectives*
- Read *Chapter Preview*
- Read text and answer *Before You Go On*
- Work *Demonstration Problem*
- Review *Summary of Study Objectives*
- Answer *Self-Study Questions*
- Complete assignments

chapter 12
Accounting for Partnerships

study objectives >>

After studying this chapter, you should be able to:

1. Describe the characteristics of the partnership form of business organization.
2. Account for partnership transactions and allocate income.
3. Prepare partnership financial statements.
4. Prepare the entries to record the admission of a partner.
5. Prepare the entries to record the withdrawal of a partner.
6. Prepare the entries to record the liquidation of a partnership.

the navigator

It is not surprising that Glen Bailey and Clare Heagy decided to use the partnership form of organization when they started their accounting practice. They saw an opportunity to combine their expertise and better leverage their resources. In this chapter, we will discuss why the partnership form of organization is often chosen. We will also explain the major issues in accounting for partnerships.

The chapter is organized as follows:

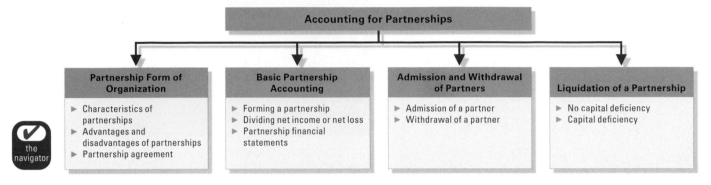

Partnership Form of Organization

study objective 1

Describe the characteristics of the partnership form of business organization.

All provinces in Canada have a *Partnership Act* that sets out the basic rules for forming and operating partnerships. These acts define a **partnership** as a relationship between people who do business with the intention of making a profit. This does not necessarily mean that there must be a profit—just that profit is the objective. Partnerships are common in professions such as accounting, advertising, law, and medicine. Professional partnerships can vary in size from two partners to thousands.

Characteristics of Partnerships

The main characteristics of the partnership form of business organization are shown in Illustration 12-1. They are explained after the illustration.

Illustration 12-1 ▶

Partnership characteristics

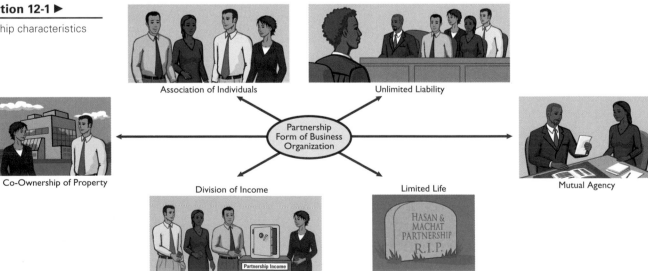

Association of Individuals

The association of two or more individuals in a partnership can be based on an act as simple as a handshake. However, it is much better to have a legal, written agreement that outlines the rights and obligations of the partners, as in the feature story. Partners who have not put their agreement in writing have found that the absence of a written agreement can some-times cause later difficulties. In fact, some *Partnership Acts* state that if you receive a share of income from a business, you will be considered a partner in the business unless there is contrary evidence. If there is no formal agreement that says who the partners of a business are, you may be part of a partnership without knowing it!

A partnership is a legal entity for certain purposes. For instance, property (land, build-ings, and equipment) can be owned in the name of the partnership. The firm can sue or be sued. A partnership is also an accounting entity for financial reporting purposes. Thus, the personal assets, liabilities, and transactions of the partners are kept separate from the ac-counting records of the partnership, just as they are in a proprietorship.

However, a partnership is not taxed as a separate entity. It must file an information tax re-turn that reports the partnership's net income and each partner's share of that net income. Each partner must then report his or her share of the partnership income on their personal income tax returns. The partner's income is taxed at his or her personal income tax rate, and does not depend on how much money the partner withdrew from the partnership during the year.

Co-Ownership of Property

Partnership assets are owned jointly by the partners. If the partnership is dissolved, an asset does not legally return to the partner who originally contributed it. The assets are normally sold and the partners share any gain or loss on disposition according to their income ratios. After partnership liabilities are paid, each partner then has a claim on any cash that re-mains: the claim is equal to the balance in the partner's capital account.

Similarly, if, in doing business, a partner invests a building in the partnership that is valued at $100,000 and the building is later sold at a gain of $20,000, that partner does not receive the entire gain. The gain becomes part of the partnership net income, which is shared among the partners, as described in the next section.

Division of Income

Just as property is co-owned, so is partnership net income (or net loss). The partners specify how the partnership net income (loss) will be divided when they form the partnership, as they did in the feature story. If the division is not specified, net income (loss) is assumed to be shared equally. We will learn more about dividing partnership income in a later section of this chapter.

Limited Life

A partnership does not have an unlimited life. Any change in ownership ends the existing partnership. There is a **partnership dissolution** whenever a partner withdraws or a new partner is admitted. When a partnership is dissolved, this does not necessarily mean that the business ends. If the continuing partners agree, operations can continue without any interruption by forming a new partnership.

Mutual Agency

Mutual agency means that each partner acts for the partnership when he or she does part-nership business. The action of any partner is binding on all other partners—in other words, the action cannot be cancelled. This is true even when partners exceed their authority, as long as the act looks appropriate for the partnership. For example, a partner of an accounting firm who purchases a building that is suitable for the business creates a binding contract in the name of the partnership. On the other hand, if a partner in a law firm decides to buy a snowmobile for the partnership, the act would not be binding on the partnership, because the purchase is unrelated to the business.

Unlimited Liability

Each partner is jointly and severally (individually) liable for all partnership liabilities. If one partner incurs a liability, the other partners are also responsible for it. For repayment, creditors first have claims on the partnership assets. If there are not enough assets to pay back the creditors, however, they can then claim the personal assets of any partner, regardless of that partner's equity in the partnership. Because each partner is responsible for all the debts of the partnership, each partner is said to have unlimited liability.

Unlimited liability and mutual agency can combine for disastrous results. An unethical or incompetent partner can commit the partnership to a deal that eventually bankrupts the partnership. The creditors may then be able to claim the partners' personal assets—the assets of all the partners, not just those of the partner who made the bad deal. As Mr. Bailey says in the feature story, "A partnership is much like a marriage." Consequently, an individual must be extremely cautious in choosing a partner.

Because of concerns about unlimited liability, there are now special forms of partnership organization that modify liability. These include limited partnerships and limited liability partnerships, discussed in the next two sections.

Limited Partnerships (LP). In a **limited partnership**, one or more of the partners have unlimited liability. This type of partner is called a general partner. A general partner normally contributes work and experience to the partnership and is authorized to manage and represent the partnership. The general partner's liability for the debts of the partnership is unlimited.

In addition to the general partner(s), one or more partners have limited liability for the debts of the partnership. This type of partner is called a limited partner. Limited partners normally give cash or assets to the partnership, but not services. The amount of debt that the limited partner is liable for in the partnership is limited to the amount of capital that he or she contributed to the partnership. In other words, a limited partner's personal assets cannot be sold to repay any partnership debt that is more than the amount that he or she contributed to the partnership.

A limited partnership is identified in its name with the words "Limited Partnership" or the abbreviation "LP." Limited partnerships are normally used by businesses that offer income tax shelters for investors, such as real estate investment trusts (REIT), rental properties, and sports ventures.

For example, the Edmonton Oilers of the National Hockey League are owned by a limited partnership called the Edmonton Investors Group Limited Partnership. In this type of partnership, sports fans (or investors) contribute money that they can use as a deduction on their personal income tax returns. With more than thirty limited partners, the Edmonton Investors Group Limited Partnership is the largest ownership group in the NHL. Among the four major North American sports leagues, only the Green Bay Packers of the National Football League have a larger ownership group.

Limited Liability Partnerships (LLP). Most professionals such as lawyers, doctors, and accountants form a **limited liability partnership** or "LLP." In the feature story, Heagy Bailey Altrogge Matchett operates as a limited liability partnership. The largest LLP in the world is PricewaterhouseCoopers. With more than 8,000 partners in 148 countries, this accounting and professional services firm earns fees of more than U.S. $20 billion annually.

A limited liability partnership is designed to protect innocent partners from the acts of other partners that result in lawsuits against the partnership. That is, partners in an LLP continue to have unlimited liability for their own negligence but have limited liability for other partners' negligence. In addition to being liable for their own actions, partners are also liable for the actions of employees who they directly supervise and control.

ACCOUNTING IN ACTION ► Ethics Insight

The legal liability of limited partners is being tested in the courts in investor lawsuits against Enron. Enron used several special purpose "partnership" entities to allegedly hide its debt and falsely increase its income. One lawsuit argues that limited partners in these partnerships should share liability with the general partners for the Enron disaster. In some precedent-setting court cases, individuals "who knowingly participate with a fiduciary in a breach of trust" have been found "liable to the beneficiary for any damage caused thereby." While there are also observers who believe that the limited partners should not be held liable, everyone agrees that in the Enron case all sorts of legal issues will be tested in the courts.

Source: Ronald Fink, "Partnership Liability: Enron's Domino Effect," *CFO Magazine*, March 1, 2002.

? **In your opinion, should the limited partners who invested in Enron's special purpose entities be liable to Enron's shareholders?**

Advantages and Disadvantages of Partnerships

Why do people choose partnerships? Often, it is to combine the skills and resources of two or more individuals. For example, the partners of Heagy Bailey Altrogge Matchett are able to work together and share office space and accounting knowledge. They can also divide among themselves different areas of responsibility and expertise—assurance, taxation, and business valuation, for example.

A partnership is easily formed and is controlled by fewer government regulations and restrictions than a corporation is. Also, decisions can be made quickly on important matters that affect the firm. This is also true in a proprietorship, but not in a corporation, where some decisions have to be approved by the board of directors.

Partnerships also have some disadvantages: mutual agency, limited life, and unlimited liability in general partnerships. Unlimited liability is particularly troublesome. Many individuals fear they may lose not only their initial investment, but also their personal assets if those assets are needed to pay partnership creditors. As a result, partnerships often have difficulty getting large amounts of investment capital. That is one reason why the largest businesses in Canada are corporations, not partnerships.

The advantages and disadvantages of the general partnership form of business organization are summarized below:

Advantages	Disadvantages
Combines skills and resources of two or more individuals	Mutual agency
Easily formed	Limited life
Fewer government regulations and restrictions	Unlimited liability
Easier decision-making	

Partnership Agreement

Ideally, when two or more individuals agree to organize a partnership, their agreement should be expressed as a written contract. Called a **partnership agreement**, this contract contains such basic information as the name and main location of the firm, the purpose of the business, and the date of inception. In addition, relationships among the partners must be specified, such as:

1. The names and capital contributions of partners
2. The rights and duties of partners
3. The basis for sharing net income or net loss
4. Provisions for a withdrawal of assets
5. Procedures for submitting disputes to arbitration
6. Procedures for the withdrawal, or addition, of a partner
7. The rights and duties of surviving partners if a partner dies
8. Procedures for the liquidation of the partnership

As discussed in our feature story, the Heagy Bailey Altrogge Matchett partnership has a detailed partnership agreement that covers all of these areas. The importance of a written contract cannot be overemphasized. If there is no partnership agreement, the provisions of the *Partnership Act* will apply, and they may not be what the partners want. The partnership agreement should be written with care so that it considers all possible situations, contingencies, and future disagreements between the partners.

BEFORE YOU GO ON . . .

▶Review It

1. What are the main characteristics of a partnership?
2. How can partners limit their liability?
3. What are the main advantages and disadvantages of a partnership?
4. What are the major items in a partnership agreement?
5. The Forzani Group Ltd. originally started as a partnership when Calgary Stampeder John Forzani and three of his teammates (two of them were his brothers) started Forzani's Locker Room in 1974. What could be the reason that it changed to the corporate form of organization in 1993? The answer to this question is at the end of the chapter.

Related exercise material: BE12–1 and E12–1.

Basic Partnership Accounting

We now turn to the basic accounting for partnerships. The major accounting issues relate to forming the partnership, dividing the income or loss, and preparing financial statements.

Forming a Partnership

Each partner's initial investment in a partnership is entered in the partnership records. These investments should be recorded at the fair market value of the assets at the date of their transfer to the partnership. The values given must be agreed to by all of the partners.

To illustrate, assume that M. Gan and K. Sin combine their proprietorships on January 2 to start a partnership named Interactive Software. Gan and Sin each have the following assets before forming the partnership:

	M. Gan		K. Sin	
	Book Value	Market Value	Book Value	Market Value
Cash	$ 8,000	$ 8,000	$ 9,000	$ 9,000
Accounts receivable			4,000	4,000
Allowance for doubtful accounts			(700)	(1,000)
Office equipment	5,000	4,000		
Accumulated amortization	(2,000)			
	$11,000	$12,000	$12,300	$12,000

The entries to record the investments are:

		Investment of M. Gan		
Jan. 2	Cash		8,000	
	Office Equipment		4,000	
	M. Gan, Capital			12,000
	To record investment of Gan.			
		Investment of K. Sin		
2	Cash		9,000	
	Accounts Receivable		4,000	
	Allowance for Doubtful Accounts			1,000
	K. Sin, Capital			12,000
	To record investment of Sin.			

A	=	L	+	PE
+8,000				+12,000
+4,000				

↑ Cash flows: +8,000

A	=	L	+	PE
+9,000				+12,000
+4,000				
−1,000				

↑ Cash flows: +9,000

Note that neither the original cost of Gan's office equipment ($5,000) nor its book value ($5,000 − $2,000) is recorded by the partnership. Instead, the equipment is recorded at its fair market value of $4,000. Because the equipment has not yet been used by the partnership, there is no accumulated amortization.

In contrast, Sin's gross claims on customers ($4,000) are carried into the partnership. The allowance for doubtful accounts is adjusted to $1,000 to arrive at a net realizable value of $3,000. A partnership may start with an allowance for doubtful accounts, because it will continue to collect existing accounts receivable and some of these are expected to be uncollectible. In addition, this procedure maintains the control and subsidiary relationship between Accounts Receivable and the accounts receivable subsidiary ledger that we learned about in Chapter 8.

After the partnership has been formed, the accounting for transactions is similar to the accounting for any other type of business organization. For example, all transactions with outside parties, such as the performance of services and payment for them, should be recorded in the same way for a partnership as for a proprietorship.

The steps in the accounting cycle that are described in Chapter 4 for a proprietorship are also used for a partnership. For example, a partnership journalizes and posts transactions, prepares a trial balance, journalizes and posts adjusting entries, and prepares an adjusted trial balance. However, there are minor differences in journalizing and posting closing entries and in preparing financial statements, as explained in the following sections. The differences occur because there is more than one owner.

Helpful hint The cost principle applies. Cash and the fair market value of noncash assets are recorded at the date of acquisition. The fair market value is what the assets would have cost if they had been purchased at that time.

Animated Tutorials
and Videos:
Accounting Cycle Tutorial

Dividing Net Income or Net Loss

Partnership net income or net loss is shared equally unless the partnership agreement indicates a different division. Usually, the same basis of division is used for both net income and net losses, and it is typically called the **income ratio**. It is also known as the income and loss ratio, or the profit and loss ratio. A partner's share of net income or net loss is recognized in the accounts through closing entries.

Closing Entries

As for a proprietorship, there are four entries to prepare closing entries for a partnership:

1. To close revenue accounts: Debit each revenue account for its balance and credit Income Summary for total revenues.
2. To close expense accounts: Debit Income Summary for total expenses and credit each expense account for its balance.
3. To close Income Summary: Debit Income Summary for its balance (which should equal the net income amount) and credit each partner's capital account for his or her share of net income. Conversely, credit Income Summary and debit each partner's capital account for his or her share of net loss.
4. To close drawings: Debit each partner's capital account for the balance in that partner's drawings account, and credit each partner's drawings account for the same amount.

The first two entries are the same as in a proprietorship. The last two entries are different because (1) it is necessary to divide net income (or net loss) among the partners, and (2) there are two or more owners' capital and drawings accounts.

To illustrate closing entries, we will assume, for simplicity, that Interactive Software has one revenue and one expense account. Sales Revenue totalled $100,000 and Operating Expenses totalled $68,000 for the year. The partners, M. Gan and K. Sin, share net income and net loss equally. Drawings for the year were $8,000 for Gan and $6,000 for Sin. The closing entries on December 31 are as follows:

A	=	L	+	PE			
				−100,000			
				+100,000			

Cash flows: no effect

Dec. 31	Sales Revenue	100,000	
	Income Summary		100,000
	To close revenue to income summary.		

A	=	L	+	PE
				−68,000
				+68,000

Cash flows: no effect

31	Income Summary	68,000	
	Operating Expenses		68,000
	To close expenses to income summary.		

A	=	L	+	PE
				−32,000
				+16,000
				+16,000

Cash flows: no effect

31	Income Summary ($100,000 − $68,000)	32,000	
	M. Gan, Capital ($32,000 × 50%)		16,000
	K. Sin, Capital ($32,000 × 50%)		16,000
	To close net income to capital accounts.		

A	=	L	+	PE
				−8,000
				−6,000
				+8,000
				+6,000

Cash flows: no effect

31	M. Gan, Capital	8,000	
	K. Sin, Capital	6,000	
	M. Gan, Drawings		8,000
	K. Sin, Drawings		6,000
	To close drawings accounts to capital accounts.		

As in a proprietorship, the partners' capital accounts are permanent accounts. Revenue, expense, income summary, and partners' drawings accounts are temporary accounts.

Income Ratios

As noted earlier, the partnership agreement should specify the basis for sharing net income or net loss. The following are typical income ratios:

1. A fixed ratio, expressed as a proportion (2:1), a percentage (67% and 33%), or a fraction ($\frac{2}{3}$ and $\frac{1}{3}$)
2. A ratio based either on capital balances at the beginning or end of the year, or on average capital balances during the year
3. Salaries to partners and the remainder in a fixed ratio

4. Interest on partners' capital balances and the remainder in a fixed ratio
5. Salaries to partners, interest on partners' capital balances, and the remainder in a fixed ratio

In each case, the goal is to share net income or net loss in a way that fairly reflects each partner's capital investment and service to the partnership.

A fixed ratio is easy to use, and it may be a fair basis in some circumstances. Assume, for example, that Hughes and Lane are partners. Each contributes the same amount of capital, but Hughes expects to work full-time in the partnership, while Lane expects to work only half-time. Accordingly, the partners agree to a fixed ratio of two-thirds to Hughes and one-third to Lane.

A ratio that is based on capital balances may be the right choice when the funds invested in the partnership are the critical factor. Capital balances may also be fair when a manager is hired to run the business and the partners do not plan to take an active role in daily operations.

The three remaining income ratios (items 3, 4, and 5 in the list above) recognize specific differences among the partners. These ratios give salary allowances for time worked and interest allowances for capital invested. Any remaining net income or net loss is divided using a fixed ratio.

The following point is very important to remember when working with these types of income ratios. These ratios are used only for the calculations that divide net income or net loss among partners. This means that salaries to partners and interest on partners' capital balances should not be recorded as expenses of the partnership. For a partnership, as with other companies, salaries expense is the cost of services performed by employees. Likewise, interest expense is the cost of borrowing from creditors. As owners, partners are neither employees nor creditors. Some partnership agreements allow partners to make monthly cash withdrawals based on their salary allowance. These may or may not be the same as the salary allowance specified in the income ratio. In such cases, the withdrawals are debited to the partner's drawings account. They are not debited to the Salaries Expense account.

ACCOUNTING IN ACTION ▶ Across the Organization

Partners in large public accounting firms can make big incomes. A few senior partners may earn as much as $1 million a year. However, the average earnings of partners are more likely to be in the $250,000 range. The compensation of partners in most large partnerships is similar to the compensation of a proprietor in a proprietorship. Like proprietors, partners are not guaranteed an annual salary—compensation depends entirely on each year's operating results, which could be positive (net income) or negative (net loss). Also, a large investment is required of each partner. This capital is at risk for the partner's entire career—often 25 to 30 years—and there is no rate of return on it. Upon leaving, the partner is simply repaid the investment without any adjustment for inflation or increase in value.

? Explain how the income earned by a partner in an accounting partnership is different from the income of a staff accountant in the same partnership.

Salaries, Interest, and Remainder in a Fixed Ratio

Under one income ratio (item 5 in the list above), salaries and interest must be allocated before the remainder is divided according to a fixed ratio. This is true even if the salary and interest provisions are more than net income. It is also true even if the partnership has suffered a net loss for the year.

To illustrate this income ratio, assume that Sara King and Ray Lee are partners in the Kingslee Company. The partnership agreement specifies (1) salary allowances of $8,400 for King and $6,000 for Lee, (2) interest allowances of 5% on capital balances at the beginning of the year, and (3) the remainder to be distributed equally. Capital balances on January 1, 2008, were King $28,000 and Lee $24,000. For the year ended December 31, 2008, partnership net income is $22,000. The division of net income for the year is shown in Illustration 12-2.

Illustration 12-2 ▶

Division of net income

KINGSLEE COMPANY Division of Net Income Year Ended December 31, 2008			
	S. King	R. Lee	Total
Net income			$22,000
Salary allowance	$ 8,400	$6,000	14,400
Remaining income			7,600
Interest allowance			
S. King ($28,000 × 5%)	1,400		
R. Lee ($24,000 × 5%)		1,200	2,600
Remaining income			5,000
Fixed ratio			
S. King ($5,000 × 50%)	2,500		
R. Lee ($5,000 × 50%)		2,500	5,000
Remaining income			0
Division of net income	$12,300	$9,700	$22,000

The entry to record the division of net income is:

A	=	L	+	PE
				−22,000
				+12,300
				+9,700

Cash flows: no effect

Dec. 31	Income Summary	22,000	
	S. King, Capital		12,300
	R. Lee, Capital		9,700
	To close net income to partners' capital accounts.		

Let's now look at a situation where the salary and interest allowances are greater than net income or where there is a loss. Assume that Kingslee Company reports a net loss of $18,000. In this case, the salary and interest allowances create a total deficiency of $35,000 ($18,000 + $14,400 + $2,600). This deficiency is divided equally among the partners as in Illustration 12-3.

Illustration 12-3 ▶

Division of net loss

KINGSLEE COMPANY Division of Net Loss Year Ended December 31, 2008			
	S. King	R. Lee	Total
Net loss			$(18,000)
Salary allowance	$ 8,400	$ 6,000	14,400
Remaining loss			(32,400)
Interest allowance			
S. King ($28,000 × 5%)	1,400		
R. Lee ($24,000 × 5%)		1,200	2,600
Remaining loss			(35,000)
Fixed ratio			
S. King ($35,000 × 50%)	(17,500)		
R. Lee ($35,000 × 50%)		(17,500)	(35,000)
Remaining loss			0
Division of net loss	$ (7,700)	$(10,300)	$(18,000)

The salary and interest allowances are calculated first, as in the previous example, whether the partnership reports a net income or a net loss. Any remaining excess or deficiency is then allocated to the partners.

The journal entry to record the division of the net loss would be as follows:

Dec. 31	S. King, Capital	7,700	
	R. Lee, Capital	10,300	
	Income Summary		18,000
	To close net loss to partners' capital accounts.		

A	=	L	+	PE
				−7,700
				−10,300
				+18,000

Cash flows: no effect

BEFORE YOU GO ON . . .

▶Review It

1. How should assets that are invested into the partnership by a partner be valued?
2. What are the closing entries for a partnership?
3. What types of income ratios may be used in a partnership?

▶Do It

LeMay Company reports net income of $72,000 for the year ended May 31, 2008. The partnership agreement specifies (1) salary allowances of $30,000 for L. Lee and $24,000 for R. May, (2) an interest allowance of 4% based on average capital account balances, and (3) sharing any remainder on a 60:40 basis (60% to Lee, 40% to May). Average capital account balances for the year were $40,000 for Lee and $30,000 for May. (a) Prepare a schedule dividing the net income between the two partners. (b) Prepare the closing entry for net income.

Action Plan

- Allocate the salary allowances first, then the interest allowances.
- Apply the partners' income ratios to the remaining income or deficiency.
- Prepare the closing entry to distribute net income or loss among the partners' capital accounts.

Solution

(a)

LEMAY COMPANY
Division of Net Income
Year Ended May 31, 2008

	L. Lee	R. May	Total
Net income			$72,000
Salary allowance	$30,000	$24,000	54,000
Remaining income			18,000
Interest allowance			
L. Lee ($40,000 × 4%)	1,600		
R. May ($30,000 × 4%)		1,200	2,800
Remaining income			15,200
Fixed ratio			
L. Lee (60% × $15,200)	9,120		
R. May (40% × $15,200)		6,080	15,200
Remaining income			0
Division of net income	$40,720	$31,280	$72,000

(b)

May 31	Income Summary		72,000	
	L. Lee, Capital			40,720
	R. May, Capital			31,280
	To close net income to partners' capital accounts.			

Related exercise material: BE12–2, BE12–3, BE12–4, BE12–5, BE12–6, BE12–7, E12–2, and E12–3.

Partnership Financial Statements

study objective 3

Prepare partnership financial statements.

The financial statements of a partnership are similar to those of a proprietorship. The differences are due to the number of owners involved.

The income statement for a partnership is identical to the income statement for a proprietorship. The division of the partnership net income or loss is often disclosed as a separate schedule or note to the statement.

The statement of equity for a partnership is called the **statement of partners' capital**. Its function is to explain the changes in each partner's capital account and in total partnership capital during the year. As in a proprietorship, changes in capital may result from three causes: additional capital investments, drawings, and each partner's share of the net income or net loss.

The statement of partners' capital for Kingslee Company is shown in Illustration 12-4. It is based on the division of $22,000 of net income in Illustration 12-2. The statement includes assumed data for the investments and drawings.

Illustration 12-4 ▶

Statement of partners' capital

	S. King	R. Lee	Total
KINGSLEE COMPANY			
Statement of Partners' Capital			
Year Ended December 31, 2008			
Capital, January 1	$28,000	$24,000	$52,000
Add: Investments	2,000	0	2,000
Net income	12,300	9,700	22,000
	42,300	33,700	76,000
Less: Drawings	7,000	5,000	12,000
Capital, December 31	$35,300	$28,700	$64,000

The statement of partners' capital is prepared from the income statement and the partners' capital and drawings accounts.

The balance sheet for a partnership is the same as for a proprietorship, except for the equity section. In a proprietorship, the equity section of the balance sheet is called owner's equity. A one-line capital account is reported for the owner. In a partnership, the capital balances of each partner are shown in the balance sheet, in a section called partners' equity. The partners' equity section in Kingslee Company's balance sheet appears in Illustration 12-5.

Illustration 12-5 ◀

Partners' equity section of a
partnership balance sheet

KINGSLEE COMPANY Balance Sheet (partial) December 31, 2008		
Liabilities and Partners' Equity		
Total liabilities (assumed amount)		$115,000
Partners' equity		
S. King, Capital	$35,300	
R. Lee, Capital	28,700	64,000
Total liabilities and partners' equity		$179,000

It is impractical for large partnerships to report each individual partner's equity separately. For reporting purposes, these amounts are usually aggregated in the balance sheet.

BEFORE YOU GO ON . . .

▶Review It

1. How are partnership financial statements similar to, and different from, proprietorship financial statements?
2. Identify the components reported in the statement of partners' capital.

▶Do It

The capital accounts of Cindy Klassen and Clara Hughes, partners in the Best Skate Company, had balances of $80,000 and $95,000, respectively, on January 1, 2008. During the year, Klassen invested an additional $15,000 and each partner withdrew $50,000. Net income for the year was $150,000 and was shared equally between the partners. Prepare a statement of partners' capital for the year ended December 31, 2008.

Action Plan

- Each partner's capital account is increased by investments and net income, and decreased by drawings.
- Allocate net income between the partners according to their income sharing agreement.

Solution

BEST SKATE COMPANY Statement of Partners' Capital Year Ended December 31, 2008			
	C. Klassen	C. Hughes	Total
Capital, January 1	$ 80,000	$ 95,000	$175,000
Add: Investments	15,000	0	15,000
Net income	75,000	75,000	150,000
	170,000	170,000	340,000
Less: Drawings	50,000	50,000	100,000
Capital, December 31	$120,000	$120,000	$240,000

Related exercise material: BE12–8 and E12–4.

the navigator

Admission and Withdrawal of Partners

We have seen how the basic accounting for a partnership works. We now look at how to account for something that happens often in partnerships—the addition or withdrawal of a partner.

Admission of a Partner

study objective 4

Prepare the entries to record the admission of a partner.

The admission of a new partner legally dissolves the existing partnership and begins a new one. From an economic standpoint, the admission of a new partner (or partners) may have only a minor impact on the continuity of the business. For example, in large public accounting or law firms, partners are admitted without any change in operating policies. To recognize the economic effects, it is only necessary to open a capital account for each new partner. In most cases, the accounting records of the old partnership will continue to be used by the new partnership.

A new partner may be admitted by either (1) purchasing the interest of an existing partner, or (2) investing assets in the partnership, as shown in Illustration 12-6. The former (purchase of an interest) involves only a transfer of capital among the partners who are part of the transaction: the total capital of the partnership is not affected. The latter (investment of assets) increases both the partnership's net assets (total assets less total liabilities) and its total capital.

Illustration 12-6 ►

Ways of adding partners

1. Purchase of a partner's interest

2. Investment of assets in the partnership

Purchase of a Partner's Interest

Helpful hint In a purchase of an interest, the partnership is not a participant in the transaction. No cash is contributed to the partnership.

The **admission by purchase of an interest** is a personal transaction between one or more existing partners and the new partner. Each party acts as an individual, separate from the partnership entity. The price paid is negotiated by the individuals involved. It may be equal to or different from the partner's capital in the accounting records of the partnership. The purchase price passes directly from the new partner to the partner who is giving up part or all of his or her ownership claims. Any money or other consideration that is exchanged is the personal property of the participants and not the property of the partnership.

Accounting for the purchase of an interest is straightforward. In the partnership, only the transfer of a partner's capital is recorded. The old partner's capital account is debited for the ownership claims that have been given up. The new partner's capital account is credited with the ownership interest purchased. Total assets, total liabilities, and total capital remain unchanged, as do all individual asset and liability accounts.

To illustrate, assume that on July 1, L. Carson agrees to pay $8,000 each to two partners, D. Arbour and D. Baker, for one-third of their interest in the ABC partnership. At the time of Carson's admission, each partner has a $30,000 capital balance. Both partners, therefore, give up $10,000 ($\frac{1}{3} \times \$30,000$) of their capital. The entry to record the admission of Carson is as follows:

July 1	D. Arbour, Capital	10,000	
	D. Baker, Capital	10,000	
	L. Carson, Capital		20,000
	To record admission of Carson by purchase.		

A	=	L	+	PE
				−10,000
				−10,000
				+20,000

Cash flows: no effect

Note that the cash paid by Carson is not recorded by the partnership because it is paid personally to Arbour and Baker. Regardless of the amount paid by Carson for the one-third interest, the entry above would be exactly the same. If Carson pays $12,000 each to Arbour and Baker for one-third of their interest in the partnership, the above entry is still made.

The effect of this transaction on the partners' capital accounts is as follows:

D. Arbour, Capital		D. Baker, Capital		L. Carson, Capital	
	Bal. 30,000		Bal. 30,000		
10,000		10,000			20,000
	Bal. 20,000		Bal. 20,000		Bal. 20,000

Each partner now has a $20,000 ending capital balance and total partnership capital is $60,000 ($20,000 + $20,000 + $20,000). Net assets (assets − liabilities) and total capital remain unchanged. Arbour and Baker continue as partners in the firm, but the capital interest of each has changed from $30,000 to $20,000.

Investment of Assets in a Partnership

The admission of a partner by an investment of assets is a transaction between the new partner and the partnership. It is often referred to simply as **admission by investment**. This transaction increases both the net assets and the total capital of the partnership. In the feature story, Richard Altrogge, Richard Matchett, Alan Ashdown, and James Schemenauer were admitted to the Heagy Bailey Altrogge Matchett partnership by investment.

To illustrate, assume that instead of purchasing a partner's interest as illustrated in the previous section, Carson invests $30,000 in cash in the ABC partnership for a one-third capital interest. In this case, the entry is:

July 1	Cash	30,000	
	L. Carson, Capital		30,000
	To record admission of Carson by investment.		

A	=	L	+	PE
+30,000				+30,000

↑ Cash flows: +30,000

Both net assets and total capital increase by $30,000. The effect of this transaction on the partners' capital accounts is as follows:

D. Arbour, Capital		D. Baker, Capital		L. Carson, Capital	
	Bal. 30,000		Bal. 30,000		
					30,000
	Bal. 30,000		Bal. 30,000		Bal. 30,000

Remember that Carson's one-third capital interest might not result in a one-third income ratio. Carson's income ratio should be specified in the new partnership agreement. It may or may not be equal to the one-third capital interest.

The before and after effects of an admission by purchase of an interest or by investment are shown in the following comparison of the net assets and capital balances:

	Before Admission of Partner	After Admission of Partner	
		Purchase of an Interest	Investment of Assets
Net assets	$60,000	$60,000	$90,000
Partners' capital			
D. Arbour	$30,000	$20,000	$30,000
D. Baker	30,000	20,000	30,000
L. Carson		20,000	30,000
Total capital	$60,000	$60,000	$90,000

When an interest is purchased, the total net assets and the total capital of the partnership do not change. In contrast, when a partner is admitted by investment, both the total net assets and the total capital change (increase) by the amount of cash invested by the new partner.

In an admission by investment, complications occur when the new partner's investment is not the same as the capital equity acquired. When those amounts are not the same, the difference is considered a bonus either (1) to the old (existing) partners or (2) to the new partner.

Bonus to Old Partners. The existing partners may not want to admit a new partner without receiving a bonus. In an established firm, existing partners may insist on a bonus as compensation for the work they have put into the partnership over the years.

Two accounting factors explain why a bonus may be necessary. First, total partners' capital equals the net book value of the recorded net assets of the partnership. When the new partner is admitted, the fair market values of assets such as land and buildings may be higher than their book values. The bonus will help make up the difference between fair market value and net book value. Second, when the partnership has been profitable, goodwill may exist. But the goodwill is not recorded among the assets or reflected in total partners' capital. In such cases, the new partner is usually willing to pay the bonus to become a partner.

A bonus to old partners results when the new partner's investment in the partnership is greater than the capital credit on the date of admittance. The bonus increases the capital balances of the old partners. It is allocated to them based on their income ratios before the admission of the new partner.

To illustrate, assume that the Bart-Simpson partnership, owned by Sam Bart and Hal Simpson, has total capital of $120,000. Bart has a capital balance of $72,000; Simpson has a capital balance of $48,000. Lisa Trent acquires a 25% ownership (capital) interest in the partnership by making a cash investment of $80,000 on November 1. The procedure for determining Trent's capital credit and the bonus to the old partners is as follows:

1. Determine the total capital of the new partnership: Add the new partner's investment to the total capital of the old partnership. In this case, the total capital of the new firm is $200,000, calculated as follows:

Total capital of existing partnership	$120,000
Investment by new partner, Trent	80,000
Total capital of new partnership	$200,000

2. Determine the new partner's capital credit: Multiply the total capital of the new partnership by the new partner's ownership interest.

Trent's capital credit ($200,000 × 25%)	$50,000

3. Determine the amount of the bonus: Subtract the new partner's capital credit from the new partner's investment.

Bonus ($80,000 − $50,000)	$30,000

4. Allocate the bonus to the old partners based on their income ratios: Assuming the ratios are Bart 60% and Simpson 40%, the allocation of the bonus to the old partners is:

To Bart ($30,000 × 60%)	$18,000
To Simpson ($30,000 × 40%)	12,000
Total bonus	$30,000

The entry to record the admission of Trent on November 1 is:

Nov. 1	Cash	80,000	
	S. Bart, Capital		18,000
	H. Simpson, Capital		12,000
	L. Trent, Capital		50,000
	To record admission of Trent and bonuses to old partners.		

A	=	L	+	PE
+80,000				+18,000
				+12,000
				+50,000

↑ Cash flows: +80,000

The before and after effects of the admission of a partner who pays a bonus to the old partners are shown in the following comparison of the net assets and capital balances:

	Bonus to Old Partners	
	Before Admission of a Partner	After Admission of a Partner
Net assets	$120,000	$200,000
Partners' capital		
S. Bart	$ 72,000	$ 90,000
H. Simpson	48,000	60,000
L. Trent		50,000
Total capital	$120,000	$200,000

In summary, $80,000 cash was invested in the partnership by Lisa Trent for a $50,000 capital credit, and the $30,000 bonus was allocated to the old partners' capital accounts as follows: $18,000 to Sam Bart and $12,000 to Hal Simpson.

Bonus to New Partner. A bonus to a new partner results when the new partner's investment in the partnership is less than his or her capital credit. This may happen when the new partner has resources or special attributes that the partnership wants. For example, the new partner may be able to supply cash that is urgently needed for expansion or to meet maturing debts. Or the new partner may be a recognized expert or authority in a relevant field. An engineering firm, for example, may be willing to give a renowned engineer a bonus to join the firm. Or the partners of a restaurant may offer a bonus to a sports celebrity in order to add the athlete's name to the partnership. A bonus to a new partner may also result when recorded net book values on the partnership books are higher than their market value.

A bonus to a new partner decreases the capital balances of the old partners. The amount of the decrease for each partner is based on the income ratios before the admission of the new partner.

To illustrate, assume that Lisa Trent invests $20,000 in cash for a 25% ownership interest in the Bart-Simpson partnership on November 1. Using the four procedures described in the preceding section, the calculations for Trent's capital credit and bonus are:

1. Determine the total capital of the new partnership:

Total capital of existing partnership	$120,000
Investment by new partner, Trent	20,000
Total capital of new partnership	$140,000

2. Determine the new partner's capital credit: Multiply the total capital of the new partnership by the new partner's ownership interest.

Trent's capital credit ($140,000 × 25%)	<u>$35,000</u>

3. Determine the amount of the bonus: Subtract the new partner's capital credit from the new partner's investment. The result in this case is $(15,000). In the Bonus to Old Partners section on the previous page, this difference was a positive amount and the bonus was allocated to the old partners. Here, the difference is a negative amount, so the bonus is allocated to the new partner from the old partners' capital accounts.

Bonus ($20,000 − $35,000)	<u>$(15,000)</u>

4. Allocate the bonus from the old partners based on their income ratios. Using the same ratios of Bart 60% and Simpson 40%, the allocation of the bonus to the new partner is:

From Bart ($15,000 × 60%)	$ 9,000
From Simpson ($15,000 × 40%)	6,000
Total bonus	<u>$15,000</u>

The entry to record the admission of Trent on November 1 in this case is:

A	=	L	+	PE
+20,000				−9,000
				−6,000
				+35,000

↑ Cash flows: +20,000

Nov. 1	Cash	20,000	
	S. Bart, Capital	9,000	
	H. Simpson, Capital	6,000	
	L. Trent, Capital		35,000
	To record Trent's admission and bonus to new partner.		

The before and after effects of the admission of a partner who is paid a bonus by the old partners are shown in the following comparison of the net assets and capital balances:

	Bonus to New Partner	
	Before Admission of a Partner	After Admission of a Partner
Net assets	<u>$120,000</u>	<u>$140,000</u>
Partners' capital		
S. Bart	$ 72,000	$ 63,000
H. Simpson	48,000	42,000
L. Trent		35,000
Total capital	<u>$120,000</u>	<u>$140,000</u>

In summary, $20,000 cash was invested in the partnership by Lisa Trent for a $35,000 capital credit, and the $15,000 bonus was allocated from the partners' capital accounts as follows: $9,000 from Sam Bart and $6,000 from Hal Simpson.

BEFORE YOU GO ON . . .

▶**Review It**

1. How is the accounting for admission in a partnership by purchase of an interest different from the accounting for admission by an investment of assets?
2. How do net assets and total capital change before and after the admission of a partner (a) by purchase of an interest, and (b) by an investment of assets?

▶Review It

I. Chandler and M. Ross have a partnership in which they share income and loss equally. There is a $40,000 balance in each capital account. Record the journal entries on September 1 for each of the independent events below:

1. Chandler and Ross agree to admit A. Rachel as a new one-fourth interest partner. Rachel pays $16,000 in cash directly to each partner.
2. Chandler and Ross agree to admit A. Rachel as a new one-fourth interest partner. Rachel contributes $32,000 to the partnership.

Action Plan

- Recognize that the admission by purchase of a partnership interest is a personal transaction between one or more existing partners and the new partner.
- In an admission by purchase, no cash is received by the partnership and the capital credit for the new partner is not based on the cash paid.
- Recognize that the admission by investment of partnership assets is a transaction between the new partner and the partnership.
- In an admission by investment, determine any bonus to old or new partners by comparing the total capital of the new partnership to the new partner's capital credit. Allocate the bonus based on the old partners' income ratios.

Solution

1.	Sept. 1	I. Chandler, Capital	10,000	
		M. Ross, Capital	10,000	
		A. Rachel, Capital		20,000[1]
		To record admission of Rachel by purchase.		
2.	Sept. 1	Cash	32,000	
		I. Chandler, Capital ($4,000[2] × 50%)		2,000
		M. Ross, Capital ($4,000[2] × 50%)		2,000
		A. Rachel, Capital		28,000
		To record admission of Rachel by investment.		

[1] Total capital of partnership: $40,000 + $40,000 = $80,000
Rachel's capital credit: $80,000 × ¼ = $20,000
[2] Total capital of partnership: $40,000 + $40,000 + $32,000 = $112,000
Rachel's capital credit: $112,000 × ¼ = $28,000
Bonus to old partners: $32,000 − $28,000 = $4,000

Related exercise material: BE12–9, BE12–10, E12–5, and E12–6.

the navigator

Withdrawal of a Partner

study objective 5

Prepare the entries to record the withdrawal of a partner.

Let's now look at the opposite situation, when a partner withdraws. A partner may withdraw from a partnership voluntarily, by selling his or her equity in the firm. He or she may withdraw involuntarily, by reaching mandatory retirement age, by expulsion, or by dying. The withdrawal of a partner, like the admission of a partner, legally dissolves the partnership. However, it is customary to record only the economic effects of the partner's withdrawal, while the partnership reorganizes itself and continues to operate.

As indicated earlier, the partnership agreement should specify the terms of withdrawal. Often, however, the withdrawal of a partner occurs outside of the partnership agreement. For example, when the remaining partners are anxious to remove an uncontrollable partner from the firm, they may agree to pay the departing partner much more than was specified in the original partnership agreement.

The withdrawal of a partner may be done by a payment from partners' personal assets or a payment from partnership assets, as shown in Illustration 12-7. The former (payment from personal assets) affects only the partners' capital accounts, not total capital. The latter (payment from partnership assets) decreases the total net assets and total capital of the partnership.

Illustration 12-7 ▶

Ways of dropping partners

1. Purchase of a partner's interest   2. Investment of assets in the partnership

After a partner has withdrawn, income ratios for the remaining partners must be reviewed and specified again. If a new income ratio is not indicated in the partnership agreement, the remaining partners are assumed to share income and losses equally.

Payment from Partners' Personal Assets

A **withdrawal by payment from partners' personal assets** is a personal transaction between the partners. It is the direct opposite of admitting a new partner who purchases a partner's interest. Payment to the departing partner is made directly from the remaining partners' personal assets. Partnership assets are not involved in any way, and total capital does not change. The effect on the partnership is limited to a transfer of the partners' capital balances.

To illustrate, assume that Javad Dargahi, Dong Kim, and Robert Viau have capital balances of $25,000, $15,000, and $10,000, respectively. The partnership equity totals $50,000 ($25,000 + $15,000 + $10,000). Dargahi and Kim agree to buy out Viau's interest. Each agrees to pay Viau $8,000 in exchange for one-half of Viau's total interest of $10,000 on February 1. The entry to record the withdrawal is as follows:

A	=	L	+	PE
				−10,000
				+5,000
				+5,000

Cash flows: no effect

Feb. 1	R. Viau, Capital	10,000	
	J. Dargahi, Capital		5,000
	D. Kim, Capital		5,000
	To record purchase of Viau's interest by other partners.		

The effect of this transaction on the partners' capital accounts is as follows:

J. Dargahi, Capital		D. Kim, Capital		R. Viau, Capital	
	Bal. 25,000		Bal. 15,000		Bal. 10,000
	5,000		5,000	10,000	
	Bal. 30,000		Bal. 20,000		Bal. 0

Net assets of $50,000 remain the same and total partnership capital is also unchanged at $50,000 ($30,000 + $20,000 + $0). All that has happened is a reallocation of capital amounts. Note also that the $16,000 paid to Robert Viau personally is not recorded. Viau's capital is debited for only $10,000, not the $16,000 cash that he received. Similarly, both Javad Dargahi and Dong Kim credit their capital accounts for only $5,000, not the $8,000 they each paid.

Payment from Partnership Assets

A **withdrawal by payment from partnership assets** is a transaction that involves the partnership. Both partnership net assets and total capital are decreased. Using partnership assets to pay for a withdrawing partner's interest is the reverse of admitting a partner through the investment of assets in the partnership.

In accounting for a withdrawal by payment from partnership assets, asset revaluations should not be recorded. Recording a revaluation to the fair market value of the assets at the time of a partner's withdrawal violates the cost principle, which requires assets to be stated at original cost. It would also ignore the going concern assumption, which assumes that the entity will continue indefinitely. The terms of the partnership contract should not dictate the accounting for this event.

To illustrate, assume that instead of Robert Viau's interest being purchased personally by the other partners as illustrated in the previous section, his interest is bought out by the partnership. In this case, the entry is:

Feb. 1	R. Viau, Capital	10,000	
	Cash		10,000
	To record purchase of Viau's interest by partnership.		

A = L + PE
−10,000   −10,000
↓ Cash flows: −10,000

Both net assets and total partnership capital decrease by $10,000. The effect of this transaction on the partners' capital accounts is as follows:

J. Dargahi, Capital	D. Kim, Capital	R. Viau, Capital
Bal. 25,000	Bal. 15,000	10,000 Bal. 10,000
Bal. 25,000	Bal. 15,000	Bal. 0

The before and after effects of the withdrawal of a partner when payment is made from personal assets or from partnership assets are shown in the following comparison of the net assets and capital balances:

	Before Withdrawal of Partner	After Withdrawal of Partner Payment from Partners' Personal Assets	Payment from Partnership Assets
Net assets	$50,000	$50,000	$40,000
Partners' capital			
J. Dargahi	$25,000	$30,000	$25,000
D. Kim	15,000	20,000	15,000
R. Viau	10,000	0	0
Total capital	$50,000	$50,000	$40,000

When payment is made from partners' personal assets, the total net assets and the total capital of the partnership do not change. In contrast, when payment is made from the partnership assets, both the total net assets and the total capital decrease.

In a payment from partnership assets, it is rare for the partnership to pay the partner the exact amount of his or her capital account balance, as was assumed above. When the amounts are not the same, the difference between the amount paid and the withdrawing partner's capital balance is considered a bonus either (1) to the departing partner, or (2) to the remaining partners.

Bonus to Departing Partner. A bonus may be paid to a departing partner in any of these situations:

1. The fair market value of partnership assets is more than their net book value.
2. There is unrecorded goodwill resulting from the partnership's superior earnings record.
3. The remaining partners are anxious to remove the partner from the firm.

The bonus is deducted from the remaining partners' capital balances based on their income ratios at the time of the withdrawal.

In our feature story, Mr. Heagy received a bonus when he retired from the partnership. In his particular case, this bonus was specified in the partnership agreement to recognize the fact that he had brought in the initial client base for the firm in 1983.

To illustrate a bonus to a departing partner, assume the following capital balances in the RST partnership: Fred Roman, $50,000; Dee Sand, $30,000; and Betty Terk, $20,000. The partners share income in the ratio of 3:2:1, respectively. Terk retires from the partnership on March 1 and receives a cash payment of $25,000 from the firm. The procedure for determining the bonus to the departing partner and the allocation of the bonus to the remaining partners is as follows:

1. Determine the amount of the bonus: Subtract the departing partner's capital balance from the cash paid by the partnership.

   Bonus ($25,000 − $20,000)   <u>$5,000</u>

2. Allocate payment of the bonus by the remaining partners based on their income ratios: The ratios of Roman and Sand are 3:2. Thus, the allocation of the $5,000 bonus is:

From Roman ($5,000 × ⅗)	$3,000
From Sand ($5,000 × ⅖)	2,000
Total bonus	<u>$5,000</u>

The entry to record the withdrawal of Terk on March 1 is as follows:

A	=	L	+	PE
−25,000				−20,000
				−3,000
				−2,000

↓ Cash flows: −25,000

Mar. 1	B. Terk, Capital	20,000	
	F. Roman, Capital	3,000	
	D. Sand, Capital	2,000	
	Cash		25,000
	To record withdrawal of, and bonus to, Terk.		

The before and after effects of the withdrawal of a partner when a bonus is paid to the departing partner are shown in the following comparison of the net assets and capital balances:

	Bonus to Departing Partner	
	Before Withdrawal of Partner	After Withdrawal of Partner
Net assets	<u>$100,000</u>	<u>$75,000</u>
Partners' capital		
F. Roman	$ 50,000	$47,000
D. Sand	30,000	28,000
B. Terk	<u>20,000</u>	<u>0</u>
Total capital	<u>$100,000</u>	<u>$75,000</u>

In summary, both net assets and capital decreased by $25,000 when $25,000 cash was paid by the partnership to Betty Terk to purchase her $20,000 equity interest. The $5,000 bonus was allocated from the remaining partners' capital accounts according to their income ratios, which reduced their total equity interest from $80,000 to $75,000. Fred Roman and Dee Sand, the remaining partners, will recover the bonus given to Terk as the undervalued assets are used or sold.

Bonus to Remaining Partners. The departing partner may give a bonus to the remaining partners in the following situations:

1. Recorded assets are overvalued.
2. The partnership has a poor earnings record.
3. The partner is anxious to leave the partnership.

In such cases, the cash paid to the departing partner will be less than the departing partner's capital balance. The bonus is allocated (credited) to the capital accounts of the remaining partners based on their income ratios.

To illustrate, assume, instead of the example above, that Terk is paid only $16,000 for her $20,000 equity when she withdraws from the partnership on March 1. In that case, the calculations are as follows:

1. Determine the amount of the bonus: Subtract the departing partner's capital balance from the cash paid by the partnership. In the Bonus to Departing Partner section above, this difference was a positive amount and the bonus was allocated to the departing partner. Here, the difference is a negative amount, so the bonus is allocated to the remaining partners:

Bonus ($16,000 − $20,000)	$(4,000)

2. Allocate the payment of the bonus to the remaining partners based on their income ratios. Roman and Sand share income in a ratio of 3:2. The allocation of the $4,000 bonus is:

To Roman ($4,000 × ⅗)	$2,400
To Sand ($4,000 × ⅖)	1,600
Total bonus	$4,000

The entry to record the withdrawal on March 1 follows:

Mar. 1	B. Terk, Capital	20,000	
	F. Roman, Capital		2,400
	D. Sand, Capital		1,600
	Cash		16,000
	To record withdrawal of Terk and bonus to remaining partners.		

A	=	L	+	PE
−16,000				−20,000
				+2,400
				+1,600

↓ Cash flows: −16,000

The before and after effects of the withdrawal of a partner when a bonus is paid by the departing partner to the remaining partners are shown in the following comparison of the net assets and capital balances:

	Bonus to Remaining Partners	
	Before Withdrawal of Partner	After Withdrawal of Partner
Net assets	$100,000	$84,000
Partners' capital		
F. Roman	$ 50,000	$52,400
D. Sand	30,000	31,600
B. Terk	20,000	0
Total capital	$100,000	$84,000

In summary, both net assets and capital decreased by $16,000 when $16,000 cash was paid by the partnership to Betty Terk to purchase her $20,000 equity interest. The $4,000 bonus was allocated to the remaining partners' capital accounts according to their income ratios, which increased their total equity interest from $80,000 to $84,000.

Death of a Partner

The death of a partner dissolves the partnership. But there is generally a provision in the partnership agreement for the surviving partners to continue operations. When a partner dies, the partner's equity at the date of death normally has to be determined. This is done by (1) calculating the net income or loss for the year to date, (2) closing the books, and (3) preparing the financial statements.

The death of the partner may be recorded by either of the two methods described earlier in the section for the withdrawal of a partner: (1) payment from the partners' personal assets or (2) payment from the partnership assets. That is, one or more of the surviving partners may agree to use his or her personal assets to purchase the deceased partner's equity. Or, partnership assets may be used to settle with the deceased partner's estate. To make it easier to pay from partnership assets, many partnerships obtain life insurance policies on each partner. The partnership is named as the beneficiary. The proceeds from the insurance policy on the deceased partner are then used to settle with the estate.

BEFORE YOU GO ON . . .

▶Review It

1. Compare the withdrawal of a partner to the admission of a partner.
2. Contrast the accounting for the withdrawal of a partner by payment from (a) personal assets, and (b) partnership assets.
3. How do net assets and total capital change before and after the withdrawal of a partner when a bonus is paid (a) to the departing partner, and (b) to the remaining partners?
4. Explain how the accounting for the death of a partner is similar to, or differs from, the accounting for the withdrawal of a partner.

▶Do It

S. Hosseinzadeh, M. Bélanger, and C. Laurin have a partnership in which they share income and loss equally. There is a $40,000 balance in each capital account. Record the journal entries on March 1 for each of the independent events below:

1. C. Laurin withdraws from the partnership. Hosseinzadeh and Bélanger each pay Laurin $25,000 out of their personal assets.
2. C. Laurin withdraws from the partnership and is paid $30,000 of partnership cash.

Action Plan

• Recognize that the withdrawal by sale of a partnership interest is a personal transaction between one or more existing partners and the withdrawing partner.
• Recognize that the withdrawal by payment of partnership assets is a transaction between the withdrawing partner and the partnership.
• In a withdrawal by payment of partnership assets, determine any bonus to the departing or remaining partners by comparing the amount paid to the amount of the withdrawing partner's capital balance. Allocate the bonus based on the old partners' income ratios.

Solution

1.	Mar. 1	C. Laurin, Capital	40,000	
		S. Hosseinzadeh, Capital ($40,000 × ½)		20,000
		M. Bélanger, Capital ($40,000 × ½)		20,000
		To record purchase of Laurin's interest.		
2.	Mar. 1	C. Laurin, Capital	40,000	
		Cash		30,000
		S. Hosseinzadeh, Capital ($10,000[1] × ½)		5,000
		M. Bélanger, Capital ($10,000[1] × ½)		5,000
		To record withdrawal of Laurin by payment of		
		partnership assets and bonus to remaining partners.		

[1] Bonus: $30,000 − $40,000 = $(10,000)

Related exercise material: BE12–11, BE12–12, E12–7, and E12–8.

Liquidation of a Partnership

study objective 6

Prepare the entries to record the liquidation of a partnership.

The liquidation of a partnership ends the business. It involves selling the assets of the business, paying liabilities, and distributing any remaining assets to the partners. Liquidation may result from the sale of the business by mutual agreement of the partners or from bankruptcy. A **partnership liquidation** ends both the legal and the economic life of the entity.

Before the liquidation process begins, the accounting cycle for the partnership must be completed for the final operating period. This includes the preparation of adjusting entries, a trial balance, financial statements, closing entries, and a post-closing trial balance. Only balance sheet accounts should be open when the liquidation process begins.

In liquidation, the sale of noncash assets for cash is called **realization**. Any difference between the net book value and the cash proceeds is called the gain or loss on realization. To liquidate a partnership, it is necessary to follow these steps:

1. Sell noncash assets for cash and recognize any gain or loss on realization.
2. Allocate any gain or loss on realization to the partners, based on their income ratios.
3. Pay partnership liabilities in cash.
4. Distribute the remaining cash to partners, based on their capital balances.

Each of the steps must be done in sequence, and creditors must be paid before partners receive any cash distributions.

It sometimes happens, when a partnership is liquidated, that all partners have credit balances in their capital accounts. This situation is called **no capital deficiency**. Alternatively, one or more of the partners' capital accounts may have a debit balance. This situation is called a **capital deficiency**.

To illustrate each of these situations, assume that Ace Company is liquidated on April 15, 2008, when its post-closing trial balance shows the assets, liabilities, and partners' equity accounts in Illustration 12-8 on the following page.

Illustration 12-8 ▶

Account balances before liquidation

ACE COMPANY
Post-Closing Trial Balance
April 15, 2008

	Debit	Credit
Cash	$ 5,000	
Accounts receivable	15,000	
Inventory	18,000	
Equipment	35,000	
Accumulated amortization—equipment		$ 8,000
Notes payable		15,000
Accounts payable		16,000
R. Aube, Capital		15,000
P. Chordia, Capital		17,800
W. Elliott, Capital		1,200
Totals	$73,000	$73,000

No Capital Deficiency

The partners of Ace Company agree to liquidate the partnership on the following terms: (1) the noncash assets of the partnership will be sold for $75,000 cash, and (2) the partnership will pay its partnership liabilities. The income ratios of the partners are 3:2:1 for R. Aube, P. Chordia, and W. Elliott. The steps in the liquidation process are as follows:

1. The noncash assets (accounts receivable, inventory, and equipment) are sold on April 18 for $75,000. The net book value of these assets is $60,000 ($15,000 + $18,000 + $35,000 − $8,000). Thus, a gain of $15,000 is realized on the sale, and the following entry is made:

```
A    =   L   +   PE
+75,000          +15,000
 +8,000
−15,000
−18,000
−35,000

↑ Cash flows: +75,000
```

	(1)		
Apr. 18	Cash	75,000	
	Accumulated Amortization—Equipment	8,000	
	Accounts Receivable		15,000
	Inventory		18,000
	Equipment		35,000
	Gain on Realization		15,000
	To record realization of noncash assets.		

2. The gain on realization of $15,000 is allocated to the partners based on their income ratios, which are 3:2:1 (or $\frac{3}{6}$, $\frac{2}{6}$, and $\frac{1}{6}$). The entry is:

```
A    =   L   +   PE
               −15,000
                +7,500
                +5,000
                +2,500

Cash flows: no effect
```

	(2)		
Apr. 18	Gain on Realization	15,000	
	R. Aube, Capital ($15,000 × $\frac{3}{6}$)		7,500
	P. Chordia, Capital ($15,000 × $\frac{2}{6}$)		5,000
	W. Elliott, Capital ($15,000 × $\frac{1}{6}$)		2,500
	To allocate gain to partners' capital accounts.		

3. Partnership liabilities consist of notes payable, $15,000; and accounts payable, $16,000. Creditors are paid in full on April 23 by a cash payment of $31,000. The entry is:

	(3)			
Apr. 23	Notes Payable		15,000	
	Accounts Payable		16,000	
	Cash			31,000
	To record payment of partnership liabilities.			

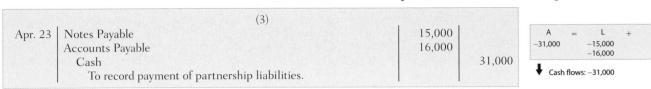

A = L + PE
−31,000   −15,000
          −16,000

↓ Cash flows: −31,000

4. The remaining cash is distributed to the partners on April 25 based on their capital balances. After the entries in the first three steps are posted, all partnership accounts will have zero balances except for four accounts: Cash $49,000; R. Aube, Capital $22,500; P. Chordia, Capital $22,800; and W. Elliott, Capital $3,700, as follows:

Cash				P. Chordia, Capital		
Bal.	5,000				Bal.	17,800
(1)	75,000	(3)	31,000		(2)	5,000
Bal.	49,000				Bal.	22,800

R. Aube, Capital				W. Elliott, Capital		
		Bal.	15,000		Bal.	1,200
		(2)	7,500		(2)	2,500
		Bal.	22,500		Bal.	3,700

The entry to record the distribution of cash on April 25 is:

	(4)			
Apr. 25	R. Aube, Capital		22,500	
	P. Chordia, Capital		22,800	
	W. Elliott, Capital		3,700	
	Cash			49,000
	To record distribution of cash to partners.			

A = L + PE
−49,000   −22,500
              −22,800
              −3,700

↓ Cash flows: −49,000

After this entry is posted, all partnership general ledger accounts will have zero balances.

A word of caution: Cash should not be distributed to partners based on their income-sharing ratios. On this basis, R. Aube would receive ⅗, or $24,500. This would produce an incorrect debit balance of $2,000. While the income ratio is the right basis for allocating net income or loss and any gains or losses on the realization of assets, it is not the right basis for making the final distribution of cash to the partners.

Capital Deficiency

A capital deficiency may be caused by recurring net losses, excessive drawings, or losses from the realization during liquidation. To illustrate, assume that Ace Company (see Illustration 12-8) is almost bankrupt. The partners decide to liquidate by having a going-out-of-business sale on April 18. Merchandise is sold at substantial discounts, and the equipment is sold at auction. Cash proceeds from these sales and collections from customers total only $42,000. The loss on liquidation is $18,000 ($60,000 in net book value − $42,000 in proceeds). The steps in the liquidation process are as follows:

1. The entry for the realization of noncash assets is recorded on April 18:

		(1)		
Apr. 18	Cash		42,000	
	Accumulated Amortization—Equipment		8,000	
	Loss on Realization		18,000	
	Accounts Receivable			15,000
	Inventory			18,000
	Equipment			35,000
	To record realization of noncash assets.			

A = L + PE
+42,000   −18,000
+8,000
−15,000
−18,000
−35,000

↑ Cash flows: +42,000

2. The loss on realization is allocated to the partners based on their income ratios of 3:2:1 and is recorded as follows:

		(2)		
Apr. 18	R. Aube, Capital ($18,000 × 3/6)		9,000	
	P. Chordia, Capital ($18,000 × 2/6)		6,000	
	W. Elliott, Capital ($18,000 × 1/6)		3,000	
	Loss on Realization			18,000
	To allocate loss to partners' capital accounts.			

A = L + PE
            −9,000
            −6,000
            −3,000
            +18,000

Cash flows: no effect

3. Partnership liabilities are paid on April 23 and recorded:

		(3)		
Apr. 23	Notes Payable		15,000	
	Accounts Payable		16,000	
	Cash			31,000
	To record payment of partnership liabilities.			

A = L + PE
−31,000 −15,000
         −16,000

↓ Cash flows: −31,000

4. After posting of the three entries, two accounts will have debit balances: Cash, $16,000; and W. Elliott, Capital $1,800. Two accounts will have credit balances: R. Aube, Capital $6,000; and P. Chordia, Capital $11,800. All four accounts follow:

Cash					P. Chordia, Capital			
Bal.	5,000				(2)	6,000	Bal.	17,800
(1)	42,000	(3)	31,000				Bal.	11,800
Bal.	16,000							

R. Aube, Capital					W. Elliott, Capital			
(2)	9,000	Bal.	15,000		(2)	3,000	Bal.	1,200
		Bal.	6,000		Bal.	1,800		

W. Elliott has a capital deficiency of $1,800. He therefore owes the partnership $1,800. R. Aube and P. Chordia have a legally enforceable claim for that amount against Elliott's personal assets. The distribution of cash is still made based on the capital balances. But the amount will vary depending on how Elliott's deficiency is settled. Two alternatives for settling are presented next.

Payment of Deficiency

If the partner with the capital deficiency pays the amount owed to the partnership, the deficiency is eliminated. This is an added step to those listed on pp. 636–637 where there was no capital deficiency.

To illustrate, assume that W. Elliott pays $1,800 to the partnership on April 24. The entry to record this payment is as follows:

	(4)			
Apr. 24	Cash		1,800	
	W. Elliott, Capital			1,800
	To record payment of capital deficiency by Elliott.			

After posting, the affected accounts show the following balances:

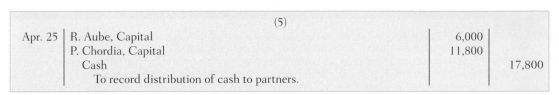

	Cash					P. Chordia, Capital		
Bal.	5,000				(2)	6,000	Bal.	17,800
(1)	42,000	(3)	31,000				Bal.	11,800
(4)	1,800							
Bal.	17,800							

	R. Aube, Capital					W. Elliott, Capital		
(2)	9,000	Bal.	15,000				Bal.	1,200
		Bal.	6,000		(2)	3,000	(4)	1,800
							Bal.	0

The cash balance of $17,800 is now equal to the credit balances in the capital accounts ($6,000 + $11,800 + $0). Cash is distributed based on these balances on April 25. This was step 4 in the list for when there was no capital deficiency on p. 637. The following entry is made:

	(5)			
Apr. 25	R. Aube, Capital		6,000	
	P. Chordia, Capital		11,800	
	Cash			17,800
	To record distribution of cash to partners.			

After this entry is posted, all accounts will have zero balances.

Nonpayment of Deficiency

If a partner with a capital deficiency is unable to pay the amount owed to the partnership, the partners with credit balances must absorb the loss. The loss is allocated based on the income ratios between the partners with credit balances. For example, the income ratios of R. Aube and P. Chordia are 3:2 (or $\frac{3}{5}$ and $\frac{2}{5}$), respectively. The following entry would be made to remove W. Elliott's capital deficiency on April 25:

	(4)			
Apr. 25	R. Aube, Capital ($1,800 × $\frac{3}{5}$)		1,080	
	P. Chordia, Capital ($1,800 × $\frac{2}{5}$)		720	
	W. Elliott, Capital			1,800
	To write off Elliott's capital deficiency.			

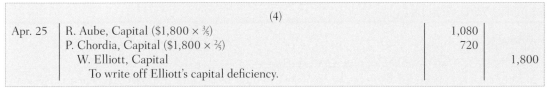

After posting this entry, the cash balance of $16,000 now equals the sum of the credit balances in the capital accounts ($4,920 + $11,080 + $0), as shown below:

Cash				P. Chordia, Capital			
Bal.	5,000			(2)	6,000	Bal.	17,800
(1)	42,000	(3)	31,000	(4)	720		
Bal.	16,000					Bal.	11,080

R. Aube, Capital				W. Elliott, Capital			
(2)	9,000	Bal.	15,000			Bal.	1,200
(4)	1,080			(2)	3,000	(4)	1,800
		Bal.	4,920			Bal.	0

The entry to record the distribution of cash is:

			(5)		
A = L + PE	Apr. 25	R. Aube, Capital		4,920	
−16,000		P. Chordia, Capital		11,080	
−4,920		Cash			16,000
−11,080		To record distribution of cash to partners.			

Cash flows: −16,000

After this entry is posted, all accounts will have zero balances.

ACCOUNTING IN ACTION ▶ Business Insight

The last thing that entrepreneurs want to think about when they are starting a business partnership is its potential divorce. But, like newlyweds who don't consider a prenuptial agreement in case of future separation, business people may be courting heartache—or at least financial disaster—if they don't sign a partnership agreement that gives detailed procedures for leaving the business, among other actions. Take for example, Andrew Patricio, who in the early 1990s began a restaurant supply business with four partners, including family members. They had a verbal agreement on how they would share profits. But, when the business grew rapidly and became an acquisition target, they couldn't agree on how to share the proceeds from the sale of the business. "I had to eventually sue my partners for my share of the business, which was $400,000. They took three years to pay me," says Mr. Patricio.

Source: Brian Christmas, "When Exchanging Vows, Write Them Down," *The Globe and Mail*, December 5, 2005.

? When most businesses start, the partners believe it will be a success. Why, then, is it important for a partnership agreement to include provisions for ending the business before it has even started?

BEFORE YOU GO ON . . .

▶Review It

1. What are the steps in liquidating a partnership?
2. What basis is used for making the final distribution of cash to the partners when there is no capital deficiency?
3. What basis is used for making the final distribution of cash to the partners when there is a capital deficiency and the deficiency is paid? And when it is not paid?

▶Review It

S. Anderson, J. Hinton, and R. Smistad LLP dissolved their partnership as of August 31. Before liquidation, the three partners shared income and losses in the ratio of 3:2:4. After the books were closed on August 31, the following summary accounts remained:

Cash	$ 6,000	S. Anderson, Capital	$30,000
Noncash assets	110,000	J. Hinton, Capital	20,000
Accounts payable	25,000	R. Smistad, Capital	41,000

On September 24, the partnership sold the remaining noncash assets for $74,000 and paid the liabilities. If there is a capital deficiency, none of the partners will be able to pay it. Prepare the journal entries to record (1) the sale of noncash assets, (2) the allocation of any gain or loss on realization, (3) the payment of liabilities, and (4) the distribution of cash to the partners.

Action Plan

- Calculate the gain or loss by comparing cash proceeds to the book value of assets.
- Allocate any gain or loss to each partner's capital account using the income ratios.
- Allocate the capital deficiency, if there is one.
- Record the final distribution of cash to each partner to eliminate the balance in each capital account. Do not distribute cash using the income ratio.

Solution

1.	Sept. 24	Cash	74,000	
		Loss on Realization	36,000	
		Noncash Assets		110,000
		To record realization of noncash assets.		
2.	Sept. 24	S. Anderson, Capital ($36,000 × ⅓)	12,000	
		J. Hinton, Capital ($36,000 × 2/9)	8,000	
		R. Smistad, Capital ($36,000 × 4/9)	16,000	
		Loss on Realization		36,000
		To allocate loss to partners' capital accounts.		
3.	Sept. 24	Accounts Payable	25,000	
		Cash		25,000
		To record payment of liabilities.		
4.	Sept. 24	S. Anderson, Capital ($30,000 − $12,000)	18,000	
		J. Hinton, Capital ($20,000 − $8,000)	12,000	
		R. Smistad, Capital ($41,000 − $16,000)	25,000	
		Cash ($6,000 + $74,000 − $25,000)		55,000
		To record distribution of cash to partners.		

Related exercise material: BE12–13, BE12–14, BE12–15, E12–9, E12–10, and E12–11.

Demonstration Problem

On January 1, 2007, the capital balances in Hollingsworth Company are Lois Holly, $26,000, and Jim Worth, $24,000. For the year ended December 31, 2007, the partnership reports net income of $32,500. The partnership agreement specifies (1) salary allowances of $12,000 for Holly and $10,000 for Worth, (2) interest allowances on opening capital account balances of 5%, and (3) the remainder to be distributed equally. Neither partner had any drawings in 2007.

In 2008, assume that the following independent transactions occur on January 2:

1. Donna Reichenbacher purchases one-half of Lois Holly's capital interest from Holly for $25,000.
2. Marsha Mears is admitted with a 25% capital interest by a cash investment of $37,500.
3. Stan Wells is admitted with a 30% capital interest by a cash investment of $32,500.

Instructions

(a) Prepare a schedule that shows the distribution of net income in 2007.
(b) Journalize the division of 2007 net income and its distribution to the partners on December 31.
(c) Journalize each of the independent transactions that occurred on January 2, 2008.

Action Plan

- Allocate the partners' salaries and interest allowances, if any, first. Divide the remaining net income among the partners, based on the income ratio.
- Journalize the division of net income in a closing entry.
- Recognize the admission by purchase of a partnership interest as a personal transaction between an existing partner and the new partner.
- Recognize the admission by investment of partnership assets as a transaction between the new partner and the partnership.
- In an admission by investment, determine any bonus to old or new partners by comparing the total capital of the new partnership to the new partner's capital credit. Allocate the bonus based on the old partners' income ratios.

Solution to Demonstration Problem

(a)

HOLLINGSWORTH COMPANY
Division of Net Income
Year Ended December 31, 2007

	L. Holly	J. Worth	Total
Net income			$32,500
Salary allowance	$12,000	$10,000	22,000
Remaining income			10,500
Interest allowance			
L. Holly ($26,000 × 5%)	1,300		
J. Worth ($24,000 × 5%)		1,200	2,500
Remaining income			8,000
Fixed ratio			
L. Holly ($8,000 × 50%)	4,000		
J. Worth ($8,000 × 50%)		4,000	8,000
Remaining income			0
Division of net income	$17,300	$15,200	$32,500

(b)

Dec. 31	Income Summary	32,500	
	L. Holly, Capital		17,300
	J. Worth, Capital		15,200
	To close net income to partners' capital accounts.		

L. Holly, Capital		J. Worth, Capital	
	26,000		24,000
	17,300		15,200
	43,300		39,200

(c)

1.	Jan. 2	L. Holly, Capital ($43,300 × 50%)	21,650	
		D. Reichenbacher, Capital		21,650
		To record purchase of one-half of Holly's interest.		

2.	Jan. 2	Cash	37,500	
		L. Holly, Capital ($7,500 × 50%)		3,750
		J. Worth, Capital ($7,500 × 50%)		3,750
		M. Mears, Capital		30,000
		To record admission of Mears by investment and bonus to old partners.		

Total capital after investment:
(L. Holly, $43,300; J. Worth $39,200; M. Mears investment, $37,500) $120,000
Mears' capital credit (25% × $120,000) $30,000
Bonus to old partners ($37,500 − $30,000) $7,500

3.	Jan. 2	Cash	32,500	
		L. Holly, Capital ($2,000 × 50%)	1,000	
		J. Worth, Capital ($2,000 × 50%)	1,000	
		S. Wells, Capital		34,500
		To record admission of Wells by investment and bonus to new partner.		

Total capital after investment:
(L. Holly, $43,300; J. Worth, $39,200; S. Wells investment, $32,500) $115,000
Wells' capital credit (30% × $115,000) $34,500
Bonus to Wells ($32,500 − $34,500) $(2,000)

Summary of Study Objectives

1. **Describe the characteristics of the partnership form of business organization.** The main characteristics of a partnership are (a) the association of individuals, (b) mutual agency, (c) co-ownership of property, (d) limited life, and (e) unlimited liability for a general partnership.

2. **Account for partnership transactions and allocate income.** When a partnership is formed, each partner's initial investment should be recorded at the fair market value of the assets at the date of their transfer to the partnership. Net income or net loss is divided based on the income ratio, which may be any of the following: (a) a fixed ratio; (b) a ratio based on beginning, ending, or average capital balances; (c) salaries allocated to partners and the remainder in a fixed ratio; (d) interest on partners' capital balances and the remainder in a fixed ratio; and (e) salaries allocated to partners, interest on partners' capital balances, and the remainder in a fixed ratio.

3. **Prepare partnership financial statements.** The financial statements of a partnership are similar to those of a proprietorship. The main differences are that (a) the statement of owners' equity is called the statement of partners' capital, and (b) each partner's capital is usually reported on the balance sheet or in a supporting schedule.

4. **Prepare the entries to record the admission of a partner.** The entry to record the admission of a new partner by purchase of a partner's interest affects only partners' capital accounts. The entry to record the admission by investment of assets in the partnership (a) increases both net assets and total capital, and (b) may result in the recognition of a bonus to either the old partners or the new partner.

5. **Prepare the entries to record the withdrawal of a partner.** The entry to record a withdrawal from the firm when payment is made from partners' personal assets affects only partners' capital accounts. The entry to record a withdrawal when payment is made from partnership assets (a) decreases net assets and total capital, and (b) may result in recognizing a bonus to either the departing partner or the remaining partners.

6. **Prepare the entries to record the liquidation of a partnership.** When a partnership is liquidated, it is necessary to record (a) the sale of noncash assets, (b) the allocation of the gain or loss on realization, (c) the payment of partnership liabilities, (d) the removal of any capital deficiency either by repayment or allocation to the other partners, and (e) the distribution of cash to the partners based on their capital balances.

Glossary

Study Aids: Glossary
Practice Tools: Key Term Matching Activity

Admission by investment Admission of a partner by an investment of assets in the partnership. Both partnership net assets and total capital increase. (p. 625)

Admission by purchase of an interest Admission of a partner through a personal transaction between one or more existing partners and the new partner. It does not change total partnership assets or total capital. (p. 624)

Capital deficiency A debit balance in a partner's capital account after the allocation of a gain or loss on liquidation of a partnership. Capital deficiencies can be repaid, or allocated among the remaining partners. (p. 635)

Income ratio The basis for dividing both net income and net loss in a partnership. (p. 617)

Limited liability partnership (LLP) A partnership in which partners have limited liability for other partners' negligence. (p. 614)

Limited partnership (LP) A partnership in which one or more general partners have unlimited liability, and one or more partners have limited liability for the obligations of the partnership. (p. 614)

No capital deficiency A situation where all partners have credit balances after the allocation of a gain or a loss on liquidation of a partnership. (p. 635)

Partnership An association of individuals who operate a business for profit. (p. 612)

Partnership agreement A written contract that expresses the voluntary agreement of two or more individuals in a partnership. (p. 616)

Partnership dissolution A change in the number of partners that dissolves (ends) the partnership. It does not necessarily end the business. (p. 613)

Partnership liquidation An event that ends both the legal and economic life of a partnership. (p. 635)

Realization The sale of noncash assets for cash in the liquidation of a partnership. (p. 635)

Statement of partners' capital The equity statement for a partnership that shows the changes in each partner's capital balance, and in total partnership capital, during the year. (p. 622)

Withdrawal by payment from partners' personal assets Withdrawal of a partner by a personal transaction between partners. It does not change total partnership assets or total capital. (p. 630)

Withdrawal by payment from partnership assets Withdrawal of a partner by a transaction that decreases both partnership net assets and total capital. (p. 631)

Self-Study Questions

Practice Tools: Self-Assessment Quizzes

Answers are at the end of the chapter.

(SO 1) K 1. Which of the following is not a characteristic of a partnership?
  (a) Taxable entity   (c) Mutual agency
  (b) Co-ownership of property (d) Limited life

(SO 2) K 2. When a partnership is formed, each partner's initial investment of assets should be recorded at its:
  (a) net book value.   (c) fair market value.
  (b) original cost.   (d) liquidation value.

(SO 2) AP 3. The ABC Company reports net income of $60,000. If partners A, B, and C have a salary allowance of $10,000 and an income ratio of 50%, 30%, and 20%, respectively, what is B's share of the net income?
  (a) $16,000   (c) $20,000
  (b) $19,000   (d) $25,000

(SO 3) K 4. Which of the following statements about partnership financial statements is true?
  (a) Details on how net income is distributed are shown in the cash flow statement.

  (b) The distribution of net income is shown on the balance sheet.
  (c) Partner capital balances are usually shown in the income statement.
  (d) The statement of owners' equity is called the statement of partners' capital.

5. R. Ranken purchases 50% of L. Lars's capital interest in the Kim & Lars partnership for $20,000. The capital balances of Kim and Lars are $40,000 and $30,000, respectively. Ranken's capital balance after the purchase is: (SO 4)
  (a) $15,000.   (c) $22,000.
  (b) $20,000.   (d) $35,000.

6. Capital balances in the DEA partnership are Delano, Capital $60,000; Egil, Capital $50,000; and Armand, Capital $40,000. The income ratio is 5:3:2. The DEAR partnership is formed by admitting Ranger to the firm with a cash investment of $60,000 for a 25% capital interest. The bonus to be credited to Armand, Capital, in admitting Ranger is: (SO 4)

(a) $1,500.　　　　　(c) $7,500.
(b) $3,750.　　　　　(d) $10,000.

SO 5) AP 7. Capital balances in the Alouette partnership are Gentille, Capital $50,000; Tête, Capital $40,000; and, Nez, Capital $30,000. The income ratio is 5:4:3. Nez withdraws from the partnership after being paid $16,000 personally by each of Gentille and Tête. Gentille's capital balance after recording the withdrawal of Nez is:
(a) $48,889.　　　　　(c) $51,111.
(b) $50,000.　　　　　(d) $65,000

SO 5) AP 8. Capital balances in the TERM partnership are Takako, Capital $50,000; Endo, Capital $40,000; Reiko, Capital $30,000; and Maeda, Capital $20,000. The income ratio is 4:3:2:1. Maeda withdraws from the firm after receiving $29,000 in cash from the partnership. Endo's capital balance after recording the withdrawal of Maeda is:
(a) $36,000.　　　　　(c) $37,300.
(b) $37,000.　　　　　(d) $40,000.

9. Fontaine and Tomah were partners in the AFN partnership, sharing income and losses in a ratio of 3:2. Fontaine's capital account balance was $30,000 and Tomah's was $20,000, immediately before the partnership liquidated on February 19. If noncash assets of $60,000 were sold for $75,000, what was Fontaine's capital account balance after the sale? **(SO 6) AP**
(a) $14,000　　　　　(c) $26,000
(b) $21,000　　　　　(d) $39,000

10. Partners Aikawa, Ito, and Mori shared an income ratio of 2:1:3 in the AIM Company. After AIM was liquidated, $12,000 cash remained and the balances in the partners' capital accounts were as follows: Aikawa, $10,000 Cr.; Ito, $5,000 Cr.; and Mori, $3,000 Dr. How much cash would be distributed to Aikawa, assuming Mori does not repay his capital deficiency? **(SO 6) AP**
(a) $8,000　　　　　(c) $9,000
(b) $8,500　　　　　(d) $10,000

Questions

(SO 1) C 1. The characteristics of a partnership include the following: (a) association of individuals, (b) limited life, and (c) co-ownership of property. Explain each of these terms.

(SO 1) C 2. Carla Cardosa is confused about mutual agency and unlimited liability in partnerships. (a) Explain these two characteristics to Carla. (b) When they are combined, how can these two characteristics create problems in a partnership?

(SO 1) C 3. K. Nasser and T. Yoko are considering a business venture. They ask you to explain the advantages and disadvantages of the partnership form of organization.

(SO 1) K 4. Because of concerns over unlimited liability, there are now special forms of partnership organization that modify that characteristic. Describe these other forms of partnership.

(SO 1) K 5. What is the difference between a general partner and a limited partner?

(SO 1) K 6. (a) What items should be specified in a partnership agreement? (b) Why is it important to have this agreement in writing?

(SO 2) K 7. (a) For accounting purposes, when a partner invests assets in a partnership, how is the value of these assets determined? (b) Is this practice consistent with the cost principle? Explain.

(SO 2) C 8. Ingrid and Hartmut are transferring the assets from each of their sole proprietorships into a partnership. These assets include equipment, net of accumulated amortization, and accounts receivable, net of allowance for doubtful accounts. (a) What amount should be used to record the transfer of the equipment to the partnership—the recorded cost, net book value, or market value? (b) What amount should be used to record the transfer of the receivables to the partnership—the recorded cost, net realizable value, or market value?

9. R. Hay, S. Innis, and L. Joyce have a partnership called Express Wings. There is a dispute among the partners. Hay has invested twice as much as the other two partners. She believes that net income and net losses should be shared according to the capital contributions. The partnership agreement does not specify the division of profits and losses. How will net income and net loss be divided? **(SO 2) C**

10. S. Hark and R. Green are discussing how income and losses should be divided in a partnership they plan to form. What factors should they consider before reaching a decision? **(SO 2) C**

11. What is the relationship between (1) a salary allowance for allocating net income among partners and (2) partners' cash withdrawals? **(SO 2) C**

12. Explain how each financial statement for a partnership is similar to, and different from, those of a proprietorship. **(SO 3) C**

13. Holly Canter decides to pay $50,000 for a one-third interest in a partnership. What effect does this transaction have on the partnership net assets? **(SO 4) AP**

14. R. Minoa decides to invest $25,000 in a partnership for a one-sixth capital interest. How much do the partnership's net assets increase? Does Minoa also acquire a one-sixth income ratio through this investment? **(SO 4) AP**

(SO 4) C 15. Explain why a new partner may agree to pay a bonus as part of the cost of investing in an existing partnership.

(SO 5) C 16. What is the impact on a partnership's financial position when (a) a partner withdraws by payment from personal assets, and (b) a partner withdraws by payment from partnership assets?

(SO 5) C 17. Under what circumstances will a partner who is leaving a partnership give the remaining partners a bonus?

(SO 5) C 18. What is the purpose of a partnership's obtaining life insurance policies on each of the partners?

19. How is the liquidation of a partnership different from the dissolution of a partnership? (SO 6)

20. Identify the steps in liquidating a partnership. (SO 6)

21. How is the cash distribution to partners in the liquidation of a partnership different when (a) there is a capital deficiency, and (b) there is no capital deficiency? (SO 6)

22. Joe and Jean are discussing the liquidation of a partnership. Joe argues that all cash should be distributed to partners based on their income ratios. Is he correct? Explain. (SO 6)

Brief Exercises

Identify partnership terminology.
(SO 1) K

BE12–1 The following terms were introduced in this chapter:

1. Admission by investment
2. Partnership liquidation
3. Salary allowance
4. Withdrawal by payment from partners' personal assets
5. Capital deficiency
6. Limited liability partnership
7. Income ratio
8. General partnership
9. Mutual agency
10. Partnership dissolution

Match the terms with the following descriptions:

(a) ___ Partners have limited liability.
(b) ___ Partners have unlimited liability.
(c) ___ It is the basis for dividing net income and loss.
(d) ___ Partnership assets and capital increase with the change in partners.
(e) ___ Partnership assets and capital stay the same with the change in partners.
(f) ___ Actions of partners are binding on all other partners.
(g) ___ It is a compensation for differences in personal effort put into the partnership.
(h) ___ Partnership is changed by the addition or withdrawal of a partner.
(i) ___ There is a debit balance in a partner's capital account.
(j) ___ Partnership is ended.

Record formation of partnership.
(SO 2) AP

BE12–2 R. Alfredo and B. Panos decide to organize the All-Star partnership. Alfredo invests $15,000 cash. Panos contributes $10,000 cash and equipment having a book value of $5,500. The equipment has an original cost of $8,000 and a fair market value of $6,000. Prepare the entry to record each partner's investment in the partnership on July 10 of the current year.

Prepare opening balance sheet.
(SO 2) AP

BE12–3 C. Held and G. Kamp decide to merge their proprietorships into a partnership called Held-Kamp Company. Immediately before the merger, the balance sheet of Kamp Co. shows the following:

Accounts receivable	$16,000	
Less: allowance for doubtful accounts	1,200	$14,800
Equipment	$20,000	
Less: accumulated amortization	7,000	13,000

The partners agree that the net realizable value of the receivables is $14,000. The fair market value of the equipment is $12,000. Indicate how these items should appear in the opening balance sheet of the partnership on March 1 of the current year.

BE12–4 Brung & Rohls Co. reports net income of $50,000 for the current year. The income ratios are A. Brung 60% and P. Rohls 40%. (a) Calculate the division of net income to each partner. (b) Prepare the entry to distribute the net income.

Calculate and record division of net income.
(SO 2) AP

BE12–5 MET Co. reports net income of $65,000 for the current year. Partner salary allowances are J. Moses $15,000; T. Eaton $5,000; and M. Talty $5,000. The income ratio is 5:3:2. Calculate the division of net income to each partner.

Calculate division of net income.
(SO 2) AP

BE12–6 The MillStone Partnership reported net income of $75,000 for the year ended February 29, 2008. Salary allowances are $25,000 for K. Mills and $20,000 for S. Stone. Interest allowances of 5% are calculated on each partner's opening capital account balance. Capital account balances at March 1, 2007, were as follows: K. Mills $80,000 (Cr.); and S. Stone $60,000 (Cr.). Any remainder is shared 60% by Mills and 40% by Stone. Calculate the division of net income to each partner.

Calculate division of net income.
(SO 2) AP

BE12–7 S & T Co. reports net income of $34,000 for the current year. Salary allowances for the partners are J. Siebrasse $15,000 and S. Tong $10,000. Interest allowances are J. Siebrasse $7,000 and S. Tong $5,000. The remainder is shared equally. Calculate the division of net income to each partner.

Calculate division of net income.
(SO 2) AP

BE12–8 The medical practice of Dr. W. Jarratt and Dr. M. Bramstrup had the following general ledger account balances at April 30, 2008, its fiscal year end:

Prepare financial statements.
(SO 3) AP

Cash	$10,000	W. Jarratt, drawings	$120,000
Equipment	35,000	M. Bramstrup, capital	33,000
Accumulated amortization		M. Bramstrup, drawings	130,000
—equipment	15,000	Fees earned	365,000
Note payable, due 2009	20,000	Operating expenses	161,000
W. Jarratt, capital	23,000		

Prepare financial statements for the partnership, assuming the doctors share income or loss equally.

BE12–9 In ABC Co., the capital balances of the partners are A. Ali $30,000; S. Babson $25,000; and K. Carter $22,000. The partners share income equally. On June 9 of the current year, D. Dutton is admitted to the partnership by purchasing one-half of K. Carter's interest for $13,000. (a) Journalize the admission of Dutton on June 9. (b) How would the entry change if Dutton paid $10,000 instead of $13,000 to be admitted to the partnership?

Record admission of partner.
(SO 4) AP

BE12–10 In the EZ Co., the capital balances of the partners are J. Edie $40,000 and K. Zane $30,000. The partners share income equally. On October 1 of the current year, when she invests $45,000 cash, J. Kerns is admitted to the partnership with a 45% interest. (a) Journalize the admission of Kerns on October 1. (b) What would the journal entry be if Kerns had paid $70,000 for a 45% interest in the partnership?

Record admission of partner.
(SO 4) AP

BE12–11 The capital balances of the partners in DEB Co. are M. Ditka $40,000; E. Embs $30,000; and B. Boyd $20,000. The partners share income equally. Boyd decides that he is going to leave the partnership. Ditka and Embs each agree to pay Boyd $12,000 from their personal assets to each receive 50% of Boyd's equity. Journalize the withdrawal of Boyd on December 31 of the current year.

Record withdrawal of partner.
(SO 5) AP

BE12–12 Data for DEB Co. are presented in BE12–11. Instead of a payment from personal assets, assume that Boyd receives $24,000 from partnership assets in withdrawing from the partnership. (a) Journalize the withdrawal of Boyd on December 31. (b) What would the journal entry be if Boyd received $16,000 cash instead of $24,000?

Record withdrawal of partner.
(SO 5) AP

BE12–13 On November 15 of the current year, the account balances in Greenscape Partnership were Cash $5,000; Other Assets $12,000; D. Dupuis, Capital $9,000; V. Dueck, Capital $6,000; and B. Veitch, Capital $2,000. The three partners share income and losses equally. The other assets are sold

Record partnership liquidation.
(SO 6) AP

for $15,000 cash. Prepare journal entries to (a) record the sale of the other assets, (b) distribute any resulting gain or loss to the capital accounts, and (c) record the final distribution of cash to the partners.

Record partnership liquidation.
(SO 6) AP

BE12–14 Data for Greenscape Partnership are presented in BE12–13. Assume that the other assets were sold for $9,000 cash instead of $15,000. Prepare journal entries to (a) record the sale of the other assets, (b) distribute any resulting gain or loss to the capital accounts, and (c) record the final distribution of cash to the partners.

Record partnership liquidation.
(SO 6) AP

BE12–15 Before the distribution of cash to the partners on September 30 of the current year, the accounts in MEL Company are as follows: Cash $31,000; M. McDonald, Capital $18,000 (Cr.); J. El Bayouni, Capital $16,000 (Cr.); and G. Lodge, Capital $3,000 (Dr.). The income ratios are 5:3:2, respectively. (a) Assuming Lodge repays his capital deficiency, prepare the entry on September 30 to record (1) Lodge's payment of $3,000 in cash to the partnership, and (2) the distribution of cash to the partners. (b) Assuming Lodge is not able to repay his capital deficiency, prepare the entry on September 30 to record (1) the absorption of Lodge's capital deficiency by the other partners, and (2) the distribution of cash to the partners.

Exercises

Determine form of organization.
(SO 1) AN

E12–1 Presented below are three independent situations:

1. Angelique Gloss and David Deutsch, two students looking for summer employment, decide to open a home meal replacement business. Each day, they prepare nutritious, ready-to-bake meals, which they sell to people on their way home from work.
2. Joe Daigle and Cathy Goodfellow own a ski repair business and a ski shop. They have decided to combine their businesses. They expect that in the coming year they will need a large amount of money to expand their operations.
3. Three business professors have formed a business to offer income tax services to the community. They expect to hire students during the busy season.
4. Myles Martin would like to organize a company that buys and leases commercial real estate. Myles will need to raise a large amount of capital so that he can buy commercial property for lease.

Instructions

In each of the above situations, explain whether the partnership form of organization is the best choice for the business. Explain your reasoning.

Record formation of partnership.
(SO 2) AP

E12–2 Ted Karl has owned and operated a proprietorship for several years. On January 1, he decides to end this business and become a partner in the firm of Kurl and Karl. Karl's investment in the partnership consists of $12,000 cash and the following assets from the proprietorship: accounts receivable of $14,000 less an allowance for doubtful accounts of $2,000, and equipment of $20,000 less accumulated amortization of $4,000. It is agreed that the net realizable value of the accounts receivable should be $11,000 for the partnership. The fair market value of the equipment is $17,500. The partnership will also assume responsibility for Karl's accounts payable of $6,000.

Instructions

Journalize Karl's admission to Kurl and Karl on January 1.

Calculate and record division of income.
(SO 2) AP

E12–3 R. Huma and W. How have capital balances on July 1, 2007, of $50,000 and $40,000, respectively. The partnership income-sharing agreement specifies (1) salary allowances of $20,000 for Huma and $12,000 for How, (2) interest at 5% on beginning capital balances, and (3) for the remaining income or loss to be shared 60% by Huma and 40% by How.

Instructions

(a) Prepare a schedule showing the division of net income for the year ended June 30, 2008, assuming net income is (1) $45,000, and (2) $32,000.
(b) Journalize the allocation of net income in each of the situations in (a).

E12–4 In Schott Co., the partners' beginning capital balances on January 1, 2008, are M. Salz $20,000 and C. Toni $18,000. During the year, drawings were $8,000 by M. Salz and $5,000 by C. Toni. Net income was $32,000 for the year ended December 31, 2008. Salz and Toni share income based on a 3:1 ratio.

Prepare partial financial statements.
(SO 3) AP

Instructions

(a) Prepare the statement of partners' capital for the year.
(b) Prepare the partners' equity section of the balance sheet at year end.

E12–5 T. Halo, K. Rose, and J. Lamp share income on a 5:3:2 basis, respectively. They have capital balances of $32,000, $26,000, and $15,000, respectively, when R. Zahn is admitted to the partnership on July 1 of the current year.

Record admission of partner.
(SO 4) AP

Instructions

Prepare the journal entry to record the admission of Zahn under each of the following independent assumptions:

(a) Zahn purchases 50% of Halo's equity for $20,000.
(b) Zahn purchases 50% of Rose's equity for $20,000.
(c) Zahn purchases 33⅓% of Lamp's equity for $10,000.

E12–6 Joe Keho and Mike McLain share income on a 4:2 basis, respectively. They have capital balances of $90,000 and $70,000, respectively, when Ed Kehler is admitted to the partnership on January 1 of the current year.

Record admission of partner.
(SO 4) AP

Instructions

Prepare the journal entry to record the admission of Kehler on January 1 under each of the following independent assumptions:

(a) Kehler invests $75,000 cash for a 25% ownership interest.
(b) Kehler invests $45,000 cash for a 25% ownership interest.

E12–7 Julie Lane, Sara Miles, and Amber Noll have capital balances of $50,000, $40,000, and $30,000, respectively. The income ratio is 5:3:2. Assume Noll withdraws from the partnership on December 31 of the current year under each of the following independent conditions:

Record withdrawal of partner.
(SO 5) AP

1. Lane and Miles agree to purchase Noll's equity by paying $17,000 each from their personal assets. Each purchaser receives 50% of Noll's equity.
2. Miles agrees to purchase all of Noll's equity by paying $35,000 cash from her personal assets.
3. Lane agrees to purchase all of Noll's equity by paying $25,000 cash from her personal assets.

Instructions

Journalize the withdrawal of Noll under each of the above assumptions.

E12–8 Dale Nagel, Keith White, and Dan Neal have capital balances of $95,000, $75,000, and $60,000, respectively. They share income or loss on a 4:3:2 basis. Assume White withdraws from the partnership on September 30 of the current year under each of the following independent assumptions:

Record withdrawal of partner.
(SO 5) AP

1. White is paid $85,000 cash from partnership assets.
2. White is paid $69,000 cash from partnership assets.

Instructions

Journalize the withdrawal of White under each of the above assumptions.

Calculate amounts paid on liquidation of partnership.
(SO 6) AP

E12–9 At December 31, Baylee Company has cash of $20,000, equipment of $140,000, accumulated amortization of $40,000, liabilities of $55,000, and the following partners' capital balances: H. Bayer $45,000 and J. Leech $20,000. The partnership is liquidated on December 31 of the current year and $120,000 cash is received for the equipment. Bayer and Leech have income ratios of 60% and 40%, respectively.

Instructions

Calculate how much will be paid to each of the partners when the company is liquidated on December 31.

Record partnership liquidation.
(SO 6) AP

E12–10 Data for the Baylee Company partnership are presented in E12–9.

Instructions

Prepare the entries to record (a) the sale of the equipment, (b) the allocation to the partners of the gain or loss on liquidation, (c) the payment of creditors, and (d) the distribution of cash to the partners.

Record partnership liquidation.
(SO 6) AP

E12–11 Ole Low, Arnt Olson, and Stig Lokum decided to liquidate the LOL partnership on December 31 of the current year, and go their separate ways. The partners share income and losses equally. As at December 31, the partnership had cash of $18,000, noncash assets of $115,000, and liabilities of $15,000. Before selling their noncash assets, the partners had capital balances of $45,000, $63,000, and $10,000, respectively. After selling the noncash assets for $82,000 and paying all creditors, $85,000 cash remained in the partnership.

Instructions

(a) Calculate the balance in each of the partners' capital accounts after allocating the loss from the sale of the noncash assets and paying the liabilities.
(b) Assume that all of the partners have the personal resources to cover a deficit in their capital accounts. Prepare journal entries to record any cash receipts from the partners to cover any existing deficit and to record the final distribution of cash.
(c) Now assume that the partners do not have the personal resources to cover a deficit in their capital accounts. Prepare journal entries to allocate any deficit to the remaining partners and to record the final distribution of cash.

Problems: Set A

Discuss partnership characteristics.
(SO 1) C

P12–1A Clearwater Limited Partnership was created in 1986 to operate a dryland lobster pound in Arichat, Nova Scotia. It also has the capacity to process lobsters and other seafood products. The general partner is Arichat Pounds Limited, which manages and operates the dryland pound. On December 31, 2005, the partnership reported total assets of $2.0 million and a partners' deficiency of $9.4 million.

Instructions

(a) What probably motivated Clearwater Limited Partnership to organize as a limited partnership?
(b) What is the impact of such a large partners' deficiency on the liability of the general partner? Of the limited partners?

Record formation of partnership and prepare balance sheet.
(SO 2, 3) AP

P12–2A Here are the post-closing trial balances of two proprietorships on January 1 of the current year:

	Visanji Company		Vanbakel Company	
	Dr.	Cr.	Dr.	Cr.
Cash	$ 9,500		$ 6,000	
Accounts receivable	15,000		23,000	
Allowance for doubtful accounts		$ 2,500		$ 4,000
Merchandise inventory	28,000		17,000	
Equipment	50,000		30,000	
Accumulated amortization—equipment		24,000		13,000
Notes payable		30,000		20,000
Accounts payable		15,000		17,000
F. Visanji, capital		31,000		
P. Vanbakel, capital				22,000
	$102,500	$102,500	$76,000	$76,000

Visanji and Vanbakel decide to form the Varsity partnership and agree on the following market values for the noncash assets that each partner is contributing:

	Visanji	Vanbakel
Accounts receivable	$15,000	$23,000
Allowance for doubtful accounts	3,500	5,000
Merchandise inventory	32,000	15,000
Equipment	28,000	15,000

All cash will be transferred to the partnership on January 1. The partnership will also assume all the liabilities of the two proprietorships. Further, it is agreed that Vanbakel will invest $15,500 cash.

Instructions

(a) Prepare separate journal entries to record the transfer of each proprietorship's assets and liabilities to the partnership on January 1.
(b) Journalize the additional cash investment.
(c) Prepare a balance sheet for the partnership at January 1.

P12–3A At the end of its first year of operations, on December 31, 2008, LBS Company's accounts show the following:

Calculate and record division of net income. Prepare statement of partners' capital.
(SO 2, 3) AP

Partner	Drawings	Capital
S. Little	$23,000	$50,000
D. Bartlet	14,000	30,000
D. Sawka	10,000	20,000

The capital balance represents each partner's initial capital investment. No closing entries have been recorded for net income (loss) or drawings as yet.

Instructions

(a) Journalize the entry to record the division of net income for the year ended December 31, 2008, under each of the following independent assumptions:
  1. Net income is shared in the ratio of their initial investments. Net income is $47,000.
  2. Net income is $34,000. Bartlet and Sawka are given salary allowances of $15,000 and $10,000, respectively. The remainder is shared equally.
  3. Net income is $23,000. Each partner is allowed interest of 5% on beginning capital balances. Sawka is given a $15,000 salary allowance. The remainder is shared equally.
(b) Journalize the entry to close each partner's drawings account.
(c) Prepare a statement of partners' capital for the year under assumption (3) in (a) above.

P12–4A Terry Lam and Chris Tan have a partnership agreement with the following provisions for sharing net income or net loss:

Calculate division of income. Prepare income statement, statement of partners' capital, and closing entries.
(SO 2, 3) AP

  1. A salary allowance of $40,000 to Lam and $25,000 to Tan
  2. An interest allowance of 6% on capital balances at the beginning of the year
  3. The remainder to be divided between Lam and Tan on a 4:2 basis

The capital balances on February 1, 2007, for T. Lam and C. Tan were $110,000 and $130,000, respectively. For the year ended January 31, 2008, the Lam Tan Partnership had sales of $445,000; cost of goods sold of $295,000; operating expenses of $100,000; T. Lam drawings of $40,000; and C. Tan drawings of $30,000.

Instructions

(a) Prepare an income statement for the Lam Tan Partnership for the year.
(b) Prepare a schedule to show how net income will be allocated to the two partners.
(c) Prepare a statement of partners' capital for the year.
(d) Prepare closing entries on January 31.

Prepare financial statements and closing entries.
(SO 3) AP

P12–5A The adjusted trial balance of the Clay and Ogletree law firm as at September 30, 2008, follows:

CLAY AND OGLETREE, LLP
Adjusted Trial Balance
September 30, 2008

	Debit	Credit
Cash	$ 7,500	
Accounts receivable	70,000	
Supplies	2,500	
Land	50,000	
Building	150,000	
Accumulated amortization—building		$ 75,000
Office equipment	40,000	
Accumulated amortization—office equipment		20,000
Accounts payable		10,000
Salaries payable		5,000
Unearned fees		25,000
Bank loan payable (short-term)		45,000
Note payable ($5,000 of this note is due within the next year)		15,000
G. Clay, Capital		50,000
M. Ogletree, Capital		25,000
G. Clay, Drawings	100,000	
M. Ogletree, Drawings	100,000	
Professional fees		450,000
Salaries expense	150,000	
Amortization expense	15,000	
Property tax expense	10,000	
Interest expense	10,000	
Other expense	6,000	
Supplies expense	5,000	
Utilities expense	4,000	
Totals	$720,000	$720,000

Additional Information: The balance in Clay's capital account includes an additional investment of $10,000 made during the year. Clay and Ogletree share income in the ratio of 2:1, respectively.

Instructions

(a) Prepare an income statement, statement of partners' capital, and balance sheet.
(b) Journalize the closing entries.

Record admission of partner.
(SO 4) AP

P12–6A At September 30 of the current year, partners' capital balances in NEW Company are A. Nolan $62,000; D. Elder $48,000; and T. Wuhan $14,000. The income-sharing ratio is 5:4:1, in the same order. On October 1, the NEWS Company is formed by admitting C. Santos to the partnership.

Instructions

Journalize the admission of C. Santos under each of the following independent assumptions:

(a) Santos purchases 50% of Wuhan's ownership interest by paying Wuhan $16,000 cash.
(b) Santos purchases 33 ⅓% of Elder's ownership interest by paying Elder $15,000 cash.
(c) Santos invests $75,000 for a 30% ownership interest.
(d) Santos invests $40,000 for a 30% ownership interest.

P12–7A   At April 30, partners' capital balances in the DLM partnership are A. Donatello $50,000; M. Leonardo $30,000; and K. Michaelangelo $20,000. The income ratio is 5:3:2, in the same order. On May 1, S. Rafael is admitted to the partnership by investment. After Rafael's admission, the total partnership capital is $117,000 and Michaelangelo's ownership interest has been reduced from 20% to 15% of total partnership capital. Donatello's ownership interest has been reduced from 50% to 37.5% and Leonardo's ownership interest has been reduced proportionately.

Calculate investment and bonus on admission of partner.
(SO 4) AN

Instructions

(a) How much was Rafael's cash investment in the partnership?
(b) What is the percentage ownership of Leonardo after Rafael's admission to the partnership? Of Rafael?
(c) What was the total bonus allocated to Rafael by the old partners?
(d) What is the balance in each partner's capital account after Rafael's admission to the partnership?

P12–8A   On December 31, the capital balances and income ratios in the VKD Company are as follows:

Record withdrawal of partner.
(SO 5) AP

Partner	Capital Balance	Income Ratio
B. Vuong	$60,000	50%
G. Khan	40,000	30%
R. Dixon	30,000	20%

Instructions

Journalize the withdrawal of Dixon under each of the following independent assumptions:

(a) Each of the continuing partners agrees to pay $18,000 cash from personal funds to purchase Dixon's ownership equity. Each partner receives 50% of Dixon's equity.
(b) Khan agrees to purchase Dixon's ownership interest for $36,000 cash.
(c) Dixon is paid $38,000 from partnership assets.
(d) Dixon is paid $26,000 from partnership assets.

P12–9A   At April 30, partners' capital balances in the Marx Company partnership are G. Harpo $60,000; F. Chico $40,000; and M. Groucho $30,000. The income ratios are 5:4:2, respectively. On May 1, Groucho withdrew from the partnership. After Groucho's exit, Chico's capital balance was $48,000.

Calculate bonus and payment on withdrawal of partner.
(SO 5) AN

Instructions

(a) What was the total partnership capital after Groucho left the partnership?
(b) What is the percentage ownership of Harpo and Chico after Groucho left the partnership?
(c) How much cash was paid by the partnership to Groucho?
(d) What was the total bonus allocated to the remaining partners?

P12–10A   The partners in Omni Company decide to liquidate the company when the post-closing trial balance shows the following:

Prepare and post entries for partnership liquidation.
(SO 6) AP

OMNI COMPANY
Post-Closing Trial Balance
May 31, 2008

	Debit	Credit
Cash	$ 27,500	
Accounts receivable	25,000	
Allowance for doubtful accounts		$ 1,000
Inventory	34,500	
Equipment	21,000	
Accumulated amortization		5,500
Notes payable		13,500
Accounts payable		27,000
Wages payable		3,800
L. Sciban, Capital		33,000
V. Subra, Capital		21,000
C. Werier, Capital		3,200
Totals	$108,000	$108,000

The partners share income and loss 5:3:2 for Sciban, Subra, and Werier, respectively. During the process of liquidation, the following transactions were completed in the sequence shown:

1. A total of $50,000 was received from converting noncash assets into cash on June 2.
2. Liabilities were paid in full on June 4.
3. Werier paid her capital deficiency on June 6.
4. Cash was paid to the partners with credit balances on June 9.

Instructions

(a) Prepare the entries to record the transactions.
(b) Post the transactions to the cash and capital accounts.
(c) Assume that Werier is unable to repay her capital deficiency. Prepare the entry to record (1) the reallocation of her deficiency, and (2) the final distribution of cash.

Record liquidation of partnership.
(SO 6) AP

P12–11A On September 1, 2008, the accounting partnership of M. Broski and B. Hazle ended and the partnership was liquidated. The partners Broski and Hazle share income and loss in a 1:3 ratio. Just before the liquidation, the post-closing trial balance showed the following:

BROSKI AND HAZLE
Post-Closing Trial Balance
September 1, 2008

	Debit	Credit
Cash	$ 80,000	
Office equipment	85,000	
Accumulated amortization		$ 50,000
Accounts payable		55,000
M. Broski, Capital		45,000
B. Hazle, Capital		15,000
Totals	$165,000	$165,000

Instructions

Journalize the liquidation of the partnership on September 2 under each of the following independent assumptions:

(a) The equipment is sold for $39,000 cash, the accounts payable are paid, and the remaining cash is paid to the two partners.
(b) The equipment is scrapped and the accounts payable are paid. Hazle pays his capital deficiency and the remaining cash is distributed to the partners.

(c) The equipment is scrapped and the accounts payable are paid. Hazle does not pay his capital deficiency. The remaining cash is distributed to Broski.

Problems: Set B

P12–1B **The Banff Rocky Mountain Resort Limited Partnership** owns and operates a resort hotel in Banff, Alberta. The general partner is Banff Rocky Mountain Resort Ltd. and the partnership has 23,000 limited partner units authorized to be issued at $1,000 each (limited partner units are similar to common shares in a corporation). The partnership reported revenue of $5.2 million for the year ended December 31, 2005, and a partners' equity of $4.3 million as at December 31.

Discuss partnership characteristics.
(SO 1) C

Instructions

(a) What probably motivated Banff Rocky Mountain Resort to organize as a limited partnership?
(b) Phoenix Capital Inc. is one of the limited partners. It owns 2,585 limited partnership units. What amount is Phoenix Capital liable for in the partnership?

P12–2B The post-closing trial balances of two proprietorships on January 1, 2008, follow:

Record formation of partnership and prepare balance sheet.
(SO 2, 3) AP

	Domic Company Dr.	Domic Company Cr.	Dasilva Company Dr.	Dasilva Company Cr.
Cash	$ 14,000		$12,000	
Accounts receivable	17,500		26,000	
Allowance for doubtful accounts		$ 3,000		$ 4,400
Merchandise inventory	26,500		18,400	
Equipment	45,000		29,000	
Accumulated amortization—equipment		24,000		11,000
Notes payable		30,000		15,000
Accounts payable		10,000		31,000
I. Domic, capital		36,000		
P. Dasilva, capital				24,000
	$103,000	$103,000	$85,400	$85,400

Domic and Dasilva decide to form a partnership on January 1 and agree on the following valuations for the noncash assets that they are each contributing:

	Domic	Dasilva
Accounts receivable	$17,500	$26,000
Allowance for doubtful accounts	4,000	4,000
Merchandise inventory	25,000	20,000
Equipment	23,000	15,000

All cash will be transferred to the partnership. The partnership will also assume all the liabilities of the two proprietorships. It is also agreed that Dasilva will invest $10,500 cash.

Instructions

(a) Prepare separate journal entries to record the transfer of each proprietorship's assets and liabilities to the partnership on January 1.
(b) Journalize the additional cash investment.
(c) Prepare a balance sheet for the partnership at January 1.

P12–3B At the end of its first year of operations, on December 31, 2008, CNW Company's accounts show the following:

Calculate and record division of net income. Prepare statement of partners' capital.
(SO 2, 3) AP

Partner	Drawings	Capital
J. Chapman	$12,000	$33,000
C. Nelson	9,000	20,000
H. Weir	4,000	10,000

The capital balance represents each partner's initial capital investment. No closing entries for net income (loss) or drawings have been recorded as yet.

Instructions

(a) Journalize the entry to record the division of net income for the year ended December 31, 2008, under each of the following independent assumptions:

1. Net income is $36,000. Income is shared 3:2:1 for Chapman, Nelson, and Weir, respectively.
2. Net income is $30,000. Nelson and Weir are given salary allowances of $10,000 and $8,000, respectively. The remainder is shared equally.
3. Net income is $30,150. Each partner is allowed interest of 5% on beginning capital balances. Nelson and Weir are each given a $15,000 salary allowance. The remainder is shared equally.

(b) Journalize the entry to close each partner's drawings account.
(c) Prepare a statement of partners' capital for the year under assumption (3) in (a) above.

Calculate division of income. Prepare income statement, statement of partners' capital, and closing entries.
(SO 2, 3) AP

P12–4B Veda Storey and Gordon Rogers have a partnership agreement with the following provisions for sharing net income or net loss:

1. A salary allowance of $20,000 to Storey and $15,000 to Rogers
2. An interest allowance of 4% on capital balances at the beginning of the year
3. The remainder to be divided between Storey and Rogers on a 3:2 basis

The capital balances on January 1, 2008, for Storey and Rogers were $80,000 and $100,000, respectively. For the year ended December 31, 2008, the Storey Rogers Partnership had sales of $330,000; cost of goods sold of $190,000; operating expenses of $100,000; V. Storey drawings of $30,000; and G. Rogers drawings of $20,000.

Instructions

(a) Prepare an income statement for Storey Rogers Partnership for the year.
(b) Prepare a schedule to show how net income will be allocated to the two partners.
(c) Prepare a statement of partners' capital for the year.
(d) Prepare closing entries on December 31.

Prepare financial statements and closing entries.
(SO 3) AP

P12–5B The adjusted trial balance of the KantAdd accounting firm as at March 31, 2008, follows:

KANTADD, LLP
Adjusted Trial Balance
March 31, 2008

	Debit	Credit
Cash	$ 8,000	
Accounts receivable	80,000	
Supplies	2,000	
Prepaid insurance	3,000	
Office equipment	30,000	
Accumulated amortization—office equipment		$ 10,000
Accounts payable		12,000
Salaries payable		8,000
Unearned fees		15,000
Demand bank loan payable		40,000
Note payable ($1,500 of this note is due within the next year)		10,000
U. Add, Capital		10,000
I. Kant, Capital		15,000
U. Add, Drawings	70,000	
I. Kant, Drawings	90,000	
Professional fees		340,000
Salaries expense	100,000	
Rent expense	24,000	
Interest expense	20,000	
Insurance expense	12,000	
Utilities expense	10,000	
Amortization expense	6,000	
Supplies expense	5,000	
Totals	$460,000	$460,000

The balance in Kant's capital account includes an additional $5,000 investment during the year. Kant and Add share income in the ratio of 60% and 40%, respectively.

Instructions

(a) Prepare an income statement, statement of partners' capital, and balance sheet.
(b) Journalize the closing entries.

P12–6B At April 30 of the current year, partners' capital balances in the SOS Company are as follows: R. Smistad $36,000; K. Osborne $24,000; and W. Smistad $60,000. The income-sharing ratio is 3:2:4, in the same order. On May 1, the SOSO Company is formed by admitting N. Ortiz to the firm as a partner.

Record admission of partner. (SO 4) AP

Instructions

Journalize the admission of Ortiz under each of the following independent assumptions:

(a) Ortiz purchases 50% of W. Smistad's ownership interest by paying W. Smistad $32,000 cash.
(b) Ortiz purchases 50% of Osborne's ownership interest by paying Osborne $20,000 cash.
(c) Ortiz invests $60,000 cash in the partnership for a 40% ownership interest.
(d) Ortiz invests $35,000 in the partnership for a 20% ownership interest.

P12–7B At February 15, partners' capital balances in the MAD partnership are L. Meechum $50,000; D. Assad $40,000; and D. Dong $30,000. The income ratios are 5:4:3, in the same order. On February 16, S. Dionne is admitted to the MADD partnership by investment. After Dionne's admission, the total partnership capital is $140,000 and Dong's ownership interest has been reduced from 25% to 22.5% of total partnership capital. Meechum's ownership interest has been reduced from 50% to 37.5% and Assad's ownership interest has been reduced proportionately.

Calculate investment and bonus on admission of partner. (SO 4) AN

Instructions

(a) How much was Dionne's cash investment in the partnership?
(b) What is the percentage ownership of Assad after Dionne's admission to the partnership? Of Dionne?
(c) What was the total bonus allocated to the old partners?
(d) What is the balance in each partner's capital account after Dionne's admission to the partnership?

Record withdrawal of partner.
(SO 5) AP

P12–8B On December 31, the capital balances and income ratios in the FJA Company are as follows:

Partner	Capital Balance	Income Ratio
H. Fercho	$70,000	60%
P. Jiang	30,000	30%
R. Antoni	24,500	10%

Instructions

Journalize the withdrawal of Antoni under each of the following independent assumptions:

(a) Each of the remaining partners agrees to pay $13,000 cash from personal funds to purchase Antoni's ownership equity. Each partner receives 50% of Antoni's equity.
(b) Jiang agrees to purchase Antoni's ownership interest for $26,000 cash.
(c) Antoni is paid $29,000 from partnership assets.
(d) Antoni is paid $19,100 from partnership assets.

Calculate bonus and payment on withdrawal of partner.
(SO 5) AN

P12–9B At April 30, partners' capital balances in the Children's partnership were K. Children $60,000; D. Picard $40,000; and V. Markle $50,000. The partners share income equally. On May 1, Picard withdrew from the partnership. After Picard's exit, Markle's capital balance was $45,000.

Instructions

(a) What was the total partnership capital after Picard left the partnership?
(b) What is the percentage ownership of Children and Markle after Picard left the partnership?
(c) How much cash was paid by the partnership to Picard?
(d) What was the total bonus allocated to Picard?

Prepare and post entries for partnership liquidation.
(SO 6) AP

P12–10B The partners in Cottage Country Company decide to liquidate the company when the post-closing trial balance shows the following:

COTTAGE COUNTRY COMPANY Post-Closing Trial Balance April 30, 2008		
	Debit	Credit
Cash	$28,000	
Accounts receivable	19,000	
Allowance for doubtful accounts		$ 1,000
Inventory	28,000	
Equipment	17,000	
Accumulated amortization		10,000
Notes payable		21,000
Accounts payable		18,000
Wages payable		5,000
A. Hoffer, Capital		25,000
K. Lonseth, Capital		11,200
D. Posca, Capital		800
Totals	$92,000	$92,000

The partners share income and loss 5:3:2 for Hoffer, Lonseth, and Posca, respectively. During the process of liquidation, the transactions below were completed in the sequence shown:

1. A total of $48,000 was received from converting noncash assets into cash on May 5.

2. Liabilities were paid in full on May 7.
3. Posca paid his capital deficiency on May 9.
4. Cash was paid to the partners with credit balances on May 12.

Instructions

(a) Prepare the entries to record the transactions.
(b) Post the transactions to the cash and capital accounts.
(c) Assume that Posca is unable to repay his capital deficiency. Prepare the entry to record (1) the reallocation of his deficiency, and (2) the final distribution of cash.

P12–11B   On June 2, 2008, the musical partnership of M. James, S. Lars, J. Kirk, and B. Robert ends and the partnership is to be liquidated. The partners have capital balances of $1 million each except for Robert, whose capital balance is $500,000. Cash, noncash assets, and liabilities total $800,000, $5.8 million, and $3.1 million, respectively. The four partners share income and loss equally.

Record liquidation of partnership.
(SO 6) AP

Instructions

Journalize the liquidation of the partnership on June 2 under each of the following independent assumptions:

(a) The noncash assets are sold for $6 million cash, the liabilities are paid, and the remaining cash is paid to the partners.
(b) The noncash assets are sold for $3.4 million cash and the liabilities are paid. The partner with the debit capital balance pays the amount owed to the partnership and the remaining cash is paid to the partners.
(c) The noncash assets are sold for $3.4 million cash and the liabilities are paid. The partner with the debit capital balance is unable to pay the amount owed to the partnership. The cash is paid to the three other partners.

Continuing Cookie Chronicle

(*Note:* This is a continuation of the Cookie Chronicle from Chapters 1 through 11.)

Natalie's high school friend, Katy Peterson, has been operating a bakery for approximately 18 months. Because Natalie has been so successful operating Cookie Creations, Katy would like to have Natalie become her partner. Katy believes that together they will create a thriving cookie-making business.

Natalie is quite happy with her current business set-up. Up until now, she had not considered joining forces with anyone. From past meetings with Katy, however, Natalie has gathered the following information about Katy's business and compared it to her own results:

The current market values of the assets and liabilities of both businesses are as follows:

	The Baker's Nook	Cookie Creations
Cash	$ 1,500	$10,000
Accounts receivable	5,000	800
Allowance for doubtful accounts	(750)	0
Merchandise inventory	450	1,200
Equipment	7,500	1,000
Bank loan payable	10,000	0

All assets would be transferred into the partnership. The partnership would assume all of the liabilities of the two proprietorships. The bank loan is due February 17, 2009.

- Katy operates her business from leased premises. She has just signed a lease for 12 months. Monthly rent will be $1,000. Katy's landlord has agreed to draw up a new lease agreement that would be signed by both partners.

- Katy graduated from cooking school. She has no assets and has a lot of student loans and credit card debt. Natalie's assets consist of investments in Canada Savings Bonds. Natalie has no personal liabilities.
- Katy is reluctant to have a partnership agreement drawn up. She thinks it's a waste of both time and money. As Katy and Natalie have been friends for a long time, Katy is confident that all problems can be easily resolved over a nice meal.

Natalie believes that it may be a good idea to establish a partnership with Katy. She comes to you with the following questions:

1. Do I really need a formalized partnership agreement drawn up? What would be the point of having one if Katy and I agree on all major decisions? What type of information should the partnership agreement contain?
2. I would like to have Katy contribute the same amount of capital as I am contributing. How much additional cash, in addition to the amount in Katy's proprietorship, would Katy have to borrow to invest in the partnership so that she and I have the same capital balances?
3. Katy has a lot of personal debt. Should this affect my decision about whether or not to go forward with this business venture? Why or why not?
4. What other issues should I consider before I say yes or no to Katy?

Instructions:

(a) Answer Natalie's questions.
(b) Assume that Natalie and Katy go ahead and form a partnership called Cookie Creations and More on November 1, 2008, and that Katy is able to borrow the additional cash she needs to contribute to the partnership. Prepare a balance sheet for the partnership on November 1.

BROADENING YOUR PERSPECTIVE

Financial Reporting and Analysis

Financial Reporting Problem

BYP12–1   The Forzani Group Ltd. originally started as a partnership when Calgary Stampeder John Forzani and three of his teammates (including two of his brothers) started Forzani's Locker Room in 1974. The business grew steadily over the next while, allowing the company to expand its initial athletic footwear business to include clothing and selected sports equipment. In 1991, the company purchased Sport-Check International Ltd., and in 1992 it purchased Hogarth's Sport & Ski. Both of these companies were sport superstores that helped Forzani expand its business to include ski, golf, and bike equipment. In 1993, the partnership was liquidated and a corporation was formed in its place.

Instructions

(a) What probably motivated the Forzani partnership to reorganize as a corporation in 1993?
(b) Explain what is involved in liquidating a partnership.
(c) Explain how the Forzani partnership would record the transfer of its assets and liabilities into the new corporation.
(d) Look at The Forzani Group Ltd.'s corporate financial statements reproduced in Appendix A at the back of this textbook. In what ways would the partnership financial statements have been different from these corporation statements?

Interpreting Financial Statements

BYP12–2 The **Sherobee Glen Limited Partnership** was formed in 1982 to purchase rental properties. The balance sheet and notes to its financial statements include the following excerpts:

SHEROBEE GLEN LIMITED PARTNERSHIP
Balance Sheet (partial)
October 31, 2005

Limited partners' equity	
Original investment, 200 limited partnership units	$2,500,000
Surplus	(1,129,063)
	$1,370,937

SHEROBEE GLEN LIMITED PARTNERSHIP
Notes to the Financial Statements (partial)
October 31, 2005

4. Liability of Limited Partners

The Limited Partnership Agreement provides that the General Partner has unlimited liability for the debts and obligations of the Limited Partnership. The liability of each Limited Partner is limited to the amount of capital contributed or agreed to be contributed plus the Limited Partner's share of undistributed income.

Instructions

(a) What are the advantages to the company of operating as a limited partnership rather than as a general partnership?

(b) Use the balance sheet information given above to determine how much the limited partners are liable for in dollars.

Critical Thinking

Collaborative Learning Activity

Note to instructor: Additional instructions and handout material for this group activity can be found on the Instructor Resource Site.

BYP12–3 In this group activity, you will review accounting for the admission of a new partner in the following situations:

1. Purchase of an existing partner's interest
2. Investment of assets in a partnership
   (a) equal to a new partner's capital interest
   (b) with a bonus to the old partners
   (c) with a bonus to the new partner

Study Aids:
Working in Groups

Instructions

(a) Your instructor will divide the class into "home" groups and distribute a package to each. Select one page from the package, which will indicate a type of admission of a new partner. Join the "expert" group for that type of admission.

(b) In the "expert" group, review and discuss accounting for the addition of a new partner in your type of situation and ensure that each group member thoroughly understands the necessary entries and their effects.

(c) Return to your "home" group and explain accounting for the admission of a new partner in your situation to the other students in your group.

(d) You may be asked by your instructor to write a short quiz on this topic.

Communication Activity

**Study Aids:
Writing Handbook**

BYP12–4   You are an expert in forming partnerships. Dr. Konu Chatterjie and Dr. Sheila Unger want to establish a partnership to practise medicine. They are going to meet with you to discuss their plans, but you have agreed to first send them a letter that outlines the issues they need to consider beforehand.

Instructions

Write a letter, in good form, to be sent to Konu and Sheila. In it, you should discuss the different types of partnership organizations and the advantages and disadvantages of each type so that the doctors can start thinking about their needs.

Ethics Case

**Study Aids:
Ethics in Accounting**

BYP12–5   Susan and Erin operate a spa as partners and share profits and losses equally. Their business has been more successful than they expected and is operating quite profitably. Erin works hard to maximize profits. She schedules appointments from 8 a.m. to 6 p.m. daily and she even works weekends to accommodate regular customers. Susan schedules her appointments from 9 a.m. to 5 p.m. and does not work weekends. Susan regularly makes much larger withdrawals of cash than Erin does, but tells Erin not to worry. "I never make a withdrawal without you knowing about it," she says to Erin, "so it's properly recorded in my drawings account and charged against my capital at the end of the year." To date, Susan's withdrawals are twice as much as Erin's.

Instructions

(a) Who are the stakeholders in this situation?

(b) Identify the problems with Susan's actions. In what ways are they unethical?

(c) What provisions could be put in the partnership agreement so that the differences in Susan's and Erin's work and withdrawal habits are no longer unfair to Erin?

ANSWERS TO CHAPTER QUESTIONS

Answers to Accounting in Action Insight Questions

Ethics Insight, p. 615

Q: In your opinion, should the limited partners who invested in Enron's special purpose entities be liable to Enron's shareholders?

A: Limited partners still have unlimited liability for their own negligence, but limited liability for other partners' negligence. It will be up to the courts to determine if the limited partners in Enron's special purpose entities were actively involved in the decision-making and promotion of the partnerships. If negligence was involved, they likely will, and should, share liability.

Across the Organization Insight, p. 619

Q: Explain how the income earned by a partner in an accounting partnership is different from the income of a staff accountant in the same partnership.

A: A staff accountant is an employee of the partnership and is paid a salary, which is generally a fixed amount for each year. A partner's income goes up and down according to how much the partnership earns during the year and the income sharing arrangements among all the partners. A partner can make withdrawals during the year, but these are recorded as reductions of capital and not as salary expense

Business Insight, p. 640

Q: When most businesses start, the partners believe it will be a success. Why, then, is it important for a partnership agreement to include provisions for ending a business before it has even started?

A: The last thing that partners want to think about when starting up a business is ending it. Still, it is much better to discuss and agree early on about what happens if the business ends and to record everyone's understanding in a partnership agreement so there is no misunderstanding in the future. There are many possibilities to consider such as what will happen if the partners agree to sell the business, have a falling-out, or if the business simply flops. Or, what happens if one of the partners wants out, becomes ill or disabled, is financially distressed, or dies?

Answer to Forzani Review It Question 5, p. 616

Mutual agency, limited life, unlimited liability, and co-ownership of property are major characteristics of a partnership. As a company like The Forzani Group grows in size, it is difficult for it to remain a partnership, because of these factors. The corporate form of organization separates ownership and management and makes it easier to raise capital. The unlimited liability of a partnership makes it harder to find investors because owners can lose not only their investment but also their personal assets if those assets are needed to pay the partnership's creditors.

Answers to Self-Study Questions

1. a   2. c   3. b   4. d   5. a   6. a   7. d   8. b   9. d   10. a

 Remember to go back to the Navigator Box at the beginning of the chapter to check off your completed work.

concepts for review >>

Before studying this chapter, you should understand or, if necessary, review:

a. The differences between the forms of business organization. (Ch. 1, pp. 9–11)

b. The content of the equity section of the balance sheet for the different forms of organization. (Ch. 1, pp. 13–14)

c. How to prepare closing entries for a proprietorship (Ch. 4, pp. 165–168) and for a partnership. (Ch. 12, p. 618)

The Double-Double Goes Public

Oakville, Ont.—Not many things are as quintessentially Canadian as a trip to Tim Hortons® for a coffee and cruller and perhaps a box of Timbits® to go. After all, it was founded by, and named after, a hockey player, and its restaurants are *everywhere* across the country. Even the term "double-double" has made it into the latest edition of the *Canadian Oxford Dictionary*.

So when the U.S. fast food giant Wendy's International Inc. bought Tim Hortons from co-founder Ron Joyce for $580 million in 1995, some Canadians certainly felt a sense of loss. The losses weren't felt at Tim Hortons, though. Still headquartered in Oakville, Ontario, it continued to grow over the next 10 years to nearly 2,600 restaurants in Canada and another 290 in the United States. By 2006, Tim Hortons had a 22-percent share of the Canadian food-service industry and 74 percent of the coffee and baked goods market.

In fact, Tim Hortons was a big source of Wendy's® overall financial health in 2005. The company reported a record U.S. $3.8 billion in revenues, with U.S. $1.2 billion of that amount coming from the Tim Hortons operations.

So Wendy's decided it was time for Tim's to go out on its own. In March 2006, the company sold 17.25 percent of its share in Tim Hortons in an "initial public offering" (IPO), with the aim of making it a fully independent public company by year end.

The IPO of 33.35 million shares raised $846.4 million, bringing the company's market capitalization to about $6 billion. On the first day of trading, the Tim Hortons share price rose as high as $37.99 and

Tim Hortons: www.timhortons.com

closed at $33.10. The net proceeds from the IPO were used to repay debt at Wendy's.

About 60 percent of the entire IPO was available to Canadian investors. So, while sipping their double-doubles over the morning paper, many Canadians can now check on the stock performance of a national icon under the symbol THI on the Toronto and New York stock exchanges. And they might also be making a profit.

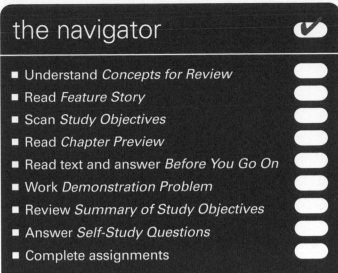

the navigator

- Understand *Concepts for Review*
- Read *Feature Story*
- Scan *Study Objectives*
- Read *Chapter Preview*
- Read text and answer *Before You Go On*
- Work *Demonstration Problem*
- Review *Summary of Study Objectives*
- Answer *Self-Study Questions*
- Complete assignments

chapter 13

Corporations: Organization and Share Capital Transactions

study objectives >>

the navigator

After studying this chapter, you should be able to:

1. Identify and discuss the major characteristics of a corporation.
2. Record common share transactions.
3. Record preferred share transactions.
4. Prepare the shareholders' equity section of the balance sheet and calculate return on equity.

Tim Hortons started in 1964 with one store in Hamilton, Ontario. Many incorporated companies start out small and grow large, as Tim Hortons has. It should not be surprising, then, that the corporation is the dominant form of business organization. In this chapter, we will explain the essential features of a corporation and the accounting for a corporation's share capital transactions. In Chapter 14, we will look at other accounting issues for corporations.

The chapter is organized as follows:

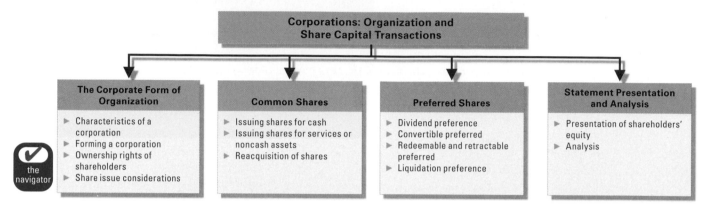

The Corporate Form of Organization

A **corporation** is a legal entity that is separate from its owners, who are known as shareholders. As a legal entity, a corporation has most of the rights and privileges of a person. Like any citizen, it also has the obligation to respect laws and pay income tax. The major exceptions in its privileges are the ones that only a living person can exercise: corporations cannot vote or hold public office.

Corporations can be classified in a variety of ways. Two common classifications are by purpose and by ownership. For example, a corporation may be organized for the purpose of making a **profit** (such as Tim Hortons in our feature story) or it may be **not-for-profit** (such as the Canadian Cancer Society). We also learned in Chapter 1 about another type of corporation that is set up for a specific or limited purpose—an **income trust** (such as the Yellow Pages Group). Recall that an income trust is set up specifically to invest in income-producing assets.

In classification by ownership, the difference is between publicly held and privately held corporations. A **publicly held corporation** may have thousands of shareholders. Its shares are usually traded in an organized securities market, such as the Toronto Stock Exchange (TSX). Most of the largest Canadian corporations are publicly held. Examples of publicly held corporations are Bombardier Inc., The Forzani Group Ltd., Sears Canada Inc., and, of course, Tim Hortons Inc.

In contrast, a **privately held corporation**, often called a closely held corporation, usually has only a few shareholders. It does not offer its shares for sale to the general public. Privately held companies are generally much smaller than publicly held companies, although there are notable exceptions such as McCain Foods, The Jim Pattison Group, and the Irving companies. Tim Hortons, in our feature story, originally was a privately held corporation that was owned 100 percent by Wendy's International, Inc. Wendy's offered its shares for sale to the public in 2006, which then made Tim Hortons publicly held.

Characteristics of a Corporation

Many characteristics make corporations different from proprietorships and partnerships. The most important ones are explained below.

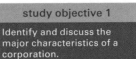

study objective 1

Identify and discuss the major characteristics of a corporation.

Separate Legal Existence

As an entity that is separate from its owners, the corporation acts under its own name rather than in the name of its shareholders. Tim Hortons, for example, may buy, own, and sell property. It may borrow money and enter into legally binding contracts in its own name. It may also sue or be sued, and it pays income tax as a separate legal entity.

Remember that in a proprietorship or partnership, the acts of the owners (partners) bind the proprietorship or partnership. In contrast, the acts of owners (shareholders) do not bind a corporation unless these individuals are also official agents of the corporation. For example, if you owned shares of Tim Hortons, you would not have the right to purchase a new production facility unless you were an official agent of the corporation.

Limited Liability of Shareholders

Since a corporation is a separate legal entity, creditors only have access to corporate assets to have their claims repaid to them. The liability of each individual shareholder is limited to the amount that he or she invested in the shares of the corporation. This means that shareholders cannot be made to pay for the company's liabilities out of their personal assets, which can be done in the case of a proprietorship and a general partnership.

Limited liability is a significant advantage for the corporate form of organization, just as it is for a limited, or limited liability, partnership. However, in certain situations, creditors may demand a personal guarantee from a controlling shareholder. This makes the controlling shareholder's personal assets available for satisfying the creditor's claim if they are needed—and it eliminates or reduces the limited liability advantage.

ACCOUNTING IN ACTION ▶ Business Insight

In two provinces—Nova Scotia and Alberta—unlimited liability corporations (ULC) can be formed. A ULC is a special type of corporation that offers income tax advantages for investors. It is used by many U.S. taxpayers for investments in Canada and by Canadian taxpayers for investments in the U.S. However, the extent of the liability in a ULC is very different in the two provinces. In Nova Scotia, a shareholder is only liable if the company is liquidated and there are not enough assets to pay its debts. In Alberta, the liability of a shareholder is "unlimited in extent and joint and several in nature." In other words, past and present shareholders are personally liable for all liabilities and acts of the corporation.

Source: David Feindel, Barry Horne, and Deborah Patterson, "NS vs. Alberta ULCs," *CAmagazine*, January/February 2006, 46.

? **Why would someone want to form an unlimited liability corporation?**

Transferable Ownership Rights

Ownership of a corporation is held in shares of capital. These are transferable units. Shareholders may dispose of part or all of their interest in a corporation simply by selling their shares. Remember that the transfer of an ownership interest in a proprietorship or partnership requires the consent of each owner or partner. In contrast, in a corporation, the transfer of shares is entirely decided by the shareholder. It does not require the approval of either the corporation or other shareholders.

The transfer of ownership rights between shareholders has no effect on the operating activities of the corporation. Nor does it affect the corporation's assets, liabilities, and total equity. The transfer of these ownership rights is a transaction between individual shareholders. The company is not involved in the transfer of ownership rights; it is only involved in the original sale of the share capital.

Ability to Acquire Capital

It is relatively easy for a large corporation to get capital by issuing shares. Buying shares in a corporation is often attractive to an investor because a shareholder has limited liability and shares are easily transferable. Also, because only small amounts of money need to be invested, many individuals can become shareholders. For these reasons, a successful corporation's ability to obtain capital is almost unlimited.

Note that the "almost unlimited" ability of a corporation to acquire capital is only true for large, publicly traded corporations. Small, or closely held, corporations can have as much difficulty getting capital as any proprietorship or partnership.

Continuous Life

Most corporations have an unlimited life. Since a corporation is a separate legal entity, its continuance as a going concern is not affected by the withdrawal, death, or incapacity of a shareholder, employee, or officer. As a result, a successful company can have a continuous and indefinite life. For example, the Hudson's Bay Co., Canada's oldest corporation, was founded in 1670 and is still going strong. Its ownership has changed over the years, but the corporation itself continues. In contrast, proprietorships end if anything happens to the proprietor and partnerships must reorganize if anything happens to one of the partners and the other partners want to continue the partnership.

Corporation Management

Shareholders legally own the corporation. But they manage the corporation indirectly through a board of directors that they elect. The board, in turn, decides on the operating policies of the company and selects officers—such as a president and one or more vice-presidents—to execute policy and to perform daily management functions. Paul House is Tim Hortons' president and chief operating officer. He, along with two of Tim Hortons' executive vice-presidents, also sit on Tim Hortons' board of directors. The other members of the Tim Hortons board of directors consist of five independent (outside) directors.

The organizational structure of a corporation makes it possible for a company to hire professional managers to run the business. On the other hand, the separation of ownership and management prevents shareholders from having an active role in managing the company, which is difficult for some shareholders to accept.

Government Regulations

Canadian companies may be incorporated federally, under the terms of the *Canada Business Corporations Act,* or provincially, under the terms of a provincial business corporations act. Federal and provincial laws specify the requirements for issuing shares, distributing income to shareholders, and reacquiring shares. Similarly, provincial securities commissions' regulations control the sale of share capital to the general public. When a corporation's shares are listed and traded on foreign securities markets, the corporation must also respect the reporting requirements of these exchanges. Respecting international, federal, provincial, and securities regulations increases costs and complexity for corporations.

Income Tax

Proprietorships, partnerships, and income trusts do not pay income tax as separate entities. Instead, each owner's (or partner's or unitholder's) share of income from these organizations is reported on his or her personal income tax return. Income tax is then paid by the individual on this amount. Note that although income trusts were not taxable entities at the time of writing this textbook, the government was proposing to tax new income trusts in the future and existing income trusts in 2011.

Corporations, on the other hand, must pay federal and provincial income taxes as separate legal entities. These taxes can be substantial. They can amount to as much as 36 percent of taxable income. There are, however, income tax deductions for some corporations. With eligible deductions, or other corporate tax incentives, a corporation's tax rate may be reduced to between 13 and 20 percent on certain kinds of active small business income. This tax rate is much lower than the tax rate for the same amount of income earned by an individual.

In some circumstances, an advantage of incorporation is being able to defer personal income tax. The shareholders of a corporation do not pay tax on corporate income until it is distributed to them. Shareholders pay tax on cash dividends, which are pro rata distributions of net income. Many people argue that corporate income is taxed twice (double taxation)—once at the corporate level and again at the individual level. This is not exactly true, however, as individuals receive a dividend tax credit to reduce some of the tax burden.

To determine whether incorporating will result in more or less income tax for a proprietorship or partnership, it is wise to get expert advice. Income tax laws are complex, and careful tax planning is essential for any business venture.

The following list summarizes the advantages and disadvantages of the corporate form of business organization:

Advantages	Disadvantages
• Corporation management—professional managers	• Corporation management—ownership separated from management
• Separate legal existence	• Increased cost and complexity to follow government regulations
• Limited liability of shareholders	• Potential for additional income tax
• Potential for deferred or reduced income tax	
• Transferable ownership rights	
• Ability to acquire capital	
• Continuous life	

As was noted earlier, many of these advantages and disadvantages depend on the size of the corporation. For example, compare Bob's Coffee Ltd. (a small, private, closely held corporation) to Tim Hortons Inc. (a large publicly traded corporation). Bob's Coffee finds it just as difficult to sell shares of ownership, or to acquire capital, as it would if it were an unincorporated business.

Forming a Corporation

As previously mentioned, a company can incorporate federally or provincially. The federal government and the majority of provinces file articles of incorporation to incorporate a company, although there are also other methods.

Articles of incorporation form the "constitution" of the company. They include information such as (1) the name and purpose of the corporation, (2) the amounts and kinds of share capital to be authorized and the number of shares, (3) the names and addresses of the incorporators, and (4) the location of the corporation's head office. Anyone can apply to incorporate a company, as long as he or she is over the age of 18, of sound mind, and not bankrupt.

After receiving its articles of incorporation, the corporation sets its by-laws. The by-laws are the internal rules and procedures for operations. Corporations that operate interprovincially must also get a licence from each province they do business in. The licence ensures that the corporation's operating activities respect the laws of the province.

The costs of forming a corporation are called **organization costs**. These costs include legal fees, accounting fees, and registration costs. It may be argued that organization costs should be capitalized as they have an asset life equal to the life of the corporation. However, most companies expense organization costs in the year they occur. Determining the amount and timing of future benefits is so difficult that the conservative approach of expensing these costs immediately is more justifiable. You will recall the discussion we had in Chapter 11 about the matching principle and the difficulty of finding a direct relationship between revenues and expenses in situations similar to this one.

ACCOUNTING IN ACTION ▶ International Insight

Corporations in North America are identified by "Ltd.," "Inc.," "Corp.," or in some cases, "Co." following their names. These abbreviations can also be spelled out. In Brazil and France, the letters used are "SA" (Sôciedade Anonima, Société Anonyme); in Japan, "KK" (Kabushiki Kaisha); in the Netherlands, "NV" (Naamloze Vennootschap); in Italy, "SpA" (Società per Azioni); and in Sweden, "AB" (Aktiebolag).

In the UK, public corporations are identified by "Plc" (Public limited company), while private corporations are denoted by "Ltd." The same designations in Germany are "AG" (Aktiengesellschaft) for public corporations and "GmbH" (Gesellschaft mit beschränkter Haftung) for private corporations.

? Why is it important to be able to identify whether or not a company is a corporation by looking at its name?

Ownership Rights of Shareholders

Shareholders purchase ownership rights in the form of shares. The shares of the company are divided into different classes, such as Class A, Class B, and so on. The rights and privileges for each class of shares are stated in the articles of incorporation. The different classes are usually identified by the generic terms *common shares* and *preferred shares*. When a corporation has only one class of shares, this class has the rights and privileges of **common shares**. Each common share gives the shareholder the ownership rights shown in Illustration 13-1.

Illustration 13-1 ▶

Ownership rights of common shareholders

Shareholders have the right to:

Vote: Shareholders have the right to vote on certain matters, such as the election of the board of directors and appointment of external auditors. Each shareholder normally has one vote for each common share owned.

Dividends: Shareholders share in the distribution of the corporate income through dividends, proportionate to the number of shares owned.

Liquidation: Shareholders share in any assets that remain after liquidation, in proportion to the number of shares owned. This is known as a residual claim because shareholders are paid only if any cash remains after all the assets have been sold and the liabilities paid.

Share Issue Considerations

When Tim Hortons first issued shares for sale, it had to make a number of decisions. How many shares should be authorized for sale? How should the shares be issued? At what initial price should the shares be issued? These kinds of questions are answered in the following sections.

Alternative terminology
Issued also means sold.

Authorized Share Capital

A corporation's **authorized shares**—that is, the total number of shares a company is allowed to sell—is indicated in its articles of incorporation. It may be specified as an unlimited number or a certain number (e.g., 500,000 shares authorized). Tim Hortons has one billion common shares authorized and 100 million preferred shares authorized. More than three-quarters of public companies with share capital in Canada have an unlimited number of authorized shares.

If a number is specified, the amount of authorized shares normally reflects the company's initial need for capital and what it expects to need in the future. **Issued shares** are the authorized shares that have been sold. At the time of writing, Tim Hortons had issued 193 million common shares and had no plans to issue any preferred shares.

If a corporation has issued all of its authorized shares, it must get legislative approval to change its articles of incorporation before it can issue additional shares. To find out how many shares can still be issued without changing the articles of incorporation, the total shares issued are subtracted from the total authorized. For example, if Tim Hortons is authorized to sell one billion common shares but has issued only 193 million shares, 807 million (1,000,000,000 – 193,000,000) shares remain unissued. If Tim Hortons had an unlimited number of common shares authorized, an unlimited number of shares would remain unissued.

The authorization of share capital does not result in a formal accounting entry, because the event has no immediate effect on either assets or shareholders' equity. However, a company must disclose in the shareholders' equity section of its balance sheet or the notes to the financial statements how many authorized shares it has and how many have been issued.

Issue of Shares

A corporation can issue common shares in two ways: either directly to investors or indirectly through an investment dealer (brokerage house) that specializes in making potential investors aware of the securities. Direct issue is typical in closely held companies. Indirect issue is typical for a publicly held corporation, such as Tim Hortons in our feature story.

The first time a corporation's shares are offered to the public, the offer is called an **initial public offering (IPO)**. In 2005, there were a total of 203 IPOs by Canadian companies. Tim Hortons' first IPO, in March 2006, issued 33.35 million shares at $27 each, for net proceeds of $846.4 million, after deducting underwriting and brokerage costs. The company receives the cash from the sale of the IPO shares whether they are issued directly or indirectly. The company's assets (cash) increase, and its shareholders' equity (share capital) also increases.

Once these shares have been issued, they then trade on the secondary market. That is, investors buy and sell shares from each other, rather than from the company. When shares are sold among investors, there is no impact on the company's financial position. The company receives no additional assets, and it issues no additional shares. The only change in the company records is the name of the shareholder, not the number of shares issued.

Tim Hortons' IPO was oversubscribed—that is, investors wanted to buy more shares than were available to purchase. While many investors were upset at not being able to buy Tim Hortons shares in the IPO, they were able to purchase the shares on the secondary market after they were issued. In Canada, shares are offered for sale to the public (whether through an IPO or through the secondary market) using organized securities exchanges, such as the Toronto Stock Exchange.

Market Value of Shares

After the initial issue of new shares, the market price per share changes according to the interaction between buyers and sellers. To some extent, the price follows the trend of a company's income and dividends. The price also depends to some extent on how well the company is expected to perform in the future. Factors that a company cannot control (such as an embargo on oil, changes in interest rates, the outcome of an election, terrorism, and war) can also influence market prices.

For each listed security, the financial press reports the highest and lowest prices of the shares for the year; the annual dividend rate; the highest, lowest, and closing prices for the day; and the net change from the previous day. The total volume of shares traded on a particular day, the dividend yield, and price-earnings ratios are also reported. A recent listing for Tim Hortons from the Toronto Stock Exchange is shown below:

| 365-day | | | | | high | low | | | vol | | pe |
high	low	stock	sym	div	/bid	/ask	close	chg	100s	yld	ratio
37.99	28.25	Tim Hortons	THI		29.24	28.80	28.95	+.04	1766		22.6

Tim Hortons' shares have traded as high as $37.99 and as low as $28.25 during the past year. The stock's ticker symbol is "THI." Tim Hortons does not pay an annual dividend, as the blank space in the "div" column shows. The highest, lowest, and closing prices for the date shown were $29.24, $28.80, and $28.95 per share, respectively. The closing share price increased $0.04 from the previous day. The trading volume was 176,600 shares. Since Tim Hortons does not pay any dividend, there is no dividend yield ("yld"). The dividend yield reports the rate of return an investor earned from dividends, and is calculated by dividing the dividend amount by the share price. The price-earnings ("pe") ratio (share price divided by earnings per share) is 22.6, which means that the share price is 22.6 times the earnings per share. We will learn more about the price-earnings ratio in the next chapter.

Legal Capital

You may recall from Chapter 1 that the shareholders' equity section of a corporation's balance sheet includes (1) share capital (contributed capital) and (2) retained earnings (earned capital). **Share capital** is amounts contributed to the corporation by shareholders in exchange for shares of ownership. **Retained earnings** are earned capital (cumulative net income less losses and amounts distributed to shareholders) that has been retained for future use. We will study retained earnings in the next chapter.

For now, it is enough to say that the distinction between retained earnings and share capital is important for both legal and financial reasons. Retained earnings can be distributed to shareholders as dividends (similar to drawings in a proprietorship or partnership) or retained in the company for operating needs. On the other hand, share capital is **legal capital** that cannot be distributed to shareholders. It must remain invested in the company for the protection of corporate creditors. This is in contrast to the capital section of an income trust. An income trust distributes most of its earnings to its unitholders, as it only retains the amount that it needs for operating purposes. Consequently, the equity of an income trust will usually be much lower than that of a corporation.

Years ago, a value—known as par or stated value—was assigned to shares to determine the amount of legal capital. Today, the use of par or stated values for shares either is not required or is prohibited for companies that incorporate federally, as well as for companies that incorporate in most Canadian provinces. Consequently, less than one percent of publicly traded companies issue par value shares. Par value shares are still issued in some other countries, though, including the United States. Tim Hortons' common shares have a par value of U.S. $0.001 per share.

In Canada, **no par value shares**—shares that have not been assigned any specific value—are normally issued. When no par value shares are issued, all of the proceeds received from the sale of the shares are considered to be legal capital. Whenever shares are issued in this chapter, we will assume that they have no par value.

BEFORE YOU GO ON . . .

▶Review It

1. What are the advantages and disadvantages of a corporation compared to a proprietorship or partnership?
2. For a corporation, why is the amount of authorized shares important? Of issued shares?
3. How does the sale of shares affect a company in an initial public offering? Afterwards, in the secondary market?
4. Distinguish between share capital and retained earnings.
5. What is legal capital?

Related exercise material: BE13–1, BE13–2, and E13–1.

Common Shares

As we learned in the preceding section, share capital is the amounts that have been contributed to the corporation by shareholders in exchange for shares of ownership. Other amounts can also be contributed by shareholders, or can accrue to them. Together, these other amounts and share capital form the total **contributed capital** of the corporation.

All corporations issue common shares. Some corporations also issue preferred shares, which have different rights and privileges than common shares. We will look at common shares in this section, and preferred shares in the next. We will also learn more about other sources of contributed capital.

study objective 2

Record common share transactions.

Issuing Shares for Cash

Most of the time, shares are issued in exchange for cash. As discussed earlier, when no par value common shares are issued, the entire proceeds from the issue become legal capital. To illustrate the issue of common shares, assume that Hydroslide, Inc. is authorized to issue an unlimited number of no par value common shares. It issues 1,000 of these shares for $1 per share on January 12. The entry to record this transaction is as follows:

Jan. 12	Cash	1,000	
	Common Shares		1,000
	To record issue of 1,000 common shares.		

A	=	L	+	SE
+1,000				+1,000

↑ Cash flows: +1,000

Issuing Shares for Services or Noncash Assets

Although it is more usual to issue common shares for cash, they are sometimes issued in exchange for services (as compensation to lawyers or consultants) or for noncash assets (land, buildings, and equipment). In such cases, what cost should be recognized in the exchange transaction? To comply with the cost principle, in a noncash transaction the cost is the cash equivalent price. This means that when there is an issue of shares in exchange for services or noncash assets, the cash equivalent price is the market value of the common shares given up.

To illustrate, assume that the lawyer who helped Hydroslide incorporate billed the company $5,000 for her services. On January 18, she agreed to accept 4,000 common shares in payment of her bill. At the time of the exchange, the market price for the shares is $1. In this case, the shares should be recorded at the market value of the consideration given up, which is 4,000 shares worth $1 per share, and not the amount of the bill, which is $5,000. What the lawyer accepted as payment for her bill were common shares valued at $4,000 on this date, and not cash of $5,000. The common shares may increase in value over time, but at the date of payment, they were worth $4,000. Accordingly, the entry is as follows:

Jan. 18	Legal Fees Expense	4,000	
	Common Shares		4,000
	To record issue of 4,000 common shares for legal services.		

Sometimes, however, common shares do not have a ready market (they cannot be easily sold) or their market value cannot be determined. In these cases, the market value of the consideration that is received would instead be used to determine the cash equivalent price, and thus the cost. To illustrate, assume that a newly incorporated company issues 10,000 shares on October 1 to acquire land with an appraised (market) value of $80,000. At the time of the acquisition, the company's shares do not have a reliable market value because they are not actively traded yet. In this case, the land would be recorded at the market value of the consideration received, $80,000, as follows:

Oct. 1	Land	80,000	
	Common Shares		80,000
	To record issue of 10,000 common shares for land.		

Reacquisition of Shares

Companies can purchase their own shares on the open market. A corporation may acquire its own shares for any number of reasons, including the following:

1. To increase trading of the company's shares in the securities market in the hope of increasing the company's market value
2. To increase earnings per share by reducing the number of shares issued
3. To eliminate hostile shareholders by buying them out
4. To have additional shares available so that they can be reissued to officers and employees through bonus and stock compensation plans, or can be used to acquire other companies
5. To comply with percentage share ownership requirements (i.e., to respect limits on foreign ownership)

When a company reacquires its own shares, the repurchased shares must be retired and cancelled. This restores the shares to the status of authorized but unissued shares. Reacquisitions of shares are common, and are often announced in the financial newspapers as "normal course issuer bids," which inform the public that a company plans to repurchase its shares.

To record a reacquisition of common (or preferred) shares, the following steps are required:

1. **Remove the cost of the shares from the share capital account:** Recall that when a long-lived asset is retired, the cost of the asset must be deleted (credited) from the appropriate asset account. Similarly, the cost of the common shares that are reacquired and retired must be determined and this amount is then deleted (debited) from the Common Shares account.

   In order to determine the cost of the common shares reacquired, it is necessary to calculate an **average cost per share**. It is impractical, and often impossible, to determine the cost of each individual common share that is reacquired. An average cost per common share is therefore calculated by dividing the balance in the Common Shares account by the number of shares issued at the transaction date.

2. **Record the cash paid:** The Cash account is credited for the amount paid to reacquire the shares. Note that a company has little choice in what it has to pay to reacquire the shares (it can only decide when to make the reacquisition). It must purchase the shares on the secondary market by paying whatever the current market price is on the date of purchase.

3. **Record the "gain" or loss" on reacquisition:** The difference between the price paid to reacquire the shares and their original cost is basically a "gain" or "loss" on reacquisition. However, because companies cannot realize a gain or suffer a loss from share transactions with their own shareholders, these amounts are not reported on the income statement. They are seen instead as an excess or deficiency that belongs to the original shareholders. As a result, the amount is reported as an increase or decrease in the shareholders' equity section of the balance sheet.

The actual accounting for the reacquisition of shares differs depending on whether the shares are reacquired by paying less than the average cost or more than the average cost. We will examine each situation in the next two sections.

Reacquisition below Average Cost

To illustrate the reacquisition of common shares at a price less than average cost, assume that Cocagne Inc. has an unlimited number of common shares authorized, and a total of 25,000 common shares issued. It has a balance in its Common Shares account of $50,000. The average cost of Cocagne's common shares is therefore $2 per share ($50,000 ÷ 25,000). On September 23, Cocagne reacquired 5,000 of its common shares at a price of $1.50 per share. Since the average cost of the shares was $2 per share, a $0.50 ($2.00 − $1.50) additional contribution to shareholders' equity results and is recorded as follows:

Sept. 23	Common Shares (5,000 × $2)	10,000	
	Contributed Capital—Reacquisition of Shares		2,500
	Cash (5,000 × $1.50)		7,500
	To record reacquisition and retirement of 5,000 common shares.		

A	=	L	+	SE
−7,500				−10,000
				+2,500

↓ Cash flows: −7,500

In this entry, the Common Shares account is debited for its average cost of $2 per share. The difference between the average cost of the shares and the amount paid to repurchase them is credited to a new shareholders' equity account for the contributed capital from the reacquisition of the shares. The balance in this account is reported as contributed capital in the shareholders' equity section of the balance sheet, along with the share capital, to indicate the total capital contributed by the shareholders. The cash in the entry was paid to the various shareholders that the shares were repurchased from.

After this entry, Cocagne still has an unlimited number of shares authorized, but only 20,000 (25,000 − 5,000) shares issued, and a balance of $40,000 ($50,000 − $10,000) in its Common Shares account. The average cost is still $2 per share ($40,000 ÷ 20,000).

Reacquisition above Average Cost

Now assume that Cocagne paid $2.50 per share to reacquire 5,000 of its common shares, rather than $1.50 per share as assumed above. In this case, there would be a debit to the shareholders' equity account for the difference between the price paid to reacquire the shares and their average cost. If there is any balance in the contributed capital account from previous reacquisitions, this amount would first be reduced (debited). However, contributed capital cannot be reduced below zero. In other words, contributed capital can never have a negative, or debit, balance. This is because of the limited liability feature of a corporation: as contributed capital is an amount that belongs to the shareholders, it cannot be put into a deficit position as that would make the shareholders liable for a deficit. Instead, if the debit amount is greater than the balance in contributed capital, the difference is recorded in Retained Earnings, which can go into a deficit position.

The journal entry to record the reacquisition and retirement of Cocagne's common shares at $2.50 per share is as follows:

A = L + SE
−12,500
−10,000
−2,500
↓ Cash flows: −12,500

Sept. 23	Common Shares (5,000 × $2)	10,000	
	Retained Earnings	2,500	
	Cash (5,000 × $2.50)		12,500
	To record reacquisition and retirement of 5,000 common shares.		

In this entry, the Common Shares account is debited for its average cost of $2 per share, just as it was in the entry in the preceding section. Because Cocagne is assumed to have no existing balance in a contributed capital account, the negative difference between the average cost of the shares and the amount paid to repurchase them is debited to the Retained Earnings account, as was explained above. After this entry, Cocagne still has 20,000 (25,000 − 5,000) shares issued and a balance of $40,000 ($50,000 − $10,000) in its Common Shares account.

In summary, then, the only difference in the accounting for a reacquisition at below or above the average cost has to do with recording the difference between the average cost of the shares and the amount of cash paid to reacquire them. If the shares are reacquired at a price below the average cost, the difference is credited to a contributed capital account. If the shares are reacquired at a price above their average cost, the difference is debited first to the contributed capital account that was used for any previous reacquisition below cost of the same class of shares, and secondly to the Retained Earnings account if there is no credit balance left in the contributed capital account.

ACCOUNTING IN ACTION ▶ Across the Organization Insight

According to a report from Standard & Poor's, $81 billion was spent by companies in the S&P 500 to buy back their own shares in the second quarter of 2005. That's an increase of 92 percent over the same quarter in 2004, which itself was a 100-percent increase over the same period in 2003. Why are companies buying back so much of their own stock? One explanation is that companies are sitting on a lot of cash after three years of good profits following the technology bubble burst of 2001. The finance department is asking "What do we do with all this cash?" and deciding that investing in themselves makes good business sense, especially if they believe the company's shares are undervalued.

Source: Jason Lee, "Taking a Little Back," *Canadian Business*, Sept. 26–Oct. 9, 2005, 90–1.

 What should a finance department consider before it spends money to reacquire the company's shares?

BEFORE YOU GO ON . . .

►Review It

1. Explain the accounting for an issue of common shares for cash.
2. Explain the accounting for an issue of common shares for services or noncash assets.
3. Distinguish between the accounting for a reacquisition of shares at a price lower than average cost and at a price higher than average cost.
4. Did The Forzani Group Ltd. repurchase any of its shares in fiscal 2006? The answer to this question is at the end of the chapter.

►Do It

Victoria Corporation begins operations on March 1 by issuing 100,000 common shares for cash at $12 per share. On March 15, it issues 5,000 common shares to its lawyers in settlement of their bill for $65,000. The shares continue to trade at $12 per share on March 15. On June 1, Victoria repurchases 10,000 of its shares at $10 per share. Record the share transactions.

Action Plan

- Credit the Common Shares account for the entire proceeds.
- Use the cash equivalent price when shares are issued for services. The cash equivalent price is equal to the market value of what is given up. If this amount cannot be determined, use the market value of what is received.
- Calculate the average cost per share by dividing the balance in the Common Shares account by the number of shares issued.
- Debit the Common Shares account for the average cost of the reacquired shares. If the reacquisition price is below the average cost, credit the difference to a contributed capital account. If the reacquisition price is above the average cost, debit the difference to Retained Earnings unless there is already a balance in a contributed capital account from previous reacquisitions and retirements.

Solution

Mar. 1	Cash	1,200,000	
	Common Shares (100,000 × $12)		1,200,000
	To record issue of 100,000 shares at $12 per share.		
15	Legal Fees Expense	60,000	
	Common Shares (5,000 × $12)		60,000
	To record issue of 5,000 shares for lawyers' fees.		
June 1	Common Shares (10,000 × $12)	120,000	
	Contributed Capital—Reacquisition of Shares		20,000
	Cash (10,000 × $10)		100,000
	To record reacquisition and retirement of 10,000 common shares at an average cost of $12 ($1,260,000 ÷ 105,000).		

Related exercise material: BE13–3, BE13–4, BE13–5, BE13–6, and E13–2.

the
navigator

Preferred Shares

study objective 3

Record preferred share transactions.

A corporation may issue preferred shares in addition to common shares. **Preferred shares** have a preference, or priority, over common shares in certain areas. Typically, preferred shareholders have priority over (1) dividends (distributions of income) and (2) assets if the company is liquidated. They generally do not have voting rights. A recent survey indicated that nearly 30 percent of Canadian companies have preferred shares.

Like common shares, preferred shares may be issued for cash or for noncash assets or services. They can also be reacquired. The entries for all these transactions are similar to the entries for common shares. When a company has more than one class of shares, the transactions for each class should be recorded in separate accounts (e.g., Preferred Shares, Common Shares). As with common shares, no par value shares are normally issued.

Some typical features of preferred shares, including dividend and liquidation preferences, are discussed next.

Dividend Preference

Preferred shareholders have the right to share in the distribution of dividends before common shareholders do. For example, if the dividend rate on preferred shares is $5 per share, common shareholders will not receive any dividends in the current year until preferred shareholders have first received $5 for every share they own. The first claim to dividends does not, however, guarantee that dividends will be paid. Dividends depend on many factors, such as having enough retained earnings and available cash. In addition, all dividends must be formally approved by the board of directors.

Preferred shares may have a **cumulative dividend** feature. This means that preferred shareholders must be paid dividends from the current year as well as any unpaid dividends from past years before common shareholders receive any dividends. When preferred shares are cumulative, preferred dividends that are not declared in a period are called **dividends in arrears**. When preferred shares are not cumulative (known as **noncumulative**), a dividend that is not paid in any particular year is lost forever. Most preferred shares that are issued today are noncumulative.

To illustrate the cumulative dividend feature, assume that Staudinger Corporation has 10,000 $3-cumulative preferred shares. The $3 is the per share dividend amount, which is usually expressed as an annual amount, similar to interest rates. So, Staudinger's annual total dividend is $30,000 (10,000 × $3 per share). If dividends are two years in arrears, preferred shareholders are entitled to receive the following dividends:

Dividends in arrears ($30,000 × 2)	$60,000
Current year dividends	30,000
Total preferred dividends	$90,000

No distribution can be made to common shareholders until this entire preferred dividend is paid. In other words, dividends cannot be paid on common shares while any preferred shares are in arrears.

Dividends in arrears are not considered a liability. There is no obligation to pay a dividend until one is declared by the board of directors. However, the amount of dividends in arrears should be disclosed in the notes to the financial statements. This allows investors to assess the potential impact of a future dividend declaration on the corporation's financial position.

Even though there is no requirement to pay an annual dividend, companies that do not meet their dividend obligations—whether cumulative or noncumulative—are not looked upon favourably by the investment community. When discussing one company's failure to pay its cumulative preferred dividend, a financial officer noted, "Not meeting your obligations on something like that is a major black mark on your record." The accounting entries for dividends are explained in Chapter 14.

Convertible Preferred

As an investment, preferred shares are even more attractive when there is a conversion privilege. Nearly half of the companies in Canada that report having preferred shares also have a conversion feature. **Convertible preferred shares** give shareholders the option of exchanging preferred shares for common shares at a specified ratio. They are purchased by investors who want the greater security of preferred shares but who also want the option of converting their preferred shares for common shares if the market value of the common shares increases significantly.

To illustrate, assume that Ross Industries Inc. issues 1,000 convertible preferred shares at $100 per share. One preferred share is convertible into 10 common shares. The current market price of the common shares is $9 per share. At this point, holders of the preferred shares would not want to convert, because they would exchange preferred shares worth $100,000 (1,000 × $100) for common shares worth only $90,000 (10,000 × $9). However, if the price of the common shares were to increase above $10 per share, it would be profitable for shareholders to convert their preferred shares to common shares.

To record the conversion, the cost of the preferred shares is transferred to the Common Shares account. As we saw earlier when shares are reacquired, it is seldom possible to determine the original cost of shares that are involved in the transaction. An average cost per share is used instead. For the preferred shares that are being converted, this is calculated by dividing the balance in the Preferred Shares account by the number of shares issued at the transaction date.

To illustrate, assume that the 1,000 preferred shares of Ross Industries Ltd. with an average cost of $100 per share are converted into 10,000 common shares when the market values of the two classes of shares are $101 and $12 per share, respectively, on June 10. The entry to record the conversion is:

June 10	Preferred Shares	100,000	
	Common Shares		100,000
	To record conversion of 1,000 preferred shares into 10,000 common shares.		

A	=	L	+	SE
				−100,000
				+100,000

Cash flows: no effect

Note that the average cost (which is the same as the original cost in this example) of the preferred shares is used to record the conversion. The market values of the shares are not considered in recording the transaction, because the corporation has not received any assets equal to market value. Therefore, the conversion of preferred shares will never result in either a gain or loss to it.

Redeemable and Retractable Preferred

Many preferred shares are issued with a redemption or call feature. **Redeemable (or callable) preferred shares** give the issuing corporation the right to purchase the shares from shareholders at specified future dates and prices. The redemption feature gives a corporation some flexibility: it allows the corporation to eliminate the preferred shares when doing this will benefit the corporation.

Often, shares that are redeemable are also convertible. Sometimes, companies will redeem or call their preferred shares to force investors to convert those preferred shares into common shares.

Retractable preferred shares are similar to redeemable preferred shares except that the shareholders can redeem shares at their option instead of the corporation redeeming the shares at its option. The redemption usually occurs at an arranged price and date.

Helpful hint The two features benefit different parties. Redeemable is at the option of the corporation. Retractable is at the option of the shareholder.

When preferred shares are redeemable or retractable, the distinction between equity and debt begins to blur. Redeemable and retractable preferred shares are similar in some ways to debt. They both offer a rate of return to the investor, and with the redemption of the shares, they both offer a repayment of the principal investment.

Contractual arrangements of this type are called **financial instruments**. A financial instrument is a contract between two or more parties that establishes financial rights or obligations. Amounts receivable and payable are simple examples of financial instruments. More complex examples include convertible bonds and redeemable or retractable preferred shares.

Financial instruments must be presented in accordance with their economic substance rather than their form. That is, redeemable and retractable preferred shares are usually presented in the *liabilities* section of the balance sheet rather than in the shareholders' equity section. This is because they have more of the features of debt than of equity.

Companies are issuing an increasing number of shares with innovative preferences. Some have the attributes of both debt and equity; others have the attributes of both common and preferred shares. Accounting for such financial instruments presents unique challenges to accountants. Further discussion of this topic is left to an intermediate accounting course.

Liquidation Preference

In addition to having a priority claim on the distribution of income over common shares, preferred shares also have a priority claim on corporate assets if the corporation fails. This means that if the company is bankrupt, preferred shareholders will get money back before common shareholders do. The preference to assets can be for the legal capital of the shares or for a specified liquidating value. So, while creditors still rank above all shareholders in terms of preference, preferred shareholders rank above the common shareholders, and this is important as the money usually runs out before everyone gets paid.

Because of these two preferential rights—the right to dividends and assets—preferred shareholders generally do not mind that they do not have the voting right that common shareholders have.

BEFORE YOU GO ON . . .

▶Review It

1. Compare the normal rights and privileges of common and preferred shareholders.
2. Distinguish between cumulative and noncumulative preferred shares.
3. Distinguish between convertible, redeemable, and retractable preferred shares.

▶Do It

Turin Corporation issued 50,000 preferred shares on February 22 for $20 each. Each share was convertible into 10 common shares. On April 12, another 30,000 preferred shares were issued for $30 each. On June 5, when the price of the common shares was $4 and the price of the preferred shares was $35, shareholders converted 20,000 of the preferred shares into common. Record the share transactions.

Action Plan

- Credit the Preferred Shares account for the entire proceeds of the share issue.
- Use the average cost to record the conversion. Market values are irrelevant.
- Calculate the average cost per share by dividing the balance in the Preferred Shares account by the number of shares issued.

Solution

Feb. 22	Cash	1,000,000	
	Preferred Shares (50,000 × $20)		1,000,000
	To record issue of 50,000 preferred shares at $20.		
Apr. 12	Cash	900,000	
	Preferred Shares (30,000 × $30)		900,000
	To record issue of 30,000 preferred shares at $30.		
June 5	Preferred Shares (20,000 × $23.75)	475,000	
	Common Shares		475,000
	To record conversion of 20,000 preferred shares into 200,000		
	(20,000 × 10) common shares at an average cost of $23.75		
	($1,900,000 ÷ 80,000).		

Related exercise material: BE13–7, BE13–8, BE13–9, E13–3, E13–4, E13–5, and E13–6.

Statement Presentation and Analysis

In this section, we will review the preparation and presentation of the shareholders' equity section of the balance sheet and then learn how to use this information to calculate an important profitability measure—the return on equity ratio.

study objective 4

Prepare the shareholders' equity section of the balance sheet and calculate return on equity.

Presentation of Shareholders' Equity

In the shareholders' equity section of the balance sheet, the following are reported: (1) contributed capital, (2) retained earnings, and (3) accumulated other comprehensive income. We have already mentioned the first two categories and will illustrate them here. Accumulated other comprehensive income is a new concept that we will briefly discuss here and look at in more detail in Chapter 16.

Contributed Capital

Recall that contributed capital is the amounts contributed by, or accruing to, the shareholders. Within contributed capital, there are two classifications:

1. **Share capital.** This category consists of preferred and common shares. Because of the additional rights they possess, preferred shares are shown before common shares. The legal value (e.g., no par value), number of shares authorized, number of shares issued, and any particular share preferences (e.g., convertible) are reported for each class of shares.
2. **Additional contributed capital.** This category includes amounts contributed from reacquiring and retiring shares. Other situations not discussed in this textbook can also result in additional contributed capital. If a company has a variety of sources of additional contributed capital, it is important to distinguish each one.

In most cases, there will be no additional contributed capital. The caption "share capital" is therefore used more often than "contributed capital."

Retained Earnings

Retained earnings are the cumulative net income (or loss) since incorporation that has been retained in the company (i.e., not distributed to shareholders). Each year, net income is added (or a net loss is deducted) and dividends are deducted from the opening retained earnings balance to determine the ending retained earnings amount. Dividends are amounts distributed to shareholders—they are similar to drawings by an owner in a proprietorship.

As in a proprietorship, revenue and expense accounts (which combine to produce net income or loss) and the Dividends account are temporary accounts which accumulate transactions for the period. At the end of each period, these accounts are closed, just as their corresponding accounts in a proprietorship are: (1) individual revenue and expense accounts are closed to Income Summary, (2) the Income Summary account is closed to Retained Earnings, and (3) Dividends is closed to Retained Earnings. Note that the Income Summary account is not closed to the owner's capital account, the way it is in a proprietorship. Instead, in a corporation, it is closed to the Retained Earnings account, as is the Dividends account.

For example, assume for simplicity that Zaboschuk Inc. has three temporary accounts at its December 31 year end: Service Revenue $500,000; Operating Expenses $290,000; and Dividends $80,000. The closing entries follow:

A	=	L	+	SE						
				−500,000 +500,000	Dec. 31	Service Revenue			500,000	
						Income Summary				500,000
						To close revenue to income summary.				

Cash flows: no effect

A	=	L	+	SE						
				−290,000 +290,000	31	Income Summary			290,000	
						Operating Expenses				290,000
						To close expenses to income summary.				

Cash flows: no effect

A	=	L	+	SE						
				−210,000 +210,000	31	Income Summary			210,000	
						Retained Earnings				210,000
						To close income summary ($500,000 − $290,000) to retained earnings.				

Cash flows: no effect

A	=	L	+	SE						
				−80,000 +80,000	31	Retained Earnings			80,000	
						Dividends				80,000
						To close dividends to retained earnings.				

Cash flows: no effect

After these entries are posted, the Retained Earnings account (a permanent account) is up to date in the general ledger. It is this ending balance that is reported as an addition in the shareholders' equity section of the balance sheet. The normal balance of the Retained Earnings account is a credit. If there is a negative, or **deficit**, balance, it is reported as a deduction from shareholders' equity, rather than as an addition.

This ending Retained Earnings balance becomes the opening balance for the next period. The statement of retained earnings, like the statement of owner's equity in a proprietorship, reconciles the opening and ending balances in each period. We will learn how to prepare the statement of retained earnings in the next chapter.

Accumulated Other Comprehensive Income

Most revenues, expenses, gains, and losses are included in net income. However, certain gains and losses bypass net income and are recorded as direct adjustments to shareholders' equity. **Comprehensive income** includes all changes in shareholders' equity during a period except for changes that result from the sale or repurchase of shares or from the payment of dividends. This means that it includes (1) the revenues, expenses, gains, and losses included in net income, *and* (2) the gains and losses that bypass net income but affect shareholders' equity. This second category is referred to as "other comprehensive income (loss)."

There are several examples of other comprehensive income. The most common example, and one that we will learn about in more detail in Chapter 16, is unrealized gains and losses on investments. If a company has debt or equity investments available for sale, they must be adjusted up or down to their market value at the end of each accounting period. This results in an unrealized gain or loss. We say "unrealized" to distinguish it from the "realized" gains and losses that occur when the investment is actually sold.

Of course, not all companies will have examples of other comprehensive income. However, if they do, they must report accumulated other comprehensive income as a separate component of shareholders' equity. Other comprehensive income is reported separately from net income and retained earnings for two important reasons: (1) it protects income from sudden changes that would simply be caused by fluctuations in market value, and (2) it informs the financial statement user of the gain or loss that would have occurred if the investment had actually been sold at year end.

Comprehensive income is a recent concept in Canada, although it has been used in the United States and internationally for many years. These new rules are part of the standards harmonization efforts we learned about in Chapter 12. Recording and reporting comprehensive income is mandatory for financial statements for any fiscal year beginning on or after October 1, 2006.

Sample Shareholders' Equity Section

The assumed shareholders' equity section of Zaboschuk Inc., shown in Illustration 13-2, includes most of the accounts discussed in this chapter. Zaboschuk's preferred shares section discloses that the dividend rate is $6 per year; 50,000 noncumulative preferred shares with no par value have been authorized; and 6,000 shares are issued. This means 44,000 shares are still available for issue at some point in the future.

The common shares are no par value with an unlimited amount of shares authorized. To date, 400,000 shares have been issued. Zaboschuk also reports additional contributed capital of $60,000 that was earned when reacquiring common shares; retained earnings of $1,058,000; and accumulated other comprehensive income of $312,000.

Illustration 13-2 ◀

Shareholders' equity section

ZABOSCHUK INC. Balance Sheet (partial) December 31, 2008		
Shareholders' equity		
Contributed capital		
Share capital		
$6-noncumulative preferred shares, no par value, 50,000		
shares authorized, 6,000 shares issued	$ 770,000	
Common shares, no par value, unlimited shares		
authorized, 400,000 shares issued	2,800,000	
Total share capital		$3,570,000
Additional contributed capital		
Contributed capital—reacquired common shares		60,000
Total contributed capital		3,630,000
Retained earnings		1,058,000
Accumulated other comprehensive income		312,000
Total shareholders' equity		$5,000,000

Analysis

There are many ratios that can be determined from the shareholders' equity section of the balance sheet. We will learn about return on equity here. In the next chapter, we will learn about others like earnings per share, price-earnings, and the payout ratio.

Return on Equity

Return on equity, also known as return on investment, is considered by many to be *the* most important measure of a company's profitability. This ratio is used by management and investors to evaluate how many dollars are earned for each dollar invested by the shareholders. It can be used to compare investment opportunities in the marketplace.

Return on equity is a widely published figure. The highest return on equity among Canada's top 500 corporations in a recent year was reported by Gateway Casinos, which reported a return on equity of 138.4 percent. The following illustration calculates the return on equity ratio for The Forzani Group ($ in thousands):

Illustration 13-3 ▶

Return on equity

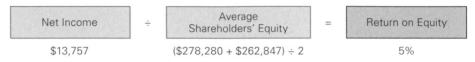

Net Income	÷	Average Shareholders' Equity	=	Return on Equity
$13,757		($278,280 + $262,847) ÷ 2		5%

Forzani's return on equity, at 5 percent, is just about the industry average, which is 5.1 percent. Return on equity can vary significantly by company and by industry.

Calculations can be done to produce a return on equity for common shareholders only. This is done by dividing net income available to common shareholders by the average common shareholders' equity. **Net income available to common shareholders** is net income less any preferred dividends. **Common shareholders' equity** is total shareholders' equity less the legal capital of any preferred shares. Recall that everything else belongs to the common, or residual, shareholders.

BEFORE YOU GO ON . . .

▶**Review It**

1. Identify the classifications found in the shareholders' equity section of a balance sheet.
2. Why is accumulated other comprehensive income reported separately from retained earnings?
3. Explain how to calculate the return on equity.

the navigator

Related exercise material: BE13–10, BE13–11, BE13–12, BE13–13, E13–7, E13–8, E13–9, E13–10, and E13–11.

Practice Tools:
Demonstration Problems

Demonstration Problem

The Rolman Corporation is authorized to issue an unlimited number of no par value common shares and 100,000 no par value, $6-noncumulative, convertible preferred shares. Each preferred share is convertible into 7.5 common shares. In its first year, the company had the following share transactions:

Jan. 10 Issued 400,000 common shares at $8 per share.

July 1 Issued 100,000 common shares in exchange for land. The land had an asking price of $900,000. The shares were selling on the Toronto Stock Exchange at $8.50 per share on that date.

Sept. 1 Issued 20,000 preferred shares at $50 each.

Oct. 12 Reacquired 50,000 common shares at $7 per share.

Dec. 1 Converted 4,000 preferred shares into 30,000 common shares. The preferred shares were selling for $55 per share and the common shares for $9 per share on that date.

Instructions

(a) Journalize the transactions.
(b) Prepare the shareholders' equity section, assuming the company has retained earnings of $900,000 and accumulated other comprehensive income of $100,000 at December 31, 2008.

Solution to Demonstration Problem

Action Plan

- Credit the appropriate share capital account for the full amount of the proceeds from the issue of no par value shares.
- Market value should be used in a noncash transaction.
- Use separate accounts for each type or class of shares.
- Record the conversion of shares at average cost, not market value.
- Keep track of the number of shares issued. Calculate the average cost per share by dividing the balance in the share account by the number of shares issued.
- Debit the common shares account for the average cost of the reacquired shares. If the reacquisition price is below the average cost, credit the difference to a contributed capital account. If the reacquisition price is above the average cost, debit the difference to Retained Earnings unless there is an existing balance in a contributed capital account from previous reacquisitions and retirements.

(a)

Jan. 10	Cash	3,200,000	
	Common Shares (400,000 × $8)		3,200,000
	To record issue of 400,000 common shares at $8.		
July 1	Land	850,000	
	Common Shares (100,000 × $8.50)		850,000
	To record issue of 100,000 common shares for land.		
Sept. 1	Cash	1,000,000	
	Preferred Shares (20,000 × $50)		1,000,000
	To record issue of 20,000 preferred shares at $50.		
Oct. 12	Common Shares (50,000 × $8.10)	405,000	
	Contributed Capital—Reacquisition of Common Shares		55,000
	Cash (50,000 × $7)		350,000
	To record reacquisition of 50,000 common shares at an average cost of $8.10 ($4,050,000 ÷ 500,000).		
Dec. 1	Preferred Shares (4,000 × $50)	200,000	
	Common Shares		200,000
	To record conversion of 4,000 preferred shares into 30,000 common shares.		

(b)

ROLMAN CORPORATION
Balance Sheet (partial)
December 31, 2008

Shareholders' equity
- Contributed capital
  - Share capital
    - Preferred shares, no par value, $6-noncumulative, convertible, 100,000 authorized, 16,000[1] issued $ 800,000[2]
    - Common shares, no par value, unlimited number of shares authorized, 480,000[3] issued 3,845,000[4]

Total share capital	$4,645,000
Contributed capital—reacquisition of common shares	55,000
Total contributed capital	4,700,000
Retained earnings	900,000
Accumulated other comprehensive income	100,000
Total shareholders' equity	$5,700,000

[1] 20,000 − 4,000 = 16,000
[2] $1,000,000 − $200,000 = $800,000
[3] 400,000 + 100,000 − 50,000 + 30,000 = 480,000
[4] $3,200,000 + $850,000 − $405,000 + $200,000 = $3,845,000

the navigator

Summary of Study Objectives

1. *Identify and discuss the major characteristics of a corporation.* The major characteristics of a corporation are as follows: separate legal existence, limited liability of shareholders, transferable ownership rights, ability to acquire capital, continuous life, corporation management, government regulations, and corporate income tax.

2. *Record common share transactions.* When no par value shares are issued for cash, the entire proceeds from the issue become legal capital and are credited to the Common Shares account. When shares are issued for assets or services, the market value of the consideration given up is used if it can be determined. If not, the market value of the consideration received is used.

When shares are reacquired, the average cost is debited to the Common Shares account. If the shares are reacquired at a price below the average cost, the difference is credited to a contributed capital account. If the shares are reacquired at a price above the average cost, the difference is debited first to a contributed capital account if a balance exists, and secondly to the Retained Earnings account.

3. *Record preferred share transactions.* The accounting for preferred shares is similar to the accounting for common shares. Preferred shares have priority over common shares in certain areas. Typically, preferred shareholders have priority over (1) dividends, and (2) assets if the company is liquidated. They usually do not have voting rights. In addition, preferred shares may be convertible, redeemable, and/or retractable. Convertible preferred shares allow their holder to convert them into common shares at a specified ratio. The redemption feature gives the issuing corporation the right to purchase the shares from shareholders at specified future dates and prices. Retractable preferred shares give shareholders the option of selling their shares to the corporation at specified future dates and prices. Redeemable and retractable preferred shares are often more like debt than equity.

4. *Prepare the shareholders' equity section of the balance sheet and calculate return on equity.* Within the shareholders' equity section, the following are reported: contributed capital, retained earnings, and accumulated comprehensive income (if any). Within contributed capital, two classifications may be shown if applicable: share capital and additional contributed capital.

Return on equity is calculated by dividing net income by average shareholders' equity. It is an important measure of a company's profitability.

Glossary

Study Aids: Glossary
Practice Tools: Key Term Matching Activity

Authorized shares The amount of share capital that a corporation is authorized to sell, as indicated in its articles of incorporation. This amount may be specified or unlimited. (p. 671)

Common shares The ownership interest represented by the shares of a corporation. (p. 670)

Comprehensive income All changes in shareholders' equity during a period except for changes resulting from the sale or repurchase of shares, or from the payment of dividends. Comprehensive income includes (1) the revenues, expenses, gains, and losses included in net income, and (2) the gains and losses that bypass net income but affect shareholders' equity. (p. 682)

Contributed capital The total amount of cash paid or other assets contributed by shareholders in exchange for share capital. (p. 673)

Convertible preferred shares Preferred shares that the shareholder can convert into common shares at a specified ratio. (p. 679)

Corporation A business organized as a legal entity that is separate and distinct from its owners under corporation law. (p. 666)

Cumulative dividend A feature of preferred shares that entitles the shareholder to receive current dividends and unpaid dividends from previous years before common shareholders receive any dividends. (p. 678)

Dividends in arrears Cumulative preferred dividends that were not declared during a period. (p. 678)

Financial instrument A contract between two or more parties that establishes financial rights or obligations. (p. 680)

Initial public offering (IPO) The initial offering of a corporation's shares to the public. (p. 671)

Issued shares The portion of authorized shares that has been sold. (p. 671)

Legal capital The amount per share that must be retained in the business for the protection of corporate creditors. (p. 672)

No par value shares Share capital that has not been given a specific value. All the proceeds from the sale of no par value shares are treated as legal capital. (p. 673)

Noncumulative Preferred shares that are entitled to the current dividend, but not to any unpaid amounts from previous years. (p. 678)

Organization costs Costs incurred in the formation of a corporation. (p. 670)

Preferred shares Shares that have contractual preferences over common shares. (p. 677)

Privately held corporation A corporation that has only a few shareholders. Its shares are not available for sale to the general public. (p. 666)

Publicly held corporation A corporation that may have thousands of shareholders. Its shares are usually traded on an organized securities market. (p. 666)

Redeemable (callable) preferred shares Preferred shares that give the issuer the right to purchase the shares from shareholders at specified future dates and prices. (p. 679)

Retained earnings Net income after subtracting net losses and dividends distributed to shareholders since incorporation. If negative (i.e., a debit balance), it is called a deficit. (p. 672)

Retractable preferred shares Preferred shares that give the shareholder the right to sell the shares to the issuer at specified future dates and prices. (p. 679)

Return on equity Net income expressed as a percentage of average shareholders' equity. (p. 684)

Share capital The amount paid to the corporation by shareholders in exchange for shares of ownership. (p. 672)

Self-Study Questions

Practice Tools: Self-Assessment Quizzes

Answers are at the end of the chapter.

(SO 1) K 1. Which of the following is not a major advantage of a corporation?
  (a) Separate legal existence
  (b) Continuous life
  (c) Government regulations
  (d) Transferable ownership rights

(SO 1) AP 2. Ilona Schiller purchased 1,000 common shares of **Bombardier Inc.** on the TSX for $2 per share. Bombardier had originally issued these shares at $3. This transaction will have what impact on Bombardier's Common Shares account?
  (a) Decrease of $1,000 (c) Decrease of $3,000
  (b) Decrease of $2,000 (d) No effect

(SO 2) AP 3. ABC Corporation issues 1,000 common shares at $12 per share. In recording the transaction, a credit is made to:
  (a) Gain on Sale of Shares for $12,000.
  (b) Common Shares for $12,000.
  (c) Investment in ABC Common Shares for $12,000.
  (d) Contributed Capital for $12,000.

(SO 2) C 4. A company will buy back its own shares:
  (a) to force the share price up.
  (b) to force the share price down.
  (c) to increase the number of shares available for dividends.
  (d) to save cash.

(SO 2) AP 5. A company has balances of Contributed Capital—Reacquisition of Shares $50,000; and Retained Earnings $500,000. It repurchases common shares for $120,000

which have an average cost of $100,000. The journal entry to record the acquisition would include:
  (a) a credit to Contributed Capital—Reacquisition of Shares for $20,000.
  (b) a debit to Contributed Capital—Reacquisition of Shares for $20,000.
  (c) a debit to Retained Earnings of $20,000.
  (d) a debit to Common Shares of $120,000.

(SO 3) K 6. Preferred shares have priority over common shares in the following areas:
  (a) dividends.
  (b) assets if the corporation is liquidated.
  (c) voting.
  (d) (a) and (b).

(SO 3) K 7. If 10,000 convertible preferred shares are converted to 20,000 common shares at a time when the average cost of the preferred is $10 per share, the market value of the preferred is $15 per share, and the market value of the common is $9 per share:
  (a) Common Shares would be credited for $180,000.
  (b) Common Shares would be credited for $100,000.
  (c) Preferred Shares would be debited for $150,000.
  (d) No entry would be recorded.

(SO 4) K 8. Which of the following is reported in the shareholders' equity section?
  (a) Accumulated other comprehensive income
  (b) Common shares
  (c) Contributed capital—reacquisition of shares
  (d) All of the above

(SO 4) AP 9. The shareholders' equity section of a balance sheet will never report:
(a) a debit balance in a contributed capital account.
(b) a debit balance in accumulated other comprehensive income.
(c) a debit balance in the Retained Earnings account.
(d) (a) and (c).

10. If a company's net income is $35,000, its share capital (SO 4) is $500,000, its retained earnings are $200,000, and its net sales are $1,000,000, its return on equity is:
(a) 3.5%.
(b) 5%.
(c) 7%.
(d) 17.5%.

Questions

(SO 1) C 1. Corporations can be classified in different ways. For example, they may be classified by purpose (e.g., profit, not-for-profit, or income trust) or by ownership (e.g., public or private). Explain the difference between each of these types of classifications.

(SO 1) C 2. Pat Kabza, a student, asks for your help in understanding the following characteristics of a corporation: (a) limited liability of shareholders, (b) transferable ownership rights, and (c) ability to acquire capital. Explain how these characteristics work together to create a significant advantage for the corporate form of organization.

(SO 1) C 3. (a) Your friend R. Cedras cannot understand how income taxation can be both an advantage and a disadvantage for a corporation. Clarify this problem.
(b) Explain how the income taxation of a corporation is different from the taxation of a proprietorship, partnership, and income trust.

(SO 1) C 4. Explain why some of the advantages of the corporate form of organization may not apply to small, privately held corporations.

(SO 1) K 5. What are the basic ownership rights of common shareholders? Of preferred shareholders?

(SO 1) C 6. Explain the difference between authorized and issued shares. Are both recorded in the general journal?

(SO 1) C 7. (a) What is legal capital?
(b) Why is it reported separately from retained earnings in the shareholders' equity section of the balance sheet? This is not done for a proprietorship.

(SO 1) C 8. Why would the retained earnings in an income trust normally be much lower than the retained earnings in a corporation?

(SO 1) AP 9. Jean-Guy LeBlanc purchases 100 common shares of Innovate.com for $10 per share from the company's initial public offering. Later, Jean-Guy purchases 200 more Innovate.com common shares for $15 each on the Toronto Stock Exchange, using his own Web Broker account. Explain the impact of each of these transactions on Innovate.com's assets, liabilities, and shareholders' equity.

10. **Abitibi-Consolidated Inc.'s** share price fell nearly 50% (SO 1 in one year from $6.83 to $3.48. Explain the effect of this decline in share price on Abitibi's financial statements.

11. Land appraised at $80,000 is purchased by issuing (SO 2 1,000 common shares. The market price of the shares at the time of the exchange is $90 per share. Should the land be recorded at $80,000 or $90,000? Explain.

12. Why would a company repurchase some of its shares? (SO 2 Give some reasons.

13. Wilmor, Inc. repurchases 1,000 of its own common (SO 2 shares. What effect does this transaction have on (a) total assets, (b) total liabilities, and (c) total shareholders' equity?

14. XYZ Corp. has reacquired some of its common shares (SO 2 at a price less than their average cost. The company's president argues that this difference is basically a gain and should be reported on the income statement. Is this appropriate? Explain.

15. Ciana Chiasson is confused. She says, "I don't under- (SO 2 stand why sometimes, when the price paid to reacquire shares is greater than their average cost, the 'loss on reacquisition' is debited to a contributed capital account. But at other times, it is debited to the Retained Earnings account. And sometimes it even is debited to both!" Help Ciana understand.

16. Explain the main differences between common shares (SO 3 and preferred shares.

17. What is the difference between noncumulative and cu- (SO 3 mulative preferred shares? Redeemable and retractable preferred shares?

18. (a) What are dividends in arrears? (SO 3
(b) How are they reported in the financial statements?

19. A preferred shareholder converts her convertible pre- (SO 3 ferred shares into common shares. What effect does this have on the corporation's (a) total assets, (b) total liabilities, and (c) total shareholders' equity?

20. Identify the main components of shareholders' equity (SO 4 and explain what each component represents.

(SO 4) C 21. Indicate how each of the following accounts should be classified in the shareholders' equity section:
   (a) Common Shares
   (b) Retained Earnings
   (c) Contributed Capital—Reacquired Shares
   (d) Accumulated Other Comprehensive Income
   (e) Preferred Shares

22. What is comprehensive income? Why is accumulated (SO 4) K other comprehensive income reported separately from retained earnings?

23. Distinguish between return on equity and return on (SO 4) C common shareholders' equity.

24. In assessing a corporation's profitability, why is it nec- (SO 4) C essary to compare net income to shareholders' equity? Why is it not enough to just examine the amount of net income?

Brief Exercises

BE13–1 For each characteristic listed, identify which type of business organization best fits the description. There may be more than one answer in some cases. The first one has been done for you as an example.

Distinguish between characteristics for different business organizations.
(SO 1) C

Characteristic	Proprietorship	Partnership	Corporation
1. Continuous life			X
2. Unlimited liability			
3. Ease of formation			
4. Income taxes			
5. Ability to acquire capital			
6. Shared skills and resources			
7. Fewer government regulations			
8. Separation of ownership and management			
9. Owners' acts are binding			
10. Easy transfer of ownership rights			

BE13–2 The **Body Shop International PLC** share price rose by €1.75 to €76.25 after L'Oréal S.A., the world's largest cosmetics maker, made an offer to purchase the company in 2006. What is the impact of this increase in share price on Body Shop's financial position? On Body Shop's shareholders?

Evaluate impact of share price on financial position.
(SO 1) C

BE13–3 On June 1, Eagle Inc. issues 2,000 common shares for $6 per share. On December 15, Eagle issues an additional 1,000 shares for $9 per share. (a) Journalize the two share issues. (b) What is the average cost per share after the December 15 transaction?

Record issue of common shares.
(SO 2) AP

BE13–4 Spiro Inc.'s common shares have a market value of $14 per share on December 20. On this same date, Spiro issues 5,000 shares to purchase land advertised for sale at $80,000. (a) Journalize the issue of the shares to acquire the land. (b) Would your answer change if the land was advertised for sale at $75,000?

Record issue of shares in noncash transaction.
(SO 2) AP

BE13–5 The Quebec-based international paper company **Cascades Inc.** repurchased 555,600 of its own common shares in 2005. The share repurchase resulted in a debit of $2 million to the Common Shares account and a debit of $4 million to the Retained Earnings account. (a) How much did Cascades pay, on average, to repurchase its shares? (b) What was the initial issue price of the shares, on average? (c) What was Cascades' likely reason for repurchasing some of its own shares?

Discuss share repurchase.
(SO 2) AP

BE13–6 Enviro Corporation reported the following information about its common shares at January 31: no par value, unlimited number of common shares authorized, 35,000 common shares issued, $122,500. On February 15 of the same year, it paid cash to reacquire 5,000 of these shares. This is the first time the company has reacquired any of its shares. (a) Journalize the reacquisition of the shares assuming the company paid (a) $15,000, and (b) $20,000, to reacquire the shares.

Record reacquisition of shares.
(SO 2) AP

Record issue of preferred shares.
(SO 3) AP

BE13–7 First Nations Inc. issues 5,000 preferred shares for $110 per share on January 28. On June 15, the company issues an additional 1,000 shares for $125 per share. (a) Journalize the two share issues. (b) What is the average cost per share after the June 15 transaction?

Record conversion of preferred shares.
(SO 3) AP

BE13–8 On March 3, Spiral Corporation issues 40,000 preferred shares for $100 each. These shares are convertible into four common shares for each preferred share. On October 1, when the preferred shares have a market value of $105 each, and the common shares $28 each, 10,000 of the preferred shares are converted into common shares. (a) Journalize the issue of the preferred shares on March 3. (b) Journalize the conversion of the preferred shares on October 1.

Determine dividends in arrears.
(SO 3) AP

BE13–9 Gushue Incorporated had 40,000 $2-cumulative preferred shares. It was unable to pay any dividend to the preferred shareholders in the current year. (a) What are the dividends in arrears, if any? (b) Would your answer change if the preferred shares were noncumulative rather than cumulative?

Prepare shareholders' equity section.
(SO 4) AP

BE13–10 Kaposi Corporation has the following shareholders' equity accounts at December 31, 2008: common shares, no par value, unlimited number of shares authorized, 5,000 shares issued, $50,000; preferred shares, $5-noncumulative, no par value, unlimited number of shares authorized, 800 shares issued, $20,000; contributed capital—reacquisition of common shares, $5,000; and retained earnings, $29,000. Prepare the shareholders' equity section of the balance sheet.

Prepare shareholders' equity section with comprehensive income.
(SO 4) AP

BE13–11 Refer to BE13–10. In addition to the information provided, assume that Kaposi Corporation also has accumulated other comprehensive income of $6,000. (a) Prepare the shareholders' equity section of the balance sheet. (b) What amount would Kaposi report as total shareholders' equity if it had an accumulated other comprehensive loss of $6,000 rather than accumulated other comprehensive income?

Record closing entries.
(SO 4) AP

BE13–12 At December 31, the Brookfield Corporation reports revenues of $2 million, expenses of $1.5 million, and dividends of $50,000. Prepare summary closing entries.

Calculate return on equity.
(SO 4) AP

BE13–13 Before it was sold to **Sapporo Breweries Ltd.**, **Sleeman Breweries Ltd.** reported the following selected information for the year ended December 31, 2005 (in thousands): net revenue $206,674; net income $8,097; beginning shareholders' equity $132,495; and ending shareholders' equity $121,784. (a) Calculate the return on equity. (b) Sleeman has no preferred shares. Would its return on common shareholders' equity be the same as, or different from, its return on equity?

Exercises

Interpret stock market listing.
(SO 1) AN

E13–1 Here is a stock market listing for **Canadian Pacific Railway Limited (CP)** common shares:

| 365-day | | stock | sym | div | high | low | close | chg | vol 100s | yld | p/e ratio |
high	low										
60.85	41.45	CPRailway	CP	0.75	60.41	59.25	59.25	-1.24	9837	1.3	17.3

Instructions

Answer the following questions:

(a) What is the highest price CP shares traded for during the last year? The lowest?
(b) What is the annual per share dividend paid on these shares?
(c) If you had purchased 1,000 common shares at CP's high price of the day in the above listing, what would be the total cost of your share purchase?
(d) What was the closing price of CP common shares on the previous day?
(e) How many CP common shares were sold on the trading day of the listing?
(f) What would be your likely motivation for purchasing these shares: dividend income or capital appreciation?

E13–2 As an accountant for the firm of Bell and Whistle, you encounter the following situations while doing the accounting for different clients:

Record issue of shares in noncash transactions.
(SO 2) AP

1. Newmarket Corporation is a closely held corporation whose shares are not publicly traded. On December 5, the corporation acquired land by issuing 5,000 common shares. The asking price for the land was $125,000. The appraised value of the land was $120,000.
2. Hache Corporation is a publicly held corporation whose common shares are traded on the Toronto Stock Exchange. On June 1, it acquired land by issuing 20,000 shares. At the time of the exchange, the land was advertised for sale at $250,000. The shares were selling at $12 per share.

Instructions

Prepare the journal entries for each situation.

E13–3 During its first year of operations, Algonquin Corporation had the following transactions related to its preferred and common shares:

Record issue of shares.
(SO 2, 3) AP

Jan. 10 Issued 75,000 common shares for $5 per share.
Feb. 24 Issued 1,000 preferred shares for $105 per share.
July   1 Issued 50,000 common shares for $6.50 per share.

Instructions

(a) Journalize the share transactions.
(b) Calculate the average cost for the (1) preferred shares and (2) common shares.

E13–4 Moosonee Co. Ltd. had the following share transactions during its first year of operations:

Record issue and reacquisition of shares.
(SO 2, 3) AP

Jan.   6 Issued 200,000 common shares for $1.50 per share.
      12 Issued 50,000 common shares for $1.75 per share.
Mar. 17 Issued 1,000 preferred shares for $105 per share.
July 18 Issued 1 million common shares for $2 per share.
Nov. 17 Reacquired 200,000 common shares for $1.95 per share.
Dec. 30 Reacquired 150,000 common shares for $1.80 per share.

Instructions

(a) Journalize the transactions.
(b) How many common shares remain at the end of the year and what is their average cost?

E13–5 Kalyani Corporation has 100,000 $4-cumulative preferred shares issued. In its first year of operations, it paid $250,000 of dividends to its preferred shareholders. In its second year, the company paid dividends of $550,000 to its preferred shareholders.

Determine dividends in arrears.
(SO 3) AP

Instructions

(a) What is the total annual preferred dividend supposed to be for the preferred shareholders?
(b) Calculate any dividends in arrears in years 1 and 2.
(c) Explain how dividends in arrears should be reported in the financial statements.
(d) If the preferred shares were noncumulative rather than cumulative, how much dividend would the company likely have paid its preferred shareholders in year 2?

E13–6 On March 1, Kerr Corporation issued 10,000 preferred shares for $100 per share. On July 15, it issued an additional 30,000 preferred shares for $120 per share. Each share is convertible into five common shares. On November 15, when the market values of the two classes of shares are $125 and $28, respectively, 2,000 preferred shares were converted into common shares.

Record conversion of preferred shares.
(SO 3) AP

Instructions

(a) Journalize the conversion of the preferred shares on November 15.
(b) How many preferred and common shares are there after the conversion on November 15?

Identify terminology.
(SO 1, 2, 3, 4) C

E13–7 Here are some of the terms discussed in this chapter:

1. Publicly held corporation
2. Authorized shares
3. Cumulative
4. Common shares
5. Issued shares
6. Retained earnings
7. Secondary market
8. Initial public offering
9. Legal capital
10. Contributed capital
11. Comprehensive income
12. Organization costs
13. Convertible

Instructions

For each description, write the number of the term it best matches.

(a) ___ The amount of share capital that must be retained in the business for the protection of the creditors

(b) ___ The type of corporation whose shares are traded in an organized security market, such as the Toronto Stock Exchange

(c) ___ Legal fees, accounting fees, and registration costs incurred in forming a company

(d) ___ The maximum number of shares a corporation is allowed to sell

(e) ___ The number of shares a corporation has actually sold

(f) ___ The first time a corporation's shares are offered to the public

(g) ___ Where investors buy and sell shares from each other, rather than from the company

(h) ___ The element of shareholders' equity that is increased by net income and decreased by net losses

(i) ___ The class of shares that normally has voting power

(j) ___ Includes all changes in shareholders' equity during a period except for changes that result from the sale or repurchase of shares or from the payment of dividends

(k) ___ The amount contributed by, or accruing to, the shareholders

(l) ___ A feature that allows preferred shareholders to exchange their shares for common shares

(m) ___ A feature that ensures that unpaid dividends on preferred shares must be paid before common shareholders can receive a dividend

Classify financial statement accounts.
(SO 4) AP

E13–8 The ledger of Val d'Or Corporation contains the following selected accounts:

1. Cash
2. Common shares
3. Contributed capital—reacquisition of common shares
4. Gain on sale of property, plant, and equipment
5. Available-for-sale security (held with the intention of selling if the need for cash arises)
6. Unrealized gain on available-for-sale security
7. Preferred shares
8. Retained earnings
9. Legal fees expense
10. Dividends

Instructions

Using the following table headings, indicate whether or not each of the above accounts should be reported in the shareholders' equity section of the balance sheet. If yes, indicate whether the account should be reported as share capital, additional contributed capital, retained earnings, or accumulated other comprehensive income. If not, indicate in which financial statement (balance sheet or income statement) and in which section the account should be reported. The first account has been done for you as an example.

| | Shareholders' Equity | | | | | |
Account	Share Capital	Additional Contributed Capital	Retained Earnings	Accumulated Other Comprehensive Income	Financial Statement	Classification
1. Cash					Balance Sheet	Current assets

E13–9 The following accounts appear in the ledger of Ozabal Inc. after the books are closed at December 31, 2008:

Prepare shareholders' equity section of balance sheet.
(SO 4) AP

Accumulated other comprehensive income	$ 75,000
Common shares (no par value, unlimited number of shares authorized, 300,000 shares issued)	300,000
Contributed capital—reacquisition of common shares	25,000
Preferred shares ($4-noncumulative, no par value, 100,000 shares authorized, 30,000 shares issued)	150,000
Retained earnings	900,000

Instructions

Prepare the shareholders' equity section of the balance sheet.

E13–10 **Reitmans** reported the following selected accounts and information, as at January 28, 2006:

Prepare shareholders' equity section of balance sheet. Calculate return on equity.
(SO 4) AP

REITMANS (CANADA) LIMITED Selected Financial Data January 28, 2006 (in thousands)	
Class A non-voting (preferred) shares, unlimited authorized, 56,747 issued	$ 16,892
Common shares, unlimited authorized, 13,440 issued	482
Contributed surplus	2,523
Dividends	29,345
Net income	84,889
Reduction of retained earnings due to reacquisition of Class A non-voting shares above average cost	1,375
Retained earnings, January 29, 2005	316,191
Total shareholders' equity, January 29, 2005	331,524

Instructions

(a) Prepare the shareholders' equity section of the balance sheet.
(b) Calculate Reitmans' return on equity.

E13–11 The shareholders' equity section of Shumway Corporation at December 31 is as follows:

Answer questions about shareholders' equity.
(SO 2, 3, 4) AN

SHUMWAY CORPORATION Balance Sheet (partial) December 31, 2008	
Shareholders' equity	
Contributed capital	
Share capital	
Preferred shares, $5-cumulative, no par value, unlimited number of shares authorized, 10,000 shares issued	$ 600,000
Common shares, no par value, 750,000 shares authorized, 600,000 shares issued	1,800,000
Total share capital	2,400,000
Contributed capital—reacquisition of common shares	100,000
Total contributed capital	2,500,000
Retained earnings	1,158,000
Total shareholders' equity	$3,658,000

Instructions

(a) What is the average cost of the preferred shares? Of the common shares?

(b) How many additional common shares can Shumway sell if it wants to raise additional equity financing?

(c) If Shumway repurchased 100,000 common shares, and that is the only transaction that affected Contributed Capital—Reacquisition of Shares, how much did it pay to repurchase the shares?

(d) What is the total annual dividend on preferred shares?

(e) If dividends of $50,000 were in arrears on the preferred shares, rather than been paid during 2008, what would be the balance reported for Retained Earnings?

Problems: Set A

Determine form of business organization.
(SO 1) AN

P13–1A Five independent situations follow:

1. Kyle Anthony, a student looking for summer employment, obtains a liquor licence to operate a beer cart on a golf course. He purchases beer from the liquor store and sells it from his cart to thirsty golfers along the golf course.

2. Joseph LeBlanc and Sabra Surkis each own separate bike shops. They have decided to combine their businesses and try to expand their operations to include skis and snowboards. They expect to need a lot of money in the coming year to expand their operations.

3. Three computer science professors have formed a business to license and sell a computer program they wrote to reduce spam e-mail. Each professor has contributed an equal amount of cash and knowledge to the venture. They expect to be able to sell this program internationally (spam has no borders!).

4. Abdur Rahim has run a successful, but small, co-operative health and organic food store for over twenty years. The increased sales of his own store have made him believe that the time is right to open a chain of health and organic food stores across the country. Of course, this will require a substantial investment in inventories and property, plant, and equipment, as well as employees and other resources. Abdur has no savings or personal assets.

5. Mary Campeau and Richard St. Pierre each speak three different languages. They have decided to start a translating business to assist companies and individuals with their translation requirements.

Instructions

In each case, explain what form of organization the business is likely to take: proprietorship, partnership, or corporation. Give reasons for your choice.

Determine impact of reacquired shares.
(SO 2) AP

P13–2A Cernavoda Limited reported the following information related to its shareholders' equity on January 1:

Common shares, 100,000 authorized, 9,000 shares issued	$270,000
Contributed capital—reacquisition of common shares	9,000
Retained earnings	180,000

During the year, the following transactions related to common shares occurred in the order listed:

1. Reacquired 400 shares at $39 per share.
2. Issued 3,500 shares at $42 per share.
3. Issued 1,200 shares at $61.50 per share.

4. Reacquired 1,000 shares at $60 per share.
5. Reacquired 1,300 shares at $34 per share.

Instructions

(a) Calculate the number of shares authorized and issued at the end of the year.

(b) Determine the ending balances in each of the following accounts: Common Shares; Contributed Capital—Reacquisition of Common Shares; and Retained Earnings.

P13–3A At the beginning of its first year of operations, Backwoods Limited has 3,000 no par value, $5 preferred shares and 50,000 no par value common shares.

Allocate dividends between preferred and common shares.
(SO 2) AP

Instructions

Using the format shown below, allocate the total dividend paid in each year to the preferred and common shareholders, assuming that the preferred shares are (a) noncumulative, and (b) cumulative. The first year has been done for you as an example.

		(a)		(b)	
Year	Dividend Paid	Noncumulative Preferred	Common	Cumulative Preferred	Common
1	$15,000	$15,000	$0	$15,000	$0
2	12,000				
3	27,000				
4	35,000				

P13–4A The following shareholders' equity accounts are reported by Talty Inc. on January 1:

Show impact of transactions on accounts.
(SO 2, 3, 4) AP

Common shares (no par value, unlimited authorized, 500,000 issued)	$4,000,000
Preferred shares ($4-noncumulative, convertible, 100,000 authorized, 4,000 issued)	600,000
Contributed capital—reacquisition of preferred shares	2,000
Retained earnings	1,958,000
Accumulated other comprehensive income	25,000

The following selected transactions occurred during the year:

1. Issued 10,000 common shares at $10 per share.
2. Issued 500 common shares in exchange for a piece of equipment. The market value of the shares was $11 per share; of the equipment, $6,000.
3. Shareholders converted 2,000 preferred shares into 20,000 common shares. The market value per preferred share was $160; per common share, $16.50.
4. Issued 1,000 preferred shares at $150 per share.
5. Reacquired 500 preferred shares at $145 per share.
6. The preferred share dividend was paid at the end of the year.
7. The company reported an unrealized loss on its available-for-sale investments of $5,000 at the end of the year.

Instructions

For each of the transactions, indicate whether it will increase (+), decrease (–), or not affect (n/a) the items in the table below and by what amount. The first transaction has been done for you as an example.

				Shareholders' Equity		
Assets	Liabilities	Preferred Shares	Common Shares	Other Contributed Capital	Retained Earnings	Accumulated Other Comprehensive Income
1. +$100,000	n/a	n/a	+$100,000	n/a	n/a	n/a

P13–5A Highland Corporation was organized on January 1, 2008. It is authorized to issue an unlimited number of $3-noncumulative, no par value preferred shares, and an unlimited number of no par value common shares. The following transactions were completed during the first year:

Record and post transactions. Prepare shareholders' equity section.
(SO 2, 3, 4) AP

Jan. 10 Issued 100,000 common shares at $2 per share.
Mar. 1 Issued 10,000 preferred shares at $42 per share.
Apr. 1 Issued 25,000 common shares for land. The appraised value of the land was $67,000 and the market value of the common shares was $2.50 per share on this date.
May 1 Issued 75,000 common shares at $3 per share.
July 24 Issued 16,800 common shares for $60,000 cash and used equipment. The equipment originally cost $15,000. It now has a net book value of $7,500 and a market value of $8,000. The common shares issued had a market value of $4 per share on this date.
Nov. 1 Issued 2,000 preferred shares at $48 per share.
Dec. 31 Reported net income of $650,000 for the year.
31 Paid $36,000 of dividends to the preferred shareholders.

Instructions

(a) Journalize the transactions and the summary closing entries.
(b) Open general ledger accounts and post to the shareholders' equity accounts.
(c) Prepare the shareholders' equity section of the balance sheet at December 31.

Record and post transactions.
Prepare shareholders' equity
section.
(SO 2, 3, 4) AP

P13–6A The shareholders' equity accounts of the MountainHi Corporation on January 1, 2008, were as follows:

Preferred shares (no par value, $4-cumulative, 50,000 shares authorized, 8,000 issued)	$ 500,000
Common shares (no par value, unlimited number of shares authorized, 1 million issued)	2,741,000
Contributed capital—reacquisition of common shares	1,500
Retained earnings	1,816,000

During 2008, the corporation had the following transactions and events related to its shareholders' equity:

Feb.   1 Issued 25,000 common shares for $75,000.
Sept. 3 Issued 5,000 common shares for $16,500.
Oct. 25 Reacquired 10,000 common shares for $30,000.
Nov.   3 Issued 2,000 preferred shares for $130,000.
Dec. 31 Reported net income of $275,000 during the year.
       31 Paid $30,000 of dividends to the preferred shareholders.

Instructions

(a) Journalize the transactions and the summary closing entries.
(b) Open general ledger accounts and post to the shareholders' equity accounts.
(c) Prepare the shareholders' equity section of the balance sheet at December 31, including the disclosure of any preferred dividends in arrears.

Record and post transactions.
Prepare shareholders' equity
section.
(SO 2, 3, 4) AP

P13–7A Denison Corporation is authorized to issue 10,000 no par value, $3-noncumulative, convertible preferred shares and an unlimited number of no par value common shares. Each preferred share is convertible into eight common shares. On January 1, 2008, the general ledger contained the following shareholders' equity balances:

Preferred shares (5,000 shares)	$ 525,000
Common shares (70,000 shares)	1,050,000
Contributed capital—reacquisition of preferred shares	18,750
Retained earnings	300,000
Accumulated other comprehensive income	25,000

During 2008, the following transactions occurred:

Feb.   6 Issued 1,000 preferred shares for a building having a market value of $132,000. The market value of the shares on this date was $111 per share.
July 15 Holders of 2,000 preferred shares converted the shares into 16,000 common shares. Market values were as follows: preferred shares, $122 per share; and common shares, $16 per share.
Aug. 22 Issued 500 preferred shares at $124 per share.
Nov.   1 Holders of 1,000 preferred shares converted the shares into 8,000 common shares. Market values were as follows: preferred shares, $130 per share; and common shares, $18 per share.
Dec. 31 Total revenues and expenses for the year were $600,000 and $540,000, respectively. No dividends were paid.

Instructions

(a) Journalize the transactions and the closing entries.

(b) Enter the beginning balances in the accounts and post the journal entries to the shareholders' equity accounts.

(c) Prepare the shareholders' equity section of the balance sheet at December 31, including the disclosure of any preferred dividends that may be in arrears.

P13–8A The adjusted trial balance of Miscou Corp., as at September 30, 2008, follows:

Record closing entries and prepare balance sheet. (SO 4) AP

MISCOU CORP.
Adjusted Trial Balance
September 30, 2008

	Debit	Credit
Cash	$ 32,500	
Accounts receivable	74,705	
Supplies	1,265	
Equipment	150,400	
Accumulated amortization—equipment		$ 60,160
Franchise	225,000	
Accounts payable		43,000
Salaries payable		8,400
Interest payable		900
Income tax payable		2,000
Unearned commission revenue		5,500
Note payable ($5,000 of this note is due within the next year)		60,000
Preferred shares ($4-noncumulative, unlimited number authorized, 500 issued)		50,000
Common shares (unlimited number authorized, 40,000 issued)		110,000
Contributed capital—reacquisition of preferred shares		1,500
Retained earnings		75,000
Dividends	2,000	
Commission revenue		314,850
Salaries expense	138,400	
Rent expense	25,000	
Amortization expense	30,080	
Supplies expense	4,860	
Utilities expense	18,200	
Interest expense	3,900	
Income tax expense	25,000	
	$731,310	$731,310

Instructions

(a) Journalize the closing entries.

(b) Prepare a balance sheet at September 30.

Prepare balance sheet and
calculate return on equity.
(SO 4) AP

P13–9A **Andrés Wines Ltd.**, headquartered in Ontario, is Canada's second largest wine producer. It has the following balance sheet accounts, in alphabetical order, as at March 31, 2006:

ANDRÉS WINES LTD.
Selected Accounts
March 31, 2006
(in thousands)

Accounts payable and accrued liabilities	$ 21,613
Accounts receivable	18,444
Accumulated amortization—property, plant, and equipment	49,100
Bank indebtedness	37,295
Class A shares, nonvoting, unlimited authorized, 3,963 issued	6,975
Class B shares, voting, convertible into Class A shares, unlimited authorized, 1,002 issued	400
Current portion of long-term debt	5,888
Dividends	3,109
Dividends payable	778
Future income tax liability (long-term)	12,381
Goodwill	35,862
Income taxes recoverable	911
Inventories	70,528
Long-term debt	50,328
Net income	6,054
Other long-term assets	8,298
Other long-term liabilities	4,224
Prepaid expenses	2,447
Property, plant, and equipment	134,697
Retained earnings	79,260

Instructions

(a) Prepare a classified balance sheet.
(b) Calculate the return on equity. Total shareholder's equity at March 31, 2005, was $87,168,000.

Calculate return on equity.
(SO 4) AP

P13–10A **Sears Canada Inc.** reported the following selected information:

SEARS CANADA INC.
December 31
(in millions)

	2005	2004	2003
Net income	$770.8	$ 128.7	$ 124.5
Shareholders' equity	645.3	1,877.4	1,780.5

Instructions

(a) Calculate Sears' return on equity for 2004 and 2005. Comment on whether its return on equity improved or worsened.
(b) The return on equity for Sears' industry was 61.1% in 2005 and 7.0% in 2004. Compare Sears' performance to the industry average.

Answer questions about
shareholders' equity section.
(SO 1, 2, 3, 4) AP

P13–11A The shareholders' equity section of Moreau Corporation reported the following information at December 31, 2008:

```
                        MOREAU CORPORATION
                        Balance Sheet (partial)
                         December 31, 2008

Shareholders' equity
  Share capital
    $5-cumulative preferred shares, no par value, unlimited
      number of shares authorized, ? shares issued                    $3,150,000
    Common shares, no par value, unlimited number of shares
      authorized, 250,000 shares issued                                1,000,000
    Total share capital                                                4,150,000
  Retained earnings
    Opening balance, January 1                          $ 500,000
    Net income                                            175,000
    Reacquisition of common shares                        (56,250)
    Dividends—preferred                                  (150,000)       468,750
  Accumulated other comprehensive loss                                  (18,750)
  Total shareholders' equity                                          $4,600,000
```

There are no dividends in arrears at the end of 2007 or 2008.

Instructions

(a) How many preferred shares were issued at December 31?

(b) What was the average cost of the preferred shares, on a per share basis? Of the common shares?

(c) Assume that the debit to retained earnings for the reacquisition of common shares was to reacquire 25,000 shares and that no new common shares were issued during the year. How much did Moreau Corporation pay to reacquire those shares?

(d) In terms of the limited liability characteristic of a corporation, what is the dollar amount that the preferred shareholders are potentially liable for? How much are the common shareholders potentially liable for?

(e) What is an "accumulated other comprehensive loss"?

Problems: Set B

P13–1B   Presented below are five independent situations:

1. Three kinesiology students have formed a business to do personal training. Each student plans on contributing an equal amount of cash and effort to this business.
2. Chris Erb, a student looking for summer employment, plans on offering his lawn maintenance services in his town.
3. Ron Cullen owns a gravel pit and plans on forming a business to excavate and sell gravel to construction companies. He will need to purchase an excavator and gravel truck, and hire drivers to deliver the gravel.
4. Hervé Gaudet wants to rent portable DVD players and DVDs in airports across the country. His idea is that customers will be able to rent equipment and DVDs at one airport, watch the DVDs on their flight, and return the equipment and DVDs at their destination airport. This will require a substantial investment in equipment and DVDs, as well as in employees and locations in each airport. Hervé has no savings or personal assets. He wants to keep control over the business.
5. Johnny Daredevil plans on purchasing a jetboat to offer extreme boat tours to tourists through the Reversing Falls. He will need to purchase liability insurance in case of accidents.

Determine form of business organization.
(SO 1) AN

Instructions

In each case, explain what form of organization the business is likely to take: proprietorship, partnership, or corporation. Give reasons for your choice.

Determine impact of
reacquired shares.
(SO 2) AP

P13–2B Harbour Limited reported the following information related to its shareholders' equity on January 1:

Common shares, 500,000 authorized, 250,000 shares issued	$1,000,000
Contributed capital—reacquisition of common shares	10,000
Retained earnings	680,000

During the year, the following transactions related to common shares occurred in the order listed:

1. Issued 25,000 shares at $5.10 per share.
2. Reacquired 5,000 shares at $4.00 per share.
3. Issued 10,000 shares at $5.50 per share.
4. Reacquired 12,000 shares at $5 per share.
5. Reacquired 68,000 shares at $4 per share.

Instructions

(a) Calculate the number of shares authorized and issued at the end of the year.
(b) Determine the ending balances in each of the following accounts: Common Shares; Contributed Capital—Reacquisition of Common Shares; and Retained Earnings.

Allocate dividends between
preferred and common
shares.
(SO 2) AP

P13–3B At the beginning of its first year of operations, Northwoods Limited has 5,000 no par value, $4 preferred shares and 50,000 no par value common shares.

Instructions

Using the format shown below, allocate the total dividend paid in each year to the preferred and common shareholders, assuming that the preferred shares are (a) noncumulative, and (b) cumulative. The first year has been done for you as an example.

		(a)		(b)	
Year	Dividend Paid	Noncumulative Preferred	Common	Cumulative Preferred	Common
1	$20,000	$20,000	$0	$20,000	$0
2	15,000				
3	30,000				
4	35,000				

Show impact of transactions
on accounts.
(SO 2, 3, 4) AP

P13–4B The following shareholders' equity accounts are reported by Branch Inc. on January 1:

Common shares (no par value, unlimited authorized, 150,000 issued)	$2,400,000
Preferred shares ($4-cumulative, convertible, 100,000 authorized, 5,000 issued)	350,000
Contributed capital—reacquisition of common shares	30,000
Retained earnings	1,275,000
Accumulated other comprehensive income	45,000

Branch Inc. had the following transactions during the year:

1. Issued 1,000 common shares at $23.55 per share.
2. Reacquired 10,000 common shares at $20 per share.
3. Shareholders converted 1,000 preferred shares into 4,000 common shares. The market value per preferred share was $80, per common share, $24.
4. Issued 1,000 common shares for land. The market value of each common share was $25, of the land, $25,500.
5. Issued 100 preferred shares at $75 per share.
6. A $15,000 dividend was paid to the preferred shareholders at the end of the year.
7. The company reported an unrealized gain on its available-for-sale investments of $2,500 at the end of the year.

Instructions

For each of the above transactions, indicate whether it increases (+), decreases (−), or does not affect (n/a) each item in the table below and by how much. The first transaction has been done for you as an example.

				Shareholders' Equity		
Assets	Liabilities	Preferred Shares	Common Shares	Other Contributed Capital	Retained Earnings	Accumulated Other Comprehensive Income
1. +$23,550	n/a	n/a	+$23,550	n/a	n/a	n/a

P13–5B   The Wetland Corporation was organized on February 1, 2007. It is authorized to issue an unlimited number of $4-noncumulative, no par value preferred shares, and an unlimited number of no par value common shares. The following transactions were completed during the first year:

Record and post transactions. Prepare shareholders' equity section.
(SO 2, 3, 4) AP

Feb. 10 Issued 80,000 common shares at $4 per share.
Mar. 1 Issued 5,000 preferred shares at $115 per share.
Apr. 1 Issued 22,000 common shares for land. The asking price of the land was $100,000 and its appraised value was $90,000. The market value of the common shares was $4.25 per share on this date.
June 20 Issued 78,000 common shares at $4.50 per share.
Aug. 1 Issued 10,000 common shares to lawyers to pay for their bill of $50,000 for services they performed in helping the company organize. The market value of the common shares was $4.75 on this date.
Sept. 1 Issued 10,000 common shares at $5 per share.
Nov. 1 Issued 1,000 preferred shares at $117 per share.
Jan. 31 Reported net income of $500,000 for the year.
    31 Paid $24,000 of dividends to the preferred shareholders.

Instructions

(a) Journalize the transactions and summary closing entries.
(b) Open general ledger accounts and post to the shareholders' equity accounts.
(c) Prepare the shareholders' equity section of the balance sheet at January 31, 2008.

P13–6B   The shareholders' equity accounts of the Cheung Corporation on January 1, 2008, were as follows:

Record and post transactions. Prepare shareholders' equity section.
(SO 2, 3, 4) AP

Preferred shares (no par value, $5-cumulative, 25,000 shares authorized, 3,000 issued)	$ 320,000
Common shares (no par value, unlimited number of shares authorized, 200,000 issued)	1,400,000
Contributed capital—reacquisition of common shares	2,500
Retained earnings	488,000

During 2008, the corporation had the following transactions and events related to its shareholders' equity:

Feb. 1 Issued 5,000 common shares for $55,500.
Sept. 3 Issued 1,000 preferred shares for $107,000.
Oct. 25 Reacquired 10,000 common shares for $75,000.
Dec. 31 Reported net income of $60,000 during the year.
    31 Paid $12,000 of dividends to the preferred shareholders.

Instructions

(a) Journalize the transactions and the summary closing entries.
(b) Open general ledger accounts and post to the shareholders' equity accounts.
(c) Prepare the shareholders' equity section of the balance sheet at December 31, including the disclosure of any preferred dividends in arrears.

Record and post transactions.
Prepare shareholders' equity
section.
(SO 2, 3, 4) AP

P13–7B Remmers Corporation is authorized to issue 10,000 no par value, $5-cumulative, convertible preferred shares and an unlimited number of no par value common shares. Each preferred share is convertible into 10 common shares. On January 1, 2008, the ledger contained the following shareholders' equity balances:

Preferred shares (4,000 shares)	$ 440,000
Common shares (70,000 shares)	1,050,000
Contributed capital—reacquisition of preferred shares	25,000
Retained earnings	300,000
Accumulated other comprehensive income	10,000

During 2008, the following transactions occurred:

Feb. 1 Issued 1,000 preferred shares for land having a market value of $125,000. The market value of the shares on this date was $120 per share.

Mar. 1 Holders of 500 preferred shares converted the shares into 5,000 common shares. Market values were as follows: preferred shares, $125 per share; and common shares, $15 per share.

July 1 Issued 1,500 preferred shares for cash at $130 per share.

Sept. 1 Holders of 1,000 preferred shares converted the shares into 10,000 common shares. Market values were as follows: preferred shares, $135 per share; and common shares, $16 per share.

Dec. 31 Total revenues and expenses for the year were $500,000 and $450,000, respectively. No dividends were paid.

Instructions

(a) Journalize the transactions and the closing entries.
(b) Enter the beginning balances in the accounts and post the journal entries to the shareholders' equity accounts.
(c) Prepare the shareholders' equity section of the balance sheet at December 31, including the disclosure of any preferred dividends that may be in arrears.

Record closing entries and
prepare balance sheet.
(SO 4) AP

P13–8B The adjusted trial balance of Moorcraft Ltd. as at December 31, 2008, is shown below:

MOORCRAFT LTD.
Adjusted Trial Balance
December 31, 2008

	Debit	Credit
Cash	$ 21,000	
Accounts receivable	69,000	
Inventory	40,000	
Prepaid insurance	10,000	
Supplies	5,000	
Land	45,000	
Building	600,000	
Accumulated amortization—building		$ 80,000
Equipment	300,000	
Accumulated amortization—equipment		90,000
Accounts payable		52,000
Salaries payable		8,000
Interest payable		2,500
Income tax payable		10,000
Unearned sales revenue		24,000
Mortgage payable ($10,000 of this mortgage is due in the next year)		350,000
Preferred shares ($4-noncumulative, unlimited number authorized, 2,500 issued)		50,000
Common shares (unlimited number authorized, 100,000 issued)		150,000
Contributed capital—reacquisition of common shares		5,000
Retained earnings		165,000
Accumulated other comprehensive income		23,500
Dividends	10,000	

	Debit	Credit
Sales revenue		596,000
Salaries expense	176,000	
Cost of goods sold	148,000	
Amortization expense	84,000	
Interest expense	31,500	
Rent expense	24,000	
Income tax expense	22,000	
Utilities expense	12,000	
Insurance expense	6,000	
Supplies expense	2,500	
	$1,606,000	$1,606,000

Instructions

(a) Journalize the closing entries.

(b) Prepare a balance sheet at December 31.

P13–9B   Magnotta Winery Corporation is Ontario's third largest winery. It has the following selected accounts, listed in alphabetical order, as at January 31, 2006:

Prepare balance sheet and calculate return on equity.
(SO 4) AP

MAGNOTTA WINERY CORPORATION
Selected Accounts
January 31, 2006

Accounts payable and accrued liabilities	$ 1,289,814
Accounts receivable	347,669
Accumulated amortization—capital assets	11,298,085
Bank indebtedness	4,757,181
Capital assets	33,129,085
Common shares, unlimited authorized, 13,670,005 issued	6,165,817
Current portion of long-term debt	1,477,404
Future income taxes (long-term liability)	1,047,517
Income taxes payable	130,754
Inventories	20,505,669
Long-term debt	8,681,328
Net income	2,574,797
Other contributed capital	210,000
Prepaid expenses and deposits	671,961
Retained earnings, February 1	17,273,203
Winery licenses	251,516

Instructions

(a) Prepare a classified balance sheet.

(b) Calculate the return on equity. Total shareholder's equity at January 31, 2005, was $23,582,360.

P13–10B   Canadian Tire Corporation reported the following selected information:

Calculate return on equity.
(SO 4) AP

CANADIAN TIRE CORPORATION
December 31
(in millions)

	2005	2004	2003
Net income	$ 330.1	$ 291.5	$ 241.2
Shareholders' equity	2,511.1	2,251.2	2,017.1

Instructions

(a) Calculate Canadian Tire's return on equity for 2004 and 2005. Comment on whether its return on equity improved or deteriorated.

(b) The return on equity for Canadian Tire's industry was 13.9% in 2005 and 13.6% in 2004. Compare Canadian Tire's performance to the industry average.

Answer questions about shareholders' equity section. (SO 2, 3, 4) AP

P13–11B The shareholders' equity section of Maple Corporation reported the following information at November 30, 2008:

MAPLE CORPORATION		
Balance Sheet (partial)		
November 30, 2008		
Shareholders' equity		
Contributed capital		
Share capital		
$3-noncumulative preferred shares, unlimited number authorized, 12,000 shares issued		$1,200,000
Common shares, no par value, 500,000 shares authorized, 100,000 shares issued		1,000,000
Total share capital		2,200,000
Additional contributed capital		
Contributed capital—reacquisition of common shares		40,000
Total contributed capital		2,240,000
Retained earnings		
December 1, 2007	$500,000	
Net income	175,000	675,000
Accumulated other comprehensive income		10,000
Total shareholders' equity		$2,925,000

Instructions

(a) What was the average cost of the preferred shares, on a per share basis? Of the common shares?

(b) What was the total amount of dividends, if any, paid by Maple Corporation for the year ended November 30, 2008?

(c) Assuming that there were no dividends in arrears at December 1, 2007, are there any dividends in arrears at November 30, 2008? If so, for what amount?

(d) Assume that the full amount in the Contributed Capital – Reacquisition of Common Shares account was for the reacquisition of 20,000 common shares and that no new common shares were issued during the year. How much did Maple Corporation pay to reacquire those shares?

(e) What is "accumulated other comprehensive income"?

Continuing Cookie Chronicle

(*Note:* This is a continuation of the Cookie Chronicle from Chapters 1 through 12.)

Natalie's friend, Curtis Lesperance, decides to meet with Natalie after hearing that her discussions about a possible business partnership with her friend Katy Peterson have failed. (Natalie had decided that forming a partnership with Katy, a high school friend, would hurt their friendship. Natalie had also concluded that she and Katy were not compatible to operate a business venture together.)

Because Natalie has been so successful with Cookie Creations and Curtis has been just as successful with his coffee shop, they both conclude that they could benefit from each other's business expertise. Curtis and Natalie next evaluate the different types of business organization, and because of the advantage of limited liability, decide to form a corporation.

Curtis has operated his coffee shop for two years. He buys coffee, muffins, and cookies from a local supplier. Natalie's business consists of giving cookie-making classes and selling fine European mixers. The plan is for Natalie to use the premises Curtis currently rents to give her cookie-making classes and demonstrations of the mixers that she sells. Natalie will also hire, train, and supervise staff to bake the cookies and muffins sold in the coffee shop. By offering her classes on the premises, Natalie will save on travel time going from one place to another. Another advantage is that the coffee shop will give one central location for selling the mixers.

The current market values of the assets of both businesses are as follows:

	Curtis's Coffee	Cookie Creations
Cash	$7,500	$10,000
Accounts receivable	100	500
Merchandise inventory	450	1,130
Equipment	2,500	1,000

Combining forces will also allow Natalie and Curtis to pool their resources and buy a few more assets to run their new business venture.

Curtis and Natalie then meet with a lawyer and form a corporation on November 1, 2008, called Cookie & Coffee Creations Ltd. The articles of incorporation state that there will be two classes of shares that the corporation is authorized to issue: common shares and preferred shares. An unlimited number of shares are authorized for the common shares; 10,000 shares with a $0.50-noncumulative dividend are authorized for the preferred shares.

The assets held by each of their sole proprietorships will be transferred into the corporation at current market value. Curtis will receive 10,550 common shares and Natalie will receive 12,630 common shares in the corporation.

Natalie and Curtis are very excited about this new business venture. They come to you with the following questions:

1. Curtis's dad and Natalie's grandmother are interested in investing $5,000 each in the business venture. We are thinking of issuing them preferred shares. What would be the advantage of issuing them preferred shares instead of common shares?

2. Our lawyer has sent us a bill for $750. When we talked the bill over with her, she said that she would be willing to receive common shares in our new corporation instead of cash. We would be happy to issue her shares, but we're a bit worried about accounting for this transaction. Can we do this? If so, how do we determine how many shares to give her?

Instructions

(a) Answer their questions.

(b) Prepare the journal entries required on November 1, 2008, the date when Natalie and Curtis transfer the assets of their respective businesses into Cookie & Coffee Creations Ltd.

(c) Assume that Cookie & Coffee Creations Ltd. issues 1,000 $0.50-noncumulative preferred shares to Curtis's dad and the same number to Natalie's grandmother, in both cases for $5,000. Also assume that Cookie & Coffee Creations Ltd. issues 750 common shares to its lawyer. Prepare the journal entries for each of these transactions. They all occurred on November 1.

(d) Prepare the opening balance sheet for Cookie & Coffee Creations Ltd. as at November 1, 2008, including the journal entries in (b) and (c) above.

Financial Reporting and Analysis

Financial Reporting Problem

BYP13–1 The shareholders' equity section for **The Forzani Group Ltd.** is shown in the Consolidated Balance Sheet in Appendix A. You will also find data related to this problem in the notes to the financial statements.

Instructions

(a) How many classes of shares does Forzani have? For each class of shares, specify how many shares are authorized and issued at January 29, 2006.

(b) Did Forzani issue any additional shares in fiscal 2006? If so, specify how many were issued and for what purpose.

(c) Did Forzani repurchase any shares in fiscal 2006? If so, how much cash did it spend to reacquire the shares?

(d) What was the average cost of the common (Class A) shares at the end of fiscal 2006?

(e) Forzani's return on equity was calculated for fiscal 2006 in Illustration 13-3. Calculate the company's return on equity for fiscal 2005. The shareholders' equity at February 1, 2004, was $233,296,000. Did this ratio improve or worsen from 2005 to 2006?

Interpreting Financial Statements

BYP13–2 **Talisman Energy Inc.**, headquartered in Calgary, is a large, international oil and gas producer. Talisman's authorized share capital includes an unlimited number of common shares.

During the 2005 fiscal year, Talisman repurchased 9,089,100 common shares for a total of $355 million. The following additional information is also available for the years ended December 31, 2005 and 2004:

	2005	2004
Profit margin	19.4%	12.2%
Asset turnover	0.4 times	0.4 times
Return on assets	10.7%	6.3%
Return on equity	29.6%	13.4%
Market price per share	$61.60	$32.35

Instructions

(a) What are some of the reasons why a company repurchases its own shares?

(b) During the year, Talisman debited Retained Earnings $290 million for the repurchase of its common shares. Were Talisman's common shares repurchased for more, or less, than their average cost? Prepare the journal entry to record this repurchase.

(c) Discuss the change in Talisman's profitability from 2004 to 2005.

(d) Is your assessment in (c) consistent with the change in market price per share? Explain why this would likely happen or not happen.

Critical Thinking

Collaborative Learning Activity

Note to instructor: Additional instructions and material for this group activity can be found on the Instructor Resource Site.

BYP13–3 In this group activity, you will take on the role of either corporation or investor. As investors, you will be given the opportunity to buy, convert, or redeem shares of four corporations during the month of November. Each company's shareholders' equity section will be available for you to make informed decisions.

Instructions

(a) Your instructor will divide the class into groups. If you are in a corporate group, your goal is to prepare the shareholder's equity section of the company's balance sheet for the end of the month. If you are in an investor group, your goal is to maximize your wealth.

(b) In the corporate groups, you will receive a one page handout showing your shareholders' equity section and other corporate information as of November 1. In the investor groups, you will receive a handout showing your investment holdings as of the same date. Using this sheet as a starting point, you will then visit each corporate group and determine which company's shares to buy, convert, or redeem.

(c) Corporate groups will complete the shareholders' equity section as of November 30. Investor groups will determine their holdings as of the same date. Together, all the investor groups will complete an overhead summary chart, as directed.

(d) Each corporate group will present its shareholders' equity section to the class and compare it to the overhead summary chart prepared by the investor groups.

Study Aids:
Working in Groups

Communication Activity

BYP13–4 Canada's standard-setters announced that companies must record and report comprehensive income in their financial statements as of October 31, 2006. Other countries, including European nations and the United States, have reported comprehensive income for years.

You are a newly graduated professional accountant, working for a large multinational company headquartered in Canada. The company has several transactions that result in comprehensive income under the new standard. The chief financial officer has asked you to explain how the new standard will affect the company's balance sheet at December 31, 2006. In particular, he would like to understand whether reporting comprehensive income will benefit the company's current and potential shareholders or not, so that he is prepared for any questions that may arise at the company's upcoming annual meeting.

Instructions

Write a memo to the chief financial officer, answering his questions.

Study Aids:
Writing Handbook

Ethics Case

BYP13–5 The R&D division of Simplex Chemical Corp. has just developed a chemical to sterilize the voracious mountain pine beetles that are invading Western Canada's forests. The president of Simplex is anxious to get the chemical to market. Simplex's profits need a boost and his job is in jeopardy because of decreasing sales and profits. Simplex has an opportunity to sell this chemical in several Central American countries, where the laws are much more relaxed than in Canada.

Study Aids:
Ethics in Accounting

The director of Simplex's R&D division strongly recommends more laboratory testing for side effects of this chemical on other insects, birds, animals, plants, and even humans. He cautions the president, "We could be sued from all sides if the chemical has tragic side effects that we didn't even test for in the labs." The president answers, "We can't wait an additional year for your lab tests. We can avoid losses from such lawsuits by establishing a separate, wholly owned corporation to protect Simplex Corp. We can't lose any more than our investment in the new corporation, and we'll invest just the patent covering this chemical. We'll reap the benefits if the chemical works and is safe, and avoid the losses from lawsuits if it's a disaster."

The following week Simplex creates a new wholly owned corporation called Pinebeetle Inc. It sells the chemical patent to it for $10 and watches the spraying begin.

Instructions

(a) Who are the stakeholders in this situation?
(b) Are the president's motives and actions ethical?
(c) Can Simplex protect itself against losses at Pinebeetle Inc.?

ANSWERS TO CHAPTER QUESTIONS

Answers to Accounting in Action Insight Questions

Business Insight, p. 667

Q: Why would someone want to form an unlimited liability corporation?
A: Unlimited liability companies are formed for the income tax advantages. In exchange for this advantage, shareholders are prepared to give up the right to limited liability.

International Insight, p. 670

Q: Why is it important to be able to identify whether or not a company is a corporation by looking at its name?
A: Creditors and investors need to know if a company is a corporation or not, because a corporation has important protections that benefit these users if the corporation goes bankrupt.

Across the Organization Insight, p. 676

Q: What should a finance department consider before it spends money to reacquire the company's shares?
A: The finance department should consider the impact that a repurchase of shares will have on share prices. That is, if the company plans to raise additional capital from the equity markets in the future, then boosting the share price will be a good thing. But this benefit has to be weighed against alternative uses of the cash—for example, perhaps cash is needed to repay debt or to fund a future expansion.

Answer to Forzani Review It Question 4, p. 677

Forzani did not repurchase any shares in 2006, but it did repurchase 135,100 common shares in 2005 for $1,510,000 (see Note 8 (b) to the financial statements).

Answers to Self-Study Questions

1. c 2. d 3. b 4. a 5. b 6. d 7. b 8. d 9. a 10. b

concepts for review >>

Before studying this chapter, you should understand or, if necessary, review:

a. How to prepare an income statement and statement of owner's equity. (Ch. 3, pp. 124–125)
b. How to account for share transactions. (Ch. 13, pp. 673–676)
c. Preferred shareholders' rights to dividends. (Ch. 13, p. 678)
d. What comprehensive income is. (Ch. 13, pp. 682–683)
e. The form and content of the shareholders' equity section of the balance sheet. (Ch. 13, pp. 681–683)
f. How to calculate return on equity. (Ch. 13, p. 684)

Financial Health Breeds Healthy Stock

MONTREAL, Que.—SNC-Lavalin Group is a world leader in engineering and construction, and a key player in facilities and operations management. It also has a hand in infrastructure ownership, operation, and maintenance, and is present in numerous projects in a variety of other industry sectors, including agrifood, aluminum, biopharmaceuticals, chemicals and petroleum, the environment, mass transit, mining and metallurgy, and power.

The resurfacing of Montreal's Jacques Cartier Bridge; the development, design, and construction of Vancouver's SkyTrain; the planning and coordination of the hospitals affiliated with the Université de Montréal; the management and construction of the Sea to Sky Corridor in British Columbia; the reconstruction of the Neptune Theatre complex in Halifax—these are just a sampling of the projects the SNC-Lavalin Group has been involved in, and that's just in Canada.

Founded in 1911, SNC-Lavalin has been active internationally for 40 years, has 30 foreign offices, and is currently working in some 100 countries. The 1991 merger of Canada's two largest engineering firms, SNC Inc. and Lavalin Inc., created a world leader with a vast international network, hundreds of experts in many industry sectors, and extensive resources in management and project financing.

SNC-Lavalin's net income increased by 24.8 percent in 2005, reaching $129.9 million, or $2.54 per share, compared to $104.1 million, or $2.04 per share in 2004. It reported a 43-percent increase in its fourth-quarter profit, at $43.9 million compared to $30.7 million for the same period in 2004.

SNC-Lavalin Group: www.snc-lavalin.com

Given the improved performance in 2005, and a positive outlook for the future, the company's board of directors announced in March 2006 that it would increase its quarterly cash dividend by 31.2 percent. It also made its shares more affordable to investors by approving a three-for-one stock split.

With the stock split, shareholders would receive two additional common shares for each common share they held. The corporation had 50.4 million shares as at December 31, 2005; after the split, the number of shares would be approximately 151.2 million. SNC-Lavalin shares were trading at $96 on March 7, 2006. The split took effect on March 10, after which the shares were trading at approximately $32.

It does not look like SNC-Lavalin's good fortunes, and thus the good fortunes of its shareholders, will be waning any time soon. Backlog, a measure of future prospects, increased to $8.1 billion at the end of 2005, from $6.3 billion at the end of 2004, with the corporation gaining new contracts in almost all industry segments.

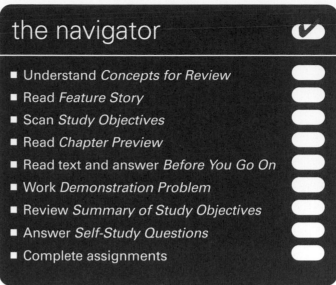

the navigator

- Understand *Concepts for Review*
- Read *Feature Story*
- Scan *Study Objectives*
- Read *Chapter Preview*
- Read text and answer *Before You Go On*
- Work *Demonstration Problem*
- Review *Summary of Study Objectives*
- Answer *Self-Study Questions*
- Complete assignments

chapter 14

Corporations: Dividends, Retained Earnings, and Income Reporting

study objectives >>

the navigator

After studying this chapter, you should be able to:

1. Prepare the entries for cash dividends, stock dividends, and stock splits, and compare their financial impact.

2. Prepare a corporate income statement.

3. Prepare a statement of retained earnings.

4. Evaluate earnings and dividend performance.

As a corporation grows, it is not unusual for its share price to rise rapidly. Many corporations split their stock—as SNC-Lavalin did in the feature story—in order to reduce their share price. A reduced share price makes a company's shares more affordable for current and potential shareholders, which should result in even more demand for the company's shares.

This chapter discusses dividends, stock splits, corporation income statements, retained earnings, and key earnings and dividend ratios. The chapter is organized as follows:

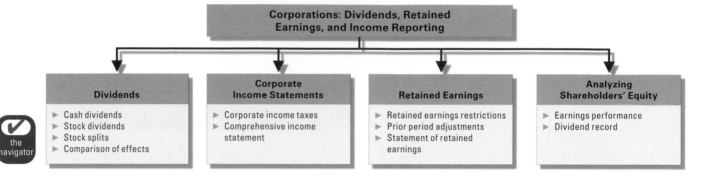

Dividends

study objective 1

Prepare the entries for cash dividends, stock dividends, and stock splits, and compare their financial impact.

A **dividend** is a pro rata distribution of a portion of a corporation's retained earnings to its shareholders. "Pro rata" means that if you own, say, 10 percent of the shares, you will receive 10 percent of the dividend. While there are different types of dividends, the most common are, first, cash dividends, and, second, stock dividends. They are the focus of our discussion on dividends.

Investors are very interested in a company's dividend practices. In a recent year, Canadian companies paid out $62 billion in dividends to shareholders—an all-time record. Bank of Montreal has the longest unbroken dividend record in Canadian history. It began paying dividends in 1829 and has not missed a year since then.

In the financial press, dividends are reported as an annual dollar amount per share, even though it is usual to pay dividends quarterly. For example, SNC-Lavalin in our feature story has an annual dividend rate of $0.28 on its common shares. The dividend is paid quarterly at a rate of $0.07 ($0.28 ÷ 4) per share. Although it is more common to have a dividend rate attached to preferred shares than common shares, SNC-Lavalin does not have any preferred shares.

Cash Dividends

A **cash dividend** is a distribution of cash to shareholders. For a corporation to pay a cash dividend, it must have all three of the following:

1. **Enough retained earnings.** Dividends are distributed from retained earnings, and therefore reduce them, so a company must have enough retained earnings to pay a dividend. Companies rarely pay out dividends equal to their retained earnings, however. They must keep a certain portion of retained earnings to finance their operations. In addition, some level of retained earnings must be kept as a cushion or buffer against possible future losses. Although the laws for cash dividends differ depending on the jurisdiction, in general a deficit cannot be created by the declaration of the dividend. Recall from Chapter 13 that a deficit is a negative, or debit, balance in retained earnings.

2. **Enough cash.** Having enough retained earnings does not necessarily mean that a company can pay a dividend. There is no direct relationship between the balance in the Retained

Earnings account and the balance in the Cash account. So, in addition to having enough retained earnings, a company must also have enough cash before it can pay a dividend.

How much cash is enough? That is hard to say, but a company must keep enough cash on hand to pay for its ongoing operations and to pay its bills as they come due. Under the *Canada Business Corporations Act*, a corporation cannot pay a dividend if it would then become unable to pay its liabilities.

For example, SNC-Lavalin had retained earnings of $446 million and cash of $1 billion at December 31, 2005. It obviously has enough retained earnings and enough cash to pay a dividend. Nonetheless, even if it had wanted to, it would not have been able to declare a $446-million cash dividend to its shareholders because that would have left the company without enough cash to pay its bills. In fact, although SNC-Lavalin had $2.6 billion of current assets (including the $1 billion cash) at year end, it also had current liabilities of $2.2 billion. Before declaring a cash dividend, a company's board of directors must carefully consider current and future demands on the company's cash resources. In some cases, current (or planned future) liabilities may make a cash dividend inappropriate.

3. **A declaration of dividends.** A company cannot pay dividends unless its board of directors decides to do so, at which point the board "declares" the dividend to be payable. The board of directors has full authority to determine the amount of retained earnings to be distributed as a dividend and the amount to keep in the business. Dividends do not accrue like interest on a note payable. Even if the preferred shares are cumulative, dividends in arrears are not a liability until they are declared.

In order to remain in business, companies must honour their interest payments to creditors, bankers, and debt holders. But the payment of dividends to shareholders is another matter. Many companies can survive, and even thrive, without such payouts. For example, high-growth companies generally do not pay dividends. Their policy is to retain all of their earnings to make it easier to grow.

Investors must keep an eye on a company's dividend policy and understand what it may mean. For example, regular increases in dividends when the company has irregular earnings can be a warning signal. Companies with high dividends and rising debt may be facing problems by borrowing money to pay shareholders. On the other hand, a small dividend or a missed dividend may lead to unhappiness among shareholders. Many shareholders purchase shares because they expect to receive a reasonable dividend payment from the company on a regular basis.

Nonetheless, low dividends are not always a bad sign. This could mean that higher returns will be earned by a rising share price rather than by receiving dividends. Presumably, investors who feel that regular dividends are important will buy shares in companies that pay periodic dividends, and those who feel that the share price is more important will buy shares in companies that retain earnings.

ACCOUNTING IN ACTION ▶ Business Insight

Share prices often follow dividend trends. Take Quebecor World Inc., for example, a commercial printer. In January 2006, it cut its dividend by almost one-third after reporting disappointing quarterly financial results. The Montreal-based company's share price immediately fell by 45 cents, or 3 percent. The company said that the dividend had to be reduced to conserve cash and that this would result in cash savings of $21 million. Quebecor World is not alone. Commercial printing has struggled with difficult market conditions and the rise of the Internet for years.

Source: Bertrand Marotte, "Quebecor World Cuts Dividend," *The Globe and Mail*, January 20, 2006, B1.

? | **What is the likely reason that Quebecor's share price fell when it cut its dividend?**

Entries for Cash Dividends

Three dates are important for dividends: (1) the declaration date, (2) the record date, and (3) the payment date. Normally, there are several weeks between each date and the next one. For example, at its February 24, 2006 (declaration date) meeting, the board of directors of SNC-Lavalin voted a quarterly dividend of $0.07 per share payable to its common shareholders. These dividends were then paid on March 24, 2006 (the payment date) to shareholders of record at the close of business on March 17, 2006 (the record date). Accounting entries were required on two of the dates—the declaration date and the payment date.

On the **declaration date**, a company's board of directors formally declares (authorizes) the cash dividend and announces it to shareholders. Declaring a cash dividend commits the corporation to a legal obligation. The obligation is binding and cannot be rescinded (reversed). An entry is required to recognize the increase in Cash Dividends (which results in a decrease in Retained Earnings) and the increase in the current liability Dividends Payable. Cash dividends can be paid to preferred or common shareholders. However, it is more usual to have regular dividends attached to preferred shares. If dividends are paid to the common shareholders, remember that preferred shareholders have to be paid first.

To illustrate a cash dividend paid to preferred shareholders, assume that on December 1 the directors of Media General declare a $0.50-per-share quarterly cash dividend on the company's 100,000 $2-noncumulative preferred shares. The dividend totals $50,000 ($2 ÷ 4 = $0.50 × 100,000) and is payable on January 23 to shareholders of record on December 30. The entry to record the declaration is as follows:

Cash flows: no effect

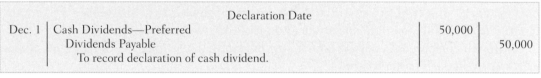

	Declaration Date		
Dec. 1	Cash Dividends—Preferred	50,000	
	Dividends Payable		50,000
	To record declaration of cash dividend.		

Note that the balance in Dividends Payable is a current liability. It will normally be paid within the next month or so. In the case of Media General, it will be paid on January 23.

On the **record date**, ownership of the shares is determined so that the corporation knows who to pay the dividend to. The records maintained by the corporation give this information. In the time between the declaration date and the record date, the corporation updates its share ownership records. Remember that shares trade among investors on organized stock markets after an initial public offering, and not between the company and its investors. For Media General, the record date is December 30. No entry is required on this date because the corporation's liability was recognized on the declaration date and is unchanged.

On the **payment date**, dividend cheques are mailed to shareholders and the payment of the dividend is recorded. The entry on January 23, the payment date, is as follows:

Helpful hint Between the declaration date and the record date, the number of shares remains the same. The purpose of the record date is to identify the persons or entities that will receive the dividend, not to determine the total amount of the dividend liability.

↓ Cash flows: –50,000

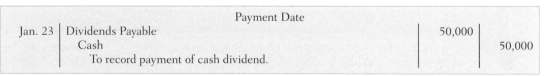

	Payment Date		
Jan. 23	Dividends Payable	50,000	
	Cash		50,000
	To record payment of cash dividend.		

Note that the declaration of a cash dividend increases liabilities and reduces shareholders' equity. The payment of the dividend reduces both assets and liabilities, but has no effect on shareholders' equity. **The cumulative effect of the declaration and payment of a cash dividend is to decrease both shareholders' equity (through the Retained Earnings account) and total assets (through the Cash account).**

Illustration 14-1 summarizes the three important dates for dividends.

Illustration 14-1 ◄

Key dividend dates

Declaration date — Board authorizes dividends

| DECEMBER | | | | | | |
S	M	Tu	W	Th	F	S
	1	2	3	4	5	6
7	8	9	10	11	12	13
14	15	16	17	18	19	20
21	22	23	24	25	26	27
28	29	30	31			

| JANUARY | | | | | | |
S	M	Tu	W	Th	F	S
				1	2	3
4	5	6	7	8	9	10
11	12	13	14	15	16	17
18	19	20	21	22	23	24
25	26	27	28	29	30	31

Record date
Registered shareholders are eligible for dividend

Payment date
Dividend cheques are issued

Stock Dividends

A **stock dividend** is a distribution of the corporation's own shares to shareholders. Whereas a cash dividend is paid in cash, a stock dividend is distributed (paid) in shares. And while a cash dividend decreases assets and shareholders' equity, a stock dividend does not change either assets or shareholders' equity. A stock dividend results in a decrease in retained earnings and an increase in share capital, but there is no change in *total* shareholders' equity.

Note that since a stock dividend neither increases nor decreases the assets in the company, investors are not receiving anything they did not already own. In a sense, it is like ordering a piece of pie and cutting it into smaller pieces. You are no better or worse off, as you have your same amount of pie.

To illustrate a stock dividend for common shareholders, assume that you have a 2-percent ownership interest in IBR Inc. You own 1,000 of its 50,000 common shares. If IBR declares a 10-percent stock dividend, it will issue 5,000 additional shares (50,000 × 10%). You will receive 100 shares (2% × 5,000 or 10% × 1,000). Will your ownership interest change? No, it will remain at 2 percent (1,100 ÷ 55,000). You now own more shares, but your ownership interest has not changed. Illustration 14-2 shows the effect of a stock dividend for shareholders.

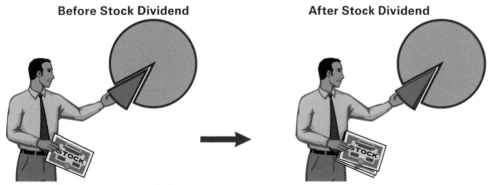

Before Stock Dividend   **After Stock Dividend**

1,000 of 50,000 shares = 2% ownership   1,100 of 55,000 shares = 2% ownership

Illustration 14-2 ◄

Effect of stock dividend for shareholders

From the company's point of view, no cash has been paid, and no liabilities have been assumed. What are the purposes and benefits of a stock dividend? A corporation generally issues stock dividends for one or more of the following reasons:

1. To satisfy shareholders' dividend expectations without spending cash.
2. To increase the marketability of the corporation's shares. When the number of shares increases, the market price per share decreases. Decreasing the market price makes it easier for investors to purchase the shares.
3. To emphasize that a portion of shareholders' equity has been permanently retained in the business and is unavailable for cash dividends.

The size of the stock dividend and the value to be assigned to each share are determined by the board of directors when the dividend is declared. The *Canada Business Corporations Act* recommends that directors of federally incorporated companies assign the market value per share for stock dividends at the declaration date, which is what most companies do.

Entries for Stock Dividends

To illustrate the accounting for stock dividends, assume that IBR Inc. has a balance of $300,000 in Retained Earnings. On June 30, it declares a 10-percent stock dividend on its 50,000 common shares, to be distributed on August 5 to shareholders of record on July 20. The market value of its shares on June 30 is $15 per share. On July 20, the market value is $16 per share and on August 5, it is $14 per share. Note that it is the market value at the declaration date that is relevant for this transaction, and not the market value on the record date or payment date. The number of shares to be issued is 5,000 (10% × 50,000). The total amount to be debited to Stock Dividends is $75,000 (5,000 × $15). The entry to record the declaration of the stock dividend is as follows:

<table>
<tr><td>A = L + SE
+75,000
−75,000

Cash flows: no effect</td><td>June 30</td><td>Stock Dividends—Common
    Common Stock Dividends Distributable
      To record declaration of 10% stock dividend.</td><td>75,000</td><td>
75,000</td></tr>
</table>

Helpful hint Note that the dividend account title uses the word "Distributable," not "Payable."

At the declaration date, the Stock Dividends account is increased by the market value of the shares issued, and Common Stock Dividends Distributable is increased by the same amount. Common Stock Dividends Distributable is a shareholders' equity account. It is not a liability, because assets will not be used to pay the dividend. Instead, it will be "paid" with common shares. If a balance sheet is prepared before the dividend shares are issued, the dividends distributable account is reported as share capital in the shareholders' equity section of the balance sheet.

As with cash dividends, no entry is required at the record date. When the dividend shares are issued on August 5, the account Common Stock Dividends Distributable is debited and the account Common Shares is credited:

<table>
<tr><td>A = L + SE
+75,000
−75,000

Cash flows: no effect</td><td>Aug. 5</td><td>Common Stock Dividends Distributable
    Common Shares
      To record issue of 5,000 common shares in a stock dividend.</td><td>75,000</td><td>
75,000</td></tr>
</table>

Note that neither of the above entries changes shareholders' equity in total. However, the composition of shareholders' equity changes because a portion of Retained Earnings is transferred to the Common Shares account. The number of shares issued has also increased. These effects are shown below for IBR Inc.:

	Before Stock Dividend	After Stock Dividend
Shareholders' equity		
Common shares	$500,000	$575,000
Retained earnings	300,000	225,000
Total shareholders' equity	$800,000	$800,000
Number of common shares	50,000	55,000

In this example, the account Common Shares is increased by $75,000 and Retained Earnings is decreased by the same amount. Total shareholders' equity remains unchanged at $800,000, the total before and after the stock dividend.

Stock Splits

Although stock splits are not dividends, we discuss them in this section because of their similarities to stock dividends. A **stock split**, like a stock dividend, involves the issue of additional shares to shareholders according to their percentage ownership. However, a stock split is usually much larger than a stock dividend. The purpose of a stock split is to increase the marketability of the shares by lowering the market value per share. A lower market value interests more investors and makes it easier for the corporation to issue additional shares.

The effect of a split on market value is generally inversely proportional to the size of the split. For example, in a two-for-one stock split, since there are twice as many shares, the market value normally will decrease by half. Sometimes, due to increased investor interest, the share price will quickly rise beyond its split value. In May 2005, Encana split its common shares two for one. Its share price fell from $82 to $41 after the stock split. Its share price had climbed to $67 just four months later.

In a stock split, the number of shares is increased by a specified proportion. For example, in a two-for-one split, one share is exchanged for two shares. A stock split does not have any effect on share capital, retained earnings, or shareholders' equity. Only the number of shares increases.

Helpful hint Some companies with penny shares do a reverse stock split, i.e., one-for-two, to increase the market value per share.

A stock split is illustrated below for IBR Inc.'s common shares. For the illustration, we assume that, instead of a 10-percent stock dividend, IBR splits its 50,000 common shares on a two-for-one basis.

	Before Stock Split	After Stock Split
Shareholders' equity		
Common shares	$500,000	$500,000
Retained earnings	300,000	300,000
Total shareholders' equity	$800,000	$800,000
Number of common shares	50,000	100,000

Because a stock split does not affect the balances in any shareholders' equity accounts, it is not necessary to journalize it. Only a memo entry explaining the details of the split is needed.

Either common or preferred shares can be split. If preferred shares that have a stated dividend rate are split, then the dividend must also be adjusted for the effects of the split. For example, if 10,000 $6 preferred shares are split three for one, then after the split there will be 30,000 shares with a $2 annual dividend. The total dividend before and after the split remains unchanged at $60,000 (10,000 × $6 before and 30,000 × $2 after). After all, it is the same shareholders that held 10,000 shares before the split that now hold 30,000 shares.

ACCOUNTING IN ACTION ▶ Business Insight

Google Inc., which operates the world's most powerful on-line search engine, has no interest in splitting its stock. The stock split is a widely used market manoeuvre that is intended to make shares more affordable. In fact, stock splits have become so commonplace that investors almost automatically expect them whenever a company's share price approaches $100. However, despite Google's shares crossing the U.S. $400 threshold recently, its management continues to defy stock market convention and show no interest in a stock split. Yahoo Inc., Google's biggest rival, has split its stock four times. If not for the splits, Yahoo's shares would be trading at U.S. $770 rather than their current price of U.S. $32.

? How would Google benefit if it split its stock?

Comparison of Effects

Significant differences between stock splits, stock dividends, and cash dividends (after payment) are shown below. In the illustration, "+" means increase, "−" means decrease, and "NE" means "no effect."

			Shareholders' Equity	
	Assets	Liabilities	Share Capital	Retained Earnings
Cash dividend	−	NE	NE	−
Stock dividend	NE	NE	+	−
Stock split	NE	NE	NE	NE

Cash dividends reduce assets (the Cash account) and shareholders' equity (the Cash Dividends account, which reduces retained earnings). Stock dividends increase share capital (the Common Shares or Preferred Shares account) and decrease retained earnings (the Stock Dividends account, which reduces retained earnings). Stock splits do not affect any of the accounts. However, both a stock dividend and stock split increase the number of shares issued.

BEFORE YOU GO ON . . .

▶**Review It**

1. What entries are made for cash dividends on (a) the declaration date, (b) the record date, and (c) the payment date?
2. What entries are made for stock dividends on (a) the declaration date, (b) the record date, and (c) the payment date?
3. What is the difference between a stock dividend and a stock split?
4. Contrast the effects of a cash dividend, stock dividend, and stock split on (a) assets, (b) liabilities, (c) shareholders' equity, and (d) the number of shares.
5. Did The Forzani Group declare any dividends or stock splits in fiscal 2006? The answer to this question is at the end of the chapter.

▶**Do It**

Sing CD Corporation has had five years of record earnings. Due to this success, the market price of its 500,000 common shares tripled from $15 to $45 per share. During this period, the Common Shares account remained the same at $2 million. Retained Earnings increased from $1.5 million to $10 million. President Bill Zerter is considering either (1) a 10-percent stock dividend, or (2) a two-for-one stock split. He asks you to show the before-and-after effects of each option on the accounts Common Shares and Retained Earnings and on the number of shares.

Action Plan

- Calculate the stock dividend effect on Retained Earnings by multiplying the stock dividend percentage by the number of existing shares to determine the number of new shares to be issued. Multiply the number of new shares by the market price of the shares.
- A stock dividend increases the number of shares and affects both Common Shares and Retained Earnings.
- A stock split increases the number of shares but does not affect Common Shares and Retained Earnings.

Solution

1. With a 10-percent stock dividend, the stock dividend amount is $2,250,000 [(500,000 × 10%) × $45]. The new balance in Common Shares is $4,250,000 ($2,000,000 + $2,250,000). In Retained Earnings it is $7,750,000 ($10,000,000 − $2,250,000).
2. With a stock split, the account balances in Common Shares and Retained Earnings after the stock split are the same as they were before: $2 million and $10 million, respectively.

   The effects in the shareholders' equity accounts of each option are as follows:

	Original Balances	After Stock Dividend	After Stock Split
Common shares	$ 2,000,000	$ 4,250,000	$ 2,000,000
Retained earnings	10,000,000	7,750,000	10,000,000
Total shareholders' equity	$12,000,000	$12,000,000	$12,000,000
Number of shares	500,000	550,000	1,000,000

the navigator

Related exercise material: BE14–1, BE14–2, BE14–3, BE14–4, BE14–5, E14–1, E14–2, and E14–3.

Corporate Income Statements

Income statements for corporations are the same as the statements for proprietorships or partnerships except for one thing: the reporting of income tax.

study objective 2

Prepare a corporate income statement.

Corporate Income Taxes

For income tax purposes, a corporation is a separate legal entity. As a result, income tax expense is reported in a separate section of the corporate income statement, just before net income. The condensed, multiple-step income statement for Leads Inc. in Illustration 14-3 shows a typical presentation.

Illustration 14-3 ◄

Corporate income statement

LEADS INC. Income Statement Year Ended December 31, 2008	
Sales	$800,000
Cost of goods sold	600,000
Gross profit	200,000
Operating expenses	50,000
Income from operations	150,000
Other revenues	10,000
Other expenses	4,000
Income before income tax	156,000
Income tax expense	46,800
Net income	$109,200

Income taxes not only affect the affect the income statement (through the Income Tax Expense account) but also the balance sheet (through the Income Tax Payable account). Companies prepare a corporate income tax return (called a T2) annually to determine their taxable income and income tax payable. However, the Canada Revenue Agency requires income tax to be estimated in advance and paid (remitted to taxing authorities) in monthly instalments, rather than waiting until the end of the company's fiscal year.

After a company determines its total income tax payable at year-end, it compares this amount to the total income tax instalments paid during the year. The difference between the income tax paid and income tax payable results in either an additional amount payable or a refund. Companies have six months after their fiscal year end to submit their corporate income tax return, or else they will incur late filing penalties on any balance due.

Once the additional liability (or receivable) has been determined, an adjusting entry is required. Assume Leads had originally estimated that its taxable income would be $140,000. It has a 30-percent income tax rate, so its income tax was anticipated to be $42,000 ($140,000 × 30%). Leads remitted monthly instalments in the amount of $3,500 per month ($42,000 ÷ 12). At year end, Leads actually reports taxable income of $156,000. Its total income tax liability is $46,800 ($156,000 × 30%), and not $42,000 as estimated. Assuming it has already recorded and remitted $42,000 of income tax, the required adjusting entry is for $4,800 ($46,800 − $42,000) and is recorded as follows:

A	=	L	+	SE
		+4,800		−4,800

Cash flows: no effect

Dec. 31	Income Tax Expense	4,800	
	Income Tax Payable		4,800
	To adjust estimated income tax expense to actual.		

Leads' income statement reports income before income tax of $156,000 and income tax expense of $46,800. The balance sheet reports a current liability of $4,800.

Income Tax Allocation

Income taxes are, in reality, more complicated than the preceding discussion implies. As discussed in earlier chapters, the objectives for revenues and expenses for accounting purposes are not the same as the objectives for income tax purposes. Because of this, there are often timing differences. Transactions can be recorded in one period for accounting purposes (in order to determine income tax expense) and in another period for income tax purposes (to determine income tax payable). These timing differences result in future income taxes which can be classified on the balance sheet as an asset (current or noncurrent) and/or a liability (current or noncurrent).

Alternative terminology
Future income taxes are also known as *deferred income taxes*.

Future income taxes are discussed at length in intermediate accounting courses. For now, it should be said that the income tax expense amount presented in many financial statements is usually divided between the amount that is due or receivable now and the amount that is due or receivable in the future. The act of dividing the amounts is called **interperiod tax allocation**. An illustration of interperiod income tax allocation is presented in the income statement of The Forzani Group in Appendix A.

Helpful hint *Intra* means within the current year's income statement; *inter* means between two or more income statements.

Intraperiod tax allocation is the process of associating income taxes in a specific period with their related item of income. Interperiod tax allocation, on the other hand, is when income taxes are allocated between two or more periods. In intraperiod tax allocation, the income tax expense or saving is associated with certain items or categories, as we will learn in the next section of this chapter for corrections of prior period errors and changes in accounting principles. Intraperiod tax allocation gives statement users useful information about the income tax effects of these adjustments. The general concept is "let the tax follow the income or loss."

Comprehensive Income Statement

Another type of income statement, called the **comprehensive income statement**, is also required in certain circumstances in addition to the other four financial statements we have studied to date: the income statement, statement of retained earnings, balance sheet, and cash flow statement. In addition to presenting net income, the comprehensive income statement also presents "comprehensive income" transactions that are reported in the shareholders' equity section of the balance sheet. By combining "traditional" income with other sources of income, the comprehensive income statement makes it easier to evaluate the profitability of a company on an "all-inclusive" basis.

As we learned in Chapter 13, comprehensive income includes all increases and decreases to shareholders' equity during a period except those changes resulting from the sale or repurchase of shares and from the payment of dividends. Examples of comprehensive income include unrealized gains and losses on the translation of foreign currency (a topic studied in advanced accounting) and unrealized gains and losses on certain types of investments (especially available-for sale securities, which we will study in Chapter 16).

There are several acceptable formats for reporting comprehensive income, including presenting it in a separate statement of comprehensive income, a combined statement of income and comprehensive income, or a statement of shareholders' equity. Illustration 14-4 presents a sample statement of comprehensive income for Leads Inc., using assumed data. Other formats are presented in advanced accounting courses.

Illustration 14-4 ◀

Statement of comprehensive income

LEADS INC. Statement of Comprehensive Income Year Ended December 31, 2008		
Net income		$109,200
Other comprehensive income		
Unrealized gains and losses on available-for-sale securities	$1,689	
Unrealized foreign currency translation adjustment	(545)	1,144
Comprehensive income		$110,344

Recall that comprehensive income is also reported on the balance sheet as a separate component of shareholders' equity, as illustrated in Chapter 13. In the case of Leads, the changes in comprehensive income for the period, $1,144, would be added to the opening balance of accumulated other comprehensive income to determine the ending balance of accumulated other comprehensive income reported on the balance sheet.

BEFORE YOU GO ON . . .

▶Review It

1. What is the unique feature of a corporate income statement?
2. What is the difference between interperiod and intraperiod tax allocation?
3. What is comprehensive income?
4. What is the difference between comprehensive income reported on the income statement and accumulated other comprehensive income reported on the balance sheet.

Related exercise material: BE14–6, BE14–7, and E14–4.

Retained Earnings

As you learned in Chapter 13, retained earnings are the cumulative total since incorporation of net income (less losses) less any declared dividends. In other words, they are the income that has been retained or kept in the business. Illustration 14-5 shows a simple statement of retained earnings for Leads Inc. In it, we have assumed that Leads had an opening Retained Earnings balance of $500,000 and declared $25,000 of cash dividends during the year.

Illustration 14-5 ▶

Statement of retained earnings

LEADS INC. Statement of Retained Earnings Year Ended December 31, 2008	
Retained earnings, January 1	$500,000
Add: Net income	109,200
	609,200
Less: Cash dividends	25,000
Retained earnings, December 31	$584,200

Each year, net income is added (or a net loss is deducted) and dividends are deducted from the opening Retained Earnings balance to determine the ending Retained Earnings amount. As in a proprietorship, revenue and expense accounts (which make up net income) and dividends accounts are temporary accounts and are closed to Retained Earnings at the end of each period to bring the Retained Earnings account up to date. The ending Retained Earnings balance at December 31 will become the opening Retained Earnings amount, dated January 1, for the 2009 fiscal year.

The balance in Retained Earnings is part of the shareholders' claim on the total assets of the corporation. However, it does not represent a claim on any specific asset. Nor can the amount of retained earnings be associated with the balance of any individual asset account. For example, a $100,000 balance in Retained Earnings does not mean that there should be $100,000 in Cash. There are many reasons for this. Not all income items generate or use cash, and any cash that was generated from income may have been used to purchase buildings, equipment, and other assets, or to pay liabilities. In addition, not all dividends are cash dividends.

To illustrate the fact that the Retained Earnings and Cash balances may be quite different, the table below shows recent amounts of retained earnings and cash for selected companies.

Company	(in millions) Retained Earnings	Cash
Canadian Tire	$1,813	$838
Reitmans	370	135
Saputo	971	92
WestJet Airlines	201	260

Retained Earnings Restrictions

The balance in Retained Earnings is generally available for dividend declarations. Of course, as mentioned earlier in the chapter, it would not be prudent for a company to declare a dividend equal to its retained earnings. A company must retain enough net assets to keep its operations going. In some cases, there may be specific **retained earnings restrictions**. These make a portion of the Retained Earnings balance unavailable for dividends. Here are two common restrictions:

1. **Contractual restrictions.** Long-term debt contracts may restrict retained earnings as a condition for the loan. These restrictions are known as **debt covenants**, which, among other things, can limit the use of corporate assets for the payment of dividends. This makes it more likely that the corporation will be able to meet required loan payments.
2. **Voluntary restrictions.** The board of directors may voluntarily create retained earnings restrictions for specific purposes. For example, the board may authorize a restriction for future plant expansion. By reducing the amount of retained earnings available for dividends, the company makes more cash available for the planned expansion.

No journal entry is necessary to record a retained earnings restriction, but these restrictions are disclosed in the notes to the financial statements. Only about 4 percent of Canadian companies reported retained earnings restrictions in a recent year.

Prior Period Adjustments

Suppose that a corporation's books have been closed and the financial statements have been issued. The corporation then discovers that a material error has been made in reporting net income of a prior year. Or suppose that the corporation changes an accounting policy that affects the comparison of prior year figures. How should these situations be recorded in the accounts and reported in the financial statements of the previous periods?

When there is a correction of an error or a change in accounting principle, the accounting treatment is similar:

1. The corrected amount or new principle should be used in reporting the results of operations of the current year.
2. The cumulative effect of the correction or change should be disclosed as an adjustment to opening retained earnings net of (after subtracting) applicable income tax. Since prior period earnings are affected, this effect must be reported on the statement of retained earnings, rather than on the current period's income statement.
3. All financial statements for prior periods should be corrected or restated to make it easier to compare them.
4. The effects of the change should be detailed and disclosed in a note to the statements.

An adjustment of financial results for prior periods is only appropriate in these two circumstances: (1) when correcting an error related to a prior period, and (2) when changing an accounting principle. Let's now look in more detail at the accounting for each of these.

Correction of Prior Period Errors

The **correction of a prior period error** in previously issued financial statements is made directly to Retained Earnings since the effect of the error is now in this account. The revenues and expenses (net income) for the previous period have been recorded in Retained Earnings through the journalizing and posting of closing entries.

To illustrate the correction of a prior period error, assume that Graber Inc. discovers in 2008 that it overstated its cost of goods sold in 2007 by $10,000 as a result of errors in counting inventory. Because cost of goods sold (an expense account) was overstated, income before income tax was understated by the same amount, $10,000. If we assume an income tax rate of 30 percent, income tax expense would also be understated, but by $3,000 ($10,000 × 30%). The overall effect on net income is to understate it by $7,000 ($10,000 − $3,000). In other words, net income is understated by the difference after tax [$10,000 × (100% − 30%)]. If net income is understated, then retained earnings would also be understated by the same amount, $7,000.

Helpful hint Normally, errors made in the year are discovered and corrected before the financial statements for the year are issued. Thus, corrections of prior period errors rarely happen.

The following table details the effect of this error on the income statement, using assumed data for revenues and expenses:

	Incorrect	Correct	Difference
Revenues	$900,000	$900,000	$ 0
Expenses	550,000	540,000	10,000
Income before income tax	350,000	360,000	10,000
Income tax expense (30%)	105,000	108,000	3,000
Net income	$245,000	$252,000	$ 7,000

In addition to overstating cost of goods sold by $10,000, the error will also result in merchandise inventory being understated by the same amount. You will recall that we learned about the pervasive impact of inventory errors in Chapter 6.

The entry for the correction of this error, discovered on February 12, is as follows:

A	=	L	+	SE
+10,000		+3,000		+7,000

Cash flows: no effect

Feb. 12	Merchandise Inventory	10,000	
	Income Tax Payable		3,000
	Retained Earnings		7,000
	To adjust for overstatement of cost of goods sold in a prior period.		

A credit to an income statement account, in this case Cost of Goods Sold, instead of Retained Earnings, would be incorrect because the error is for a prior year. Recall that income statement accounts are temporary accounts that are closed at the end of each year to the Retained Earnings account.

Change in Accounting Principle

Ethics note

Changes in accounting principles should only be made to make financial statements more informative for statement users. They should not be used to artificially improve the company's reported performance and financial position.

To make comparisons easier, financial statements for the current period should be prepared using the same accounting principles that were used for the preceding period. This improves comparability, an important characteristic of accounting information that we learned about in Chapter 11. This does not mean, however, that accounting principles can never change. A **change in accounting principle** (also known as a change in accounting policy) occurs when the principle used in the current year is different from the one used in the previous year. These changes may be voluntary or prescribed.

A voluntary change in accounting principle is allowed when the new generally accepted accounting principle results in a more reliable and relevant presentation of a company's events or transactions in its financial statements. Examples of a voluntary change in accounting principle include a change in amortization method (e.g., declining-balance to straight-line) and a change in inventory cost flow assumption (e.g., FIFO to average cost).

Often the CICA prescribes a change in accounting principle. Ideally the application of a new accounting principle can be applied retroactively, but there are times when it may be impractical to do so. One of the more recent changes required by the CICA was the introduction of comprehensive income. This change was applied retroactively and financial statements restated for comparative purposes.

To illustrate the accounting for a voluntary change in accounting principle, assume that at the beginning of 2008, Graber changes from the straight-line method of amortization for equipment to the declining-balance method. The equipment was purchased on January 2, 2004. The cumulative effect of this change is to increase amortization expense and accumulated amortization by $24,000 for the years 2004 to 2007.

Retained earnings are affected by the change in amortization expense as is income tax expense. Both affect net income of the prior periods. If amortization expense has increased, then income before income tax would decrease by the same amount, $24,000. Since the company has a 30-percent tax rate, income tax expense would also decrease by $7,200 ($24,000 × 30%). The after-tax effect of the change on net income, and retained earnings, is $16,800 ($24,000 − $7,200), This can also be calculated by multiplying $24,000 by the after-tax rate of 70% (100% − 30%).

The entry to record this change in accounting principle on January 2 is as follows:

Jan. 2	Income Tax Payable (or Recoverable)	7,200	
	Retained Earnings	16,800	
	Accumulated Amortization		24,000
	To record retroactive effect of change in amortization method.		

A	=	L	+	SE
−24,000		−7,200		−16,800

Cash flows: no effect

Presentation of Prior Period Adjustments

Prior period adjustments—whether they are for corrections of prior period errors or changes in accounting principles—are reported in the statement of retained earnings, less the associated income tax. The adjustment is added to (or deducted from, depending on the direction of the adjustment) the beginning Retained Earnings balance. This results in an adjusted beginning balance.

Assuming Graber had reported $800,000 of retained earnings at December 31, 2007, the two adjustments we journalized above—the correction for the overstatement of cost of goods sold and the change in amortization method—would be reported as in Illustration 14-6.

GRABER INC.
Statement of Retained Earnings (partial)
Year Ended December 31, 2008

Balance, January 1, as previously reported	$800,000
Add: Correction for overstatement of cost of goods sold in 2007, net of $3,000 income tax expense	7,000
Less: Cumulative effect of change in amortization method, net of $7,200 income tax savings	(16,800)
Balance, January 1, as adjusted	790,200

Illustration 14-6 ◀

Statement presentation of prior period adjustments

Any financial statements from prior years which are presented for comparison would be restated using the correct cost of goods sold expense and inventory amounts, and using the declining-balance method to amortize equipment. Graber's income statement would also show amortization expense for the current year on a declining-balance basis (i.e., using the new method of amortization). Accumulated amortization on the balance sheet would be calculated as though declining-balance had always been used. There would also be a note that is cross-referenced to the statements: it would give details about the impact of both the correction of the error and the change in principle and it would say that statements from previous years have been restated.

Statement of Retained Earnings

The **statement of retained earnings** shows the changes in retained earnings during the year. The statement is prepared from the Retained Earnings account. Transactions and events that affect retained earnings are summarized in Illustration 14-7.

Illustration 14-7 ▶

Debits and credits to retained earnings

Retained Earnings	
Debits (Decreases)	Credits (Increases)
1. Correction of a prior period error that overstated income	1. Correction of a prior period error that understated income
2. Cumulative effect of a change in accounting principle that decreased income	2. Cumulative effect of a change in accounting principle that increased income
3. Net loss	3. Net income
4. Cash dividends	
5. Stock dividends	
6. Reacquisition of shares	

As indicated, net income increases retained earnings and a net loss decreases retained earnings. Prior period adjustments—a correction of an error or a change in accounting principle—may either increase or decrease retained earnings. Both cash and stock dividends decrease retained earnings. Stock splits do not affect retained earnings, so they do not appear in this list of transactions.

You will recall from Chapter 13 that gains and losses from the reacquisition of shares are reported as shareholders' equity transactions, not income statement transactions. Gains, which occur when shares are reacquired at a price lower than the average issue price, create contributed capital. Losses, which occur when shares are reacquired at a price higher than the average issue price, first reduce contributed capital until the balance is exhausted. Then, any remaining loss is debited to Retained Earnings. There are also other transactions that can sometimes affect retained earnings—these are left to another accounting course.

Illustration 14-8 shows the statement of retained earnings for Graber, using assumed data for net income and dividends, and incorporating the prior period adjustments just discussed.

Illustration 14-8 ▶

Statement of retained earnings

GRABER INC.
Statement of Retained Earnings (partial)
Year Ended December 31, 2008

Balance, January 1, as previously reported		$ 800,000
Add: Correction for overstatement of cost of goods sold in 2007, net of $3,000 income tax expense		7,000
Less: Cumulative effect of change in amortization method, net of $7,200 income tax savings		(16,800)
Balance, January 1, as adjusted		790,200
Add: Net income		549,800
		1,340,000
Less: Cash dividends	$100,000	
Stock dividends	200,000	
Reacquisition of common shares	15,000	315,000
Balance, December 31		$1,025,000

Some companies combine the statement of retained earnings with their income statement instead of presenting them separately. For example, The Forzani Group does this in its Consolidated Statements of Operations and Retained Earnings, as shown in Appendix A. However, most companies present a separate statement of retained earnings.

BEFORE YOU GO ON . . .

▶Review It

1. How are retained earnings restrictions reported?
2. What is the difference between a correction of a prior period error and a change in accounting principle?
3. What are the principal sources of debits and credits to the Retained Earnings account?

▶Review It

Vega Corporation reported retained earnings of $5,130,000 at December 31, 2007. In 2008, the company earns $2,000,000 of net income. It declares and pays a $250,000 cash dividend. Vega also records a pre-tax adjustment of $275,000 for an overstatement resulting from a mathematical error that affected 2007 ending inventory. The company also incurs a $25,500 charge to retained earnings for the reacquisition of common shares. Its income tax rate is 30 percent. Prepare a statement of retained earnings for the year ended December 31.

Action Plan

- A statement of retained earnings begins with retained earnings as reported at the end of the previous year.
- Add or subtract any prior period adjustments, net of applicable income tax, to arrive at the adjusted opening Retained Earnings balance.
- Add net income and subtract dividends declared and any other debits (e.g., from a reacquisition of shares) to arrive at the ending balance in Retained Earnings.

Solution

VEGA CORPORATION
Statement of Retained Earnings
Year Ended December 31, 2008

Balance, January 1, as previously reported		$5,130,000
Less: Correction for overstatement of ending inventory, net of $82,500[1] applicable income tax		(192,500)
Balance, January 1, as adjusted		4,937,500
Add: Net income		2,000,000
		6,937,500
Less: Cash dividend	$250,000	
Reacquisition of common shares	25,500	275,500
Balance, December 31		$6,662,000

[1] $275,000 × 30% = $82,500

Related exercise material: BE14–8, BE14–9, BE14–10, E14–5, E14–6, E14–7, E14–8, and E14–9.

the navigator

Analyzing Shareholders' Equity

Shares are generally purchased by investors for potential capital gains (increases in the shares' market price) or for potential income (dividends). Consequently, investors are interested in both a company's earnings performance and its dividend record.

study objective 4
Evaluate earnings and dividend performance.

Earnings Performance

When shareholders want to analyze their investment in a company, they can measure the company's earnings performance, or profitability, in several different ways. We learned about one measure in Chapter 13—the return on equity ratio. Two other ratios are widely used by existing shareholders and potential investors: earnings per share and the price-earnings ratio.

Earnings per share is useful because shareholders usually think in terms of the number of shares they own—or plan to buy or sell—so determining net income per share makes it easier for the shareholder to understand the return on his or her investment.

Investors and others also link earnings per share to the market price per share. This relationship produces the second ratio—the price-earnings ratio.

Earnings Per Share

Earnings per share (EPS) indicates the net income earned by each common share. Thus, earnings per share is reported only for common shares. When a company has both preferred and common shares, the current year's dividend declared on preferred shares is subtracted from net income to determine the income available to common shareholders. Illustration 14-9 shows the formula for calculating EPS.

Illustration 14-9 ▶

Earnings per share formula

Net Income Minus Preferred Dividends	÷	Weighted Average Number of Common Shares	=	Earnings per Share
($13,757 – $0)	÷	32,755	=	$0.42

To show the calculation of earnings per share, the illustration uses data (in thousands) from Forzani's 2006 financial statements reproduced in Appendix A. Forzani's net income of $13,757,000 is divided by the weighted average number of common shares, 32,755,000, to determine its earnings per share of $0.42.

In determining the numerator of the earnings per share calculation ($13,757,000), note that Forzani had no preferred dividends to subtract from net income. If it did, any preferred dividends declared for the current year would be subtracted from net income to determine the income available for the common shareholders. In addition, note that if preferred shares are cumulative, the dividend is deducted whether or not it is declared.

For the denominator of the earnings per share calculation (32,755), the **weighted average number of shares** is used instead of the ending balance, or a straight average. If there is no change in the number of common shares issued during the year, the weighted average number of shares will be the same as the ending balance. If new shares are issued in the year, these shares are adjusted for the fraction of the year they are outstanding to determine the weighted average number of shares. This is done because the issue of shares during the period changes the amount of net assets that income can be earned on.

To illustrate the calculation of the weighted average number of common shares, assume that a company had 100,000 common shares on January 1, and issued an additional 10,000 shares on October 1. The weighted average number of shares for the year would be calculated as follows:

Date	Actual Number	Fraction of Year	Weighted Average
Jan. 1	100,000	$\times \frac{12}{12} =$	100,000
Oct. 1	10,000	$\times \frac{3}{12} =$	2,500
	110,000		102,500

As illustrated, 110,000 shares were actually issued by the end of the year. Of these, 100,000 were outstanding for the full year and are allocated a full weight, 12 months out of 12. As 10,000 of the shares have only been outstanding for three months (from October 1 to December 31), they are weighted for $^3/_{12}$ of the year, resulting in 2,500 weighted shares. In total, the company's weighted average number of shares is 102,500 for the year. In the next calendar year, the 110,000 shares would receive a full weight (unless some of these shares are repurchased) because all 110,000 shares would be outstanding for the entire year.

The disclosure of the earnings per share is required for publicly held companies and recommended for private companies. This disclosure is so important that EPS must be reported directly on the income statement, and it also has to be explained in the notes to the financial statements. It is the only ratio that is reported in this way.

Complex Capital Structure. When a corporation has securities that may be converted into common shares, it has what is called a complex capital structure. One example of a convertible security is convertible preferred shares. When the preferred shares are converted into common shares, the additional common shares will result in a reduced, or diluted, earnings per share figure.

Two earnings per share figures are calculated when a corporation has a complex capital structure. The first earnings per share figure is called **basic earnings per share**. The earnings per share amount we calculated in Illustration 14-9, $0.42, is known as basic earnings per share, which is what Forzani reported on its income statement for fiscal 2006.

The second earnings per share figure is called **fully diluted earnings per share**. This figure calculates *hypothetical* earnings per share as though *all* securities that can be converted into, or exchanged for, common shares have been (even though they really have not). Forzani, which has other securities that can be converted into common shares (stock options, in this case) is considered to have a complex capital structure. It reports fully diluted earnings per share of $0.42 for fiscal 2006. Note that fully diluted earnings per share will never be higher than basic earnings per share.

The calculation of fully diluted earnings per share is complex. In addition, the determination of the weighted average number of shares for both basic and fully diluted earnings per share becomes more complicated when there are stock dividends and stock splits during the year. Further discussion of these and other earnings per share complexities is left to an intermediate accounting course.

ACCOUNTING IN ACTION ▶ Business Insight

Earnings performance matters. When Sears missed its estimated earnings per share figure by five cents, its share price fell by 14 cents. Although it is not unusual for a company's share price to be affected by earnings announcements, what was unusual in the case of Sears was that the share prices of other companies also fell as a result of the news. Investors reacted because Sears' financial health is viewed as a good indicator of the strength of the economy as a whole. In other words, investors were expressing their concern that difficult times for retailers were on the horizon.

? Why does a company's earnings per share affect its share price?

Price-Earnings Ratio

Comparing the earnings per share amounts of different companies is not very helpful, because there are big differences in the numbers of shares in companies and in the share prices. In order to compare earnings across companies, we instead calculate the **price-earnings (PE) ratio**.

The price-earnings ratio is a frequently quoted statistic that gives the ratio of the market price of each common share to its earnings per share.

To illustrate, we will calculate the price-earnings ratio for The Forzani Group Ltd. Forzani's earnings per share for the year ended January 29, 2006, was $0.42 as shown in Illustration 14-9. Its market price at year end was $14.30. Illustration 14-10 shows Forzani's price-earnings ratio.

Illustration 14-10 ▶

Price-earnings ratio formula

Market Price per Share	÷	Earnings per Share	=	Price-Earnings Ratio
$14.30	÷	$0.42	=	34 times

This ratio indicates that Forzani's shares are trading at 34 times earnings. The PE ratio reflects investors' assessment of a company's future earnings. The ratio of price to earnings will be higher if investors think that current income levels will continue or increase. It will be lower if investors think that income will decrease.

Dividend Record

One way that companies reward shareholders for their investment is to pay dividends. The **payout ratio** tells you what percentage of income the company is distributing to its shareholders. If the number is very high, it could be a warning signal—it could mean the company is failing to reinvest enough of its income in its operations. A high payout ratio can also mean the company's income is falling or that it is trying to attract investors who find little else to get excited about.

The payout ratio is calculated by dividing cash dividends by net income. This ratio can also be expressed on a per share basis by dividing dividends per share by earnings per share. The payout ratio can be calculated for total dividends, for common dividends, or for preferred dividends. The formula to calculate the payout ratio is shown in Illustration 14-11.

Illustration 14-11 ▶

Payout ratio formula

Cash Dividends	÷	Net Income	=	Payout Ratio

Forzani's payout ratio is zero. As mentioned earlier, it paid no dividends during the year ended January 29, 2006.

Like most ratios, the payout ratio varies with the industry. Income trusts pay out almost all their income because of a provision in the law that exempts them from income tax if they do this. You will recall, as we discussed in Chapters 1 and 13, that this provision is currently in the process of changing at the time of writing this textbook. Utilities also have high payout ratios. By contrast, companies that have high growth rates generally have low payout ratios because they reinvest most of their net income in the company.

BEFORE YOU GO ON . . .

▶Review It

1. Why is net income available to common shareholders not always the same as net income?
2. Explain how to calculate earnings per share.
3. How is the weighted average number of shares calculated?
4. Explain how the price-earnings ratio relates to the earnings per share ratio.
5. What ratio gives information about a company's dividend record?

▶Do It

Shoten Limited reported net income of $249,750 on its October 31, year-end income statement. The shareholders' equity section of its balance sheet reported 3,000 $2-noncumulative preferred shares and

50,000 common shares. Of the common shares, 40,000 had been issued since the beginning of the year, 15,000 were issued on March 1, and 5,000 were repurchased on August 1. The preferred dividend was declared and paid during the year. Calculate Shoten's earnings per share.

Action Plan

- Subtract the preferred dividends from net income to determine the income available for common shareholders.
- Adjust the shares for the fraction of the year they were outstanding to determine the weighted average number of shares.
- Divide the income available for common shareholders by the weighted average number of shares to calculate the earnings per share.

Solution

Weighted average number of common shares:

Date	Actual Number	Fraction of Year	Weighted Average
Nov. 1	40,000	$\times\ ^{12}/_{12} =$	40,000
Mar. 1	15,000	$\times\ ^{8}/_{12} =$	10,000
Aug. 1	(5,000)	$\times\ ^{3}/_{12} =$	(1,250)
	50,000		48,750

Earnings per share: $\dfrac{\$249{,}750 - \$6{,}000\ [3{,}000 \times \$2]}{48{,}750} = \$5$

Related exercise material: BE14–11, BE14–12, BE14–13, BE14–14, E14–10, E14–11, and E14–12.

the navigator

Demonstration Problem

On January 1, 2008, Fuso Corporation had the following shareholders' equity accounts:

Preferred shares, $5-noncumulative, no par value, unlimited number authorized, 10,000 issued	$1,000,000
Common shares, no par value, unlimited number authorized, 260,000 issued	3,120,000
Retained earnings	3,200,000
Accumulated other comprehensive income	30,000

During the year, the following transactions occurred:

Mar. 10 Declared quarterly cash dividend to preferred shareholders of record on March 31, payable April 15.

June 1 Announced a 2-for-1 stock split of the preferred shares. Immediately before the split, the share price was $100 per share. After the split, the dividend was adjusted from $5 to $2.50 per share.

10 Declared quarterly cash dividend to preferred shareholders of record on June 30, payable July 15.

Sept. 10 Declared quarterly cash dividend to preferred shareholders of record on September 30, payable October 15.

Nov. 30 Declared a 5-percent stock dividend to common shareholders of record on December 20, distributable January 8. On November 30, the share price was $15 per share. On December 20, it was $16 per share and on January 8, it was $17 per share.

Dec. 10 Declared quarterly cash dividend to preferred shareholders of record on December 31, payable January 15.

31 Determined that net income for the year was $600,000.

31 A loan agreement entered into on December 31 restricts the payment of future dividends to 75 percent of net income.

Practice Tools:
Demonstration Problems

Instructions

(a) Record the transactions and the closing entries.
(b) Prepare the shareholders' equity section of the balance sheet at December 31.

Action Plan

- Keep a running total of the number of shares issued.
- Remember that dividend rates are expressed as annual amounts.
- Make journal entries for dividends on the declaration and payment dates, but not on the record date.
- Adjust the number of shares for the stock split, but make no journal entry.
- Apply the stock dividend percentage to the number of shares issued. Multiply the new shares to be issued by the market value of the shares.

Solution to Demonstration Problem

(a)

Mar. 10	Cash Dividend—Preferred	12,500	
	Dividend Payable		12,500
	To record quarterly preferred dividend		
	($5 ÷ 4 = $1.25; $1.25 × 10,000).		
Apr. 15	Dividend Payable	12,500	
	Cash		12,500
	To record payment of quarterly preferred dividend.		
June 1	Memo entry only about 2-for-1 stock split. Now 20,000 (10,000 × 2) preferred shares.		
10	Cash Dividend—Preferred	12,500	
	Dividend Payable		12,500
	To record quarterly preferred dividend		
	($2.50 ÷ 4 = $0.625; $0.625 × 20,000).		
July 15	Dividend Payable	12,500	
	Cash		12,500
	To record payment of quarterly preferred dividend.		
Sept.10	Cash Dividend—Preferred	12,500	
	Dividend Payable		12,500
	To record quarterly preferred dividend		
	($2.50 ÷ 4 = $0.625; $0.625 × 20,000).		
Oct. 15	Dividend Payable	12,500	
	Cash		12,500
	To record payment of quarterly preferred dividend.		
Nov. 30	Stock Dividend—Common	195,000	
	Stock Dividend Distributable		195,000
	To record stock dividend to common shareholders		
	(260,000 × 5% = 13,000; 13,000 × $15).		
Dec. 10	Cash Dividend—Preferred	12,500	
	Dividend Payable		12,500
	To record quarterly preferred dividend		
	($2.50 ÷ 4 = $0.625; $0.625 × 20,000).		
31	Income Summary	600,000	
	Retained Earnings		600,000
	To close net income.		
31	Retained Earnings	245,000	
	Cash Dividend—Preferred		50,000
	Stock Dividend—Common		195,000
	To close dividend accounts. Cash dividend account =		
	$50,000 ($12,500 + $12,500 + $12,500 + $12,500).		
31	No entry required		

(b)

FUSO CORPORATION
Balance Sheet (partial)
December 31, 2008

Shareholders' equity	
Share capital	
Preferred shares, $2.50-noncumulative, no par value, unlimited number authorized, 20,000 issued	$1,000,000
Common shares, no par value, unlimited number authorized, 260,000 issued	3,120,000
Common stock dividend distributable, 13,000 shares	195,000
	4,315,000
Retained earnings ($3,200,000 + $600,000 − $245,000) (*Note X*)	3,555,000
Accumulated other comprehensive income	30,000
Total shareholders' equity	$7,900,000

Note X: A loan agreement contains a restrictive covenant that limits the payment of future dividends to 75 percent of net income.

Summary of Study Objectives

1. *Prepare the entries for cash dividends, stock dividends, and stock splits, and compare their financial impact.* Entries for both cash and stock dividends are required at the declaration date and the payment or distribution date. There is no entry for a stock split. Cash dividends reduce assets and shareholders' equity (retained earnings). Stock dividends reduce retained earnings and increase common shares, but have no impact on total shareholders' equity. Both stock dividends and stock splits increase the number of shares issued. Stock splits reduce the market price of the shares, but have no impact on the financial position of the company.

2. *Prepare a corporate income statement.* Corporate income statements are similar to the income statements for proprietorships and partnerships with one exception. Income tax expense must be reported in a separate section before net income in the corporation's income statement. The comprehensive income statement reports all increases and decreases to shareholders' equity during a period except changes resulting from the sale or repurchase of shares and from the payment of dividends.

3. *Prepare a statement of retained earnings.* Additions to retained earnings include net income, corrections of understatements of prior years' net income, and increases due to the cumulative effect of a change in accounting principle. Deductions consist of net loss, corrections of overstatements of prior years' net income, decreases due to the cumulative effect of a change in accounting principle, cash and stock dividends, and losses from the reacquisition of shares.

4. *Evaluate earnings and dividend performance.* Profitability measures that are used to analyze shareholders' equity include return on equity (discussed in Chapter 13), earnings per share, the price-earnings ratio, and the payout ratio.

Earnings (loss) per share is calculated by dividing net income (loss) available to the common shareholders by the weighed average number of common shares. The price-earnings ratio is calculated by dividing the market price per share by the earnings per share. The payout ratio is calculated by dividing cash dividends by net income.

Glossary

Study Aids: Glossary
Practice Tools: Key Term Matching Activity

Basic earnings per share The net income (or loss) earned by each common share. It is calculated by subtracting any preferred dividends declared from net income and dividing the result by the weighted average number of common shares. (p. 729)

Cash dividend A pro rata (equal) distribution of cash to shareholders. (p. 712)

Change in accounting principle The use of a generally accepted accounting principle in the current year that is different from the one used in the preceding year. (p. 724)

Comprehensive income statement A statement that reports all increases and decreases to shareholders' equity during a period except changes resulting from the sale or repurchase of shares and from the payment of dividends. (p. 721)

Correction of a prior period error The correction of an error in previously issued financial statements. (p. 723)

Debt covenant A restriction in a loan agreement which, among other things, may limit the use of corporate assets for the payment of dividends. (p. 723)

Declaration date The date when the board of directors formally declares a dividend and announces it to shareholders. (p. 714)

Dividend A distribution of cash or shares by a corporation to its shareholders on a pro rata basis. (p. 712)

Earnings per share (EPS) The net income (or loss) earned by each common share. (p. 728)

Fully diluted earnings per share Earnings per share adjusted for the maximum possible dilution that would occur if securities were converted, or changed, into common shares. (p. 729)

Interperiod tax allocation The allocation of income tax expense between two or more periods to record the amount that is currently due and the amount that is due in the future (deferred). (p. 720)

Intraperiod tax allocation The procedure of associating income tax expense with the specific item that directly affects the income tax for the period. (p. 720)

Payment date The date when cash dividend cheques are mailed to shareholders. For a stock dividend, the date when the shares are distributed to shareholders. (p. 714)

Payout ratio Measures the percentage of income distributed as cash dividends. It is calculated by dividing cash dividends by net income. (p. 730)

Price-earnings (PE) ratio The ratio of the price of a common share to earnings per common share. (p. 729)

Record date The date when ownership of shares is determined for dividend purposes. (p. 714)

Retained earnings restrictions Circumstances that make a portion of retained earnings currently unavailable for dividends. (p. 722)

Statement of retained earnings A financial statement that shows the changes in retained earnings during the year. (p. 725)

Stock dividend A pro rata distribution of the corporation's own shares to shareholders. (p. 715)

Stock split The issue of additional shares to shareholders in a multiple such as two for one. A two-for-one stock split means that two new shares are issued in exchange for one old share. (p. 717)

Weighted average number of shares The number of common shares outstanding during the year, with any shares purchased or issued during the year weighted by the fraction of the year that they have been outstanding. (p. 728)

Self-Study Questions

Practice Tools: Self-Assessment Quizzes

Answers are at the end of the chapter.

(SO 1) K 1. Entries for cash dividends are required on the:
(a) declaration date and payment date.
(b) record date and payment date.
(c) declaration date, record date, and payment date.
(d) declaration date and record date.

(SO 1) K 2. Which of the following statements about stock dividends is true?
(a) A stock dividend increases total shareholders' equity.
(b) A stock dividend decreases total shareholders' equity.

(c) Market value per share is usually assigned to the dividend shares.
(d) A stock dividend ordinarily will have no effect on total share capital.

3. Which of the following statements about a 3-for-1 stock split is true? (SO 1)
(a) It will triple the market value of the shares.
(b) It will triple the amount of total shareholders' equity.
(c) It will have no effect on total shareholders' equity.
(d) It requires the company to distribute cash.

SO 2) K 4. Corporate income statements are the same as the income statements for unincorporated companies, except for:
(a) gross profit.   (c) operating income.
(b) income tax expense.   (d) net sales.

SO 2) K 5. The statement of comprehensive income can include all of the following except:
(a) Net income
(b) Unrealized gains and losses from available-for-sale securities
(c) Gains and losses from the reacquisition of shares
(d) Unrealized translation gains and losses from foreign currency

SO 3) K 6. Which of the following can cause a restriction in retained earnings?
(a) A covenant in a long-term debt agreement
(b) A change in accounting principle
(c) A correction of a prior period error
(d) All of the above

SO 3) K 7. A prior period adjustment is:
(a) reported in the income statement.
(b) reported directly in the shareholders' equity section.
(c) reported in the statement of retained earnings as an adjustment to the opening balance of retained earnings.
(d) reported in the statement of retained earnings as an adjustment to the ending balance of retained earnings.

8. Wreck Cove Inc. had 100,000 common shares on January 1. It issued an additional 24,000 shares on June 1 and repurchased 10,000 shares on October 1. What is Wreck Cove's weighted average number of shares? (SO 4) AP
(a) 57,000   (c) 114,000
(b) 111,500   (d) 116,500

9. The Breau Corporation reported net income of $24,000; its weighted average number of common shares as 6,000; and a market price per share of $60. It had no preferred shares. What were its earnings per share and price-earnings ratios? (SO 4) AP
(a) $4 and 15 times   (c) $10 and 6 times
(b) $6 and 10 times   (d) $15 and 4 times

10. Bernard Dupuis is nearing retirement and would like to invest in shares that will give him a steady income. Bernard should choose shares with a: (SO 4) C
(a) high earnings per share.
(b) high price-earnings ratio.
(c) high payout ratio.
(d) high return on equity.

Questions

SO 1) K 1. A dividend is a "pro rata" distribution of retained earnings. Explain what "pro rata" means.

SO 1) C 2. Robin O'Malley argues that having enough cash is the only requirement for the declaration of a cash dividend. Is Robin correct? Explain.

SO 1) K 3. Three dates are important in connection with cash dividends. Identify these dates and explain their significance to the corporation and its shareholders.

SO 1) C 4. Jill Simmons asks, "Since stock dividends don't change anything, why declare them?" What is your answer to Jill?

SO 1) C 5. "The only thing more exciting than **Apple Computer's** wildly popular iPod music player is its stock," said one financial analyst in early 2006. At that time, Apple's share price was expected to reach U.S. $103 and many analysts speculated that Apple will split its stock. Why should Apple consider splitting its stock?

SO 1) C 6. Contrast the effects of a cash dividend, stock dividend, and stock split on a company's (a) assets, (b) liabilities, (c) share capital, (d) retained earnings, and (e) number of shares.

7. What is the difference between income statements for corporations and income statements for proprietorships and partnerships? Why does this difference exist? (SO 2) C

8. Explain the difference between interperiod tax allocation and intraperiod tax allocation. (SO 2) C

9. How is comprehensive income different from net income? (SO 2) C

10. Explain how comprehensive income is reported on (a) the statement of comprehensive income, and (b) the balance sheet. (SO 2) K

11. Under what circumstances is it appropriate to record an adjustment of the results of prior periods? How are these adjustments reported in the financial statements? (SO 3) C

12. "I don't understand the difference between a correction of a prior period error and a change in accounting principle," Joss said. "It looks to me like they're accounted for and reported in exactly the same way." Explain the similarities and differences to Joss. (SO 3) C

13. What is the purpose of a retained earnings restriction? How are retained earnings restrictions generally reported in the financial statements? (SO 3) K

14. Identify the events that result in increases (credits) and decreases (debits) to Retained Earnings. (SO 3) K

(SO 3) C 15. Omar Radhah believes that both the beginning and ending balances in Retained Earnings are shown in the shareholders' equity section of the balance sheet. Is Omar correct? Explain.

(SO 3) AP 16. Indicate whether each of the following accounts should be classified in the statement of retained earnings (RE) or in the contributed capital section of the balance sheet (BS): (a) Common Shares, (b) Cash Dividends—Preferred, (c) Stock Dividends Distributable, (d) Contributed Capital—Reacquisition of Shares, (e) opening Retained Earnings, and (f) correction of a prior period error.

(SO 4) C 17. Why is the weighted average number of common shares used in earnings per share calculations rather than the average number of common shares?

(SO 4) C 18. The Hanwell Corporation has both common and preferred shares. The company's accountant argues that it is only necessary to subtract the preferred share dividends from net income in the earnings per share calculation if preferred share dividends have been declared that year. Is the accountant correct? Discuss.

(SO 4) 19. Company A has a price-earnings ratio of 12 times and a payout ratio of 3.5%. Company B has a price-earnings ratio of 62 times and a payout ratio of 0%. Which company's shares would be better for an investor interested in a steady dividend income?

(SO 4) 20. If all other factors stay the same, indicate whether each of the following is generally considered favourable or unfavourable by a potential investor: (a) a decrease in return on equity, (b) an increase in earnings per share, (c) a decrease in the price-earnings ratio, and (d) an increase in the payout ratio.

Brief Exercises

Record cash dividend.
(SO 1) AP

BE14–1 The Boudin Corporation has 50,000 $2-noncumulative preferred shares. It declares the annual preferred share dividend on November 15 to shareholders of record on December 1, to be paid on December 21. Prepare the entries on the appropriate dates to record the cash dividend.

Record stock dividend.
(SO 1) AP

BE14–2 Patina Corporation has 80,000 common shares. It declares a 10% stock dividend on December 1 to shareholders of record on December 15, to be distributed on December 31. The market value per share was $15 on December 1, $14 on December 15, and $12 on December 31. Prepare the entries on the appropriate dates to record the stock dividend.

Analyze impact of stock dividend.
(SO 1) AP

BE14–3 The shareholders' equity section of Chew Corporation's balance sheet consists of 100,000 common shares for $1 million, and retained earnings of $400,000. A 10% stock dividend is declared when the market value per share is $8. Show the before-and-after effects of the dividend on (a) share capital, (b) retained earnings, (c) total shareholders' equity, and (d) the number of shares.

Identify impact of stock split.
(SO 1) AP

BE14–4 In February 2005, **Apple Computer** announced a 2-for-1 stock split. Before the split, Apple had 900 million shares authorized and 421 million shares issued. Its share price was U.S. $82 per share. (a) After the split, how many shares were authorized and issued? (b) What was the approximate market price per share?

Compare cash dividend, stock dividend, and stock split.
(SO 1) AP

BE14–5 Indicate whether each of the following transactions would increase (+), decrease (–), or have no effect (NE) on total assets, total liabilities, total shareholders' equity, and the number of shares:

Transaction	Assets	Liabilities	Shareholders' Equity	Number of Shares

(a) Declared a cash dividend.
(b) Paid the cash dividend declared in (a).
(c) Declared a stock dividend.
(d) Distributed the stock dividend declared in (c).
(e) Split stock 2-for-1.

BE14–6 For the year ended May 31, 2008, Osbern Inc. earned $2 million in revenues and had $1.6 million of expenses. The company has a 25% income tax rate. Prepare (a) the journal entry to record income taxes, assuming that $92,000 had been previously accrued, and (b) the income statement.

Record income tax and prepare income statement.
(SO 2) AP

BE14–7 Nike, Inc. reported the following selected information (in U.S. millions) for the year ended May 31, 2005: net income $1,211.6; unrealized gain on foreign currency translation $70.1; and unrealized gain on certain securities $89.6. (a) Prepare a comprehensive income statement. (b) Nike had an accumulated other comprehensive loss of $86.3 at April 1, 2004. What amount would it report in the shareholders' equity section of its balance sheet on May 31, 2005?

Prepare statement of comprehensive income.
(SO 2) AP

BE14–8 For the year ending December 31, 2008, Cadien Inc. reports net income of $200,000; a cash dividend of $25,000; a stock dividend of $60,000; and a loss from the reacquisition of common shares of $15,000. Prepare the statement of retained earnings for the year, assuming the balance in Retained Earnings on January 1, 2008, was $260,000.

Prepare statement of retained earnings.
(SO 3) AP

BE14–9 On January 1, 2008, Ouellet, Inc. changed from the declining-balance method of amortization to the straight-line method. The cumulative effect of the change was to decrease prior years' amortization by $70,000. The income tax rate is 30%. Prepare the journal entry to record this change in accounting principle.

Record change in accounting principle.
(SO 3) AP

BE14–10 Ouellet, Inc. reported retained earnings of $337,000 on December 31, 2007. For the year ended December 31, 2008, the company had net income of $195,000, and it declared and paid dividends of $20,000. Using this information and the data for Ouellet in BE14–9, prepare a statement of retained earnings.

Prepare statement of retained earnings with prior period adjustment.
(SO 3) AP

BE14–11 Ménard Corporation has this account information at December 31, 2008: common shares, no par value, unlimited number authorized, 50,000 issued, $500,000; preferred shares, $6-noncumulative, no par value, unlimited number authorized, 500 issued, $40,000; common stock dividend distributable, 2,500 shares, $25,000; contributed capital—reacquisition of common shares, $5,000; and retained earnings, $290,000. Of the retained earnings, $50,000 has been restricted because of loan agreements. Prepare the shareholders' equity section of the balance sheet.

Prepare shareholders' equity section.
(SO 4) AP

BE14–12 Lake Limited had 40,000 common shares on January 1, 2008. On April 1, 8,000 shares were repurchased. On August 31 and November 30, 12,000 and 6,000 shares were issued, respectively. Calculate (a) the number of shares issued, and (b) the weighted average number of shares at December 31.

Calculate weighted average number of shares.
(SO 4) AP

BE14–13 Darlin Corporation reports net income of $370,000 and 200,000 common shares. (a) Calculate the earnings per share. (b) Assume that Darlin also has 10,000 $2-cumulative preferred shares, on which the dividend for the current year was declared and paid. Recalculate the earnings per share. (c) Assume that the preferred dividends referred to in part (b) were not declared and paid. What difference would this make in calculating the earnings per share?

Calculate earnings per share.
(SO 4) AP

BE14–14 Wang, Inc. reported earnings per share of $5. Its common shares were selling at $52.50 per share. During the same year, the company paid a $0.50 per share cash dividend. Calculate the price-earnings ratio and the payout ratio.

Calculate price-earnings and payout ratios.
(SO 4) AP

Exercises

E14–1 Laine Inc. is considering one of three options: (1) paying a $0.50 cash dividend, (2) distributing a 5% stock dividend, or (3) effecting a 2-for-1 stock split. The current market price is $14 per share.

Compare cash dividend, stock dividend, and stock split.
(SO 1) AP

Instructions

Help Laine decide what to do by completing the following chart (treat each possibility independently):

	Before Action	After Cash Dividend	After Stock Dividend	After Stock Split
Total assets	$1,250,000			
Total liabilities	$ 50,000			
Common shares	800,000			
Retained earnings	400,000			
Total shareholders' equity	1,200,000			
Total liabilities and shareholders' equity	$1,250,000			
Number of common shares	80,000			

Record share and dividend transactions; prepare shareholders' equity section.
(SO 1) AP

E14–2 On January 1, 2008, Knowledge Corporation had an unlimited number of no par value common shares authorized, and 150,000 of them issued for $1,500,000; it also had retained earnings of $750,000. The company issued 50,000 common shares at $14 per share on July 1, and declared a 3-for-2 stock split on September 30 when the market value was $18 per share. On December 10, it declared a 5% stock dividend to common shareholders of record at December 31 and distributable on January 15, 2009. At the declaration date, the market value of the common shares was $20 per share. The company earned net income of $410,000 for the year.

Instructions

(a) Journalize the transactions.
(b) Prepare the shareholders' equity section of the balance sheet at December 31.

Prepare correcting entries for dividends and stock split.
(SO 1) AP

E14–3 Before preparing financial statements for the current year, the chief accountant for Kaufel Ltd. discovered the following errors in the accounts:

1. Kaufel has 10,000 $5-noncumulative preferred shares issued. It paid the preferred shareholders the quarterly dividend, and recorded it as a debit to Dividends Expense and a credit to Cash.
2. A 5% stock dividend (1,000 shares) was declared on the common shares when the market value per share was $10. To record the declaration, Retained Earnings was debited and Dividends Payable was credited. The shares have not been issued yet.
3. The company declared a 2-for-1 stock split on its 10,000 $5-noncumulative preferred shares. The average cost of the preferred shares before the split was $60. The split was recorded as a debit to Retained Earnings of $600,000 and a credit to Preferred Shares of $600,000.
4. After the stock split described in (3) above, the declaration of the quarterly dividend was recorded as a debit to Cash Dividends—Preferred for $25,000 and a credit to Dividends Payable for $25,000.

Instructions

Prepare any correcting entries that are needed.

Prepare income statement.
(SO 2) AP

E14–4 The Aquatic Centre Limited reported the following selected information for the year ended March 31, 2008:

Advertising expense	$ 6,000	Interest expense	$ 6,000
Amortization expense	5,000	Other operating expenses	20,000
Cash dividends	4,000	Rent revenue	34,000
Fees earned	50,000	Retained earnings, April 1, 2007	23,000
Gain on sale of equipment	2,000	Training programs expense	15,000
Income tax payable	5,700	Travel expense	3,000

The company's income tax rate is 20%.

Instructions

Prepare an income statement for The Aquatic Centre.

E14–5 On January 1, Wei Corporation had 75,000 common shares. During the year, the following occurred:

Record share and dividend transactions; indicate statement presentation.
(SO 1, 3) AP

Apr. 1 Issued 5,000 additional common shares for $10 per share.
June 15 Declared a cash dividend of $0.25 per share to common shareholders of record on June 30 and payable on July 10.
Aug. 21 Declared a 5% stock dividend to the common shareholders of record on September 5 and distributable on September 20. The market value of the shares was $12 on August 21, $13 on September 5, and $15 on September 20.
Dec. 1 Issued 3,000 additional common shares for $18 per share.
15 Declared a cash dividend of $0.25 per share to common shareholders of record on December 31 and payable on January 10.

Instructions

(a) Journalize the transactions.
(b) Prepare the entry to close dividends at December 31, Wei's year end.
(c) Explain where each of the following would be reported in the financial statements: (1) cash, (2) common shares, (3) dividends, (4) dividends payable, and (5) retained earnings.

E14–6 Kettle Creek Corporation had the following transactions and events:

Indicate effects of transactions on shareholders' equity.
(SO 1, 3) AP

1. Declared a cash dividend.
2. Paid the cash dividend declared in (1).
3. Issued common shares for cash.
4. Completed a 2-for-1 stock split of the common shares.
5. Declared a stock dividend on the common shares.
6. Distributed the stock dividend declared in (5).
7. Made a prior period correction for an understatement of net income.
8. Adopted a new accounting principle which resulted in the recording of an unrealized gain on available-for-sale securities.
9. Repurchased common shares for less than their initial issue price.
10. Restricted $50,000 of retained earnings.

Instructions

Indicate the effect(s) of each of the above items on the subdivisions of shareholders' equity. Present your answer in tabular form with the following columns. Use "I" for increase, "D" for decrease, and "NE" for no effect. Item 1 is given as an example.

	Contributed Capital			Accumulated Other	Total
Item	Share Capital	Additional	Retained Earnings	Comprehensive Income	Shareholders' Equity
1.	NE	NE	D	NE	D

E14–7 On January 1, 2008, Windsor Corporation had retained earnings of $580,000. During the year, Windsor had the following selected transactions:

Prepare statement of retained earnings.
(SO 1, 3) AP

1. Declared and paid cash dividends, $20,000.
2. Corrected a prior period amortization error of $35,000, which resulted in an understatement of 2007 net income.
3. Earned income before income taxes, $390,000.
4. Declared and distributed stock dividends, $50,000.
5. Reacquired 20,000 common shares for $15,000 more than the original issue price. This was the first time the company had ever reacquired its own shares.
6. Restricted $65,000 of retained earnings for a future plant expansion.

Instructions

Prepare a statement of retained earnings for the year ended December 31, 2008. The company has a 30% income tax rate.

Prepare combined income
statement and statement of
retained earnings.
(SO 2, 3) AP

E14–8 Coaldale Ltd. has an August 31 fiscal year end. On August 31, 2008, Coaldale had retained earnings of $285,000. The company has a 20% income tax rate. The following are in the company's trial balance at August 31, 2008:

Cost of goods sold	$512,000	Interest expense	$ 9,200
Cash dividends	7,000	Operating expenses	233,000
Dividends payable	1,750	Sales	931,000
Contributed capital—		Unrealized gain on available-for-	
reacquisition of common shares	3,500	sale securities	5,000

Instructions

Prepare a combined multiple-step income statement and statement of retained earnings for the year.

Prepare statement of
comprehensive income,
statement of retained
earnings, and shareholders'
equity section.
(SO 2, 3) AP

E14–9 Research in Motion Limited reported the following selected accounts and information (dollars in U.S. thousands), as at March 4, 2006:

Accumulated other comprehensive loss, February 26, 2005	$ 2,771
Retained earnings, February 26, 2005	94,181
Net income	382,078
Unrealized losses on available-for-sale investments	5,888
Other comprehensive income items	6,685
Common shares, unlimited number authorized, 186,001,765 issued	1,852,713
Reduction in retained earnings from reacquisition of common shares	328,231

Instructions

Prepare a statement of comprehensive income, statement of retained earnings, and the shareholders' equity section of the balance sheet.

Calculate earnings per share.
(SO 4) AP

E14–10 Chinook Corporation reported net income of $343,125 for its November 30, 2008, year end. Cash dividends of $75,000 on the common shares and of $45,000 on the noncumulative preferred shares were declared and paid during the year. There were also the following changes in common shares:

Dec. 1, 2007	The opening number of common shares was 60,000.
Feb. 28, 2008	Sold 10,000 common shares for $200,000 cash.
May 31, 2008	Reacquired 5,000 shares for $90,000 cash.
Nov. 1, 2008	Issued 15,000 common shares in exchange for land with a market value of $310,000.

Instructions

(a) Calculate the income available for the common shareholders.
(b) Calculate the weighted average number of common shares for the year.
(c) Calculate the earnings per share for the year.
(d) Why is it necessary to calculate a weighted average number of shares? Why not use the average number of shares (beginning balance plus ending balance divided by two)? After all, we use averages for other ratio calculations.

Calculate earnings per share.
(SO 4) AP

E14–11 At December 31, Morse Corporation has 2,000 $4 preferred shares and 100,000 common shares. Morse's net income for the year is $547,000.

Instructions

Calculate the earnings per share under each of the following independent assumptions.

(a) Assume that the preferred shares are cumulative and that the dividend to the preferred shareholders was (1) declared, and (2) not declared.
(b) Assume that the preferred shares are noncumulative and that the dividend to the preferred shareholders was (1) declared, and (2) not declared.

Calculate ratios.
(SO 4) AP

E14–12 The following financial information is available for **Bank of Montreal** as at October 31 (in millions, except for per share amounts):

	2005	2004	2003
Net income	$2,400	$2,306	$1,781
Preferred share dividends (total)	$30	$31	$38
Weighted average number of common shares	500	502	496
Dividends per common share	$1.85	$1.59	$1.32
Market price per common share	$57.81	$57.55	$49.33

Instructions

(a) Calculate the earnings per share, price-earnings ratio, and payout ratio for the common share-holders for each of the three years.

(b) Using the information in (a), comment on Bank of Montreal's earnings performance and dividend record.

Problems: Set A

P14–1A Gull Lake Enterprises Inc. had 100,000 common shares at July 1, 2007, the beginning of its fiscal year. Mark Bradbury is the president and largest shareholder, owning 25% of the common shares. On July 1, the common shares were trading on the Toronto Stock Exchange for $25 per share. Gull Lake Enterprises' Common Shares and Retained Earnings accounts had opening balances of $2,000,000 and $350,000, respectively.

Indicate impact of share and dividend transactions.
(SO 1) AP

You have the following information about selected events and transactions that occurred during the year ended June 30, 2008:

Aug. 31 The company declared a 4% stock dividend to shareholders of record on September 15, distributable on September 30. The shares were trading at $28 per share on August 31, $30 on September 15, and $29 on September 30.

Dec. 1 The company issued 20,000 common shares for $30 per share. Mark Bradbury acquired 5,000 of these shares to keep his 25% interest in the company.

Mar. 31 The company's shares were trading at $26 per share and the company effected a 2-for-1 stock split. After the split, each share was trading at $13.

June 30 The share price at the close of business on June 30 was $15.

Instructions

Starting with the July 1 opening balances, indicate the impact of each transaction on the following:

(a) The balance in the Common Shares account
(b) The number of common shares issued by the company
(c) The balance in the Retained Earnings account
(d) The number of shares held by Mark Bradbury
(e) The share price
(f) The market value of Mark Bradbury's portfolio of common shares

Compare impact of cash
dividend, stock dividend, and
stock split.
(SO 1) AP

P14–2A The condensed balance sheet of Erickson Corporation reports the following:

ERICKSON CORPORATION
Balance Sheet (partial)
January 31, 2008

Total assets		$9,000,000
Liabilities and shareholders' equity		
Liabilities		$2,500,000
Shareholders' equity		
Common shares, no par value, unlimited number		
authorized, 500,000 issued	$3,000,000	
Retained earnings	3,500,000	6,500,000
Total liabilities and shareholders' equity		$9,000,000

The market price of the common shares is currently $30 per share. Erickson wants to assess the impact of three possible alternatives on the corporation and its shareholders. The alternatives are:

1. Payment of a $1.50 per share cash dividend
2. Distribution of a 5% stock dividend
3. A 2-for-1 stock split

Instructions

(a) For each alternative, determine the impact on (1) assets, (2) liabilities, (3) common shares, (4) retained earnings, (5) total shareholders' equity, and (6) the number of shares.
(b) Assume an Erickson shareholder currently owns 2,000 common shares at a cost of $50,000. What is the impact of each alternative for the shareholder, assuming that the market price of the shares changes proportionately with the alternative?

Record and post transactions;
prepare shareholders' equity
section.
(SO 1, 2) AP

P14–3A On December 31, 2007, Asaad Corporation had the following shareholders' equity accounts:

ASAAD CORPORATION
Balance Sheet (partial)
December 31, 2007

Shareholders' equity	
Common shares (no par value, unlimited number	
of shares authorized, 75,000 shares issued)	$1,700,000
Retained earnings	600,000
Total shareholders' equity	$2,300,000

During the year, the following transactions occurred:

Feb. 1 Declared a $1 cash dividend to shareholders of record on February 15 and payable March 1.
Apr. 1 Announced a 2-for-1 stock split. The market price per share was $36 on the date of the announcement.
Dec. 1 Declared a 5% stock dividend to shareholders of record on December 20, distributable January 5. On December 1, the market price of the shares was $16 per share; on December 20, it was $18 per share; and on January 5, it was $15 per share.
     31 Determined that net income before income taxes for the year was $400,000. The company has a 25% income tax rate.

Instructions

(a) Journalize the transactions and closing entries.
(b) Enter the beginning balances, and post the entries in (a) to the shareholders' equity accounts. (*Note:* Open additional shareholders' equity accounts as needed.)
(c) Prepare the shareholders' equity section of the balance sheet at December 31, 2008.

P14–4A The post-closing trial balance of Michaud Corporation at December 31, 2008, contains the following shareholders' equity accounts:

Reproduce accounts and prepare statement of retained earnings.
(SO 1, 2, 3) AP

$4-cumulative preferred shares (15,000 shares issued)	$ 850,000
Common shares (250,000 shares issued)	3,200,000
Contributed capital—reacquisition of common shares	20,000
Retained earnings	1,418,000

A review of the accounting records reveals the following:

1. The January 1 opening balance in Common Shares was $3,210,000 (255,000 shares) and in Retained Earnings was $980,000.
2. On March 1, 20,000 common shares were sold for $15.50 per share.
3. On July 1, 25,000 common shares were reacquired for $12 per share.
4. On September 1, the company discovered a $60,000 error that understated amortization expense in 2007. The net-of-tax effect was properly debited to Retained Earnings. The company has a 30% income tax rate.
5. The preferred shareholders' dividend was declared and paid in 2008 for three quarters. Due to a cash shortage, the last quarter's dividend was not paid.
6. Net income for the year before income taxes was $750,000.
7. On December 31, the directors authorized a $200,000 restriction of retained earnings for a plant expansion.

Instructions

(a) Starting with the January 1 balance, reproduce the Common Shares and Retained Earnings general ledger accounts for the year.
(b) Prepare a statement of retained earnings for the year.

P14–5A The shareholders' equity accounts of Kanada Inc. at September 30, 2007, are as follows:

Prepare statement of retained earnings.
(SO 1, 2, 3) AP

KANADA INC.
Balance Sheet (partial)
September 30, 2007

Shareholders' equity	
Preferred shares, $5-noncumulative, no par value, unlimited number authorized, 6,000 issued	$ 465,000
Common shares, no par value, unlimited number authorized, 225,000 issued	900,000
Retained earnings	540,000
Accumulated other comprehensive income	95,000
Total shareholders' equity	$2,000,000

Kanada has a 30% income tax rate. During the following fiscal year ended September 30, 2008, Kanada had the following transactions and events:

Mar. 14 Declared a 4% common stock dividend to shareholders of record at March 31, distributable on April 5. The market value of the common shares was $10 per share on March 14, $11 on March 31, and $12 on April 5.
July   7 Changed from declining-balance amortization to straight-line amortization. The cumulative effect of the change on prior years' net income was an increase of $33,000 before income tax.
Aug.   1 Discovered a $54,000 overstatement of cost of goods sold in the prior year's income statement.
Sept. 20 Declared the annual dividend payable to the preferred shareholders of record on October 5, payable on October 31.
      25 Announced a 2-for-1 common stock split. The market price of the common shareholders at the date of announcement was $15 per share.
      30 Determined that net income before income taxes was $325,000.

Instructions

Prepare a statement of retained earnings for the year ended September 30, 2008.

Record and post transactions; prepare statement of retained earnings and shareholders' equity section.
(SO 1, 3) AP

P14–6A The shareholders' equity accounts of Fryman Ltd. at December 31, 2007, are as follows:

FRYMAN LTD.
Balance Sheet (partial)
December 31, 2007

Shareholders' equity	
Preferred shares, $4-noncumulative, no par value, unlimited number authorized, 12,000 issued	$ 800,000
Common shares, no par value, unlimited number authorized, 250,000 issued	500,000
Contributed capital—reacquired common shares	100,000
Retained earnings	900,000
Accumulated other comprehensive loss	(50,000)
Total shareholders' equity	$2,250,000

During 2008, the company had the following transactions and events:

Aug. 1 Discovered a $45,000 understatement of 2007 amortization expense. The company has a 30% income tax rate.

Oct. 15 Declared a 10% stock dividend to common shareholders of record on October 31, distributable November 10. The market value of the common shares was $18 per share on October 15, $19 per share on October 31, and $20 per share on November 10.

Dec. 15 Declared the annual cash dividend to the preferred shareholders of record on December 31, payable January 15, 2006.

31 Determined that net income for the year was $395,000.

31 Recognized a $200,000 restriction of retained earnings for a plant expansion.

Instructions

(a) Journalize the transactions and summary closing entries.
(b) Enter the beginning balances in the accounts and post to the shareholders' equity accounts. (*Note:* Open additional shareholders' equity accounts as needed.)
(c) Prepare a statement of retained earnings for the year.
(d) Prepare the shareholders' equity section of the balance sheet at December 31, 2008.

Prepare statement of comprehensive income, statement of retained earnings, and shareholders' equity section.
(SO 2, 3) AP

P14–7A Canadian National Railway Company reported the following selected accounts and information (in millions) for the year ended December 31, 2005:

Accumulated other comprehensive loss, January 1	$ 148
Common shares	4,580
Dividends	275
"Loss" on reacquisition of shares	1,116
Net income	1,556
Other comprehensive loss items	51
Retained earnings, January 1	4,726
Unrealized losses on investments	23

Instructions

Prepare a statement of comprehensive income, statement of retained earnings, and the shareholders' equity section of the balance sheet.

Prepare income statement, including EPS, and statement of retained earnings.
(SO 2, 3, 4) AP

P14–8A The ledger of Coquitlam Corporation at December 31, 2008, contains the following summary data:

Cash dividends—common	$ 125,000	Other revenues	$ 47,000
Cost of goods sold	1,088,000	Retained earnings,	
Operating expenses	551,000	January 1, 2008	642,000
Other expenses	28,000	Net sales	1,750,000

Your analysis reveals the following additional information:

1. The company has a 30% income tax rate.
2. In 2007, the company incorrectly recorded sales revenue of $62,000 that should have been recorded as revenue in 2008. This error has not been corrected in the above amounts.
3. There were 100,000 common shares on January 1, 2008. On April 1, Coquitlam issued an additional 25,000 shares for $25 per share.

Instructions

(a) Prepare a multiple-step income statement for the year, including the disclosure of earnings per share.
(b) Prepare a statement of retained earnings for the year.

P14–9A The shareholders' equity accounts of Gualtieri Inc. on August 1, 2007, the beginning of its fiscal year, are as follows:

Calculate earnings per share.
(SO 4) AP

$4-preferred shares (25,000 issued)	$1,250,000
Common shares (350,000 issued)	3,750,000
Retained earnings	2,250,000
Total shareholders' equity	$7,250,000

During the year, the following transactions occurred:

Nov. 30 Issued 37,500 common shares for $12 per share.
Feb.   1 Reacquired 6,000 common shares for $10 per share.
Mar.   1 Issued 30,000 common shares in exchange for equipment. The market value of the common shares issued was $13 per share.
July 31 Net income for the year ended July 31, 2008, was $1,022,800.

Instructions

(a) Calculate the weighted average number of common shares for the year.
(b) Assume the preferred shares are cumulative and one year in arrears:
   1. Calculate the earnings per share if no preferred dividends are declared during the year.
   2. Calculate the earnings per share if the preferred share dividends for the current and prior year are declared during the year.
(c) Assume the preferred shares are noncumulative:
   1. Calculate the earnings per share if no preferred share dividends are declared during the year.
   2. Calculate the earnings per share if the company declares a preferred share dividend of $60,000.
(d) Why is it important to use a weighted average number of shares in the earnings per share calculations? Why not just use the average number of shares during the year?

P14–10A The following selected information is available for **National Bank of Canada** for the year ended October 31:

Calculate ratios and comment.
(SO 4) AN

(in millions, except market price)	2005	2004
Weighted average number of common shares	166	171
Net income	$ 855	$ 725
Total common cash dividends	286	243
Total preferred cash dividends	26	23
Average common shareholders' equity	4,013	3,776
Market price per common share	$59.14	$48.78

Instructions

(a) Calculate the following ratios for 2005 and for 2004:
   1. Return on common shareholders' equity   3. Price-earnings ratio
   2. Earnings per share   4. Payout ratio for common shareholders
(b) Comment on the above ratios for 2005 compared to the results for 2004.

Problems: Set B

Indicate impact of share and dividend transactions.
(SO 1) AP

P14–1B Savary Island Development Inc. has 200,000 common shares issued on November 1, 2007, the beginning of its fiscal year. Juanita Tolentino is the president and largest shareholder, owning 20% of the common shares. On November 1, the shares were trading on the Toronto Stock Exchange for $8 per share. The November 1 balances in Common Shares and Retained Earnings were $1,000,000 and $500,000, respectively.

You have the following information about selected events and transactions that occurred during the fiscal year ended October 31, 2008:

Jan. 2 Savary Island issued 50,000 common shares for $10 per share in order to finance a new development project. Juanita purchased 10,000 of these shares in order to keep her 20% interest in the company.

May 1 The company effected a 3-for-2 stock split when the company's shares were trading at $12 per share. After the split, each share was trading at $8.

Aug. 31 Savary Island declared and issued a 3% stock dividend. The shares were trading at $9 on that day.

Oct. 31 The share price at the close of business was $11.

Instructions

Starting with the November 1 opening balances, indicate the impact of each transaction on the following:

(a) The balance in the Common Shares account
(b) The number of common shares issued by the company
(c) The balance in the Retained Earnings account
(d) The number of shares held by Juanita Tolentino
(e) The share price
(f) The market value of Juanita Tolentino's portfolio of common shares

Compare impact of cash dividend, stock dividend, and stock split.
(SO 1) AP

P14–2B The condensed balance sheet of Laporte Corporation reports the following:

LAPORTE CORPORATION Balance Sheet (partial) June 30, 2008	
Total assets	$16,000,000
Liabilities and shareholders' equity	
Total liabilities	$ 6,000,000
Shareholders' equity	
Common shares, no par value, unlimited number authorized, 400,000 issued	2,000,000
Retained earnings	8,000,000
Total shareholders' equity	10,000,000
Total liabilities and shareholders' equity	$16,000,000

The market price of the common shares is currently $30 per share. Laporte wants to assess the impact of three possible alternatives on the corporation and its shareholders. The alternatives are:

1. Payment of a $1.50 per share cash dividend
2. Distribution of a 5% stock dividend.
3. A 3-for-2 stock split

Instructions

(a) For each alternative, determine the impact on (1) assets, (2) liabilities, (3) common shares, (4) retained earnings, (5) total shareholders' equity, and (6) the number of shares.

(b) Assume a Laporte shareholder currently owns 1,000 common shares at a cost of $28,000. What is the impact of each alternative for the shareholder, assuming that the market price of the shares changes proportionately with the alternative?

P14–3B On December 31, 2007, LeBlanc Corporation had the following shareholders' equity accounts:

Record and post transactions; prepare shareholders' equity section.
(SO 1, 2) AP

LEBLANC CORPORATION Balance Sheet (partial) December 31, 2007	
Shareholders' equity	
Common shares (no par value, unlimited number of shares authorized, 90,000 issued)	$1,100,000
Retained earnings	540,000
Total shareholders' equity	$1,640,000

During the year, the following transactions occurred:

Jan. 15 Declared a $1 cash dividend per share to shareholders of record on January 31, payable February 15.

July 1 Announced a 3-for-2 stock split. The market price per share on the date of the announcement was $15.

Dec. 15 Declared a 10% stock dividend to shareholders of record on December 30, distributable January 15. On December 15, the market price of each share was $10; on December 30, $12; and on December 15, $11.

31 Determined that net income before income taxes for the year was $450,000. The company has a 25% income tax rate.

Instructions

(a) Journalize the transactions and closing entries.
(b) Enter the beginning balances and post the entries in part (a) to the shareholders' equity accounts. (*Note:* Open additional shareholders' equity accounts as needed.)
(c) Prepare the shareholders' equity section of the balance sheet at December 31, 2008.

P14–4B The post-closing trial balance of Jajoo Corporation at December 31, 2008, contains the following shareholders' equity accounts:

Reproduce accounts and prepare statement of retained earnings.
(SO 1, 2, 3) AP

$5-noncumulative preferred shares (10,000 issued)	$1,100,000
Common shares (400,000 issued)	2,000,000
Common stock dividend distributable	180,000
Retained earnings	2,966,000

A review of the accounting records reveals the following:

1. The January 1 balance in the Common Shares was $1,280,000 (320,000 shares), in Contributed Capital—Reacquisition of Shares was $30,000, and in Retained Earnings was $2,443,500.
2. On January 15, 20,000 common shares were reacquired for $7 per share.
3. On July 1, the company adopted a new accounting principle which resulted in a cumulative increase to the Investments account, as well as to prior years' net income of $250,000 before income taxes. The company has a 25% income tax rate.
4. On October 1, 100,000 common shares were sold for $8 per share.
5. The preferred shareholders' dividend was declared and paid in 2008 for two quarters. Due to a cash shortage, the last two quarters' dividends were not paid.
6. On December 15, a 5% stock dividend (20,000 shares) was declared to common shareholders of record on December 30, to be distributed on January 12, 2009. The market price per share was $9 on December 15, $10 on December 30, and $9.50 on January 12.
7. Net income for the year before income taxes was $760,000.
8. On December 31, the directors authorized a $500,000 restriction of retained earnings as required by a debt covenant.

Instructions

(a) Starting with the January 1 balance, reproduce the Common Shares, Contributed Capital—Reacquisition of Common Shares, and Retained Earnings general ledger accounts for the year.

(b) Prepare a statement of retained earnings for the year.

Prepare statement of retained earnings.

(SO 1, 2, 3) AP

P14–5B The shareholders' equity accounts of Tmao, Inc. at December 31, 2007, are as follows:

TMAO INC.
Balance Sheet (partial)
December 31, 2007

Shareholders' equity
Preferred shares, $3-noncumulative, no par value, unlimited number authorized, 4,000 issued	$ 400,000
Common shares, no par value, unlimited number authorized, 160,000 issued	800,000
Retained earnings	450,000
Accumulated other comprehensive loss	(50,000)
Total shareholders' equity	$1,600,000

Tmao has a 25% income tax rate. During the following fiscal year, ended December 31, 2008, the company had the following transactions and events:

Feb. 1 Discovered a $70,000 understatement of 2007 amortization expense.

July 12 Announced a 2-for-1 preferred stock split. The market price of the preferred shares at the date of announcement was $150.

Oct. 1 Adopted a new accounting principle which resulted in a cumulative decrease to prior years' net income of $30,000 before income tax.

Dec. 1 Declared a 10% stock dividend to common shareholders of record at December 20, distributable January 12. The market value of the common shares was $12 per share.

18 Declared the annual cash dividend ($1.50 post-split) to the preferred shareholders of record on January 10, 2009, payable January 31, 2009.

31 Determined that net income before income taxes for the year was $350,000.

Instructions

Prepare a statement of retained earnings for the year ended December 31.

Record and post transactions; prepare statement of retained earnings and shareholders' equity section.

(SO 1, 3) AP

P14–6B The shareholders' equity accounts of Cedeno Inc. at December 31, 2007, are as follows:

CEDENO INC.
Balance Sheet (partial)
December 31, 2007

Shareholders' equity
Common shares, no par value (unlimited number of shares authorized, 1,000,000 issued)	$3,000,000
Stock dividends distributable	400,000
Contributed capital—reacquired common shares	5,000
Retained earnings	1,200,000
Total shareholders' equity	$4,605,000

During 2008, the following transactions and events occurred:

Jan. 20 Issued 100,000 common shares as a result of a 10% stock dividend declared on December 15, 2007. The market value of the shares was $4 on December 15 and $5 on January 20.

Feb. 12 Issued 50,000 common shares for $5 per share.

Mar. 31 Corrected an error that had overstated the cost of goods sold for 2007 by $60,000. The company has a 30% income tax rate.

Nov. 2 Reacquired 25,000 shares for $2.50 each.

Dec. 31 Declared a cash dividend to the common shareholders of $0.50 per share to shareholders of record at January 15, payable January 31.

31 Earned net income of $400,000.

31 Recognized a $250,000 restriction of retained earnings for a future acquisition.

Instructions

(a) Journalize the transactions and summary closing entries.

(b) Enter the beginning balances, and post the entries in (a) to the shareholders' equity accounts. (*Note:* Open additional shareholders' equity accounts as needed.)

(c) Prepare a statement of retained earnings for the year.

(d) Prepare the shareholders' equity section of the balance sheet at December 31, 2008.

P14–7B   Suncor Energy Inc. reported the following selected accounts and information (in U.S. millions), for the year ended December 31, 2005:

Prepare statement of comprehensive income, statement of retained earnings, and shareholders' equity section.
(SO 2, 3) AP

Accumulated other comprehensive loss, January 1	$ 229
Contributed surplus	88
Net income	1,274
Other comprehensive income items	99
Other shareholders' equity items	(81)
Retained earnings, January 1	4,293
Share capital	780

Instructions

Prepare a statement of comprehensive income, statement of retained earnings, and the shareholders' equity section of the balance sheet.

P14–8B   The ledger of Hyperchip Corporation at November 30, 2008, contains the following summary data:

Prepare income statement, including EPS, and statement of retained earnings.
(SO 2, 3, 4) AP

Amortization expense	$ 355,000	Other expenses	$ 83,000
Cash dividends	162,500	Other revenues	48,000
Common shares	325,000	Net sales	9,124,000
Cost of goods sold	7,280,000	Retained earnings,	
Operating expenses	1,120,000	December 1, 2007	755,000

Your analysis reveals the following additional information:

1. The company has a 25% income tax rate.

2. During the year, Hyperchip changed its amortization method from declining-balance to straight-line. The cumulative effect of the change on prior years' income was an increase of $57,000 before income tax. (Assume that amortization under the new method is correctly included for the current year in the above data.)

3. The company had 25,000 common shares on December 1, 2007, and issued an additional 10,000 shares on June 1, 2008.

Instructions

(a) Prepare a multiple-step income statement for the year, including the disclosure of earnings per share.

(b) Prepare a statement of retained earnings for the year ended November 30, 2008.

P14–9B   The shareholders' equity accounts of Blue Bay Logistics Ltd. on April 1, 2007, the beginning of the fiscal year, are as follows:

Calculate earnings per share.
(SO 4) AP

$6-preferred shares (20,000 issued)	$1,800,000
Common shares (500,000 issued)	3,750,000
Retained earnings	1,550,000
Total shareholders' equity	$7,100,000

During the year, the following transactions occurred:

June   1 Reacquired 12,000 common shares for $9 per share.
July   1 Issued 50,000 common shares for $10 per share.
Sept. 30 Reacquired 8,000 common shares for $9.50 per share.
Jan. 31 Issued 60,000 common shares in exchange for land. The market value of the common shares issued was $10 per share.
Mar. 31 Net income for the year ended March 31, 2008, was $973,600.

Instructions

(a) Calculate the weighted average number of common shares for the year.
(b) Assume the preferred shares are cumulative and one year in arrears:
   1. Calculate the earnings per share if no preferred dividends are declared during the year.
   2. Calculate the earnings per share if the preferred share dividends for the current and prior year are declared during the year.
(c) Assume the preferred shares are noncumulative:
   1. Calculate the earnings per share if no preferred share dividends are declared during the year.
   2. Calculate the earnings per share if the company declares a preferred share dividend of $80,000.
(d) Why is it important to use a weighted average number of shares in the earnings per share calculations? Why not just use the ending balance?

Calculate ratios and comment.

(SO 4) AN

P14–10B   The following selected information is available for **Saputo Inc.** for the year ended March 31:

(in millions, except market price)	2006	2005
Weighted average number of common shares	105	104
Net income	$192	$ 232
Total common cash dividends	72	59
Average shareholders' equity	1,359	1,236
Market price per common share	$32.70	$36.15

Saputo has no preferred shares.

Instructions

(a) Calculate the following ratios for 2006 and for 2005:
   1. Return on equity   3. Price-earnings ratio
   2. Earnings per share   4. Payout ratio
(b) Comment on the above ratios for 2006 compared to the results for 2005.

Continuing Cookie Chronicle

(*Note:* This is a continuation of the Cookie Chronicle from Chapters 1 through 13.)

After deciding that their company's fiscal year end was going be October 31, Natalie and Curtis begin operating Cookie & Coffee Creations Ltd. on November 1, 2008. As at that date, after the issue of shares, the share capital section of the company's balance sheet is as follows:

Share capital	
Preferred shares, $0.50-noncumulative, no par value,	
10,000 shares authorized, 2,000 issued	$10,000
Common shares, no par value, unlimited number of shares	
authorized, 23,930 issued	23,930

Cookie & Coffee Creations then has the following selected transactions during its first year of operations:

Dec.   1 Issues an additional 500 preferred shares to Natalie's brother for $2,500.

Apr. 30 Declares a semi-annual dividend to the preferred shareholders of record on May 15, payable on June 1.

June 30 Repurchases 750 shares issued to the lawyer, for $500. Recall that these were originally issued for $750. The lawyer had decided to retire and wanted to liquidate all of her assets.

Oct. 31 The company has had a very successful first year of operations. It earned revenues of $462,500 and incurred expenses of $370,000 (excluding income tax).

       31 Records income tax expense (the company has a 20% income tax rate).

       31 Declares a semi-annual dividend to the preferred shareholders of record on November 15, payable on December 1.

Instructions

(a) Prepare the journal entries to record the above transactions.

(b) Prepare the statement of retained earnings for the year ended October 31, 2009.

(c) Prepare the shareholders' equity section of the balance sheet as at October 31, 2009.

(d) Prepare closing entries.

(e) Calculate the earnings per share and dividend payout ratio.

Cumulative Coverage—Chapters 13 and 14

Cyber Force Corp.'s post-closing trial balance at December 31, 2007, follows:

CYBER FORCE CORP. Post-Closing Trial Balance December 31, 2007		
	Debit	Credit
Cash	$ 10,820	
Accounts receivable	45,500	
Allowance for doubtful accounts		$ 1,500
Inventory	138,485	
Equipment	144,950	
Accumulated amortization—equipment		42,135
Accounts payable		26,950
Income taxes payable		3,500
6% Note payable (due on July 1, 2010)		75,000
Common shares, no par value, unlimited number authorized, 100,000 issued		100,000
Retained earnings		90,670
	$339,755	$339,755

The following transactions (in summary form) occurred during 2008:

1. Cash sales were $200,750; sales on account were $645,000; and cost of goods sold was $507,450. (Cyber Force uses a perpetual inventory system.)

2. Cash purchases of inventory were $125,000 and purchases on account were $410,650.

3. Collected $600,000 from customers on account.

4. Cash received in advance from customers for deliveries in January 2009 was $48,000.

5. Cash payments for operating expenses were $194,855.

6. Paid $400,000 on accounts payable.

7. Six months of interest on the note payable, $2,250, was paid July 1.

8. The income taxes payable from December 31, 2007, were paid.

9. The company issued 350 $4 preferred shares for $25,000. The preferred share are no par value, noncumulative, and with an unlimited number authorized.

10. On October 1, 10,000 common shares were reacquired for $1.65 per share.

11. On December 1, the annual preferred share dividend was declared to shareholders of record at December 20, payable on January 10, 2009.

Adjustment data:

1. Cyber Force uses straight-line amortization. The equipment has a total estimated 10-year useful life and a residual value of $4,500.
2. Interest was accrued for the six months ended December 31 on the note payable. It is due January 1.
3. Bad debt expense of $3,025 was recorded.
4. The company has a 20% income tax rate.

Instructions

(a) Prepare and post journal entries for the above events.
(b) Prepare an adjusted trial balance at December 31, 2008.
(c) Prepare a multiple-step income statement, a statement of retained earnings, and a classified balance sheet.
(d) Prepare closing entries.
(e) Calculate the earnings per share.

BROADENING YOUR PERSPECTIVE

Financial Reporting and Analysis

Financial Reporting Problem

BYP14–1   Refer to the consolidated financial statements and accompanying notes for **The Forzani Group Ltd.** reproduced in Appendix A.

Instructions

(a) Did Forzani pay, or distribute, any dividends in fiscal 2006? If yes, how much? If no, why might a company choose *not* to pay dividends?
(b) Did Forzani report any of the following in fiscal 2006: (1) comprehensive income, (2) prior period adjustments, or (3) restricted retained earnings?
(c) Basic earnings per share of $0.42 for 2006 was reported in the chapter in Illustration 14-9. How much was basic earnings per share for 2005? Did earnings per share improve or weaken in 2006?
(d) Did Forzani report any fully diluted earnings per share in fiscal 2006 and 2005? If yes, what was the difference between these amounts and the basic earnings per share in each year?
(e) Forzani's price-earnings ratio for 2006 was reported in the chapter in Illustration 14-10. Its price-earnings ratio for 2005 was 18.6 times. Did the price-earnings ratio improve or weaken in 2006? Is your answer consistent with your findings in part (c)? Explain.

Interpreting Financial Statements

BYP14–2   On March 3, 2006, **The RBC Financial Group** declared, for the fourth time in its history, a 2-for-1 stock split to common shareholders of record on March 27, to be distributed April 6. Financial information for RBC for the quarter ended January 31, 2006 follows (in thousands, except share price data):

Net income	$ 1,171
Average common shareholders' equity	19,300
Common share cash dividends	412
Preferred share cash dividends	10
Common share price	89
Weighted average number of shares	642

Instructions

(a) Explain the different effects that a cash dividend and stock split have on RBC's assets, liabilities, shareholders' equity, and the number of shares.

(b) What is the likely reason that RBC has split its common shares in the past?

(c) If the market price for a common share before the stock split in March 2006 was $98, what do you think the market price for a common share would be immediately after the stock split?

(d) If the cash dividend on the common shares was $0.72 before the stock split, how much will it be after the stock split?

(e) Calculate the return on common shareholders' equity, earnings per share, and payout ratio for the common shareholders for 2006. Comment on the company's profitability.

Critical Thinking

Collaborative Learning Activity

Note to instructor: Additional instructions and material for this group activity can be found on the Instructor Resource Site.

BYP14–3   In this group activity, you will review the transactions for cash dividends and stock dividends.

Instructions

(a) Without consulting your classmates, record the transactions given to you by your instructor.

(b) Your instructor will divide the class into groups. One member of your group will take on the role of team recorder. As a group, record the transactions used in part (a). You can refer to your individual journal entries for answers during the group activity but you should not change these answers. Where your answers differ, you must explain your reasoning to the other members of the group. You may refer to the text at this point in the activity.

(c) Each group will hand in the group journal entries along with the individual entries of each member.

Study Aids:
Working in Groups

Communication Activity

BYP14–4   Earnings per share is the most commonly cited financial ratio. Indeed, share prices rise and fall in reaction to a company's earnings per share. The price-earnings ratio is also published in many newspapers' stock market listings.

Instructions

Write a memo explaining why earnings per share and the price-earnings ratio are so important to investors. Explain how both ratios are calculated and how they relate to each other. Include in your memo an explanation of how to interpret a high or low price-earnings ratio.

Study Aids:
Writing Handbook

Ethics Case

Study Aids:
Ethics in Accounting

BYP14–5 Flambeau Corporation has paid 40 consecutive quarterly cash dividends (10 years' worth). The last six months, however, have been a real cash drain on the company as profit margins have been greatly squeezed by increasing competition. With only enough cash to meet day-to-day operating needs, the president, Vince Ramsey, has decided that a stock dividend instead of a cash dividend should be declared. He tells Flambeau's financial vice-president, Janice Rahn, to issue a press release stating that the company is extending its consecutive dividend record with the issue of a 5-percent stock dividend. "Write the press release to convince the shareholders that the stock dividend is just as good as a cash dividend," he orders. "Just watch our share price rise when we announce the stock dividend. It must be a good thing if that happens."

Instructions

(a) Who are the stakeholders in this situation?
(b) Is there anything unethical about Ramsey's intentions or actions?
(c) As a shareholder, which would you rather receive—a cash dividend or a stock dividend? Why?

ANSWERS TO CHAPTER QUESTIONS

Answers to Accounting in Action Insight Questions

Business Insight, p. 713

Q: What is the likely reason that Quebecor's share price fell when it cut its dividend?

A: If shareholders had purchased Quebecor's shares for the dividend income, they would be disappointed when the dividend was cut. They likely expected the dividend to stay at its historical level, or even at a higher level. In addition, cutting a dividend can often signal financial difficulties at a company. Consequently, some investors would sell their shares after the announcement, and others would no longer be interested in purchasing Quebecor's shares. This reduced demand would then lead to a drop in the share price.

Business Insight, p. 718

Q: How would Google benefit if it split its stock?

A: Although at first there would be no direct impact on Google's financial position if it split its stock, its shares would be more affordable to more people. This normally leads to a higher share price than would otherwise have been the case, because of the increased demand. In addition, with a wider distribution of ownership (that is, with more people buying the shares), more people would be interested in using and promoting Google. Concentrated ownership also makes a company more vulnerable to hostile takeovers.

Business Insight, p. 729

Q: Why does a company's earnings per share affect its share price?

A: Although share prices are influenced by many factors, they usually follow a company's income levels. If income falls, as it did in Sears' case, shareholders may be worried about the company's future prospects and are likely to be less interested in holding onto the shares, or in purchasing shares.

Answer to Forzani Review It Question 5, p. 718

Forzani did not declare any dividends or stock splits in 2006.

Answers to Self-Study Questions

1. a   2. c   3. c   4. b   5. c   6. a   7. c   8. b   9. a   10. c

 Remember to go back to the Navigator Box at the beginning of the chapter to check off your completed work.

concepts for review >>

Before studying this chapter, you should understand or, if necessary, review:

a. How to record adjusting entries for interest expense. (Ch. 3, pp. 117–118)

b. What a current liability is, and what a long-term liability is. (Ch. 4, pp. 178–179 and Ch. 10, p. 518)

c. How to record entries for the issue of notes payable and related interest expense. (Ch. 10, pp. 519–520)

d. How to calculate return on equity and earnings per share. (Ch. 13, p. 684 and Ch. 14, pp. 728–729)

Investing in Higher Education

MONTREAL, Que.—Concordia University has undergone some major changes in recent years, and in the process new life has been injected into a neglected part of downtown Montreal. "Quartier Concordia" features the new Engineering, Computer Science and Visual Arts Integrated Complex and will soon be the home of the John Molson School of Business, which is going up on the corner of Guy and de Maisonneuve streets. At the same time, the university's Loyola Campus in the city's west end has expanded with the construction of the Richard J. Renaud Science Complex. In all, the $400-million project involves three new buildings and a variety of improvements to existing facilities.

In 2002, when Concordia needed cash for this expansion project, the institution did something it had never done before—it raised part of the funds by selling bonds. At $200 million, Concordia's issue was the largest Canadian university bond offering at that time, although it was not the first or last of its kind.

The trend began in 2001 with the University of Toronto, which raised $160 million, followed by UBC's offering worth $125 million. Faced with rising enrolments and shrinking resources from provincial governments, post-secondary institutions are turning to the private sector to help finance upgrades and repairs. By 2006, 12 universities were listed on the Dominion Bond Rating Service, including the University of Ottawa, Queens, York, and Simon Fraser.

By issuing bonds, universities pay less interest than they would have to pay with a bank loan. And unlike bank loans, which usually have to be renegotiated every few years, the interest rate for a bond offering is locked in for the whole term.

Concordia University: www.concordia.ca

Concordia offered a series of 40-year unsecured bonds with an interest rate of 6.55% paid semi-annually. The university also required a minimum purchase of $150,000—which made the debenture something that only large institutional investors could consider, such as pension and mutual funds.

Dominion Bond Rating Service has given Concordia a credit rating of A, while Moody's Investors Service assigned it an A1. Just like credit ratings for individuals, these ratings reflect a school's ability to meet its financial obligations. They are affected by many factors, including its age, size, and location, as well as factors affecting its regular funding from tuition fees, government grants, and donations.

Some universities have considered the bond option and rejected it, and critics point out that not-for-profit organizations in general should not be going into debt. But so far investors have decided otherwise. Canadian university bond offerings have sold out fast—in some cases within hours.

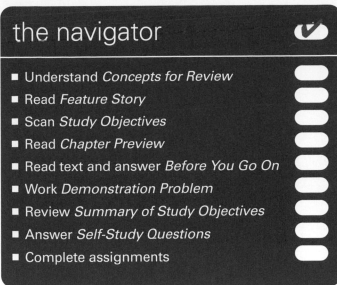

the navigator

- Understand *Concepts for Review*
- Read *Feature Story*
- Scan *Study Objectives*
- Read *Chapter Preview*
- Read text and answer *Before You Go On*
- Work *Demonstration Problem*
- Review *Summary of Study Objectives*
- Answer *Self-Study Questions*
- Complete assignments

chapter 15

Long-Term Liabilities

study objectives >>

the navigator

After studying this chapter, you should be able to:

1. Compare the impact of issuing debt instead of equity.
2. Account for bonds payable.
3. Account for long-term notes payable.
4. Account for leases.
5. Explain and illustrate the methods for the presentation and analysis of long-term liabilities.
6. Apply the effective-interest method of amortizing bond discounts and premiums (Appendix 15A).

As you can see from the feature story, Concordia University chose to issue bonds to fund its building projects. The bonds are classified as long-term liabilities because they are obligations that are not due within the next year. In this chapter, we will explain the accounting for the major types of long-term liabilities reported on the balance sheet. These liabilities include bonds, long-term notes, and lease obligations.

The chapter is organized as follows:

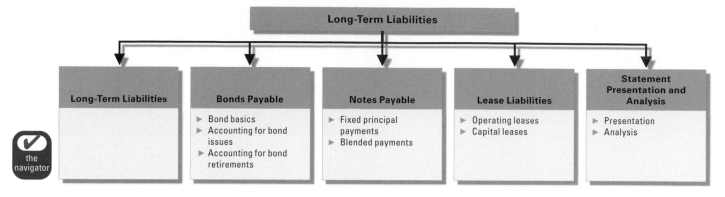

Long-Term Liabilities

study objective 1

Compare the impact of issuing debt instead of equity.

You will recall from Chapter 10 that a current liability is a debt with two key features: (1) It is likely to be paid within one year. (2) It will be paid from existing current assets (e.g., cash) or by creating other current liabilities. Debt that does not meet both criteria is a **long-term liability**. Common examples of long-term liabilities include bonds payable, notes payable, and capital leases. These are all examples of financial instruments, which were introduced in Chapter 13. More specifically, long-term liabilities such as these are referred to as financial liabilities because there is a contract between two or more parties to pay cash in the future.

Just as people need money for long periods of time, so do companies. A problem that large corporations can sometimes have is that they need much more money than the average bank can lend for certain types of projects, such as purchasing another company or constructing new buildings like Concordia University did. The solution is to raise money by issuing debt securities (e.g., bonds payable) or equity securities (e.g., common shares) to the investing public. In this way, thousands of investors each lend part of the capital that is needed.

Whenever a company decides that it needs long-term financing, it must first decide if it should issue debt or equity. For a corporation that wants long-term financing, debt offers some advantages over equity, as shown in Illustration 15-1 on the following page.

To show the potential effect on earnings per share and return on equity, assume that Microsystems Inc. is considering two plans for financing the construction of a new $5-million plant. Plan A is to use equity by issuing 200,000 common shares for $25 per share. Plan B is to use debt by issuing $5 million of 6-percent bonds payable. Once the new plant is built, Microsystems expects to earn an additional $1.5 million of income before interest and income tax. The income tax rate is expected to be 30 percent. Microsystems has 100,000 common shares and shareholders' equity of $2.5 million, before including the common shares and net income expected to be generated by each plan.

Illustration 15-1 ◀

Advantages of debt over equity financing

	1. Shareholder control is not affected. Debt holders do not have voting rights, so shareholders keep full control of the company.
	2. Income tax savings result. Interest expense is deductible for income tax purposes. Dividends are not.
	3. Earnings per share may be higher. Although interest expense reduces net income, earnings per share is often higher under debt financing because no additional common shares are issued.
	4. Return on equity may be higher. Although net income is lower, return on equity is often higher under debt financing because shareholders' equity is proportionately lower than net income.

The effects on earnings per share and return on equity for each plan are shown in Illustration 15-2:

Illustration 15-2 ◀

Comparison of effects of issuing equity vs. debt

	Plan A Issue Equity	Plan B Issue Debt
Income before interest and income tax	$1,500,000	$1,500,000
Interest expense	0	300,000 [6]
Income before income tax	1,500,000	1,200,000
Income tax expense	450,000 [1]	360,000 [7]
Net income	$1,050,000	$ 840,000
Number of shares	300,000 [2]	100,000
Earnings per share	$3.50 [3]	$8.40 [8]
Shareholders' equity	$8,550,000 [4]	$3,340,000 [9]
Return on equity	12% [5]	25% [10]

Calculations:

[1] $30\% \times \$1,500,000 = \$450,000$
[2] $100,000 + 200,000 = 300,000$
[3] $\$1,050,000 \div 300,000 = \$3.50$
[4] $\$2,500,000 + \$5,000,000 + \$1,050,000 = \$8,550,000$
[5] $\$1,050,000 \div \$8,550,000 = 12\%$

[6] $\$5,000,000 \times 6\% = \$300,000$
[7] $30\% \times \$1,200,000 = \$360,000$
[8] $\$840,000 \div 100,000 = \$8.40$
[9] $\$2,500,000 + \$840,000 = \$3,340,000$
[10] $\$840,000 \div \$3,340,000 = 25\%$

Net income is $210,000 ($1,050,000 − $840,000) lower with long-term debt financing. But when this net income is spread over 200,000 fewer shares, earnings per share jumps from $3.50 per share to $8.40 per share. We learned about earnings per share in Chapter 14. Earnings per share is calculated by dividing the net income available for the common shareholders by the weighted average number of shares. For this illustration, we have assumed that the shares were issued for the entire period.

After seeing the effect of debt on earnings per share, one might ask why companies do not rely exclusively on debt financing rather than equity financing. The answer is that debt is riskier than equity because interest must be paid regularly each period and the principal (face value) of the debt must be paid at maturity. If a company is unable to pay its interest or principal, creditors could force the company to sell its assets to repay its liabilities. In contrast, if equity is issued, a company is not required to pay dividends or repay the shareholders' investment.

Even if it is riskier, most companies still choose to issue debt. They do this because money that is borrowed increases earnings per share and it also produces a higher return on equity for the shareholders. You may have heard the saying about "using other people's money to make money." In general, debt can increase the return on equity if the company can borrow at one rate and invest the borrowed money in company operations that earn a higher rate. Borrowing at one rate and investing at a different rate is known as **financial leverage**. Financial leverage is said to be "positive" if the rate of return is higher than the rate of borrowing. It is said to be "negative" if the rate of return is lower than the rate of borrowing.

As we can see in Illustration 15-2, Microsystems' return on equity increases from 12 percent in Plan A, where equity financing is used, to 25 percent in Plan B, where debt financing is used. Even though net income is lower under debt financing, there is much less equity to spread the income across. If equity financing is used, shareholders' equity is $8,550,000. If debt financing is used, shareholders' equity is only $3,340,000. In Chapter 13, we learned that the return on equity ratio is calculated by dividing net income by average shareholders' equity. For this illustration, we have assumed that the shareholders' equity is the average amount.

Each company must decide what the right mix of debt and equity is for its particular circumstances. There is a risk with debt financing, and the risk increases with the amount of debt a company has. The risk that goes with debt must be compared to the return that can be generated by using debt. As we have just seen, earnings per share and the return on equity can improve with the use of debt. Later in this chapter, we will introduce some ratios that will help us evaluate whether a company has too much debt or if the debt is reasonable.

BEFORE YOU GO ON . . .

▶Review It

1. What is the difference between a current and a long-term liability?
2. What are the advantages of debt financing over equity financing?
3. Why can debt financing result in an improved earnings per share and return on equity ratio?

Related exercise material: BE15–1 and E15–1.

Bonds Payable

Animated Tutorials and Videos: Bond Tutorial

Like other kinds of long-term debt, **bonds** represent a promise to repay a principal amount at a specific maturity date. In addition, periodic interest is paid (normally semi-annually) at a specified rate on the principal amount. Bonds are also similar to shares: they are sold to, and purchased by, investors on organized securities exchanges. Unlike Concordia University's bonds, which had a minimum purchase of $150,000 and were aimed at large investors, bonds are usually sold in small denominations ($1,000 or multiples of $1,000). As a result, bonds attract many investors.

Bond credit-rating agencies help investors assess the risk level or creditworthiness of bonds. The highest-quality bonds are graded as AAA bonds; superior quality as AA; and good quality as A. The Dominion Bond Rating Service gave the Concordia University bonds in the feature story an A rating. The credit-rating scale goes down to C, and finally to the D or default category. Generally, bonds rated below BBB (or its equivalent) are called junk bonds. Junk bonds are considered speculative and have a higher risk of default (of not being repaid).

Moody's Investors Service also adds numbers (1, 2, and 3) to each grade category from A to C to distinguish credit risk even more. The Concordia University bonds were rated A1 by Moody's, which indicates that the bonds are of good quality and have a low credit risk.

Credit ratings are linked to interest rates. Normally, the higher the credit rating, the lower the interest rate. For example, banks normally pay 2 or 3 percent on a term deposit, because there is almost no risk. On the other hand, a corporate bond rated AAA might pay 5 or 6 percent. A corporate bond rated BBB will likely have to pay an even higher rate—say 9 or 10 percent—because the risk is higher. Interest rates vary with risk, but they also vary with duration, the general state of the economy, and many other factors. So, although some interest rates have been given here as examples, they may be quite different right now in practice.

ACCOUNTING IN ACTION ▶ Business Insight

In the debt markets, 2005 will go down as the year the rest of the world discovered Canadian bonds. In fact, it was a record-setting year, with $96.5 billion of corporate bonds sold in 305 separate bond issues. Banks dominated the corporate bond deals, as they issued 67 percent of the bonds that were sold. Almost all the bonds that were sold were of high investment quality—less than 4 percent were rated as junk (less than BBB).

Source: Andrew Willis, "World Beat a Path to Canadian Bonds in 2005," *The Globe and Mail*, January 19, 2006, B9.

? **What is the likely reason that corporations, and banks in particular, were so interested in selling bonds in 2005?**

Bond Basics

In the next few sections, we will look at some basic questions about bonds, including how they are issued and traded. We will also show you how to calculate market value and introduce you to some different types of bonds.

Issuing Procedures

In a corporation, approval by the board of directors is required before bonds can be issued. In authorizing the bond issue, the board of directors must state the number of bonds to be authorized, the total face value, the contractual interest rate, and the maturity date. As happens with issues of share capital, the total bond authorization is often more than the number of bonds actually issued. This is done intentionally to help ensure that the company will have the flexibility it needs to meet future cash requirements by selling more bonds.

The **face value** is the amount of principal that the company (known as the issuer) must pay at the maturity date. The **contractual interest rate** is the rate that is used to determine the amount of interest the borrower pays and the investor receives. Usually, the contractual rate is stated as an annual rate and interest is paid semi-annually. For example, the contractual interest rate on Concordia University's bonds is 6.55 percent a year, but interest is paid semi-annually at a rate of 3.275 percent ($6.55\% \times \frac{6}{12}$). The **maturity date** is the date when the final payment is due to the investor from the company. The maturity date for Concordia University's bonds is September 2, 2042. All of these details are included in a **bond certificate**, which is issued to investors to provide evidence of an investor's credit claim against the company.

Alternative terminology
Face value is also called *par value*. The contractual interest rate is commonly known as the *coupon interest rate* or *stated interest rate*.

Bond Trading

Corporate bonds, like share capital, are traded on organized securities exchanges. Thus, bondholders have the opportunity to convert their bonds into cash at any time by selling the bonds at the current market price. The following illustration shows one example of bond prices and yields, which are published daily in the financial press:

Issuer	Coupon	Maturity Date	Price	Yield
Bell CDA	6.100	2035-Mar-16	103.20	5.87

This bond listing for Bell Canada (Bell CDA) bonds indicates that these bonds have a contractual (coupon) interest rate of 6.1 percent per year. However, as is the norm, interest is paid semi-annually at a rate of 3.05 percent (6.1% × %₁₂). The listing also states that the bonds mature on March 16, 2035.

Bond prices are quoted as a percentage of the face value of the bonds, which are usually sold in denominations of $1,000. You can assume that bonds are issued in $1,000 denominations unless you are told otherwise. In this particular case, the price of 103.2 means $1,032 ($1,000 × 103.2%) was the selling price of the bonds on the date of the above listing. The yield, or market interest rate, on the bonds is 5.87 percent. Note that because the market interest rate is lower than the contractual interest rate, these bonds are currently selling at a premium. We will learn more about market interest rates and bond premiums in the next section.

As is the case with share transactions, transactions between a bondholder and other investors are not journalized by the issuing corporation. If Vinod Thakkar sells his Bell Canada bonds to Julie Tarrel, the issuing corporation, Bell Canada, does not journalize the transaction. While the issuer (or its trustee) does keep records of the names of bondholders in the case of registered bonds, a corporation only makes journal entries when it issues or buys back bonds and pays interest.

Helpful hint Bonds are normally in denominations of $1,000, but they can be of any value, such as $100 or $5,000 or $10,000.

Determining the Market Value of Bonds

If you were an investor wanting to purchase a bond, how would you determine how much to pay? To be more specific, assume that Candlestick Inc. issues a zero-interest bond (pays no interest) with a face value of $1 million due in five years. For this bond, the only cash you receive is a million dollars at the end of five years. Would you pay a million dollars for this bond? We hope not! A million dollars received five years from now is not the same as a million dollars received today.

The reason you should not pay a million dollars relates to the **time value of money**. If you had a million dollars today, you could invest it. From that investment, you would earn interest. At the end of five years, your investment would be worth much more than a million dollars. If someone were going to pay you a million dollars five years from now, you would want to find out its equivalent today. In other words, you would want to determine how much must be invested today at current interest rates to have a million dollars in five years. That amount—what must be invested today at a specific rate of interest over a specific amount of time—is called the **present value**.

The present value of a bond is the value at which it should sell in the marketplace. Market value, therefore, depends on the three factors that determine present value: (1) the dollar amounts to be received, (2) the length of time until the amounts are received, and (3) the market interest rate. The **market interest rate** is the rate that investors demand for lending their money. This rate is also commonly known as the effective interest rate or yield. The process of finding the present value is called discounting the future amounts.

To illustrate, assume that on January 1, 2008, Candlestick issues $1 million of 5-percent bonds due in five years, with interest payable semi-annually. The purchaser of the bonds would receive two cash inflows: (1) the principal of $1 million to be paid at maturity, and (2) ten $25,000 interest payments ($1,000,000 × 5% × %₁₂) received semi-annually over the term of the bonds. Illustration 15-3 shows the time diagram for both cash flows.

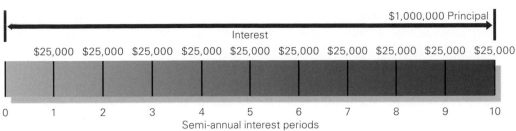

Illustration 15-3 ◀

Time diagram of bond cash flows

The current market value of a bond is equal to the present value of all the future cash flows promised by the bond. If we assume that the contractual interest rate on the Candlestick bonds is the same as the market interest rate, the present values of these amounts are as shown below:

Present value of $1 million received in 10 periods	
$1,000,000 × 0.78120 (n = 10, i = 2.5%)*	$ 781,200
Present value of $25,000 received for each of 10 periods	
$25,000 × 8.75206 (n = 10, i = 2.5%)	218,800
Present value (market price) of bonds	$1,000,000
* Where *n* = number of interest periods and *i* = interest rate.	

There are standard tables to determine the present value factors that are used (e.g., 0.78120 and 8.75206). We have reproduced these tables in Appendix 15B and you should look at them as you read the following procedures for calculating the present value of a bond:

1. Use table 1 (the present value of $1) to determine the right factor to use to calculate the present value of the principal, which is a single sum.
2. Use table 2 (the present value of an annuity of $1) to calculate the present value of the interest, which recurs periodically (annuity).
3. To find the right factor in each table, locate the factor at the intersection of the number of periods and the interest rate. When interest is paid semi-annually, remember to double the number of periods and halve the annual interest rate. For example, in our Candlestick example above, the five-year term of the bonds means that there are 10 semi-annual interest periods. In addition, the annual interest rate of 5 percent becomes 2.5 percent (5% × $\frac{6}{12}$) when adjusted for the semi-annual period.
4. The face value of the bonds and the contractual interest rate are used to calculate the interest payment. Note that while the contractual interest rate is used to determine the interest payment, the market interest rate is what is used to determine the present value.

Present value can also be determined mathematically using a financial calculator or spreadsheet program such as Excel. There is further discussion of present value concepts in the website for this textbook.

The present value illustration above assumed that the contractual interest rate paid on the bonds and the market interest rate were the same. The present value of the bonds always equals the face value when the two rates are the same, as was assumed in this case. However, market interest rates change daily. They are influenced by the type of bond issued, the state of the economy, current industry conditions, and the company's performance. The contractual and market interest rates are often quite different. As a result, bonds sell below or above face value.

To illustrate, suppose that investors have one of two options: (1) purchase bonds that have just been issued with a contractual interest rate of 6 percent, or (2) purchase bonds issued at an earlier date with a lower contractual interest rate of 5 percent. If the bonds are of equal risk,

Study Aids:
Present Value Concepts

investors will choose the 6-percent investment. To make the investments equal, investors will therefore demand a rate of interest higher than the 5-percent contractual interest rate provided in option 2. But investors cannot change the contractual interest rate. What they can do, instead, is pay less than the face value for the bonds. By paying less for the bonds, investors can effectively get the market interest rate of 6 percent. In these cases, bonds sell at a **discount**.

On the other hand, the market interest rate may be lower than the contractual interest rate. In that case, investors will have to pay more than face value for the bonds. That is, if the market interest rate is 4 percent and the contractual interest rate is 5 percent, the issuer will require more funds from the investors. In these cases, bonds sell at a **premium**. You will recall that the Bell Canada bonds described earlier in the chapter sold at a premium because the market interest rate was 5.87 percent while the contractual interest rate was 6.1 percent. The relationship between bond contractual interest rates and market interest rates, and the resultant selling price, is shown in Illustration 15-4.

Illustration 15-4 ▶

Interest rates and bond prices

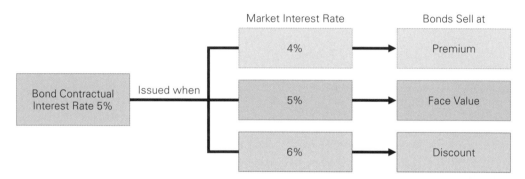

Issuing bonds at an amount different from face value is quite common. By the time a company prints the bond certificates and markets the bonds, it will be a coincidence if the market rate and the contractual rate are the same. Thus, the sale of bonds at a discount does not mean that the issuer's financial strength is suspect. Nor does the sale of bonds at a premium indicate superior financial strength.

Types of Bonds

There are many different kinds of bonds. Some of the more common types of bonds are described below.

Secured and Unsecured Bonds. Secured bonds have specific assets of the issuer pledged as collateral for the bonds. **Unsecured bonds** are issued against the general credit of the borrower. There are no assets used as collateral. These bonds, also called **debenture bonds**, are used by large corporations with good credit ratings. For example, Concordia University's bonds are unsecured debenture bonds.

Term and Serial Bonds. Bonds that mature (are due for payment) at a single specified future date are called **term bonds**. In contrast, bonds that mature in instalments are called **serial bonds**. The Concordia University bonds in the feature story are term bonds, due in 40 years.

Registered and Bearer Bonds. Bonds issued with the name of the owner are called **registered bonds**. Interest payments on registered bonds are made by cheque or direct deposit to registered bondholders. Canada Savings Bonds, issued by the federal government each fall, are an example of registered bonds. Bonds that are not registered are called **bearer (or coupon) bonds**. Holders of bearer bonds must send in coupons to receive interest payments. Bearer bonds may be transferred directly to another party. In contrast, the transfer of registered bonds requires the cancellation of the bonds by the institution and the issue of new bonds. Most bonds that are issued today are registered bonds.

Convertible Bonds. Bonds that can be converted into shares by the bondholder are called **convertible bonds**. Convertible bonds have features that are attractive to both the bondholder and the issuer. The conversion gives bondholders an opportunity to benefit if the market price of the common shares increases. The bondholder also receives interest on the bond until a decision is made to convert it. For the issuer, the bonds sell at a higher price and pay a lower rate of interest than similar debt securities that do not have a conversion option.

Because convertible bonds have both debt and equity features, these are considered to be a complex type of financial instrument. Accounting for complex financial instruments such as these is left to an intermediate accounting course.

Redeemable/Retractable Bonds. Bonds that can be retired (redeemed) by the issuer at a stated dollar amount before they mature are known as **redeemable bonds** or callable bonds. **Retractable bonds** are bonds which can be retired before maturity by the bondholder. Both redeemable and retractable bonds can be retired at a specified amount before they mature. The key distinction is that redeemable bonds can be retired at the option of the issuer (the borrower) and retractable bonds can be retired at the option of the bondholder (the investor).

Accounting for Bond Issues

Bonds can be issued at face value, below face value (at a discount), or above face value (at a premium).

Issuing Bonds at Face Value

To illustrate the accounting for bonds, let's continue the example discussed in the last section, where Candlestick Inc. issues five-year, 5-percent, $1 million bonds on January 1, 2008, to yield a market interest rate of 5 percent. We say that these bonds are issued at 100 (100% of face value) because the contractual interest rate and the market interest rate are the same.

The entry to record the sale is as follows:

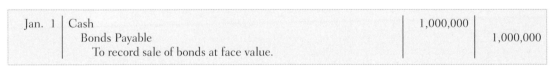

Jan. 1	Cash	1,000,000	
	Bonds Payable		1,000,000
	To record sale of bonds at face value.		

A = L + SE
+1,000,000 +1,000,000

⬆ Cash flows: +1,000,000

These bonds payable are reported in the long-term liabilities section of the balance sheet because the maturity date (January 1, 2013) is more than one year away.

Over the term (life) of the bonds, entries are required for bond interest. The interest payment on bonds payable is calculated in the same way as interest on notes payable, as explained in Chapter 10. Interest is payable semi-annually on January 1 and July 1 on the bonds described above. Interest of $25,000 ($1,000,000 × 5% × $\frac{6}{12}$) must be paid on July 1, 2008, the first interest payment date. The entry for the interest payment, assuming no previous accrual of interest, is:

July 1	Bond Interest Expense	25,000	
	Cash		25,000
	To record payment of bond interest.		

A = L + SE
−25,000   −25,000

⬇ Cash flows: −25,000

At December 31, Candlestick's year end, an adjusting entry is needed to recognize the $25,000 of interest expense incurred since July 1. The entry is as follows:

A	=	L	+	SE
		+25,000		−25,000

Cash flows: no effect

Dec. 31	Bond Interest Expense	25,000	
	Bond Interest Payable		25,000
	To accrue bond interest.		

Bond interest payable is classified as a current liability because it is scheduled for payment within the next year (in fact, it is due the next day in this case). When the interest is paid on January 1, 2009, Bond Interest Payable is debited and Cash is credited for $25,000.

Issuing Bonds at a Discount

To illustrate the issue of bonds at a discount (below face value), assume that on January 1, 2008, the Candlestick bonds are issued to yield a market interest rate of 6 percent rather than 5 percent, as we assumed in the previous section.

Using the present value tables in Appendix 15B, we can determine that the bonds will sell for $957,345. The selling price (present value) is determined as follows:

Present value of $1 million received in 10 periods	
$1,000,000 × 0.74409 ($n = 10$, $i = 3\%$)*	$744,090
Present value of $25,000 received for each of 10 periods	
$25,000 × 8.53020 ($n = 10$, $i = 3\%$)	213,255
Present value (market price) of bonds	$957,345
*Where n = number of interest periods and i = interest rate	

Sometimes you will be asked to calculate the market price as we have done above. Other times, you will be told that the bonds have been issued at a stated percentage amount (95.7345 in this situation), in which case you can calculate the market price by multiplying this percentage by the face value ($1 million × 95.7345% = $957,345). Regardless, you will end up with the same issue price—$957,345 in this case.

The market price of $957,345 results in a bond discount of $42,655 ($1,000,000 − $957,345). The entry to record the bond issue is as follows:

A	=	L	+	SE
+957,345		−42,655		
		+1,000,000		

↑ Cash flows: +957,345

Jan. 1	Cash	957,345	
	Discount on Bonds Payable ($1,000,000 − $957,345)	42,655	
	Bonds Payable		1,000,000
	To record sale of bonds at a discount.		

Although the Discount on Bonds Payable account has a debit balance, it is not an asset. Rather, it is a contra liability account. This account is deducted from bonds payable on the balance sheet, as shown below:

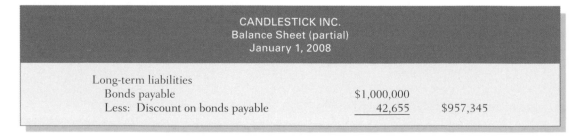

CANDLESTICK INC.
Balance Sheet (partial)
January 1, 2008

Long-term liabilities		
Bonds payable	$1,000,000	
Less: Discount on bonds payable	42,655	$957,345

The $957,345 represents the carrying (or book) value of the bonds. On the date of issue, this amount equals the market price of the bonds.

When a corporation issues bonds at a discount, the total cost of borrowing is higher than the bond interest paid. That is, the issuing corporation must pay not only the contractual interest rate over the term of the bonds, but it must also repay the face value (rather than the issue price) at maturity. Therefore, the difference between the issue price ($957,345) and the face value ($1,000,000) of the bonds—the discount ($42,655)—is an additional cost of borrowing. Candlestick must repay $1 million at maturity even though it only received $957,345 from the sale of the bonds.

To follow the matching principle, the total cost of borrowing—the interest payment and bond discount—must be allocated to interest expense over the life of the bonds. The interest payment, $25,000, is recorded as one component of the interest expense every semi-annual period for five years (10 semi-annual periods). The bond discount is also allocated to interest expense over the 10 semi-annual periods—this allocation is called **amortizing the discount**.

The discounts (and premiums, which will be discussed in the next section) on all financial liabilities, such as bonds payable, must be amortized using the effective-interest method of amortization. We will explain this method in detail in Appendix 15A of this chapter. For now, we will assume that the discount amortization is 3,720 for the first interest period. Consequently, interest expense is the total of the interest payment ($25,000) and the discount amortization (3,720).

We record the interest expense, amortization of the discount, and payment of interest on the first interest payment date, July 1, as follows:

July 1	Interest Expense	28,720	
	Discount on Bonds Payable		3,720
	Cash		25,000
	To record semi-annual interest payment.		

As the discount is amortized, its balance will decline until it reaches zero at maturity. Therefore, the carrying value of the bonds will increase until at maturity the carrying value of the bonds equals their face value.

Issuing Bonds at a Premium

To illustrate the issue of bonds at a premium (above face value), assume that on January 1, 2008, the Candlestick bonds are issued to yield a market interest rate of 4 percent rather than 5 percent, as we assumed in the previous section. Using the present value tables in Appendix 15B, we can determine that the bonds will sell for $1,044,915. The selling price (present value) is determined as follows:

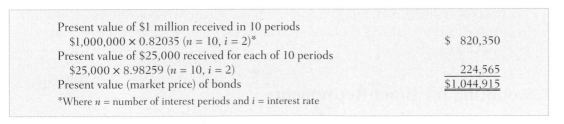

We could also say that these bonds have been issued at 104.4915 (104.4915% of face value). This market price results in a premium of $44,915 ($1,044,915 − $1,000,000).

The entry to record the sale would be as follows:

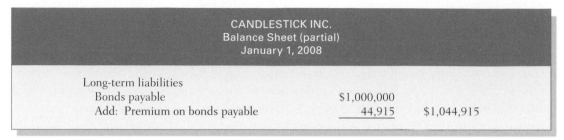

Jan. 1	Cash	1,044,915	
	Bonds Payable ($1,044,915 – $1,000,000)		1,000,000
	Premium on Bonds Payable		44,915
	To record sale of bonds at a premium.		

A premium on bonds payable is added to bonds payable on the balance sheet, as shown below:

Helpful hint A discount account is a contra account (its balance is deducted from Bonds Payable). A premium account is an adjunct account (its balance is added to the balance of Bonds Payable).

CANDLESTICK INC.
Balance Sheet (partial)
January 1, 2008

Long-term liabilities		
Bonds payable	$1,000,000	
Add: Premium on bonds payable	44,915	$1,044,915

The sale of bonds above face value causes the total cost of borrowing to be less than the bond interest paid. The bond premium is considered a reduction in the cost of borrowing. Candlestick must only repay $1 million at maturity, even though it received $1,044,915 from the sale of the bonds.

To follow the matching principle, the total cost of borrowing—the interest payment and bond premium—must be allocated to interest expense over the life of the bonds. The interest payment, $25,000, is recorded as one component of the interest expense every semi-annual period for five years (10 semi-annual periods). The bond premium is also allocated as a reduction of interest expense over the 10 semi-annual periods—this allocation is called **amortizing the premium**.

To illustrate the recording of the interest expense and amortization of the premium on the first interest payment date, we will assume that the premium amortization is $4,102. Consequently, interest expense is the interest payment ($25,000) reduced by the premium amortization ($4,102). It is recorded as follows:

A = L + SE
–25,000 –4,102 –20,898

↓ Cash flows: –25,000

July 1	Interest Expense	20,898	
	Premium on Bonds Payable	4,102	
	Cash		25,000
	To record semi-annual interest payment.		

The same method—the effective-interest method—used to allocate bond discounts is also used to allocate bond premiums to interest expense. This method is described in Appendix 15A of this chapter, where we also show how the $4,102 premium amortization amount is calculated.

As the premium is amortized, its balance will decline until it reaches zero at maturity. Therefore, the carrying value of the bonds will decrease until at maturity the carrying value of the bonds equals their face value.

Accounting for Bond Retirements

Bonds may be retired either (1) when they mature, or (2) when the issuing corporation purchases them from the bondholders on the open market before they mature. Some bonds have special redemption provisions that allow them to be retired before they mature. As we learned earlier in this chapter, **redeemable bonds** can be retired at a stated dollar amount at the option of the company.

These retirement options are explained in the following sections.

Redeeming Bonds at Maturity

Regardless of the issue price of bonds, the carrying value of the bonds at maturity will equal their face value. By the time the bonds mature, any discount or premium will be fully amortized and will have a zero balance.

Assuming that the interest for the last interest period has been paid and recorded, the entry to record the redemption of the Candlestick bonds at maturity, January 1, 2013, is as follows:

Jan. 1	Bonds Payable	1,000,000	
	Cash		1,000,000
	To record redemption of bonds at maturity.		

Because the carrying value of the bonds equals the face value at maturity, there is no gain or loss.

Redeeming Bonds before Maturity

Why would a company want to have the option to retire its bonds early? If interest rates drop, it can be a good idea financially to retire the bond issue and replace it with a new bond issue at a lower interest rate. Or, a company may become financially able to repay its debt earlier than expected. When a company purchases non-redeemable bonds on the open market, it pays the going market price. If the bonds are redeemable, the company will pay the bondholders an amount that was specified at the time of issue, known as the redemption (or call) price. To make the bonds more attractive to investors, the redemption price is usually a few percentage points above the face value.

To record the redemption of bonds, it is necessary to (1) update any unrecorded interest, (2) eliminate the carrying value of the bonds at the redemption date, (3) record the cash paid, and (4) recognize the gain or loss on redemption.

Interest must be updated if the bonds are redeemed between semi-annual interest payment dates. The carrying value of the bonds is the face value of the bonds less the unamortized bond discount, or plus the unamortized bond premium, at the redemption date. So two accounts must be removed from the books in order to eliminate the carrying value: the Bonds Payable account and any related discount or premium account. There is a gain on redemption when the cash paid is less than the carrying value of the bonds. There is a loss on redemption when the cash paid is more than the carrying value of the bonds.

To illustrate, assume that Candlestick sells its bonds at a premium as described in the last section. It retires its bonds at 103 at the end of the fourth year (eighth period) after paying the semi-annual interest. Assume also that the carrying value of the bonds at the redemption date is $1,009,709. That is, the face value of the bonds is $1,000,000 and the unamortized premium is $9,709. The entry to record the redemption on January 1, 2012 (end of the eighth interest period) is:

Jan. 1	Bonds Payable	1,000,000	
	Premium on Bonds Payable	9,709	
	Loss on Bond Redemption	20,291	
	Cash ($1,000,000 × 103%)		1,030,000
	To record redemption of bonds at 103.		

The loss of $20,291 is the difference between the cash paid of $1,030,000 and the carrying value of the bonds of $1,009,709. This is very similar to the calculation of a loss or gain on the sale of property, plant, and equipment. In both cases, cash is compared to carrying value. However, the determination of whether a loss or a gain results is of course different, depending on whether you are selling property, plant, and equipment (assets) or purchasing bonds (liabilities). For example, when you sell an asset, you gain when the cash received is greater than the carrying value. When you retire a liability, you gain when the cash paid is less than the carrying value. These differences are shown in Illustration 15-5.

Illustration 15-5 ▶

Comparison of asset and liability gain and loss

Property, Plant, and Equipment	Bonds Payable
Sale price	Redemption price
– Carrying value	– Carrying value
Gain (loss)	Loss (gain)

Similar to gains and losses on the sale of property, plant, and equipment, gains and losses on bond redemption are reported separately in the income statement as other expenses or other revenues.

BEFORE YOU GO ON . . .

▶Review It

1. How is the market price of bonds determined?
2. Why do bonds sell at a discount? At a premium? At face value?
3. Explain the differences between each of these types of bonds: secured versus unsecured, term versus serial, registered versus bearer, and redeemable versus retractable.
4. Explain why bond discounts and premiums are amortized.
5. Explain the accounting for the redemption of bonds at maturity and before maturity.

▶Do It

On January 1, 2005, R & B Inc. issues $500,000 of 10-year, 4% bonds at 92.2. Interest is paid semi-annually on January 1 and July 1. On July 1, 2009, the company records the semi-annual interest and amortization (the semi-annual amortization amount for this period is $1,859). On this same date, the company redeems the bonds at 99. The carrying value of the bonds is $476,214 on this date. Prepare the entry to record (a) the issue of the bonds on January 1, 2005, (b) the payment of interest and amortization of any bond discount or premium on July 1, 2009, and (c) the redemption of the bonds on July 1, 2009.

Action Plan

- Apply the issue price as a percentage (e.g., 92.2%) to the face value of the bonds to determine the proceeds that are received.
- Record a discount as a contra liability (debit) account and a premium as an adjunct liability (credit) account.
- Amortization of a bond discount increases interest expense while amortization of a bond premium decreases interest expense.
- To record the redemption, do the following: (1) Update any partial period interest and amortization, if required. (2) Eliminate the carrying value of the bonds and remove the balances from the Bonds Payable account and any discount or premium account. (3) Record the cash paid. (4) Calculate and record the gain or loss (the difference between the cash paid and the carrying value).

Solution

(a)

Jan. 1, 2005	Cash ($500,000 × 92.2%)	461,000	
	Discount on Bonds Payable	39,000	
	Bonds Payable		500,000
	To record issue of bonds at 92.2.		

(b)

July 1, 2009	Interest Expense ($10,000 + $1,859)	11,859	
	Discount on Bonds Payable		1,859
	Cash ($500,000 × 4% × $^6\!/_{12}$)		10,000
	To record payment of interest and amortization of		
	discount.		

(c)

July 1, 2009	Bonds Payable	500,000	
	Loss on Bond Redemption ($495,000 − $476,214)	18,786	
	Discount on Bonds Payable ($500,000 − $476,214)		23,786
	Cash ($500,000 × 99%)		495,000
	To record redemption of bonds at 99.		

Related exercise material: BE15–2, BE15–3, BE15–4, BE15–5, BE15–6, E15–2, E15–3, E15–4, and E15–5.

the navigator

Notes Payable

You will recall that we first learned about notes payable in Chapter 10, where they were included as an example of a current liability. Long-term notes payable are similar to short-term notes payable except that the terms of the notes are for more than one year.

Notes and bonds are also quite similar. Both have a fixed maturity date and pay interest. However, whereas bonds have a contractual or fixed interest rate, notes may have either a fixed interest rate or a floating interest rate. A **fixed interest rate** is constant for the entire term of the note. A **floating (or variable) interest rate** changes as market rates change. A floating interest rate is often based on the prime borrowing rate. Prime is the interest rate that banks charge their most creditworthy customers. This rate is usually increased by a specified percentage that matches the risk profile of the company—in other words, it depends on how risky the company is judged to be.

Similar to bonds, a long-term note may be unsecured or secured. A secured note pledges title to specific assets as security for the loan, often known as collateral. Secured notes are commonly known as mortgages. A **mortgage note payable** is widely used by individuals to purchase homes. It is also used by many companies to acquire property, plant, and equipment. Unsecured notes are issued against the general credit of the borrower. There are no assets used as collateral.

One difference between notes and bonds is that bonds are often traded on a stock exchange as shares are. Notes are rarely traded on stock exchanges. Small and large corporations issue notes, whereas only large corporations issue bonds. You will recall that bonds help a company borrow when the amount of financing is too large for one lender.

While short-term notes and bonds are normally repayable in full at maturity, most long-term notes are repayable in a series of periodic payments. These payments are known as instalments and are paid monthly, quarterly, semi-annually, or at another defined period. Each payment consists of (1) interest on the unpaid balance of the loan, and (2) a reduction of loan principal. Payments generally take one of two forms: (1) fixed principal payments plus interest, or (2) blended principal and interest payments. Let's look at each of these payment patterns in more detail.

Fixed Principal Payments

Instalment notes with fixed principal payments are repayable in **equal periodic amounts, plus interest**. To illustrate, assume that on January 1, 2008, Bélanger Ltée issues a $120,000, 5-year, 7-percent note payable to finance a new research laboratory. The entry to record the issue of the note payable is as follows:

A	=	L	+	SE
+120,000		+120,000		

↑ Cash flows: +120,000

Jan. 1	Cash	120,000	
	Notes Payable		120,000
	To record 5-year, 7% note payable.		

The terms of the note provide for equal monthly instalment payments of $2,000 ($120,000 ÷ 60 monthly periods) on the first of each month, plus interest of 7 percent on the outstanding principal balance. Monthly interest expense is calculated by multiplying the outstanding principal balance by the interest rate. The calculation of interest expense for notes payable is similar to that of bonds payable—both use the effective-interest method.

For the first payment date—February 1—interest expense is $700 ($120,000 × 7% × $\frac{1}{12}$). Note that the 7 percent is an annual interest rate and must be adjusted for the monthly time period. The cash payment of $2,700 for the month of February is the sum of the instalment payment, $2,000, which is applied against the principal, plus the interest, $700.

The entry to record the first instalment payment on February 1 is as follows:

A	=	L	+	SE
−2,700		−2,000		−700

↓ Cash flows: −2,700

Feb. 1	Interest Expense ($120,000 × 7% × $\frac{1}{12}$)	700	
	Notes Payable	2,000	
	Cash ($2,000 + $700)		2,700
	To record monthly payment on note.		

An instalment payment schedule is a useful tool to help organize this information and assist in the preparation of journal entries. The instalment payment schedule for the first few months for Bélanger Ltée, rounded to the nearest dollar, is shown in Illustration 15-6.

Illustration 15-6 ▶

Instalment payment schedule—fixed principal payments

	BÉLANGER LTÉE			
	Instalment Payment Schedule—Fixed Principal Payments			
	(A)	(B)	(C)	(D)
Interest Period	Cash Payment (B + C)	Interest Expense (D × 7% × $\frac{1}{12}$)	Reduction of Principal ($120,000 ÷ 60)	Principal Balance (D − C)
Jan. 1				$120,000
Feb. 1	$2,700	$700	$2,000	118,000
Mar. 1	2,688	688	2,000	116,000
Apr. 1	2,677	677	2,000	114,000

Column A, the cash payment, is the total of the instalment payment, $2,000, plus the interest. The cash payment changes each period because the interest amount changes. Column B determines the interest expense, which decreases each period because the principal balance, on which interest is calculated, decreases. Column C is the instalment payment of $2,000, which is applied against the principal. The instalment payment (the reduction of the principal) is constant each period in a "fixed principal payment" pattern. Column D is the principal balance, which decreases each period by the amount of the instalment payment.

In summary, with fixed principal payments, the interest decreases each period (as the principal decreases). The portion applied to the reduction of loan principal stays constant, but because of the decreasing interest, the total cash payment decreases.

Blended Payments

Instalment notes with blended payments are repayable in **equal periodic amounts that include the principal and the interest**. With blended payments, the amount of interest and principal that is applied to the loan changes with each payment. Specifically, as happens with fixed principal payments, the interest decreases each period (as the principal decreases). In contrast to fixed principal payments, however, the portion that is applied to the loan principal increases each period.

To illustrate, assume that instead of fixed principal payments, Bélanger Ltée repays its $120,000 note payable in blended payments of $2,376 each month. As with the fixed principal payments illustrated in the previous section, monthly interest expense is calculated by multiplying the outstanding principal balance by the interest rate. For the first payment date— February 1—interest expense is $700 ($120,000 × 7% × 1/12 months). The instalment payment of $2,376 is fixed for each month, and includes interest and principal amounts which will vary. In February, the principal balance will be reduced by $1,676, which is the difference between the instalment payment of $2,376 and the interest amount of $700.

The entry to record the issue of the note payable is the same as in the previous section. The amounts in the journal entry to record the instalment payment on February 1 change as follows:

Feb. 1	Interest Expense ($120,000 × 7% × 1/12)	700	
	Notes Payable ($2,376 − $700)	1,676	
	Cash		2,376
	To record monthly payment on note.		

A	=	L	+	SE
−2,376		−1,676		−700

↓ Cash flows: −2,376

An instalment payment schedule can also be prepared for blended principal and interest payments. Illustration 15-7 shows the instalment payment schedule for the first few months for Bélanger Ltée, rounded to the nearest dollar.

BÉLANGER LTÉE Instalment Payment Schedule—Blended Payments				
Interest Period	(A) Cash Payment	(B) Interest Expense (D × 7% × 1/12)	(C) Reduction of Principal (A − B)	(D) Principal Balance (D − C)
Jan. 1				$120,000
Feb. 1	$2,376	$700	$1,676	118,324
Mar. 1	2,376	690	1,686	116,638
Apr. 1	2,376	680	1,696	114,942

Illustration 15-7 ◄

Instalment payment schedule—blended payments

Column A, the cash payment, is specified and is the same for each period. The amount of this cash payment can be calculated using present value techniques discussed earlier in the chapter and in the companion website to this textbook. Column B determines the interest expense, which decreases each period because the principal balance on which interest is

Study Aids:
Present Value Concepts

calculated also decreases. Column C is the amount by which the principal is reduced. This is the difference between the cash payment of $2,376 and the interest for the period. Consequently, this amount will increase each period. Column D is the principal balance, which decreases each period by an increasing amount, that is, by the reduction of the principal amount from Column C.

In summary, with blended payments, the interest decreases each period as the principal decreases. The cash payment stays constant, but because of the decreasing interest, the reduction of principal increases.

There are two key differences between a fixed principal payment and a blended payment schedule. With a fixed principal payment, the cash payment varies; with a blended payment, it is constant. Second, with a fixed principal payment, the reduction of principal is a constant amount; with a blended payment, it increases. The interest expense changes each period in both payment situations because the principal balance varies.

With both types of instalment notes payable, as with any other long-term note payable, the reduction in principal for the next year must be reported as a current liability, and is normally called "Current portion of long-term note payable." The remaining unpaid principal is classified as a long-term liability. No journal entry is necessary; it is simply a reclassification of amounts for the balance sheet.

BEFORE YOU GO ON . . .

▶Review It

1. What is the difference between short-term and long-term notes payable?
2. What is the difference between bonds and notes payable?
3. Why is the cash payment different each period for a note with fixed principal payments?
4. How is the reduction of principal different in a note with fixed principal payments compared to a note with blended payments?

▶Do It

On December 31, 2007, Tian Inc. issued a $500,000, 15-year, 8% mortgage note payable. The terms provide for semi-annual blended payments of $28,915, on June 30 and December 31. (a) Prepare an instalment payment schedule for the first two years of the note (through to December 31, 2009). (b) Prepare the journal entries required to record the issue of the note on December 31, 2007, and the first two instalment payments. (c) Show the presentation of the liability on the balance sheet at December 31, 2008.

Action Plan

- For the instalment payment schedule, multiply the interest rate by the principal balance at the beginning of the period to determine the interest expense. Remember to adjust for the partial period ($^6/_{12}$ months). The reduction of principal is the difference between the cash payment and the interest expense.
- Record the mortgage payments, recognizing that each blended payment consists of (1) interest on the unpaid loan balance, and (2) a reduction of the loan principal.
- Remember to separate the current and long-term portions of the note so that they are presented correctly in the balance sheet. The current portion is the amount of principal that will be repaid in the next year.

Solution

(a)

Interest Period	Cash Payment	Interest Expense	Reduction of Principal	Principal Balance
Dec. 31, 2007				$500,000
June 30, 2008	$28,915	$20,000	$8,915	491,085
Dec. 31, 2008	28,915	19,643	9,272	481,813
June 30, 2009	28,915	19,273	9,642	472,171
Dec. 31, 2009	28,915	18,887	10,028	462,143

(b)

Dec. 31, 2007	Cash	500,000	
	Mortgage Note Payable		500,000
	To record issue of 15-year, 8% mortgage note payable.		
June 30, 2008	Interest Expense ($500,000 × 8% × $\frac{6}{12}$)	20,000	
	Mortgage Note Payable ($28,915 − $20,000)	8,915	
	Cash		28,915
	To record semi-annual payment on note.		
Dec. 31, 2008	Interest Expense [($500,000 − $8,915) × 8% × $\frac{6}{12}$]	19,643	
	Mortgage Note Payable ($28,915 − $19,643)	9,272	
	Cash		28,915
	To record semi-annual payment on note.		

(c)

TIAN INC.
December 31, 2008
Balance Sheet (partial)

Current liabilities
   Current portion of mortgage note payable ($9,642 + $10,028) $ 19,670
Long-term liabilities
   Mortgage note payable   462,143
Total liabilities $481,813

Related exercise material: BE15–7, BE15–8, BE15–9, E15–6, E15–7, and E15–8.

the navigator

Lease Liabilities

study objective 4
Account for leases.

A lease is a contractual arrangement between two parties. A party that owns an asset (the **lessor**) agrees to allow another party (the **lessee**) to use the specified property for a series of cash payments over an agreed period of time. Why would anyone want to lease property rather than buy it? There are many advantages to leasing an asset instead of purchasing it:

1. **Reduced risk of obsolescence.** Obsolescence is the process by which an asset becomes out of date before it physically wears out. Frequently, lease terms allow the party using the asset (the lessee) to exchange the asset for a more modern or technologically capable asset if it becomes outdated. This is much easier than trying to sell an obsolete asset.
2. **100-percent financing.** To purchase an asset, most companies must borrow money, which usually requires a down payment of at least 20 percent. Leasing an asset does not require any money down, which helps to conserve cash. In addition, interest payments are often fixed for the term of the lease, unlike other financing, which often has a floating interest rate.
3. **Income tax advantages.** When a company owns an amortizable asset, it can only deduct the amortization expense (called capital cost allowance for income tax purposes)

on its income tax return. However, when a company leases an asset, it can deduct 100 percent of the lease payment on its income tax return.

The two main types of leases are operating leases and capital leases, which we will discuss in the next sections.

 ACCOUNTING IN ACTION ▶ Business Insight

British cable company NTL Group Ltd. agreed to buy billionaire entrepreneur Richard Branson's mobile phone company, Virgin Mobile, for U.S. $1.67 billion, just after buying competitor Telewest. This made it Britain's first company to provide cable, wired telephone, high-speed Internet, and cellular telephone services combined. But Virgin Mobile isn't actually a phone company; it is essentially a marketing company. It doesn't really own anything, apart from a brand name and office space with marketing and sales people. Virgin is a "mobile virtual network operator" or MVNO. It doesn't own any network capacity or lines of its own; it leases space on a real phone company's network, in this case T-Mobile, and resells it under its own name. The risk with this type of arrangement is that the MVNO is relying on another company to provide the service it is selling, in most cases, a competitive telecom carrier. If an MVNO gets too large, the carrier might decide to change the terms of the deal. That's why successful MVNOs like Virgin usually offer their telecom partners an equity stake in the company.

Source: Mathew Ingram, "MVNOs: Phone Companies Without the Equipment," *The Globe and Mail*, May 11, 2006.

> **?** What are the advantages to Virgin Mobile of leasing space on a phone company's network rather than developing its own network infrastructure?

Operating Leases

Helpful hint *Financial Reporting in Canada* reports that 75 percent of the companies surveyed have operating leases and 40% have capital leases.

Rental of an apartment and rental of a car are examples of **operating leases**. An operating lease is when there is a temporary use of the property by the lessee, while the lessor continues to own it. The lease (or rental) payments are recorded as an expense by the lessee and as revenue by the lessor. For example, assume that a sales representative for Western Inc. leases a car from Hertz Car Rental at the airport on July 17. Hertz charges a total of $275. The entry by the lessee, Western Inc., would be as follows:

A	=	L	+	SE
−275				−275

↓ Cash flows: −275

July 17	Car Rental Expense	275	
	Cash		275
	To record payment of lease rental charge.		

Many operating leases are short-term, such as the rental of an apartment or car as described above. Others are for an extended period of time. Operating leases that cover a long period of time are sometimes seen as a form of off–balance sheet financing. **Off–balance sheet financing** occurs when liabilities are kept off of a company's balance sheet. Many people argue that if an operating lease results in the long-term use of an asset and an unavoidable obligation, it should be recorded as an asset and a liability. To reduce these concerns, companies are required to report their operating lease obligations in detail in a note to the financial statements. This allows analysts and other financial statement users to adjust ratios such as debt to total assets (which we will learn about later in the next section of this chapter) by adding leased assets and lease liabilities if this treatment is considered more appropriate.

Capital Leases

While operating leases do not result in a recorded asset and liability, capital leases do. In a capital lease contract, all of the benefits and risks of ownership are essentially transferred to the lessee. This kind of lease basically results in a purchase of the property, so it is called a **capital lease**. The name comes from the fact that the present value of the cash payments for the lease is capitalized and recorded as an asset. This is essentially the same as if the company had purchased an asset and financed the purchase by issuing debt.

Capital leases are a good example of the application of the "reliability" characteristic of accounting information. You will recall that we learned about the importance of recording the economic substance of a transaction in Chapter 11. In order for accounting information to be reliable, it must be a faithful representation of the economic substance, and not just the legal form, of the transaction.

The lessee must classify the lease as a capital lease and record the purchase as an asset if any of the following conditions exists:

1. **Transfer of ownership:** If, during or at the end of the lease term, the lease transfers ownership of the asset to the lessee, the leased asset should be recorded as an asset on the lessee's books.
2. **Option to buy:** If, during the term of the lease, the lessee has an option to purchase the asset at a price that is much below its market value (called a bargain purchase option), we can assume that the lessee will choose to use this option. Thus, the leased asset should be recorded as an asset on the lessee's books.
3. **Lease term:** If the lease term is equal to 75 percent or more of the economic life of the leased property, the asset has effectively been purchased and should be recorded as an asset by the lessee.
4. **Purchase price:** If the present value of the lease payments equals or is more than 90 percent of the fair market value of the leased property, the lessee has essentially paid for the asset. As a result, the leased asset should be recorded on the books of the lessee.

To illustrate, assume that Fortune Ltd. decides to lease new equipment on November 27. The lease period is four years and the economic life of the leased equipment is estimated to be five years. The present value of the lease payments is $190,000 and the fair market value of the equipment is $200,000. There is no transfer of ownership during the lease term.

In this example, Fortune has essentially purchased the equipment. Conditions (3) and (4) have both been met. First, the lease term is 80 percent (4 ÷ 5), which is ≥ 75 percent of the economic life of the asset. Second, the present value of cash payments is 95 percent ($190,000 ÷ $200,000), which is ≥ 90 percent of the equipment's fair market value. The present value of the cash payments in a capital lease is calculated in the same way as was explained earlier in the chapter for bond interest payments.

Note that while two conditions were met in this case, only one condition has to be met for the lease to be treated as a capital lease. The entry to record the transaction is as follows:

Nov. 27	Leased Asset—Equipment	190,000	
	Lease Liability		190,000
	To record leased asset and lease liability.		

A	=	L	+	SE
+190,000		+190,000		

Cash flows: no effect

The leased asset is reported on the balance sheet under property, plant, and equipment. The portion of the lease liability that is expected to be paid in the next year is reported as a current liability. The remainder is classified as a long-term liability.

After it is acquired, the leased asset is amortized just as any other long-lived asset is. In addition, the liability is reduced each period by the lease payment. Usually, the payment is allocated between interest expense and the principal amount of the lease liability, which is like what was shown earlier in the chapter for blended principal and interest payments on notes payable.

Illustration 15-8 summarizes the major difference between an operating and a capital lease.

Illustration 15-8 ▶

Types of leases

Operating Lease	Capital Lease
Lessor has substantially all of the benefits and risks of ownership.	**Lessee** has substantially all of the benefits and risks of ownership.

For an operating lease, no asset or liability is reported in the balance sheet. The only expense that is reported in the income statement is rental expense. For a capital lease, both an asset and a liability are reported in the balance sheet. Two expenses—amortization expense and interest expense related to the lease liability—are reported in the income statement.

BEFORE YOU GO ON . . .

▶Review It

1. What is the difference in accounting for an operating lease and a capital lease?
2. Why is an operating lease sometimes considered to be an example of off–balance sheet financing?
3. Does The Forzani Group have any capital and/or operating leases? The answer to this question is at the end of the chapter.

▶Do It

The Alert Company has the following two leasing options to acquire a new machine:

	Lease Option 1	Lease Option 2
Transfer of ownership	No	No
Bargain purchase option	No	No
Lease term	4 years	3 years
Estimated useful life	5 years	5 years
Fair market value	$20,000	$20,000
Present value	$15,000	$15,000

Discuss how each lease option would affect Alert's financial statements.

Action Plan

- Know the four criteria to distinguish between an operating and a capital lease. A lease is considered to be a capital lease if any one of the following conditions are met: (1) transfer of ownership, (2) option to buy, (3) lease term (≥ 75% of economic life), and (4) purchase price (≥ 90% of fair market value).
- Understand the impact of an operating and a capital lease on the income statement and balance sheet. With an operating lease, no asset or liability is recorded; with a capital lease, both an asset and a liability are recorded.

Solution

Lease option 1 would be recorded as a capital lease because the lease term is 80% (4 ÷ 5), which is ≥ 75 percent of the economic life of the machinery. Because of this, an asset and a liability would be reported on the balance sheet. Amortization expense and interest expense would be reported on the income statement.

Lease option 2 would be recorded as an operating lease as none of the four conditions have been met. There would be no impact on the balance sheet, but the lease payments would be reported as rental expense on the income statement.

Related exercise material: BE15–10, BE15–11, and E15–9.

Statement Presentation and Analysis

Liabilities are a significant amount on the financial statements and they have to be disclosed in detail so they can be properly understood by creditors. These and other users are very interested in assessing a company's solvency (its ability to pay) with regard to its long-term liabilities. We will look at the presentation and analysis of liabilities in the next sections.

Presentation

Long-term liabilities are reported in a separate section of the balance sheet, immediately after current liabilities, as here with assumed data:

ANY COMPANY LTD. Balance Sheet (partial) December 31, 2008		
Long-term liabilities		
Bonds payable, 6%, due in 2012	$1,000,000	
Less: Discount on bonds payable	80,000	$ 920,000
Mortgage notes payable, 8%, due in 2018		500,000
Lease liability		540,000
Total long-term liabilities		$1,960,000

Full disclosure of debt is very important. Summary data are usually presented in the balance sheet, and detailed data (interest rate, maturity date, redemption price, convertibility, and any assets pledged as collateral) are shown in a supporting schedule or in the notes to the financial statements. The current maturities of long-term debt should be reported under current liabilities.

Analysis

A company's creditors are interested in analyzing its liquidity and solvency. Short-term creditors are more interested in liquidity ratios, which measure the ability of a company to repay its short-term debt and to meet unexpected needs for cash. We learned about liquidity ratios such as the current ratio, inventory turnover, and receivables turnover in earlier chapters.

Long-term creditors are more interested in solvency ratios, which measure the ability of a company to repay its long-term debt and survive over a long period of time. They are particularly interested in a company's ability to pay interest when it is due and to repay its debt at maturity. Two examples of solvency ratios are debt to total assets and the interest coverage ratio. They are explained next.

Debt to Total Assets

Helpful hint Some users measure the percentage of the total assets that is financed by shareholders. This ratio is called the debt to equity ratio.

Debt to total assets measures the percentage of the total assets that is financed by creditors rather than by shareholders. Financing provided by creditors is riskier than financing provided by shareholders, because debt must be repaid at specific points in time whether the company is doing well or not.

Illustration 15-9 shows how the debt to total assets ratio is calculated. Using data from Forzani's financial statements (in thousands), the ratio is calculated by dividing total liabilities (both current and long-term) by total assets.

Illustration 15-9 ▶

Debt to total assets

This means that 57 percent of Forzani's assets is financed by creditors. The remainder, 43 percent (100% − 57%), has been financed by shareholders. In general, the higher the percentage of debt to total assets, the greater the risk that the company may be unable to meet its maturing obligations.

While you may assume that having no, or a low, debt to total assets ratio is ideal, recall that we learned at the beginning of this chapter that some debt may be good for a company. In some circumstances, a company can increase its earnings per share and return on equity by increasing how much debt financing it relies on.

Interest Coverage

The debt to total assets ratio must be interpreted in light of the company's ability to handle its debt. That is, a company might have a high debt to total assets ratio but still be able to easily pay its interest payments. Alternatively, a company may have a low debt to total assets ratio and struggle to cover its interest payments.

Alternative terminology The interest coverage ratio is also commonly known as the *times interest earned ratio.*

The **interest coverage ratio** indicates the company's ability to meet interest payments as they come due. It is calculated by dividing net income before interest expense and income tax expense by interest expense. The numerator is often abbreviated and called **EBIT**, which stands for "earnings before interest and tax." EBIT can be calculated by adding back interest expense and income tax expense to net income. Because these amounts were originally deducted to determine net income, adding them back has the effect of cancelling them.

Illustration 15-10 calculates interest coverage for Forzani ($ in thousands).

Illustration 15-10 ▶

Interest coverage

Even though Forzani's debt to total assets ratio is 57 percent, the company appears well equipped to handle its interest payments in 2005. Its EBIT can cover interest charges 4.5 times.

ACCOUNTING IN ACTION ▶ Business Insight

Most investors agree that a company's ability to handle its debt has a big impact on its share price. Two analysts at CIBC World Markets tested a number of ratios over a 20-year period to determine which ones were most useful in predicting future stock performance. They found that companies with high interest coverage ratios have a stronger ability to repay their debt and that this was an important ratio in predicting future stock performance. "The market rewards those companies with higher returns," the analysts said.

Source: David Berman and Jason Kirby, "Cash Flow/Debt Best Indicator," *National Post*, December 13, 2005, FP9.

? What is the likely reason that a high interest coverage ratio might result in a high share price?

BEFORE YOU GO ON . . .

▶Review It

1. How are liabilities presented on the balance sheet?
2. What information about long-term liabilities should be disclosed in the notes to the financial statements?
3. How are the debt to total assets and interest coverage ratios calculated? Explain why they should always be interpreted together.

Related exercise material: BE15–12, BE15–13, E15–10, E15–11, and E15–12.

APPENDIX 15A ▶ EFFECTIVE-INTEREST AMORTIZATION

We learned earlier in the chapter that bond discounts and premiums must be allocated to expense over the life of the bonds using the **effective-interest method of amortization**, in accordance with the matching principle. There is also another method of amortization, known as the straight-line method, which is sometimes used for simplicity. However, this method is not permitted under GAAP and is not illustrated here.

> **study objective 6**
>
> Apply the effective-interest method of amortizing bond discounts and premiums.

There are three steps required to calculate amortization using the effective-interest method:

1. **Bond interest paid (or accrued):** Calculate the bond interest paid by multiplying the face value of the bonds by the contractual interest rate.
2. **Bond interest expense:** Calculate interest expense by multiplying the carrying value of the bonds at the beginning of the interest period by the market (effective) interest rate.
3. **Amortization amount:** The amortization amount is the difference between the amounts calculated in steps (1) and (2).

Illustration 15A-1 shows how amortization is calculated with the effective-interest method.

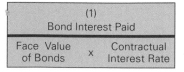 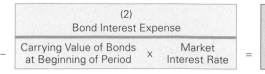

(1) Bond Interest Paid		(2) Bond Interest Expense		(3)
Face Value of Bonds	× Contractual Interest Rate	Carrying Value of Bonds at Beginning of Period	× Market Interest Rate	Amortization Amount

Illustration 15A-1 ◀

Calculation of amortization using effective-interest method

We will explain each of these steps in the next two sections—first for a bond discount and then for a bond premium.

Amortizing a Bond Discount

To illustrate the effective-interest method of bond discount amortization, we will continue to use Candlestick Inc. from earlier in the chapter as our example. As you recall from the "Issuing Bonds at a Discount" section, Candlestick issued $1 million of five-year, 5% bonds at $957,345 to yield a market interest rate of 6 percent. This resulted in a bond discount of $42,655 ($1,000,000 − $957,345). Interest is payable semi-annually on July 1 and January 1.

The interest payment, $25,000, is calculated by multiplying the face value of the bonds by the contractual interest rate ($1,000,000 × 5% × $\frac{6}{12}$). For the first interest period, the bond interest expense is $28,720, calculated by multiplying the carrying value of the bonds at the beginning of the period by the market interest rate ($957,345 × 6% × $\frac{6}{12}$). The discount amortization is then calculated as the difference between the interest paid and the interest expense ($25,000 − $28,720 = $3,720). Don't worry about whether this number is a negative or a positive difference—it is the difference that is important here. A negative amount indicates that a discount is being amortized while a positive amount indicates that a premium is being amortized, as we will see in the next section.

A bond discount amortization schedule, as shown in Illustration 15A-2, makes it easier to record the interest expense and the discount amortization. For simplicity, amounts have been rounded to the nearest dollar in this schedule.

Illustration 15A-2 ▼

Bond discount amortization schedule—effective-interest method

CANDLESTICK INC. Bond Discount Amortization Schedule Effective-Interest Method					
Semi-Annual Interest Period	(A) Interest Payment ($1,000,000 × 5% × $\frac{6}{12}$)	(B) Interest Expense (E × 6% × $\frac{6}{12}$)	(C) Discount Amortization (B − A)	(D) Unamortized Discount (D − C)	(E) Bond Carrying Value ($1,000,000 − D)
Issue date (Jan. 1, 2008)				$42,655	$ 957,345
1 (July 1)	$ 25,000	$ 28,720	$ 3,720	38,935	961,065
2 (Jan. 1, 2009)	25,000	28,832	3,832	35,103	964,897
3 (July 1)	25,000	28,947	3,947	31,156	968,844
4 (Jan. 1, 2010)	25,000	29,065	4,065	27,091	972,909
5 (July 1)	25,000	29,187	4,187	22,904	977,096
6 (Jan. 1, 2011)	25,000	29,313	4,313	18,591	981,409
7 (July 1)	25,000	29,442	4,442	14,149	985,851
8 (Jan. 1, 2012)	25,000	29,576	4,576	9,573	990,427
9 (July 1)	25,000	29,713	4,713	4,860	995,140
10 (Jan. 1, 2013)	25,000	29,860*	4,860	0	1,000,000
	$250,000	$292,655	$42,655		

* $6 difference due to rounding

We have highlighted columns A, B, and C in the amortization schedule shown in Illustration 15A-2 to emphasize their importance. These three columns give the numbers for each period's journal entries. They are the main reason for preparing the schedule, although all the columns give useful information:

- Column A gives the amount of the credit to Cash (or Interest Payable). Note that the amounts in this column stay the same because the face value of the bonds ($1,000,000) is multiplied by the same semi-annual contractual interest rate each period.

- Column B shows the debit to Bond Interest Expense. It is calculated by multiplying the bond carrying value at the beginning of the period by the semi-annual market interest rate. Note that while the semi-annual market interest rate (3%) stays constant each interest period, the interest expense increases because the bond carrying value increases.
- Column C is the credit to Discount on Bonds Payable. It is the difference between the interest payment and the interest expense. The amounts in this column increase throughout the amortization period because the interest expense increases.
- Column D shows the unamortized discount. It decreases each period by the discount amortization amount from Column C until it reaches zero at maturity.
- Column E is the bond's carrying value (its face value less the unamortized discount amount from column D). Note that the carrying value of the bonds increases by the discount amortization amount each period until it reaches the face value of $1 million at the end of period 10 (January 1, 2013).

Columns A, B, and C give information for the required journal entries. For the first interest period, the entry to record the payment of interest and amortization of the bond discount by Candlestick is as follows:

July 1	Bond Interest Expense ($957,345 × 6% × ½)	28,720	
	Discount on Bonds Payable		3,720
	Cash ($1,000,000 × 5% × ½)		25,000
	To record payment of bond interest and amortization of bond discount.		

A = L + SE
−25,000 +3,720 −28,720

↓ Cash flows: −25,000

Recall from our chapter discussion that a bond discount increases the cost of borrowing. Consequently, the interest expense includes both the interest payment ($25,000) and the bond discount amortization ($3,720).

For the second interest period, at Candlestick's year end, the following adjusting entry is made:

Dec. 31	Bond Interest Expense ($961,065 × 6% × ½)	28,832	
	Discount on Bonds Payable		3,832
	Bond Interest Payable ($1,000,000 × 5% × ½)		25,000
	To record accrued bond interest and amortization of bond discount.		

A = L + SE
+3,832 −28,832
+25,000

Cash flows: no effect

Note that Bond Interest Payable is credited rather than Cash because the next interest payment date is January 1. On January 1, the Bond Interest Payable account will be debited and the Cash account credited.

Amortizing a Bond Premium

Using our previous example, we will now assume that Candlestick Inc. issues its bonds at $1,044,915. You will recall from the "Issuing Bonds at a Premium" section in the chapter, that this price resulted in a market interest rate of 4 percent and a premium of $44,915 ($1,044,915 − $1,000,000). Interest is payable semi-annually on July 1 and January 1.

The amortization of a bond premium by the effective-interest method is similar to the procedures described for a bond discount. The bond premium amortization schedule is shown in Illustration 15A-3 on the following page. Figures have been rounded to the nearest dollar for simplicity.

CANDLESTICK INC.
Bond Premium Amortization Schedule
Effective-Interest Method

Semi-Annual Interest Period	(A) Interest Payment ($1,000,000 × 5% × %₂)	(B) Interest Expense (E × 4% × %₂)	(C) Premium Amortization (A – B)	(D) Unamortized Premium (D – C)	(E) Bond Carrying Value ($1,000,000 + D)
Issue date (Jan. 1, 2008)				$44,915	$1,044,915
1 (July 1)	$ 25,000	$ 20,898	$ 4,102	40,813	1,040,813
2 (Jan. 1, 2009)	25,000	20,816	4,184	36,629	1,036,629
3 (July 1)	25,000	20,733	4,267	32,362	1,032,362
4 (Jan. 1, 2010)	25,000	20,647	4,353	28,009	1,028,009
5 (July 1)	25,000	20,560	4,440	23,569	1,023,569
6 (Jan. 1, 2011)	25,000	20,471	4,529	19,040	1,019,040
7 (July 1)	25,000	20,381	4,619	14,421	1,014,421
8 (Jan. 1, 2012)	25,000	20,288	4,712	9,709	1,009,709
9 (July 1)	25,000	20,194	4,806	4,903	1,004,903
10 (Jan. 1, 2013)	25,000	20,097*	4,903	0	1,000,000
	$250,000	$205,085	$44,915		

* $1 difference due to rounding

Illustration 15A-3 ▲

Bond premium amortization schedule—effective-interest method

Each column in the premium amortization schedule gives the following information:

- Column A gives the amount of the credit to Cash (or Interest Payable). The amounts in this column stay the same because the face value of the bonds ($1,000,000) is multiplied by the same semi-annual contractual interest rate each period.
- Column B shows the debit to Bond Interest Expense. It is calculated by multiplying the bond carrying value at the beginning of the period by the semi-annual market interest rate. Note that while the semi-annual market interest rate (2%) stays constant each interest period, the interest expense decreases because the bond carrying value decreases. When we amortized a discount in Illustration 15A-2, the interest expense *increased* because the bond carrying value also increased.
- Column C is the debit to Premium on Bonds Payable. It is the difference between the interest payment and the interest expense. The amounts in this column increase throughout the amortization period because the interest expense increases.

  Note that for both a discount and a premium, the amortization amount is calculated as the difference between the interest payment (column A) and the interest expense (column B). However, for a discount, because the interest expense is greater than the interest payment, we subtract column A from column B. For a premium, where the interest payment is greater than the interest expense, we subtract column B from column A.

- Column D shows the unamortized premium. It decreases each period by the premium amortization amount from Column C until it reaches zero at maturity.
- Column E is the bond's carrying value (its face value plus the unamortized premium amount from column D). Note that the carrying value of the bonds decreases by the premium amortization amount each period until it reaches the face value of $1 million at the end of period 10 (January 1, 2013). In the discount situation shown in Illustration 15A-2, the carrying value *increased* but both amortization schedules end up with the same face value amount at maturity.

The entry on the first interest payment date is as follows:

July 1	Bond Interest Expense ($1,044,915 × 4% × %₁₂)	20,898	
	Premium on Bonds Payable	4,102	
	Cash ($1,000,000 × 5% × %₁₂)		25,000
	To record payment of bond interest and amortization of bond premium.		

A	=	L	+	SE
−25,000		−4,102		−20,898

↓ Cash flows: −25,000

As we learned earlier in the chapter, a bond premium reduces the cost of borrowing. Consequently, the interest expense account is basically increased (debited) for the interest payment ($25,000) and decreased (credited) for the bond premium amortization ($4,102) in the same entry. Note that interest expense is credited, rather than a revenue or other account.

For the second period, the following adjusting entry is made. While the interest expense and amortization amounts vary, the cash payment is a constant $25,000 every interest period.

Dec. 31	Bond Interest Expense ($1,040,813 × 4% × %₁₂)	20,816	
	Premium on Bonds Payable	4,184	
	Bond Interest Payable ($1,000,000 × 5% × %₁₂)		25,000
	To record accrued bond interest and amortization of bond premium.		

A	=	L	+	SE
		−4,184		−20,816
		+25,000		

Cash flows: no effect

Illustration 15A-4 summarizes some of the differences between a discount and a premium under the effective-interest method of amortization.

	Discount	Premium
Periodic interest payment	Same	Same
Periodic interest expense	Increases each period	Decreases each period
Bond carrying value	Increases to face value at maturity	Decreases to face value at maturity

Illustration 15A-4 ◀

Differing effects of a discount and premium

Under the effective-interest method, the interest payment is the same whether the bonds were issued at a discount or at a premium. This is because the interest payment is calculated by multiplying the face value of the bonds by the contractual interest rate.

However, interest expense is calculated by multiplying the bond carrying value by the market interest rate. Consequently, interest expense changes proportionately with the carrying value. It increases with a discount because the carrying value also increases. It decreases with a premium because the carrying value also decreases.

APPENDIX 15B ► PRESENT VALUE TABLES

Table 1: Present Value of $1

TABLE 1

Present Value of $1

(n) Periods	1%	1.5%	2%	2.5%	3%	3.5%	4%	4.5%	5%	6%	7%	8%	9%	10%
1	0.99010	0.98522	0.98039	0.97561	0.97087	0.96618	0.96154	0.95694	0.95238	0.94340	0.93458	0.92593	0.91743	0.90909
2	0.98030	0.97066	0.96117	0.95181	0.94260	0.93351	0.92456	0.91573	0.90703	0.89000	0.87344	0.85734	0.84168	0.82645
3	0.97059	0.95632	0.94232	0.92860	0.91514	0.90194	0.88900	0.87630	0.86384	0.83962	0.81630	0.79383	0.77218	0.75131
4	0.96098	0.94218	0.92385	0.90595	0.88849	0.87144	0.85480	0.83856	0.82270	0.79209	0.76290	0.73503	0.70843	0.68301
5	0.95147	0.92826	0.90573	0.88385	0.86261	0.84197	0.82193	0.80245	0.78353	0.74726	0.71299	0.68058	0.64993	0.62092
6	0.94205	0.91454	0.88797	0.86230	0.83748	0.81350	0.79031	0.76790	0.74622	0.70496	0.66634	0.63017	0.59627	0.56447
7	0.93272	0.90103	0.87056	0.84127	0.81309	0.78599	0.75992	0.73483	0.71068	0.66506	0.62275	0.58349	0.54703	0.51316
8	0.92348	0.88771	0.85349	0.82075	0.78941	0.75941	0.73069	0.70319	0.67684	0.62741	0.58201	0.54027	0.50187	0.46651
9	0.91434	0.87459	0.83676	0.80073	0.76642	0.73373	0.70259	0.67290	0.64461	0.59190	0.54393	0.50025	0.46043	0.42410
10	0.90529	0.86167	0.82035	0.78120	0.74409	0.70892	0.67556	0.64393	0.61391	0.55839	0.50835	0.46319	0.42241	0.38554
11	0.89632	0.84893	0.80426	0.76214	0.72242	0.68495	0.64958	0.61620	0.58468	0.52679	0.47509	0.42888	0.38753	0.35049
12	0.88745	0.83639	0.78849	0.74356	0.70138	0.66178	0.62460	0.58966	0.55684	0.49697	0.44401	0.39711	0.35553	0.31863
13	0.87866	0.82403	0.77303	0.72542	0.68095	0.63940	0.60057	0.56427	0.53032	0.46884	0.41496	0.36770	0.32618	0.28966
14	0.86996	0.81185	0.75788	0.70773	0.66112	0.61778	0.57748	0.53997	0.50507	0.44230	0.38782	0.34046	0.29925	0.26333
15	0.86135	0.79985	0.74301	0.69047	0.64186	0.59689	0.55526	0.51672	0.48102	0.41727	0.36245	0.31524	0.27454	0.23939
16	0.85282	0.78803	0.72845	0.67362	0.62317	0.57671	0.53391	0.49447	0.45811	0.39365	0.33873	0.29189	0.25187	0.21763
17	0.84438	0.77639	0.71416	0.65720	0.60502	0.55720	0.51337	0.47318	0.43630	0.37136	0.31657	0.27027	0.23107	0.19784
18	0.83602	0.76491	0.70016	0.64117	0.58739	0.53836	0.49363	0.45280	0.41552	0.35034	0.29586	0.25025	0.21199	0.17986
19	0.82774	0.75361	0.68643	0.62553	0.57029	0.52016	0.47464	0.43330	0.39573	0.33051	0.27651	0.23171	0.19449	0.16351
20	0.81954	0.74247	0.67297	0.61027	0.55368	0.50257	0.45639	0.41464	0.37689	0.31180	0.25842	0.21455	0.17843	0.14864

Table 2: Present Value of an Annuity of $1

TABLE 2

Present Value of an Annuity of $1

(n) Periods	1%	1.5%	2%	2.5%	3%	3.5%	4%	4.5%	5%	6%	7%	8%	9%	10%
1	0.99010	0.98522	0.98039	0.97561	0.97087	0.96618	0.96154	0.95694	0.95238	0.94340	0.93458	0.92593	0.91743	0.90909
2	1.97040	1.95588	1.94156	1.92742	1.91347	1.89969	1.88609	1.87267	1.85941	1.83339	1.80802	1.78326	1.75911	1.73554
3	2.94099	2.91220	2.88388	2.85602	2.82861	2.80164	2.77509	2.74896	2.72325	2.67301	2.62432	2.57710	2.53129	2.48685
4	3.90197	3.85438	3.80773	3.76197	3.71710	3.67308	3.62990	3.58753	3.54595	3.46511	3.38721	3.31213	3.23972	3.16987
5	4.85343	4.78264	4.71346	4.64583	4.57971	4.51505	4.45182	4.38998	4.32948	4.21236	4.10020	3.99271	3.88965	3.79079
6	5.79548	5.69719	5.60143	5.50813	5.41719	5.32855	5.24214	5.15787	5.07569	4.91732	4.76654	4.62288	4.48592	4.35526
7	6.72819	6.59821	6.47199	6.34939	6.23028	6.11454	6.00205	5.89270	5.78637	5.58238	5.38929	5.20637	5.03295	4.86842
8	7.65168	7.48593	7.32548	7.17014	7.01969	6.87396	6.73274	6.59589	6.46321	6.20979	5.97130	5.74664	5.53482	5.33493
9	8.56602	8.36052	8.16224	7.97087	7.78611	7.60769	7.43533	7.26879	7.10782	6.80169	6.51523	6.24689	5.99525	5.75902
10	9.47130	9.22218	8.98259	8.75206	8.53020	8.31661	8.11090	7.91272	7.72173	7.36009	7.02358	6.71008	6.41766	6.14457
11	10.36763	10.07112	9.78685	9.51421	9.25262	9.00155	8.76048	8.52892	8.30641	7.88687	7.49867	7.13896	6.80519	6.49506
12	11.25508	10.90751	10.57534	10.25776	9.95400	9.66333	9.38507	9.11858	8.86325	8.38384	7.94269	7.53608	7.16073	6.81369
13	12.13374	11.73153	11.34837	10.98318	10.63496	10.30274	9.98565	9.68285	9.39357	8.85268	8.35765	7.90378	7.48690	7.10336
14	13.00370	12.54338	12.10625	11.69091	11.29607	10.92052	10.56312	10.22283	9.89864	9.29498	8.74547	8.24424	7.78615	7.36669
15	13.86505	13.34323	12.84926	12.38138	11.93794	11.51741	11.11839	10.73955	10.37966	9.71225	9.10791	8.55948	8.06069	7.60608
16	14.71787	14.13126	13.57771	13.05500	12.56110	12.09412	11.65230	11.23402	10.83777	10.10590	9.44665	8.85137	8.31256	7.82371
17	15.56225	14.90765	14.29187	13.71220	13.16612	12.65132	12.16567	11.70719	11.27407	10.47726	9.76322	9.12164	8.54363	8.02155
18	16.39827	15.67256	14.99203	14.35336	13.75351	13.18968	12.65930	12.15999	11.68959	10.82760	10.05909	9.37189	8.75563	8.20141
19	17.22601	16.42617	15.67846	14.97889	14.32380	13.70984	13.13394	12.59329	12.08532	11.15812	10.33560	9.60360	8.95011	8.36492
20	18.04555	17.16864	16.35143	15.58916	14.87747	14.21240	13.59033	13.00794	12.46221	11.46992	10.59401	9.81815	9.12855	8.51356

Demonstration Problem 1

On January 1, 2003, Feng Inc. issued $500,000 of 10-year, 7% bonds at 93.205. This resulted in a market interest rate of 8%. Interest is payable semi-annually on January 1 and July 1. Feng's year end is June 30. Five years later, on January 1, 2008, Feng redeemed all of these bonds at 98. The carrying value of the bonds at that time was $479,724.

Practice Tools:
Demonstration Problems

Instructions

(a) Calculate the issue price of the bonds using (1) the stated percentage rate, and (2) the present value tables. Round your answers to the nearest dollar.

(b) Prepare the journal entry to record the issue of the bonds on January 1, 2003.

(c) Prepare the journal entry to accrue the first interest payment on June 30. Assume that the amortization amount for the first interest period is $1,141.

(d) Show the presentation of the liability on Feng's balance sheet on June 30, 2003.

(e) Prepare the journal entry to record the redemption of the bonds on January 1, 2008.

Solution to Demonstration Problem

(a) (1) $500,000 × 93.205% .... <u>$466,025</u>

(2) Present value of $500,000 received in 20 periods

$500,000 × 0.45639 (*n* = 20, *i* = 4%) $228,195

Present value of $17,500 received for each of 20 periods

$500,000 × 7% × %12 = $17,500;

$17,500 × 13.59033 (*n* = 20, *i* = 4%) 237,830

Present value (market price) of bonds .... <u>$466,025</u>

(b)

2003			
Jan. 1	Cash	466,025	
	Discount on Bonds Payable ($500,000 − $466,025)	33,975	
	Bonds Payable		500,000
	To record issue of 10-year, 7% bonds.		

(c)

June 30	Bond Interest Expense ($17,500 + $1,141)	18,641	
	Discount on Bonds Payable		1,141
	Bond Interest Payable ($500,000 × 7% × %12)		17,500
	To record accrual of semi-annual interest.		

(d)

FENG INC.
Balance Sheet (partial)
June 30, 2003

Long-term liabilities		
Bonds payable		$500,000
Less: Discount on bonds payable ($33,975 − $1,141)		<u>32,834</u>
		<u>$467,166</u>

(e)

2008			
Jan. 1	Bonds Payable	500,000	
	Loss on Bond Redemption ($490,000 − $479,724)	10,276	
	Cash ($500,000 × 98%)		490,000
	Discount on Bonds Payable ($500,000 − $479,724)		20,276
	To record redemption of bonds.		

Action Plan

- To calculate the proceeds using the stated percentage rate, multiply the face value by the issue price expressed as a percentage (e.g., 93.205%).

- To calculate the proceeds using present value tables, use Table 1 for the face value and Table 2 for the interest payment. Don't forget to double the number of interest periods and halve the interest rate for semi-annual interest.

- If the proceeds are greater than the face value, the difference is a premium. If the proceeds are less than the face value, the difference is a discount.

- Record and report a discount as a contra liability account and a premium as an adjunct liability account.

- Amortization of a bond discount increases interest expense; amortization of a bond premium decreases interest expense.

- To record the redemption, (1) update any partial period interest and amortization, if required. (2) Eliminate the carrying value of the bonds and remove the balances from the Bonds Payable account and any discount or premium account. (3) Record the cash paid. (4) Calculate and record the gain or loss (the difference between the cash paid and the carrying value).

the navigator

Practice Tools:
Demonstration Problems

Demonstration Problem 2

Note: This demonstration problem uses the same facts as those shown in the "Do It" problem on p. 774, but the nature and amount of the payment are changed.

On December 31, 2007, Tian Inc. issued a $500,000, 15-year, 8% mortgage note payable. The terms provide for semi-annual fixed principal payments of $16,667 on June 30 and December 31. Tian's year end is December 31.

Instructions

Round your answers to the nearest dollar.

(a) Prepare a payment schedule for the first two years of the note (through to December 31, 2009).

(b) Prepare the journal entries to record the issue of the note on December 31, 2007, and the first two instalment payments.

(c) Indicate the current and noncurrent amounts for the mortgage note payable at December 31, 2008.

(d) What is the difference between your results here using a fixed principal payment and the results shown using a blended payment for the same situation illustrated in the "Do It" problem on p. 774.

Action Plan

- Determine the interest expense for the mortgage by multiplying the semi-annual interest rate by the principal balance at the beginning of the period. The cash payment is the total of the principal payment and interest expense. The reduction of principal is the amount of the fixed principal payment.
- Record the reduction of principal and interest expense separately.
- The current portion of the mortgage note payable is the amount of principal that will be repaid in the next year. The long-term portion is the remaining balance.

Solution to Demonstration Problem

(a)

Semi-Annual Interest Period	Cash Payment	Interest Expense	Reduction of Principal	Principal Balance
Issue Date (Dec. 31, 2007)				$500,000
1 (June 30, 2008)	$36,667[1]	$20,000[2]	$16,667[3]	483,333[4]
2 (Dec. 31)	36,000	19,333	16,667	466,666
3 (June 30, 2009)	35,334	18,667	16,667	449,999
4 (Dec. 31)	34,667	18,000	16,667	433,332

[1] $20,000 + $16,667 = $36,667
[2] $500,000 × 8% × $\frac{6}{12}$ = $20,000
[3] $500,000 ÷ 30 periods = $16,667
[4] $500,000 − $16,667 = $483,333

(b)

Dec. 31, 2007	Cash	500,000	
	Mortgage Note Payable		500,000
	To record issue of 15-year, 8% mortgage note payable.		
June 30, 2008	Interest Expense ($500,000 × 8% × $\frac{6}{12}$)	20,000	
	Mortgage Note Payable	16,667	
	Cash		36,667
	To record semi-annual payment on note.		
Dec. 31, 2008	Interest Expense ($483,333 × 8% × $\frac{6}{12}$)	19,333	
	Mortgage Note Payable	16,667	
	Cash		36,000
	To record semi-annual payment on note.		

(c) The current liability is $33,334 ($16,667 + $16,667).

The long-term liability is $433,332.

The total liability is $466,666, the balance at the end of the second period, December 31, 2008.

(d) In a blended payment situation, the cash payment stays constant. In a fixed principal payment situation, the reduction of the principal stays constant. In both situations, the same amount of principal is repaid over the same period of time—just in a different payment pattern.

the navigator

Summary of Study Objectives

1. Compare the impact of issuing debt instead of equity. Debt offers the following advantages over equity: (a) shareholder control is not affected, (b) income tax savings result, (c) earnings per share may be higher, and (d) return on equity may be higher.

2. Account for bonds payable. The market value of bonds is determined using present value factors: these factors determine the value of the interest and principal cash flows generated by the bond relative to the current market interest rate.

When bonds are issued, the Bonds Payable account is credited for the face value of the bonds. If the bonds are issued for less than their face value, there will also be a contra liability account for the bond discount (debit). If the bonds are issued for more than their face value, there will instead be an adjunct liability account for the bond premium (credit). Bond discounts and bond premiums are amortized to interest expense over the life of the bond using the effective-interest method of amortization. The amortization of a bond discount increases interest expense. The amortization of a bond premium decreases interest expense.

When bonds are retired at maturity, Bonds Payable is debited and Cash is credited. There is no gain or loss at retirement. When bonds are redeemed before maturity, it is necessary to (a) update any unrecorded interest, (b) eliminate the carrying value of the bonds at the redemption date, (c) record the cash paid, and (d) recognize any gain or loss on redemption.

3. Account for long-term notes payable. Long-term notes payable are repayable in a series of instalments. Each payment consists of (1) interest on the unpaid balance of the note, and (2) a reduction of the principal balance. These payments can be either (1) fixed principal plus interest payments or (2) blended principal and interest payments. With fixed principal payments, the reduction in principal is constant but the cash payment and interest decreases each period (as the principal decreases). Blended payments result in a constant cash payment but changing amounts of interest and principal.

4. Account for leases. For an operating lease, lease (or rental) payments are recorded as an expense by the lessee (renter). For a capital lease, the transaction is considered to be equivalent to a purchase and the lessee records the asset and related obligation at the present value of the future lease payments. The income statement reflects both the interest expense and amortization expense.

5. Explain and illustrate the methods for the presentation and analysis of long-term liabilities. The current portion of the long-term debt is reported as a current liability in the balance sheet, and the remaining portions are reported as long-term liabilities. The nature of each liability should be described in the notes accompanying the financial statements. The long-term solvency of a company may be analyzed by calculating two ratios. Debt to total assets indicates the proportion of company assets that is financed by debt. Interest coverage measures a company's ability to meet its interest payments as they come due.

6. Apply the effective-interest method of amortizing bond discounts and premiums (Appendix 15A). Amortization is calculated under the effective-interest method as the difference between the interest paid and the interest expense. Interest paid is calculated by multiplying the face value of the bonds by the contractual interest rate. Interest expense is calculated by multiplying the carrying value of the bonds at the beginning of the interest period by the market interest rate.

Glossary

Study Aids: Glossary
Practice Tools: Key Term Matching Activity

Bearer (coupon) bonds Bonds that are not registered. (p. 764)

Bond A debt security that is traded on an organized securities exchange, is issued to investors, and has these properties: the principal amount will be repaid at a designated maturity date and periodic interest is paid (normally semi-annually) at a specified rate on the principal amount. (p. 760)

Bond certificate A legal document indicating the name of the issuer, the face value of the bond, and other data such as the contractual interest rate and maturity date of the bond. (p. 761)

Capital lease A contractual arrangement that transfers all the benefits and risks of ownership to the lessee, so that the lease effectively results in a purchase of the property. (p. 777)

Contractual interest rate The rate that determines the amount of interest the borrower pays and the investor receives. (p. 761)

Convertible bonds Bonds that permit bondholders to convert them into common shares. (p. 765)

Debenture bonds Bonds issued against the general credit of the borrower. Also called unsecured bonds. (p. 764)

Debt to total assets The ratio of total liabilities to total assets. Indicates the proportion of assets that is financed by debt. (p. 780)

Discount (on bonds payable) The difference that results when the selling price of the bonds is less than the face value of the bonds. This occurs when the market interest rate is greater than the contractual interest rate. (p. 764)

EBIT Earnings before interest and tax, calculated as net income + interest expense + income tax expense. (p. 780)

Effective-interest method of amortization A method of amortizing a bond discount or bond premium that results in periodic interest expense equal to a constant percentage of the carrying value of the bonds. (p. 781)

Face value The amount of principal that the issuer must pay at the maturity date of the bond. (p. 761)

Financial leverage Borrowing at one rate and investing at a different rate. (p. 760)

Fixed interest rate An interest rate that is constant (unchanged) over the term of the debt. (p. 771)

Floating (or variable) interest rate An interest rate that changes over the term of the debt with fluctuating market rates. (p. 771)

Interest coverage ratio A measure of a company's ability to meet its interest obligations. It is calculated by dividing income before interest expense and income tax expense (EBIT) by interest expense. (p. 780)

Lessee The renter of a property. (p. 775)

Lessor The owner of a property for rent. (p. 775)

Market (effective) interest rate The rate that investors require for lending money to a corporation. (p. 762)

Maturity date The date on which the final payment on a debt security is due to be repaid by the issuer to the investor. (p. 761)

Mortgage note payable A long-term note that pledges title to specific assets as security for a loan. (p. 771)

Off–balance sheet financing The intentional effort by a company to structure its financing arrangements so as to avoid showing liabilities on its books. (p. 776)

Operating lease A contractual arrangement that gives the lessee temporary use of the property, but the lessor continues to own the property. (p. 776)

Premium (on bonds payable) The difference that results when the selling price of the bonds is greater than the face value of the bonds. This occurs when the market interest rate is less than the contractual interest rate. (p. 764)

Present value The value today of an amount to be received at some date in the future after taking interest rates into account. (p. 762)

Redeemable bonds Bonds that the issuer can redeem at a stated dollar amount before maturity. Also known as callable bonds. (p. 765)

Registered bonds Bonds issued in the name of the owner. (p. 764)

Retractable bonds Bonds that the bondholder can redeem at a stated dollar amount before maturity. (p. 765)

Secured bonds Bonds that have specific assets of the issuer pledged as collateral. (p. 764)

Serial bonds Bonds that mature in instalments. (p. 764)

Term bonds Bonds that mature at a single specified future date. (p. 764)

Unsecured bonds Bonds that are issued against the general credit of the borrower. Also called debenture bonds. (p. 764)

Note: All questions, exercises, and problems below with an asterisk (*) relate to material in the appendices to this chapter.

Self-Study Questions

Practice Tools: Self-Assessment Quizzes

Answers are at the end of the chapter.

(SO 1) K 1. Which of the following are advantages of issuing debt securities instead of equity securities?
   (a) Voting control of the company is not affected.
   (b) Savings in income tax result because interest expense is tax deductible.
   (c) Earnings per share and return on equity will be higher.
   (d) All of the above

(SO 2) K 2. If bonds are issued at a premium, it indicates that:
   (a) the contractual interest rate is higher than the market interest rate.

   (b) the market interest rate is higher than the contractual interest rate.
   (c) the contractual interest rate and the market interest rate are the same.
   (d) None of the above.

3. On January 1, Scissors Corp. issues $200,000 of five- (SO 2) year, 7% bonds at 97. The entry to record the issue of the bonds would include a:
   (a) debit to Cash for $200,000.
   (b) debit to Bonds Payable for $200,000.
   (c) debit to Discount on Bonds Payable for $6,000.
   (d) credit to Premium on Bonds Payable for $6,000.

(SO 2) AP 4. The Marshlands Corporation has bonds issued at a premium. The entry to record the payment of semi-annual interest would include a:
(a) debit to Amortization Expense and credit to Cash.
(b) debit to Interest Expense, a debit to Premium on Bonds Payable, and a credit to Cash.
(c) debit to Interest Expense, a credit to Premium on Bonds Payable, and a credit to Cash.
(d) debit to Cash, credit to Interest Revenue, and a credit to Premium on Bonds Payable.

(SO 2) AP 5. Gester Corporation redeems its $100,000 face value bonds at 105 on January 1, after the payment of semi-annual interest. The carrying value of the bonds at the redemption date is $103,745. The entry to record the redemption will include a:
(a) credit of $3,745 to Premium on Bonds Payable.
(b) debit of $1,255 to Loss on Bond Redemption.
(c) credit of $1,255 to Gain on Bond Redemption.
(d) debit of $105,000 to Cash.

(SO 3) AP 6. Zhang Inc. issues a $497,000, three-year, 7% instalment note payable on January 1. The note will be paid in three annual blended payments of $189,383 each. What is the amount of interest expense that should be recognized by Zhang in the second year?
(a) $11,597 (c) $23,968
(b) $23,193 (d) $34,790

(SO 3) AP 7. Assume that the note issued by Zhang Inc. in question 5 above will be paid with fixed principal payments of $165,667 each. What is the amount of interest expense that should be recognized by Zhang in the second year?
(a) $11,597 (c) $23,968
(b) $23,193 (d) $34,790

(SO 4) C 8. The lease term for Lease A is equal to 90% of the estimated economic life of the leased property. The lease term for Lease B is equal to 60% of the estimated economic life of the leased property. Assuming no other conditions are met, how should the lessee classify these leases?

	Lease A	Lease B
(a)	Operating lease	Capital lease
(b)	Operating lease	Operating lease
(c)	Capital lease	Operating lease
(d)	Capital lease	Capital lease

(SO 5) AP 9. In a recent year, Yung Kee Corporation had net income of $150,000, interest expense of $30,000, and income tax expense of $20,000. What was Yung Kee's interest coverage ratio?
(a) 5.0 times (c) 6.0 times
(b) 5.7 times (d) 6.7 times

(SO 6) AP *10. On January 1, Dias Corporation issued $2 million of five-year, 7% bonds with interest payable on July 1 and January 1. The bonds sold for $1,918,880. The market rate of interest for these bonds was 8%. Assuming the effective-interest method is used, on the first interest date the debit entry to Bond Interest Expense (rounded to the nearest dollar) is for:
(a) $67,161. (c) $76,755.
(b) $70,000. (d) $80,000.

Questions

(SO 1) C 1. What is the difference between a current liability and a long-term liability? Give two examples of each type of liability.

(SO 1) C 2. As a source of long-term financing, what are the major advantages of using debt over equity? Disadvantages?

(SO 1) C 3. Explain how a company can increase its earnings per share and return on equity by issuing debt instead of equity.

(SO 2) C 4. Explain how bonds are similar to (a) notes payable and (b) common shares.

(SO 2) C 5. (a) Explain the difference between a contractual interest rate and market interest rate. (b) Explain why one rate changes over the term of the bonds and the other stays the same.

(SO 2) C 6. Explain how the market value of a bond is determined using present value factors.

(SO 2) AP 7. Assume that Stoney Inc. sold bonds with a face value of $100,000 for $98,000. Was the market interest rate equal to, less than, or greater than the bonds' contractual interest rate? Explain.

(SO 2) C 8. How will the total cost of borrowing be affected if a bond is sold (a) at a discount and (b) at a premium? Explain when this cost of borrowing should be recorded and identify the related generally accepted accounting principle.

(SO 2) C 9. Why is there no gain or loss when bonds are redeemed at maturity, but there usually is a gain or loss when bonds are redeemed before maturity?

(SO 3) C 10. What are the similarities and differences between short-term and long-term notes payable?

(SO 3) C 11. What is the difference between a fixed interest rate and a floating interest rate?

(SO 3) C 12. What is the difference between instalment notes payable with fixed principal payments and those with blended payments?

(SO 3) C 13. When students borrow money for their post-secondary education under the Canada Student Loans Program, they sign an instalment note payable, which must be repaid, starting six months following graduation, in equal monthly amounts including principal and interest. Is this a fixed or blended pattern?

(SO 3) AP 14. Doug Bareak, a friend of yours, has recently purchased a home for $200,000. He paid $20,000 down and financed the remainder with a 20-year, 5% mortgage, payable in blended payments of $1,290 per month. At the end of the first month, Doug received a statement from the bank indicating that only $390 of the principal was paid during the month. At this rate, he calculated that it will take over 38 years to pay off the mortgage. Explain why this is not true.

(SO 4) C 15. (a) What is a lease? (b) Distinguish between the different types of leases.

(SO 4) C 16. What is off–balance sheet financing? Why are operating leases considered to be a form of off–balance sheet financing?

(SO 4) AP 17. What is the impact on a company's balance sheet and income statement if it accounts for a lease as an operating lease instead of as a capital lease?

(SO 5) K 18. In general, what are the requirements for the financial statement presentation of long-term liabilities?

19. In the liabilities section of the balance sheet, how is the (SO 5) presentation of a bond payable issued at a discount different from the presentation of a bond payable issued at a premium?

20. How are the current and noncurrent portions of a mort- (SO 5) gage note payable determined for presenting them in the liabilities section of the balance sheet?

21. Huan Yue is wondering why the debt to total assets (SO 5) and interest coverage ratios are calculated. Answer her question and explain why the debt to total assets ratio should never be interpreted without also referring to the interest coverage ratio.

*22. Explain how amortization is calculated using the ef- (SO 6) fective-interest method of amortization when bonds are issued at a discount, and at a premium.

*23. Compare the effects of the effective-interest method (SO 6) of amortization on interest paid, interest expense, and the bond carrying value when bonds are issued at (a) a discount, and (b) a premium.

*24. Explain why the bond carrying value (a) decreases (SO 6) when the effective-interest method of amortization is applied to bonds issued at a premium, and (b) increases when the effective-interest method of amortization is applied to bonds issued at a discount.

Brief Exercises

Compare debt and equity financing alternatives.
(SO 1) AP

BE15–1 Olga Inc. is considering two alternatives to finance its construction of a new $2-million plant at the beginning of the year:

(a) Issue 200,000 common shares at a market price of $10 per share.
(b) Issue $2 million of 8% bonds at face value.

It has 500,000 common shares and $5 million of shareholders' equity before the new financing. Complete the following table for the year, and indicate which alternative is better:

	(a) Issue Equity	(b) Issue Debt
Income before interest and income tax	$1,000,000	$1,000,000
Interest expense		
Income before income tax		
Income tax expense (25%)		
Net income		
Number of shares		
Earnings per share		
Shareholders' equity		
Return on equity		

Calculate present value of bond.
(SO 2) AP

BE15–2 Carvel Corp. issued $500,000 of five-year, 6% bonds with interest payable semi-annually. How much did Carvel receive from the sale of these bonds if the market interest rate was (a) 5%, (b) 6%, and (c) 7%?

BE15–3 Keystone Corporation issued $1 million of five-year, 5% bonds dated March 1, 2008, at 100. Interest is payable semi-annually on September 1 and March 1. Keystone has a December 31 year end. (a) Prepare the journal entry to record the sale of these bonds on March 1, 2008. (b) Prepare the journal entry to record the first interest payment on September 1, 2008. (c) Prepare the adjusting journal entry on December 31, 2008, to accrue the interest expense. (d) Prepare the journal entry to record the second interest payment on March 1, 2009.

Record bond transactions.
(SO 2) AP

BE15–4 Refer to data presented in BE15–3 for Keystone Corporation's bond issue.

(a) Record the sale of these bonds assuming that the bonds were issued at 99, rather than 100.
(b) Record the sale of these bonds assuming that the bonds were issued at 101, rather than 100.
(c) Show the balance sheet presentation of the bonds on March 1, 2008, if the bonds were issued at (1) 100, (2) 99, and (3) 101.
(d) What will the carrying value be at maturity, March 1, 2013, under each of the three different issue prices?

Record issue of bonds; show balance sheet presentation.
(SO 2) AP

BE15–5 The Town of Moosonee issued $1 million of five-year, 4% bonds dated January 1. Interest is payable semi-annually on July 1 and January 1.

(a) Record the sale of these bonds on January 1 and the first interest payment on July 1, assuming that the bonds were issued at 95 and that the semi-annual amortization amount for the first interest period is $3,900.
(b) Record the sale of these bonds on January 1 and the first interest payment on July 1, assuming that the bonds were issued at 100.
(c) Record the sale of these bonds on January 1 and the first interest payment on July 1, assuming that the bonds were issued at 104 and that the semi-annual amortization amount for the first interest period is $4,100.

Record bond transactions.
(SO 2) AP

BE15–6 The balance sheet for Hathaway Corporation reports the following information on July 1, 2008:

Record redemption of bonds.
(SO 2) AP

HATHAWAY CORPORATION		
Balance Sheet (partial)		
July 1, 2008		
Long-term liabilities		
Bonds payable	$1,000,000	
Less: Discount on bonds payable	60,000	$940,000

Interest is payable semi-annually on June 30 and December 31. Assuming Hathaway redeems these bonds at 102 on July 1, prepare the journal entry to record the redemption.

BE15–7 You qualify for a $10,000 loan from the Canada Student Loans Program to help finance your education. Once you graduate, you start repaying this note payable at an interest rate of 7%. The monthly cash payment is $116.11, principal and interest, for 120 payments (10 years). Prepare an instalment payment schedule for the first three payments.

Prepare instalment schedule.
(SO 3) AP

BE15–8 Eyre Inc. issues a $300,000, 10-year, 8%, mortgage note payable on November 30, 2007, to obtain financing for a new building. The terms provide for monthly instalment payments. Prepare the journal entries to record the mortgage loan on November 30, 2007, and the first two payments on December 31, 2007, and January 31, 2008, assuming the payment is (a) a fixed principal payment of $2,500, and (b) a blended payment of $3,640.

Record note transactions.
(SO 3) AP

BE15–9 Bow River Inc. issues a $400,000, four-year, 5% note payable on March 31, 2007. The terms provide for fixed principal payments annually of $100,000. (a) Prepare the journal entries to record the note on March 31, 2007, and the first payment on March 31, 2008. (b) Show the balance sheet presentation of the current and long-term liability related to the note as at March 31, 2008.

Record note transaction; show balance sheet presentation.
(SO 3) AP

Record lease.
(SO 4) AP

BE15–10 P. Paquin leases an apartment for $1,000 per month from Privateer Landing Apartments Ltd. (a) Prepare the journal entry to record the monthly lease payment by the lessee. (b) Prepare the journal entry to record the receipt of the monthly lease payment by the lessor.

Record lease.
(SO 4) AP

BE15–11 Chang Corp. leases a new building from Bracer Construction, Inc. The present value of the lease payments is $600,000 and the fair market value is $650,000. (a) Which company is the lessor and which company the lessee? (b) Prepare the journal entry to record the lease for the lessee.

Prepare liabilities section of balance sheet.
(SO 5) AP

BE15–12 Selected liability items for Waugh Corporation at December 31, 2008, follow. Prepare the liabilities section of Waugh's balance sheet.

Accounts payable	$ 55,000	Income tax payable	$12,000
Bonds payable, due 2028	900,000	Lease liability	50,000
Current portion of notes payable	15,000	Notes payable, due 2015	
Premium on bonds payable	35,000	(net of current portion)	80,000

Calculate debt ratios.
(SO 5) AP

BE15–13 **The Jean Coutu Group (PJC) Inc.** reported the following selected data at May 27, 2006 (in U.S. millions):

Total assets	$5,591.0
Total liabilities	4,025.3
Interest expense	190.0
Income tax recovery	(44.0)
Net income	103.8

Calculate Jean Coutu's (a) debt to total assets, and (b) interest coverage ratios.

Prepare amortization schedule.
(SO 6) AP

*BE15–14 Niagara Corporation issued $100,000 of five-year, 8.5% bonds on April 1, 2008, with interest payable semi-annually on October 1 and April 1. The bonds were issued at $106,237 to yield a market interest rate of 7%. Prepare an amortization schedule to April 1, 2009.

Complete amortization schedule and answer questions.
(SO 2, 6) AP

*BE15–15 A partial bond discount amortization schedule for Chiasson Corp. is presented below:

Semi-Annual Interest Period	Interest Payment	Interest Expense	Discount Amortization	Unamortized Discount	Bond Carrying Value
Issue Date				$62,311	$937,689
1 (Apr. 30)	$45,000	(1)	$1,884	(2)	939,573
2 (Oct. 31)	45,000	$46,979	(3)	58,448	(4)

(a) Fill in the missing amounts for items (1) through (4).
(b) What is the face value of the bonds?
(c) What is the contractual interest rate on the bonds? The market interest rate?
(d) Explain why interest expense is greater than interest paid.
(e) Explain why interest expense will increase each period.
(f) Prepare the journal entry to record the payment of interest on April 30 and October 31.

Record bond transactions using effective-interest amortization.
(SO 2, 6) AP

*BE15–16 On May 1, 2008, the Jianhua Corporation issued $120,000 of 10-year, 8% bonds, with interest payable semi-annually on November 1 and May 1. The bonds were issued to yield a market interest rate of 6%. Jianhua uses the effective-interest method of amortization.

(a) Calculate the issue price of the bonds.
(b) Record the issue of the bonds on May 1, 2008.
(c) Record the payment of interest on November 1, 2008 and May 1, 2009.

Exercises

E15–1   Charter Airlines is considering two alternatives to finance the purchase of a fleet of air-planes. These alternatives are (1) to issue 60,000 common shares at $45 per share, and (2) to issue 10-year, 6% bonds for $2.7 million.

Compare debt and equity financing alternatives.
(SO 1) AP

It is estimated that the company will earn $600,000 before interest and income tax as a result of this purchase. The company has an income tax rate of 30%. It has 90,000 common shares issued and shareholders' equity of $6 million before the new financing.

Instructions

(a) Calculate the net income for each financing alternative.
(b) Calculate the earnings per share and return on equity for each alternative.

E15–2   Central College is about to issue $1 million of 10-year bonds that pay a 7% annual interest rate, with interest payable semi-annually.

Calculate present value of bonds.
(SO 2) AP

Instructions

Calculate how much Central will receive from the sale of these bonds if the market interest rate is (a) 6%, (b) 7%, and (c) 8%.

E15–3   The following information about two independent bond issues was recently reported in the financial press:

Analyze and record bond issues.
(SO 2) AP

1. **Canadian Tire** 6.25% bonds, maturing April 13, 2028, were trading at 103.
2. **Bell Canada** 6.25% bonds, maturing April 12, 2012, were trading at 106.

Instructions

(a) Are the Canadian Tire bonds trading at a premium or a discount?
(b) Are the Bell Canada bonds trading at a premium or a discount?
(c) Explain how bonds, both paying the same contractual interest rate (6.25%), could be trading at different prices on the same date.
(d) Record the issue of $1,000 of each of these two bonds.

E15–4   On July 31, 2007, Laramie Corporation issued $400,000 of 10-year, 5% bonds at 101. In-terest is payable semi-annually on July 31 and January 31.

Record bond transactions; show balance sheet presentation.
(SO 2) AP

Instructions

(a) Record the issue of the bonds on July 31, 2007.
(b) Record the payment of interest on January 31, 2008, assuming the semi-annual amortization amount for this interest period is $910.
(c) Show how the bonds would be reported on Laramie's balance sheet on January 31, 2008.

E15–5   The following independent transactions occurred on June 30, 2008:

Record redemption of bonds.
(SO 2) AP

1. Ernst Corporation redeemed $120,000 of 7% bonds at 103. The carrying value of the bonds at the date of redemption was $117,500.
2. Takase Corporation redeemed $150,000 of 5% bonds at 96. The carrying value of the bonds at the redemption date was $152,000.
3. Young, Inc. redeemed $150,000 of 8% bonds at their maturity date, June 30, 2008.

Instructions

Record the transactions.

E15–6   Ste. Anne Corp. receives $150,000 on December 31, 2008, when it issues a 20-year, 6% mortgage note payable to finance the construction of a building. The terms provide for semi-annual instalment payments on June 30 and December 31.

Record mortgage note payable.
(SO 3) AP

Instructions

Prepare the journal entries to record the mortgage note payable and the first two instalment payments assuming the payment is (a) a fixed principal payment of $3,750, and (b) a blended payment of $6,489.

Analyze instalment payment schedule. Identify balance sheet presentation.
(SO 3) AP

E15–7 The following instalment payment schedule is for a long-term note payable:

Interest Period	Cash Payment	Interest Expense	Reduction of Principal	Principal Balance
Issue date				$50,000
1	$13,500	$3,500	$10,000	40,000
2	12,800	2,800	10,000	30,000
3	12,100	2,100	10,000	20,000
4	11,400	1,400	10,000	10,000
5	10,700	700	10,000	0

Instructions

(a) Is this a fixed principal or blended payment schedule?
(b) Assuming payments are made annually, what is the interest rate on the note?
(c) Prepare the journal entry to record the first instalment payment.
(d) What are the long-term and current portions of the note at the end of period 2?

Prepare instalment payment schedule and record note payable. Identify balance sheet presentation.
(SO 3) AP

E15–8 On January 1, 2008, Wolstenholme Corp. borrows $9,000 by signing a three-year, 7% note payable. The note is repayable in three annual blended payments of $3,429.46 on December 31 of each year.

Instructions

(a) Prepare an instalment payment schedule for the note.
(b) Prepare journal entries to record the note and the first instalment payment.
(c) What amounts would be reported as current and long-term in the liabilities section of Wolstenholme's balance sheet on December 31, 2008?

Analyze and record leases.
(SO 4) AP

E15–9 Two independent situations follow:

1. Ready Car Rental leased a car to Dumfries Company for one year. Terms of the lease agreement call for monthly payments of $525, beginning on May 21, 2008.
2. On January 1, 2008, InSynch.com entered into an agreement to lease 60 computers from Hi-Tech Electronics. The terms of the lease agreement require three annual payments of $39,648 (including 9.5% interest) beginning on December 31, 2008. The present value of the three payments is $99,474 and the market value of the computers is $100,000.

Instructions

(a) What kind of lease—operating or capital—should be recorded in each of the above situations? Explain your rationale.
(b) Prepare the journal entry, if any, that each company must make to record the lease agreement.

Analyze solvency.
(SO 4, 5) AP

E15–10 **Maple Leaf Foods Inc.'s** December 31 financial statements contain the following selected data (in millions):

	2005	2004
Total assets	$3,189.8	$3,038.1
Total liabilities	2,103.7	2,058.5
Net income	94.2	102.3
Income tax expense	51.3	57.0
Interest expense	98.3	89.8

Instructions

(a) Calculate the debt to total assets and interest coverage ratios for 2005 and 2004. Did Maple Leaf's solvency improve, worsen, or remain unchanged in 2005?

(b) The notes to Maple Leaf Foods' financial statements show that the company has future operating lease commitments totalling $203.2 million. What is the significance of these unrecorded obligations in an analysis of Maple Leaf Foods' solvency?

E15–11 The Utopia Paper Company requires $4 million of financing to upgrade its production facilities. It has a choice to finance the upgrade with a 9% long-term loan or to issue additional shares. The company currently has total assets of $10 million, total liabilities of $6 million, shareholders' equity of $4 million, and net income of $1 million. It projects that net income will be $1,098,000 if debt is issued and $1,350,000 if shares are issued.

Calculate ratios under financing alternatives.
(SO 1, 5) AP

Instructions

(a) Calculate the debt to total assets and return on equity ratios under each financing alternative.

(b) Which financing alternative would you recommend for Utopia Paper? Why?

E15–12 The adjusted trial balance for Priya Corporation at July 31, 2008, contained the following:

Prepare long-term liabilities section of balance sheet.
(SO 5) AP

Interest payable	$295,000	Bonds payable, due 2018	$180,000
Note payable	75,000	Discount on bonds payable	3,600
Lease liability	79,500		

Of the lease liability amount, $11,000 is due within the next year. Of the note payable amount, $15,000 is due on January 31, 2009.

Instructions

(a) Prepare the long-term liabilities section of the balance sheet as at July 31, 2008.

(b) Some of the accounts above belong in the balance sheet but not in its long-term liabilities section. What is the correct classification for them?

*E15–13 Creek Corporation issued 10-year bonds on January 1, 2005. Interest is paid semi-annually on January 1 and July 1 and the company's year-end is December 31. Below is a partial amortization schedule for the first few years of the bond issue.

Answer questions about amortization schedule.
(SO 2, 6) AP

Semi-Annual Interest Period	Interest Payment	Interest Expense	Amortization	Unamortized Amount	Bond Carrying Value
Issue date				$6,795	$93,205
1	$3,500	$3,728	$228	6,567	93,433
2	3,500	3,737	237	6,330	93,670
3	3,500	3,747	247	6,083	93,917
4	3,500	3,757	257	5,826	94,174
5	3,500	3,767	267	5,559	94,441
6	3,500	3,778	278	5,281	94,719

Instructions:

(a) What is the face value of the bonds?

(b) Were the bonds issued at a discount or at a premium?

(c) What will the bond carrying value be at the maturity date?

(d) What is the contractual interest rate on the bonds? The market interest rate?

(e) What will be the total interest payment over the ten-year life of the bonds? Total interest expense?

(f) Would your answers in (e) change if the bonds had been issued at a premium instead of a discount or at a discount instead of a premium? Explain.

*E15–14 Québec Corporation issued $650,000 of 10-year, 7% bonds on January 1, 2007, to yield a market interest rate of 6%. Interest is payable semi-annually on July 1 and January 1. Québec has a December 31 year end.

Prepare amortization schedule. Show balance sheet presentation.
(SO 2, 6) AP

Instructions

(a) Calculate the issue price of the bonds.
(b) Prepare an amortization schedule through to December 31, 2008 (four interest periods).
(c) Show the balance sheet presentation of the bonds at December 31, 2008.

Record bond transactions.
(SO 2, 6) AP

*E15–15   Tagawa Corporation issued $600,000 of 10-year, 7% bonds on January 1, 2008, for $559,231. This price resulted in a market interest rate of 8% on the bonds. Interest is payable semi-annually on July 1 and January 1. Tagawa has a December 31 year end. On January 1, 2009, the bonds were redeemed at 90.

Instructions

(a) Record the issue of the bonds on January 1, 2008.
(b) Record the payment of interest on July 1, 2008.
(c) Record the accrual of interest on December 31, 2008.
(d) Record the redemption of the bonds on January 1, 2009.

Problems: Set A

Record bond transactions.
(SO 2) AP

P15–1A   The following selected information is from Peppermint Patty's balance sheet:

PEPPERMINT PATTY LTD. Balance Sheet (partial) December 31, 2007	
Current liabilities	
Bond interest payable	$ 7,000
Long-term liabilities	
Bonds payable, 7%, due January 1, 2012	200,000

Interest is payable semi-annually on January 1 and July 1.

Instructions

(a) Record the payment of the bond interest on January 1, 2008.
(b) Assume that on January 1, 2008, after paying interest, Peppermint Patty redeems $75,000 of the bonds at 101. Record the redemption of the bonds.
(c) Record the payment of the bond interest on July 1, 2008, on the remaining bonds.
(d) Prepare the adjusting entry on December 31, 2008, to accrue the interest on the remaining bonds.

Record bond transactions;
show balance sheet
presentation.
(SO 2) AP

P15–2A   On October 1, 2007, PFQ Corp. issued $600,000 of 10-year, 6% bonds at 98. The bonds pay interest annually on October 1. PFQ's year end is September 30.

Instructions

(a) Record the issue of the bonds on October 1, 2007.
(b) Record the accrual of interest on September 30, 2008, assuming the amortization amount is $2,127.
(c) Show the balance sheet presentation on September 30, 2008.
(d) Record the payment of interest on October 1, 2008.
(e) Assume that on October 1, 2008, after payment of the interest, PFQ redeems all of the bonds at 102. Record the redemption of the bonds.

Record note transactions.
(SO 3) AP

P15–3A   Peter Furlong has just approached a venture capitalist for financing for his sailing school. The lenders are willing to lend Peter $50,000 in exchange for a note payable at a high-risk interest rate of 12%. The note is payable over three years in blended payments of $3,335. Payments are due at the end of every other month (that is, six times per year). Peter receives the $50,000 on May 1, 2008, the first day of his fiscal year and makes the first payment on June 30.

Instructions

(a) Record the issue of the note payable on May 1.
(b) Record the first two instalment payments on June 30 and August 31.
(c) If the note had been repayable in fixed principal payments, rather than in blended payments, calculate how much the cash payment would have been on June 30 and August 31.

P15–4A On September 30, 2007, Atwater Corporation purchased a new piece of equipment for $550,000. The equipment was purchased with a $50,000 down payment and the issue of a $500,000, three-year, 8%, mortgage note payable for the balance. The terms provide for quarterly blended payments of $47,280 starting on December 31. Atwater's year end is December 31.

Record note transactions.
(SO 3) AP

Instructions

(a) Record the purchase of equipment on September 30, 2007.
(b) Record the first two instalment payments on December 31, 2007, and March 31, 2008.
(c) Repeat part (b) assuming that the terms provided for quarterly fixed principal payments of $41,667, rather than blended payments of $47,280.

P15–5A Elite Electronics issues a $350,000, 10-year, 7.5% mortgage note payable on December 31, 2007. The terms of the note provide for semi-annual fixed principal payments of $17,500, plus interest, on June 30 and December 31. Elite Electronics' year end is December 31.

Prepare instalment payment schedule and record note transactions. Show balance sheet presentation.
(SO 3) AP

Instructions

(a) Prepare an instalment payment schedule for the first two years. Round all calculations to the nearest dollar.
(b) Record the issue of the mortgage note payable on December 31, 2007.
(c) Show how the mortgage liability should be reported on the balance sheet at December 31, 2007. (*Hint:* Remember to report any current portion separately from the long-term liability.)
(d) Record the first two instalment payments on June 30, 2008, and December 31, 2008.

P15–6A Presented below are three different lease transactions that occurred for Klippert Inc. Assume that all lease contracts start on January 1, 2008. Klippert does not receive title to any of the properties, either during the lease term or at the end of it.

Analyze lease situations. Discuss financial statement presentation.
(SO 4) AP

	Manufacturing Equipment	Delivery Equipment	Automobile
Annual lease rental payment	$8,000	$4,200	$6,000
Lease term	6 years	4 years	2 years
Estimated economic life	7 years	7 years	5 years
Fair market value of lease asset	$44,000	$19,000	$20,000
Present value of the lease rental payments	$41,000	$13,000	$10,400

Instructions

(a) Which of the leases above are operating leases and which are capital leases? Explain.
(b) How should the lease transaction for each of the above assets be recorded in 2008?
(c) Describe how the lease transaction would be reported on the income statement and balance sheet for each of the above assets for 2008.

P15–7A **Shoppers Drug Mart Corporation** reported the following selected information (in millions):

Calculate and analyze debt ratios.
(SO 4, 5) AN

	2005	2004
Total assets	$4,375.4	$4,117.4
Total liabilities	1,872.4	1,921.0
Interest expense	48.6	60.9
Income tax expense	186.1	168.5
Net income	364.5	307.3

Instructions

(a) Calculate Shoppers Drug Mart's debt to total assets and interest coverage ratios for each year.

(b) Based on the ratios calculated in (a), what conclusions can you make about Shoppers Drug Mart's solvency?

(c) Shoppers Drug Mart had total operating lease commitments of nearly $2.2 billion in 2005 and $1.8 billion in 2004. Explain the impact that an operating lease has on a company's solvency ratios. Does this information change any of your conclusions in (b)?

Analyze leverage.
(SO 1, 5) AN

P15–8A Two competitors in the oil industry, **Petro-Canada** and **Suncor Energy**, recently reported the following selected ratios:

	Petro-Canada	Suncor Energy
Debt to total assets	23.7%	33.3%
Interest coverage	21.7 times	13.4 times
Return on equity	18.6%	22.6%

Instructions

(a) Based on the debt to total assets and interest coverage ratios, which company is more solvent? Explain.

(b) Which company is making better use of debt to produce a higher return? Explain.

Record bond transactions and prepare amortization schedule. Show balance sheet presentation.
(SO 2, 6) AP

*P15–9A On July 1, 2007, Ponasis Corporation issued $1.5 million of 10-year, 6% bonds to yield a market interest rate of 7%. The bonds pay semi-annual interest on July 1 and January 1, and Ponasis has a December 31 year end.

Instructions

(a) Calculate the issue price of the bonds.

(b) Record the issue of the bonds on July 1, 2007.

(c) Prepare an amortization schedule through December 31, 2008 (three interest periods) for this bond issue.

(d) Record the accrual of interest on December 31, 2008.

(e) Show the balance sheet presentation of the bonds at December 31, 2008.

Record bond transactions. Answer questions.
(SO 2, 6) AP

*P15–10A On July 1, 2007, Waubonsee Ltd. issued $2.2 million of 10-year, 5% bonds at $2,379,863. This price resulted in a market interest rate of 4%. The bonds pay semi-annual interest on July 1 and January 1, and Waubonsee has a December 31 year end.

Instructions

(a) Record the following transactions:

1. The issue of the bonds on July 1, 2007
2. The accrual of interest on December 31, 2007
3. The payment of interest on January 1, 2008
4. The payment of interest on July 1, 2008

(b) Answer the following questions:
1. What amount of interest expense is reported for 2007?
2. Would the bond interest expense reported in 2007 be the same as, greater than, or less than the amount that would be reported if the bonds had been issued at a discount rather than at a premium? Explain.
3. Determine the total cost of borrowing over the life of the bonds.
4. Would the total bond interest expense be greater than, the same as, or less than the total interest expense that would be reported if the bonds had been issued at a discount rather than at a premium? Explain.

Problems: Set B

P15–1B The following is from Disch Corp.'s balance sheet:

Record bond transactions. (SO 2) AP

DISCH CORP.
Balance Sheet (partial)
December 31, 2007

Current liabilities	
Bond interest payable	$ 48,000
Long-term liabilities	
Bonds payable, 6%, due January 1, 2014	1,600,000

Interest is payable semi-annually on January 1 and July 1.

Instructions

(a) Record the payment of the bond interest on January 1, 2008.
(b) Assume that on January 1, 2008, after paying interest, Disch redeems $400,000 of the bonds at 99. Record the redemption of the bonds.
(c) Record the payment of the bond interest on July 1, 2008, on the remaining bonds.
(d) Prepare the adjusting entry on December 31, 2008, to accrue the interest on the remaining bonds.

P15–2B On May 1, 2007, MEM Corp. issued $800,000 of five-year, 9% bonds at 104. The bonds pay interest annually on May 1. MEM's year end is April 30.

Record bond transactions; show balance sheet presentation. (SO 2) AP

Instructions

(a) Record the issue of the bonds on May 1, 2007.
(b) Record the accrual of interest on April 30, 2008, assuming the amortization amount is $5,445.
(c) Show the balance sheet presentation on April 30, 2008.
(d) Record the payment of interest on May 1, 2008.
(e) Assume that on May 1, 2008, after payment of the interest, MEM redeems all of the bonds at 98. Record the redemption of the bonds.

P15–3B A local company has just approached a venture capitalist for financing to develop a ski hill. On April 1, 2007, the venture capitalist loaned the company $100,000 at an interest rate of 10%. The loan is repayable over four years in fixed principal payments of $25,000 a year. The first payment is due March 31, 2008. The ski hill operator's year end will be March 31.

Record note transactions. (SO 3) AP

Instructions

(a) Record the issue of the note payable on April 1, 2007.
(b) Record the first two instalment payments on March 31, 2008, and March 31, 2009.
(c) Explain how the interest expense and reduction of the note payable would change in (b) if the note had been repayable in blended payments of $31,547, rather than in fixed principal payments.

P15–4B On July 31, 2008, Myron Corporation purchased a piece of equipment for $750,000. The equipment was purchased with a $50,000 down payment and through the issue of a $700,000, four-year, 6% mortgage note payable for the balance. The terms provide for the mortgage to be repaid with monthly blended payments of $16,440 starting on August 31.

Instructions

(a) Record the issue of the note payable on July 31.

(b) Record the first two instalment payments on August 31 and September 30.

(c) Repeat part (b) assuming that the terms provided for monthly fixed principal payments of $14,583, rather than blended payments of $16,440.

P15–5B Kinyae Electronics issues a $500,000, 10-year, 7% mortgage note payable on December 31, 2007, to help finance a plant expansion. The terms of the note provide for blended payments of $35,181. Payments are due on June 30 and December 31.

Instructions

(a) Prepare an instalment payment schedule for the first two years. Round all calculations to the nearest dollar.

(b) Record the issue of the mortgage note payable on December 31, 2007.

(c) Show how the mortgage liability should be reported on the balance sheet at December 31, 2007. (*Hint:* Remember to report any current portion separately from the long-term liability.)

(d) Record the first two instalment payments on June 30, 2008, and December 31, 2008.

P15–6B Three different lease transactions are presented below for Manitoba Enterprises. Assume that all lease transactions start on January 1, 2008. Manitoba does not receive title to the properties, either during the lease term or at the end of it.

	Bulldozer	Truck	Photocopier
Lease term	5 years	6 years	3 years
Estimated economic life	15 years	7 years	6 years
Yearly rental	$13,000	$15,000	$4,000
Fair market value of leased asset	$80,000	$85,000	$17,500
Present value of the lease rental payments	$55,000	$79,000	$10,500

Instructions

(a) Which of the above leases are operating leases and which are capital leases? Explain.

(b) How should the lease transaction for each of the above assets be recorded in 2008?

(c) Describe how the lease transaction would be reported on the income statement and balance sheet for each of the above assets for 2008.

P15–7B **Loblaw Companies Limited** reported the following selected information (in millions):

	2005	2004
Total assets	$13,761	$12,949
Total liabilities	7,875	7,535
Interest expense	252	239
Income tax expense	400	445
Net income	746	968

Instructions

(a) Calculate Loblaw's debt to total assets and interest coverage ratios for each year.

(b) Based on the ratios calculated in (a), what conclusions can you make about Loblaw's solvency?

(c) Loblaw has total operating lease commitments of $1,424 million in 2005 and $1,104 million in 2004. Explain the impact that an operating lease has on a company's solvency ratios. Does this information change any of your conclusions in (b)?

P15–8B Two competitors in the retail industry, **Sears Canada** and **Wal-Mart**, recently reported the following selected ratios:

	Sears Canada	Wal-Mart
Debt to total assets	53.7%	42.2%
Interest coverage	20.6 times	17.1 times
Return on equity	61.1%	21.9%

Instructions

(a) Based on the debt to total assets and interest coverage ratios, which company is more solvent? Explain.
(b) Which company is making better use of debt to produce a higher return? Explain.

*P15–9B On July 1, 2007, Global Satellites issued $1.2 million of 10-year, 7% bonds to yield a market interest rate of 8%. Global uses the effective-interest method of amortization. The bonds pay semi-annual interest on July 1 and January 1, and Global has a December 31 year end.

Instructions

(a) Calculate the issue price of the bonds.
(b) Record the issue of the bonds on July 1, 2007.
(c) Prepare an amortization table through December 31, 2008 (three interest periods) for this bond issue.
(d) Record the accrual of interest on December 31, 2008.
(e) Show the balance sheet presentation of the bonds at December 31, 2008.

*P15–10B On July 1, 2007, Webhancer Corp. issued $2 million of 10-year, 6% bonds at $2,155,890. This price resulted in a 5% market interest rate on the bonds. The bonds pay semi-annual interest on July 1 and January 1, and Webhancer has a December 31 year end.

Instructions

(a) Record the following transactions:
  1. The issue of the bonds on July 1, 2007
  2. The accrual of interest on December 31, 2007
  3. The payment of interest on January 1, 2008
  4. The payment of interest on July 1, 2008
(b) Answer the following questions:
  1. What amount of interest expense is reported for 2007?
  2. Would the bond interest expense reported in 2007 be the same as, greater than, or less than the amount that would be reported if the bonds had been issued at a discount rather than at a premium? Explain.
  3. Determine the total cost of borrowing over the life of the bond.
  4. Would the total bond interest expense be greater than, the same as, or less than the total interest expense that would be reported if the bonds had been issued at a discount rather than at a premium? Explain.

Continuing Cookie Chronicle

(*Note:* This is a continuation of the Cookie Chronicle from Chapters 1 through 14.)

Natalie and Curtis anticipate great demand for their cookies and muffins. As a result, they are making plans to purchase a commercial oven. The cost of this oven is estimated at $14,000, and the company already has $5,000 set aside for the purchase. Natalie and Curtis have met with their bank manager. She is willing to lend Cookie & Coffee Creations Ltd. $9,000 on November 1, 2008, for a period of three years at a 5% interest rate. The bank manager has set out the following two payment alternatives:

Alternative 1: The terms provide for fixed principal payments of $1,500, on May 1 and November 1 of each year.

Alternative 2: The terms provide for blended payments of $1,634, on May 1 and November 1 of each year.

Natalie and Curtis ask you to help them decide which alternative is better for them.

Instructions

(a) Prepare instalment payment schedules for each of the alternatives for the full term of the loan.

(b) Prepare the journal entry for the purchase of the oven and the issue of the note payable on November 1, 2008.

(c) Prepare the journal entries for the first two instalment payments under each alternative.

(d) Determine the current portion of the note payable and the long-term portion of the note payable as at October 31, 2009, under each alternative.

(e) Which payment plan alternative do you recommend? Why?

BROADENING YOUR PERSPECTIVE

Financial Reporting and Analysis

Financial Reporting Problem

BYP15–1 Refer to the consolidated financial statements and notes of **The Forzani Group Ltd.** in Appendix A.

Instructions

(a) What was Forzani's long-term debt at January 29, 2006? By how much has Forzani's total long-term debt increased (decreased) since January 30, 2005?

(b) Does Forzani separate the current portion of its debt from its long-term debt? If so, how much of its long-term debt is currently due?

(c) What kind of long-term debt does Forzani have?

(d) Does Forzani have any off–balance sheet financing that you can determine?

(e) Forzani's debt to total assets and interest coverage ratios for fiscal 2006 were calculated in Illustrations 15-9 and 15-10 in the chapter. Calculate these ratios for fiscal 2005. Comment on whether Forzani's solvency improved or worsened in 2005.

Interpreting Financial Statements

BYP15–2 **Reitmans (Canada) Limited** and **La Senza Corporation** are two specialty women's clothing merchandisers. Here are financial data for both companies for 2006 (in thousands):

	Reitmans	La Senza
Balance sheet data		
Total assets	$523,233	$232,744
Total liabilities	132,976	89,562
Income statement data		
Interest expense	1,132	191
Income tax expense	40,122	11,171
Net income (loss)	84,889	17,737

Instructions

(a) Calculate the debt to total assets and interest coverage ratios for each company. Discuss the solvency of each company compared to the other.

(b) The notes to the financial statements indicate that many of the retail stores' furniture, fixtures, and other such items are leased using operating leases. Discuss the implications of these operating leases for each company's solvency.

Critical Thinking

Collaborative Learning Activity

Note to instructor: Additional instructions and material for this group activity can be found on the Instructor Resource Site.

BYP15–3 In this group activity, you will review accounting for bonds selling at a discount or bonds selling at a premium. You will review the entries for your situation at:

1. Issue of the bonds
2. Payment of interest
3. Redemption of the bonds before maturity

Instructions

(a) Your instructor will divide the class into "home" groups. Each member of your group will select either bonds selling at a discount or bonds selling at a premium and then move to join the "expert" group for that particular situation.

(b) In the "expert" group, you will be given a handout to help you in your discussion of the accounting for the issue of bonds, payment of interest, and redemption of bonds. Ensure that each group member thoroughly understands these three journal entries for your situation.

(c) Return to your "home" group and explain your entries to the other students in the group.

(d) You may be asked by your instructor to write a short quiz on this topic.

Study Aids:
Working in Groups

Communication Activity

BYP15–4 Financial statement users are interested in the obligations that a company has from past transactions. It is important to determine which liabilities are current and which are long-term. Some company obligations are not recorded on the balance sheet itself, however; instead they are disclosed in the notes to the financial statements.

Instructions

Write a memorandum to a friend of yours who has inherited some money and would like to invest in some companies. Your friend plans to get professional advice before investing but would like you to review some basics with her. For instance, she is trying to determine the amount of cash that a

Study Aids:
Writing Handbook

company will have to pay within the next five years. She knows she should start with the liabilities that are on the balance sheet, but she is wondering if any of those can be settled without the company having to write a cheque. She would also like to know what kinds of liabilities could be buried somewhere in the notes to the financial statements.

Ethics Case

**Study Aids:
Ethics in Accounting**

BYP15–5 Enron Corporation—once the world's largest electronic trader in natural gas and electricity—was one of the largest corporate bankruptcies in American history. Just weeks before it filed for bankruptcy, the company admitted that it had shifted billions of dollars of debt off its balance sheets and into a variety of complex partnerships.

One journalist wrote: "The Enron practice of shifting liabilities off the books to more than 3,500 subsidiaries raised so many red flags that you'd think you were in a military parade somewhere in China." Yet, Enron and its auditors argued vehemently that the "special purpose entity" partnerships they used were in accordance with GAAP and fully disclosed, even if they were not recorded in the books.

Instructions

(a) Who are the stakeholders in this situation?

(b) Explain how shifting debt off the balance sheet might mislead investors.

(c) Do you think that management has an obligation to ensure that a company's accounting and disclosure is relevant to users, over and above following GAAP?

ANSWERS TO CHAPTER QUESTIONS

Answers to Accounting in Action Insight Questions

Business Insight, p. 761

Q: What is the likely reason that corporations, and banks in particular, were so interested in selling bonds in 2005?

A: The bonds were of high investment quality, so the risk and interest rates were relatively low. Consequently, corporations were able to raise additional financing, or replace old financing that had higher interest rates, with a better interest rate. In addition, debt financing likely resulted in improved earnings per share and return on equity ratios.

Business Insight, p. 776

Q: What are the advantages to Virgin Mobile of leasing space on a phone company's network, rather than developing its own network infrastructure?

A: In leasing space on T-Mobile's network, Virgin Mobile avoids the upfront capital costs that would be required to develop its own network infrastructure as well as later ongoing technological and other upgrades. In addition, Virgin Mobile can likely purchase the space at a cheaper rate from T-Mobile (because it is purchasing a large amount of space) than it can resell it for to its many customers each renting smaller amounts of space.

Business Insight, p. 781

Q: What is the likely reason that a high interest coverage ratio might result in a high share price?

A: Companies with high interest coverage ratios have a greater ability to handle their debt, so they are considered less risky than other companies. Investors would be more interested in purchasing the shares of less risky companies, if all other factors are equal.

Answer to Forzani Review It Question 3, p. 778

Forzani does not have any capital leases. It does, however, have an operating lease for land (see Building on Leased Land reported in note 3). Note 10 reports the company's commitments for this lease, as well as for equipment leases, over the next five years.

Answers to Self-Study Questions

1. d   2. a   3. c   4. b   5. b   6. c   7. b   8. c   9. d   *10. c

Remember to go back to the Navigator Box at the beginning of the chapter to check off your completed work.

concepts for review >>

Before studying this chapter, you should understand or, if necessary, review:

a. How to calculate and record interest. (Ch. 3, pp. 117–118, Ch. 8, p. 410, and Ch. 15, pp. 765–768 and 772–774)

b. Where short- and long-term investments are classified on a balance sheet. (Ch. 4, pp. 176–177)

c. What comprehensive income is. (Ch. 13, pp. 682–683)

d. The comprehensive income statement. (Ch. 14, p. 721)

e. How to record bond transactions. (Ch. 15, pp. 765–770)

Building a Global Player on B.C.'s Coast

DUNCAN, B.C.—Up until 2006, Western Forest Products Inc., based in Duncan, B.C., was the second-largest coastal woodland operator in British Columbia. Things changed that year, however, when it purchased Cascadia Forest Products Ltd. for $220 million from a subsidiary of Brookfield Asset Management Inc., and Englewood Logging Division for $45 million from Canfor Corporation.

Cascadia Forest Products, a producer of valuable, high-quality wood products harvested from sustainably managed certified forests, was the largest lumber producer on the B.C. coast, with more than 2,000 employees and sales offices and agencies overseas.

Western Forest Products Inc.: westernforest.com

Englewood Logging Division, located on Northern Vancouver Island next to Western's main logging operations, comprised Tree Farm Licence 37 (TFL 37), which includes approximately 6,800 hectares of private lands. Western's acquisition included timber licences, existing capital improvements and infrastructure, machinery, equipment, and railway rolling stock. Western took on specific contracts and equipment leases and planned to keep the approximately 270 employees currently involved in harvesting operations.

"The acquisition of TFL 37 represents an important milestone in the restructuring of the coastal forest industry and obtaining a secure source of logs for our lumber mills," said president and CEO Reynold Hert. "With the transaction now closed, we can begin to move forward to integrate TFL 37 with our own operations."

Western Forest Products' main activities include timber harvesting, reforestation, sawmilling logs into lumber and wood chips, and value-added manufacturing. More than 95 percent of its logging is done on government-owned timberlands in B.C. And, while all of its operations, employees, and corporate facilities are located in the B.C. coastal region, its products are sold in more than 20 countries worldwide.

With the acquisition of Englewood and Cascadia, Western has become the largest coastal woodland operator and lumber producer in British Columbia, with an annual allowable cut of approximately 7.7 million cubic metres and nine sawmills producing a lumber capacity of 1.5 billion board feet.

"Closing the acquisition of Cascadia is a significant milestone in executing our strategic plan of creating a coastal lumber producer capable of competing in the global softwood markets," Mr. Hert said.

By setting out and following a strategic investment plan, Western moved from being number two to number one.

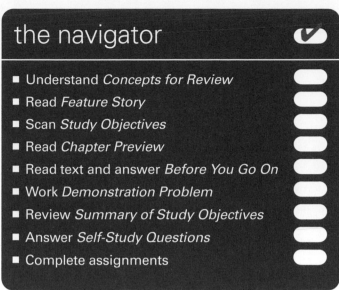

the navigator

- Understand *Concepts for Review*
- Read *Feature Story*
- Scan *Study Objectives*
- Read *Chapter Preview*
- Read text and answer *Before You Go On*
- Work *Demonstration Problem*
- Review *Summary of Study Objectives*
- Answer *Self-Study Questions*
- Complete assignments

c h a p t e r   1 6
Investments

study objectives >>

After studying this chapter, you should be able to:

1. Classify investments.
2. Account for debt investments.
3. Account for equity investments.
4. Indicate how investments are valued.
5. Indicate how investments are reported in the financial statements.

Investments can include debt and equity, and can be made by individuals or corporations. Investments can be either passive or for strategic purposes, as in our feature story. They can be bought for a short or long period of time. As you will see in this chapter, the way in which a company accounts for its investments is determined by several factors.

The chapter is organized as follows:

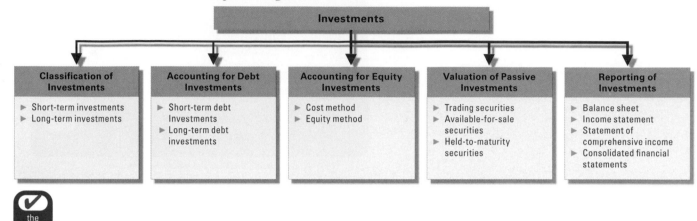

Classification of Investments

study objective 1

Classify investments.

Corporations generally purchase investments in debt securities (money-market instruments, bonds, commercial paper, or similar items) and equity securities (preferred and common shares) for one of two reasons. The investment may be purchased as a **passive investment** to generate investment income. Or, it might be purchased as a **strategic investment** to influence or control the operations of another company in some way.

There are several reasons for a company to purchase debt or equity securities of another company as a **passive investment**. A corporation may have cash that it does not immediately need. For example, many companies have seasonal fluctuations in sales which can lead to idle cash until purchases are made for the next busy season. Until the cash is needed, these companies may decide to invest it to earn a higher return than they would get if they just kept the excess cash in the bank.

When investing excess cash for short periods of time, corporations invest in debt securities—usually money-market instruments which are low-risk and highly liquid. Money-market instruments include money-market funds, bankers acceptances, term deposits, and treasury bills. It is not wise to invest short-term excess cash in equity securities, because share prices can drop suddenly and dramatically. If a company does invest excess cash in shares and the price of the shares falls just before the company needs the cash again, it will be forced to sell its equity investment at a loss. Money-market instruments do not change in market value. Their value comes from the interest they generate.

Excess cash may also be invested for the longer term in debt securities to generate a steady source of interest income (e.g., bonds). Or, it may be invested in equity securities to generate dividend income. Preferred shares are usually purchased for dividend purposes, but both common and preferred shares can and do pay dividends. Companies also invest in debt and equity securities hoping that they can sell them at a higher price than they originally paid for them. They speculate that the investment will increase in value and result in a gain when it is sold.

Some companies, such as financial institutions, are in the business of actively buying and selling securities in the hope of generating investment income from price fluctuations.

Debt and equity securities that are purchased for this purpose are known as trading securities, which we will discuss later in the chapter.

While either debt or equity securities can be purchased as a passive investment, only equity securities (normally common shares) can be purchased as a **strategic investment**. For example, a company may buy some or all of the common shares of another company in a related or new industry to become part of that industry. Or a company might buy another company in the same industry as itself. In particular, it may buy an interest in a supplier to ensure an uninterrupted source of raw materials as Western Forest Products did when it purchased the Englewood Logging Division. As described in our feature story, this purchase secured a source of logs for its lumber mills.

The acquisition of Englewood is known as a vertical acquisition. The purchase of a company that is in the industry, but involved in a different activity, is called a vertical acquisition. In contrast, the purchase of Cascadia Forest Products is known as a horizontal acquisition. In a horizontal acquisition, the purchased company is in the same activity as the company buying it.

In summary, businesses invest in debt and equity securities of other companies for the reasons shown in Illustration 16-1.

Reason	Purpose	Type of Investment
Passive investment	To generate investment income	Debt securities (money-market instruments, bonds, commercial paper) and equity securities (preferred and common shares)
Strategic investment	To influence or control another company	Equity securities (common shares)

Illustration 16-1 ◄

Why businesses invest

ACCOUNTING IN ACTION ▶ Business Insight

Lots of cash, an attractive Canadian dollar, high commodity prices, and a healthy economy drove acquisitions of Canadian companies to record levels in the second quarter of 2006. A total of 480 acquisitions were announced in the second quarter with a value of $86.1 billion. This value was triple that of the first quarter and set a new record, surpassing even the dot.com boom. The largest deal in the second quarter was Swiss mining giant Xstrata's purchase of Canadian mining powerhouse Falconbridge for $19.2 billion. The combination of the two companies will result in the fifth largest mining company in the world spanning 18 countries.

Source: Richard Blackwell, "Major Mining M&As Fuel a Record Quarter," *The Globe and Mail*, August 24, 2006, B11.

? Was the acquisition of Falconbridge by Xstrata a passive or strategic investment? What are some advantages that Xstrata might now have because of its acquisition of Falconbridge?

Short-Term Investments

Once a company decides to invest in debt or equity securities, for any of the reasons described in the preceding section, it must also determine whether the investment will be short- or long-term. **Short-term investments** are debt or equity securities that (1) are readily marketable, *or* (2) mature within the next year. Note that only one of these two criteria must be met for the investment to be classified as short-term, not both. Short-term investments are always passive investments.

An investment is "readily marketable" if it is capable of reasonably prompt liquidation. That means it can be sold easily whenever cash is needed. Money-market instruments meet this criterion because they can easily be sold to other investors. Shares and bonds that are traded on organized securities exchanges, such as the Toronto Stock Exchange, are readily marketable. They can be bought and sold daily. In contrast, there may be only a limited market for the securities issued by small corporations and no market at all for the securities of a privately held company.

You will recall that we learned about cash equivalents in Chapter 7. Cash equivalents are highly liquid investments. They normally have maturities of three months or less from the date they were purchased. Some companies combine this type of investment with cash and report the total as cash and cash equivalents, rather than as a short-term investment on their balance sheet.

Classifying Short-Term Investments

Short-term investments can be further classified as either trading securities or available-for-sale securities. **Trading securities** are debt or equity securities that are purchased and held for resale in the short term, hopefully at a gain. "Trading" in this context means frequent buying and selling for the purpose of generating a gain (hopefully) from short-term differences in prices. Trading securities are often found in financial institutions, such as banks, which actively manage an investment portfolio as part of their normal business operations.

Available-for-sale securities are debt and equity securities that are *not* trading securities and that are *not* held-to-maturity securities. We have just learned what trading securities are and we will learn what held-to-maturity securities are in the next section. For now, it is enough to say that the available-for-sale classification is kind of a catch-all for investments that do not fit in any other classification.

Let's move away now from what available-for-sale securities are not, and talk instead about what they are. Available-for-sale securities are debt or equity securities that are held with the intention of selling them sometime in the future. During the time that available-for-sale securities are held, they will likely generate investment revenue through interest or dividends. When available-for-sale securities are sold, they will generate a gain or loss on sale.

Trading securities are normally considered to be short-term investments. Available-for-sale securities can be either short- or long-term, depending on whether they are readily marketable and their maturity date.

Long-Term Investments

Long-term investments can also consist of debt and equity securities that are purchased for either passive or strategic reasons. To determine whether a debt or equity security is long-term, we test the investment against the short-term investment criteria. Investments that are not readily marketable and do not mature within the next year are **long-term investments**.

Classifying Long-Term Investments

As we discussed in the previous section, available-for-sale securities can be classified as long-term investments. Held-to-maturity securities are another example of a long-term investment.

Held-to-maturity securities are debt securities issued by companies to raise financing for an expansion, acquisitions, or other reasons. A debt security is classified as held-to-maturity if the investor has the intention and ability to hold the investment until it matures. Naturally, held-to-maturity securities are always long-term investments, except when they are less than one year away from their maturity date.

Note that held-to-maturity securities are always debt securities. Equity securities cannot be held-to-maturity as they have no maturity date. Available-for-sale and held-to-maturity securities are always passive investments.

Equity investments purchased for strategic reasons, such as to have influence or control over a company, are also classified as long-term investments. Western Forest Products' acquisition of Cascadia Forest Products and Englewood Logging Division are both long-term equity investments. We will learn more about these types of investments later in the chapter.

Illustration 16-2 summarizes the different types of short- and long-term investments that can be purchased as passive investments.

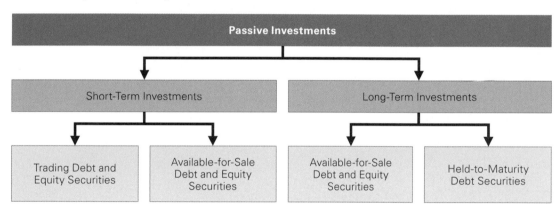

Illustration 16-2 ◀

Classification of passive investments

BEFORE YOU GO ON...

▶Review It

1. What are the reasons that corporations invest in debt and equity securities?
2. What criteria must be met for an investment to be classified as short-term? As long-term?
3. What are the differences between trading securities, available-for-sale securities, and held-to-maturity securities?
4. Are trading securities normally classified as short- or long-term investments? What about available-for-sale securities? Held-to-maturity securities?

Related exercise material: BE16–1, BE16–2, and E16–1.

the
navigator

Accounting for Debt Investments

Debt investments are investments in money-market instruments (that are not classified as cash equivalents), as well as investments in bonds, commercial paper, and a large variety of other debt securities. The accounting for debt investments can be different depending on whether the investments are short- or long-term.

study objective 2

Account for debt investments.

Short-Term Debt Investments

If a company actively manages and trades its debt securities to sell them in the near term, these debt investments are classified as trading securities. Otherwise, they are classified as available-for-sale securities, which is more common for most companies.

In accounting for short-term debt investments, entries are required to record (1) the acquisition, (2) the interest revenue, and (3) the sale. We will look at the accounting for two types of debt investments—money-market instruments and bonds—in the next sections.

Money-Market Instruments

As we have learned, money-market instruments can be reasonably safe investments that allow a company to earn a higher interest rate than can normally be earned on a regular bank account balance. Companies often buy and sell money-market instruments as a way to manage their cash flow.

Recording Acquisitions of Money-Market Instruments. Assume that Cheung Corporation has an excess of cash on hand. On November 30, 2007, it purchases a $5,000, three-month, two-percent term deposit. Most term deposits pay a fixed interest rate on maturity, although variable interest rates are also possible. We will assume, for the purpose of this example, that the money-market instrument has been classified as an available-for-sale investment. The entry to record the investment is as follows:

A = L + SE
+5,000
−5,000

↓ Cash flows: −5,000

Nov. 30	Available-for-Sale—Term Deposit	5,000	
	Cash		5,000
	To record purchase of 3-month, 2% term deposit.		

Note that in the debit entry above, we have placed the classification of the security—"available-for-sale" in this instance—before the account name Term Deposit. Some companies simply maintain each investment account separately in their general ledger, and then group them into the right investment portfolio category at year end for reporting purposes. Other companies maintain a subsidiary ledger for each category of investment.

You will recall that we learned about the use of subsidiary ledgers for inventory and accounts receivable in Part 1 of this textbook. To help you become more familiar with subsidiary ledger classifications, we will identify each entry by its subsidiary ledger account name where appropriate. In our example above, we have assumed that Cheung Corporation has a general ledger account called Available-for-Sale Securities, with a supporting subsidiary ledger that gives details for each individual investment.

These names, "Available-for-Sale," "Trading," or "Held-to-Maturity" need not be used in the financial statements. In most cases, investments are grouped together for reporting purposes as "Financial Assets" or some other general descriptor. We use the specific terms here to help you distinguish between the different types of investments for accounting purposes.

Recording Interest Revenue. Cheung Corporation's year end is December 31, so it is necessary to accrue $8 of interest for the month of December ($5,000 × 2% × $\frac{1}{12}$, rounded to the nearest dollar).

A = L + SE
+8   +8

Cash flows: no effect

Dec. 31	Interest Receivable	8	
	Interest Revenue		8
	To accrue interest on term deposit.		

Recording the Maturity of Money-Market Instruments. On February 28, 2008, when the term deposit matures, it is necessary to (1) update the interest for the latest period, and (2) record the receipt of cash and the elimination of the term deposit. Most banks credit the company's bank account directly for the interest and principal amounts when a term deposit matures unless they have been asked to do something else.

Feb. 28	Cash	5,025	
	Interest Receivable		8
	Interest Revenue ($5,000 × 2% × ²⁄₁₂)		17
	Available-for-Sale—Term Deposit		5,000
	To record maturity of term deposit.		

A	=	L	+	SE
+5,025				+17
−8				
−5,000				

↑ Cash flows: +5,025

If the company does not need the money when the term deposit matures, it may reinvest it by buying another term deposit. In such cases, two separate entries should be recorded. One entry, as above, records the maturation of the first term deposit and interest earned. The second entry records the acquisition of the new term deposit, which will have a different maturity date and may also have a different interest rate.

If a term deposit, or other money-market instrument, is sold before it matures, it does not usually result in any gain or loss—just less interest revenue. Some term deposits are not cashable before their maturity date and some are. Before purchasing them, it is wise to look carefully at any penalties or conditions attached to money-market instruments that will be purchased for short-term use.

Bonds

We learned about bonds in Chapter 15 from the liability side—i.e., from the issuer's perspective. There we saw that corporations, governments, and universities issue bonds which are then purchased by investors. The issuer of the bonds is known as the **investee**. The purchaser of the bonds, or the bondholder, is known as the **investor**. Investments in bonds can be classified as trading securities or as available-for-sale securities, depending on the intent to sell. The accounting for each type of security is the same.

The recording of investments in bonds is different from the recording of money-market instruments in three ways: (1) the determination of cost, (2) the timing of the receipt of interest, and (3) the sale of the bond. First, the cost of the bond may include a discount or a premium, whereas money-market instruments are purchased at face value. Second, bond investments receive interest semi-annually, while money-market investments receive interest only at maturity. Third, bonds are usually for a much longer term than money-market instruments, which means that they are often sold before they mature if cash is needed, and a gain or loss can result.

Recording Acquisitions of Bonds. At acquisition, the bond is recorded at its purchase price or cost. Debt (and equity) securities are supposed to be recorded at market value at acquisition. Generally, cost does equal the market value at the acquisition date. We will learn how to deal with situations where the market value moves away from the acquisition cost later in this chapter.

Note that it does not matter if the bonds are purchased at face value or at a discount or premium. You will recall from Chapter 15 that a discount occurs when a bond is purchased below its face value and a premium occurs when a bond is purchased above its face value. It is the actual cost that is recorded in the investment account. While the cost is affected by whether the company has to pay more or less for the bonds than their face value, a bond discount or premium is not recorded separately for the short-term investor as it would be for the issuer, for whom it is a liability. In other words, any premium or discount is netted with the face value when recording a short-term investment.

Transaction costs, such as brokerage fees, are sometimes incurred when debt (or equity) investments are purchased. Companies have a choice as to whether to expense or capitalize transaction costs on available-for-sale or held-to-maturity securities, but they must expense transaction costs incurred on trading securities. We will ignore the accounting for transaction costs in this textbook for simplicity—this topic will be discussed in detail in an intermediate accounting course.

To illustrate the accounting for a short-term investment in bonds, assume that Kuhl Corporation acquires $50,000 face value of Doan Inc. 10-year, six-percent bonds on January 1, 2008, for $49,000. Kuhl Corporation, as the bondholder, is the investor. Doan Inc., as the issuer of the bonds, is the investee. Assuming that Kuhl is holding these bonds as a short-term available-for-sale security, the entry to record the investment is as follows:

	Jan. 1	Available-for-Sale—Doan Bonds	49,000	
		Cash		49,000
		To record purchase of Doan bonds.		

The bonds are recorded at their acquisition cost of $49,000. Note that the $1,000 discount on the bonds ($50,000 − $49,000) is not recorded separately, as mentioned above. It is included (hidden) in the Available-for Sale account entry.

Recording Interest Revenue. The bonds pay interest of $1,500 ($50,000 × 6% × $\frac{6}{12}$) semi-annually on July 1 and January 1. As we learned in Chapter 15, interest is paid on face value and not on acquisition cost or carrying value. The following entry records the receipt of interest on July 1:

	July 1	Cash	1,500	
		Interest Revenue		1,500
		To record receipt of interest on Doan bonds.		

Note that any premium or discount on bonds (recorded net as part of the acquisition cost as shown in the January 1 journal entry above) is not amortized to interest revenue in a short-term debt investment situation. This is in contrast to what we learned in Chapter 15 for long-term liabilities. In Chapter 15, any premium or discount on bonds for the issuer was amortized to interest expense. The reason for this difference in accounting treatment is because the bonds are held for a short period of time and any misstatement of interest revenue is not considered to be significant.

Recording Sales of Bonds. When the bonds are sold, it is necessary to (1) update any unrecorded interest up to the date of sale, (2) debit Cash for the proceeds received, (3) credit the investment account for the cost of the bonds, and (4) record any gain or loss on sale. Any difference between the proceeds from the sale of the bonds and their original cost is recorded as a gain or loss.

Assume, for example, that Kuhl receives $50,500 on the sale of the Doan bonds on July 1, 2008, after receiving (and recording) the interest due. Since the debt securities cost $49,000, a gain of $1,500 has been realized. The entry to record the sale follows:

July 1	Cash	50,500	
	Available-for-Sale—Doan Bonds		49,000
	Gain on Sale of Available-for-Sale Securities		1,500
	To record sale of Doan bonds.		

A	=	L	+	SE
+50,500				+1,500
−49,000				

↑ Cash flows: +50,500

We call the gain on sale a *realized* gain in this situation because the sale has actually happened. This is to distinguish **realized gains and losses** from *unrealized* gains or losses, which we will discuss later in the chapter when we learn how to revalue investments to market value for reporting purposes.

A realized gain on the sale of available-for-sale securities is reported as other revenue in the income statement.

Recording Bonds for Investor and Investee. Using the Kuhl Corporation example, Illustration 16-3 compares the recording of the bonds as a short-term investment for Kuhl (the investor) and the recording of the bonds as a long-term liability for Doan (the investee). For the purpose of this illustration, we have assumed that the discount amortization for the first interest period is $150.

Illustration 16-3 ▼

Comparison of short-term investment and long-term liability

	Kuhl Corporation (Investor)		
Jan. 1	Available-for-Sale—Doan Bonds	49,000	
	Cash		49,000
July 1	Cash	1,500	
	Interest Revenue		1,500
1	Cash	50,500	
	Available-for-Sale—Doan Bonds		49,000
	Gain on Sale of Available-for-Sale Securities		1,500

	Doan Inc. (Investee)		
Jan. 1	Cash	49,000	
	Discount on Bonds Payable	1,000	
	Bonds Payable		50,000
July 1	Interest Expense	1,650	
	Discount on Bonds Payable		150
	Cash		1,500
1	No entry		

Recording a short-term investment in bonds (an asset) for an investor differs from the recording of bonds payable (a liability) for an investee in several ways. First, premiums and discounts are not recorded separately for the investor as they are for the investee. Second, any premium or discount is not amortized by the investor as it is for the investee. Lastly, assuming that Kuhl sold its bonds on the open market, the issuer, Doan Inc., is not affected by this transaction. It would only be affected if the bonds were redeemed before maturity or repaid at maturity.

Long-Term Debt Investments

The accounting for short- and long-term debt investments is similar. The accounting at acquisition is the same. For an investment in bonds, if there is a bond premium or discount, it is not recorded separately; instead, the amount recorded in the debt investment account is net of any premium or discount for both short- and long-term investments.

Long-term debt investments can be classified as either available-for-sale securities or held-to-maturity securities, depending on whether the company's intent is to sell the bonds sometime in the future or to hold them until they mature. Either way, the initial accounting is the same for both types of long-term debt investments.

To illustrate the recording of a long-term investment in bonds, we will use the following example where Khadr Inc. purchases $100,000 of ABC Corporation five-year, seven-percent bonds at 101 on January 1. Khadr intends to hold this investment until it matures.

Jan. 1	Held-to-Maturity—ABC Bonds	101,000	
	Cash		101,000
	To record purchase of ABC bonds.		

Note that the investment is recorded net of any premium or discount, similar to that illustrated earlier for the recording of a short-term investment.

The recording of interest revenue differs for short- and long-term investments. As we learned above, premiums and discounts are not amortized to interest revenue for short-term investments. This is because the bonds are held for a short period of time. In contrast, for long-term investments, any premium or discount recorded in the investment account is amortized to interest revenue over the remaining term of the bonds. A premium occurs when a bond is issued for more than its face value. If there is a bond premium, interest revenue is reduced by the amortization amount. A discount occurs when a bond is issued for less than its face value. If there is a bond discount, interest revenue is increased by the amortization amount. Like the issuer of the bonds, the investor uses the effective-interest method of amortization (explained in Chapter 15 in Appendix 15A).

To continue our Khadr example, assume that interest is payable semi-annually on July 1 and January 1. The semi-annual amortization of the premium is assumed to be $290 for the first interest period in this example. The entry required to record the receipt of the interest and amortization of the premium on July 1 is as follows:

July 1	Cash	3,500	
	Held-to-Maturity—ABC Bonds		290
	Interest Revenue		3,210
	To record receipt of interest on ABC bonds.		

The interest received is $3,500 ($100,000 × 7% × $\frac{6}{12}$). Interest revenue includes the interest received, $3,500, less the amortization of the premium, $290. While a premium account would be separately recorded and amortized for the issuer of the bonds, the investment account "Held-to-Maturity—ABC Bonds" is reduced for the amortization of the premium for the investor in the bonds.

Illustration 16-4 compares the recording of the bonds as an investment for Khadr Inc. (the investor) and as a liability for ABC Corporation (the investee) for the bond issue and first interest payment date.

Illustration 16-4 ▼

Comparison of long-term investment and liability

Khadr Inc. (Investor)				ABC Corporation (Investee)		
Jan. 1	Held-to-Maturity—ABC Bonds	101,000		Jan. 1	Cash	101,000	
	Cash		101,000		Premium on Bonds		1,000
					Bonds Payable		100,000
July 1	Cash	3,500		July 1	Interest Expense	3,210	
	Held-to-Maturity—ABC Bonds		290		Premium on Bonds	290	
	Interest Revenue		3,210		Cash		3,500

The accounting for the sale of a long-term debt investment is the same as that for a short-term debt investment except that the long-term debt investment is often held, as is intended here, until it matures rather than sold before its maturity.

BEFORE YOU GO ON . . .

▶**Review It**

1. What entries are required for a short-term investment in money-market instruments? In bonds?
2. How is the accounting for a short-term debt investment different from the accounting for a long-term debt investment?
3. Compare the accounting for short-term bond investments and long-term bond liabilities.
4. How is the recording of a long-term bond investment by an investor different from the recording of a long-term bond issue by an investee?

▶**Do It**

Wang Corporation had the following transactions for debt investments in trading securities:

Jan. 1 Purchased 5%-interest Hillary Corp. bonds with a face value of $30,000 for $30,400. Interest is payable semi-annually on July 1 and January 1.
July 1 Received semi-annual interest on Hillary Corp. bonds.
  1 Sold Hillary Corp. bonds with a face value of $15,000 for $14,250.

(a) Record the above transactions for Wang Corporation.
(b) Prepare the adjusting entry for the accrual of interest on December 31, Wang's year end.

Action Plan

• When bonds are purchased as a short-term investment, any premium or discount is recorded in the investment account rather than recorded separately as an adjunct or contra asset account.
• When bonds are sold, (1) update any unrecorded interest and (2) credit the investment account for the cost of the bonds.
• Record any difference between the proceeds and the cost as a realized gain or loss: Gain = proceeds > cost; loss = proceeds < cost.

Solution

(a)

Jan. 1	Trading Securities—Hillary Bonds	30,400	
	Cash		30,400
	To record purchase of Hillary bonds.		
1	Cash ($30,000 × 5% × $\frac{6}{12}$)	750	
	Interest Revenue		750
	To record receipt of semi-annual interest on Hillary bonds.		
1	Cash	14,250	
	Loss on Sale of Trading Securities	950	
	Trading Securities—Hillary Bonds ($30,400 × ½)		15,200
	To record sale of Hillary Corp. bonds.		

(b)

Dec. 31	Interest Receivable	375	
	Interest Revenue ($15,000 × 5% × $\frac{6}{12}$)		375
	To accrue semi-annual interest on Hillary bonds.		

Related exercise material: BE16–3, BE16–4, BE16–5, E16–2, E16–3, and E16–4.

the navigator

Accounting for Equity Investments

Equity investments are investments in the share capital—common and/or preferred—of other corporations. Preferred shares are usually held to earn dividend income. Either common or preferred shares can also be held for share price appreciation (an increase in value). Common shares can also be held to influence relationships between companies.

The accounting for equity investments is based on how much influence the investor has over the operating and financial affairs of the issuing corporation (the investee). Illustration 16-5 shows the guidelines for the levels of influence.

Illustration 16-5 ▶

Accounting guidelines for equity investments

Investor's Ownership Interest in Investee's Common Shares	Presumed Influence on Investee	Accounting Guidelines
Less than 20 percent	Insignificant	Cost method
20 percent or more	Significant	Equity method

All short-term equity investments are accounted for using the cost method. Long-term equity investments are accounted for by either the cost method or the equity method, depending on the amount of influence.

When an investor owns 20 percent or more of the common shares of another company, the investor is generally presumed to have a significant influence over the decisions of the investee company. The investor probably also has a representative on the investee's board of directors. Through that representative, the investor begins to exercise some influence over the investee. The investee company, to some extent, becomes part of the investor company.

Of course, when an investor owns more than 50 percent of the common shares of a corporation, it has more than significant influence—it has control. Either way, when an investor owns more than 20 percent of the common shares of another company, it is normal to expect that it will be able to exercise significant or total influence over the investee. In our feature story, Western Forest Products purchased 100 percent of the common shares of Cascadia Forest Products and now controls the company.

The influence that an investor is assumed to have may be weakened by other circumstances. For example, a company that acquires a 25-percent interest in a "hostile" takeover may not have significant influence over the investee. Among the questions that should be answered to determine an investor's influence are these: (1) Does the investor have representation on the investee's board of directors? (2) Does the investor participate in the investee's policy-making process? (3) Are there material transactions between the investor and investee? (4) Are the common shares that are held by other shareholders concentrated among a few investors or dispersed among many? In other words, companies are required to use judgement instead of blindly following the guidelines. On the following pages, we will explain and illustrate how each guideline is applied.

Cost Method

To account for equity investments where there is no significant influence (normally holdings of less than 20 percent), the cost method is used. Under the **cost method**, the investment is recorded at its original purchase price (cost) and revenue is only recognized when cash dividends are received, as explained in the next sections. The cost method is applied in the same way regardless of whether the investment is classified as short- or long-term, or as trading or available-for-sale. Note that "cost" is the same as market value at the acquisition date so trading and available-for-sale securities are essentially recorded at market value initially.

We will talk more about trading and available-for-sale securities and valuing them at market value later in this chapter.

Recording Acquisitions of Shares

As it does for debt investments, cost for equity investments includes the price paid to acquire the equity securities. Assume, for example, that on July 1, 2007, St. Amand Corporation (the investor) acquires 1,000 common shares of Beal Corporation (the investee) at $40 per share. If Beal has a total of 10,000 common shares, then St. Amand has a 10-percent ownership interest in Beal that it plans to hold as an available-for-sale investment. This would be recorded using the cost method, since it is unlikely that there is significant influence.

The entry to record the equity investment is as follows:

Helpful hint The entries for investments in common shares are also used for investments in preferred shares.

July 1	Available-for-Sale—Beal Common Shares	40,000	
	Cash (1,000 × $40)		40,000
	To record purchase of 1,000 Beal common shares.		

This investment would be reported as a current asset on the balance sheet if it met one of the short-term investment criteria: (1) readily marketable, or (2) matures within the next year. Otherwise, it would be classified as a noncurrent asset on the balance sheet.

While the investor, St. Amand Corporation, must record this acquisition, there is no entry required for Beal Corporation. Recall that shares, once issued, are traded among investors. St. Amand Corporation did not purchase these shares directly from Beal Corporation. It purchased them from investors on organized stock exchanges, such as the Toronto Stock Exchange.

Recording Dividend Revenue

During the time the shares are held, entries are required for any cash dividends that are received. If a $2 per share dividend is received by St. Amand Corporation on December 1, the entry is as follows:

Dec. 1	Cash (1,000 × $2)	2,000	
	Dividend Revenue		2,000
	To record receipt of cash dividend.		

Dividend revenue is reported under other revenues in the income statement. Unlike interest, dividends do not accrue before they are declared. There are therefore no adjusting entries to accrue dividends.

Recording Sales of Shares

When shares are sold, the difference between the proceeds from the sale and the cost of the shares is recognized as a realized gain or loss. Assume that St. Amand receives proceeds of $39,000 on the sale of its Beal common shares on October 10, 2008. Because the shares cost $40,000, there is a loss of $1,000 ($40,000 – $39,000). The entry to record the sale follows:

Oct. 10	Cash	39,000	
	Loss on Sale of Available-for-Sale Securities	1,000	
	Available-for-Sale—Beal Common Shares		40,000
	To record sale of Beal common shares.		

This realized loss is reported under other expenses in the income statement. A realized gain on sale would be reported as other revenue.

Equity Method

When an investor company owns only a small portion of the shares of another company, the investor cannot exercise any influence over the investee. But when an investor owns at least 20 percent of the common shares of a corporation, it is presumed that the investor has significant influence over the financial and operating activities of the investee and plans to hold the investment for the long term. In these circumstances, the **equity method**, rather than the cost method, is used to account for the investment. These equity investments are neither trading nor available-for-sale, nor, of course, held-to-maturity.

Helpful hint Under the equity method, revenue is recognized on the accrual basis—i.e., when it is earned by the investee.

Under the equity method, the investment in common shares is initially recorded at cost. After that, the investment account is adjusted annually to show the investor's equity in the investee. An alternative might be to delay recognizing the investor's share of net income until a cash dividend is declared. But doing that would ignore the fact that the investor and investee are, in some sense, one company, which means the investor benefits from the investee's net income.

Each year, the investor adjusts the investment account to do the following:

1. **Record its share of the investee's net income (loss):** Increase (debit) the investment account and increase (credit) revenue for the investor's share of the investee's net income. Conversely, when the investee has a net loss, the investor increases (debits) a loss account and decreases (credits) the investment account for its share of the investee's net loss.
2. **Record the dividends received:** Decrease (credit) the investment account when dividends are received. The investment account is reduced for dividends received because the net assets of the investee are decreased when a dividend is paid.

Recording Acquisitions of Shares

Assume that Milar Corporation (the investor) acquires 30 percent of the common shares of Beck Corporation (the investee) for $120,000 on January 1, 2008. Milar is assumed to have significant influence over Beck. The following entry records this transaction:

A	=	L	+	SE
+120,000				
−120,000				

↓ Cash flows: −120,000

Jan. 1	Equity Investment—Beck Common Shares	120,000	
	Cash		120,000
	To record purchase of Beck common shares.		

Recording Investment Revenue

For the year ended December 31, 2008, Beck reports net income of $100,000. It declares and pays a $40,000 cash dividend. Milar is required to record (1) its share of Beck's income, $30,000 (30% × $100,000), and (2) the reduction in the investment account for the dividends received, $12,000 ($40,000 × 30%). The entries are as follows:

A	=	L	+	SF
+30,000				+30,000

Cash flows: no effect

	(1)		
Dec. 31	Equity Investment—Beck Common Shares	30,000	
	Revenue from Equity Investment in Beck		30,000
	To record 30% equity in Beck's net income.		

A	=	L	+	SE
+12,000				
−12,000				

↑ Cash flows: +12,000

	(2)		
31	Cash	12,000	
	Equity Investment—Beck Common Shares		12,000
	To record dividends received.		

After the transactions for the year have been posted, the investment and revenue accounts will show the following:

Equity Investment—Beck Common Shares				Revenue from Equity Investment in Beck	
Jan. 1	120,000			Dec. 31	30,000
Dec. 31	30,000	Dec. 31	12,000		
Dec. 31 Bal.	138,000				

During the year, the investment account has increased by $18,000 ($138,000 – $120,000). This $18,000 is Milar's 30-percent equity in the $60,000 increase in Beck's retained earnings ($100,000 – $40,000). In addition, Milar will report $30,000 of revenue from its investment, which is 30 percent of Beck's net income of $100,000.

The difference between income reported under the cost method and under the equity method can be significant. For example, if Milar were assumed not to have significant influence, it would report only $12,000 of dividend revenue (30% × $40,000) using the cost method.

Illustration 16-6 compares the journal entries used to record these investment transactions under the cost and equity methods. On the left-hand side of the illustration, we assume that Milar had no significant influence and used the cost method. We also assume that it classified this investment as an available-for-sale investment. On the right-hand side of the illustration, we assume that Milar did have significant influence and used the equity method (as we just illustrated in this section).

Illustration 16-6 ▼

Comparison of cost and equity method journal entries

Cost Method			Equity Method		
Acquisition			*Acquisition*		
Available-for-Sale—Beck Common	120,000		Equity Investment—Beck Common	120,000	
Cash		120,000	Cash		120,000
Investee reports net income			*Investee reports net income*		
No entry			Equity Investment—Beck Common	30,000	
			Revenue from Equity Investment in Beck		30,000
Investee pays dividends			*Investee pays dividends*		
Cash	12,000		Cash	12,000	
Dividend Revenue		12,000	Equity Investment—Beck Common		12,000

BEFORE YOU GO ON . . .

▶Review It

1. Is there any difference in the accounting for short- and long-term equity investments under the cost method?
2. Compare the accounting entries for long-term equity investments when the investor (a) has no significant influence, and (b) has significant influence.

▶Do It

CJW Inc. acquired 20 percent of the 400,000 common shares of Stillwater Corp. for $6 per share on January 2, 2008. On August 30, Stillwater paid a $0.10 per share dividend. On December 31, Stillwater reported net income of $244,000 for the year. Prepare all necessary journal entries for 2008 assuming (a) there is no significant influence and the investment is classified as an available-for-sale security, and (b) there is significant influence.

Action Plan

- Use the cost method for ownership when there is no significant influence (normally ownership of less than 20 percent of the common shares of another corporation).
- Under the cost method, recognize investment revenue when dividends are declared.
- Use the equity method for ownership when there is significant influence (normally ownership of 20 percent or more of the common shares of another corporation).
- Under the equity method, recognize investment revenue when the investee declares net income. The distribution of dividends is not income; rather, it does reduce the equity investment.

Solution

(a)

Cost Method

Jan. 2	Available-for-Sale—Stillwater Common Shares (400,000 × 20% = 80,000; 80,000 × $6)	480,000	
	Cash		480,000
	To record purchase of 80,000 Stillwater common shares.		
Aug. 30	Cash	8,000	
	Dividend Revenue ($0.10 × 80,000)		8,000
	To record receipt of cash dividend.		

(b)

Equity Method

Jan. 2	Equity Investment—Stillwater Common Shares (400,000 × 20% = 80,000; 80,000 × $6)	480,000	
	Cash		480,000
	To record purchase of 80,000 Stillwater common shares.		
Aug. 30	Cash	8,000	
	Equity Investment—Stillwater Common Shares ($0.10 × 80,000)		8,000
	To record receipt of cash dividend.		
Dec. 31	Equity Investment—Stillwater Common Shares ($244,000 × 20%)	48,800	
	Revenue from Equity Investment in Stillwater		48,800
	To record 20% equity in Stillwater's net income.		

Related exercise material: BE16–6, BE16–7, BE16–8, E16–5, E16–6, and E16–7.

Valuation of Passive Investments

study objective 4

Indicate how investments are valued.

As we have just seen, debt and equity investments are initially recorded at cost. But what happens if the value of debt and equity investments changes after they have been purchased? Bond and share prices often jump dramatically or drop drastically depending on whether changes in the economy are favourable or unfavourable. For example, in a recent one-year period, Forzani's share price hit a low of $10.10 and a high of $16.70—a percentage change of more than 66 percent. If prices fluctuate so much, at what value should investments that are held for passive (income) purposes be carried?

A recent change in accounting standards has determined that valuing certain kinds of investments at market value after they are acquired is the preferred approach, especially for investments that are purchased to be resold. The advantage of doing this is that it allows users to better assess the impact of changing prices on a company's liquidity and solvency. In addition, the market values of these types of investments can be obtained easily. This does not mean that the market values will not change again; rather, it simply means that at any specific point in time, market value can be objectively determined from stock market quotes.

When investments are valued at market value, any increase or decrease in the market value is recorded in the investment account, with a corresponding gain or loss. The difference between the cost and market value while an investment is held is called an **unrealized gain or loss**. This is distinguished from a realized gain or loss, which results when the proceeds exceed the cost of the investment when it is actually sold.

Whether market or cost is used to value the investment depends on the classification of the security. You will recall that we learned earlier in this chapter that there are three categories of securities that can be held as passive investments:

1. **Trading securities** are securities held mainly for sale in the near term to generate earnings on short-term price differences.
2. **Available-for-sale securities** are securities that are held with the intention of selling them sometime in the future. These securities do not fit in either the trading or held-to-maturity securities category.
3. **Held-to-maturity securities** are debt securities that the investor has the intention and ability to hold to maturity.

Note that management has some flexibility in its initial classification of securities as trading or available-for-sale. For simplicity, we have assumed in this textbook that management will designate as "trading" only those securities it plans to actively trade prior to their due date.

Trading and available-for-sale securities are valued at market value, while held-to-maturity securities are valued at cost (after any discounts or premiums have been amortized), as shown in Illustration 16-7.

Illustration 16-7 ◄

Investment valuation guidelines

Trading: At market value with unrealized gains or losses reported as other revenue

Available-for-sale: At market value with unrealized gains or losses reported as other comprehensive income

Held-to-maturity: At amortized cost

Of course, this discussion does not apply to equity investments that are purchased for strategic purposes. These investments are purchased to influence or control another company, and not for resale. These investments are carried at cost, and are later adjusted for the investor's share of undistributed income.

We will discuss the valuation of trading, available-for-sale, and held-to-maturity securities in the next sections.

Trading Securities

Since trading securities are purchased with the intention of selling them in the near future, it is not surprising that they are valued at market value, as was shown in Illustration 16-7. This valuation approach is also referred to as mark-to-market accounting.

To illustrate the valuation of trading securities, assume that on December 31, 2008, Skaweniio Corporation has the following costs and market values in its trading securities subsidiary ledger:

Trading Securities	Cost	Market Value	Unrealized Gain (Loss)
Bell Canada bonds	$ 50,000	$ 48,000	$(2,000)
Norbord shares	90,000	95,000	5,000
Total	$140,000	$143,000	$3,000

Skaweniio's trading securities would be reported at their market value of $143,000 at December 31 in the current assets section of the balance sheet.

In addition, Skaweniio would report an unrealized gain of $3,000 as other revenue in its income statement. It has an unrealized gain of $3,000 because the total market value ($143,000) is $3,000 greater than the total cost ($140,000). This unrealized gain indicates that the securities have changed in value and are still being held. Note that any unrealized gain or loss is assessed on the total portfolio of trading securities, and not on each individual debt or equity security.

We indicated above that unrealized gains are reported as other revenue in the income statement. Unrealized losses are reported as other expenses in the income statement. This means that **unrealized gains and losses for trading securities are reported in exactly the same way as realized gains and losses**. Recognizing a gain or loss in the income statement before it is realized is a major exception to past practice where the cost principle was followed. However, accounting standard-setters in Canada, as well as in other countries, believe that this is an appropriate way to treat trading securities since they are highly marketable and intended to be sold in the near future.

The revaluation of the trading securities to market value and the recognition of any unrealized gain or loss is usually done through an adjusting journal entry at year end. The adjusting entry for Skaweniio is:

A	=	L	+	SE
+3,000				+3,000

Cash flows: no effect

Dec. 31	Allowance to Adjust Trading Securities to Market Value	3,000	
	Unrealized Gain—Trading Securities		3,000
	To record unrealized gain on trading securities.		

In this entry, a valuation allowance account, Allowance to Adjust Trading Securities to Market Value, is used to record the difference between the total cost and the total market value of the trading securities investment portfolio. This enables the company to keep a record of the historical investment cost of each individual debt or equity security recorded in its subsidiary ledger, which will be needed to determine the gain or loss realized when the securities are sold.

The allowance account is carried forward into future accounting periods—in the same way that Allowance for Doubtful Accounts is—and therefore offsets the general ledger control account Trading Securities. No entries are made to Allowance to Adjust Trading Securities to Market Value during the period. Rather, at the end of each reporting period, the balance in the account is adjusted to the difference between cost and market value.

Available-for-Sale Securities

Available-for-sale securities are also valued at market value at year end. The procedure for determining and recording any change in market value and any unrealized gain or loss is the same as for trading securities.

However, the reporting of an unrealized gain or loss is different for available-for-sale securities. There is a reporting difference because, while trading securities will be sold in the near term, available-for-sale securities may or may not be sold in the near term. Thus, before the actual sale, it is more likely that changes in market value may reverse any unrealized gain or loss at a specific point in time. Consequently, an unrealized gain or loss on available-for-sale securities is not reported as part of net income. Instead, it is separately reported as other comprehensive income. As we learned in Chapter 13, comprehensive income includes all changes to shareholders' equity during a period except for changes that result from dividends and other investments by shareholders.

Held-to-Maturity Securities

Recall that a debt security is classified as held-to-maturity if the investor intends and is able to hold the investment until it matures. If the company intends to hold the security until it matures and has no plans to sell it, market values are irrelevant. Consequently, these investments are valued at cost, and their values are not adjusted to reflect changes in market value. We usually say that held-to-maturity investments are valued at *amortized* cost, because any premiums or discounts for long-term investments must be amortized, as we have previously learned.

If the market value falls greatly below cost, and the decline is considered permanent, then (and only then) will a held-to-maturity debt security be adjusted to its market value. This value becomes the debt investment's new cost base. Any write-down to market value is directly credited to the investment account because no future recovery in value is expected. This write-down results in an impairment loss and applies to equity investments as well as to other long-lived assets. You will recall that we learned about impairment losses in Chapter 9.

ACCOUNTING IN ACTION ▶ International Insight

The Accounting Standards Board issued new standards for financial instruments that affected nearly every company in Canada, small and large, in 2006. These standards are extensive, and the result of many years of consultation with Canadian users and international standard-setters. Changes to requirements to recognize and measure financial instruments have moved companies away from reporting certain types of investments on their balance sheets at historical cost, or at the lower of cost and market. Investments that are purchased for resale are now reported at their market value, which many observers believe is far more relevant to decision-makers. With the implementation of these new accounting standards, Canadian accounting practices for investments now match what is done internationally and in the U.S.

? **How will reporting trading and available-for-sale securities at their market value be more relevant to financial statement users?**

BEFORE YOU GO ON . . .

▶Review It

1. What is the proper valuation for (a) trading securities, (b) available-for-sale securities, and (c) held-to-maturity securities?
2. Why are strategic investments not reported at market value?
3. Distinguish between the reporting of realized gains and losses and unrealized gains and losses for (a) trading securities, and (b) available-for-sale securities.

Related exercise material: BE16–9, BE16–10, E16–8, E16–9, and E16–10.

the navigator

Reporting of Investments

In this section, we will review the presentation of investments in the balance sheet, income statement, and statement of comprehensive income. We will also learn about consolidated financial statements.

Balance Sheet

In the balance sheet, investments must be classified as short- or long-term. In addition, within each category the investments are further categorized as trading, available-for-sale, or held-to-maturity securities purchased as passive investments, or as equity investments purchased as strategic investments.

Short-Term Investments

Cash, the most liquid asset, is listed first in the current assets section of the balance sheet. Highly liquid investments that are very near maturity (usually less than three months) are viewed as "near" cash. This type of short-term investment is generally combined with cash and reported as a single line item called "Cash and Cash Equivalents."

Other short-term investments rank next in order of liquidity. As we learned earlier in the chapter, investments that are held for trading purposes are usually classified as short-term investments. Available-for-sale securities may be classified as short- or long-term, depending on their marketability and term to maturity.

Trading or available-for-sale securities are reported at their market value. The valuation allowance to adjust cost to market value may be added or deducted directly on the balance sheet, or it can be disclosed in the notes to the financial statements. The allowance account is added as an **adjunct asset account** (a debit), if the market value is greater than cost. The allowance account is deducted as a **contra asset account** (a credit), if the market value is less than cost.

Illustration 16-8 shows one possible presentation of trading securities on the balance sheet for Skaweniio Corporation.

Illustration 16-8 ▶

Presentation of trading securities

SKAWENIIO CORPORATION Balance Sheet (partial) December 31, 2008		
Assets		
Current assets		
Cash and cash equivalents		$ 28,000
Trading securities, at cost	$140,000	
Add: Allowance to adjust trading securities to market value	3,000	
Trading securities, at market		143,000

Long-Term Investments

Available-for-sale securities that are held for the long term are also reported on the balance sheet at their market value. As is done for short-term available-for-sale securities, the valuation allowance to adjust cost to market value may be added or deducted directly on the balance sheet, or it can be disclosed in the notes to the financial statements.

Held-to-maturity securities are debt securities that are classified as long-term investments until they are about to mature. Any portion that is expected to mature within the year is classified as a current asset. Held-to-maturity securities are reported at their amortized cost.

In addition, certain equity securities that are purchased to have significant influence or control are also classified as long-term investments, and supporting details are given in the notes to the financial statements.

Illustration 16-9 summarizes the reporting and valuation requirements of both short- and long-term investments on the balance sheet.

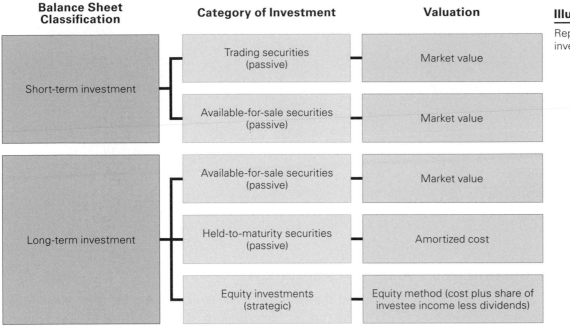

Balance Sheet Classification	Category of Investment	Valuation
Short-term investment	Trading securities (passive)	Market value
	Available-for-sale securities (passive)	Market value
Long-term investment	Available-for-sale securities (passive)	Market value
	Held-to-maturity securities (passive)	Amortized cost
	Equity investments (strategic)	Equity method (cost plus share of investee income less dividends)

Illustration 16-9 ◀
Reporting and valuation of investments

Accumulated Other Comprehensive Income

Accumulated other comprehensive income is presented in the shareholders' equity section of the balance sheet. It is the cumulative total of each period's comprehensive income (or loss) reported in the statement of comprehensive income. Recall that comprehensive income is created when unrealized gains and losses are recorded for available-for-sale securities.

Although we have concentrated on comprehensive income that is generated from available-for-sale securities in this chapter, there are other sources of comprehensive income. These include certain translation gains or losses on foreign currency, unrealized gains and losses from cash flow hedges, and unrealized pension cost from a minimum pension liability adjustment—which are all topics for more advanced accounting courses.

Income Statement

Realized gains and losses on investments are presented as other revenue or other expense in the income statement. In addition, unrealized gains and losses from trading securities are also presented in the income statement.

These gains and losses, as well as other investment-related accounts such as those for interest and dividend revenue, are reported in the non-operating section of the income statement.

Statement of Comprehensive Income

We learned in Chapters 13 and 14 that the comprehensive income statement includes not only net income reported on the traditional income statement but also "comprehensive income" transactions, such as unrealized gains and losses from available-for-sale securities. By combining items that are traditionally reported in the income statement with other income items that are presented elsewhere, it is easier to determine the profitability of a company on an "all-inclusive" basis. The comprehensive income statement was illustrated in Chapter 14 and is not shown again here.

Illustration 16-10 summarizes the presentation of investments and investment-related accounts on the balance sheet, income statement, and statement of comprehensive income.

Illustration 16-10 ▼

Presentation of investments

Balance Sheet	Income Statement	Statement of Comprehensive Income
Assets	Other revenue	Unrealized gains or losses on available-for-sale securities
Current assets	Realized gains on sale of securities	
Trading securities	Unrealized gains on trading securities	
Available-for-sale securities	Interest revenue	
Long-term investments	Dividend revenue	
Available-for-sale securities	Other expenses	
Held-to-maturity securities	Realized losses on sale of securities	
Equity investments, at equity	Unrealized losses on trading securities	
Shareholders' equity		
Accumulated other comprehensive income		

Consolidated Financial Statements

Earlier in the chapter, we learned that when one company has significant influence over another company it uses the equity method of accounting. This is true whether a company owns 20 percent or 100 percent of another company. If a company owns between 20 percent and 50 percent of the common shares of another company, the investment is reported in the investor's balance sheet as a long-term equity investment.

However, when a company owns more than 50 percent of, or controls, the common shares of another company, an additional set of financial statements is required. Remember that a company can also sometimes have control when it owns less than 50 percent of another company's shares, depending on the factors that were mentioned earlier in the chapter.

When one company (known as the **parent company**) controls another company (known as the **subsidiary company**), **consolidated financial statements** must be prepared for financial reporting purposes. Consolidated financial statements present the total assets and liabilities controlled by the parent company. They indicate the size and scope of operations under common control. Most publicly traded companies in Canada present consolidated financial statements.

Consolidated statements are prepared in addition to the financial statements for the parent company and each subsidiary company. For example, Western Forest Products uses the equity method to account for its investment in Cascadia Forest Products in its own individual statements. But, for external reporting, Western Forest Products consolidates Cascadia Forest Products' results with its own financial statements. Under this approach, the individual assets and liabilities of Cascadia Forest Products are included with those of Western Forest Products.

Consolidation is a complex topic and is discussed in greater detail in advanced accounting courses.

ACCOUNTING IN ACTION ▶ Business Insight

The top five subsidiary companies in Canada, ranked by revenue, are listed below. In all cases, the major shareholder controls the subsidiary's shares. The percentage ownership is in parentheses.

Rank	Subsidiary	Parent
1	Imperial Oil (69.6%)	Exxon Mobil
2	Manufacturers Life Insurance (100%)	Manulife Financial
3	Great-West Lifeco (74.8%)	Power Financial
4	Bell Canada (100%)	BCE
5	Power Financial (66.4%)	Power Corporation

> **?** Why is it important for a company such as Exxon Mobil to consolidate the results of its subsidiary Imperial Oil in its own financial statements?

BEFORE YOU GO ON . . .

▶Review It

1. What investment or investment-related accounts are reported on the balance sheet? Income statement? Statement of comprehensive income?
2. What is the purpose of consolidated financial statements?
3. Are The Forzani Group's financial statements consolidated? If they are, what percentage does Forzani own of its subsidiary companies? The answers to these questions are at the end of the chapter.

▶Do It

Zaboschuk Corporation has the following asset account balances at December 31, 2008. Prepare the assets section of Zaboschuk's balance sheet at December 31.

Accounts receivable	$ 84,000
Accumulated amortization—buildings	200,000
Accumulated amortization—equipment	54,000
Allowance for doubtful accounts	4,000
Allowance to adjust short-term available-for-sale securities to market value (contra account)	5,000
Allowance to adjust long-term available-for-sale securities to market value (adjunct account)	10,000
Available-for-sale securities (short-term), at cost	65,000
Available-for-sale securities (long-term), at cost	90,000
Buildings	800,000
Cash	10,000
Equipment	180,000
Equity investments, at equity	150,000
Goodwill	170,000
Held-to-maturity investments, at amortized cost	50,000
Inventory	130,000
Land	200,000
Money-market instruments	11,000
Prepaid insurance	23,000

Action Plan

- Organize each asset account into its proper classification: current assets; long-term investments; property, plant, and equipment; and intangible assets.
- Remember that contra asset accounts reduce the related account balance and adjunct asset accounts increase the related account balance.

Solution

ZABOSCHUK CORPORATION
Balance Sheet (partial)
December 31, 2008

Assets

Current assets			
Cash and cash equivalents ($10,000 + $11,000)			$ 21,000
Available-for-sale securities, at cost		$ 65,000	
Less: Allowance to adjust available-for-sale securities to market value		5,000	60,000
Accounts receivable		$ 84,000	
Less: Allowance for doubtful accounts		4,000	80,000
Inventory			130,000
Prepaid insurance			23,000
Total current assets			314,000
Long-term investments			
Available-for-sale securities, at cost		$ 90,000	
Add: Allowance to adjust available-for-sale securities to market value		10,000	$100,000
Held-to-maturity investments, at amortized cost			50,000
Equity investments, at equity			150,000
Total long-term investments			300,000
Property, plant, and equipment			
Land			$200,000
Buildings	$800,000		
Less: Accumulated amortization	200,000		600,000
Equipment	$180,000		
Less: Accumulated amortization	54,000		126,000
Total property, plant, and equipment			926,000
Intangible assets			
Goodwill			170,000
Total assets			$1,710,000

Related exercise material: BE16–11, BE16–12, BE16–13, E16–11, E16–12, E16–13, and E16–14.

Demonstration Problem

In its first year of operations, which ended December 31, 2008, Northstar Finance Corporation had the following selected transactions in trading securities:

Mar. 14 Purchased $10,000 of treasury bills.

June 1 Purchased 600 Sanburg common shares for $24.50 per share.

  29 Sold treasury bills for $10,000, plus $50 interest.

July 1 Purchased 800 Cey common shares for $33.75 per share.

Sept. 1 Received a $1 per share cash dividend from Cey Corporation.

Nov. 1 Sold 200 Sanburg common shares for $26.25 per share.

Dec. 15 Received a $0.50 per share cash dividend on Sanburg common shares.

  31 The market values per share were $25 for Sanburg and $30 for Cey.

Instructions

(a) Record the transactions.

(b) Prepare the adjusting entry at December 31 to report the securities at their market value.

(c) Show the presentation of the trading securities, and related accounts, in the balance sheet and income statement.

Solution to Demonstration Problem

Action Plan

• Keep a running balance of the number of shares purchased and sold.
• Calculate the realized gain or loss by subtracting the cost of the securities from the proceeds.
• Determine the adjustment to market value based on the difference between the total cost and total market value of the securities.

(a)

Date	Account	Debit	Credit
Mar. 14	Trading Securities—Treasury Bills	10,000	
	Cash		10,000
	To record purchase of treasury bills.		
June 1	Trading Securities—Sanburg Common Shares	14,700	
	Cash (600 × $24.50)		14,700
	To record purchase of 600 Sanburg common shares.		
29	Cash ($10,000 + $50)	10,050	
	Trading Securities—Treasury Bills		10,000
	Interest Revenue		50
	To record sale of treasury bills.		
July 1	Trading Securities—Cey Common Shares	27,000	
	Cash (800 × $33.75)		27,000
	To record purchase of 800 Cey common shares.		
Sept. 1	Cash (800 × $1)	800	
	Dividend Revenue		800
	To record receipt of $1 per share cash dividend from Cey.		
Nov. 1	Cash (200 × $26.25)	5,250	
	Trading Securities—Sanburg Common Shares		4,900
	[(200 ÷ 600) × $14,700)]		
	Gain on Sale of Trading Securities		350
	To record sale of 200 Sanburg common shares.		
Dec. 15	Cash [(600 − 200) × $0.50]	200	
	Dividend Revenue		200
	To record receipt of $0.50 per share dividend from Sanburg.		

(b)

Trading Securities	Cost	Market Value	Unrealized Gain (Loss)
Sanburg common shares (400)	$ 9,800	$10,000	$ 200
Cey common shares (800)	27,000	24,000	(3,000)
Total	$36,800	$34,000	$(2,800)

Date	Account	Debit	Credit
Dec. 31	Unrealized Loss—Trading Securities	2,800	
	Allowance to Adjust Trading Securities to Market Value		2,800
	To record unrealized loss on trading securities.		

(c)

NORTHSTAR FINANCE CORPORATION
Balance Sheet (partial)
December 31, 2008

Assets

Current assets		
Trading securities, at cost		$36,800
Less: Allowance to adjust trading securities to market value		2,800
Trading securities, at market		34,000

Note: This information could also be presented in the current assets section net of the allowance, with details disclosed in the notes to the financial statements.

NORTHSTAR FINANCE CORPORATION
Income Statement (partial)
Year Ended December 31, 2008

Other revenue	
Dividend revenue ($800 + $200)	$1,000
Gain on sale of trading securities	350
Interest revenue	50
	1,400
Other expenses	
Unrealized loss on trading securities	2,800

the navigator

Summary of Study Objectives

1. **Classify investments.** Companies purchase debt and equity securities of other companies for two main reasons: (a) They purchase the investment for passive reasons as a source of investment revenue. (b) They purchase the investment for strategic reasons, such as gaining control of a competitor, influencing strategic alliances, or moving into a new line of business.

Short-term investments are debt and equity securities that are held by a company as a passive investment. They are readily marketable or investments whose term matures within the next year. Investments that do not meet these criteria are classified as long-term investments. Long-term investments can be purchased for either passive or strategic reasons.

2. **Account for debt investments.** Debt investments include money-market instruments, bonds, commercial paper, and similar items. Entries are required to record the (1) acquisition, (2) interest revenue, and (3) maturity or sale. The accounting for short-term debt investments is similar to that for long-term debt investments, except that premiums and discounts must be amortized for long-term investments in bonds.

3. **Account for equity investments.** Equity investments are investments in the share capital of other corporations. Entries are required to record the (1) acquisition, (2) investment revenue, and (3) sale.

When the investor company does not have significant influence (ownership is usually less than 20 percent) over the investee company, the cost method should be used. The cost method records dividends as investment revenue. When there is significant influence (ownership is usually 20 percent or more), the equity method should be used. The equity method records investment revenue when net income is reported by the investee and increases the investor's investment account accordingly. Dividends that are received reduce the value of the investment account.

4. **Indicate how investments are valued.** Trading securities are valued at market value, and unrealized gains and losses that result from adjusting cost to market value are reported as other revenue in the income statement. Available-for-sale securities are valued at market value, and unrealized gains and losses that result from adjusting cost to market value are reported as other comprehensive income in the statement of comprehensive income. Held-to-maturity securities are valued at amortized cost. Long-term equity investments that are held for influence or control are not adjusted for changes in market value. They are carried at cost, and subsequently adjusted for the investee's share of undistributed net income.

5. **Indicate how investments are reported in the financial statements.** Trading securities are presented in the current assets section of the balance sheet. Available-for-sale securities may be classified as short- or long-term, depending on their marketability and term. Held-to-maturity securities and equity investments that are purchased for strategic reasons are classified as long-term investments. Accumulated other comprehensive income, which includes unrealized gains or losses from available-for-sale securities, is presented in the shareholders' equity section of the balance sheet.

Realized gains and losses are presented as other revenue and other expenses in the income statement. Unrealized gains and losses for trading securities are presented in the income statement, while unrealized gains and losses for available-for-sale securities are presented as comprehensive income in the statement of comprehensive income.

When a company controls (ownership usually greater than 50 percent) the common shares of another company, consolidated financial statements that give details about the financial position of the combined entity must also be prepared.

Glossary

Available-for-sale securities Debt or equity securities that are held with the intention of selling them sometime in the future and that are neither trading securities nor held-to-maturity securities. They are reported at market value on the balance sheet. (p. 812)

Consolidated financial statements Financial statements that present the assets and liabilities controlled by the parent company, and the total profitability of the combined companies. (p. 830)

Cost method An accounting method in which the equity investment in shares is recorded at cost. Investment revenue is only recognized when cash dividends are received. (p. 820)

Debt investments Investments in money-market instruments, bonds, commercial paper, and similar items. (p. 813)

Equity investments Investments in the share capital of other corporations. (p. 819)

Equity method An accounting method in which the investment in common shares is initially recorded at cost. The investment account is then adjusted annually to show the investor's equity in the investee. (p. 822)

Held-to-maturity securities Debt securities that the investor has the intention and ability to hold until their maturity date. They are reported at amortized cost on the balance sheet. (p. 813)

Investee The corporation that issues (sells) the debt or equity securities. (p. 815)

Investor The corporation that buys (owns) the debt or equity securities. (p. 815)

Long-term investments Investments that are not readily marketable and do not mature within the next year. (p. 812)

Parent company A company that controls, or owns more than 50 percent of the common shares of, another company. (p. 830)

Passive investment An investment that is purchased mainly to generate investment income. (p. 810)

Realized gain or loss The difference between market value and cost when an investment is actually sold. (p. 817)

Short-term investments Investments that are readily marketable or whose term matures within the next year. (p. 812)

Strategic investment An investment that is purchased to influence or control another company. (p. 810)

Subsidiary company A company whose common shares are controlled by another company (usually more than 50 percent of its common shares are owned by the other company). (p. 830)

Trading securities Debt or equity securities that are bought and held for sale in the near term, mainly to generate earnings from short-term price differences. They are reported at market value on the balance sheet. (p. 812)

Unrealized gain or loss The difference between the market value and cost of an investment still being held. (p. 825)

Self-Study Questions

Answers are at the end of the chapter.

(SO 1) K   1. Short-term investments are investments:
(a) which are readily marketable.
(b) whose term matures within the next year.
(c) which are readily marketable, or whose term matures within the next year.
(d) that are not held-to-maturity securities.

(SO 1) K   2. Which of the following statements is true?
(a) Trading securities are purchased as a strategic investment.
(b) Trading securities can be short- or long-term investments.
(c) Available-for-sale securities can be short- or long-term investments.
(d) Held-to-maturity securities that do not mature within the next year can be short- or long-term investments.

3. Short-term investments in bonds: (SO 2) C
(a) are recorded net of any premium or discount.
(b) record premiums or discounts separately from the investment.
(c) are always Held-to-Maturity securities.
(d) receive interest at maturity only.

4. Pryor Corp. receives proceeds of $42,000 on the sale   (SO 2) AP
of a short-term investment in bonds that cost $39,500. This transaction should be reported in the income statement as a:
(a) loss of $2,500 under other expenses.
(b) loss of $2,500 under operating expenses.
(c) gain of $2,500 under other revenues.
(d) gain of $2,500 under operating revenues.

(SO 3) K 5. The equity method of accounting for an investment in common shares is normally used when the investor owns:
  (a) less than 20 percent of the investee's common shares.
  (b) 20 percent or more of the investee's common shares.
  (c) 20 percent or more of the investeee's preferred shares.
  (d) more than 50 percent of the investee's common shares.

(SO 4) AP 6. The Big K Ranch owns 20 percent of the Little L Ranch's common shares. The Little L Ranch reported net income of $150,000 and paid dividends of $40,000 this year. How much investment revenue would the Big K Ranch report if it used the cost method to account for this equity investment? If it used the equity method?
  (a) $8,000 cost method; $22,000 equity method
  (b) $8,000 cost method; $30,000 equity method
  (c) $40,000 cost method; $110,000 equity method
  (d) $150,000 under both methods

(SO 5) AP 7. Which securities are valued at market value?
  (a) Trading securities
  (b) Available-for-sale securities
  (c) Held-to-maturity securities
  (d) Both (a) and (b)

(SO 5) AP 8. At the end of the first year of operations, the total cost of the trading securities investment portfolio is $120,000. Total market value is $115,000. The journal entry to adjust the trading securities at year end is as follows:

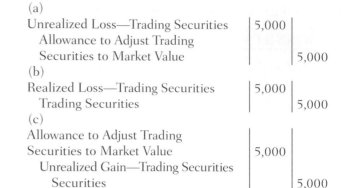

(a)

| Unrealized Loss—Trading Securities | 5,000 | |
| Allowance to Adjust Trading Securities to Market Value | | 5,000 |

(b)

| Realized Loss—Trading Securities | 5,000 | |
| Trading Securities | | 5,000 |

(c)

| Allowance to Adjust Trading Securities to Market Value | 5,000 | |
| Unrealized Gain—Trading Securities Securities | | 5,000 |

  (d) No journal entry is required until the investments are sold.

(SO 6) 9. When the market value of available-for-sale securities is less than cost, the unrealized loss is reported in the:
  (a) liability section of the balance sheet.
  (b) other revenues section of the income statement.
  (c) comprehensive income statement.
  (d) All of the above

(SO 6) 10. Which of the following is *false*? Consolidated financial statements are useful to determine the:
  (a) profitability of specific subsidiaries.
  (b) total profitability of companies under common control.
  (c) range of a parent company's operations.
  (d) full extent of the total obligations of companies that are under common control.

Questions

(SO 1) C 1. What are the differences between (a) passive and strategic investments, and (b) short- and long-term investments?

(SO 1) K 2. Japan's **Sapporo Breweries** purchased 100 percent of the common shares of **Sleeman Breweries** in 2006. Was this (a) a passive investment or a strategic investment, and (b) a short- or a long-term investment?

(SO 1) K 3. What are the differences between trading, available-for-sale, and held-to-maturity securities?

(SO 1) C 4. Explain why trading securities can only be classified as short-term investments but available-for-sale securities can be classified as either short- or long-term investments.

(SO 2) C 5. What are the differences between the accounting for short-term investments in money-market instruments versus bonds?

(SO 2) C 6. Osborne Corp. is considering making an investment in Bank of Canada bonds. If Osborne considers this to be a long-term investment instead of a short-term investment, will this have an impact on Osborne's recognition of interest revenue from the investment? Explain why or why not.

(SO 2) 7. What are the differences in accounting for a long-term investment in bonds versus a bond payable?

(SO 2) 8. Ann Adler is confused about gains and losses realized on the sale of an available-for-sale debt security. Explain to Ann (a) how the gain or loss is calculated, and (b) the statement presentation of the gains and losses.

(SO 3) 9. What constitutes "significant influence"? Is it safe to conclude that there is significant influence when a company owns 20 percent of the common shares of another company?

(SO 3) 10. When should a long-term investment in common shares be accounted for using the (a) cost method, and (b) equity method?

(SO 3) 11. Explain why the equity method cannot be applied to trading and available-for-sale securities.

(SO 3) 12. Identify what is included in the carrying value of an equity investment using (1) the cost method, and (2) the equity method. Explain why the carrying value will differ.

(SO 4) 13. At what value—cost or market—are each of the following reported: (a) trading securities, (b) available-for-sale securities, and (c) held-to-maturity securities?

(SO 4) C 14. Assad says, "I understand why market value is used to report certain investments—it is more relevant to statement users. But I don't understand why market value is only used to report certain investments and not all investments." Identify which investments are not reported at market value and explain why they are reported this way and others are not.

(SO 4) K 15. What is the difference between a realized gain or loss and an unrealized gain or loss?

(SO 4) K 16. What are the similarities and differences between the account Allowance to Adjust Securities to Market Value and the account Allowance for Doubtful Accounts?

(SO 5) K 17. Identify the proper statement presentation of the following accounts: (a) Trading Securities, (b) Available-for-Sale Securities, and (c) Held-to-Maturity Securities.

(SO 5) K 18. Identify the proper statement presentation of the following accounts: (a) Unrealized Loss on Trading Securities, (b) Realized Gain on Trading Securities, (c) Unrealized Loss on Available-for-Sale Securities, and (d) Realized Gain on Available-for-Sale Securities.

(SO 5) AP 19. **China Mobile (Hong Kong) Limited** reported the following selected data (in RMB millions) at December 31, 2005: cash and cash equivalents 64; available-for-sale equity securities 77; equity investments, at cost 468,222; equity investments, at equity 1,771; dividend income 51; and interest income 1,615. Identify on which financial statement each of these amounts should be reported and give the most likely classification.

(SO 5) C 20. **Onex Corporation** owns 99 percent of the common shares of **Celestica Inc.**—an electronics manufacturing business. (a) What method—cost or equity—should Onex use to account for this investment? (b) Which company is the parent? Which one is the subsidiary? (c) What kind of financial statements should Onex prepare to properly present this investment?

Brief Exercises

BE16–1   The following terms were introduced in this chapter:

1. Short-term investments
2. Passive investments
3. Strategic investments
4. Trading securities
5. Available-for-sale securities
6. Held-to-maturity securities

Identify terminology.
(SO 1) K

Match each term with the following definitions:

(a) ___ Debt or equity securities that are not trading securities and that are not held-to-maturity securities
(b) ___ Investments purchased to influence or control another company
(c) ___ Investments that are readily marketable or whose term matures within the next year.
(d) ___ Debt or equity securities that are bought and held for sale in the near term at a profit
(e) ___ Debt securities that the investor has the intent and ability to hold until they mature
(f) ___ Investments purchased mainly to generate investment income

BE16–2   Identify whether each of the following is most likely (a) a passive or strategic investment, (b) a short- or long-term investment, and (c) a trading, available-for-sale, or held-to-maturity security. You may assume that none of the following are cash equivalents. The first one has been done for you as an example.

Classify investments.
(SO 1) C

	(a) Passive or Strategic?	(b) Short- or Long-Term?	(c) Type of Security?
1. Treasury bill	Passive	Short-term	Available-for-sale
2. Common shares purchased by a bank for resale at a profit in the near future			
3. Common shares purchased on the TSX by a manufacturing company for resale in a few years			
4. Common shares purchased to control another company			
5. Money-market fund			
6. Five-year bonds intended to be held for the entire term of the bonds			

Record debt investment.
(SO 2) AP

BE16–3 On March 1, Toyworks Ltd. invested $100,000 in the ADR Canadian Money-Market Fund as a short-term, available-for-sale investment. On March 31, it received notification that $250 of interest had been earned for the month and added to the fund. On April 15, it cashed in the fund and received $100,375 in cash, which included $125 of interest earned in April. Record each of these transactions.

Record debt investment.
(SO 2) AP

BE16–4 On January 1, Phelps Corporation purchased $40,000 face value of Cullen Ltd. bonds as a short-term, available-for-sale investment for $41,500. On July 1, Phelps received interest of $1,245. On October 1, it sold the securities for $43,000, plus accrued interest of $623. Record each of these transactions.

Record debt investment and liability.
(SO 2) AP

BE16–5 On June 30, $150,000 of 5-year, 5% Plaza bonds are issued at 101. Interest is payable semi-annually each June 30 and December 31. The semi-annual amortization amount for the first interest period is $225. (a) Record the purchase of $150,000 of these bonds as a held-to-maturity investment on June 30 and the receipt of the first interest payment on December 31 on the books of the investor. (b) Record the issue of the debt on June 30 and the first interest payment on December 31 on the books of the investee (issuer).

Record equity investment.
(SO 3) AP

BE16–6 On August 1, McLain Finance Inc. buys 1,000 Datawave common shares as a trading investment for $36,000 cash. On October 15, McLain receives a cash dividend of $1 per share from Datawave. On December 1, McLain sells the shares for $38,000 cash. Record these three transactions.

Record equity investment, using cost and equity methods.
(SO 3) AP

BE16–7 On January 1, Loop Limited purchases 20% of Hook Corporation for $150,000. For the year ended December 31, Hook reports net income of $180,000 and pays a $5,000 cash dividend. Record each of these transactions, assuming Loop (a) does not have significant influence over Hook, and (b) does have significant influence over Hook.

Compare impact of cost and equity methods.
(SO 3) AP

BE16–8 Chan Inc. owns 20% of Dong Ltd.'s common shares. During the year, Dong reported net income of $250,000 and paid a dividend of $15,000. Indicate whether using the equity method instead of the cost method would result in an increase (+), a decrease (−), or no effect (NE) in each of the following categories:

Balance Sheet			Income Statement		
Assets	Liabilities	Shareholders' Equity	Revenues	Expenses	Net Income

Adjust trading securities.
(SO 4) AP

BE16–9 Cost and market value for the trading securities of Deal Inc. at December 31, 2008, are $64,000 and $61,000, respectively. Prepare the adjusting entry to record the securities at market value.

Adjust available-for-sale securities.
(SO 4) AP

BE16–10 Cost and market value for the available-for-sale securities of Leafblower Ltd. at December 31, 2008, are $72,000 and $75,000, respectively. Prepare the adjusting entry to record the securities at market value.

Prepare statement of comprehensive income.
(SO 5) AP

BE16–11 Atwater Corporation reported net income of $750,000, an unrealized gain of $36,000 on its available-for-sale securities, an unrealized loss of $60,000 on its trading securities, and a realized gain of $42,000 on its available-for-sale securities for the year ended April 30, 2008. Prepare a statement of comprehensive income.

Classify accounts.
(SO 5) AP

BE16–12 Indicate on which financial statement (i.e., balance sheet, income statement, or statement of comprehensive income) each of the following accounts would be reported. Also give the appropriate financial statement classification (e.g., current assets, long-term investments, other revenue, etc.).

Account	Financial Statement	Classification
Available-for-sale securities (short-term)		
Dividend revenue		
Equity investment, at equity		
Held-to-maturity securities		
Realized gain on available-for-sale securities		
Trading securities		

Account	Financial Statement	Classification
Unrealized gain on trading securities		
Unrealized loss on available-for-sale securities		

BE16–13 Sabre Corporation has the following investments at November 30, 2008:

1. Trading securities: common shares of National Bank, cost $25,000, market value $26,000.
2. Available-for-sale securities (short-term): common shares of Sword Corp., cost $108,000, market value $105,000.
3. Equity investment: common shares of Epee Inc. (30% ownership), cost $210,000, equity $250,000.
4. Held-to-maturity securities: bonds of Ghoti Ltd., amortized cost $150,000, market value $175,000.

Show how the investments would be reported in the assets section of the balance sheet.

Report investments on balance sheet.
(SO 5) AP

Exercises

E16–1 Kroshka Holdings Corporation has several investments in the debt and equity securities of other companies:

Classify investments.
(SO 1) C

1. 10-year BCE bonds, intended to be held for the duration of the bonds
2. 10-year GE bonds, intended to be sold if interest rates go down
3. 1-year Government of Canada bonds, intended to be held until maturity
4. 180-day treasury bill, intended to be held until maturity
5. Bank of Montreal preferred shares, purchased for the dividend income
6. Tim Hortons common shares, purchased to sell in the near term at a profit. These shares are part of an investment portfolio that is actively traded

Instructions

(a) Indicate whether each of the above investments is a passive or strategic investment.
(b) Indicate whether each of the above investments would be classified as a short- or long-term investment on Kroshka Holdings' balance sheet.
(c) Identify the type of investment that each of the above investments is: trading security, available-for-sale security, or held-to-maturity security.

E16–2 During the year ended November 30, 2008, Jackson Corporation had the following transactions for money-market instruments that were held as short-term, available-for-sale investments:

Record debt investments.
(SO 2) AP

Jan. 2 Purchased a 120-day treasury bill maturing on May 1 for $9,900.
May 1 The treasury bill matured. Jackson received $10,000 cash, which included the interest earned.
June 1 Invested $40,000 in a money-market fund.
      30 Received notification that $75 of interest had been earned and added to the fund.
July 31 Received notification that $75 of interest had been earned and added to the fund.
Aug. 15 Cashed the money-market fund and received $40,188.
Oct. 31 Purchased a 3-month, 2.5% term deposit for $24,000.

Instructions

(a) Record the above transactions.
(b) Prepare any required adjusting entries at November 30.

E16–3 Piper Corporation had the following transactions with short-term, available-for-sale securities:

Record debt investment.
(SO 2) AP

Jan. 1 Purchased $60,000 of Harris Corp. 6% bonds at 101. Interest is payable semi-annually on July 1 and January 1.
July 1 Received semi-annual interest on Harris bonds.

July 1 Sold half of the Harris bonds for $32,000.
Dec. 31 Accrued interest at Piper's year end.

Instructions

Record the above transactions.

Record debt investment and liability.
(SO 2) AP

E16–4 On June 30, 2008, Imperial Inc. purchased $250,000 of Acme Corp. 10-year, 5% bonds at 98 as a held-to-maturity security. The bonds pay interest semi-annually on December 31 and June 30. Both companies have a December 31 year end.

Instructions

(a) Record the purchase of the bonds on June 30 for (1) Imperial, the investor, and (2) Acme, the investee (issuer).
(b) Record the first interest payment on December 31 for (1) Imperial, and (2) Acme. The semi-annual amortization amount for the first interest period is $750.

Record equity investment.
(SO 3) AP

E16–5 McCormick Inc. had the following long-term, available-for-sale investment transactions:

Jan. 1 Purchased 1,000 Starr Corporation $5-noncumulative preferred shares for $105,000.
Apr. 1 Received the quarterly cash dividend.
July 1 Received the quarterly cash dividend.
2 Sold 500 Starr shares for $55,000.
Oct. 1 Received the quarterly cash dividend.

Instructions

Record the above transactions.

Record equity investment, using cost and equity methods.
(SO 3) AP

E16–6 Here are two transactions for Visage Cosmetics Inc. in 2008:

1. Visage Cosmetics acquires 40% of Diner Limited's 30,000 common shares for $9 per share on January 2, 2008. On June 15, Diner pays a cash dividend of $15,000. On December 31, Diner reports net income of $195,000 for the year.
2. Visage Cosmetics acquires 10% of Image Fashion Inc.'s 200,000 common shares for $12 per share on March 18, 2008. On June 30, Image Fashion pays a cash dividend of $22,000. On December 31, Image Fashion reports net income of $252,000 for the year.

Instructions

Record the above transactions for the year ended December 31, 2008, assuming the company does not intend to sell either investment at this time.

Record equity investment; determine balance sheet presentation.
(SO 3) AP

E16–7 On January 1, Diversity Corporation buys 20% of Bellingham Corporation's common shares for $180,000. At December 31, Bellingham pays a $10,000 cash dividend and reports net income of $200,000. Assume Diversity has significant influence over Bellingham.

Instructions

(a) Record the above transactions.
(b) Determine the amount to be reported on Diversity's balance sheet and income statement for the investment in Bellingham shares at December 31.
(c) Repeat (b) assuming Diversity does not have significant influence over Bellingham.

Record debt and equity investments.
(SO 2, 3, 4) AP

E16–8 On November 1, 2007, Lalonde Lteé buys 2,000 shares of Lyman Corporation for $35 per share and $100,000 of Kaur Inc. 6%-bonds at face value as short-term, available-for-sale investments. The bonds pay interest semi-annually on May 1 and November 1. On December 15, Lalonde sells 800 Lyman shares for $50 per share. At December 31, the company's year end, the Lyman shares are trading at $45 per share and the Kaur bonds are trading at 98. On March 31, 2008, Lalonde sells the remaining Lyman shares for $40 per share. On December 31, the Kaur bonds are trading at 100 again.

Instructions

Record the above transactions, including any required adjusting entries, for 2007 and 2008.

E16–9   At December 31, 2008, the trading securities for Yanik, Inc., are as follows:

Record adjusting entry for trading securities; show statement presentation.
(SO 4) AP

Security	Cost	Market Value
A	$18,500	$16,000
B	12,500	14,000
C	23,000	19,000
Totals	$54,000	$49,000

Instructions

(a) Prepare the adjusting entry at December 31 to report the investment portfolio at market value.
(b) Show the financial statement presentation of the trading securities and any related accounts at December 31, 2008.

E16–10   Kouchibouquac Inc. reports the following cost and market values for its investment portfolio of available-for-sale securities on June 30:

Record adjusting entry for available-for-sale securities for multiple years.
(SO 4) AP

	Cost	Market Value
2006	$275,000	$263,500
2007	325,600	354,000
2008	475,700	589,500

Instructions

For each year, prepare the required adjusting entry to report the investment portfolio at market value.

E16–11   Data for investments classified as trading securities by Yanik, Inc. are presented in E16–9. Assume that the investments are classified as short-term, available-for-sale securities with the same costs and market values.

Record adjusting entry for available-for-sale securities; show statement presentation.
(SO 4, 5) AP

Instructions

(a) Prepare the adjusting entry at December 31 to report the investment portfolio at market value.
(b) Show the financial statement presentation of the available-for-sale securities and any related accounts at December 31, 2008.

E16–12   Lai Inc. had the following investment transactions:

Identify impact of investment transactions.
(SO 2, 3, 4, 5) AP

1. Purchased Regina Corporation common shares for cash as an available-for-sale investment.
2. Received a cash dividend on Regina preferred shares.
3. Sold one-third of the Regina preferred shares at a price more than originally paid.
4. Bought Government of Canada bonds for cash as a held-to-maturity investment.
5. Accrued interest on Government of Canada bonds.
6. The Government of Canada bonds matured. Interest was previously accrued.
7. Bought 30% of Black Tickle Ltd. common shares for cash as an equity investment with significant influence.
8. Received Black Tickle's financial statements, which reported a net loss for the year.
9. Black Tickle paid a cash dividend.
10. Prepared an adjusting entry to record an increase in the market value of the available-for-sale investment portfolio above cost.

Instructions

Using the following table format, indicate whether each of the above transactions would result in an increase (+), decrease (–), or no effect (NE) in each category. The first one has been done for you as an example.

	Balance Sheet			Income Statement			Statement of Comprehensive Income
			Shareholders'				Other Comprehensive
Assets	Liabilities		Equity	Revenues	Expenses	Net Income	Income
1. NE (+ / –)	NE		NE	NE	NE	NE	NE

Classify balance sheet accounts.
(SO 5) AP

E16–13 You are provided with the following balance sheet accounts of New Bay Inc. as at December 31, 2008:

Accounts payable	$ 35,000	Common shares, 10,000, no par value	$100,000
Accounts receivable	60,000	Computers	12,000
Accumulated amortization—computers	8,000	Equipment	49,000
Accumulated amortization—equipment	32,000	Equity investment (Hemosol Inc.	
Allowance for doubtful accounts	10,000	common shares), at equity	71,000
Allowance to adjust available-for-sale securities		Held-to-maturity investment (Aliant Inc. bonds)	180,000
to market value (contra account)	9,000	Income tax payable	12,000
Available-for-sale securities (short-term), at cost	65,000	Interest receivable	5,000
Bond interest payable	8,000	Merchandise inventory	64,000
Bonds payable, 8%, due 2012	250,000	Premium on bonds payable	18,000
Cash and cash equivalents	22,000	Retained earnings	53,000
		Unearned sales revenue	7,000

Instructions

Indicate where each of the above accounts would be classified on New Bay's balance sheet at December 31.

Record acquisition and explain accounting for consolidation.
(SO 5) AP

E16–14 In 2006, 100% of the common shares of **Hudson's Bay Company (HBC)** were acquired by U.S.-based **Maple Leaf Heritage Investments Acquisition Corporation** for $957 million.

Instructions

(a) Prepare the journal entry to record the acquisition of HBC on Maple Leaf Heritage's books. What entry would HBC have made on its books?

(b) Which method—equity or cost—should Maple Leaf Heritage use to account for its investment in HBC?

(c) Which company is the parent company and which is the subsidiary company?

(d) After the acquisition, the HBC stores continued to operate under the HBC name. But HBC shares are no longer traded on the stock exchange and the company's financial results have been consolidated with Maple Leaf Heritage's for reporting purposes. Explain why.

Problems: Set A

Record debt investment and liability; show statement presentation.
(SO 2, 4, 5) AP

P16–1A The following bond transactions occurred during 2008 for College of Higher Learning (CHL) and Otutye Ltd. Both companies have a July 31 year end.

Feb. 1 CHL issued $10 million of 5-year, 6% bonds at 101. The bonds pay interest semi-annually on August 1 and February 1.

1 Otutye purchased all ($10 million) of CHL's bonds at 101 on the TSX.

July 31 Both companies prepared entries to accrue the bond interest. The semi-annual amortization amount was $15,625.

31 The bonds were trading at 100 on this date .

Aug. 1 The semi-annual interest on the bonds was paid.

Instructions

(a) Prepare the journal entries for CHL (investee) to record the above transactions.

(b) Show how the bond liability would be presented on CHL's July 31, 2008, balance sheet.

(c) Prepare the journal entries for Otutye to record the above transactions, assuming that it purchased the bonds as an available-for-sale investment classified as (1) short-term, and (2) long-term.

(d) Show how the debt investment would be presented on Otutye's July 31, 2008, balance sheet under each assumption used in (c).

P16–2A Givar Corp. had the following transactions in short-term, available-for-sale securities during the year ended December 31, 2008:

Record debt investments; show statement presentation.
(SO 2, 4, 5) AP

Feb. 1 Purchased $100,000 of Lesley Corporation 5% bonds at 101. Interest is paid semi-annually on August 1 and February 1.

Aug. 1 Received semi-annual interest on Lesley bonds.

2 Sold $40,000 of the Lesley bonds at 99.

Sept. 25 Purchased a treasury bill for $49,600.

Dec. 25 The treasury bill matured and Givar received $50,000 cash.

31 Accrued interest at year end on Lesley bonds.

31 The market value of the remaining bonds was $61,000 on this date.

Instructions

(a) Record the transactions.

(b) Show the financial statement presentation of the available-for-sale securities and any related accounts at December 31.

P16–3A During the year ended December 31, 2008, Mead Investment Corporation had the following transactions in trading securities:

Record debt and equity investments; show statement presentation.
(SO 2, 3, 4, 5) AP

Feb. 1 Purchased 600 CBF common shares for $31,800.

Mar. 1 Purchased 800 RSD common shares for $20,000.

Apr. 1 Purchased $50,000 of MRT 6% bonds at 100. Interest is payable semi-annually on April 1 and October 1.

July 1 Received a cash dividend of $1 per share on the CBF common shares.

Aug. 1 Sold 200 CBF common shares at $50 per share.

Oct. 1 Received the semi-annual interest on the MRT bonds.

2 Sold the MRT bonds for 102.

Dec. 31 The market values of the CBF and RSD common shares were $45 and $27 per share, respectively.

Instructions

(a) Record the transactions.

(b) Show the financial statement presentation of the trading securities and any related accounts at December 31.

P16–4A Lai Inc. had the following investment transactions:

Identify impact of investments on financial statements.
(SO 2, 3, 4, 5) AP

1. Purchased Chang Corporation preferred shares as an available-for-sale security.
2. Received a stock dividend on the Chang preferred shares.
3. Purchased Government of Canada bonds for cash as a trading security.
4. Accrued interest on the Government of Canada bonds.
5. Sold half of the Chang preferred shares at a price less than originally paid.
6. Purchased 25% of Xing Ltd.'s common shares as a long-term equity investment, with significant influence.
7. Received Xing's financial statements, which reported a net loss for the year.
8. Xing paid a cash dividend.
9. The market value of Chang's preferred shares was lower than cost at year end.
10. The market value of the Government of Canada bonds was higher than cost at year end.

Instructions

Using the following table format, indicate whether each of the above transactions would result in an increase (+), a decrease (−), or no effect (NE) in each category. The first one has been done for you as an example.

Balance Sheet			Income Statement			Statement of Comprehensive Income
Assets	Liabilities	Shareholders' Equity	Revenues	Expenses	Net Income	Other Comprehensive Income
1. NE (+ / −)	NE	NE	NE	NE	NE	NE

Record equity investment, using cost and equity methods; compare balances.
(SO 3) AP

P16–5A DFM Services Ltd. acquired 20% of the common shares of BNA Corporation on January 1, 2008, by paying $800,000 for 50,000 shares. BNA paid a $0.50 per share semi-annual cash dividend on June 15 and December 15. BNA reported net income of $350,000 for the year ended December 31, 2008. The market value of the shares equalled their cost at year-end.

Instructions

(a) Prepare the journal entries for DFM Services for 2008, assuming DFM (1) does not have significant influence, and (2) has significant influence.

(b) Compare the investment and revenue account balances at December 31, 2008, under each method of accounting used in (a).

(c) What factors help determine whether a company has significant influence over another company?

Record equity investments; show statement presentation.
(SO 3, 4, 5) AP

P16–6A The following investments are in Head Financial Corporation's portfolio of trading securities at December 31, 2007:

	Quantity	Cost
Alta Corporation common shares	500	$18,500
Brunswick Corporation common shares	700	35,000
Flon Corporation preferred shares	300	27,000
		$80,500

On December 31, 2007, the total cost of the portfolio equalled its total market value. Head Financial had the following transactions for the securities during 2008:

Jan.   7 Sold all 500 Alta common shares for $41 per share.
    10 Purchased 200 common shares of Econo Corporation at $53 per share.
Feb.   2 Received a cash dividend of $6 per share on Flon preferred shares.
    10 Sold all 300 Flon preferred shares at $85 per share.
Mar. 15 Received 70 additional Brunswick common shares as a result of a 10% stock dividend when the shares were trading at $45 per share.
June 23 Received 400 additional Econo common shares as a result of a 3-for-1 stock split.
Dec. 31 The market value of the Brunswick common shares was $42 per share and the market value of the Econo common shares was $18 per share.

Instructions

(a) Record the transactions.

(b) Show the financial statement presentation of the securities and any related accounts at December 31.

(c) Explain how your answer to (b) would change if the securities were classified as available-for-sale securities rather than as trading securities.

Record equity investment, using cost and equity methods; show statement presentation.
(SO 3, 5) AP

P16–7A Hat Limited has 200,000 common shares. On October 1, 2007, Cat Inc. purchased a block of these shares in the open market at $40 per share to hold as a long-term equity investment. Hat reported net income of $375,000 for the year ended September 30, 2008, and paid a $0.20 per share dividend. This problem assumes three independent situations that relate to how Cat would account for its investment:

Situation 1: Cat purchased 20,000 Hat common shares.
Situation 2: Cat purchased 60,000 Hat common shares.
Situation 3: Cat purchased 200,000 Hat common shares.

Instructions

(a) For each situation, identify whether Cat should use the cost or equity method to account for its investment in Hat.

(b) For each situation, record all transactions for Cat related to the investment for the year ended September 30, 2008.

(c) For each situation, compare Cat's nonconsolidated balance sheet and income statement accounts that relate to this investment at September 30.

(d) In situation 3, what kind of financial statements should be prepared to report the combined operations of Cat and Hat? Whose name will be on the financial statements?

P16–8A On December 31, 2008, Val d'Or Ltée held the following debt and equity investments:

Determine valuation of investments.

(SO 4, 5) AP

	Quantity	Cost Per Unit	Market Value Per Unit
Debt Securities			
Money-market instruments	10,000	$ 1	$ 1
CIBC bonds	2,000	98	100
Government of Canada bonds	1,000	100	140
Equity Securities			
Bank of Montreal	1,000	$31	$57
Bombardier	5,000	15	3
Nortel	5,000	55	3

Instructions

(a) Calculate the total cost and total market value of Val d'Or's investment portfolio at December 31.

(b) If Val d'Or considers its entire portfolio to be trading securities, at what value should the investments be reported on the balance sheet at December 31? At what amount, and where, should any unrealized gains or losses be reported?

(c) If Val d'Or considers its entire portfolio to be available-for-sale securities, at what value should the investments be reported on the balance sheet at December 31? At what amount, and where, should any unrealized gains or losses be reported?

(d) If Val d'Or decides to classify the Bombardier and Nortel shares as available-for-sale securities and the Bank of Montreal and debt securities as trading securities, what would be the impact on the income statement? On the statement of comprehensive income? On the balance sheet?

P16–9A Presented in alphabetical order, the following data are from the accounting records of Vladimir Corporation at December 31, 2008:

Prepare balance sheet.

(SO 5) AP

Accounts payable	$231,000	Held-to-maturity securities, at amortized cost	$100,000
Accounts receivable	140,000	Income tax payable	53,000
Accumulated amortization—buildings	100,000	Interest payable	5,000
Accumulated amortization—equipment	52,000	Interest receivable	8,000
Accumulated other comprehensive loss	97,000	Land	500,000
Allowance for doubtful accounts	14,000	Long-term equity investment—	
Allowance to adjust trading securities		Huston common shares, at equity	330,000
to market value (contra account)	20,000	Merchandise inventory, at FIFO cost	170,000
Bonds payable	250,000	Mortgage payable	670,000
Buildings	950,000	Patent	200,000
Cash	72,000	Premium on bonds payable	40,000
Common shares (no par value,		Prepaid insurance	10,000
unlimited authorized, 220,000 issued)	817,000	Retained earnings	713,000
Current portion of mortgage payable	27,000	Unearned service revenue	15,000
Dividends payable	40,000	Trading securities, at cost	195,000
Equipment	275,000		

Instructions

Prepare a balance sheet at December 31.

Prepare income statement
and statement of
comprehensive income.

(SO 5) AP

P16–10A Selected condensed information (in millions) for **Canadian National Railway Company** follows for the year ended December 31, 2005:

Equity in earnings of English			Investment income	$ 3
Welsh and Scottish Railway	$ 4		Operating expenses	4,616
Gain on disposal of properties	26		Other comprehensive income items	194
Income tax expense	781		Other comprehensive loss items	268
Interest expense	299		Other expenses	21
			Revenues	7,240

Instructions

(a) Prepare an income statement and statement of comprehensive income for the year ended December 31, 2005.
(b) The Canadian National Railway had an opening balance in its Accumulated Other Comprehensive Loss account of $148 million. What is the ending balance it would report in the shareholders' equity section of its balance sheet at December 31, 2005?

Problems: Set B

Record debt investment and
liability; show statement
presentation.

(SO 2, 4, 5) AP

P16–1B The following bond transactions occurred during 2008 for CASB Incorporated and Densmore Consulting Ltd. Both companies have a December 31 year end.

Jan. 1 CASB issued $1 million of 10-year, 7% bonds at 98. The bonds pay interest semi-annually on June 30 and December 31.
  1 Densmore Consulting purchased all $1 million of CASB's bonds at 98 on the TSX.
June 30 The semi-annual interest on the bonds was paid. The semi-annual amortization was $1,750.
Dec. 31 The semi-annual interest on the bonds was paid. The semi-annual amortization amount was $1,815.
  31 The bonds were trading at 99 on this date.

Instructions

(a) Prepare the journal entries for CASB (investee) to record the above transactions.
(b) Show how the bond liability would be presented on CASB's December 31, 2008, balance sheet.
(c) Prepare the journal entries for Densmore Consulting to record the above transactions assuming that it purchased the bonds as an available-for-sale investment classified as (1) short-term, and (2) long-term.
(d) Show how the debt investment would be presented on Densmore Consulting's December 31, 2008, balance sheet under each assumption used in (c).

P16–2B Liu Corporation had the following transactions in short-term, available-for-sale securities during the year ended December 31, 2008:

Jan. 1 Purchased $50,000 of RAM Corp. 6% bonds at 99. Interest is paid semi-annually on July 1 and January 1.
July 1 Received semi-annual interest on the RAM bonds.
  1 Sold $25,000 of RAM bonds at 101.
  5 Purchased a money-market fund for $25,000.
Oct. 1 Cashed in the money-market fund, receiving $25,000 plus $185 interest.
Dec. 31 Accrued semi-annual interest on the RAM bonds.
  31 The market value of the remaining bonds was $24,000 on this date.

Instructions

(a) Record the transactions.
(b) Show the financial statement presentation of the available-for-sale securities and any related accounts at December 31.

P16–3B During the year ended December 31, 2008, Rakai Corporation had the following transactions in trading securities:

Record debt and equity investments; show statement presentation.
(SO 2, 3, 4, 5) AP

Feb.	1	Purchased 850 IBF common shares for $40,800.
Mar.	1	Purchased 500 RST common shares for $18,000.
Apr.	1	Purchased $70,000 of CRT 6% bonds for $69,000. Interest is payable semi-annually on April 1 and October 1.
July	1	Received a cash dividend of $1 per share on the IBF common shares.
Aug.	1	Sold 350 IBF common shares at $45 per share.
Oct.	1	Received the semi-annual interest on the CRT bonds.
	1	Sold the CRT bonds for $70,000.
Dec.	31	The market values of the IBF and RST common shares were $42 and $38 per share, respectively.

Instructions

(a) Record the transactions.
(b) Show the financial statement presentation of the trading securities and any related accounts at December 31.

P16–4B Olsztyn Inc. had the following investment transactions:

Identify impact of investments on financial statements.
(SO 2, 3, 4, 5) AP

1. Purchased Arichat Corporation common shares as a trading security.
2. Received a cash dividend on Arichat common shares.
3. Purchased Bombardier bonds as an available-for-sale security.
4. Received interest on Bombardier bonds.
5. Sold half of the Bombardier bonds at a price greater than originally paid.
6. Purchased 40% of LaHave Ltd.'s common shares as a long-term equity investment, with significant influence.
7. Received LaHave's financial statements, which reported net earnings for the year.
8. LaHave paid a cash dividend.
9. The market value of Arichat's common shares was higher than cost at year end.
10. The market value of Bombardier's bonds was lower than cost at year end.

Instructions

Using the following table format, indicate whether each of the above transactions would result in an increase (+), a decrease (–), or no effect (NE) in each category. The first one has been done for you as an example.

Balance Sheet			Income Statement			Statement of Comprehensive Income
Assets	Liabilities	Shareholders' Equity	Revenues	Expenses	Net Income	Other Comprehensive Income
1. NE (+ / –)	NE	NE	NE	NE	NE	NE

P16–5B Cardinal Concrete Limited acquired 20% of the common shares of Edra, Inc., on January 1, 2008, by paying $1.2 million for 50,000 shares. Edra paid a $0.50 per share semi-annual cash dividend on June 30 and again on December 31. Edra reported net income of $750,000 for the year. The market value of the shares equalled their cost at year-end.

Record equity investment, using cost and equity methods; compare balances.
(SO 3) AP

Instructions

(a) Prepare the journal entries for Cardinal Concrete for 2008, assuming Cardinal (1) does not have significant influence, and (2) has significant influence.

(b) Compare the investment and revenue account balances at December 31, 2008, under each method of accounting used in (a).

(c) Are there any advantages to a company having significant influence over another? Explain.

Record equity investments; show statement presentation.

(SO 3, 4, 5) AP

P16—6B   The following are in Hi-Tech Inc.'s portfolio of trading securities at December 31, 2007:

	Quantity	Cost
Aglar Corporation common shares	500	$26,000
BAL Corporation common shares	700	42,000
Hicks Corporation preferred shares	600	16,800
		$84,800

On December 31, 2007, the total cost of the portfolio equalled its total market value. Hi-Tech had the following transactions related to the securities during 2008:

Jan. 7 Sold 500 Aglar common shares at $55 per share.
   10 Purchased 200 common shares of Miley Corporation at $78 per share.
Feb. 2 Received a cash dividend of $1 per share on the Hicks preferred shares.
   10 Sold all 600 Hicks preferred shares at $27 per share.
Apr. 30 Received 700 additional BAL common shares as a result of a 2-for-1 stock split.
Aug. 3 Received 20 additional Miley common shares as the result of a 10% stock dividend.
Sept. 1 Purchased an additional 800 common shares of Miley at $70 per share.
Dec. 31 The market value of the BAL common shares was $32 per share and the market value of the Miley common shares was $72 per share.

Instructions

(a) Record the transactions.

(b) Show the financial statement presentation of the securities and any related accounts at December 31.

(c) Explain how your answer to (b) would change if the securities were classified as available-for-sale securities rather than trading securities.

Record equity investment, using cost and equity methods. Show statement presentation.

(SO 3, 5) AP

P16—7B   Sub Corporation has 500,000 common shares. On January 10, 2007, Par Inc. purchased a block of these shares in the open market at $10 per share to hold as a long-term equity investment. Sub reported net income of $260,000 for the year ended December 31, 2008, and paid a $0.25 per share dividend.

This problem assumes three independent situations that relate to how Par would account for its investment:

Situation 1: Par purchased 50,000 Sub common shares.
Situation 2: Par purchased 150,000 Sub common shares.
Situation 3: Par purchased 500,000 Sub common shares.

Instructions

(a) For each situation, identify whether Par should use the cost or equity method to account for its investment in Sub.

(b) For each situation, record all transactions related to the investment for Par for the year ended December 31, 2008.

(c) For each situation, compare Par's unconsolidated balance sheet and income statement accounts that relate to this investment at December 31.

(d) In situation 3, what kind of financial statements should be prepared to report the combined operations of Par and Sub? Whose name will be on the financial statements?

Determine valuation of investments.

(SO 4, 5) AP

P16—8B   On June 30, 2008, Sturge Enterprises Inc. held the following debt and equity investments:

	Quantity	Cost Per Unit	Market Value Per Unit
Debt Securities			
Money-market instruments	25,000	$ 1	$ 1
BCE bonds	50,000	101	99
Government of Canada bonds	100,000	100	105
Equity Securities			
Scotiabank	1,000	$39	$45
Barrick Gold	5,000	26	33
Tim Hortons	5,000	37	30

Instructions

(a) Calculate the total cost and total market values of Sturge's investment portfolio at June 30.

(b) If Sturge considers its entire portfolio to be trading securities, at what value should the investments be reported on the balance sheet at June 30? At what amount, and where, should any unrealized gains or losses be reported?

(c) If Sturge considers its entire portfolio to be available-for-sale securities, at what value should the investments be reported on the balance sheet at June 30? At what amount, and where, should any unrealized gains or losses be reported?

(d) If Sturge decides to classify the BCE bonds and Tim Hortons shares as available-for-sale securities and the others as trading securities, what would be the impact on the income statement? On the statement of comprehensive income? On the balance sheet?

P16–9B Presented in alphabetical order, the following data are from the accounting records of Stinson Corporation at April 30, 2008:

Prepare balance sheet.
(SO 5) AP

Accounts payable	$ 200,000	Equipment	$275,000
Accounts receivable	90,000	Goodwill	200,000
Accumulated amortization—building	180,000	Held-to-maturity securities, at amortized cost	24,000
Accumulated amortization—equipment	72,000	Income tax payable	120,000
Accumulated other comprehensive income	20,000	Interest payable	12,000
Allowance for doubtful accounts	6,000	Land	500,000
Allowance to adjust available-for-sale securities to market value (adjunct account)	10,000	Long-term equity investment—Indira common shares, at equity	270,000
Available-for-sale securities (short-term), at cost	350,000	Merchandise inventory, at average cost	170,000
Bonds payable	400,000	Notes payable (due 2009)	70,000
Buildings	900,000	Preferred shares (no par value, $5-noncumulative,	
Cash and cash equivalents	100,000	unlimited authorized, 5,000 issued)	200,000
Common shares (no par value, unlimited		Retained earnings	665,000
authorized, 300,000 issued)	1,000,000	Supplies	6,000
Discount on bonds payable	20,000	Trademark	100,000
Dividends payable	70,000		

Instructions

Prepare a balance sheet at April 30.

P16–10B **Barrick Gold Corporation**, headquartered in Toronto, is the world's number one gold producer. Selected condensed information (in U.S. millions) for Barrick Gold follows for the year ended December 31, 2005:

Prepare income statement and statement of comprehensive income.
(SO 5) AP

Cost of sales	$1,214	Other comprehensive income items	128
Equity (loss) in investee earnings	(6)	Other comprehensive loss items	171
Gold sales	2,350	Other expenses	67
Income tax expense	60	Other revenues	6
Interest expense	7	Unrealized gains on available-	
Interest income	38	for-sale securities	12
Operating expenses	$639		

Instructions

(a) Prepare an income statement and statement of comprehensive income for the year ended December 31, 2005.
(b) Barrick Gold had an opening balance in its Accumulated Other Comprehensive Income account of $69 million. What is the ending balance it would report in the shareholders' equity section of its balance sheet at December 31, 2005?

Continuing Cookie Chronicle

(*Note*: This is a continuation of the Cookie Chronicle from Chapters 1 through 15.)

Natalie and Curtis have been approached by Ken Thornton, a shareholder of The Beanery Coffee Ltd. Ken wants to retire and would like to sell his 1,000 shares in The Beanery Coffee, which represent 20% of all shares issued. The Beanery is currently operated by Ken's twin daughters, who each own 40% of the common shares. The Beanery not only operates a coffee shop but also roasts and sells beans to retailers, under the name "Rocky Mountain Beanery."

The business has been operating for approximately five years, and in the last two years Ken has lost interest and left the day-to-day operations to his daughters. Both daughters at times find the work at the coffee shop overwhelming. They would like to have a third shareholder involved to take over some of the responsibilities of running a small business. Both feel that Natalie and Curtis are entrepreneurial in spirit and that their expertise would be a welcome addition to the business operation. The twins have also said that they plan to operate this business for another 10 years and then retire.

Ken has met with Curtis and Natalie to discuss the business operation. All have concluded that there would be many advantages for Cookie & Coffee Creations Ltd. to acquire an interest in The Beanery Coffee. One of the major advantages would be volume discounts for purchases of coffee bean inventory.

Despite the apparent advantages, Natalie and Curtis are still not convinced that they should participate in this business venture. They come to you with the following questions:

1. We are a little concerned about how much influence we would have in the decision-making process for The Beanery Coffee. Would the amount of influence we have affect how we would account for this investment?
2. Can you think of other advantages of going ahead with this investment?
3. Can you think of any disadvantages of going ahead with this investment?

Instructions

(a) Answer Natalie and Curtis's questions.
(b) Assume that Ken wants to sell his 1,000 shares of The Beanery Coffee for $15,000. Prepare the journal entry required if Cookie & Coffee Creations Ltd. buys Ken's shares.
(c) Assume that Cookie & Coffee Creations Ltd. buys the shares and in the following year The Beanery Coffee earns $50,000 net income and pays $25,000 in dividends. Prepare the journal entries required under both the cost method and the equity method of accounting for this investment.
(d) Identify where this investment would be classified on the balance sheet of Cookie & Coffee Creations Ltd. and explain why. What amount would appear on the balance sheet under each of the methods of accounting for the investment?

Cumulative Coverage—Chapters 13 to 16

Plankton Corporation's trial balance at December 31, 2008, is presented on the following page. All transactions and adjustments for 2008 have been recorded except for the items described below.

Jan. 7 Issued 1,000 preferred shares for $25,000. In total, 100,000 $2-noncumulative, convertible, preferred shares are authorized. Each preferred share is convertible into five common shares.

Mar. 16 Purchased 800 common shares of Osborne Inc. for $24 per share. This investment is intended to be held as a short-term, available-for-sale investment.

Aug. 2 Sold the Osborne common shares for $25 per share (see March 16 transaction).

5 Invested $20,000 in a money-market fund.

Sept. 25 Five hundred of the preferred shares were converted into common shares (see January 7 transaction).

Oct. 24 Cashed in the money-market fund, receiving $20,000 plus $200 interest (see August 5 transaction).

Nov. 30 Obtained a $50,000 bank loan by issuing a 3-year, 6% note payable. Plankton is required to make equal blended principal and interest instalment payments of $1,521 at the end of each month. The first payment was made on December 31. Note that at December 31, $15,757 of the note payable is due within the next year.

Dec. 1 Declared the annual dividend on the preferred shares on December 1 to shareholders of record on December 23, payable on January 15.

31 Plankton owns 40% of RES, which it has accounted for using the equity method. RES earned $20,000 and paid dividends of $1,200 in 2008.

31 Semi-annual interest is due on the bonds January 1, 2009. The amortization amount for this period is $200.

31 The market value of the company's available-for-sale securities portfolio was $28,000.

PLANKTON CORPORATION
Trial Balance
December 31, 2008

	Debit	Credit
Cash	$ 18,000	
Accounts receivable	51,000	
Allowance for doubtful accounts		$ 2,550
Merchandise inventory	22,700	
Available-for-sale securities, at cost	25,000	
Allowance to adjust available-for-sale securities to market value	5,000	
Held-to-maturity securities, at amortized cost	10,000	
Equity investment in RES common shares, at equity	85,000	
Land	120,000	
Building	200,000	
Accumulated amortization—building		40,000
Equipment	40,000	
Accumulated amortization—equipment		15,000
Accounts payable		18,775
Income tax payable		4,500
Bonds payable (6%, due January 1, 2016)		130,000
Discount on bonds payable	3,750	
Common shares, unlimited number of no par value shares authorized, 100,000 issued		100,000
Retained earnings		120,500
Accumulated other comprehensive income		5,000
Sales		750,000
Cost of goods sold	370,000	
Operating expenses	180,000	
Interest revenue		375
Interest expense	6,250	
Income tax expense	50,000	
Total	$1,186,700	$1,186,700

Instructions

(a) Record the transactions.

(b) Prepare an updated trial balance at December 31, 2008, that includes the above transactions.

(c) Using the income statement accounts in the trial balance, calculate income before income tax. Assuming Plankton has a 27% income tax rate, prepare the journal entry to adjust income taxes for the year. Note that Plankton has recorded $50,000 of income tax expense for the year to date. Update the trial balance for this additional entry.

(d) Prepare the following financial statements for Plankton: (1) income statement, (2) statement of retained earnings, (3) statement of comprehensive income, and (4) balance sheet.

BROADENING YOUR PERSPECTIVE

Financial Reporting and Analysis

Financial Reporting Problem

BYP16–1 Refer to the financial statements and accompanying notes for **The Forzani Group Ltd.** presented in Appendix A.

Instructions

(a) What information about investments is reported in Forzani's financial statements in fiscal 2006?

(b) Does Forzani report any investment-related income in its financial statements in fiscal 2006?

Interpreting Financial Statements

BYP16–2 **American Express Company** is the world's number one travel company, with operations in more than 200 countries. The company reported the following selected information for its investment portfolio for the year ended December 31, 2005 (in U.S. millions):

	2005	2004
Trading securities, at market value	$ 231	$ 240
Available-for-sale securities, at market value	21,103	21,435
	$21,334	$21,675

The following additional information was available for the company's available-for-sale investment portfolio:

	Cost	Unrealized Gains	Unrealized Losses	Market Value
2005	$20,884	$403	$184	$21,103
2004	20,912	621	98	21,435

Instructions

(a) Why does American Express most likely have an investment portfolio consisting of both trading and available-for-sale securities?

(b) Out of its total investment portfolio, American Express has a significant amount invested in available-for-sale securities. Why do you suppose it has such a high percentage of its portfolio invested in available-for-sale securities?

(c) Explain where American Express would report its trading securities, available-for-sale securities, and unrealized gains and losses for is trading and available-for-sale securities in its financial statements.

Critical Thinking

Collaborative Learning Activity

Note to instructor: Additional instructions and material for this group activity can be found on the Instructor Resource Site.

BYP16–3   In this group activity, you will compare the accounting for long-term debt investments to that for long-term bonds payable (Chapter 15).

Instructions

(a) Your instructor will divide the class into groups of two and distribute a package to each. With your partner, determine who will be the investor and who will be the issuer (borrower). Select the pages associated with your role from the package. Review the notes and complete the requirements.

(b) With your partner, compare your answers and when different, explain how your answers were determined.

Study Aids:
Working in Groups

Communication Activity

BYP16–4   In 2006, accounting standards changed so that trading securities and available-for-sale securities were reported at market values, rather than at cost (or lower of cost and market).

Instructions

Discuss whether reporting investments at their market value rather than at cost gives better information for investors to evaluate the performance of a company's investment portfolio. Outline the advantages and disadvantages of this new approach. Describe any additional data that investors would need to have in order to properly evaluate a company's investment performance.

Study Aids:
Writing Handbook

Ethics Case

BYP16–5   Kreiter Financial Services Limited holds a large portfolio of debt and equity investments. The total market value of the portfolio at December 31, 2008, is greater than its total cost. Some securities have increased in value and others have decreased. Vicki Lemke, the financial vice-president, and Ula Greenwood, the controller, are busy classifying the securities in the portfolio for the first time.

Lemke suggests classifying the securities that have increased in value as trading securities in order to increase net income for the year. She wants to classify the securities that have decreased in value as available-for-sale securities so that the decreases in value will not affect net income.

Greenwood disagrees. She recommends classifying the securities that have decreased in value as trading securities and those that have increased in value as available-for-sale securities. Greenwood argues that the company is having a good year and that recognizing the losses now will help to smooth income for the year. Moreover, for future years, when the company may not be as profitable, it will have built-in gains "held in reserve."

Study Aids:
Ethics in Accounting

Instructions

(a) Will classifying the securities as Lemke and Greenwood suggest actually affect income the way they think it will?

(b) Is there anything unethical in what Lemke and Greenwood propose?

(c) Who are the stakeholders affected by their proposals?

(d) Assume that Lemke and Greenwood classify the portfolio properly. Now, at year end, Greenwood proposes to sell the available-for-sale securities that will decrease net income for 2008. Is this unethical?

Answers to Accounting in Action Insight Questions

Business Insight, p. 811

Q: Was the acquisition of Falconbridge by Xstrata a passive or strategic investment? What are some advantages that Xstrata might now have because of its acquisition of Falconbridge?

A: The acquisition of Falconbridge was a strategic investment. By acquiring Falconbridge, Xstrata created a larger company that should be able to compete better in the global marketplace. That is, the value and performance of the two companies combined is expected to be greater than the sum of them operating individually. In addition, major cost savings are expected to result from the combination of the two companies.

International Insight, p. 827

Q: How will reporting trading and available-for-sale securities at their market value be more relevant to financial statement users?

A: Because trading and available-for-sale securities are purchased with the intent of selling them in the future and generating investment income, it will be more relevant to users to have these investments reported at their market value. Users can then better understand the amount of value that could be created by each of these types of securities.

Business Insight, p. 831

Q: Why is it important for a company such as Exxon Mobil to consolidate the results of its subsidiary Imperial Oil in its own financial statements?

A: It is important for the user to understand the scope and financial impact of all operations controlled by Exxon Mobil. If Exxon Mobil controls Imperial Oil, then it is more relevant to show their combined results as though they were one company.

Answer to Forzani Review It Question 3, p. 831

The Forzani Group's financial statements are consolidated. It owns 100 percent of its subsidiary companies (see Note 2 (a)).

Answers to Self-Study Questions

1. c   2. c   3. a   4. c   5. b   6. a   7. d   8. a   9. c   10. a

Remember to go back to the Navigator Box at the beginning of the chapter to check off your completed work.

concepts for review >>

Before studying this chapter, you should understand or, if necessary, review:

a. The difference between the accrual basis and the cash basis of accounting. (Ch. 3, pp. 106–107)

b. The major items included in a corporation's balance sheet. (Ch. 4, pp. 175–180 and Ch. 13, pp. 681-683)

c. The major items included in a corporation's income statement. (Ch. 14, pp. 719–721)

Looking for the Big Picture in Small Business Loans

HALIFAX, N.S.—If you're a company trying to borrow money from a bank, what determines whether not your loan application is approved? What, exactly, is the person on the other side of that desk looking for?

If that person is Shelley LeBrun, manager of Small Business Banking at TD Canada Trust in Halifax, the answer is—all kinds of things.

The first thing a loan officer usually asks to see, says Ms. LeBrun, is the balance sheet, "to see how much equity the company has, then the income statement, to see if it's actually making any money." But the process, she insists, shouldn't stop there.

The rest of the company's financial statements also help clarify the picture, especially the cash flow statement. Sometimes, for example, a company may not look profitable from its income statement, but its cash flow statement will show that it actually has significant resources available.

"For example, when certain expenses, such as amortization expense, are recorded on the income statement, they can reduce the profit as it appears on the income statement," explains Ms. LeBrun. "However, this has no impact on the amount of cash generated by the business since the asset being amortized was purchased and paid for in prior periods."

There could also be timing differences between the recording on the income statement of revenue earned on a project, for instance, and the actual receipt of cash from the customer.

The bottom line, Ms. LeBrun says, is that "we need to know that the company is able to service the debt. The cash flow statement can show us that. It also gives the

TD Canada Trust: www.tdcanadatrust.com

bank a good idea of what type of operating line of credit a company may require going forward."

If the cash flow statement, together with previous years' statements and a good business plan, shows the bank that the company is financially sound and can meet its loan payments, then the application is likely to be approved.

"At TD Canada Trust, we try to see the big picture," she explains. Factors like a sound business plan, signed contracts for major orders in the near future, and, in a small business, the owner's personal financial situation—including credit history, net worth, and previous business experience— can all make the difference in getting the small business loan needed for the next step.

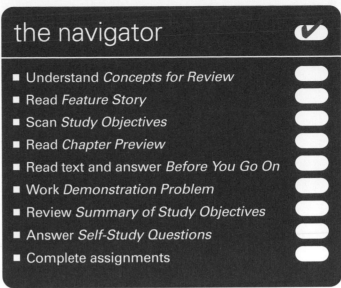

the navigator ✔

- Understand *Concepts for Review*
- Read *Feature Story*
- Scan *Study Objectives*
- Read *Chapter Preview*
- Read text and answer *Before You Go On*
- Work *Demonstration Problem*
- Review *Summary of Study Objectives*
- Answer *Self-Study Questions*
- Complete assignments

chapter 17
The Cash Flow Statement

study objectives >>

After studying this chapter, you should be able to:

1. Describe the purpose and content of the cash flow statement.
2. Prepare a cash flow statement using one of two approaches: (a) the indirect method or (b) the direct method.
3. Analyze the cash flow statement.

As Shelley LeBrun in our feature story indicates, the cash flow statement gives information for decision-making that is not always available from the other financial statements, including the balance sheet, income statement, statement of comprehensive income, and statement of retained earnings. In fact, looking at the financial statements for some well-known companies, a thoughtful reader might have questions like the following: How did Andrés Wines pay dividends in a year when it had no cash and instead had bank indebtedness? How did the Students' Association of Mount Royal College fund the expansion of its student centre? What did Wendy's do with the money it received from the sale of its Tim Hortons shares? This chapter, which presents the cash flow statement, will answer these and similar questions.

The chapter is organized as follows:

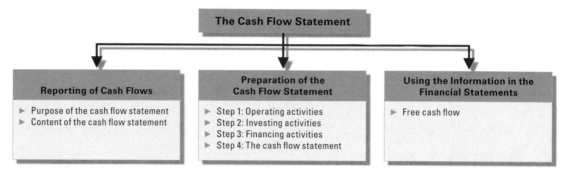

Reporting of Cash Flows

The financial statements we have studied so far present only partial information about a company's cash flows (cash receipts and cash payments). For example, comparative balance sheets show the increase in property, plant, and equipment during the year, but they do not show how the additions were financed or paid for. The income statement shows net income, but it does not indicate the amount of cash that was generated by operating activities. Similarly, the statement of retained earnings shows the amount of cash dividends that was declared, but not the amount of cash dividends that was actually paid during the year.

Note that the statement of comprehensive income, which we studied in Chapter 14, does not affect cash flow since unrealized gains and losses are only "paper" gains and losses. No cash is generated until an investment is actually sold.

Purpose of the Cash Flow Statement

The **cash flow statement** gives information about the cash receipts, cash payments, and net change in cash that result from operating, investing, and financing activities during a period. Reporting the causes of changes in cash helps investors, creditors, and other interested parties understand what is happening to a company's most liquid resource—its cash. As the feature story indicates, in order to determine whether a company is financially sound or not, it is essential to understand its cash flows.

The information in a cash flow statement should help investors, creditors, and others evaluate the following aspects of the company's financial position:

1. **Ability to generate future cash flows.** Investors and others examine the relationships between items in the cash flow statement. From these, users can predict the amounts, timing, and uncertainty of future cash flows better than they can from accrual-based data.

2. **Ability to pay dividends and meet obligations.** If a company does not have enough cash, employees cannot be paid, debts settled, or dividends paid. Employees, creditors, and shareholders are particularly interested in this statement because it is the only one that shows the flow of cash in a company.
3. **Investing and financing transactions during the period.** By examining a company's investing and financing transactions, users can better understand why assets and liabilities changed during the period.
4. **Difference between net income and cash provided (used) by operating activities.** Net income gives information about the success or failure of a business. However, some people are critical of accrual-based net income because it requires many estimates, allocations, and assumptions. As a result, the reliability of the net income amount is often challenged. This is not true of cash. If readers of the cash flow statement understand the reasons for the difference between net income and net cash provided by operating activities, they can then decide for themselves how reliable the net income amount is.

Content of the Cash Flow Statement

Before we can start preparing the cash flow statement, we must first understand what it includes and why. We will begin by reviewing the definition of cash used in the cash flow statement and then discuss how cash receipts and payments are classified within the statement.

Definition of Cash

The cash flow statement is generally prepared using **cash and cash equivalents** as its basis. You will recall from Chapter 7 that cash equivalents are highly liquid investments that are both:

1. readily convertible to known amounts of cash, and
2. so near to their maturity that their market value is not significantly affected by changes in interest rates.

Generally, only money-market instruments that are due within three months fit this definition. Because of the varying definitions of "cash" that can be used in this statement, companies must give a clear definition of "cash" as it is used in their particular statement.

Since cash and cash equivalents (e.g., money-market instruments) are viewed as being the same, transfers between cash and cash equivalents are not treated as cash receipts and cash payments. That is, such transfers are not reported in the cash flow statement.

Classification of Cash Flows

The cash flow statement classifies cash receipts and cash payments into three types of activities: (1) operating, (2) investing, and (3) financing activities. The transactions and other events for each kind of activity are as follows:

1. **Operating activities** include the cash effects of transactions that create revenues and expenses. They affect net income.
2. **Investing activities** include (a) acquiring and disposing of investments and long-lived assets, and (b) lending money and collecting the loans. They generally affect long-term asset accounts.
3. **Financing activities** include (a) obtaining cash from issuing debt and repaying the amounts borrowed, and (b) obtaining cash from shareholders and paying them dividends. Financing activities generally affect long-term liability and shareholders' equity accounts.

Illustration 17-1 lists typical cash receipts and cash payments in each of the three classifications.

Illustration 17-1 ▶

Cash receipts and payments classified by activity

Types of Cash Inflows and Outflows

Operating activities—income statement items and changes in noncash working capital accounts
  Cash inflows:
    From the sale of goods or services
    From returns on debt investments (interest) and on equity investments (dividends)
  Cash outflows:
    To suppliers for inventory
    To employees for services
    To governments for taxes
    To lenders for interest
    To others for expenses
Investing activities—changes in long-term asset accounts
  Cash inflows:
    From the sale of property, plant, and equipment
    From the sale of debt or equity investments
    From the collection of principal on loans to other companies
  Cash outflows:
    To purchase property, plant, and equipment
    To purchase debt or equity investments
    To make loans to other companies
Financing activities—changes in long-term liability and equity accounts
  Cash inflows:
    From the sale of shares (preferred and common)
    From the issue of debt (bonds and notes)
  Cash outflows:
    To shareholders as dividends
    To repay long-term debt or reacquire share capital

As you can see, some cash flows that are related to investing or financing activities are classified as operating activities. For example, receipts of investment revenue (interest and dividends) earned from debt or equity securities are classified as operating activities. So are payments of interest to lenders of debt. Why are these considered operating activities? Because these items are reported in the income statement where results of operations are shown.

Note the following general guidelines:

1. **Operating activities** involve income statement items. These items are also affected by noncash working capital accounts (current assets and current liabilities) on the balance sheet.
2. **Investing activities** involve cash flows resulting from changes in long-term asset accounts.
3. **Financing activities** involve cash flows resulting from changes in long-term liability and shareholders' equity accounts.

Illustration 17-2 ▼

Operating, investing, and financing activities

Illustration 17-2 shows these general guidelines.

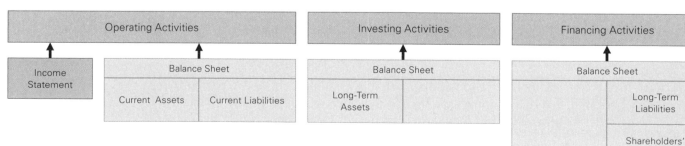

There are always exceptions to general guidelines such as those shown above. For example, changes in short-term investments that are not cash equivalents are reported as investing activities. Changes in short-term notes receivable that result from non-trade (i.e., lending) transactions are also reported as investing activities rather than as operating activities. And changes in short-term notes payable that result from non-trade (i.e., borrowing) transactions are reported as financing activities.

Significant Noncash Activities. Not all of a company's significant investing and financing activities involve cash. The following are examples of significant noncash activities:

1. An issue of debt to purchase assets
2. An issue of common shares to purchase assets
3. A conversion of debt or preferred shares to common shares
4. Exchanges of property, plant, and equipment

Significant investing and financing activities that do not affect cash are not reported in the body of the cash flow statement. These noncash activities are reported in a separate note, which satisfies the full disclosure principle.

Note that this disclosure requirement also includes the noncash portion of a partial cash transaction, as the following example shows. Assume that a building is purchased for $10 million. A $1-million down payment was made and the remainder was financed with a mortgage note payable. The cash flow statement would disclose only the $1 million cash paid (as an investing activity). The acquisition of the building (a $9-million investing activity) by a mortgage note payable (a $9-million financing activity) would be disclosed in the notes and cross referenced to the $1-million cash outflow reported in the investing activities section of the cash flow statement.

BEFORE YOU GO ON . . .

▶**Review It**

1. How does the cash flow statement help users understand a company's financial position?
2. What are cash equivalents?
3. What are the three types of activities reported in the cash flow statement? Give an example of each.
4. In its cash flow statement for the year ended January 29, 2006, what amounts are reported by The Forzani Group for (a) cash provided by operating activities, (b) cash used by investing activities, and (c) cash provided by financing activities? The answer to this question is at the end of the chapter.

▶**Do It**

During its first week of existence, Carrier Molding Ltd. had the following transactions:

1. Issued common shares.
2. Sold an available-for-sale security.
3. Purchased a tractor trailer truck. Made a cash down payment, and financed the remainder with a mortgage note payable.
4. Paid interest on the mortgage note payable.
5. Collected cash for services provided.

Classify each of these transactions by type of cash flow activity. Indicate whether the transaction would be reported as a cash inflow or cash outflow.

Action Plan

- Identify the three types of activities that are used to report all cash inflows and outflows.
- Report as operating activities the cash effects of transactions that create revenues and expenses, and which are included when net income is determined.

- Report as investing activities transactions to (a) acquire and dispose of investments and long-lived assets, and (b) lend money and collect loans.
- Report as financing activities transactions to (a) obtain cash by issuing debt and repay the amounts borrowed, and (b) obtain cash from shareholders and pay them dividends.

Solution

1. Financing activity; cash inflow
2. Investing activity; cash inflow
3. Investing activity; cash outflow for down payment. The remainder is a noncash investing (tractor trailer truck) and financing (mortgage note payable) activity.
4. Operating activity; cash outflow
5. Operating activity; cash inflow

the
navigator

Related exercise material: BE17–1, BE17–2, E17–1, and E17–2.

Preparation of the Cash Flow Statement

study objective 2

Prepare a cash flow statement using one of two approaches: (a) the indirect method or (b) the direct method.

You may recall that we first illustrated the cash flow statement in Chapter 1, in Illustration 1-8. The cash flow statement covers the same period of time as the income statement and statement of retained earnings (e.g., for the year ended). The general format of the statement focuses on the three types of activities (operating, investing, and financing) that we discussed in the preceding section. The operating activities section is always presented first. It is followed by the investing activities and financing activities sections. Finally, any significant noncash investing and financing activities are reported in a note to the statement.

The reported operating, investing, and financing activities result in net cash being either provided or used by each activity. These amounts are totalled to determine the net increase (decrease) in cash for the period. This amount is then added to, or subtracted from, the beginning-of-period cash balance. This gives the end-of-period cash balance. The end-of-period cash balance should agree with the cash balance reported on the balance sheet.

Now that we understand the content and format of a cash flow statement, where do we find the information to prepare it? There are no specific accounts in the general ledger for the types of operating activities, investing activities, or financing activities shown in Illustration 17-1. This is because the cash flow statement is prepared differently from the other financial statements. First, it is not prepared from an adjusted trial balance. The statement requires detailed information about the changes in account balances that occurred between two periods of time. An adjusted trial balance will not provide the necessary data. Second, the cash flow statement deals with cash receipts and payments. As a result, the accrual concept is not used in the preparation of a cash flow statement.

The information to prepare this statement usually comes from three sources:

1. **Comparative balance sheet.** Information in the comparative balance sheet indicates the amount of the changes in assets, liabilities, and shareholders' equity from the beginning to the end of the period.
2. **Current income statement.** Information in the income statement helps determine the amount of cash provided or used by operating activities during the period.
3. **Additional information.** This includes transaction data that are needed to determine how cash was provided or used during the period.

There are four steps to prepare the cash flow statement from these data sources, as Illustration 17-3 shows.

Illustration 17-3 ◀

Steps in preparing the cash flow statement

Step 1: Determine the net cash provided (used) by operating activities by converting net income from an accrual basis to a cash basis.

The current year's income statement is analyzed, as well as the relevant current assets and current liabilities accounts from the comparative balance sheet, and selected additional information.

Step 2: Determine the net cash provided (used) by investing activities by analyzing changes in long-term asset accounts.

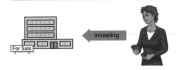

Comparative balance sheet data and selected additional information are analyzed for their effects on cash.

Step 3: Determine the net cash provided (used) by financing activities by analyzing changes long-term liability and equity accounts.

Comparative balance sheet data and selected additional information are analyzed for their effects on cash.

Step 4: Prepare the cash flow statement and determine the net increase (decrease) in cash.

Compare the net change in cash reported on the cash flow statement with the change in cash reported on the balance sheet to make sure the amounts agree.

To explain and illustrate the preparation of a cash flow statement, we will use financial information from Computer Services Corporation. Illustration 17-4 on the following page presents Computer Services' current- and prior-year balance sheet, its current-year income statement, and related financial information.

Illustration 17-4 ▶

Computer Services' financial information

COMPUTER SERVICES CORPORATION
Balance Sheet
December 31

Assets	2008	2007	Increase (Decrease)
Current assets			
Cash	$ 55,000	$ 33,000	$ 22,000
Accounts receivable	20,000	30,000	(10,000)
Inventory	15,000	10,000	5,000
Prepaid expenses	5,000	1,000	4,000
Property, plant, and equipment			
Land	130,000	20,000	110,000
Building	160,000	40,000	120,000
Accumulated amortization—building	(11,000)	(5,000)	6,000
Equipment	27,000	10,000	17,000
Accumulated amortization—equipment	(3,000)	(1,000)	2,000
Total assets	$398,000	$138,000	
Liabilities and Shareholders' Equity			
Current liabilities			
Accounts payable	$ 28,000	$ 12,000	$ 16,000
Income tax payable	6,000	8,000	(2,000)
Long-term liabilities			
Bonds payable	130,000	20,000	110,000
Shareholders' equity			
Common shares	70,000	50,000	20,000
Retained earnings	164,000	48,000	116,000
Total liabilities and shareholders' equity	$398,000	$138,000	

COMPUTER SERVICES CORPORATION
Income Statement
Year Ended December 31, 2008

Sales revenue		$507,000
Cost of goods sold		150,000
Gross profit		357,000
Operating expenses	$111,000	
Amortization expense	9,000	120,000
Income from operations		237,000
Other expenses		
Loss on sale of equipment	$ 3,000	
Interest expense	42,000	45,000
Income before income tax		192,000
Income tax expense		47,000
Net income		$145,000

Additional information for 2008:

1. A $29,000 cash dividend was paid.
2. Land was acquired by issuing $110,000 of long-term bonds.
3. Equipment costing $25,000 was purchased for cash.
4. Equipment with a book value of $7,000 (cost of $8,000, less accumulated amortization of $1,000) was sold for $4,000 cash.
5. Amortization expense consists of $6,000 for the building and $3,000 for equipment.

We will now apply the four steps using the above information for Computer Services Corporation.

Step 1: Operating Activities

Determine the Net Cash Provided (Used) by Operating Activities by Converting Net Income from an Accrual Basis to a Cash Basis

In order to perform step 1 and determine the cash provided (used) by operating activities, net income must be converted from an accrual basis to a cash basis. Why is this necessary? Under generally accepted accounting principles, companies use the accrual basis of accounting. As you have learned, this basis requires that revenue be recorded when it is earned and that expenses be matched against the revenue that they helped generate. Earned revenues may include credit sales that have not been collected in cash. Some expenses incurred, such as amortization, have not been paid in cash. Thus, under the accrual basis of accounting, net income is not the same as net cash provided by operating activities.

Net income can be converted to net cash provided (used) by operating activities by one of two methods: (1) the indirect method or (2) the direct method. The **indirect method** converts total net income from an accrual basis to a cash basis. The **direct method** converts each individual revenue and expense account from an accrual basis to a cash basis, identifying specific cash receipts and payments. **Both methods arrive at the same total amount** for "Net cash provided (used) by operating activities." The only difference is which items they disclose.

On the following pages, in two separate sections, we describe the use of the two methods. Section 1 explains the indirect method. Section 2 explains the direct method. These sections are independent of each other. When you have finished the section(s) assigned by your instructor, turn to the next topic after these sections, "Step 2: Investing Activities."

ACCOUNTING IN ACTION ▶ Business Insight

Variations between net income and cash provided by operating activities can be seen in the following results for three companies. Note how big the differences are among these three companies that are all in retail merchandising.

Company	Net Income (Loss)	Cash Provided by Operating Activities
Canadian Tire	$330.1	$438.1
Hudson's Bay	(174.9)	279.0
Sears Canada	770.8	270.7

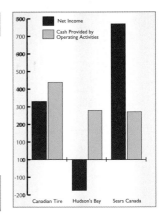

? Why are there differences between net income and cash provided by operating activities?

Section 1: Indirect Method

Most companies use the indirect method. They prefer this method for three reasons: (1) it is easier to prepare, (2) it focuses on the differences between net income and net cash flow from operating activities, and (3) it reveals less detail to competitors. To determine net cash provided (used) by operating activities under the indirect method, net income is adjusted for items that did not affect cash.

Illustration 17-5 on the following page shows three types of adjustments that are made to adjust net income for items that affect accrual-based net income but do not affect cash. The first two types of adjustments are found on the income statement. The last type of adjustment—changes to current asset and current liability accounts—is found on the balance sheet.

Illustration 17-5 ▶

Adjustments to convert net income to net cash provided (used) by operating activities

| Net Income | ± | Adjustments | = | Net Cash Provided (Used) by Operating Activities |

+ Add noncash expenses, such as amortization expense.

± Add losses and deduct gains that result from investing and financing activities.

± Analyze changes to noncash current asset and current liability accounts. Add decreases in current asset and increases in current liability accounts. Deduct increases in current asset and decreases in current liability accounts.

The next three sections explain each type of adjustment.

Noncash Expenses

Helpful hint Expenses with no cash outflows are added back to net income.

The income statement includes expenses that do not use cash, such as amortization expense. For example, Computer Services' income statement reports an amortization expense of $9,000. Recall that the entry to record amortization is:

A	=	L	+	SE
−6,000				−9,000
−3,000				

Cash flows: no effect

Amortization Expense	9,000	
Accumulated Amortization—Building		6,000
Accumulated Amortization—Equipment		3,000

This entry has no effect on cash, so amortization expense is added back to net income in order to arrive at net cash provided (used) by operating activities. It is important to understand that amortization expense is not added to operating activities as if it were a source of cash. As shown in the journal entry above, amortization does not involve cash. It is added to cancel the deduction that was created by the amortization expense when net income was determined.

A partial operating activities section of the cash flow statement for Computer Services is shown below, with the addition of the noncash expense to net income highlighted in red.

Operating activities	
Net income	$145,000
Adjustments to reconcile net income to net cash	
provided (used) by operating activities:	
Amortization expense	9,000

Other examples of noncash expenses include the amortization of bond discounts and premiums for a bond issuer. The amortization of a bond discount increases interest expense but does not use cash. Recall from Chapter 15 that the journal entry to amortize a bond discount for the issuer results in a debit to the Interest Expense account and a credit to the Discount on Bonds Payable account. So any portion of interest expense that is related to the amortization of a bond discount must be added to net income to determine the net cash provided (used) by operating activities.

The amortization of a bond premium for the issuer reduces interest expense but does not reduce cash. The journal entry to amortize a bond premium results in a debit to the Premium on Bonds Payable account and a credit to the Interest Expense account. So any portion of interest expense that is related to the amortization of a bond premium must be deducted from net income to determine the net cash provided (used) by operating activities.

Just as a bond issuer can incur amortization for a bond discount or premium, so can a bond investor who is holding the bonds as a held-to-maturity security. You will recall that we learned about amortizating bond discounts and premiums for investors in Chapter 16. Adjusting net income for the effects of the amortization on bond discounts and premiums is similar to the procedure that is used in the next section to adjust for gains and losses.

Gains and Losses

Illustration 17-1 states that cash received from the sale of long-lived assets should be reported in the investing activities section of the cash flow statement. Consequently, all gains and losses from investing activities must be eliminated from net income to arrive at net cash from operating activities. Why is this necessary? Perhaps it will help if we review the accounting for the sale of a long-lived asset.

Helpful hint Gains are deducted from, and losses are added to, net income.

The sale of a long-lived asset is recorded by (1) recognizing the cash proceeds that are received, (2) removing the asset and accumulated amortization account, and (3) recognizing any gain or loss on the sale. To illustrate, recall that Computer Services' income statement reported a $3,000 loss on the sale of equipment. With the additional information provided in Illustration 17-4, we can reconstruct the journal entry to record the sale of equipment:

Cash	4,000	
Accumulated Amortization	1,000	
Loss on Sale of Equipment	3,000	
Equipment		8,000

A	=	L	+	SE
+4,000				−3,000
+1,000				
−8,000				

↑ Cash flows: +4,000

The cash proceeds of $4,000 that are received are not considered part of operating activities; rather they are part of investing activities. Selling long-lived assets is not part of a company's primary activities. *There is therefore no cash inflow (or outflow) from operating activities.* Logically, then, to calculate the net cash provided (used) by operating activities, we have to eliminate the gain or loss on the sale of an asset from net income.

In our example, Computer Services' $3,000 loss is eliminated from the operating activities section of the cash flow statement by adding the $3,000 back to net income. Adding back the loss cancels the original deduction.

The partial operating activities section of Computer Services' cash flow statement is shown below, illustrating the addition of the noncash expense discussed previously and the addition of the loss discussed above.

Operating activities	
Net income	$145,000
Adjustments to reconcile net income to net cash provided (used) by operating activities:	
Amortization expense	9,000
Loss on sale of equipment	3,000

If a gain on sale occurs, the gain is deducted from net income in order to determine net cash provided (used) by operating activities. For both a gain and a loss, the actual amount of cash received from the sale of the asset is reported as a source of cash in the investing activities section of the cash flow statement.

Gains and losses are also possible in other circumstances, such as when debt is retired. The same adjustment guidelines apply to debt as described for gains and losses on the sale of assets, except that the other side of the transaction is reported in financing activities, rather than investing activities.

Changes in Noncash Current Asset and Current Liability Accounts

Another type of adjustment in converting net income to net cash provided (used) by operating activities involves changes in noncash current asset and current liability accounts. Most current asset and current liability accounts include transactions that result in revenues or expenses. For example, the Accounts Receivable account includes credit sales recorded as revenue before the cash has actually been received. Prepaid expenses include assets that have been paid in advance, but which have not yet expired or been used up, and have therefore not yet been recorded as an expense. An example is Prepaid Insurance, which is only recorded as Insurance Expense at the end of each month as it expires. Similarly, Income Tax Payable includes income tax expense that a company has incurred but not yet paid.

Thus, because these accruals and prepayments change asset and liability accounts but the changes do not involve cash, we need to adjust net income to determine the net cash provided (used) by operating activities. We do this by analyzing the change in each current asset and current liability account to determine each change's impact on net income and cash.

As was mentioned previously in the chapter, there are situations when current asset and current liability accounts do not result from operating activities. Short-term investments in trading or available-for-sale securities are an example of a current asset that does not relate to operating activities. Investments are shown in the investing activities section of the cash flow statement if they are not part of cash equivalents. Short-term notes receivable that do not relate to sales transactions (i.e., are non-trade as we learned about in Chapter 8) are another example of a current asset shown in the investing activities section. Similarly, short-term notes payable that do not relate to purchase transactions (i.e., are non-trade as we learned about in Chapter 10) are an example of a current liability that does not relate to operating activities. These are shown instead in the financing activities section of the cash flow statement.

Changes in Noncash Current Assets

Helpful hint Increases in current assets are deducted from, and decreases in current assets are added to, net income.

The adjustments that are required for changes in noncash current asset accounts are as follows: increases in these accounts are deducted from net income and decreases in these accounts are added to net income, to arrive at net cash provided (used) by operating activities. We will look at these relationships by analyzing Computer Services' current asset accounts.

Decrease in Accounts Receivable. When accounts receivable decrease during the year, revenues on an accrual basis are lower than revenues on a cash basis. In other words, more cash was collected during the period than was recorded as revenue. Computer Services' accounts receivable decreased by $10,000 (from $30,000 to $20,000) during the year. For Computer Services, this means that cash receipts were $10,000 higher than revenues.

Illustration 17-4 indicated that Computer Services had $507,000 in sales revenue reported on its income statement. To determine how much cash was collected in connection with this revenue, it is useful to analyze the accounts receivable account:

Accounts Receivable			
Jan. 1 Balance	30,000		
Sales revenue	507,000	Receipts from customers	517,000
Dec. 31 Balance	20,000		

$10,000 net decrease

If sales revenue (assumed to be sales on account) journalized during the period was $507,000 (Dr. Accounts Receivable; Cr. Sales Revenue), and the change in Accounts Receivable during the period was a decrease of $10,000, then cash receipts from customers must have been $517,000 (Dr. Cash; Cr. Accounts Receivable).

Consequently, revenue as reported on the accrual-based income statement was less than cash collections. To convert net income to net cash provided (used) by operating activities, the $10,000 decrease in accounts receivable must be added to net income because $10,000 more cash was collected than was reported as accrual-based revenue in the income statement.

When the accounts receivable balance increases during the year, revenues on an accrual basis are higher than cash receipts. Therefore, the amount of the increase in accounts receivable is deducted from net income to arrive at net cash provided (used) by operating activities.

Increase in Inventory. Assuming a perpetual inventory system is being used, the Inventory account is increased by the cost of goods purchased. It is decreased by the cost of goods sold. When the Inventory account increases during the year, the cost of goods purchased is greater than the cost of goods sold expense recorded in the income statement. Any increase in the Inventory account must be deducted from net income, just as we did for an increase in the Accounts Receivable account above.

Inventory increased by $5,000 for Computer Services Corporation. Because the inventory account is increased by the purchase of goods (Dr. Inventory; Cr. Accounts Payable) and is decreased by the cost of goods sold (Dr. Cost of Goods Sold; Cr. Inventory), Computer Services must have purchased $5,000 more inventory than it sold. Therefore, because cost of goods sold reported on the income statement is $150,000, purchases of inventory during the year must have been $155,000:

Inventory				
Jan. 1 Balance	10,000			
Purchases	155,000	Cost of goods sold	150,000	$5,000 net increase
Dec. 31 Balance	15,000			

To convert net income to net cash provided (used) by operating activities, the $5,000 increase in inventory must be deducted from net income. The increase in inventory means that the cash-based expense must be increased, which has the effect of reducing net income.

This deduction does not completely convert an accrual-based figure to a cash-based figure. It does not tell us how much cash was paid to suppliers for the goods purchased. It just converts the cost of goods sold to the cost of goods purchased during the year. The analysis of accounts payable—shown later—completes the calculation of payments made to suppliers by converting the cost of goods purchased from an accrual basis to a cash basis.

Increase in Prepaid Expenses. Prepaid expenses increased during the period by $4,000. This means that the cash paid for expenses is higher than the expenses reported on the accrual basis. In other words, cash payments were made in the current period, but expenses will not be recorded until future periods. To determine how much cash was paid for operating expenses, it is useful to analyze the Prepaid Expenses account. Operating expenses, as reported on the income statement, at $111,000. Accordingly, payments for expenses must have been $115,000:

Prepaid Expenses				
Jan. 1 Balance	1,000			
Payments for expenses	115,000	Operating expenses	111,000	$4,000 net increase
Dec. 31 Balance	5,000			

Computer Services reported amortization expense separately from its operating expenses on its income statement in Illustration 17-4. Sometimes, amortization expense is combined and reported in the operating expenses category rather than reported separately. If Computer Services had combined amortization expense with operating expenses for reporting purposes, operating expenses would also have to be reduced by the amount of the amortization expense included. Other charges that do not require the use of cash, such as the amortization of bond discounts and premiums, are treated in the same way as amortization of long-lived assets.

To adjust net income to net cash provided (used) by operating activities, the $4,000 increase in prepaid expenses must be deducted from net income to determine the cash paid for expenses. If prepaid expenses decrease, reported expenses are higher than the expenses paid. Therefore, the decrease in prepaid expenses is added to net income to arrive at net cash provided (used) by operating activities.

These adjustments may not completely convert accrual-based expenses to cash-based expenses. For example, if Computer Services Corporation had any accrued expenses payable, these would also have to be considered before we could completely determine the amount of cash paid for operating expenses. We will look at changes in current liability accounts in the next section.

Changes in Current Liabilities

Helpful hint Increases in current liabilities are added to, and decreases in current liabilities are deducted from, net income.

The adjustments that are required for changes in current liability accounts are as follows: increases in these accounts are added to net income, and decreases are deducted from net income, to arrive at net cash provided (used) by operating activities. We will observe these relationships by analyzing Computer Services' current liability accounts Accounts Payable and Income Tax Payable.

Increase in Accounts Payable. In some companies, the Accounts Payable account is used only to record purchases of inventory on account. An accrued expenses payable account is used to record other credit purchases. In other companies, the Accounts Payable account is used to record all credit purchases.

For simplicity, in this chapter we have assumed that Accounts Payable is used only to record purchases of inventory on account. Computer Services' Accounts Payable account is therefore increased by purchases of inventory (Dr. Inventory; Cr. Accounts Payable) and decreased by payments to suppliers (Dr. Accounts Payable; Cr. Cash). We determined the amount of purchases made by Computer Services in the analysis of the Inventory account earlier: $155,000. Using this figure, we can now determine that payments to suppliers must have been $139,000:

Accounts Payable			
		Jan. 1 Balance	12,000
Payments to suppliers	139,000	Purchases	155,000
		Dec. 31 Balance	28,000

$16,000 net increase

To convert net income to net cash provided (used) by operating activities, the $16,000 increase in accounts payable must be added to net income. The increase in accounts payable means that less cash was paid for the purchases than was deducted in the accrual-based expenses section of the income statement. The addition of $16,000 completes the adjustment that is required to convert the cost of goods purchased to the cash paid for these goods.

In summary, the conversion of the cost of goods sold on the accrual-based income statement to the cash paid for goods purchased involves two steps: (1) The change in the Inventory account adjusts the cost of goods sold to the accrual-based figure cost of goods purchased. (2) The change in the Accounts Payable account adjusts the accrual-based cost of goods purchased to the cash-based payments to suppliers. These changes for Computer Services are summarized as follows:

Cost of goods sold	$150,000
Add: Increase in inventory	5,000
Cost of goods purchased	155,000
Less: Increase in accounts payable	16,000
Cash payments to suppliers	$139,000

If a periodic inventory system was used instead of a perpetual inventory system, the accounts for purchases and related expenses, rather than cost of goods sold, would be adjusted in the same way for any change in accounts payable. There would be no change in the Inventory account throughout the period in a periodic inventory system.

Decrease in Income Tax Payable. When a company incurs income tax expense but has not yet paid its taxes, it records income tax payable. A change in the Income Tax Payable account is due to the difference between the income tax expense incurred and the income tax actually paid during the year.

Computer Services' Income Tax Payable account decreased by $2,000. This means that the $47,000 of income tax expense reported on the income statement was $2,000 less than the amount of taxes actually paid during the period ($49,000), as shown in the following T account:

		Income Tax Payable			
		Jan. 1 Balance		8,000	
Payments for income tax	49,000	Income tax expense		47,000	$2,000 net decrease
		Dec. 31 Balance		6,000	

To adjust net income to net cash provided (used) by operating activities, the $2,000 decrease in income tax payable must be deducted from net income. If the amount of income tax payable had increased during the year, the increase would be added to net income because the income tax expense deducted on the accrual-based income statement was higher than the cash paid during the period.

If Computer Services had any accrued expenses payable, they would be treated just as income tax payable was. Income tax payable is actually an example of an accrued expense payable; however, it is dealt with separately because income tax expense is reported by itself on the income statement.

The partial cash flow statement that follows shows the impact on operating activities of the changes in current assets and current liability accounts (the changes are highlighted in red). It also shows the adjustments that were described earlier for noncash expenses and gains and losses. The operating activities section of the cash flow statement is now complete.

Helpful hint Whether the indirect or direct method (Section 2) is used, net cash provided (used) by operating activities will be the same.

COMPUTER SERVICES CORPORATION
Cash Flow Statement (partial)
Year Ended December 31, 2008

Operating activities		
Net income		$145,000
Adjustments to reconcile net income to net cash		
provided (used) by operating activities:		
Amortization expense	$ 9,000	
Loss on sale of equipment	3,000	
Decrease in accounts receivable	10,000	
Increase in inventory	(5,000)	
Increase in prepaid expenses	(4,000)	
Increase in accounts payable	16,000	
Decrease in income tax payable	(2,000)	27,000
Net cash provided by operating activities		172,000

In summary, the operating activities section of Computer Services' cash flow statement shows that the accrual-based net income of $145,000 resulted in net cash provided by operating activities of $172,000, after adjustments for noncash items.

Summary of Conversion to Net Cash provided (used) by Operating Activities—Indirect Method

As shown in the previous pages, the cash flow statement prepared by the indirect method starts with net income. It then adds or deducts items to arrive at net cash provided (used) by operating activities. The adjustments are generally for three types of items: (1) noncash expenses, (2) gains and losses, and (3) changes in related noncash current asset and current liability accounts.

A summary of these changes is given in Illustration 17-6.

Illustration 17-6 ▼

Adjustments required to convert net income to net cash provided (used) by operating activities

Adjustment Item	Example	To Convert Net Income to Net Cash Provided (Used) by Operating Activities
Noncash expenses	Amortization expense	Add
Gains and losses	Gain on sale of asset	Deduct
	Loss on sale of asset	Add
Changes in noncash current asset	Increase in current asset account	Deduct
and current liability accounts	Decrease in current asset account	Add
	Increase in current liability account	Add
	Decrease in current liability account	Deduct

BEFORE YOU GO ON . . .

▶Review It

1. What is the format of the operating activities section of the cash flow statement when the indirect method is used?

2. Why are amortization expense and losses added to net income in the operating activities section when the indirect method is used?

3. Explain why increases in noncash current asset account balances are deducted from net income and increases in noncash current liability account balances are added to net income when preparing the operating activities section using the indirect method.

▶Do It

Selected financial information follows for Reynolds Ltd. at December 31. Prepare the operating activities section of the cash statement using the indirect method.

	2008	2007	Increase (Decrease)
Current assets			
Cash	$54,000	$37,000	$ 17,000
Accounts receivable	68,000	26,000	42,000
Inventories	54,000	10,000	44,000
Prepaid expenses	4,000	6,000	(2,000)
Current liabilities			
Accounts payable	23,000	50,000	(27,000)
Accrued expenses payable	10,000	0	10,000

REYNOLDS LTD.
Income Statement
Year Ended December 31, 2008

Sales revenue		$890,000
Cost of goods sold		465,000
Gross profit		425,000
Operating expenses	$188,000	
Amortization expense	33,000	221,000
Income from operations		204,000
Other expenses		
Loss on sale of equipment	$ 2,000	
Interest expense	12,000	14,000
Income before income tax		190,000
Income tax expense		65,000
Net income		$125,000

Action Plan

- Operating activities relate to items shown on the income statement, which are generally affected by changes in the related noncash current assets and current liabilities in the balance sheet, and noncash items in the income statement.
- Start with net income to determine the net cash provided (used) by operating activities. Add noncash expenses, losses, decreases in noncash current asset accounts, and increases in noncash current liability accounts. Deduct gains, increases in noncash current asset accounts, and decreases in noncash current liability accounts.

Solution

REYNOLDS LTD.
Cash Flow Statement (partial)
Year Ended December 31, 2008

Operating activities		
Net income		$125,000
Adjustments to reconcile net income to net cash provided by operating activities:		
Amortization expense	$ 33,000	
Loss on sale of equipment	2,000	
Increase in accounts receivable	(42,000)	
Increase in inventories	(44,000)	
Decrease in prepaid expenses	2,000	
Decrease in accounts payable	(27,000)	
Increase in accrued expenses payable	10,000	(66,000)
Net cash provided by operating activities		59,000

Related exercise material: BE17–3, BE17–4, BE17–5, E17–3, E17–4, and E17–5.

the navigator

Section 2: Direct Method

Although both the indirect and direct method are acceptable choices to determine cash flows from operating activities, the direct method is preferred by the CICA. Under the direct method, net cash provided (used) by operating activities is calculated by adjusting each individual revenue and expense item in the income statement from the accrual basis to the cash basis.

To simplify and condense the operating activities section, only major classes of operating cash receipts and cash payments are reported. The difference between these cash receipts and cash payments for these major classes is the net cash provided (used) by operating activities. These relationships are shown in Illustration 17-7.

Illustration 17-7 ▶

Major classes of cash receipts and payments

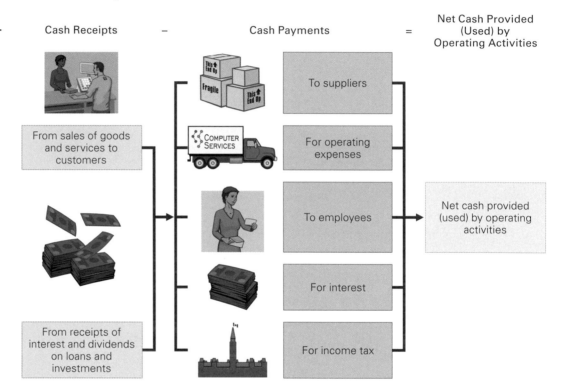

An efficient way to apply the direct method is to analyze the items reported in the income statement in the order in which they are listed. The cash receipts and cash payments that relate to these revenues and expenses are then determined by adjusting for changes in the related current asset and current liability accounts. Most current asset and current liability accounts include transactions that result in revenues or expenses. For example, the Accounts Receivable account records credit sales as revenue before the cash has actually been received. Prepaid expenses record assets that have been paid in advance, but which have not yet expired or been used up, and have therefore not yet been recorded as an expense. An example is Prepaid Insurance, which is only recorded as insurance expense at the end of each month as it expires. Similarly, Income Tax Payable records income tax expense that a company has incurred but not yet paid.

Thus, because these accruals and prepayments change asset and liability accounts but the changes do not involve cash, we need to adjust revenues and expenses reported on the income statement to determine the net cash provided (used) by operating activities. We do this by analyzing the change in each noncash current asset and current liability account to determine each change's impact on the related revenue or expense account.

Once the change and related account are identified, increases in current asset accounts are deducted from revenues and added to expenses to convert accrual-based income statement amounts to cash-based amounts. Conversely, decreases in current asset accounts are added to revenues and deducted from expenses.

Increases in current liability accounts are added to revenues and deducted from expenses to convert accrual-based income statement amounts to cash-based amounts. Conversely, decreases in current liability accounts are deducted from revenues and added to expenses. The adjustments that are required to convert revenues and expenses from an accrual system to a cash system are summarized in Illustration 17-8.

	Revenues	Expenses
Current assets		
Increase in account balance	Deduct	Add
Decrease in account balance	Add	Deduct
Current liabilities		
Increase in account balance	Add	Deduct
Decrease in account balance	Deduct	Add

Illustration 17-8 ◄

Summary of adjustments required to convert from accrual to cash

We explain the reasoning behind these adjustments for Computer Services Corporation, first for cash receipts and then for cash payments, in the following sections.

Cash Receipts

Computer Services has only one source of cash receipts—its customers.

Cash Receipts from Customers

The income statement for Computer Services reported sales revenue from customers of $507,000. How much of that was received in cash? To answer that, it is necessary to look at the change in accounts receivable during the year.

When accounts receivable decrease during the year, revenues on an accrual basis are lower than revenues on a cash basis. In other words, more cash was collected during the period than was recorded as revenue. Computer Services' accounts receivable decreased by $10,000 (from $30,000 to $20,000) during the year. This means that cash receipts were $10,000 higher than revenues. To determine the amount of cash receipts, the decrease in accounts receivable is added to sales revenue.

Thus, cash receipts from customers were $517,000, calculated as in Illustration 17-9.

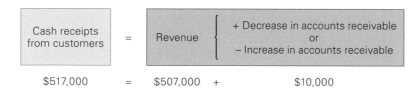

| Cash receipts from customers | = | Revenue | { + Decrease in accounts receivable or − Increase in accounts receivable |

$517,000 = $507,000 + $10,000

Illustration 17-9 ◄

Formula to calculate cash receipts from customers— direct method

Alternatively, when the Accounts Receivable account balance increases during the year, revenues on an accrual basis are higher than cash receipts. In other words, revenues have increased, but not all of these revenues resulted in cash receipts. Therefore, the amount of the increase in accounts receivable is deducted from sales revenues to arrive at cash receipts from customers.

Cash receipts from customers can also be determined by analyzing the Accounts Receivable account as follows:

Accounts Receivable			
Jan. 1 Balance	30,000		
Sales revenue	507,000	Receipts from customers	517,000
Dec. 31 Balance	20,000		

$10,000 net decrease

Cash Receipts from Interest and Dividends

Computer Services does not have cash receipts from any source other than customers. If an income statement details other revenue, such as interest and/or dividend revenue, these amounts must be adjusted for any accrued amounts receivable to determine the actual cash receipts. As in Illustration 17-9, increases in accrued receivables would be deducted from accrual-based revenues. Decreases in accrued receivable accounts would be added to accrual-based revenues.

Cash Payments

Computer Services has many sources of cash payments—to suppliers and for operating expenses, interest, and income taxes. We will analyze each of these in the next sections.

Cash Payments to Suppliers

Using the perpetual inventory system, Computer Services reported a cost of goods sold of $150,000 on its income statement. How much of that was paid in cash to suppliers? To answer that, it is necessary to find the cost of goods purchased for the year. To find purchases, the cost of goods sold is adjusted for the change in inventory. When the Inventory account increases during the year, the cost of goods purchased is higher than the cost of goods sold. To determine the cost of goods purchased, the increase in inventory is added to the cost of goods sold. Any decrease in inventory would be deducted from the cost of goods sold. Computer Services' inventory increased by $5,000 so its cost of goods purchased is $155,000 ($150,000 + $5,000).

After the cost of goods purchased is calculated, cash payments to suppliers can be determined. This is done by adjusting the cost of goods purchased for the change in accounts payable. In some companies, the Accounts Payable account is used only to record purchases of inventory on account. An accrued expenses payable account is used to record other credit purchases. In other companies, the Accounts Payable account is used to record all credit purchases. For simplicity, we have assumed in this chapter that Accounts Payable is only used to record purchases of inventory on account.

Consequently, when accounts payable increase during the year, purchases on an accrual basis are higher than they are on a cash basis. To determine cash payments to suppliers, an increase in accounts payable is deducted from the cost of goods purchased. On the other hand, there may be a decrease in accounts payable. That would occur if cash payments to suppliers amounted to more than the purchases. In that case, the decrease in accounts payable is added to the cost of goods purchased.

For Computer Services, cash payments to suppliers were $139,000 ($150,000 + $5,000 = $155,000 − $16,000), as calculated in Illustration 17-10.

Illustration 17-10 ▶

Formula to calculate cash payments to suppliers—direct method

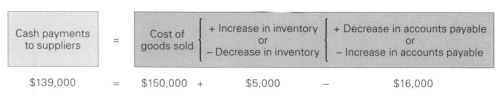

Cash payments to suppliers (also known as creditors) can also be determined from an analysis of the Inventory and Accounts Payable accounts as follows:

Inventory				
Jan. 1 Balance	10,000			
Purchases	155,000	Cost of goods sold	150,000	} $5,000 net increase
Dec. 31 Balance	15,000			

Accounts Payable				
		Jan. 1 Balance	12,000	
Payments to suppliers	139,000	Purchases	155,000	} $16,000 net increase
		Dec. 31 Balance	28,000	

Cash Payments for Operating Expenses

Computer Services' income statement includes $111,000 of operating expenses. To determine the cash paid for operating expenses, we need to adjust this amount for any changes in prepaid expenses and accrued liabilities.

If prepaid expenses increase during the year, the cash paid for operating expenses will be higher than the operating expenses reported on the income statement. To adjust operating expenses to cash payments for services, any increase in prepaid expenses must be added to operating expenses. On the other hand, if prepaid expenses decrease during the year, the decrease must be deducted from operating expenses.

Operating expenses must also be adjusted for changes in accrued liability accounts (e.g., accrued expenses payable). While for simplicity we have assumed in this chapter that accrued liabilities are recorded separately from accounts payable, some companies do combine them with accounts payable. This is one reason that using the direct method can be difficult in real life. If accrued liabilities and accounts payable are combined and recorded in one account, you have to figure out what proportion of accounts payable relate to purchases of inventory, and what relates to other payables, in order to determine the cash payments to suppliers and cash payments for operating expenses.

At this point, Computer Services does not have any accrued expenses payable related to its operating expenses. If it did, any changes in the Accrued Expenses Payable account would affect operating expenses as follows: When accrued expenses payable increase during the year, operating expenses on an accrual basis are higher than they are on a cash basis. To determine cash payments for operating expenses, an increase in accrued expenses payable is deducted from operating expenses. On the other hand, a decrease in accrued expenses payable is added to operating expenses because the cash payments are greater than the operating expenses.

Computer Services' cash payments for operating expenses were $115,000, calculated as in Illustration 17-11.

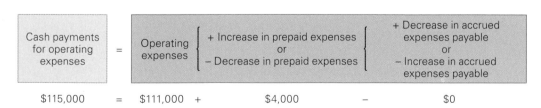

Illustration 17-11 ◄

Formula to calculate cash payments for operating expenses—direct method

Cash payments for operating expenses can also be determined by analyzing the Prepaid Expenses account as follows:

Prepaid Expenses			
Jan. 1 Balance	1,000		
Payments for expenses	115,000	Operating expenses	111,000
Dec. 31 Balance	5,000		

$4,000 net increase

Computer Services reported amortization expense separately from its operating expenses on its income statement in Illustration 17-4. Sometimes, amortization expense is combined and reported in the operating expenses category rather than reported separately. If Computer Services had combined amortization expense with operating expenses for reporting purposes, operating expenses would also have to be reduced by the amount of the amortization expense included. Other charges that do not require the use of cash, such as the amortization of bond discounts and premiums, are treated in the same way as amortization of long-lived assets.

Cash Payments to Employees

Some companies report payments to employees separately, removing these payments from their operating expenses. To determine payments to employees, you would have to know the salary expense amount on the income statement and any salaries payable on the comparative balance sheets. Cash payments to employees would equal the salary expense, plus any decrease (or less any increase) during the period in salaries payable.

Other companies condense their income statements in such a way that cash payments to suppliers and employees cannot be separated from cash payments for operating expenses (i.e., they do not disclose their cost of goods sold or salary expense separately). Although the disclosure will not be as informative, for reporting purposes it is acceptable to combine these sources of cash payments.

Cash Payments for Interest

Computer Services reports $42,000 of interest expense on its income statement in Illustration 17-4. This amount equals the cash paid, since the comparative balance sheet indicated no interest payable at the beginning or end of the year. The relationship among cash payments for interest, interest expense, and changes in interest payable (if any) is shown in Illustration 17-12.

Illustration 17-12 ▶

Formula to calculate cash payments for interest—direct method

$42,000 = $42,000 + $0

Cash Payments for Income Tax

The income statement for Computer Services shows an income tax expense of $47,000 and a decrease in income tax payable of $2,000. When a company incurs income tax expense but has not yet paid its taxes, it records income tax payable. A change in the Income Tax Payable account is due to the difference between the income tax expense that was incurred and the income tax that was actually paid during the year.

The relationship among cash payments for income tax, income tax expense, and changes in income tax payable is shown in Illustration 17-13.

Cash payments for income tax	=	Tax expense	{ + Decrease in income tax payable or − Increase in income tax payable
$49,000	=	$47,000 +	$2,000

Computer Services' Income Tax Payable account decreased by $2,000. This means that the $47,000 of income tax expense reported on the income statement was $2,000 less than the $49,000 of taxes paid during the period, as detailed in the following T account:

Income Tax Payable			
		Jan. 1 Balance	8,000
Payments for income tax	49,000	Income tax expense	47,000
		Dec. 31 Balance	6,000

$2,000 net decrease

All of the revenues and expenses in the income statement have now been adjusted to a cash basis. The operating activities section of the cash flow statement is as follows:

COMPUTER SERVICES CORPORATION
Cash Flow Statement (partial)
Year Ended December 31, 2008

Operating activities		
Cash receipts from customers		$517,000
Cash payments		
To suppliers	$(139,000)	
For operating expenses	(115,000)	
For interest	(42,000)	
For income tax	(49,000)	(345,000)
Net cash provided by operating activities		172,000

Helpful hint Note that in the operating activities section, positive numbers indicate cash inflows (receipts) and negative numbers indicate cash outflows (payments). As well, whether the direct or indirect method is used, net cash provided (used) by operating activities will be the same.

As mentioned earlier, the CICA allows the use of both the indirect and direct methods, but encourages companies to use the direct method of reporting operating activities. Despite the CICA's preference for the direct method, less than one percent of Canadian companies use it. The authors of *Financial Reporting in Canada* state: "We continue to be surprised by the failure to use the direct method for presenting this important figure. It is difficult to believe that investors would not find information on the various functional cash flows (e.g., payments to employees) more useful than the information on adjustments required to convert net income into cash flows from operating activities (e.g., amortization expense)."

ACCOUNTING IN ACTION ▶ Across the Organization Insight

The cash flow statement should be one of the most important tools for any user across the organization, whether internal or external. But, all too often, the cash flow statement adds little insight to a company's operations. Take, for example, Hudson's Bay Company. The Bay's business is pretty simple. It buys clothes, housewares, and other products, puts them in its stores, and sells them.

When you look at the operating activities section of The Bay's cash flow statement, however, you find references to amortization and "net change in operating working capital." Nowhere does it tell you how much cash The Bay received from shoppers or how much it paid its suppliers.

So why do companies not report this information in their cash flow statements? "It gives material information, so managements don't want to use it," says Richard Rooney, president of Burgundy Asset Management. Mr. Rooney would like to see the direct method of preparing the operating activities

section of the cash flow statement be made mandatory. "Something like this is comprehensible, easy to understand and I think it would be harder to fudge—though where there's a will, there's a way."

Source: Derek DeCloet, "Show Investors the Cash Flow," *Financial Post*, March 28, 2002, IN3.

You are the sales manager of a company that sells inventory to The Bay and are looking at its cash flow statement, among other financial information, to determine whether to give additional credit. Which method of preparing the operating activities section of the cash flow statement—indirect or direct—would you find more helpful in making your decision?

BEFORE YOU GO ON . . .

▶Review It

1. What is the format of the operating activities section of the cash flow statement for the direct method?
2. Give the formulae to calculate cash receipts from customers, cash payments to suppliers, and cash payments for operating expenses.
3. If both the indirect and direct methods arrive at the same net cash provided (used) by operating activities, why does it matter which method is used?

▶Do It

Selected financial information follows for Reynolds Ltd. at December 31. Prepare the operating activities section of the cash statement using the direct method.

	2008	2007	Increase (Decrease)
Current assets			
Cash	$54,000	$37,000	$ 17,000
Accounts receivable	68,000	26,000	42,000
Inventories	54,000	10,000	44,000
Prepaid expenses	4,000	6,000	(2,000)
Current liabilities			
Accounts payable	23,000	50,000	(27,000)
Accrued expenses payable	10,000	0	10,000

REYNOLDS LTD.
Income Statement
Year Ended December 31, 2008

Sales revenue		$890,000
Cost of goods sold		465,000
Gross profit		425,000
Operating expenses	$188,000	
Amortization expense	33,000	221,000
Income from operations		204,000
Other expenses		
Loss on sale of equipment	$ 2,000	
Interest expense	12,000	14,000
Income before income tax		190,000
Income tax expense		65,000
Net income		$125,000

Action Plan

- Determine the net cash provided (used) by operating activities by adjusting each individual revenue and expense item for changes in the related current asset and current liability account.
- Report cash receipts and cash payments by major sources and uses: cash receipts from customers and cash payments to suppliers, for operating expenses, to employees, for interest, and for income taxes.

Solution

REYNOLDS LTD.
Cash Flow Statement (partial)
Year Ended December 31, 2008

Operating activities		
Cash receipts from customers		$ 848,000ᵃ
Cash payments		
To suppliers	$(536,000)ᵇ	
For operating expenses	(176,000)ᶜ	
For interest	(12,000)	
For income tax	(65,000)	(789,000)
Net cash provided by operating activities		59,000

Calculations:
a Cash receipts from customers: $890,000 – $42,000 = $848,000
b Payments to suppliers: $465,000 + $44,000 + $27,000 = $536,000
c Payments for operating expenses: $188,000 – $2,000 – $10,000 = $176,000

---

the navigator

Related exercise material: BE17–6, BE17–7, BE17–8, BE17–9, BE17–10, E17–6, E17–7, and E17–8.

Step 2: Investing Activities

Determine the Net Cash Provided (Used) by Investing Activities by Analyzing Changes in Long-Term Asset Accounts

Regardless of whether the indirect or direct method is used to calculate operating activities, investing and financing activities are measured and reported in the same way. Investing activities affect long-term asset accounts, such as long-term investments, property, plant, and equipment, and intangible assets. There are, of course, exceptions. Short-term investments (except for the ones that are classified as cash equivalents) are generally reported as investing activities as are short-term notes receivable issued for loans rather than for trade transactions.

To determine the investing activities, the balance sheet and additional information in Illustration 17-4 must be examined. The change in each long-term asset account (and the short-term investment accounts) is analyzed to determine what effect, if any, the change had on cash. Computer Services has no short-term investments or notes receivable but does have three long-term asset accounts that must be analyzed: Land, Building, and Equipment.

Land

Land increased by $110,000 during the year, as reported in Computer Services' balance sheet. The additional information in Illustration 17-4 states that this land was purchased by issuing long-term bonds. Issuing bonds for land has no effect on cash, but it is a significant noncash investing and financing activity that must be disclosed in a note to the statement.

Building

The Building account increased by $120,000 during the year. What caused this increase? No additional information has been given for this change. Whenever unexplained differences in accounts occur, we assume the transaction was for cash. That is, we would assume in this case that a building was acquired, or expanded, for $120,000 cash.

Accumulated Amortization—Building

Accumulated Amortization increased by $6,000 during the year. As explained in the additional information in Illustration 17-4, this increase resulted from the amortization expense reported on the income statement for the building:

$6,000 net increase {

Accumulated Amortization—Building		
	Jan. 1 Balance	5,000
	Amortization expense	6,000
	Dec. 31 Balance	11,000

As was explained earlier, amortization expense is a noncash charge and does not affect the cash flow statement.

Equipment

Computer Services' Equipment account increased by $17,000. The additional information in Illustration 17-4 explains that this was a net increase resulting from two different transactions: (1) a purchase of equipment for $25,000 cash, and (2) a sale of equipment that cost $8,000 for $4,000 cash. The T account below shows the reasons for the change in this account during the year:

$17,000 net increase {

Equipment				
Jan. 1 Balance	10,000			
Purchase of equipment	25,000	Cost of equipment sold	8,000
Dec. 31 Balance	27,000			

In the above example, you were given additional information about both the purchase and the sale of equipment. Often, in analyzing accounts, you will be given just one piece of information and are expected to deduce the information that is missing. For example, if you knew the beginning and ending balances of the Equipment account as well as the fact that the cost of the equipment sold was $8,000, you could determine that the cost of the equipment purchased must have been $25,000.

The following entries show the details of the equipment transactions shown in the above T account:

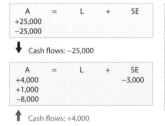

A	=	L	+	SE
+25,000				
−25,000				

↓ Cash flows: −25,000

A	=	L	+	SE
+4,000				−3,000
+1,000				
−8,000				

↑ Cash flows: +4,000

Equipment	25,000	
Cash		25,000
Cash	4,000	
Accumulated Amortization	1,000	
Loss on Sale of Equipment	3,000	
Equipment		8,000

Each transaction should be reported separately on the cash flow statement. When a net change in a long-term balance sheet account has occurred during the year, the individual items that caused the net change should be reported separately. This is different than what we do for current asset and current liability accounts, where we report only the net change.

In this particular case, the purchase of equipment should be reported as a $25,000 outflow of cash. The sale of equipment should be reported as a $4,000 inflow of cash. Note that it is the cash proceeds that are reported on the cash flow statement, not the cost of the equipment sold.

Accumulated Amortization—Equipment

The accumulated amortization for equipment increased by $2,000. This change does not represent the overall amortization expense for the year. The additional information in Illustration 17-4 helps us determine the details of this change.

Accumulated Amortization—Equipment			
		Jan. 1 Balance	1,000
Sale of equipment	1,000	Amortization expense	3,000
		Dec. 31 Balance	3,000

$2,000 net increase

This account was decreased (debited $1,000) as a result of the sale of equipment, as described earlier. The account was also increased by $3,000 of amortization expense for the current period, as indicated in the additional information in Illustration 17-4.

As we have seen, the sale of the equipment affects one account on Computer Services' income statement (Loss on Sale of Equipment) and three accounts on its balance sheet (Cash, Equipment, and Accumulated Amortization). We ignored the Loss on Sale of Equipment in our preparation of the operating activities section of the cash flow statement because losses (and gains) have no effect on cash.

In addition, it is important to combine the effects of this sale in one place—in the investing activities section. The overall result, then, is that the sale of the equipment ends up having no impact on the operating activities section of the cash flow statement. Instead, the cash proceeds received from the sale of the equipment are shown fully in the investing activities section.

The investing activities section of Computer Services' cash flow statement is shown below and reports the changes in the three accounts Land, Building, and Equipment:

COMPUTER SERVICES CORPORATION
Cash Flow Statement (partial)
Year Ended December 31, 2008

Investing activities		
Purchase of building	$(120,000)	
Purchase of equipment	(25,000)	
Sale of equipment	4,000	
Net cash used by investing activities		$(141,000)
Note x: Significant noncash investing and financing activities		
Issue of bonds to purchase land		$110,000

Helpful hint Note that in the investing activities section, positive numbers indicate cash inflows (receipts) and negative numbers indicate cash outflows (payments).

BEFORE YOU GO ON . . .

▶**Review It**

1. What are some examples of items reported in the investing activities section of the cash flow statement?
2. Since short-term investments such as available-for-sale securities are a current asset, why aren't they reported in the operating activities section rather than the investing activities section of the cash flow statement?
3. Why isn't any gain or loss on the sale of equipment reported in the operating activities section and the book value of equipment sold reported in the investing activities section of the cash flow statement?

▶Do It

Umiujaq Corporation reported an opening balance of $146,000 and an ending balance of $135,000 in its Equipment account; and an opening balance of $47,000 and an ending balance of $62,000 in its Accumulated Amortization—Equipment account. During the year, it sold equipment for cash with a cost of $21,000 and a gain on the sale of $1,000. It also purchased equipment for cash. It recorded amortization expense of $31,000. Calculate the cash received from the sale of equipment and the cash paid for equipment.

Action Plan

- Use journal entries and T accounts to reconstruct the transactions affecting the Equipment and Accumulated Amortization accounts.

Solution

Cash received from sale of equipment = $6,000

Cash	6,000	
Accumulated Amortization	16,000	
Gain on Sale of Equipment		1,000
Equipment		21,000

Cash paid for equipment = $10,000

Equipment	10,000	
Cash		10,000

Equipment

Opening bal.	146,000		
Purchase of equipment	10,000	Sale of equipment	21,000
Ending bal.	135,000		

Accumulated Amortization—Equipment

		Opening balance	47,000
Sale of equipment	16,000	Amortization expense	31,000
		Ending balance	62,000

the navigator

Related exercise material: BE17–11.

Step 3: Financing Activities

Determine the Net Cash Provided (Used) by Financing Activities by Analyzing Changes in Long-Term Liability and Equity Accounts

The third step is to analyze the changes in long-term liability and equity accounts. If short-term notes are issued for lending purposes rather than for trade, they should also be reported in the financing activities section. Computer Services has no notes payable but has one long-term liability account, Bonds Payable, and two shareholders' equity accounts, Common Shares and Retained Earnings.

Bonds Payable

Bonds Payable increased by $110,000. As indicated earlier, land was acquired from the issue of these bonds. This noncash transaction is reported as a note to the cash flow statement because it is a significant financing activity.

Common Shares

Computer Services' Common Shares account increased by $20,000. Since there is no additional information about any reacquisition of shares, we assume that this change is due entirely to the issue of additional common shares for cash. This cash inflow is reported in the financing activities section of the cash flow statement.

Retained Earnings

What caused the net increase of $116,000 in Retained Earnings? This increase can be explained by two factors. First, net income increased retained earnings by $145,000. Second, the additional information in Illustration 17-4 indicates that a cash dividend of $29,000 was paid. This information could have also been deduced by analyzing the T account:

		Retained Earnings		
		Jan. 1 Balance	48,000	
Cash dividend	29,000	Net income	145,000	} $116,000 net increase
		Dec. 31 Balance	164,000	

The cash dividend paid is reported as a cash outflow in the financing activities section of the cash flow statement. Note that the Retained Earnings account above only reports the dividend declared. This amount must be adjusted to determine the dividend paid, if there is any balance in the Dividend Payable account reported in the current liabilities section of the balance sheet. There was none in the case of Computer Services.

If you were told the beginning and ending balances in the Retained Earnings account as well as the amount of the net income, you could have calculated the amount of the cash dividend, or vice versa. In this case, both the net income and cash dividend were described in Illustration 17-4. You will often be asked to deduce missing information in the end-of-chapter material, which will help you determine how well you understand account relationships.

The financing activities section of Computer Services' cash flow statement is shown below and reports the issue of common shares and payment of a dividend:

COMPUTER SERVICES CORPORATION		
Cash Flow Statement (partial)		
Year Ended December 31, 2008		
Financing activities		
Issue of common shares	$ 20,000	
Payment of cash dividend	(29,000)	
Net cash used by financing activities		$ (9,000)
Note x: Significant noncash investing and financing activities		
Issue of bonds to purchase land		$110,000

Helpful hint Note that in the financing activities section, positive numbers indicate cash inflows (receipts) and negative numbers indicate cash outflows (payments).

BEFORE YOU GO ON . . .

▶Review It

1. What are some examples of items reported in the financing activities section of the cash flow statement?

2. When should short-term notes payable be reported in the operating activities section and when should they be reported in the financing activities section of the cash flow statement?
3. If you know the opening and ending retained earnings balances and the amount of net income, explain how you can figure out the amount of dividends paid to report in the financing activities section of the cash flow statement.
4. What are some significant noncash investing and financing activities shown in a cash flow statement? Give some examples.

▶Do It

La Tuque Corporation reported an opening balance of $80,000 and an ending balance of $95,000 in its Common Shares account and an opening balance of $15,000 and an ending balance of $20,000 in its Contributed Capital—Reacquisition of Common Shares account. During the year, it issued $50,000 of common shares for cash and reacquired common shares for cash. Calculate the cash paid to reacquire the shares.

Action Plan

- Use journal entries and T accounts to reconstruct the transactions affecting the Common Shares and Contributed Capital accounts.

Solution

Cash paid to reacquire shares = $30,000

Common Shares	35,000	
Contributed Capital—Reacquisition of Common Shares		5,000
Cash		30,000

Common Shares

		Opening balance	80,000
Reacquisition of shares	35,000	Issue of shares	50,000
		Ending balance	95,000

Contributed Capital—Reacquisition of Common Shares

	Opening balance	15,000
	Reacquisition of shares	5,000
	Ending balance	20,000

Related exercise material: BE17–12 and E17–9.

Step 4: The Cash Flow Statement

Prepare the Cash Flow Statement and Determine the Net Increase (Decrease) in Cash

Using the information presented in the previous sections, we can now present a complete cash flow statement for Computer Services Corporation. Illustration 17-14 presents the statement using the indirect method of preparing the operating activities section; Illustration 17-15 presents the statement using the direct method of preparing the operating activities section. Notice that while the operating activities sections differ between the indirect and direct methods, the investing and financing activities sections are exactly the same.

Illustration 17-14 ◄

Cash flow statement—
indirect method

COMPUTER SERVICES CORPORATION
Cash Flow Statement
Year Ended December 31, 2008

Operating activities		
Net income		$145,000
Adjustments to reconcile net income to net cash		
provided (used) by operating activities:		
Amortization expense	$ 9,000	
Loss on sale of equipment	3,000	
Decrease in accounts receivable	10,000	
Increase in inventory	(5,000)	
Increase in prepaid expenses	(4,000)	
Increase in accounts payable	16,000	
Decrease in income tax payable	(2,000)	27,000
Net cash provided by operating activities		172,000
Investing activities		
Purchase of building	$(120,000)	
Purchase of equipment	(25,000)	
Sale of equipment	4,000	
Net cash used by investing activities		(141,000)
Financing activities		
Issue of common shares	$ 20,000	
Payment of cash dividend	(29,000)	
Net cash used by financing activities		(9,000)
Net increase in cash		22,000
Cash, January 1		33,000
Cash, December 31		$ 55,000
Note x: Significant noncash investing and financing activities		
Issue of bonds to purchase land		$110,000

Illustration 17-15 ◄

Cash flow statement—direct
method

COMPUTER SERVICES CORPORATION
Cash Flow Statement
Year Ended December 31, 2008

Operating activities		
Cash receipts from customers		$517,000
Cash payments		
To suppliers	$(139,000)	
For operating expenses	(115,000)	
For interest	(42,000)	
For income tax	(49,000)	(345,000)
Net cash provided by operating activities		172,000
Investing activities		
Purchase of building	$(120,000)	
Purchase of equipment	(25,000)	
Sale of equipment	4,000	
Net cash used by investing activities		(141,000)
Financing activities		
Issue of common shares	$ 20,000	
Payment of cash dividend	(29,000)	
Net cash used by financing activities		(9,000)
Net increase in cash		22,000
Cash, January 1		33,000
Cash, December 31		$ 55,000
Note x: Significant noncash investing and financing activities		
Issue of bonds to purchase land		$110,000

Computer Services' cash flow statement shows the following: Operating activities provided $172,000 of cash. Investing activities used $141,000 of cash. Financing activities used $9,000 of cash. There was a significant noncash investing and financing activity for $110,000.

Notice how the cash flow statement links the income statement with the beginning and ending balance sheets. The revenues and expenses reported on the income statement and the changes in the balance sheet accounts are explained in terms of their impact on cash. These changes lead to the end-of-period cash balances on the balance sheet and on the cash flow statement.

As our final step in preparing this statement, we can prove our cash balance. The comparative balance sheets in Illustration 17-4 indicate that the net change in cash during the period was an increase of $22,000. The $22,000 net increase in cash reported in the cash flow statement above agrees with this change.

BEFORE YOU GO ON . . .

▶Review It

1. How do you determine the net increase or decrease in cash?
2. Explain how the income statement, statement of retained earnings, and balance sheet are interrelated with the cash flow statement.

▶Do It

Selected information follows for Reynolds Ltd. at December 31. Prepare a cash flow statement.

	2008	2007	Increase (Decrease)
Property, plant, and equipment			
Land	$ 45,000	$ 70,000	$(25,000)
Buildings	200,000	200,000	0
Accumulated amortization—buildings	(21,000)	(11,000)	10,000
Equipment	193,000	68,000	125,000
Accumulated amortization—equipment	(28,000)	(10,000)	18,000
Long-term liabilities and shareholders' equity			
Bonds payable	110,000	150,000	(40,000)
Common shares	220,000	60,000	160,000
Retained earnings	206,000	136,000	70,000

Additional information:

1. Cash provided from operating activities was $59,000.
2. Equipment was bought for cash. Equipment with a cost of $41,000 and a book value of $36,000 was sold at a loss of $2,000.
3. Bonds of $40,000 were redeemed at their face value for cash.
4. Net income was $125,000 and a cash dividend was paid.

Action Plan

• Determine the net cash provided (used) by investing activities. Investing activities generally relate to changes in long-term asset accounts.
• Determine the net cash provided (used) by financing activities. Financing activities generally relate to changes in long-term liability and shareholders' equity accounts.
• Determine the net increase (decrease) in cash. Verify that this amount agrees with the end-of-period cash balance reported on the balance sheet.

Solution

REYNOLDS LTD.
Cash Flow Statement
Year Ended December 31, 2008

Operating activities		
Net cash provided by operating activities		$ 59,000
Investing activities		
Sale of land	$ 25,000	
Sale of equipment	34,000 [a]	
Purchase of equipment	(166,000) [b]	
Net cash used by investing activities		(107,000)
Financing activities		
Redemption of bonds	$ (40,000)	
Issue of common shares	160,000	
Payment of dividends	(55,000) [c]	
Net cash provided by financing activities		65,000
Net increase in cash		17,000
Cash, January 1		37,000
Cash, December 31		$ 54,000

Calculations:

[a] $36,000 − $2,000 = $34,000

[b] $68,000 − $41,000 − $193,000 = $166,000

[c] $136,000 + $125,000 − $206,000 = $55,000

the
navigator

Related exercise material: BE17–13, E17–10, E17–11, and E17–12.

Using the Information in the Financial Statements

The cash flow statement gives information about a company's financial health that cannot be found in the other financial statements. None of the other financial statements give enough information for decision-making by themselves. The income statement, statement of retained earnings, and balance sheet must be read along with the cash flow statement in order to fully understand a company's financial position.

For example, the income statement might show a profitable company. However, a rapidly growing company might also find it difficult to pay its current liabilities because its cash is being used to finance its growth. Both successful and unsuccessful companies can have problems with cash flow. However, the reasons can be quite different.

Consider the condensed income and cash flow data shown below for three different companies, each operating in the same industry.

	Company A	Company B	Company C
Net income (loss)	$ 75,000	$ 25,000	$(50,000)
Cash provided (used) by operating activities	$100,000	$(25,000)	$(25,000)
Cash provided (used) by investing activities	(50,000)	(25,000)	35,000
Cash provided (used) by financing activities	(25,000)	75,000	15,000
Net increase in cash	$ 25,000	$ 25,000	$ 25,000

In this example, we have assumed that each company has the same change in cash, an increase of $25,000. However, this increase in cash is generated quite differently by each company. Company A reports net income of $75,000 and a positive cash flow from operating activities of $100,000. How can Company A's cash provided from operating activities be higher than its net income? This could occur in any of these three situations: if it has noncash expenses such as amortization, reduced current assets such as receivables or inventory, or increased current liabilities such as accounts payable. It is important to analyze the components of each section as well as the net result, along with the information in the other financial statements. Depending on which of the situations created Company's A higher cash flow from operating activities, there could be different implications. For example, if receivables are lower, this could be because the company is collecting them faster. If so, this is a good thing. Alternatively, receivables could have decreased because sales decreased. This is not good, and has implications for future profitability.

For now, we know that Company A's operating activities produced a positive cash flow of $100,000, which allowed it to invest $50,000 in its long-lived assets and repay $25,000 of its debt and/or pay dividends. Based only on this information, Company A appears to be in a strong financial position.

Company B, which also produced a positive net income, used $25,000 in its operating activities. How could Company B's net income result in a negative operating cash flow? Company B may be in the early start-up stages of its development. It may have quickly increasing receivables and inventories, with lower amounts of noncash expenses. It was able to end up with the same cash balance as Company A only because it borrowed money. If Company B is indeed a new and rapidly growing company, this is fine. If not, this type of cash flow pattern would not be sustainable in the long run.

Assuming Company B is a start-up company, its cash flow figures appear to be reasonable. For example, early in its operations, during its growth stage, one would expect a company to generate a small amount of net income (or net loss) and negative cash from its operating activities. It will likely also be spending large amounts to purchase productive assets, and will finance these purchases by issuing debt or equity securities. Thus, during its early years, cash from operating and investing activities will likely be negative, while cash from financing activities will be positive.

Company C, which reported both a net loss and a negative cash flow from operating activities, is able to produce a positive change in cash only by selling long-lived assets and borrowing additional debt. A company that generates cash mainly from investing activities is usually in a downsizing or restructuring situation. This is fine if the assets being disposed of are unnecessary or unprofitable. However, if the company is in the position where it must sell off income-producing assets to generate cash, then this will affect future revenue and profitability.

As you can see from the above example, analyzing cash flows from different activities along with the information in the other financial statements can provide significant information about the overall financial health and activities of a company.

Free Cash Flow

Another way of evaluating cash flows is to determine how much discretionary cash flow a company has—in other words, how much cash it has available to expand, repay debt, pay dividends, or do whatever it best determines. This discretionary cash flow is a measure of solvency known as "free cash flow."

Free cash flow describes the cash remaining from operating activities after making cash outlays for capital expenditures. Using net cash provided by operating activities as a proxy for free cash flow is not sufficient as it does not take into account the fact that a company must invest in productive assets, such as property, plant, and equipment, just to maintain its current level of operations. However, the cash flow statement rarely separates investing activities into those required for maintenance and those used for expansion. So we are forced to use the net cash used by investing activities rather than capital expenditures incurred to maintain productive capacity when calculating free cash flow.

To calculate free cash flow, the net cash used for investing activities is deducted from the net cash provided by operating activities. Illustration 17-16 uses data from Forzani's cash flow statement (in thousands) to illustrate the calculation of free cash flow.

Cash Provided (Used) by Operating Activities	−	Cash Used (Provided) by Investing Activities	=	Free Cash Flow
$45,858	−	$50,837	=	$(4,979)

Illustration 17-16 ◄

Free cash flow

Forzani's free cash flow is not "free" at all. It is a negative $4,979 thousand. The cash Forzani produces from operating activities is not enough to cover its current year's investing activities. We are not able to determine whether these investing activities were incurred by Forzani to maintain its existing productive capacity, to expand, or for both purposes. However, we do know that Forzani must finance any shortage of cash between its operating and investing activities with debt and equity. What we do not know is if Forzani deliberately chose to invest in long-lived assets and finance them with debt or equity for other reasons, such as those we discussed in Chapter 15. Without additional information, it is important to be cautious in interpreting any single measure.

ACCOUNTING IN ACTION ▶ Business Insight

Amazon.com, Inc., which used to be the Earth's biggest bookstore, is now the Earth's biggest anything store. Amazon.com's website offers millions of books and videos (which still account for most of the company's sales), not to mention toys, tools, electronics, home furnishings, apparel, health and beauty goods, prescription drugs, gourmet foods, and services, including film processing.

The company states in its annual report: "Our financial focus is on long-term, sustainable growth in free cash flow." In fact, Amazon.com considers free cash flow to be so important that it includes a reconciliation of net cash provided (used) by operating activities to free cash flow in its annual report. For the year ended December 31, 2005, its net cash provided by operating activities increased 130 percent while its free cash flow increased 110 percent. During the same period, its net income declined by 61 percent.

? What is the likely reason that free cash flow so important to Amazon.com?

BEFORE YOU GO ON . . .

▶Review It

1. How is it possible for a company to report a positive net income but report a negative cash flow from operating activities?
2. How is it possible for different companies to report the same net change in cash but different amounts for cash provided (used) by operating activities?
3. What is free cash flow?
4. What does it mean if a company has a negative free cash flow?

Related exercise material: BE17–14, BE17–15, E17–13, and E17–14.

the navigator

Demonstration Problem

The income statement for the year ended December 31, 2008, for Kosinski Manufacturing Ltd. contains the following condensed information:

KOSINSKI MANUFACTURING LTD.
Income Statement
Year Ended December 31, 2008

Sales		$6,583,000
Cost of goods sold		3,572,000
Gross profit		3,011,000
Operating expenses		2,349,000
Income from operations		662,000
Other revenues and expenses		
Gain on sale of machinery	$24,000	
Interest expense	25,000	1,000
Income before income tax		661,000
Income tax expense		180,000
Net income		$ 481,000

The following selected account balances are reported on Kosinski's comparative balance sheet at December 31:

	2008	2007
Cash	$327,000	$130,000
Accounts receivable	775,000	610,000
Inventories	834,000	867,000
Accounts payable	521,000	501,000
Interest payable	2,000	0

Additional information:

1. Operating expenses include an amortization expense of $880,000.
2. Machinery was sold for $270,000 at a gain of $24,000.
3. New machinery was purchased during the year for $1,750,000. It was partially financed by a note payable issued for $500,000.
4. Dividends paid in 2008 totalled $50,000.

Instructions

Prepare the cash flow statement using (a) the indirect method or (b) the direct method, as assigned by your instructor.

Solution to Demonstration Problem

(a) Indirect Method

KOSINSKI MANUFACTURING LTD.
Cash Flow Statement
Year Ended December 31, 2008

Operating activities		
Net income		$ 481,000
Adjustments to reconcile net income to net cash		
provided by operating activities:		
Amortization expense	$ 880,000	
Gain on sale of machinery	(24,000)	
Increase in accounts receivable	(165,000)	
Decrease in inventories	33,000	
Increase in accounts payable	20,000	
Increase in interest payable	2,000	746,000
Net cash provided by operating activities		1,227,000
Investing activities		
Sale of machinery	$ 270,000	
Purchase of machinery (see Note x)	(1,250,000)	(980,000)
Financing activities		
Payment of cash dividends		(50,000)
Net increase in cash		197,000
Cash, January 1		130,000
Cash, December 31		$ 327,000

Note x: Machinery was purchased for $1,750,000 and partially financed by the issue of a $500,000 mortgage note payable.

(b) Direct Method

KOSINSKI MANUFACTURING LTD.
Cash Flow Statement
Year Ended December 31, 2008

Operating activities		
Cash receipts from customers		$ 6,418,000 [a]
Cash payments to suppliers		(3,519,000) [b]
Cash payments for operating expenses		(1,469,000) [c]
Cash payments for interest		(23,000) [d]
Cash payment for income tax		(180,000)
Net cash provided by operating activities		1,227,000
Investing activities		
Sale of machinery	$ 270,000	
Purchase of machinery (see Note x)	(1,250,000)	(980,000)
Financing activities		
Payment of cash dividends		(50,000)
Net increase in cash		197,000
Cash, January 1		130,000
Cash, December 31		$ 327,000

Note x: Machinery was purchased for $1,750,000 and partially financed by the issue of a $500,000 mortgage note payable.

Calculations:
[a] $6,583,000 - $165,000 = $6,418,000
[b] $3,572,000 - $33,000 - $20,000 = $3,519,000
[c] $2,349,000 - $880,000 = $1,469,000
[d] $25,000 - $2,000 = $23,000

Action Plan

- Determine the net cash provided (used) by operating activities. Operating activities generally relate to revenues and expenses shown on the income statement, which are affected by changes in related noncash current assets and current liabilities in the balance sheet, and noncash items in the income statement.
- Determine the net cash provided (used) by investing activities. Investing activities generally relate to changes in long-term assets.
- Determine the net cash provided (used) by financing activities. Financing activities generally relate to changes in long-term liability and shareholders' equity accounts.
- Determine the net increase (decrease) in cash. Verify that this amount agrees with the end-of-period cash balance reported on the balance sheet.
- Note the similarities and differences between the indirect and direct methods: Both methods report the same total amount of cash provided (used) by operating activities but report different detail in this section. The information in the investing and financing sections is the same in both methods.

Summary of Study Objectives

1. **Describe the purpose and content of the cash flow statement.** The cash flow statement gives information about the cash receipts and cash payments resulting from the operating, investing, and financing activities of a company during the period.

In general, operating activities include the cash effects of transactions that affect net income. Investing activities generally include cash flows resulting from changes in long-term asset items. Financing activities generally include cash flows resulting from changes in long-term liability and shareholders' equity items.

2. **Prepare a cash flow statement using one of two approaches: (a) the indirect method or (b) the direct method.** There are four steps to prepare a cash flow statement: (1) Determine the net cash provided (used) by operating activities. In the indirect method, this is done by converting net income from an accrual basis to a cash basis. In the direct method, this is done by converting each individual revenue and expense from an accrual basis to a cash basis.

(2) Analyze the changes in long-term asset accounts and record them as investing activities, or as significant noncash transactions. (3) Analyze the changes in long-term liability and equity accounts and record them as financing activities, or as significant noncash transactions. (4) Prepare the cash flow statement and determine the net increase or decrease in cash.

3. **Analyze the cash flow statement.** The cash flow statement must be read along with the other financial statements in order to adequately assess a company's financial position. In addition, it is important to understand how the net change in cash is affected by each type of activity—operating, investing, and financing—especially when different companies are being compared. Free cash flow is a measure of solvency: it indicates how much cash that was generated from operating activities during the current year is available after making necessary payments for capital expenditures. It is calculated by subtracting the cash used by investing activities from the cash provided by operating activities.

Glossary

Study Aids: Glossary
Practice Tools: Key Term Matching Activity

Cash flow statement A financial statement that gives information about the cash receipts and cash payments of a company during a period and classifies them as operating, investing, and financing activities. (p. 858)

Direct method A method of determining the net cash provided (used) by operating activities by adjusting each item in the income statement from the accrual basis to the cash basis. (p. 865)

Financing activities Cash flow activities from long-term liability and equity accounts. These include (a) obtaining cash by issuing debt and repaying the amounts borrowed, and (b) obtaining cash from shareholders and providing them with a return on their investment. (p. 859)

Free cash flow Cash provided by operating activities less cash used by investing activities. (p. 890)

Indirect method A method of preparing a cash flow statement in which net income is adjusted for items that did not affect cash, to determine net cash provided (used) by operating activities. (p. 865)

Investing activities Cash flow activities from long-term asset accounts. These include (a) acquiring and disposing of investments and long-lived assets, and (b) lending money and collecting on those loans. (p. 859)

Operating activities Cash flow activities that include the cash effects of transactions that create revenues and expenses, and thus affect net income. (p. 859)

Self-Study Questions

Practice Tools: Self-Assessment Quizzes

Answers are at the end of the chapter.

(SO 1) C 1. Which of the following is an example of a cash flow from an operating activity?
    (a) A payment of cash to lenders for interest
    (b) A receipt of cash from the sale of common shares
    (c) A payment of cash dividends to shareholders
    (d) A receipt of cash from the issue of a mortgage payable

2. Which of the following is an example of a cash flow from an investing activity? (SO 1)
    (a) A receipt of cash from the issue of bonds
    (b) A payment of cash to purchase a cash equivalent
    (c) A receipt of cash from the sale of equipment
    (d) The acquisition of land by issuing bonds

3. Which of the following is an example of a cash flow from a financing activity? (SO 1)

(a) A receipt of cash from the sale of land
(b) An issue of debt for land
(c) A payment of dividends
(d) A purchase of inventory on credit

2a) AP 4. Net income is $132,000. During the year, accounts payable increased by $10,000, inventory decreased by $6,000, and accounts receivable increased by $12,000. Under the indirect method, net cash provided by operating activities is:
(a) $102,000.   (c) $136,000.
(b) $128,000.   (d) $148,000.

O 2a) K 5. In determining cash provided (used) by operating activities under the indirect method, the items that are added to net income do not include:
(a) amortization expense.
(b) a gain on the sale of equipment.
(c) a decrease in inventory.
(d) a loss on the sale of equipment.

) 2b) AP 6. The beginning balance in Accounts Receivable is $44,000. The ending balance is $42,000. Sales during the period are $129,000. Cash receipts from customers are:
(a) $127,000.   (c) $131,000.
(b) $129,000.   (d) $141,000.

O 2) AP 7. Retained earnings were $197,000 at the beginning of the year and $386,500 at the end of the year, and net income was $200,000. Dividends payable were $2,000 at the beginning of the year and $2,500 at the end of the year. What

amount should be reported in the financing activities section of the cash flow statement for dividend payments?
(a) $500   (c) $10,500
(b) $10,000   (d) $11,000

8. Which of the following items is an example of a noncash (SO 2) C
investing and financing activity?
(a) A loss on the sale of a building
(b) The purchase of a building, financed by a mortgage payable
(c) Amortization expense on the building
(d) The refinancing of interest rate on the mortgage

9. If a company is in the early years of its development and (SO 3) C
is rapidly growing, it would be normal to see:
(a) negative cash from operating and investing activities, and positive cash from financing activities.
(b) negative cash from operating activities, and positive cash from investing and financing activities.
(c) positive cash from operating activities, and negative cash from investing and financing activities.
(d) positive cash from operating and financing activities, and negative cash from investing activities.

10. Free cash flow gives an indication of a company's ability (SO 3) K
to:
(a) generate sales.
(b) generate net income.
(c) generate cash for discretionary uses.
(d) generate cash for investments.

the navigator

Questions

SO 1) C 1. In preparing a cash flow statement, why is it necessary to use the balance sheet, income statement, and statement of retained earnings, but not the statement of comprehensive income?

SO 1) K 2. How is the cash flow statement useful to investors, creditors, and others in assessing a company's financial position?

SO 1) C 3. Elisa Botelho maintains that the cash flow statement is an optional financial statement. Do you agree? Explain.

SO 1) C 4. What are "cash equivalents"? How do the purchases and sales of cash equivalents affect the cash flow statement?

SO 1) C 5. Identify, and describe the differences among, the three types of activities reported in the cash flow statement.

SO 1) K 6. What are some examples of significant noncash investing and financing transactions? How should they be disclosed?

SO 1) C 7. At a shareholders' meeting, one of Osman Corporation's shareholders asks why the company's cash flow statement

ends with cash at the end of the period on the balance sheet date and yet the date on the cash flow statement is not the same as the one on the balance sheet—it seems to cover the entire year. Explain why the dates of the two statements are not the same.

8. Why is it necessary to convert accrual-based net income (SO 2) C
to cash-based income when preparing a cash flow statement?

9. How can a company's cash balance decrease when the (SO 2) C
company has earned net income? Conversely, how can cash increase when a company has incurred a net loss?

10. Describe the indirect method for determining net cash (SO 2a) C
provided (used) by operating activities.

11. Identify three items under the indirect method that (SO 2a) K
could be adjustments to reconcile net income to net cash provided (used) by operating activities.

12. Why and how is amortization expense reported in a cash (SO 2a) C
flow statement prepared using the indirect method?

(SO 2b) C 13. Describe the direct method for determining net cash provided (used) by operating activities.

(SO 2b) C 14. If a company reports $500,000 of cash collected from customers on its cash flow statement, would it also report $500,000 of sales on its income statement? Explain why or why not.

(SO 2b) C 15. Under the direct method, why is amortization expense not reported in the cash flow from operating activities section?

(SO 2a, 2b) C 16. (a) Contrast the advantages and disadvantages of the direct and indirect methods of preparing the cash flow statement. (b) Are both methods acceptable? (c) Which method is preferred by the CICA? (d) Which method is more popular? Why?

(SO 2a, 2b) C 17. Goh Corporation changed its method of reporting operating activities from the indirect method to the direct method in order to make its cash flow statement more informative to its readers. Will this change increase, decrease, or not affect the net cash provided (used) by operating activities?

(SO 2) C 18. Explain how the sale of equipment at a gain is reported on a cash flow statement. The sale of equipment at a loss?

(SO 2) C 19. Explain how the redemption of bonds payable at a loss is reported on a cash flow statement. The redemption of bonds payable at a gain?

(SO 2) C 20. Explain why short-term notes receivable and note payable are sometimes reported as operating activities and sometimes as financing activities?

21. David, Barbara, and Zofia were discussing the preparation of the cash flow statement of Rock Candy Corp. Rock Candy had purchased $25,000 of machinery during the year. It paid for it with $10,000 cash and financed the remainder with a note payable. David thinks that the purchase of the machinery should be disclosed as a cash outflow of $25,000 in the investing activities section of the cash flow statement and the note payable should be disclosed as a cash inflow of $15,000 in the financing activities section. Barbara thinks this transaction should be recorded as a cash outflow of $10,000 in the investing activities section for the purchase of equipment and the remainder as a significant noncash investing and financing activity in the notes to the statement. Zofia thinks that this transaction should only be disclosed as a significant noncash investing and financing activity in the notes to the statement. Who is correct? Explain. (SO 2

22. Why is it important to understand the pattern of a company's cash flows—that is, how much cash is generated from, or used by, operating activities, investing activities, and financing activities? (SO 3

23. Explain how a company's cash flows can indicate whether it is in the early stages of its development or not. (SO 3

24. What does free cash flow indicate, and how is it calculated? (SO 3

25. How is it possible for a company to report positive net cash from operating activities but have a negative free cash flow? (SO 3

Brief Exercises

Indicate impact of transactions on cash.
(SO 1) AP

BE17–1   For each of the following transactions, indicate whether it will increase (+), decrease (−), or have no effect (NE) on a company's cash flows:

(a) ____ A repayment of a bank loan
(b) ____ The sale of land for cash
(c) ____ A reacquisition of common shares
(d) ____ A purchase of an available-for-sale investment
(e) ____ The acquisition of a building by an issue of common shares
(f) ____ An issue of preferred shares for cash
(g) ____ The distribution of a previously declared stock dividend
(h) ____ A collection of accounts receivable
(i) ____ The recording of amortization expense
(j) ____ Payment of a cash dividend

Classify transactions by activity.
(SO 1) C

BE17–2   Classify each of the transactions listed in BE17–1 as an operating, investing, financing, or significant noncash investing and financing activity. If a transaction does not belong in any of these classifications, explain why.

BE17–3 Indicate whether each of the following transactions would be added to (+) or subtracted from (–) net income in determining the cash provided (used) by operating activities using the indirect method:

(a) ___ Amortization expense
(b) ___ An increase in accounts receivable
(c) ___ A decrease in inventory
(d) ___ An increase in accounts payable
(e) ___ A decrease in income tax payable
(f) ___ A gain on sale of equipment
(g) ___ A loss on the sale of an available-for-sale security
(h) ___ An impairment loss for goodwill

Indicate impact on cash from operating activities—indirect method.
(SO 2a) AP

BE17–4 Crystal Inc. reported net income of $775,000 for the year ended November 30, 2008. Amortization expense for the year was $260,000, accounts receivable decreased by $350,000, prepaid expenses increased by $95,000, accounts payable decreased by $280,000, and the company incurred a gain on sale of equipment of $10,000. Calculate the net cash provided (used) by operating activities using the indirect method.

Calculate cash from operating activities—indirect method.
(SO 2a) AP

BE17–5 The comparative balance sheet for Dupigne Corporation shows the following noncash current asset and current liability accounts at March 31:

Calculate cash from operating activities—indirect method.
(SO 2a) AP

	2008	2007
Accounts receivable	$60,000	$40,000
Inventory	64,000	70,000
Prepaid expenses	6,000	4,000
Accounts payable	35,000	40,000
Income tax payable	22,000	12,000

Dupigne's income statement reported the following selected information for the year ended March 31, 2008: net income was $250,000 and amortization expense was $60,000. Calculate the net cash provided (used) by operating activities using the indirect method.

BE17–6 Westcoast Corporation has accounts receivable of $14,000 at December 31, 2007, and of $24,000 at December 31, 2008. Sales revenues were $270,000 for 2008. Calculate the cash receipts from customers.

Calculate cash receipts from customers—direct method.
(SO 2b) AP

BE17–7 Winter Sportswear Inc. reported a cost of goods sold of $89,000 on its income statement. It also reported a decrease in inventory of $3,600 and an increase in accounts payable of $5,400 for the same period. Calculate the cash payments to suppliers.

Calculate cash payments to suppliers—direct method.
(SO 2b) AP

BE17–8 For the current year, Linux Corporation reports operating expenses of $100,000, including an amortization expense of $15,000. During the year, prepaid expenses increased by $6,600 and accrued expenses payable decreased by $2,600. Calculate the cash payments for operating expenses.

Calculate cash payments for operating expenses—direct method.
(SO 2b) AP

BE17–9 ICE Inc. reported salary expense of $189,000 on its 2008 income statement. It also reported salaries payable of $2,500 at December 31, 2007, and of $3,000 at December 31, 2008. Calculate the cash payments to employees.

Calculate cash payments to employees—direct method.
(SO 2b) AP

BE17–10 Home Grocery Corporation reported income tax expense of $90,000 in its 2008 income statement. It also reported income tax payable of $7,000 at December 31, 2007, and of $8,000 at December 31, 2008. Calculate the cash payments for income tax.

Calculate cash payments for income tax—direct method.
(SO 2b) AP

Calculate cash received for equipment.
(SO 2) AP

BE17–11 The T accounts for equipment and the related accumulated amortization for Trevis Corporation are as follows:

	Equipment				Accumulated Amortization—Equipment	
Beg. bal.	80,000				Beg. bal.	44,500
Acquisitions	41,600	Disposals	22,000	Disposals 5,500	Amortization	12,000
End. bal.	99,600				End. bal.	51,000

In addition, Trevis' income statement reported a loss on the sale of equipment of $1,500. (a) What amount was reported on the cash flow statement as "cash flow provided by sale of equipment"? (b) In what section(s) of the cash flow statement would this transaction be reported if Trevis uses (1) the indirect method, and (2) the direct method?

Calculate cash paid for dividends.
(SO 2) AP

BE17–12 Canadian Tire Corporation, Limited reported net income of $330.1 million for the year ended December 31, 2005. Its retained earnings were $1,546.9 million on December 31, 2004, and $1,812.6 million on December 31, 2005. It also repurchased shares, which resulted in a $17-million reduction to retained earnings in 2005. Calculate the dividends paid by Canadian Tire in 2005, assuming there were no dividends payable at the beginning or end of the year.

Prepare cash flow statement.
(SO 2) AP

BE17–13 The following information is available for Baker Corporation for the year ended April 30, 2008:

Cash and cash equivalents, May 1, 2007	$ 7,000
Cash provided by operating activities	52,000
Cash receipts	
Sale of equipment	6,000
Issue of non-trade note payable	20,000
Issue of $75,000 mortgage note payable to	
partially finance purchase of land for $100,000	75,000
Cash payments	
Dividends	25,000
Reacquisition of common shares	19,000
Purchase of land for $100,000, partially financed	
by issuing a $75,000 mortgage note payable	100,000

Prepare a cash flow statement for the year, including any required note disclosure.

Use cash flows to identify new company.
(SO 3) AN

BE17–14 Two companies reported the following information.

	Company A	Company B
Net income (loss)	$ (5,000)	$100,000
Cash provided (used) by operating activities	(10,000)	30,000
Cash provided (used) by investing activities	(40,000)	50,000
Cash provided (used) by financing activities	120,000	(100,000)

Which company is more likely to be in the early stages of its development? Explain.

Calculate free cash flow.
(SO 3) AP

BE17–15 Svetlana Limited reported cash provided by operating activities of $300,000, cash used by investing activities of $250,000, and cash provided by financing activities of $70,000. Calculate Svetlana's free cash flow.

Exercises

Classify transactions by activity.
(SO 1) AP

E17–1 Fisher Corp. reported the following transactions. Assume all items involve cash unless there is information to the contrary.

(a) ___ A purchase of land
(b) ___ The payment of dividends
(c) ___ The sale of a building
(d) ___ The retirement of bonds at maturity
(e) ___ Payment of employee salaries
(f) ___ The issue of a mortgage note payable in partial payment of land
(g) ___ Payment of interest on a mortgage note payable
(h) ___ The sale of inventory
(i) ___ Collection of accounts receivable
(j) ___ A conversion of preferred shares into common shares

Instructions

Indicate how the above items should be classified in the cash flow statement using these classifications: operating activity (O), investing activity (I), financing activity (F), and noncash investing and financing activity (NC).

E17–2 Eng Corporation had the following transactions:

Classify transactions by activity.
(SO 1) AP

Transaction	(a) Classification	(b) Cash Inflow or Outflow
1. Sold inventory for $1,000.	O	+$1,000
2. Purchased a machine for $30,000. Made a $5,000 down payment and issued a long-term note for the remainder.		
3. Issued common shares for $50,000.		
4. Collected $16,000 of accounts receivable.		
5. Paid a $25,000 cash dividend.		
6. Sold an available-for-sale security with a cost of $15,000 for $10,000.		
7. Redeemed bonds having a carrying value of $200,000 for $175,000.		
8. Paid $18,000 on accounts payable.		
9. Purchased inventory for $28,000 on account.		
10. Purchased a held-to-maturity security for $100,000.		

Instructions

Complete the above table indicating whether each transaction (a) should be classified as an operating activity (O), investing activity (I), financing activity (F), or noncash transaction (NC); and (b) represents a cash inflow (+), cash outflow (–), or has no effect (NE) on cash, and in what amount. The first one has been done for you as an example.

E17–3 IROC Corporation had the following transactions.

Indicate impact on net income and cash from operating activities.
(SO 2a) AP

Transaction	Net Income	Net Cash Provided (Used) by Operating Activities
1. Sold inventory for cash at a price higher than cost.	+	+
2. Sold inventory on account at a price higher than cost.		
3. Purchased inventory on account.		
4. Accrued income tax payable.		
5. Paid income taxes.		
6. Purchased supplies for cash.		
7. Recorded amortization expense.		
8. Paid an amount owing on account.		
9. Collected an amount owing from a customer.		
10. Paid a one-year insurance policy in advance.		

Instructions

Identify whether each of the above transactions will increase (+), decrease (–), or have no effect (NE) on net income and net cash provided (used) by operating activities in a cash flow statement prepared using the indirect method. The first one has been done for you as an example.

Prepare operating activities section—indirect method. (SO 2a) AP

E17–4 Pesci Limited reported net income of $195,000 for the year ended July 31, 2008. Pesci also reported an amortization expense of $25,000 and a loss of $5,000 on the sale of equipment. The comparative balance sheet shows an increase in accounts receivable of $15,000 for the year, an increase in accounts payable of $10,000, a decrease in prepaid expenses of $4,000, and a decrease in accrued liabilities of $3,500.

Instructions

Prepare the operating activities section of the cash flow statement, using the indirect method.

Prepare operating activities section—indirect method. (SO 2a) AP

E17–5 The current assets and liabilities sections of Barth Inc.'s comparative balance sheets at December 31 are presented below:

	2008	2007
Current assets		
Cash	$105,000	$ 99,000
Accounts receivable	120,000	89,000
Inventory	161,000	186,000
Prepaid expenses	27,000	32,000
Total current assets	$413,000	$406,000
Current liabilities		
Accrued expenses payable	$ 15,000	$ 5,000
Accounts payable	85,000	92,000
Total current liabilities	$100,000	$ 97,000

Barth's net income for 2008 was $135,000. Amortization expense was $19,000.

Instructions

Prepare the operating activities section of the cash flow statement, using the indirect method.

Indicate impact on cash from operating activities—direct method. (SO 2b) AP

E17–6 You are provided with the following transactions:

Transaction	(a) Related Income Statement Account(s)	(b) Add to (+) or Deduct from (–) Income Statement Account	(c) Related Cash Receipt or Payment
1. Increase in accounts receivable	Sales revenue	–	Cash receipts from customers
2. Decrease in accounts receivable			
3. Increase in accounts payable			
4. Decrease in interest payable			
5. Increase in prepaid expenses			
6. Increase in inventory			
7. Decrease in inventory			
8. Increase in income tax payable			
9. Increase in salaries payable			
10. Decrease in accrued expenses payable			

Instructions

Under the direct method, net cash provided (used) by operating activities is calculated by adjusting each item in the income statement from the accrual basis to the cash basis. For each transaction, do the following: (a) Identify the related income statement account. (b) Indicate if the transaction should be added to or deducted from the related income statement account to convert net income to cash from operating activities. (c) State the title of the resulting cash receipt or payment category that is reported on the cash flow statement. The first transaction has been done for you as an example.

E17–7 McGillis Ltd. completed its first year of operations on December 31, 2008. Its income statement showed that McGillis had revenues of $182,000, operating expenses of $88,000, and income tax expense of $21,000. Accounts receivable, accounts payable, and income tax payable at year end were $42,000, $33,000, and $1,500, respectively. Assume that the accounts payable related to operating expenses.

Calculate cash from operating activities—direct method.
(SO 2b) AP

Instructions

Calculate the net cash provided (used) by operating activities, using the direct method.

E17–8 The following information is taken from the general ledger of Robinson Limited:

Calculate operating cash flows—direct method.
(SO 2b) AP

Sales:	Sales revenue	$190,000
	Accounts receivable, January 1	12,000
	Accounts receivable, December 31	7,000
Inventory:	Cost of goods sold	$114,000
	Inventory, January 1	4,500
	Inventory, December 31	5,900
	Accounts payable, January 1	2,500
	Accounts payable, December 31	3,750
Operating expenses:	Operating expenses	$ 50,000
	Amortization expense	11,000
	Prepaid expenses, January 1	2,500
	Prepaid expenses, December 31	3,000
	Accrued expenses payable, January 1	4,500
	Accrued expenses payable, December 31	5,500

Instructions

Using the direct method, calculate (a) the cash receipts from customers, (b) the cash payments to suppliers, and (c) the cash payments for operating expenses.

E17–9 Selected general ledger accounts follow for Dupré Corp. during the year ended December 31, 2008:

Prepare investing and financing activities sections.
(SO 2) AP

Equipment

Date		Debit	Credit	Balance
Jan. 1	Balance			160,000
July 31	Purchase of equipment	70,000		230,000
Sept. 2	Purchase of equipment, partially financed through			
	issue of note	53,000		283,000
Nov. 10	Cost of equipment sold		39,000	244,000

Accumulated Amortization—Equipment

Date		Debit	Credit	Balance
Jan. 1	Balance			71,000
Nov. 10	Accumulated amortization on equipment sold	30,000		41,000
Dec. 31	Amortization expense		28,000	69,000

Notes Payable

Date		Debit	Credit	Balance
Jan. 1	Balance			0
Sept. 2	Issue of note to purchase equipment		43,000	43,000

Retained Earnings

Date		Debit	Credit	Balance
Jan. 1	Balance			105,000
Aug. 23	Dividends (cash)	4,000		101,000
Dec. 31	Net income		67,000	168,000

Additional information:

A loss of $3,000 was incurred on the sale of equipment.

Instructions

Prepare the investing and financing activities sections of the cash flow statement, including any required note disclosure.

Prepare cash flow statement—indirect method. (SO 2a) AP

E17–10 Savary Limited's comparative balance sheet at December 31 is as follows:

SAVARY LIMITED Balance Sheet December 31		
	2008	2007
Assets		
Cash	$ 164,000	$ 85,000
Accounts receivable	750,000	600,000
Inventory	500,000	330,000
Prepaid insurance	18,000	25,000
Equipment and vehicles	1,250,000	1,000,000
Accumulated amortization	(350,000)	(280,000)
Total assets	$2,332,000	$1,760,000
Liabilities and Shareholders' Equity		
Accounts payable	$ 226,000	$ 200,000
Salaries payable	30,000	40,000
Interest payable	26,000	20,000
Notes payable (non-trade)	500,000	350,000
Preferred shares	250,000	0
Common shares	400,000	400,000
Retained earnings	900,000	750,000
Total liabilities and shareholders' equity	$2,332,000	$1,760,000

Additional information:

1. Net income for 2008 was $200,000.
2. Equipment was purchased during the year. No equipment was sold.
3. Cash dividends were paid to the preferred shareholders during the year.

Instructions

Prepare the cash flow statement, using the indirect method.

Prepare cash flow statement—direct method. (SO 2b) AP

E17–11 The accounting records of Flypaper Airlines Inc. reveal the following transactions and events for the year ended March 31, 2008:

Payment of interest	$ 10,000	Payment of salaries	$ 53,000
Cash sales	48,000	Amortization expense	16,000
Receipt of dividend revenue	14,000	Proceeds from sale of aircraft	212,000
Payment of income tax	7,500	Purchase of equipment for cash	22,000
Net income	38,000	Loss on sale of aircraft	3,000
Payment of accounts payable	110,000	Payment of dividends	14,000
Payment for land	174,000	Payment of operating expenses	28,000
Collection of accounts receivable	192,000		

Additional information:

Flypaper Airlines' cash and cash equivalents on April 1, 2007, were $35,000.

Instructions

Prepare a cash flow statement, using the direct method.

E17–12 The comparative balance sheet for Puffy Ltd. follows:

Prepare cash flow statement—indirect and direct methods.
(SO 2a, 2b) AP

PUFFY LTD.
Balance Sheet
December 31

	2008	2007
Assets		
Cash	$ 63,000	$ 22,000
Accounts receivable	85,000	76,000
Inventories	180,000	189,000
Land	75,000	100,000
Equipment	260,000	200,000
Accumulated amortization	(66,000)	(32,000)
Total assets	$597,000	$555,000
Liabilities and Shareholders' Equity		
Accounts payable	$ 38,000	$ 47,000
Bonds payable	120,000	200,000
Common shares	209,000	174,000
Retained earnings	230,000	134,000
Total liabilities and shareholders' equity	$597,000	$555,000

Additional information:

1. Net income for 2008 was $115,000.
2. Bonds payable amounting to $80,000 were retired at maturity.
3. Common shares were issued for $35,000.
4. Land was sold at a gain of $5,000.
5. No equipment was sold during 2006.
6. Net sales for the year were $978,000.
7. Cost of goods sold for the year was $751,000.
8. Operating expenses (not including amortization expense) were $43,000.
9. Income tax expense was $40,000.

Instructions

Prepare a cash flow statement using (a) the indirect method or (b) the direct method, as assigned by your instructor.

E17–13 Condensed cash flow statements are as follows for two companies operating in the same industry:

Compare cash flows for two companies.
(SO 3) AN

	Company A	Company B
Cash provided (used) by operating activities	$100,000	$(90,000)
Cash provided (used) by investing activities	(10,000)	(10,000)
Cash provided (used) by financing activities	(30,000)	160,000
Increase in cash	60,000	60,000
Cash, beginning of period	15,000	15,000
Cash, end of period	$ 75,000	$ 75,000

Instructions

Which company is in better financial shape? Explain why.

E17–14 Selected information follows for **Bank of Montreal** and **Scotiabank** (in millions):

Calculate and discuss free cash flow.
(SO 3) AN

	Bank of Montreal	Scotiabank
Net income	$ 2,400	$ 3,209
Cash used by operating activities	(6,285)	(3,322)
Cash provided by investing activities	24,053	31,474

Instructions

(a) Calculate the free cash flow for each company.
(b) Which company appears to be in a stronger financial position? Explain.
(c) In what way might a bank's free cash flow be different from the free cash flow of a manufacturing company?

Problems: Set A

Classify transactions by activity. Indicate impact on cash and net income.
(SO 1) AP

P17–1A You are provided with the following transactions that took place during a recent fiscal year:

Transaction	(a) Classification	(b) Cash	(c) Net Income
1. Paid wages to employees.	O	–	–
2. Sold land for cash, at a gain.			
3. Acquired land by issuing common shares.			
4. Paid a cash dividend to preferred shareholders.			
5. Recorded cash sales.			
6. Recorded sales on account.			
7. Purchased inventory for cash.			
8. Purchased inventory on account.			
9. Paid income tax.			
10. Made principal repayment on a trade note payable.			

Instructions

Complete the above table for each of the following requirements, assuming none of the transactions were previously accrued. The first one has been done for you as an example.

(a) Classify each transaction as an operating activity (O), an investing activity (I), a financing activity (F), or a noncash transaction (NC) on the cash flow statement.
(b) Specify whether the transaction will result in an increase (+), decrease (–), or have no effect (NE) on cash reported on the balance sheet.
(c) Specify whether the transaction will increase (+), decrease (–), or have no effect (NE) on net income reported on the income statement.

Indicate impact of transactions on cash, net income, and cash from operating activities.
(SO 1) AP

P17–2A You are provided with the following transactions that took place during a recent fiscal year:

Transaction	Cash	Net Income	Cash from Operating Activities
1. Paid insurance for the month.	–	–	–
2. Paid semi-annual bond interest.			
3. Received rent from a tenant in advance.			
4. Recorded amortization expense.			
5. Sold equipment for cash, at a loss.			
6. Reacquired common shares.			
7. Declared and paid a cash dividend to common shareholders.			
8. Performed services on account.			
9. Collected cash from customers on account.			
10. Issued a non-trade note payable.			

Instructions

In the above table, indicate whether each transaction increases (+), decreases (–), or has no effect (NE) on cash reported on the balance sheet, net income reported on the income statement, and cash provided (used) by operating activities on the cash flow statement. The first one has been done for you as an example.

P17–3A The income statement of Gum San Ltd. follows:

Prepare operating activities section—indirect and direct methods.
(SO 2a, 2b) AP

GUM SAN LTD.
Income Statement
Year Ended April 30, 2008

Sales		$5,400,000
Cost of goods sold		3,290,000
Gross profit		2,110,000
Operating expenses	$925,000	
Amortization expense	145,000	1,070,000
Income from operations		1,040,000
Other revenues		
Gain on sale of equipment		12,000
Income before income taxes		1,052,000
Income tax expense		263,000
Net income		$ 789,000

Additional information:

1. Accounts receivable increased by $510,000 during the year.
2. Inventory decreased by $220,000 during the year.
3. Prepaid expenses increased by $170,000 during the year.
4. Accounts payable to suppliers increased by $50,000 during the year.
5. Accrued expenses payable decreased by $165,000 during the year.
6. Income tax payable decreased by $16,000 during the year.

Instructions

Prepare the operating activities section of the cash flow statement, using (a) the indirect method or (b) the direct method, as assigned by your instructor.

P17–4A Sable Island Ltd.'s income statement contained the following condensed information:

Prepare operating activities section—indirect and direct methods.
(SO 2a, 2b) AP

SABLE ISLAND LTD.
Income Statement
Year Ended December 31, 2008

Fee revenue		$900,000
Operating expenses	$624,000	
Amortization expense	60,000	684,000
Income from operations		216,000
Other expenses		
Interest expense	$ 5,000	
Loss on sale of equipment	26,000	31,000
Income before income tax		185,000
Income tax expense		46,250
Net income		$138,750

Sable Island's balance sheet contained the following comparative data at December 31:

	2008	2007
Accounts receivable	$47,000	$57,000
Prepaid expenses	8,000	6,500
Accounts payable	41,000	36,000
Income tax payable	4,000	9,250
Interest payable	1,000	550
Unearned revenue	12,000	9,000

Additional information: Accounts payable relate to operating expenses.

Instructions

Prepare the operating activities section of the cash flow statement, using (a) the indirect method or (b) the direct method, as assigned by your instructor.

Calculate cash flows for property, plant, and equipment.
(SO 2) AP

P17–5A The following selected account balances relate to the property, plant, and equipment accounts of Bird Corp. at year end:

	2008	2007
Accumulated amortization—buildings	$ 675,000	$ 600,000
Accumulated amortization—equipment	288,000	192,000
Amortization expense	203,000	171,000
Buildings	1,250,000	1,250,000
Equipment	500,000	480,000
Land	250,000	200,000
Loss on sale of equipment	5,000	0

Additional information:

1. Purchased land, making a $25,000 down payment and financing the remainder with a mortgage note payable.
2. Equipment was purchased for $80,000 cash. Equipment was also sold during the year.

Instructions

(a) Determine the amounts of any cash inflows or outflows related to the property, plant, and equipment accounts in 2008.
(b) Indicate where each of the cash inflows or outflows identified in (a) would be classified on the cash flow statement.

Calculate cash flows for shareholders' equity.
(SO 2) AP

P17–6A The following selected account balances relate to the shareholders' equity accounts of Wood Corp. at year end:

	2008	2007
Preferred shares: 5,000 shares	$125,000	$125,000
Common shares: 9,000 shares in 2008; 10,000 in 2007	122,000	140,000
Contributed capital—reacquisition of common shares	1,500	0
Cash dividends—preferred	6,250	6,250
Stock dividends—common	14,000	0
Retained earnings	300,000	240,000

Additional information:

1. The company reacquired 2,000 common shares in 2008, with an average cost of $32,000.
2. During the year, 1,000 common shares were issued as a stock dividend.

Instructions

(a) What was the amount of net income reported by Wood in 2008?
(b) Determine the amounts of any cash inflows or outflows related to the shareholders' equity accounts in 2008.
(c) Indicate where each of the cash inflows or outflows identified in (b) would be classified on the cash flow statement.

Prepare cash flow statement—indirect and direct methods.
(SO 2a, 2b) AP

P17–7A Condensed financial data follow for Galenti, Inc.:

GALENTI, INC.
Balance Sheet
December 31

	2008	2007
Assets		
Cash	$ 92,700	$ 47,250
Accounts receivable	80,800	21,000
Inventory	121,900	102,650
Prepaid expenses	10,000	16,000
Available-for-sale securities	84,500	107,000
Property, plant, and equipment	290,000	205,000
Accumulated amortization	(49,500)	(40,000)
Total assets	$630,400	$458,900
Liabilities and Shareholders' Equity		
Accounts payable	$ 52,700	$ 48,280
Accrued expenses payable	12,100	18,830
Notes payable	140,000	70,000
Common shares	250,000	200,000
Retained earnings	175,600	121,790
Total liabilities and shareholders' equity	$630,400	$458,900

GALENTI, INC.
Income Statement
Year Ended December 31, 2008

Revenues		
Sales		$297,500
Gain on sale of equipment		8,750
		306,250
Expenses		
Cost of goods sold	$99,460	
Operating expenses	14,670	
Amortization expense	58,700	
Interest expense	2,940	
Loss on sale of available-for-sale securities	7,500	183,270
Income before income tax		122,980
Income tax expense		32,670
Net income		$ 90,310

Additional information:

1. Available-for-sale securities were sold for $15,000, resulting in a realized loss of $7,500. There were no unrealized gains or losses in 2008.
2. New equipment costing $141,000 was purchased for $71,000 cash and a $70,000 note payable.
3. Equipment with an original cost of $56,000 was sold for $15,550, resulting in a gain of $8,750.

Instructions

Prepare a cash flow statement, using (a) the indirect method or (b) the direct method, as assigned by your instructor.

Prepare cash flow
statement—indirect and
direct methods.
(SO 2a, 2b) AP

P17–8A The financial statements of Milk River Ltd. follow:

MILK RIVER LTD.
Balance Sheet
December 31

Assets	2008	2007
Cash	$ 13,000	$ 15,000
Money-market instruments	16,000	5,000
Accounts receivable	32,000	4,000
Inventory	33,000	30,000
Property, plant, and equipment	80,000	78,000
Accumulated amortization	(30,000)	(24,000)
Total assets	$144,000	$108,000
Liabilities and Shareholders' Equity		
Accounts payable	$ 17,000	$ 15,000
Income taxes payable	1,000	8,000
Notes payable	47,000	33,000
Common shares	18,000	14,000
Retained earnings	61,000	38,000
Total liabilities and shareholders' equity	$144,000	$108,000

MILK RIVER LTD.
Income Statement
Year Ended December 31, 2008

Sales		$242,000
Cost of goods sold		180,000
Gross profit		62,000
Operating expenses		24,000
Income from operations		38,000
Other revenues and expenses		
Gain on sale of equipment	$1,000	
Interest expense	2,000	1,000
Income before income tax		37,000
Income tax expense		9,250
Net income		$ 27,750

Additional information:

1. Equipment costing $20,000 was purchased with a $6,000 down payment and the remainder was financed with a note payable.
2. During the year, equipment was sold for $9,500 cash. This equipment had cost $18,000 originally and had a book value of $8,500 at the time of sale.
3. All amortization expenses are in the operating expenses category.
4. The money-market instruments are highly liquid and should be considered cash equivalents for this statement.

Instructions

(a) Prepare a cash flow statement for the year, using (1) the indirect method or (2) the direct method, as assigned by your instructor.
(b) Explain why Milk River should combine its money-market instruments with cash when preparing the cash flow statement.

P17–9A Selected information (in thousands) for two close competitors, **Reitmans (Canada) Limited** and **La Senza Corporation,** follows for fiscal 2006:

	Reitmans	La Senza
Net income	$ 84,889	$ 17,737
Cash provided by operating activities	106,349	46,610
Cash used by investing activities	(43,509)	(14,895)
Cash used by financing activities	(29,380)	(5,938)
Cash and cash equivalents, end of period	135,399	28,899

Instructions

(a) Calculate the free cash flow for each company.

(b) Which company appears to be in the stronger financial position?

(c) By comparing the company's cash flows, can you tell which company is likely in a growth stage? Explain.

Problems: Set B

P17–1B   You are provided with the following transactions that took place during a recent fiscal year:

Classify transactions by activity. Indicate impact on cash and net income. (SO 1) AP

Transaction	(a) Classification	(b) Cash	(c) Net Income
1. Paid telephone bill for the month.	O	–	–
2. Sold equipment for cash, at a loss.			
3. Sold an available-for-sale security, at a gain.			
4. Acquired a building by paying 10% in cash and signing a mortgage payable for the balance.			
5. Made principal repayments on the mortgage.			
6. Paid interest on the mortgage.			
7. Sold inventory on account, at a price greater than cost.			
8. Paid wages owing (previously accrued) to employees.			
9. Declared and distributed a stock dividend to common shareholders.			
10. Paid rent in advance.			

Instructions

Complete the above table for each of the following requirements. The first one has been done for you as an example.

(a) Classify each transaction as an operating activity (O), an investing activity (I), a financing activity (F), or a noncash transaction (NC) on the cash flow statement

(b) Specify whether the transaction will result in an increase (+), decrease (–), or have no effect (NE) on cash reported on the balance sheet.

(c) Specify whether the transaction will increase (+), decrease (–), or have no effect (NE) on net income reported on the income statement.

Indicate impact of
transactions on cash, net
income, and cash from
operating activities.
(SO 1) AP

P17–2B You are provided with the following transactions that took place during a recent fiscal year:

Transaction	Cash	Net Income	Cash from Operating Activities
1. Recorded cash sales.	+	+	+
2. Received semi-annual bond interest.			
3. Wrote down the value of inventory to market, which was lower than cost.			
4. Received dividends on an available-for-sale equity investment.			
5. Sold equipment for cash, at a gain.			
6. Issued common shares.			
7. Paid a cash dividend to common shareholders.			
8. Sold inventory on account at a price greater than cost.			
9. Collected cash from customers on account.			
10. Collected rent in advance.			

Instructions

In the above table, indicate whether each transaction increases (+), decreases (–), or has no effect (NE) on cash reported on the balance sheet, net income reported on the income statement, and cash provided (used) by operating activities on the cash flow statement. The first one has been done for you as an example.

Prepare operating activities
section—indirect and direct
methods.
(SO 2a, 2b) AP

P17–3B The income statement of Breckenridge Ltd. follows:

BRECKENRIDGE LTD.
Income Statement
Year Ended November 30, 2008

Sales		$8,200,000
Cost of goods sold		
Beginning inventory	$1,900,000	
Purchases	4,400,000	
Goods available for sale	6,300,000	
Ending inventory	1,400,000	4,900,000
Gross profit		3,300,000
Operating expenses	$2,060,000	
Amortization expense	90,000	2,150,000
Income before income tax		1,150,000
Income tax expense		300,000
Net income		$ 850,000

Additional information:

1. Accounts receivable increased by $200,000 during the year.
2. Prepaid expenses increased by $150,000 during the year.
3. Accounts payable to suppliers decreased by $300,000 during the year.
4. Accrued expenses payable decreased by $100,000 during the year.
5. Income tax payable increased by $20,000 during the year.

Instructions

Prepare the operating activities section of the cash flow statement, using (a) the indirect method or (b) the direct method, as assigned by your instructor.

P17–4B The income statement of Hanalei International Inc. contained the following condensed information:

Prepare operating activities section—indirect and direct methods.

(SO 2a, 2b) AP

HANALEI INTERNATIONAL INC. Income Statement Year Ended December 31, 2008		
Revenue		$545,000
Operating expenses	$325,000	
Amortization expense	45,000	370,000
Income from operations		175,000
Other revenues and expenses		
Gain on sale of equipment	$ 25,000	
Interest expense	(10,000)	15,000
Income before income taxes		190,000
Income tax expense		47,500
Net income		$142,500

Hanalei's balance sheet contained the following comparative data at December 31:

	2008	2007
Accounts receivable	$50,000	$60,000
Prepaid insurance	8,000	5,000
Accounts payable	30,000	41,000
Interest payable	2,000	750
Income tax payable	4,000	3,500
Unearned revenue	10,000	14,000

Additional information: Accounts payable relate to operating expenses.

Instructions

Prepare the operating activities section of the cash flow statement, using (a) the indirect method or (b) the direct method, as assigned by your instructor.

P17–5B The following selected account balances relate to the property, plant, and equipment accounts of Trudeau Inc. at year end:

Calculate cash flows for property, plant, and equipment.

(SO 2) AP

	2008	2007
Accumulated amortization—buildings	$337,500	$300,000
Accumulated amortization—equipment	144,000	96,000
Amortization expense	101,500	85,500
Buildings	750,000	750,000
Equipment	293,000	240,000
Gain on sale of equipment	1,000	0
Land	100,000	60,000

Additional information:

1. Purchased $75,000 of equipment for $10,000 cash and a note payable for the remainder. Equipment was also sold during the year.
2. Purchased land for $40,000 cash.

Instructions

(a) Determine the amounts of any cash inflows or outflows related to the property, plant, and equipment accounts in 2008.
(b) Indicate where each of the cash inflows or outflows identified in (a) would be classified on the cash flow statement.

P17–6B The following selected account balances relate to the shareholder's equity accounts of Valerio Corp. at year end:

	2008	2007
Preferred shares: 2,250 shares in 2008; 2,750 in 2007	$225,000	$275,000
Common shares: 55,000 shares in 2008; 40,000 in 2007	550,000	410,000
Retained earnings	200,000	100,000
Cash dividends	25,000	10,000
Dividends payable	6,250	2,500

Additional information for 2008:

1. Converted 500 preferred shares to 5,000 common shares.
2. Common shares were issued for cash. The company did not reacquire any shares during the year.

Instructions

(a) What was the amount of net income reported by Valerio in 2008?
(b) Determine the amounts of any cash inflows or outflows related to the shareholders' equity and dividends payable accounts in 2008.
(c) Indicate where each of the cash inflows or outflows identified in (b) would be classified on the cash flow statement.

P17–7B Condensed financial data follow for E-Perform Ltd.:

E-PERFORM LTD.
Balance Sheet
December 31

	2008	2007
Assets		
Cash	$ 78,800	$ 48,400
Accounts receivable	95,800	33,000
Inventory	112,500	102,850
Prepaid expenses	18,400	6,000
Available-for-sale securities	94,000	94,000
Allowance to adjust available-for-sale securities to market value	19,000	0
Property, plant, and equipment	270,000	242,500
Accumulated amortization	(50,000)	(52,000)
Total assets	$638,500	$474,750
Liabilities and Shareholders' Equity		
Accounts payable	$102,000	$ 77,300
Accrued expenses payable	16,500	17,000
Notes payable (non-trade)	85,000	100,000
Common shares	182,000	175,000
Retained earnings	234,000	105,450
Accumulated other comprehensive income	19,000	0
Total liabilities and shareholders' equity	$638,500	$474,750

E-PERFORM LTD.
Income Statement
Year Ended December 31, 2008

Sales		$392,780
Cost of goods sold		135,460
Gross profit		257,320
Operating expenses	$12,410	
Amortization expense	46,500	58,910
Income from operations		198,410
Other expenses		
Interest expense	$4,730	
Loss on sale of equipment	7,500	12,230
Income before income tax		186,180
Income tax expense		45,000
Net income		$141,180

Additional information:

1. New equipment costing $85,000 was purchased for $35,000 cash and a $50,000 note payable.
2. Equipment with an original cost of $57,500 was sold for $1,500, resulting in a loss of $7,500.
3. Notes payable matured during the year and were repaid.

Instructions

Prepare a cash flow statement for the year, using (a) the indirect method or (b) the direct method, as assigned by your instructor.

P17–8B The financial statements of Wetaskiwin Ltd. follow:

Prepare cash flow statement—indirect and direct methods.

(SO 2a, 2b) AP

WETASKIWIN LTD.
Balance Sheet
December 31

	2008	2007
Assets		
Cash	$ 9,000	$ 10,000
Money-market instruments	14,000	23,000
Accounts receivable	28,000	14,000
Inventory	38,000	25,000
Property, plant, and equipment	73,000	78,000
Accumulated amortization	(30,000)	(24,000)
Total assets	$132,000	$126,000
Liabilities and Shareholders' Equity		
Accounts payable	$ 29,000	$ 43,000
Income tax payable	15,000	20,000
Notes payable	20,000	10,000
Common shares	25,000	25,000
Retained earnings	43,000	28,000
Total liabilities and shareholders' equity	$132,000	$126,000

WETASKIWIN LTD.
Income Statement
Year Ended December 31, 2008

Sales		$286,000
Cost of goods sold		194,000
Gross profit		92,000
Operating expenses		34,000
Income from operations		58,000
Other expenses		
Loss on sale of equipment	$2,000	
Interest expense	5,000	7,000
Income before income tax		51,000
Income tax expense		15,000
Net income		$ 36,000

Additional information:

1. The money-market instruments are highly liquid and should be considered cash equivalents for this statement.
2. Equipment was sold during the year for $8,000 cash. This equipment cost $15,000 originally and had a book value of $10,000 at the time of sale.
3. Equipment costing $10,000 was purchased in exchange for a $10,000 note payable.
4. Amortization expense is included in operating expenses.

Instructions

(a) Prepare a cash flow statement for the year, using (1) the indirect method, and (2) the direct method, as directed by your instructor.
(b) Explain why Wetaskiwin should combine its money-market instruments with cash when preparing the cash flow statement.

Calculate free cash flow and evaluate cash.
(SO 3) AN

P17–9B Selected information (in U.S. millions) for two close competitors, **Potash Corporation of Saskatchewan Inc.** and **Agrium Inc.**, follows for fiscal 2006:

	Potash	Agrium
Net income	$ 543	$ 283
Cash provided by operating activities	865	450
Cash used by investing activities	(555)	(212)
Cash used by financing activities	(675)	(363)
Cash and cash equivalents, end-of-period	94	300

Instructions

(a) Calculate the free cash flow for each company.
(b) Which company appears to be in the stronger financial position?
(c) By comparing the company's cash flows, can you tell which company is likely in a growth stage? Explain.

Continuing Cookie Chronicle

(*Note*: This is a continuation of the Cookie Chronicle from Chapters 1 through 16.)

Natalie has prepared the balance sheet and income statement of Cookie & Coffee Creations Ltd. for the first year of operations, but does not understand how to prepare the cash flow statement. The income statement and balance sheet follow. Recall that the company started operations on November 1, 2008, so all of the opening balances are nil (zero).

COOKIE & COFFEE CREATIONS LTD.
Income Statement
Year Ended October 31, 2009

Sales		$462,500
Cost of goods sold		231,250
Gross profit		231,250
Operating expenses		
Amortization expense	$ 9,850	
Salaries and wages expense	92,500	
Other operating expenses	35,987	138,337
Income from operations		92,913
Other expenses		
Interest expense		413
Income before income tax		92,500
Income tax expense		18,500
Net income		$ 74,000

COOKIE & COFFEE CREATIONS LTD.
Balance Sheet
October 31, 2009

Assets

Current assets			
Cash		$29,294	
Accounts receivable		3,250	
Inventory		17,897	
Prepaid expenses		6,300	$ 56,741
Property, plant, and equipment			
Furniture and fixtures	$12,500		
Accumulated amortization—furniture and fixtures	(1,250)	$11,250	
Computer equipment	$ 4,200		
Accumulated amortization—computer equipment	(600)	3,600	
Kitchen equipment	$80,000		
Accumulated amortization—kitchen equipment	(8,000)	72,000	86,850
Total assets			$143,591

Liabilities and Shareholders' Equity

Current liabilities			
Accounts payable		$ 5,848	
Income tax payable		18,500	
Dividends payable		625	
Salaries payable		2,250	
Interest payable		188	
Note payable—current portion		3,000	$ 30,411
Long-term liabilities			
Note payable—long-term portion			4,500
Total liabilities			34,911
Shareholders' equity			
Contributed capital			
Preferred shares, 2,500 shares issued	$12,500		
Common shares, 23,180 shares issued	23,180		
Contributed capital—reacquisition of shares	250	$35,930	
Retained earnings		72,750	108,680
Total liabilities and shareholders' equity			$143,591

Additional information:

1. Recall from Chapter 15 that kitchen equipment (a commercial oven) was bought for $14,000 on November 1, 2008, and a $9,000 note payable was signed to help pay for it. The terms provide for

semi-annual fixed principal payments of $1,500 on May 1 and November 1 of each year, plus interest of 5%. All other furniture, fixtures, and equipment were purchased during the year for cash.

2. Recall from Chapter 14 that 23,930 common shares were originally issued for $23,930, of which 750 shares were repurchased from the lawyer for $500.
3. Recall from Chapter 14 that a semi-annual dividend was declared to the preferred shareholders on April 30 and was paid on June 1. The second semi-annual dividend was declared to the preferred shareholders on October 31, to be paid on December 1.
4. Prepaid expenses relate only to operating expenses.

Instructions

Prepare a cash flow statement, using (a) the indirect method or (b) the direct method, as assigned by your instructor.

BROADENING YOUR PERSPECTIVE

Financial Reporting and Analysis

Financial Reporting Problem

BYP17–1   Refer to the consolidated financial statements for **The Forzani Group Ltd.**, which are reproduced in Appendix A at the end of the textbook.

Instructions

(a) How does Forzani define "cash" for the purpose of its cash flow statement?
(b) What was the amount of the increase or decrease in cash for the year ended January 29, 2006?
(c) What were the significant investing activities reported in Forzani's 2006 cash flow statement?
(d) What were the significant financing activities reported in Forzani's 2006 cash flow statement?
(e) Did Forzani report any significant noncash investing and financing activities in 2006?

Interpreting Financial Statements

BYP17–2   Andrés Wines Ltd.'s 2006 balance sheet reported current assets of $92.3 million and current liabilities of $65.6 million, including bank indebtedness (negative cash balance) of $37.3 million. Andrés Wines' net income declined in 2006, from $8.5 million in 2005 to $6.1 million in 2006. Andrés Wines reported on its cash flow statement that it generated $19.0 million of cash from operating activities, used $45.5 million of cash in investing activities, and generated $26.5 million of cash in financing activities in 2006.

Instructions

(a) Do you believe that Andrés Wines' creditors should be worried about its lack of cash? Explain why or why not.
(b) How is it possible for Andrés Wines to generate $19.0 million of cash from its operating activities but have only $6.1 million of net income?
(c) What is the likely reason that Andrés Wines generated $19.0 million of cash from operating activities but has no cash?
(d) Calculate Andrés Wines' free cash flow for 2006. Explain what this free cash flow means.

Critical Thinking

Collaborative Learning Activity

Note to instructor: Additional instructions and material for this group activity can be found on the Instructor Resource Site.

BYP17–3 In this group activity, you will prepare cash flow statements using the:

1. Indirect method
2. Direct method

Instructions

(a) Your instructor will divide the class into groups. Each group will split into two smaller groups. Using information provided by your instructor, one of these groups will prepare the cash flow statement using the indirect method; the other will prepare it using the direct method. Record the results of your small group discussion.
(b) In your larger group, compare the subtotals of the two cash flow statements. If any subtotals are different, explain to the group how the statements were prepared and correct any error(s).
(c) Based on the cash flow statements, answer the following questions about the company:
  1. Will the company be able to meet its current obligations in the next 12 months?
  2. Where did the major portion of cash come from during the year?
  3. Where was the major portion of cash spent during the year?

Study Aids:
Working in Groups

Communication Activity

BYP17–4 Many investors today prefer the cash flow statement over the income statement. They believe that cash-based data are a better measure of performance than accrual-based data because it is harder to manage income using cash-based data.

Instructions

Write a brief memo explaining whether or not it is harder for management to manage income using cash-based data than accrual-based data. In your answer, say which financial statement, in your opinion, is the best measure of a company's performance, and explain why.

Study Aids:
Writing Handbook

Ethics Case

BYP17–5 Paradis Corporation is a wholesaler of automotive parts. It has 10 shareholders who have been paid a total of $1 million in cash dividends for eight years in a row. In order for this dividend to be declared, the board of directors' policy requires that net cash provided by operating activities, as reported in Paradis's cash flow statement, must be more than $1 million. President and CEO Phil Monat's job is secure as long as he produces annual operating cash flows to support the usual dividend.

 At the end of the current year, controller Rick Rodgers presents president Monat with some disappointing news. The net cash provided by operating activities is only $970,000. The president says to Rick, "We must get that amount above $1 million. Isn't there some way to increase operating cash flow by another $30,000?" Rick answers, "These figures were prepared by my assistant. I'll go back to my office and see what I can do." The president replies, "I know you won't let me down, Rick."

 After examining the cash flow statement carefully, Rick concludes that he can get the operating cash flows above $1 million by reclassifying a two-year, $60,000 non-trade note payable that is listed in the financing activities section as "Proceeds from bank loan—$60,000." He will report the note as a note arising from trade transactions instead in the operating activities section. He returns to the president, saying, "You can tell the board to declare its usual dividend. Our net cash

Study Aids:
Ethics in Accounting

flow provided by operating activities is $1.03 million." "Good man, Rick! I knew I could count on you," exults the president.

Instructions

(a) Who are the stakeholders in this situation?
(b) Was there anything unethical about the president's actions? Was there anything unethical about the controller's actions?
(c) Are the board members or anyone else likely to discover the misclassification?

ANSWERS TO CHAPTER QUESTIONS

Answers to Accounting in Action Insight Questions

Business Insight, p. 865

Q: Why are there differences between net income and cash provided by operating activities?
A: The differences are because of differences in the timing of the reporting of revenues and expenses under accrual accounting compared to cash accounting. Under accrual accounting, companies report revenues when they are earned, even if cash has not been received, and they report expenses when they are incurred, even if cash has not been paid.

Across the Organization Insight, p. 879

Q: You are the sales manager of a company that sells inventory to The Bay and are looking at its cash flow statement, among other financial information, to determine whether to give additional credit. Which method of preparing the operating activities section of the cash flow statement—indirect or direct—would you find more helpful in making your decision?
A: The direct method is easier to understand. It also discloses more information about where cash came from and where it went to than does the indirect method. The direct method would be a more useful format for you as a sales manager to assess The Bay's ability to generate future cash flows from operating activities and to understand the nature of its operations.

Business Insight, p. 891

Q: What is the likely reason that free cash flow is so important to Amazon.com?
A: Free cash flow results from cash generated by operating activities (through increases in sales and/or decreases in operating costs), and from effective management of capital expenditures to maintain productivity. Free cash flow is important to Amazon.com because it measures the discretionary cash flow that is available for it to expand operations, repay debt, pay dividends, or use for other purposes.

Answer to Forzani Review It Question 4, p. 861

Forzani reports the following (in thousands): (a) $45,858 cash provided by operating activities, (b) $65,499 cash used by investing activities, and (c) $12,889 cash provided by financing activities.

Answers to Self-Study Questions

1. a   2. c   3. c   4. c   5. b   6. c   7. b   8. b   9. a   10. c

Remember to go back to the Navigator Box at the beginning of the chapter to check off your completed work.

concepts for review >>

Before studying this chapter, you should understand or, if necessary, review:

a. The various types of users of financial statement information. (Ch. 1, pp. 4–5)

b. The content and classification of a balance sheet. (Ch. 4, pp. 175–180 and Ch. 16, pp. 828–829)

c. The content and classification of an income statement. (Ch. 5, pp. 239–243)

d. The ratios introduced in previous chapters: working capital, current ratio (Ch. 4, p. 182); gross profit margin, profit margin (Ch. 5, pp. 244–245); inventory turnover, days sales in inventory (Ch. 6, pp. 304–305); receivables turnover, collection period (Ch. 8, p. 427); asset turnover, return on assets (Ch. 9, pp. 488–489); return on equity (Ch. 13, p. 684); earnings per share, price-earnings, payout (Ch. 14, pp. 728–730); debt to total assets, interest coverage (Ch. 15, p. 780); and free cash flow (Ch. 17, pp. 890–891).

Presenting the Whole Picture

TORONTO, Ont.—In the high-stakes world of investments, it's not "who you know" that counts, but "what you know." Strong communication lets investors, creditors, and others know if a company is doing well, what its past performance has been, and what its future prospects are. The annual report plays a big part in keeping a company's stakeholders informed.

While most annual reports use the same basic format, they can be very different in their presentation, content, and most importantly, the quality of the information they give. That's where the annual Corporate Reporting Awards play an important role. Jointly sponsored in 2005 by the Canadian Institute of Chartered Accountants (CICA), the Toronto Stock Exchange, PricewaterhouseCoopers LLP, and Fasken Martineau DuMoulin LLP, the Awards recognize the best reporting models in Canada and, by doing this, aim to strengthen corporate reporting in the country.

"The expectation of users and complexity of financial reporting has certainly increased since the award program started [more than 50 years ago]," said CICA's president and CEO, David Smith. "The winning companies have raised the bar in terms of financial reporting excellence, with disclosure that goes beyond financial results."

Canadian Tire Corporation, Limited has won the overall award of excellence in past years. Although it didn't win in 2005, it did receive an honourable mention for excellence in financial reporting in each of the four judging categories—financial reporting, corporate governance disclosure, electronic disclosure, and sustainable development reporting.

Most annual reports include a message from the chairman and CEO, the year's financial statements, a management discussion and analysis (MD&A), and information

Canadian Institute of Chartered Accountants: www.cica.ca

about the company directors. The judges described Canadian Tire's annual report as "detailed and informative." They went on to say the "letter to shareholders includes an introduction to the new strategy with an outline of initiatives and strengths." In addition, they noted the company's MD&A was "very comprehensive and there is no ambiguity in the financial statements."

The judges also consider things like a statement of objectives, a discussion of the company's performance relative to its objectives, some comparative industry information, information on corporate governance, and layout and design. They said Canadian Tire has "excellent detail on key performance indicators and actual vs. target reporting" and that the "performance scorecard by business line is very effective." They also stated that the "What Sets Us Apart" and "Where We're Headed" sections were helpful, as was the use of photos in the annual report.

Communication, after all, is what it's all about. With full disclosure being more important now than ever before, communicating everything—both good news and bad—is the only way for investors to make well-informed decisions.

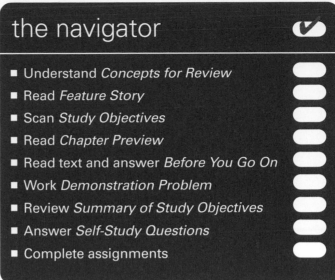

the navigator

- Understand *Concepts for Review*
- Read *Feature Story*
- Scan *Study Objectives*
- Read *Chapter Preview*
- Read text and answer *Before You Go On*
- Work *Demonstration Problem*
- Review *Summary of Study Objectives*
- Answer *Self-Study Questions*
- Complete assignments

chapter 18
Financial Statement Analysis

study objectives >>

After studying this chapter, you should be able to:

1. Explain and apply horizontal analysis.
2. Explain and apply vertical analysis.
3. Identify and use ratios to analyze a company's liquidity, profitability, and solvency.
4. Recognize and illustrate the limitations of financial statement analysis.

the navigator

An important lesson can be learned from Canadian Tire's annual report described in our feature story. Effective communication is the key to understanding. The purpose of this chapter is to take you through a comprehensive review of financial statements—a company's main way of communicating its results. We review all of the decision tools presented in this text and use them to analyze Canadian Tire—Canada's most shopped-at general merchandise retailer.

In addition, we also show how difficult it can be to develop high-quality financial numbers because of the complexities of financial reporting. In particular, we will examine the impact of certain irregular items on financial results and analysis.

The chapter is organized as follows:

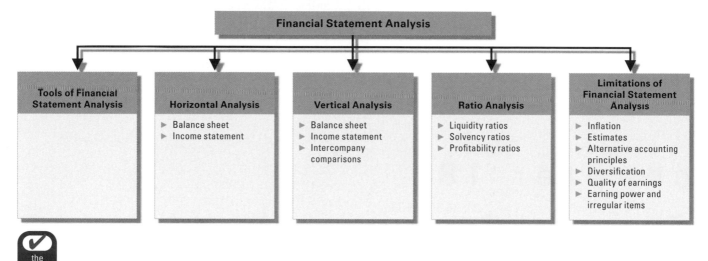

Tools of Financial Statement Analysis

In analyzing financial statements, investors and creditors are interested in making comparisons from period to period. Every item reported in a financial statement has significance. When Canadian Tire reports accounts receivable of $652.8 million on its balance sheet dated December 31, 2005, we know that the company had that amount of accounts receivable on that date. However, we do not know if the amount is an increase or decrease compared to past years, or if Canadian Tire is collecting its receivables on a timely basis. To get this information, the amount of receivables must be compared to other financial statement data.

Comparisons can be made on several different bases. The following three are illustrated in this chapter:

1. **Intracompany basis.** This basis compares an item or financial relationship inside a company in the current year with one or more prior years. Intracompany comparisons are useful for finding changes in financial relationships and discovering significant trends. For example, Canadian Tire can compare its accounts receivable balance at the end of the current year with last year's balance to find the amount of the increase or decrease. Likewise, Canadian Tire can compare the percentage of accounts receivable to current assets at the end of the current year with the percentage in one or more prior years.
2. **Intercompany basis.** This basis compares an item or financial relationship of one company with the same item or relationship in one or more competing companies. Intercompany comparisons are useful for understanding a company's competitive position. For example, Canadian Tire's total sales for the year can be compared with the total sales of one of its major competitors.

Who are its competitors? Don't be fooled by the name: Canadian Tire sells much more than tires. It sells home, car, sports, and leisure products, in addition to work clothes and casual attire through its subsidiary, Mark's Work Wearhouse. Consequently, it competes with other stores in the retail industry, such as Sears and Wal-Mart.

3. **Industry averages.** This basis compares an item or financial relationship of a company with industry averages. These averages are determined and published by financial ratings organizations, such as Bloomberg, Dun & Bradstreet, *The Financial Post*, and Statistics Canada. Comparisons with industry averages give information about how well a company is performing within its industry. For example, Canadian Tire's net income can be compared with the average net income of all companies in the retail industry.

To analyze a company, we usually start with its financial statements. However, it is important to also review other financial and non-financial information in the company's annual report. Other financial information includes a management discussion and analysis of the company's financial position and a summary of key financial figures and ratios from prior years. As mentioned in our feature story, Canadian Tire's MD&A was described as "very comprehensive."

Non-financial information includes a discussion of the company's mission, goals, and objectives, and its market position, people, and products. Some analysts argue that non-financial, or qualitative, information is even more important than financial, or quantitative, information in determining how successful a company is. Financial information can only evaluate past performance. Non-financial information may predict future performance better. For example, the section on "Where We're Headed" in Canadian Tire's annual report was considered to be very useful by the judges for the corporate reporting awards.

We must also consider the economic circumstances that a company is operating in. Economic measures such as the rates of interest, inflation, unemployment, and changes in supply and demand can have a significant impact on a company's performance. For example, suppose a company's performance has been declining and it is operating in an industry that is being affected by an economic recession. An analyst could not reach a proper conclusion about the reasons for the company's weaker results if the analyst does not know about the recession.

While non-financial information is important, the focus of this chapter is on financial information and the various tools that are used to evaluate what the financial data mean. Three commonly used tools follow:

1. **Horizontal analysis.** This tool evaluates a series of financial statement data over a period of time.
2. **Vertical analysis.** This tool evaluates financial statement data by expressing each item in a financial statement as a percentage of a base amount that covers the same period of time as the item.
3. **Ratio analysis.** This tool expresses the relationship among selected items of financial statement data.

Horizontal analysis is used mainly in intracompany comparisons. Vertical analysis is used in both intracompany and intercompany comparisons. Ratio analysis is used in all three types of comparison. In the following sections, we will explain and illustrate each of the three types of analysis.

Horizontal Analysis

Horizontal analysis, also called trend analysis, is a technique for comparing a series of financial statement data over a period of time. Two features in annual reports make this type of comparison easier. First, the data in each of the financial statements found in the annual report are presented in comparison to data for one or more previous years. Second, a summary of selected financial data is presented in the annual report for a series of five to ten years or more.

The purpose of horizontal analysis is to determine the increase or decrease that has taken place. This change may be expressed as either an amount or a percentage. For example, operating revenue figures and percentages for Canadian Tire are as follows:

CANADIAN TIRE CORPORATION, LIMITED Year Ended December 31 (in millions)					
	2005	2004	2003	2002	2001
Operating revenue	$7,774.6	$7,153.6	$6,552.8	$5,944.5	$5,374.7
% of base-period amount	144.7%	133.1%	121.9%	110.6%	100.0%
% change for period	8.7%	9.2%	10.2%	10.6%	—

Helpful hint Percentage of base period amount = Analysis period amount ÷ Base period amount

If we assume that 2001 is the base year, we can express operating revenue as a percentage of the base-year amount. This is done by dividing the amount for the specific year we are analyzing by the base-year amount. For example, we can determine that operating revenue in 2005 is 144.7 percent of the operating revenue in 2001 by dividing $7,774.6 million by $5,374.7 million. In other words, operating revenue in 2005 is 44.7 percent greater than sales five years earlier, in 2001. From this horizontal analysis, shown in the second row of the above table, we can easily see Canadian Tire's revenue trend. Revenue has increased each year since 2001.

Helpful hint Percentage change for period = Dollar amount of change since base period ÷ Base period amount

We can also use horizontal analysis to measure the percentage change for any one specific period. This is done by dividing the dollar amount of the change between the specific year under analysis and the base year by the base-year amount. For example, if we set the previous year, 2004 in this case, as our base year, we can determine that operating revenue increased by $621 million ($7,774.6 million – $7,153.6 million) between 2004 and 2005. This increase can then be expressed as a percentage, 8.7 percent, by dividing the amount of the change between the two years, $621 million, by the amount in the base year, $7,153.6 million. That is, in 2005, operating revenue increased by 8.7 percent compared to 2004. The percentage change in operating revenues for each period is presented in the last row of the above table.

Balance Sheet

To further illustrate horizontal analysis, we will use the financial statements of Hometown Tires and More Inc. Hometown Tires and More is a small, local retail store that directly competes with Canadian Tire. Its two-year condensed balance sheet, which shows dollar and percentage changes, is presented in Illustration 18-1.

Illustration 18-1 ◄

Horizontal analysis of balance sheet

HOMETOWN TIRES AND MORE INC.
Balance Sheet
December 31

	2005	2004	Increase (Decrease) Amount	Percentage
Assets				
Current assets				
Cash	$ 50,000	$ 55,000	$ (5,000)	(9.1%)
Available-for-sale securities	20,000	35,000	(15,000)	(42.9%)
Accounts receivable	72,500	50,000	22,500	45.0%
Inventory	372,500	325,000	47,500	14.6%
Prepaid expenses	30,000	20,000	10,000	50.0%
Total current assets	545,000	485,000	60,000	12.4%
Property, plant, and equipment	400,000	450,000	(50,000)	(11.1%)
Intangible assets	55,000	65,000	(10,000)	(15.4%)
Total assets	$1,000,000	$1,000,000	$ 0	0.0%
Liabilities and Shareholders' Equity				
Liabilities				
Current liabilities	$ 337,700	$ 313,500	$ 24,200	7.7%
Long-term liabilities	400,000	475,000	(75,000)	(15.8%)
Total liabilities	737,700	788,500	(50,800)	(6.4%)
Shareholders' equity				
Share capital	90,000	90,000	0	0.0%
Retained earnings	172,300	121,500	50,800	41.8%
Total shareholders' equity	262,300	211,500	50,800	24.0%
Total liabilities and shareholders' equity	$1,000,000	$1,000,000	$ 0	0.0%

Note that, in a horizontal analysis, while the amount column of the increase or decrease is additive (e.g., the change in total liabilities totals to a net decrease of $50,800), the percentage column is not additive (6.4 percent is not a total).

The horizontal analysis of Hometown Tires and More's comparative balance sheet shows that several changes have occurred between 2004 and 2005. In the current assets section, accounts receivable increased by $22,500, or 45 percent, while available-for-sale securities decreased by $15,000, or 42.9 percent. Note that there were no changes in market value for the available-for-sale securities, so all of this decrease relates to sales of short-term investments. It looks like Hometown Tires and More may be financing its increase in receivables by selling its investments. We will look at the income statement in the next section to determine whether sales increased by the same proportion as receivables. If not, this may indicate that the receivables are slow-moving.

Inventory increased by the largest dollar amount, $47,500, but not the largest percentage, 14.6 percent. Inventory may have changed because of increased sales—we will investigate this further when we analyze the income statement. Prepaid expenses also increased by 50 percent in 2005. One has to be careful in interpreting percentage changes like this. Because it is a proportionately large change ($10,000) on a small amount ($20,000), the percentage change is not as meaningful as it first appears. Despite these changes, it is interesting to note that total assets are unchanged from 2004 to 2005.

Current liabilities increased by 7.7 percent. The increase in current liabilities may be due to the increase in inventory. Changes in current assets and current liabilities usually move in the same direction—that is, normally both will increase or both will decrease. In this case, both have risen, although current assets have increased more than current liabilities.

Long-term liabilities decreased by $75,000, or 15.8 percent, in 2005. Hometown Tires and More appears to be using some of its profits to repay its debt. Retained earnings increased by

41.8 percent in the shareholders' equity section of the balance sheet. This suggests that Hometown Tires and More is financing its business by retaining income, rather than by adding to its long-term debt.

Income Statement

Illustration 18-2 presents a horizontal analysis of Hometown Tires and More's condensed income statement for the years 2004 and 2005.

Illustration 18-2 ▶

Horizontal analysis of income statement

	2005	2004	Increase (Decrease) Amount	Increase (Decrease) Percentage
HOMETOWN TIRES AND MORE INC. Income Statement Year Ended December 31				
Sales	$2,095,000	$1,960,000	$135,000	6.9%
Sales returns and allowances	90,000	123,000	(25,000)	(20.3%)
Net sales	1,997,000	1,837,000	160,000	8.7%
Cost of goods sold	1,381,000	1,240,000	141,000	11.4%
Gross profit	616,000	597,000	19,000	3.2%
Operating expenses	457,000	440,000	17,000	3.9%
Income from operations	159,000	157,000	2,000	1.3%
Other revenues and expenses				
Investment revenue	9,000	11,000	(2,000)	(18.2%)
Interest expense	36,000	40,500	(4,500)	(11.1%)
Income before income tax	132,000	127,500	4,500	3.5%
Income tax expense	50,000	52,500	(2,500)	(4.8%)
Net income	$ 82,000	$ 75,000	$ 7,000	9.3%

Horizontal analysis of the income statement shows the following changes: Net sales increased by 8.7 percent, while the cost of goods sold increased by 11.4 percent.

Sales do not appear to have increased at the same rate as receivables. Recall from Illustration 18-1 that receivables increased by 45 percent. Here we learn that net sales increased by only 8.7 percent. Later in the chapter, we will look at the receivables turnover ratio to determine whether receivables are being collected more slowly or not. However, we must be cautious in over-interpreting this increase. This type of business relies a lot on cash sales, not credit sales. Therefore, a relatively small change in receivables can produce a large percentage change.

Recall also that in Illustration 18-1 we observed that inventory increased by 14.6 percent. The cost of goods sold reported on the income statement also appears to have increased, by 11.4 percent, even though net sales only increased by 8.7 percent. We will look at the inventory turnover ratio later in the chapter to determine if these increases are reasonable.

To continue with our horizontal analysis of the income statement, we note that gross profit increased by 3.2 percent. Operating expenses outpaced this percentage increase at 3.9 percent. Normally, management tries to control operating expenses wherever possible, so we would hope to see operating expenses change at the same rate, or a lower rate, than gross profit. Other revenues and expenses declined. Overall, gross profit and net income both increased, so Hometown Tires and More's profit trend looks good.

A horizontal analysis of changes from period to period is pretty straightforward and is quite useful. But complications can occur in making the calculations. If an item has no value in a base year and a value in the next year, no percentage change can be calculated. Or, if an item has a small value in a base year and a large value in the next year, the percentage change may not be meaningful. In addition, if a negative amount appears in the base year and there is a positive amount the following year, or vice versa, no percentage change can be calculated.

We have not included a horizontal analysis of Hometown Tires and More's statement of retained earnings or cash flow statement and Hometown Tires and More does not have a statement of comprehensive income. An analysis of these three statements is not as useful as the horizontal analyses performed on the balance sheet and income statement. The amounts presented in the statement of retained earnings, cash flow statement, and statement of comprehensive income give details about the changes between two periods. The value of these statements comes from the analysis of the changes during the year, and not from percentage comparisons of these changes against a base amount.

BEFORE YOU GO ON . . .

▶Review It

1. What are the differences between intracompany, intercompany, and industry comparisons?
2. What are the three different tools that are used to compare financial information?
3. How is a percentage of a base-period amount calculated? How is a percentage change for a period calculated?

▶Do It

Selected, condensed information (in thousands) from Bonora Ltd.'s income statements for four years ended June 30 follows:

	2008	2007	2006	2005
Revenues	$5,035	$6,294	$9,468	$8,646
Gross profit	936	1,077	2,146	1,900
Net income	251	110	546	428

(a) Calculate the percentage of the base-year amount for each year, assuming that 2005 is the base year.
(b) Calculate the percentage change between the following years: 2005 and 2006; 2006 and 2007; and 2007 and 2008.

Action Plan

- Set the base-year (2005) dollar amounts at 100. Express each later year's amount as a percentage of the base period.
- Find the percentage of the base-year amount by dividing the dollar amount for the year under analysis by the base-year amount.
- Find the percentage change between two periods by dividing the dollar amount of the change between the prior year and the current year by the prior-year amount.

Solution

(a) Percentage of the base-year amount

	2008	2007	2006	2005
Revenues	58.2%	72.8%	109.5%	100%
Gross profit	49.3%	56.7%	112.9%	100%
Net income	58.6%	25.7%	127.6%	100%

(b) Percentage change for each year

	2008	2007	2006
Revenues	(20.0)%	(33.5)%	9.5%
Gross profit	(13.1)%	(49.8)%	12.9%
Net income	128.2%	(80.0)%	27.6%

Related exercise material: BE18–1, BE18–2, and E18–1.

the navigator

Vertical Analysis

study objective 2

Explain and apply vertical analysis.

Vertical analysis, also called common size analysis, is a technique for evaluating financial statement data that expresses each item in a financial statement as a percentage of a base amount. While horizontal analysis compares data across more than one year, vertical analysis compares data within the same year.

Using vertical analysis, we might say that current assets are 54.5 percent of total assets (total assets being the base amount) on the balance sheet. Or, on the income statement, we might say that operating expenses are 22.9 percent of net sales (net sales being the base amount).

Balance Sheet

Illustration 18-3 shows a vertical analysis of Hometown Tires and More's comparative balance sheet. The base amount for the asset items is *total assets*. The base amount for the liability and shareholders' equity items is *total liabilities and shareholders' equity*, which equals total assets.

Illustration 18-3 ▶

Vertical analysis of balance sheet

Helpful hint

% = $\frac{\text{Each item on balance sheet}}{\text{Total assets}}$

HOMETOWN TIRES AND MORE INC.
Balance Sheet
December 31

	2005 Amount	2005 Percentage	2004 Amount	2004 Percentage
Assets				
Current assets				
Cash	$ 50,000	5.0%	$ 55,000	5.5%
Available-for-sale securities	20,000	2.0%	35,000	3.5%
Accounts receivable	72,500	7.2%	50,000	5.0%
Inventory	372,500	37.3%	325,000	32.5%
Prepaid expenses	30,000	3.0%	20,000	2.0%
Total current assets	545,000	54.5%	485,000	48.5%
Property, plant, and equipment	400,000	40.0%	450,000	45.0%
Intangible assets	55,000	5.5%	65,000	6.5%
Total assets	$1,000,000	100.0%	$1,000,000	100.0%
Liabilities and Shareholders' Equity				
Liabilities				
Current liabilities	$ 337,700	33.8%	$ 313,500	31.4%
Long-term liabilities	400,000	40.0%	475,000	47.5%
Total liabilities	737,700	73.8%	788,500	78.9%
Shareholders' equity				
Share capital	90,000	9.0%	90,000	9.0%
Retained earnings	172,300	17.2%	121,500	12.1%
Total shareholders' equity	262,300	26.2%	211,500	21.1%
Total liabilities and shareholders' equity	$1,000,000	100.0%	$1,000,000	100.0%

Vertical analysis shows the size of each item in the balance sheet compared to a base amount. It can also show the percentage change in the individual asset, liability, and shareholders' equity items. For example, we can see that current assets increased from 48.5 percent of total assets in 2004 to 54.5 percent of total assets in 2005. We can also see that the biggest change was in inventory, which increased from 32.5 percent of total assets in 2004 to 37.3 percent in 2005. This is contrary to what we first observed in Illustration 18-1, where it appeared that prepaid expenses had the greatest percentage increase. In Illustration 18-3, prepaid expenses increased only by one percentage point of total assets, from 2 percent in 2004 to 3 percent in 2005. You will recall our earlier words of caution about interpreting such a large percentage change as what was presented for prepaid expenses in Illustration 18-1.

Property, plant, and equipment and intangible assets both decreased as relative percentages of total assets—45 percent in 2004 to 40 percent in 2005 for property, plant, and equipment and 6.5 percent in 2004 to 5.5 percent in 2005 for intangible assets. This decrease is likely due to increased accumulated amortization.

Long-term liabilities decreased from 47.5 percent to 40 percent, while retained earnings increased from 12.1 percent to 17.2 percent of total liabilities and shareholders' equity between 2004 and 2005. These results reinforce the earlier observation that Hometown Tires and More is financing its growth by retaining earnings, rather than by issuing additional debt.

Income Statement

A vertical analysis of Hometown Tires and More's income statement is shown in Illustration 18-4. The base amount is usually net sales on the income statement.

HOMETOWN TIRES AND MORE INC.
Income Statement
Year Ended December 31

	2005 Amount	2005 Percentage	2004 Amount	2004 Percentage
Sales	$2,095,000	104.9%	$1,960,000	106.7%
Sales returns and allowances	98,000	4.9%	123,000	6.7%
Net sales	1,997,000	100.0%	1,837,000	100.0%
Cost of goods sold	1,381,000	69.2%	1,240,000	67.5%
Gross profit	616,000	30.8%	597,000	32.5%
Operating expenses	457,000	22.9%	440,000	24.0%
Income from operations	159,000	7.9%	157,000	8.5%
Other revenues and expenses				
Investment revenue	9,000	0.5%	11,000	0.6%
Interest expense	36,000	1.8%	40,500	2.2%
Income before income tax	132,000	6.6%	127,500	6.9%
Income tax expense	50,000	2.5%	52,500	2.9%
Net income	$ 82,000	4.1%	$ 75,000	4.0%

Illustration 18-4 ◄

Vertical analysis of income statement

Helpful hint
$$\% = \frac{\text{Each item on income statement}}{\text{Net sales}}$$

We can see that the cost of goods sold as a percentage of net sales increased by 1.7 percent (from 67.5 percent to 69.2 percent). Operating expenses declined as a percentage of net sales by 1.1 percent (from 24 percent to 22.9 percent). As a result, income from operations did not change substantially between 2004 and 2005: it declined by 0.6 percent (from 8.5 percent to 7.9 percent). Net income remained relatively unchanged as a percentage of net sales from 2004 to 2005: it increased by 0.1 percent. Although we saw Hometown Tires and More's net income increase by 9.3 percent in Illustration 18-2, its profitability is unchanged in comparison to net sales.

A vertical analysis can also be performed on the statement of retained earnings, cash flow statement, and statement of comprehensive income. However, this is rarely done, because each statement already gives details that show changes between two periods.

Intercompany Comparisons

Another benefit of vertical analysis is that it makes it possible to compare companies of different sizes. For example, Hometown Tires and More's main competitor is Canadian Tire. Using vertical analysis, the condensed balance sheet (or the income statement) of the small local retail company Hometown Tires and More can be more meaningfully compared with the balance sheet (or income statement) of the giant retailer Canadian Tire, as shown in Illustration 18-5.

Illustration 18-5 ▶

Intercompany balance sheet comparison—vertical analysis

BALANCE SHEETS
December 31, 2005
(in thousands)

	Hometown Tires and More		Canadian Tire	
	Amount	Percentage	Amount	Percentage
Assets				
Current assets	$ 545	54.5%	$2,981,000	50.0%
Long-term receivables and other assets	0	0.0%	132,100	2.2%
Property, plant, and equipment	400	40.0%	2,743,900	46.1%
Intangible assets	55	5.5%	98,600	1.7%
Total assets	$1,000	100.0%	$5,955,600	100.0%
Liabilities and Shareholders' Equity				
Liabilities				
Current liabilities	$ 338	33.8%	$1,821,000	30.6%
Long-term liabilities	400	40.0%	1,623,500	27.2%
Total liabilities	738	73.8%	3,444,500	57.8%
Shareholders' equity				
Share capital	90	9.0%	698,500	11.7%
Retained earnings	172	17.2%	1,812,600	30.5%
Total shareholders' equity	262	26.2%	2,511,100	42.2%
Total liabilities and shareholders' equity	$1,000	100.0%	$5,955,600	100.0%

Canadian Tire's total assets are nearly 6,000 times greater than the total assets of the much smaller Hometown Tires and More. Vertical analysis eliminates this difference in size. For example, although Hometown Tires and More has fewer dollars of property, plant, and equipment compared to Canadian Tire ($400,000 compared to $2,743.9 million), using percentages, the proportion of property, plant, and equipment for each company is relatively similar (40 percent compared to 46.1 percent).

Although Hometown Tires and More has fewer dollars of debt compared to Canadian Tire ($738,000 compared to $3,444.5 million), it has a higher debt percentage than does Canadian Tire (73.8 percent compared to 57.8 percent). This is not surprising given that Hometown Tires and More does not have the same access to equity financing as does Canadian Tire. Hometown Tires and More is a privately owned business, with limited share distribution. Accordingly, Hometown Tires and More has a lower equity base than Canadian Tire (26.2 percent compared to 42.2 percent).

As you can see from this limited example, there are many things that can be learned by looking at vertically analyzed financial statements even when comparing companies of vastly different sizes.

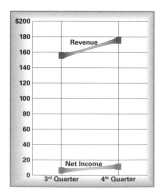

ACCOUNTING IN ACTION ▶ Business Insight

Many companies report financial information using percentages. For example, Groupe Laperrière & Verreault Inc., based in Montreal, reported the following in a recent press release announcing its fourth quarter results: Net income rose 75 percent to $11.4 million from $6.5 million. Revenue grew 12.7 percent to $175.3 million from $155.6 million. Growth was driven primarily by an 80.9-percent increase in revenue generated by the company's water treatment group, as a result of acquisitions.

Source: "Laperrière Sees Profit Jump 75% in Quarter," *The Globe and Mail*, May 30, 2006, B5.

? Are the percentage changes for Laperrière based on horizontal or vertical analysis?

BEFORE YOU GO ON . . .

▶Review It

1. What is vertical analysis?
2. How is vertical analysis different from horizontal analysis?
3. What base amount is used to calculate the percentage size of an amount reported in a vertically analyzed balance sheet? Income statement?

▶Do It

Summary financial information for Boyko Corporation at May 31 is as follows:

	2008	2007
Current assets	$234,000	$180,000
Property, plant, and equipment	756,000	420,000
Total assets	$990,000	$600,000

Calculate the percentage sizes of each category, for each year, using vertical analysis.

Action Plan

- The base amount is total assets in a balance sheet.
- Find the relative percentage by dividing the specific asset amount by the base amount for each year.

Solution

	2008		2007	
	Amount	Percentage	Amount	Percentage
Current assets	$234,000	23.6%	$180,000	30.0%
Property, plant, and equipment	756,000	76.4%	420,000	70.0%
Total assets	$990,000	100.0%	$600,000	100.0%

Related exercise material: BE18–3, BE18–4, BE18–5, E18–2, E18–3, and E18–4.

Ratio Analysis

Ratio analysis expresses the relationships between selected financial statement items. Ratios are generally classified into three types:

1. **Liquidity ratios.** These measure the short-term ability of the company to pay its maturing obligations and to meet unexpected needs for cash.
2. **Solvency ratios.** These measure the ability of the company to survive over a long period of time.
3. **Profitability ratios.** These measure the operating success of a company for a specific period of time.

In earlier chapters, we presented liquidity, solvency, and profitability ratios for evaluating the financial condition of a company. In this section, we give a summary list of these ratios. Chapter and page numbers of the earlier discussions are included so you can review any individual ratio.

In addition, in the appendix to this chapter there is an example of a comprehensive financial analysis using these ratios. This analysis uses three bases for comparisons: (1) intracompany, comparing two years of data for Canadian Tire, (2) intercompany, comparing Canadian Tire to Hometown Tires and More, and (3) industry, comparing both companies to industry averages for the retail industry.

Liquidity Ratios

Liquidity ratios measure the short-term ability of a company to pay its maturing obligations and to meet unexpected needs for cash. Short-term creditors, such as bankers and suppliers, are particularly interested in assessing liquidity. Illustration 18-6 lists the liquidity ratios we have seen in this textbook.

Illustration 18-6 ▶

Summary of liquidity ratios

Ratio	Formula	Purpose	Discussion
Working capital	Current assets − Current liabilities	Measures short-term debt-paying ability.	Ch. 4, p. 182
Current ratio	$\dfrac{\text{Current assets}}{\text{Current liabilities}}$	Measures short-term debt-paying ability.	Ch. 4, p. 182
Inventory turnover	$\dfrac{\text{Cost of goods sold}}{\text{Average inventory}}$	Measures liquidity of inventory.	Ch. 6, p. 304
Days sales in inventory	$\dfrac{\text{Days in year}}{\text{Inventory turnover}}$	Measures number of days inventory is on hand.	Ch. 6, p. 305
Receivables turnover	$\dfrac{\text{Net credit sales}}{\text{Average gross receivables}}$	Measures liquidity of receivables.	Ch. 8, p. 427
Collection period	$\dfrac{\text{Days in year}}{\text{Receivables turnover}}$	Measures number of days receivables are outstanding.	Ch. 8, p. 427

ACCOUNTING IN ACTION ▶ Business Insight

The apparently simple current ratio can have real-world limitations because adding equal amounts to both the numerator and denominator causes this ratio to decrease.

Assume, for example, that a company has $2 million of current assets and $1 million of current liabilities. Its current ratio is 2:1. If it purchases $1 million of inventory on account, it will have $3 million of current assets and $2 million of current liabilities. Its current ratio now decreases to 1.5:1.

If, instead, the company pays $500,000 of its current liabilities, it will have $1.5 million of current assets and $500,000 of current liabilities. Its current ratio now increases to 3:1. Any comparisons over time should therefore be done with care: this ratio can change quickly and is easily influenced by management.

 What could management do to influence a company's current ratio?

Solvency Ratios

Solvency ratios measure the ability of a company to survive over a long period of time. Long-term creditors and shareholders are interested in a company's long-term solvency, particularly its ability to pay interest as it comes due and to repay the face value of debt at maturity. Illustration 18-7 lists the solvency ratios we have seen in this textbook.

Ratio	Formula	Purpose	Discussion
Debt to total assets	$\dfrac{\text{Total liabilities}}{\text{Total assets}}$	Measures percentage of total assets provided by creditors.	Ch. 15, p. 780
Interest coverage	$\dfrac{\text{Net income} + \text{Interest expense} + \text{Income tax expense (EBIT)}}{\text{Interest expense}}$	Measures ability to meet interest payments.	Ch. 15, p. 780
Free cash flow	Cash provided (used) by operating activities − Cash used (provided) by investing activities	Measures cash available from operating activities that management can use after paying capital expenditures.	Ch. 17, p. 891

Illustration 18-7 ▲

Summary of solvency ratios

Profitability Ratios

Profitability ratios measure the operating success of a company for a specific period of time. A company's income, or lack of it, affects its ability to obtain debt and equity financing, its liquidity position, and its growth. Both creditors and investors are therefore interested in evaluating profitability. Profitability is often used as the ultimate test of management's operating effectiveness. Illustration 18-8 lists the profitability ratios we have seen in the textbook.

Illustration 18-8 ▼

Summary of profitability ratios

Ratio	Formula	Purpose	Discussion
Gross profit margin	$\dfrac{\text{Gross profit}}{\text{Net sales}}$	Measures margin between selling price and cost of goods sold.	Ch. 5, p. 244
Profit margin	$\dfrac{\text{Net income}}{\text{Net sales}}$	Measures net income generated by each dollar of sales.	Ch. 5, p. 245
Asset turnover	$\dfrac{\text{Net sales}}{\text{Average total assets}}$	Measures how efficiently assets are used to generate sales.	Ch. 9, p. 488
Return on assets	$\dfrac{\text{Net income}}{\text{Average total assets}}$	Measures overall profitability of assets.	Ch. 9, p. 489
Return on equity	$\dfrac{\text{Net income}}{\text{Average shareholders' equity}}$	Measures profitability of shareholders' investment.	Ch. 13, p. 684
Earnings per share	$\dfrac{\text{Net income} - \text{Preferred dividends}}{\text{Weighted average number of common shares}}$	Measures net income earned on each common share.	Ch. 14, p. 728
Price-earnings ratio	$\dfrac{\text{Market price per share}}{\text{Earnings per share}}$	Measures relationship between market price per share and earnings per share.	Ch. 14, p. 730
Payout ratio	$\dfrac{\text{Cash dividends}}{\text{Net income}}$	Measures percentage of income distributed as cash dividends.	Ch. 14, p. 730

It is important to remember that the ratios shown in Illustrations 18-6, 18-7, and 18-8 are only examples of commonly used ratios. You will find more examples as you learn more about financial analysis.

As analysis tools, ratios can give clues to underlying conditions that may not be visible from the individual financial statement components of a particular ratio. However, a single ratio by itself is not very meaningful. Accordingly, ratios must be interpreted alongside the information gained from a detailed review of the financial information, including horizontal and vertical analyses, and non-financial information, as described earlier in the chapter.

BEFORE YOU GO ON . . .

▶**Review It**

1. What are liquidity ratios? Explain working capital, current ratio, inventory turnover, days sales in inventory, receivables turnover, and collection period.
2. What are solvency ratios? Explain debt to total assets, interest coverage, and free cash flow.
3. What are profitability ratios? Explain gross profit margin, profit margin, asset turnover, return on assets, return on equity, earnings per share, price-earnings ratio, and payout ratio.

Related exercise material: BE18–6, BE18–7, BE18–8, BE18–9, BE18–10, BE18–11, E18–5, E18–6, E18–7, E18–8, E18–9, E18–10, and E18–11.

Limitations of Financial Analysis

Business decisions are frequently made by using one or more of the analytical tools illustrated in this chapter. But you should be aware of the limitations of these tools and of the financial statements they are based on.

Inflation

Our accounting information system does not adjust data for price-level changes. For example, a five-year comparison of Canadian Tire's operating revenues shows growth of 144.7 percent. But this growth trend would be misleading if the general price-level had increased or decreased greatly during the same period. In actuality, inflation was 13 percent during this same period, so while Canadian Tire's revenues have indeed increased, they have not increased as much as it first appears. Still, our comparisons are relevant because data that have not been adjusted for inflation are being used consistently for both revenues and expenses, and for each period.

Some countries experience "hyper," or extremely rapid, inflation. Hyperinflation refers to situations where the cumulative inflation rate, over a three-year period, reaches or exceeds 100 percent. One such example is Zimbabwe, where inflation was 624 percent in 2004, 586 percent in 2005, and 1,043 percent in 2006. In countries where hyperinflation exists, financial statements are adjusted for the effects of inflation in order to make the financial information more meaningful for decision-making.

Estimates

Financial statements contain many estimates. For example, estimates are used to determine the allowance for uncollectible receivables, periodic amortization, warranty costs, and the market values of trading and available-for-sale securities. To the extent that these estimates are inaccurate or biased, the financial ratios and percentages will be inaccurate or biased.

Alternative Accounting Principles

Companies use different generally accepted accounting principles. These variations may reduce comparability. For example, Canadian Tire uses the average inventory cost flow assumption. Wal-Mart, one of its competitors, uses LIFO. If inventory is a significant asset for both companies, it is unlikely that their current or inventory turnover ratios can be compared. Recall, however, that although the current assets may be different in one or more periods because of the choice of inventory cost flow assumption, in total, over the life of the inventory, there is no difference. We call differences created from alternative accounting principles "artificial" or timing differences.

Also, in more and more industries, competition is global. To evaluate a company's standing, an investor or analyst must make comparisons to companies from other countries. However, due to the many differences in accounting practices, these comparisons can be both difficult and misleading. Although it might be possible to detect differences in accounting principles by reading the notes to the financial statements, adjusting the financial data to compensate for the different principles can be very difficult.

Diversification

Diversification in Canadian industry also can limit the usefulness of financial analysis. Many firms today are so diversified that they cannot be classified by industry. Canadian Tire, for example, sells home, car, sports, and leisure products. In addition, it is the country's largest independent gasoline retailer. Canadian Tire also sells work clothes and casual attire through its subsidiary, Mark's Work Wearhouse. Consequently, deciding what industry a company is in is actually one of the main challenges to an effective evaluation of its results.

Other companies may appear to be comparable but are not. McCain Foods and Irving-owned Cavendish Farms compete in the frozen potato product field. Yet McCain produces other food products besides french fries, and Irving has many other interests, including oil, newspapers, tissue products, transportation, and forestry.

When companies have significant operations in different lines of business, they are required to report additional disclosures in a segmented information note to their financial statements. Segmented information includes services or product lines and segments located in different countries. Operating income, revenues, and identifiable assets are also reported. Many analysts say that segmented information is the most important data in the financial statements. Without it, a comparison of diversified companies is very difficult. In our feature story, the judges praised Canadian Tire for reporting its performance scorecard and other sections of its annual report by business line (segment).

Quality of Earnings

In evaluating the financial performance of a company, the quality of earnings is extremely important. A company that has a high quality of earnings gives full and transparent information that will not confuse or mislead users of the financial statements. Canadian Tire has a high quality of earnings. The corporate reporting award judges stated that there was "no ambiguity in the financial statements" in our feature story.

Other companies may limit what they disclose or make it confusing to try to hide information and mislead users of the financial statements. In such cases, the quality of the information content will decrease.

Fortunately, the chief executive officer and chief financial officer of a publicly traded company must ensure, and personally declare, that the reported financial information is accurate, relevant, and understandable. In addition, audit committees are held responsible for quizzing management on the degree of aggressiveness/conservatism applied to the information and the quality of the underlying estimates, accounting principles, and judgements.

A strong corporate governance process, including an active board of directors and audit committee, is essential to ensuring the quality of earnings. PotashCorp, the overall winner of the 2005 corporate reporting awards, received top scores for its corporate governance disclosure. Betty-Ann Heggie, senior vice-president of corporate relations at PotashCorp, stated, "Reputation is the most valuable asset any business can have and only by disclosing entirely transparent corporate information can we hope to win people's trust and, in the course of events, enhance our value with investors."

 ACCOUNTING IN ACTION ▶ Ethics Insight

Al and Mark Rosen recommend the following five steps in analyzing a company: (1) read the company's quarterly and annual financial statements, including all the notes and the management discussion and analysis, (2) watch for too-good-to-be-true situations, (3) be careful about who you trust, (4) watch for specific accounting games and poor financial statement disclosures, and (5) look out for executive compensation schemes that base management performance bonuses on slippery accounting figures.

Source: Al Rosen and Mark Rosen, "Dig Deeper," Canadian Business, January 17, 2005, 27.

> **?** The Rosens warn analysts to watch for "too-good-to-be-true" situations and accounting games. Can you give an example of what they might be referring to?

Earning Power and Irregular Items

Users of financial statements are interested in the concept of "earning power," or the normal level of income. In order to determine **earning power**, net income must be adjusted for any irregular, or non-typical, items. Why? If we compare the performance of one company without irregular items to another company with irregular items, comparability will be affected. Consequently, financial statement items are normally adjusted for the impact of irregular items before analyzing them horizontally, vertically, or through ratios.

For example, suppose that Li Corporation reports that this year's net income is $500,000, but a once-in-a-lifetime gain of $400,000 is included in that amount. Using the $500,000 to perform horizontal, vertical, and ratio analyses would be misleading, because the company's earning power is really only $100,000, not $500,000 as reported.

To help determine earning power, irregular items are reported separately on the financial statements and net of income tax. You will recall that we learned about one type of irregular item in Chapter 14—a change in accounting principle. Changes in accounting principle are reported on the statement of retained earnings. In the next section, we will learn about another type of irregular item, which is reported on the income statement—discontinued operations.

There is a third type of irregular item known as extraordinary items, that are sometimes found on U.S. corporate income statements. However, they are rarely found on Canadian corporate income statements as the criteria for recognizing extraordinary items are different in the U.S. and Canada. *Financial Reporting in Canada* notes that no public company has reported an extraordinary item in Canada since 2001. Consequently, we do not cover extraordinary items in this text but rather leave them for an intermediate accounting course.

Discontinued Operations

Discontinued operations refer to the disposal of an identifiable reporting or operating segment of the business. An **identifiable business segment** is a part of a company that can be clearly distinguished, for financial reporting and operating purposes, from the rest of the company. A segment can be a separate subsidiary company, an operating division within the company, or even a group of assets, as long as it is a separate business that can be clearly distinguished from the company as a whole.

Most large corporations have multiple business segments or divisions. For example, Canadian Tire has four business segments that it reports financial and operating information about:

Canadian Tire Retail, Canadian Tire Petroleum, Mark's Work Wearhouse, and Canadian Tire Financial Services.

When an identifiable business segment is disposed of, the disposal is reported separately on the income statement as a nonrecurring item called discontinued operations. The income (or loss) reported in the discontinued operations section consists of two parts: the income (loss) from these operations and the gain (loss) on disposal of the segment. Both items are presented net of applicable income tax so that the income tax related to continuing operations is clearly separated from the income tax for discontinued operations.

To illustrate, assume that Hwa Energy Inc. has revenues of $2.5 million and expenses of $1.7 million from continuing operations in 2008. The company therefore has income before income tax of $800,000. If we assume that Hwa has a 30-percent income tax rate, it would report $240,000 of income tax ($800,000 × 30%), resulting in $560,000 ($800,000 − $240,000) of income from continuing operations.

During 2008, Hwa discontinues and sells its unprofitable chemical division. The loss from chemical operations is $140,000 ($200,000 less $60,000 in income tax savings). The loss on disposal of the chemical division is $70,000 ($100,000 less $30,000 in income tax savings). Illustration 18-9 shows how this information is reported in the income statement.

Illustration 18-9 ◄

Statement presentation of discontinued operations

HWA ENERGY INC. Income Statement (partial) Year Ended December 31, 2008		
Revenues		$2,500,000
Expenses		1,700,000
Income before income tax		800,000
Income tax expense		240,000
Income from continuing operations		560,000
Discontinued operations		
Loss from operations of chemical division, net of $60,000 income tax savings	$140,000	
Loss on disposal of chemical division, net of $30,000 income tax savings	70,000	210,000
Net income		$ 350,000

Note that the caption "Income from continuing operations" is used, and that a section called "Discontinued operations" is added. In the new section, both the operating loss and the loss on disposal are reported net of applicable income tax. This presentation clearly indicates the separate effects of continuing operations and discontinued operations on net income.

Discontinued operations are pretty common. In a recent year, nearly 35 percent of the companies surveyed by *Financial Reporting in Canada* reported discontinued operations.

BEFORE YOU GO ON . . .

►Review It

1. What are some of the limitations of financial analysis?
2. What factors can reduce the quality of earnings?
3. What is "earning power"?
4. What impact do irregular items have on the analysis of financial information?
5. Did The Forzani Group report any irregular items in fiscal 2006? The answer to this question is at the end of the chapter.

▶Do It

In its 2008 income statement, Qu Ltd. reported income before income tax of $400,000; a pre-tax loss on discontinued operations of $75,000; and a pre-tax gain on the disposal of the assets from the discontinued operations of $30,000. The company has a 25-percent income tax rate. Prepare an income statement, beginning with income before income tax.

Action Plan

- Allocate income tax between income from continuing operations and income from atypical (discontinued) items.
- Note that two disclosures are required for discontinued operations: separately disclose (1) the results of operations of the discontinued division, and (2) the disposal of the operation.

Solution

QU LTD.
Income Statement (partial)
Year Ended December 31, 2008

Income before income tax		$400,000
Income tax expense		100,000 [1]
Income from continuing operations		300,000
Discontinued operations		
Loss from operations, net of $18,750 [2] income tax savings	$56,250	
Gain on disposal of assets, net of $7,500 [3] income tax expense	22,500	33,750
Net income		$266,250

[1] $400,000 × 25% = $100,000
[2] $75,000 × 25% = $18,750
[3] $30,000 × 25% = $7,500

the navigator

Related exercise material: BE18–12, BE18–13, BE18–14, E18–12, and E18–13.

APPENDIX 18A ▶ COMPREHENSIVE ILLUSTRATION OF RATIO ANALYSIS

In previous chapters, we calculated many ratios that are used to evaluate the liquidity, solvency, and profitability of a company. In this appendix, we do a comprehensive review of those ratios and discuss some important relationships among them. In this review, we use the following comparisons:

1. Intracompany comparisons covering two years (2004 and 2005) for Hometown Tires and More
2. Intercompany comparisons for the year ended December 31, 2005, for Canadian Tire, Hometown Tires and More's main competitor
3. Industry average comparisons for 2005 for the retail department store industry. For some of the ratios that we use, industry comparisons are not available. These are indicated by "n/a."

You will recall that Hometown Tires and More's balance sheet was presented earlier in the chapter in Illustration 18-1 and its income statement in Illustration 18-2. We will use the information in these two financial statements, in addition to the following data, to calculate Hometown Tires and More's ratios:

	2005	2004
Cash provided by operating activities	$86,200	$ 80,000
Cash provided (used) by investing activities	15,000	(20,000)
Dividends	31,200	30,000
Market price of common shares	5	5
Number of common shares	30,000	30,000

You can use these data to review the calculations for each ratio to make sure you understand where the numbers came from. Detailed calculations are not shown for either Canadian Tire or the industry.

Liquidity Ratios

Liquidity ratios measure the ability of a company to pay its current liabilities. Consequently, liquidity ratios focus mainly on the relationships between current assets and current liabilities that are reported on the income statement for balance sheet and related accounts. Cash provided by operating activities, reported on the cash flow statement, is also useful in assessing liquidity. Liquidity ratios include working capital, the current ratio, receivables turnover, collection period, inventory turnover, and days sales in inventory.

Working Capital

Working capital is the difference between current assets and current liabilities. The 2004 and 2005 working capital figures for Hometown Tires and More, and data for comparison, are shown in Illustration 18A-1.

Working capital = Current assets − Current liabilities

Illustration 18A-1 ◄

Working capital

Hometown Tires and More

2005	2004
$545,000 − $337,700 = $207,300	$485,000 − $313,500 = $171,500

Industry Average	Canadian Tire
n/a	$160.0 million

Hometown Tires and More has a positive and increasing working capital: $207,300 in 2005 and $171,500 in 2004. It is not very meaningful to compare this amount to that of the much larger Canadian Tire. In addition, no industry average is available for working capital, and working capital amounts are not comparable within the industry.

It is difficult to compare absolute dollar amounts. As we learned in Chapter 4, the current ratio—which expresses current assets and current liabilities as a ratio rather than as an amount—is a more useful indicator of liquidity. In addition, two companies with the same amount of working capital may have very different current ratios.

Current Ratio

The current ratio is a widely used measure of a company's liquidity and short-term debt-paying ability. The ratio is calculated by dividing current assets by current liabilities. The 2005 and 2004 current ratios for Hometown Tires and More, and data for comparison, are shown in Illustration 18A-2 on the following page.

Illustration 18A-2 ▶

Current ratio

$$\text{Current ratio} = \frac{\text{Current assets}}{\text{Current liabilities}}$$

Hometown Tires and More

2005	2004
$\dfrac{\$545,000}{\$337,700} = 1.6:1$	$\dfrac{\$485,000}{\$313,500} = 1.5:1$

Industry Average	Canadian Tire
2.1:1	1.6:1

What does the ratio actually mean? The 2005 ratio of 1.6:1 means that for every dollar of current liabilities, Hometown Tires and More has $1.60 of current assets. Hometown Tires and More's current ratio has increased slightly in 2005. Its 2005 ratio is the same as Canadian Tire's current ratio of 1.6:1 and quite a bit lower than the industry average of 2.1:1.

The current ratio is only one measure of liquidity. It does not consider what the current assets are composed of. For example, a satisfactory current ratio does not disclose the fact that a portion of the current assets may be tied up in uncollectible accounts receivable or in slow-moving inventory. A dollar of cash is more available to pay bills than a dollar of an overdue account receivable or a dollar of slow-moving inventory that has not yet been sold.

Receivables Turnover

Liquidity may be measured by how quickly certain assets can be converted to cash. How liquid, for example, are the receivables? The receivables turnover ratio is used to assess the liquidity of the receivables. It measures the number of times, on average, that receivables are collected during the period. The receivables turnover is calculated by dividing net credit sales (net sales less cash sales) by the average gross receivables.

Assuming that all sales are credit sales, that there is no allowance for doubtful accounts, and that the balance of accounts receivable at the beginning of 2004 is $45,000, the receivables turnover figures for Hometown Tires and More, and data for comparison, are shown in Illustration 18A-3.

Illustration 18A-3 ▶

Receivables turnover

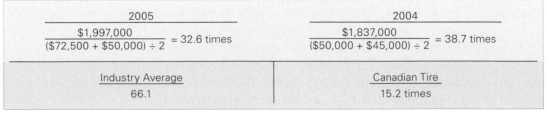

$$\text{Receivables turnover} = \frac{\text{Net credit sales}}{\text{Average gross receivables}}$$

Hometown Tires and More

Helpful hint Whenever an end-of-period (e.g., balance sheet) figure is compared to a period (e.g., income statement or cash flow statement) figure, the end-of-period figure must be averaged so that it is for approximately the same period of time. Comparisons of end-of-period figures to end-of-period figures, or period figures to period figures, do not require averaging.

2005	2004
$\dfrac{\$1,997,000}{(\$72,500 + \$50,000) \div 2} = 32.6$ times	$\dfrac{\$1,837,000}{(\$50,000 + \$45,000) \div 2} = 38.7$ times

Industry Average	Canadian Tire
66.1	15.2 times

Hometown Tires and More's receivables turn over (i.e., are collected) 32.6 times a year. In general, the faster the turnover, the more reliable the current ratio is for assessing liquidity.

Hometown Tires and More's receivables turnover declined from 38.7 times in 2004 to 32.6 times in 2005. It is still much higher than Canadian Tire's receivables turnover of 15.2 times a year, but slower than the industry average of 66.1 times a year in 2005.

Why is Hometown Tires and More's receivables turnover so much higher than that of Canadian Tire? Hometown Tires and More likely has few credit sales and therefore few receivables. Most of its sales are for cash. Canadian Tire, on the other hand, has receivables from its franchise stores.

It is important to be careful in interpreting this ratio. We assumed that all sales were credit sales, when in fact, this is not a reasonable assumption. Companies do not separately disclose their credit and cash sales. However, intracompany, intercompany, and industry comparisons can still be made, since the same assumption—all sales were credit sales—was applied to Canadian Tire and the industry average.

Collection Period

A popular variation of the receivables turnover is to convert it into a collection period stated in days. This is done by dividing the number of days in a year (365 days) by the receivables turnover, as shown in Illustration 18A-4.

$$\text{Collection period} = \frac{\text{Days in year}}{\text{Receivables turnover}}$$

Hometown Tires and More

2005	2004
$\dfrac{365 \text{ days}}{32.6} = 11 \text{ days}$	$\dfrac{365 \text{ days}}{38.7} = 9 \text{ days}$
Industry Average	Canadian Tire
6 days	24 days

The effectiveness of a company's credit and collection policies is much easier to interpret using the collection period, rather than the receivables turnover ratio. Hometown Tires and More's receivables were collected every 11 days in 2005. Although weaker than in 2004, and not as good as the industry average, this collection period is still excellent and well under the normal 30-day payment period. The general rule is that the collection period should not be more than the credit-term period (the time allowed for payment). Even Canadian Tire's collection period of 24 days is still a reasonable one.

So, despite earlier concerns, receivables management appears to be in good shape for both companies, and the industry. Because of the large proportion of cash sales, this is to be expected.

Inventory Turnover

Inventory turnover measures the average number of times that the inventory is sold during the period. Its purpose is to measure the liquidity of the inventory. The inventory turnover is calculated by dividing the cost of goods sold by the average inventory.

Assuming that the inventory balance for Hometown Tires and More at the beginning of 2004 was $300,000, its inventory turnover figures, and data for comparison, are shown in Illustration 18A-5 on the following page.

$$\text{Inventory turnover} = \frac{\text{Cost of goods sold}}{\text{Average inventory}}$$

Hometown Tires and More

2005	2004
$\dfrac{\$1,381,000}{(\$372,500 + \$325,000) \div 2} = 4.0$ times	$\dfrac{\$1,240,000}{(\$325,000 + \$300,000) \div 2} = 4.0$ times

Industry Average	Canadian Tire
6.8 times	9.6 times

Hometown Tires and More turns over (sells) its entire inventory 4 times a year. Its inventory turnover was unchanged between 2004 and 2005. Hometown Tires and More's turnover ratio of 4 times is low compared to the industry average of 6.8 times and that of Canadian Tire at 9.6 times. Generally, the faster inventory is sold, the less cash there is tied up in inventory and the less chance there is of inventory becoming obsolete.

Days Sales in Inventory

A variant of inventory turnover is the days sales in inventory. This is calculated by dividing the inventory turnover into the number of days in a year (365 days). Hometown Tires and More's days sales in inventory ratios for 2005 and 2004, and data for comparison, are shown in Illustration 18A-6.

$$\text{Days sales in inventory} = \frac{\text{Days in year}}{\text{Inventory turnover}}$$

Hometown Tires and More

2005	2004
$\dfrac{365 \text{ days}}{4.0} = 91$ days	$\dfrac{365 \text{ days}}{4.0} = 91$ days

Industry Average	Canadian Tire
54 days	38 days

Hometown Tires and More's inventory turnover of 4 times divided into 365 days is approximately 91 days. In other words, Hometown Tires and More has 91 days' worth of inventory on hand. This is relatively slow compared to the industry average of 54 days.

It is important to use judgement in interpreting both the inventory turnover and days sales in inventory ratios. Remember that Hometown Tires and More is only one store, while Canadian Tire has 464 stores and the industry is composed of large box stores. Canadian Tire, and other stores in the industry, are large enough to take advantage of just-in-time and other computerized inventory management techniques, whereas Hometown Tires and More likely does not have such sophisticated inventory options.

Nonetheless, Hometown Tires and More must keep a close eye on its inventory. It runs the risk of being left with unsaleable inventory, not to mention the additional costs of financing and carrying this inventory over a longer period of time.

Liquidity Conclusion

On an intracompany comparison, Hometown Tires and More's current ratio improved slightly from 2004 to 2005. Although its receivables turnover ratio declined, it is still a strong ratio, and well within the normal collection period. The proportionate increase in the dollar amount of receivables (and prepaid expenses) is likely the reason that Hometown Tires and More's current ratio increased. Its inventory turnover remained unchanged.

On an intercompany comparison, Hometown Tires and More's current ratio is the same as Canadian Tire's, its receivables turnover is better than Canadian Tire's, but its inventory turnover is lower than Canadian Tire's. Hometown Tires and More's liquidity is lower than the industry's.

Nonetheless, its receivables management is still strong, and well within normal collection periods. Hometown Tires and More's inventory turnover is significantly below that of the industry, although this may be mainly because of the type of goods on hand and the size of the store. To conclude, Hometown Tires and More's liquidity is good, but it should keep a close eye on its inventory.

Solvency Ratios

While liquidity ratios measure the ability of a company to pay its current liabilities, solvency ratios measure the ability of a company to pay its total liabilities. The debt to total assets and interest coverage ratios give information about debt-paying ability. In addition, free cash flow gives information about the company's ability to invest in new projects, repay debt, or pay dividends.

Debt to Total Assets

Debt to total assets measures the percentage of the total assets that is provided by creditors. It is calculated by dividing total liabilities (both current and long-term) by total assets. This ratio indicates the company's degree of leverage. It also gives some indication of the company's ability to absorb losses without hurting the interests of its creditors. The higher the percentage of total debt to total assets, the greater the risk that the company may be unable to meet its maturing obligations. The lower the debt to total assets ratio, the more net assets there are to repay creditors if the company becomes insolvent. So, from a creditor's point of view, a low ratio of debt to total assets is desirable.

Helpful hint A popular variation of this ratio is the debt to equity ratio. It is calculated by dividing total debt by shareholders' equity. It compares the percentage of assets provided by creditors to that provided by shareholders.

Hometown Tires and More's 2005 and 2004 ratios, and data for comparison, are shown in Illustration 18A-7.

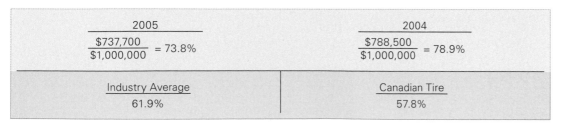

$$\text{Debt to total assets} = \frac{\text{Total liabilities}}{\text{Total assets}}$$

Illustration 18A-7 ◀

Debt to total assets

Hometown Tires and More

2005	2004
$\dfrac{\$737,700}{\$1,000,000} = 73.8\%$	$\dfrac{\$788,500}{\$1,000,000} = 78.9\%$

Industry Average	Canadian Tire
61.9%	57.8%

A ratio of 73.8% means that creditors have provided 73.8% of Hometown Tires and More's total assets. Although its ratio improved in 2005, Hometown Tires and More's debt to total assets ratio is much higher than Canadian Tire's 57.8%, and that of the industry, 61.9%.

However, as mentioned in the chapter, Hometown Tires and More does not have access to the equity markets since it is privately owned. Consequently, it is not surprising that it relies on debt financing. A more relevant calculation is whether or not it can afford this level of debt. The debt to total assets ratio should never be interpreted without also looking at the interest coverage ratio. A company may have a low debt to total assets ratio but be unable to cover its interest payments. Alternatively, a company may have a high debt to total assets ratio but easily be able to cover its interest payments.

Interest Coverage

Alternative terminology
The interest coverage ratio is also called the *times interest earned ratio*.

The interest coverage ratio gives an indication of the company's ability to make its interest payments as they come due. It is calculated by dividing income before interest expense and income tax expense by interest expense. Note that the interest coverage ratio uses income before interest expense and income tax expense. This is often abbreviated as EBIT, which stands for earnings before interest and tax. EBIT represents the amount that is available to cover interest.

The 2005 and 2004 ratios for Hometown Tires and More, and data for comparison, are shown in Illustration 18A-8.

Illustration 18A-8 ▶

Interest coverage

$$\text{Interest coverage} = \frac{\text{Net income} + \text{Interest expense} + \text{Income tax expense}}{\text{Interest expense}}$$

Hometown Tires and More

2005	2004
$\dfrac{\$82,000 + \$36,000 + \$50,000}{\$36,000} = 4.7$ times	$\dfrac{\$75,000 + \$40,500 + \$52,500}{\$40,500} = 4.2$ times

Industry Average	Canadian Tire
13.6 times	7.3 times

Despite Hometown Tires and More's high debt to total assets ratio, it is able to cover its interest payments. Its income before interest and taxes was 4.7 times the amount needed for interest expense in 2005. Hometown Tires and More's interest coverage improved slightly in 2005, although it is still below that of Canadian Tire at 7.3 times and that of the industry at 13.6 times.

Free Cash Flow

One indication of a company's solvency, as well as of its ability to expand operations, repay debt, or pay dividends is the amount of excess cash it generates after paying to maintain its current productive capacity. This amount is referred to as free cash flow.

Hometown Tires and More's free cash flow figures for 2005 and 2004, and data for comparison, are shown in Illustration 18A-9.

Free cash flow = Cash provided (used) by operating activities − Cash used (provided) by investing activities

Hometown Tires and More

2005	2004
$86,200 + $15,000 = $101,200	$80,000 − $20,000 = $60,000

Industry Average	Canadian Tire
n/a	$(180.3) million

Note that the $15,000 of cash provided by investing activities is *added to* cash provided by operating activities in 2005, compared to the $20,000 used by investing activities *deducted from* cash provided by operating activities in 2004.

Hometown Tires and More has "free" cash to invest in additional property, plant, and equipment, repay debt, and pay its dividends. Hometown Tires and More did not acquire additional property, plant, and equipment and intangibles in 2005, but it did sell some of its available-for-sale securities. This sale of investments provided $15,000 of additional cash for management to use at its discretion in addition to the $86,200 provided by operating activities.

In contrast, Canadian Tire reported a negative amount of free cash in 2005. It spent $180.3 million more on investing activities than it generated from operating activities. There is no industry average available for free cash flow. And, as noted earlier, it is hard to make a meaningful comparison of absolute dollar amounts for two companies of such different sizes.

Solvency Conclusion

In an intracompany comparison, all of Hometown Tires and More's ratios improved in 2005. Despite this improvement inside the company, in intercompany and industry comparisons, Hometown Tires and More's solvency was significantly lower than that of Canadian Tire and the industry with the exception of its free cash flow.

It is important to distinguish between Hometown Tires and More and Canadian Tire in this analysis, as they are very different types of companies. Hometown Tires and More, as a small, privately held company, relies mainly on debt for its financing and has to generate enough income to cover its interest payments. In contrast, Canadian Tire, a large public company, relies more on equity for its financing needs.

Profitability Ratios

Profitability ratios measure the income or operating success of a company for a specific period of time. Income, or the lack of it, affects the company's ability to obtain debt and equity financing. It also affects the company's liquidity position and its ability to grow. Consequently, both creditors and investors are interested in evaluating profitability. Profitability is often used as the real test of management's operating effectiveness. Profitability ratios include the gross profit margin, profit margin, asset turnover, return on assets, return on equity, earnings per share, price-earnings, and payout ratios.

Gross Profit Margin

The gross profit margin is determined by dividing gross profit (net sales less cost of goods sold) by net sales. This ratio indicates a company's ability to keep a selling price that is high enough above its cost of goods sold. Gross profit margins should be watched closely over time.

Hometown Tires and More's gross profit margin figures for 2005 and 2004, and data for comparison, are shown in Illustration 18A-10.

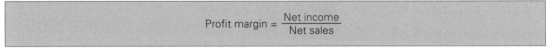

$$\text{Gross profit margin} = \frac{\text{Gross profit}}{\text{Net sales}}$$

Hometown Tires and More

2005	2004
$\frac{\$616,000}{\$1,997,000} = 30.8\%$	$\frac{\$597,000}{\$1,837,000} = 32.5\%$

Industry Average	Canadian Tire
23.5%	20%

Hometown Tires and More's gross profit margin for 2005 means that 30.8 cents of each dollar of its sales that year went to cover operating expenses and generate a profit. Hometown Tires and More's gross profit margin declined slightly, from 32.5% in 2004 to 30.8% in 2005.

Hometown Tires and More's gross profit margin is higher than Canadian Tire's and the industry average of 23.5%. This could be the result of several factors. It may be that Hometown Tires and More sells higher quality merchandise than do Canadian Tire and other competitors. In addition, prices may be higher in general not only because of increased costs, but also because the company offers a higher level of personal service.

Profit Margin

Profit margin is a measure of the percentage of each dollar of sales that results in net income. It is calculated by dividing net income by net sales. Hometown Tires and More's profit margin figures, and data for comparison, are shown in Illustration 18A-11.

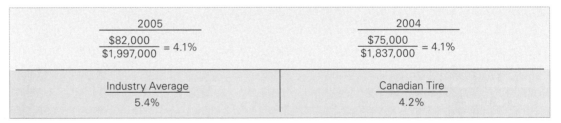

$$\text{Profit margin} = \frac{\text{Net income}}{\text{Net sales}}$$

Hometown Tires and More

2005	2004
$\frac{\$82,000}{\$1,997,000} = 4.1\%$	$\frac{\$75,000}{\$1,837,000} = 4.1\%$

Industry Average	Canadian Tire
5.4%	4.2%

Hometown Tires and More's profit margin is unchanged from 2004 to 2005, at 4.1% of net sales. It is a bit lower than that of Canadian Tire and the industry. This is not what we would expect given that we found Hometown Tires and More's gross profit margin, analyzed above, to be higher than that of Canadian Tire and the industry. This suggests that Hometown Tires and More is not able to control its operating expenses as well as Canadian Tire and the industry do.

Asset Turnover

Asset turnover measures how efficiently a company uses its assets to generate sales. It is determined by dividing net sales by average total assets. The resulting number shows the dollars of sales produced by each dollar of assets. Assuming that total assets at the beginning of 2004 were $1,090,000, the 2005 and 2004 asset turnover ratios for Hometown Tires and More, and data for comparison, are shown in Illustration 18A-12.

Illustration 18A-12 ◄

Asset turnover

$$\text{Asset turnover} = \frac{\text{Net sales}}{\text{Average total assets}}$$

Hometown Tires and More

2005	2004
$\dfrac{\$1,997,000}{(\$1,000,000 + \$1,000,000) \div 2} = 2.0 \text{ times}$	$\dfrac{\$1,837,000}{(\$1,000,000 + \$1,090,000) \div 2} = 1.8 \text{ times}$
Industry Average 2.4 times	Canadian Tire 1.4 times

In 2005, Hometown Tires and More generated $2 of sales for each dollar it had invested in assets. This ratio improved from 2004, when its asset turnover was 1.8 times, or $1.80 of sales for each dollar of assets. Although its 2005 asset turnover is below that of the industry, it is higher than Canadian Tire's asset turnover of 1.4 times.

Return on Assets

An overall measure of profitability is return on assets. This ratio is calculated by dividing net income by average total assets. Hometown Tires and More's return on assets figures for 2005 and 2004, and data for comparison, are shown in Illustration 18A-13.

Illustration 18A-13 ◄

Return on assets

$$\text{Return on assets} = \frac{\text{Net income}}{\text{Average total assets}}$$

Hometown Tires and More

2005	2004
$\dfrac{\$82,000}{(\$1,000,000 + \$1,000,000) \div 2} = 8.2\%$	$\dfrac{\$75,000}{(\$1,000,000 + \$1,090,000) \div 2} = 7.2\%$
Industry Average 12.3%	Canadian Tire 5.9%

Hometown Tires and More's return on assets improved from 2004 to 2005. Its 2005 return of 8.2% is lower than the industry average. However, it is high in comparison to Canadian Tire's return of 5.9%. Although the percentage is high, it must be analyzed in perspective. Hometown Tires and More's income improved, and it was strong to begin with. However, it is being compared to a relatively small asset base, so small dollar increases result in large percentage increases.

The return on assets can be further analyzed by looking at the profit margin and asset turnover ratios in combination, as shown in Illustration 18A-14 on the following page.

Return on Assets		Profit Margin		Asset Turnover
$\dfrac{\text{Net income}}{\text{Average total assets}}$	=	$\dfrac{\text{Net income}}{\text{Net sales}}$	×	$\dfrac{\text{Net sales}}{\text{Average total assets}}$

2005	8.2%	=	4.1%	×	2.0 times
2004	7.2%	=	4.1%	×	1.8 times

With a rounded figure of 1.8 times used for the asset turnover, the calculation for the year 2004 does not work out precisely. If we use Hometown Tires and More's unrounded asset turnover of 1.76 instead of the rounded amount of 1.8, we can prove the above calculation.

From this breakdown of the return on assets, we learn that Hometown Tires and More's return on assets increased because of the improved asset turnover. That is, Hometown Tires and More's assets generated more efficient sales, which resulted in an improved return on assets. The profitability of each dollar of sales remained unchanged.

Return on Equity

For shareholders, a popular measure of profitability is the return on equity ratio. This ratio shows how many dollars of net income were earned for each dollar invested by the shareholders. It is calculated by dividing net income by average total shareholders' equity. Although we calculate this ratio using total shareholders' equity, it can also be calculated using only the common shareholders' equity if there is more than one class of shares. In such cases, net income is reduced by any preferred dividends to determine the income available for common shareholders. The denominator is the average common shareholders' equity.

Assuming that total shareholders' equity at the beginning of 2004 was $166,500, the return on equity figures for Hometown Tires and More for 2005 and 2004, and data for comparison, are shown in Illustration 18A-15.

$$\text{Return on equity} = \frac{\text{Net income}}{\text{Average shareholders' equity}}$$

Hometown Tires and More

2005	2004
$\dfrac{\$82,000}{(\$262,300 + \$211,500) \div 2} = 34.6\%$	$\dfrac{\$75,000}{(\$211,500 + \$166,500) \div 2} = 39.7\%$

Industry Average	Canadian Tire
23.9%	13.9%

Although it declined in 2005, Hometown Tires and More's return on equity is unusually high at 34.6%. The return on equity figures for Canadian Tire and the industry are much lower at 13.9% and 23.9%, respectively.

Note that Hometown Tires and More's 2005 return on equity (34.6%) is much higher than its return on assets (8.2%). The reason is that Hometown Tires and More has made effective use of leveraging, or trading on the equity. Trading on the equity means that the company can earn a higher rate of interest by using borrowed money in its operations than it has to pay on the borrowed money. This enables Hometown Tires and More to use money supplied by creditors to increase the return to the shareholders. Recall that Hometown Tires and More has substantially more debt than Canadian Tire, so it is not surprising that its return on equity is higher than Canadian Tire's.

A comparison of the rate of return on total assets to the rate of interest paid for borrowed money indicates the profitability of trading on the equity. Note, however, that trading on the equity is a two-way street. For example, if you borrow money at 7 percent and earn only 4 percent on it, you're trading on the equity at a loss rather than at a gain. Hometown Tires and More earns more on its borrowed funds than it has to pay in the form of interest. Thus, the return to shareholders is higher than the return on assets, which indicates that shareholders are benefiting from positive leveraging or trading on the equity.

Earnings Per Share (EPS)

Earnings per share is a measure of the net income earned on each common share. It is calculated by dividing the net income available to common shareholders (net income less preferred dividends) by the weighted average number of common shares.

Shareholders usually think in terms of the number of shares they own or plan to buy or sell. Reducing net income to a per share basis gives a useful measure of profitability. This measure is widely used and reported. Because of the importance of the earnings per share ratio, most companies are required to present it directly on the income statement.

Hometown Tires and More has 30,000 common shares issued. There has been no change in this number over the past three years, so the weighted average number of shares is the same. As mentioned previously, Hometown Tires and More's shares are not traded publicly and have a limited ownership market. The earnings per share figures for Hometown Tires and More for 2005 and 2004, and data for comparison, are shown in Illustration 18A-16.

Illustration 18A-16 ◀

Earnings per share

$$\text{Earnings per share} = \frac{\text{Net income} - \text{Preferred dividends}}{\text{Weighted average number of common shares}}$$

Hometown Tires and More

2005	2004
$\dfrac{\$82{,}000 - \$0}{30{,}000} = \$2.73$	$\dfrac{\$75{,}000 - \$0}{30{,}000} = \$2.50$

Industry Average	Canadian Tire
n/a	$4.04

Hometown Tires and More's earnings per share increased by $0.23 per share in 2005. This represents a 9-percent increase over the 2004 earnings per share figure of $2.50. Comparisons to the industry average or Canadian Tire are not meaningful, because of the large differences in the number of shares issued by companies. The only meaningful EPS comparison is an intracompany one.

Price-Earnings (PE) Ratio

The price-earnings (PE) ratio is an often-quoted measure of the ratio of the market price of each common share to the earnings per share. The price-earnings ratio reflects investors' assessments of a company's future earnings. It is calculated by dividing the market price per share by earnings per share. The price-earnings ratios for Hometown Tires and More for 2005 and 2004, and data for comparison, are shown in Illustration 18A-17.

$$\text{Price-earnings ratio} = \frac{\text{Market price per share}}{\text{Earnings per share}}$$

Hometown Tires and More

2005	2004
$\dfrac{\$5}{\$2.73}$ = 1.8 times	$\dfrac{\$5}{\$2.50}$ = 2.0 times
Industry Average 15.0	Canadian Tire 17.2 times

In 2005, Hometown Tires and More's shares traded at 1.8 times their earnings. This ratio is really not meaningful for Hometown Tires and More, because of the restricted trading market for its shares. Hometown Tires and More is a family-owned, privately held company. Its shares are not available to the general public for sale.

Canadian Tire's price-earnings ratio is 17.2 times, which is higher than Hometown Tires and More's average of 1.8 times and higher than that of the industry.

In general, a higher price-earnings ratio means that investors favour the company. They are willing to pay more for the shares because they believe the company has good prospects for growth and income in the future.

Some investors carefully study price-earnings ratios over time to help them determine when to buy or sell shares. If the highs and lows of a particular share's PE ratio remain constant over several stock market cycles, then these highs and lows can indicate selling and buying points for the shares. They could also mean other things, however, so investors should be very cautious in interpreting PE ratios.

Payout Ratio

The payout ratio measures the percentage of income distributed as cash dividends. It is calculated by dividing cash dividends by net income. The 2005 and 2004 payout ratios for Hometown Tires and More, and data for comparison, are shown in Illustration 18A-18.

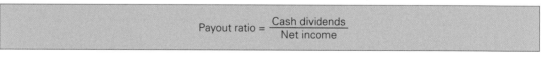

$$\text{Payout ratio} = \frac{\text{Cash dividends}}{\text{Net income}}$$

Hometown Tires and More

2005	2004
$\dfrac{\$31,200}{\$82,000}$ = 38.0%	$\dfrac{\$30,000}{\$75,000}$ = 40.0%
Industry Average 15.3%	Canadian Tire 14.3%

Hometown Tires and More's 2005 payout ratio of 38% is more than double the payout ratio of Canadian Tire and the industry. Once again, recall that Hometown Tires and More is a private company, and has discretion as to how much it pays in dividends. It is likely that dividends are high because they are part of management's compensation.

Many companies with stable earnings have high payout ratios. For example, BCE Inc. currently has a 66% payout ratio. Companies that are expanding rapidly normally have low, or no, payout ratios. Research in Motion, for example, has a zero payout ratio.

Profitability Conclusion

In an intracompany comparison, except for the gross profit margin and return on equity, Hometown Tires and More's profitability measures generally improved or remained relatively constant from 2004 to 2005. Some of its market-based ratios declined, such as the price-earnings and payout ratios. However, these ratios do not really say much because of the restricted trading of Hometown Tires and More's shares. We therefore ignore these market-based ratios in our intercompany and industry comparisons.

In an intercompany comparison, Hometown Tires and More's profitability measures were generally close to or better than those of Canadian Tire. In an industry comparison, Hometown Tires and More's profitability was generally weaker than that of the industry.

Demonstration Problem

Practice Tools:
Demonstration Problems

A vertical analysis of the condensed financial statements of Mukhin Inc. for the years 2005 to 2008 follows:

MUKHIN INC.
Percentage Balance Sheet
May 31

	2008	2007	2006	2005
Assets				
Current assets	11.1%	11.1%	13.9%	11.4%
Current assets of discontinued operations	0.2%	2.1%	0.6%	4.2%
Noncurrent assets	88.0%	77.0%	84.8%	81.2%
Noncurrent assets of discontinued operations	0.7%	9.8%	0.7%	3.2%
Total assets	100.0%	100.0%	100.0%	100.0%
Liabilities and Shareholders' Equity				
Current liabilities	19.3%	17.5%	19.0%	15.0%
Current liabilities of discontinued operations	0.0%	1.4%	0.2%	4.1%
Noncurrent liabilities	52.4%	52.1%	46.0%	45.3%
Noncurrent liabilities of discontinued operations	2.3%	4.8%	1.8%	3.4%
Total liabilities	74.0%	75.8%	67.0%	67.8%
Shareholders' equity	26.0%	24.2%	33.0%	32.2%
Total liabilities and shareholders' equity	100.0%	100.0%	100.0%	100.0%

MUKHIN INC.
Percentage Income Statement
Year Ended May 31

	2008	2007	2006	2005
Revenues	100.0%	100.0%	100.0%	100.0%
Expenses	87.8%	89.5%	104.0%	96.0%
Income (loss) before income taxes	12.2%	10.5%	(4.0%)	4.0%
Income tax expense (recovery)	3.8%	3.1%	(0.3%)	2.3%
Income (loss) from continuing operations	8.4%	7.4%	(3.7%)	1.7%
Income (loss) from discontinued operations	0.0%	(0.2%)	1.4%	9.0%
Net income (loss)	8.4%	7.2%	(2.3%)	10.7%

Instructions

Discuss the significant changes between 2005 and 2008 for the company.

Action Plan

- Exclude the impact of irregular items in your analysis.
- Look at the percentage comparisons both vertically (within the year) and horizontally (across the years).

Solution to Demonstration Problem

Current assets increased in 2006, declined in 2007, and remained stable in 2008. Mukhin's current liabilities are a higher percentage of total assets than are its current assets. Current liabilities have generally been increasing, except for in 2007. Except for during that same year, 2007, Mukhin's noncurrent assets have also been increasing as a percentage of total assets. Noncurrent liabilities have been increasing. The company likely increased its long-term liabilities to help finance increasing purchases of noncurrent assets.

Mukhin's liquidity and solvency appear to be declining over recent years, with increasing percentages of liabilities. We would have to perform further analyses (e.g., ratio analysis) to determine the reasons for this decline.

In terms of profitability, Mukhin appears to be controlling its expenses, which have declined, except in 2006. Except for this same year, its profitability (income from continuing operations) also appears to be on the increase.

It is interesting to note the impact that discontinued operations have on Mukhin's financial position. While these should be excluded from our comparative analysis, one might question whether they are a nonrecurring item or not since discontinued operations appear to be the norm over the last four years rather than the exception. However, except for in 2005, the discontinued operations have not significantly impacted Mukhin's profitability.

Summary of Study Objectives

1. *Explain and apply horizontal analysis.* Horizontal analysis is a technique for evaluating a series of data over a period of time. The increase or decrease that has taken place is determined, and is expressed as either an amount or a percentage.

2. *Explain and apply vertical analysis.* Vertical analysis is a technique for expressing each item in a financial statement as a percentage of a relevant total (base amount).

3. *Identify and use ratios to analyze a company's liquidity, profitability, and solvency.* The formula and purpose of each ratio are presented in Illustrations 18-6 (liquidity), 18-7 (solvency), and 18-8 (profitability).

4. *Recognize and illustrate the limitations of financial statement analysis.* The usefulness of analytical tools is limited by price-level changes, the use of estimates, the application of alternative accounting principles, diversification of companies, the quality of earnings, and irregular items.

One example of an irregular item is discontinued operations, which is a disposal of an identifiable business segment. Discontinued operations are presented on the income statement, net of tax, below "Income from continuing operations" to highlight the fact that they are unusual.

Study Aids: Glossary
Practice Tools: Key Term Matching Activity

Glossary

Discontinued operations The disposal of an identifiable segment of a business. (p. 936)

Earning power Net income adjusted for irregular, or atypical, items. (p. 936)

Horizontal analysis A technique for evaluating a series of financial statement data over a period of time to determine the increase (decrease) that has taken place. This increase (decrease) is expressed as either an amount or a percentage. (p. 924)

Identifiable business segment A division or part of a company that can be clearly distinguished, for financial reporting and operating purposes, from the rest of the company. (p. 936)

Liquidity ratios Measures of the short-term ability of a company to pay its maturing obligations and to meet unexpected needs for cash. (p. 932)

Profitability ratios Measures of the operating success of a company for a specific period of time. (p. 933)

Ratio analysis A technique for evaluating financial statements that expresses the relationship between selected financial statement data. (p. 931)

Solvency ratios Measures of a company's ability to survive over a long period of time. (p. 932)

Vertical analysis A technique for evaluating financial statement data within a period. Each item in a financial statement is expressed as a percentage of the base amount. (p. 928)

Self-Study Questions

Practice Tools: Self-Assessment Quizzes

Answers are at the end of the chapter.

(SO 1) K 1. In horizontal analysis, each item is expressed as a percentage of the:
(a) net sales amount.
(b) shareholders' equity amount.
(c) total assets amount.
(d) base-year amount.

(SO 1) AP 2. Rankin Inlet Corporation reported net sales of $300,000, $330,000, and $360,000 in the years 2006, 2007, and 2008, respectively. If 2006 is the base year, what is the percentage of the base-period amount for 2008?
(a) 77%   (c) 120%
(b) 108%   (d) 130%

(SO 2) K 3. In a vertical analysis, the base amount for amortization expense is generally:
(a) net sales.
(b) amortization expense in a previous year.
(c) total assets.
(d) total property, plant, and equipment.

O 2, 3) K 4. The following schedule shows what type of analysis?

	Amount	Percentage
Current assets	$200,000	25%
Long-lived assets	600,000	75%
Total assets	$800,000	100%

(a) Horizontal analysis   (c) Vertical analysis
(b) Differential analysis   (d) Ratio analysis

(SO 3) K 5. Which of the following is not a liquidity ratio?
(a) Current ratio
(b) Asset turnover
(c) Inventory turnover
(d) Receivables turnover

SO 3 AN 6. Which of the following situations would be the most likely indicator that Wang Corporation might have a solvency problem?

(a) Increasing debt to total assets and interest coverage ratios
(b) Increasing debt to total assets and decreasing interest coverage ratios
(c) Decreasing debt to total assets and interest coverage ratios
(d) Decreasing debt to total assets and increasing interest coverage ratios

7. Which of the following situations is a likely indicator of **(SO 3) AN** profitability?
(a) An increasing price-earnings ratio
(b) Increasing return on assets, asset turnover, and profit margin ratios
(c) Decreasing return on equity and payout ratios
(d) A decreasing gross profit margin and increasing profit margin

8. Which of the following is generally *not* considered to be **(SO 4) K** a limitation of financial analysis?
(a) Use of estimates
(b) A high quality of earnings
(c) Diversification
(d) Use of alternative accounting principles

9. The income statement should be adjusted for the impact **(SO 4) C** of which of the following before performing a financial analysis?
(a) Changes in accounting principles
(b) Discontinued operations
(c) Inflation
(d) Unrealized gains and losses on available-for-sale securities

10. In reporting discontinued operations, a special section **(SO 4) K** in the income statement should show:
(a) gains and losses on disposal of the discontinued segment.
(b) gains and losses from operations of the discontinued segment.
(c) neither (a) nor (b).
(d) both (a) and (b).

the navigator

Questions

(SO 1) C 1. (a) What are the differences among the following bases of comparison: (1) intracompany, (2) intercompany, and (3) industry averages? (b) Explain whether these three bases of comparison should be used individually or together.

(SO 1) K 2. Explain how the percentage of a base-period amount and the percentage change for a period are calculated in horizontal analysis.

(SO 1) C 3. Explain how a horizontal analysis is affected if an account (a) has no value in a base year and a value in the next year, or (b) has a negative value in the base year and a positive value in the next year.

(SO 1, 2) C 4. Horizontal analysis and vertical analysis are two methods of financial statement analysis. Explain the difference between these two methods.

(SO 1, 2) C 5. **Tim Hortons Inc.** reported $242,651 thousand of sales for its first quarter ended April 2, 2006. It became a publicly traded company at the beginning of 2006, after separating from Wendy's International. Can a meaningful horizontal and vertical analysis be prepared, comparing the first quarter ended April 2, 2006, with the first quarter of the prior year? Explain.

(SO 2) K 6. What items are usually assigned a 100% value in a vertical analysis of (a) the balance sheet and (b) the income statement?

(SO 2) C 7. Can vertical analysis be used to compare two companies of different sizes and using different currencies, such as **InBev**, the world's largest brewer, headquartered in Belgium, and **Molson Coors Brewing Company**, the fifth largest brewer, headquartered in the U.S.? Explain.

(SO 3) K 8. What do the following classes of ratios measure: (a) liquidity ratios, (b) profitability ratios, and (c) solvency ratios?

(SO 3) C 9. Which ratio(s) should be used to help answer each of the following questions?
   (a) How efficient is a company at using its assets to produce sales?
   (b) How near to sale is the inventory on hand?
   (c) How many dollars of net income were earned for each dollar invested by the shareholders?
   (d) How able is a company to pay interest charges as they come due?
   (e) How able is the company to repay a short-term loan?

(SO 3) AN 10. Does a high current ratio always indicate that a company has a strong liquidity position? Describe two situations in which a high current ratio might be hiding liquidity problems.

(SO 3) AN 11. Aubut Corporation, a retail store, has a receivables turnover of 4.5 times. The industry average is 6.5 times. Does Aubut have a collection problem with its receivables?

12. Wong Ltd. reported debt to total assets of 37% and an (SO 3) interest coverage ratio of 3 times in the current year. The industry average is 39% for debt to total assets and 2.5 times for interest coverage. Is Wong's solvency better or worse than that of the industry?

13. Laser Corp.'s cash provided by operating activities was (SO 3) double the amount of the prior year, but its free cash flow was one-half the amount. Discuss whether or not the decline in free cash flow indicates a decline in the company's solvency.

14. **Saputo Inc.'s** return on assets is 12%. During the same (SO 3) year, it reported a return on equity of 19%. Has Saputo made effective use of leverage? Explain.

15. If you were an investor interested in buying the shares (SO 3) of a company with growth potential, would you look for a company that had high or low price-earnings and payout ratios? If you were interested in buying the shares of a company with income potential, would your answer change? Explain why.

16. In an effort to increase its profitability, Medicine Hat (SO 3) Inc. revised its sales strategy by reducing the selling price of its merchandise. The result was that sales and net income both increased but the gross profit margin and profit margin decreased. Discuss whether the president of Medicine Hat Inc. should be concerned about the decline in these ratios.

17. Identify and briefly explain the limitations of financial (SO 4) analysis.

18. Give an example of how management might deliberately (SO 4) try to increase income by changing an accounting estimate. How would this affect the quality of the earnings reported?

19. Explain how the choice of one of the following account- (SO 4) ing principles over the other increases or decreases a company's net income:
   (a) Use of FIFO instead of average cost for the inventory cost flow assumption during a period of continuing inflation (rising prices)
   (b) Use of a three-year estimated useful life to calculate amortization for machinery instead of a five-year life
   (c) Use of straight-line amortization instead of declining-balance amortization

20. In 2007, Lai Inc. reported a profit margin of 5% before (SO 4) discontinued operations and a profit margin of 8% after discontinued operations. In 2008, the company had no discontinued operations and reported a profit margin of 8%. Has Lai's profit margin improved, weakened, or remained constant? Explain.

(SO 4) C 21. Explain the concept of earning power. In financial analysis, what is the relationship between this concept and the treatment of irregular items?

22. What are discontinued operations? Why is it important (SO 4) C to report discontinued operations separately from income from continuing operations?

Brief Exercises

BE18–1   Use the following data (in thousands) from the comparative balance sheet of Federer Ltd. as at December 31 to prepare a horizontal analysis:

Prepare horizontal analysis. (SO 1) AP

	2008	2007
Cash	$ 24	$ 45
Accounts receivable	268	257
Inventory	499	481
Prepaid expenses	22	0
Property, plant, and equipment	3,216	3,246
Intangible assets	532	532
Total assets	$4,561	$4,561

BE18–2   Horizontal analysis percentages from Tilden Ltd.'s income statement follow:

Use horizontal analysis to determine change in net income. (SO 1) AP

	2008	2007	2006
Sales	96%	107%	100%
Cost of goods sold	102%	97%	100%
Operating expenses	111%	95%	100%
Income tax expense	76%	132%	100%

Did Tilden's net income increase, decrease, or remain unchanged over the three-year period? Explain.

BE18–3   Use the following data from the comparative balance sheet of Rioux Ltd. as at December 31 to prepare horizontal and vertical analyses:

Prepare horizontal and vertical analyses. (SO 1, 2) AP

	2008	2007
Cash	$ 150,000	$ 175,000
Accounts receivable	600,000	400,000
Inventory	780,000	600,000
Property, plant, and equipment	3,130,000	2,800,000
Total assets	$4,660,000	$3,975,000

BE18–4   Use the following data (in thousands) from the comparative income statement of JTI Inc. for the year ended May 31 to prepare a vertical analysis:

Prepare vertical analysis. (SO 2) AP

	2008	2007
Net sales	$1,914	$2,073
Cost of goods sold	1,612	1,674
Gross profit	302	399
Operating expenses	218	210
Income before income tax	84	189
Income tax expense	30	68
Net income	$ 54	$ 121

BE18–5   Vertical analysis percentages for Waubons Corp.'s sales, cost of goods sold, and operating expenses follow:

Use vertical analysis to determine change in net income. (SO 2) AP

	2008	2007	2006
Sales	100%	100%	100%
Cost of goods sold	59%	62%	64%
Operating expenses	25%	27%	28%
Income tax expense	3%	2%	2%

Did Waubons' net income as a percentage of sales increase, decrease, or remain unchanged over the three-year period? Explain.

Interpret changes in ratios.
(SO 3) C

BE18–6 For each of the following independent situations, indicate whether this change would be viewed as an improvement or deterioration:

(a) A decrease in the receivables turnover
(b) An increase in the days sales in inventory
(c) A decrease in debt to total assets
(d) A decrease in interest coverage

(e) An increase in the gross profit margin
(f) A decrease in asset turnover
(g) An increase in return on equity
(h) An increase in the payout ratio

Evaluate liquidity.
(SO 3) AP

BE18–7 Holysh Inc. reported a current ratio of 1.5:1 in the current fiscal year, which is higher than last year's current ratio of 1.3:1. It also reported a receivables turnover of 8 times, which is less than last year's receivables turnover of 9 times, and an inventory turnover of 6 times, which is less than last year's inventory turnover of 7 times. Is Holysh's liquidity improving or deteriorating? Explain.

Calculate and evaluate receivables ratios.
(SO 3) AN

BE18–8 The following data are taken from **Maple Leaf Foods Inc.'s** financial statements:

> **MAPLE LEAF FOODS INC.**
> **December 31**
> **(in thousands)**
>
> | | 2005 | 2004 | 2003 |
> |---|---|---|---|
> | Accounts receivable | $ 247,014 | $ 292,462 | $ 242,306 |
> | Sales[1] | 6,462,581 | 6,364,983 | 5,041,896 |
>
> [1] Assume that all sales are on account, with credit terms of n/30.

Calculate for each of 2005 and 2004 (a) the receivables turnover, and (b) the collection period. What conclusion about the management of accounts receivable can be drawn from these data?

Calculate and evaluate inventory ratios.
(SO 3) AN

BE18–9 The following data are taken from Shumway Ltd.'s financial statements:

	2008	2007	2006
Sales	$6,420,000	$6,240,000	$5,430,000
Cost of goods sold	4,540,000	4,550,000	3,950,000
Inventory	1,020,000	960,000	840,000

Calculate for each of 2008 and 2007 (a) the inventory turnover, and (b) the days sales in inventory. Based on these ratios, what conclusion can be drawn about the management of the inventory?

Calculate solvency ratios.
(SO 3) AP

BE18–10 **Shoppers Drug Mart Corporation** reported the following selected financial data (in thousands) for the year ended December 31, 2005:

Interest expense	$ 48,649
Income tax expense	186,102
Net income	364,494
Total assets	4,375,383
Total liabilities	1,872,374
Cash provided by operating activities	450,575
Cash used by investing activities	274,182

Calculate the following: (a) debt to total assets, (b) interest coverage, and (c) free cash flow.

BE18–11   Staples, Inc. reported net income of U.S. $834.4 million and net revenue of U.S. $16,078.1 million for the year ended January 28, 2006. Its total assets were U.S. $7,071.1 million at the beginning of the year and U.S. $7,676.1 million at the end of the year. Calculate the following: (a) asset turnover and (b) profit margin.

Calculate profitability ratios.
(SO 3) AP

BE18–12   Write the numbers of the following income statement classifications beside the correct letters to show where each of the items in the second list would be reported:

Classify income statement items.
(SO 4) C

1. Gross profit section
2. Operating expenses section
3. Other revenues section

4. Other expenses section
5. Discontinued operations section
6. Not reported on income statement

(a) ___ A loss on the sale of trading securities
(b) ___ Sales revenue
(c) ___ A change in accounting principle
(d) ___ Salaries expense
(e) ___ Cost of goods sold
(f) ___ Investment revenue
(g) ___ A loss from operations of a discontinued wholesale business
(h) ___ Amortization expense
(i) ___ Accumulated amortization
(j) ___ A gain on the sale of assets of a discontinued wholesale business

BE18–13   Lima Corporation reported the following pre-tax amounts for the current year: income from continuing operations, $500,000; loss from operations of discontinued operations, $154,000; and gain on disposal of assets of discontinued operations, $60,000. Lima is subject to a 25% income tax rate. Calculate (a) the income tax expense on continuing operations, (b) any income tax expense or savings on discontinued operations, and (c) net income.

Calculate income tax on continuing and discontinued operations.
(SO 4) AP

BE18–14   Osborn Corporation discontinued a business segment of its operations in Mexico in 2008. The operating loss from these operations was $300,000 before income tax. The loss on the disposal of these operations was $160,000 before income tax. Osborn's income from continuing operations before income tax was $950,000. The tax rate is 25%. Prepare a partial income statement for Osborn, starting with income from continuing operations before income tax, for the year ended December 31, 2008.

Prepare discontinued operations section.
(SO 4) AP

Exercises

E18–1   Financial information follows for Dressaire Inc. as at December 31:

Prepare horizontal analysis.
(SO 1) AP

	2008	2007	2006
Current assets	$120,000	$ 80,000	$100,000
Noncurrent assets	400,000	350,000	300,000
Current liabilities	90,000	70,000	100,000
Noncurrent liabilities	145,000	95,000	100,000
Shareholders' equity	285,000	265,000	200,000

Instructions

(a) Calculate the percentage change since the base year, using 2006 as the base year.
(b) Calculate the percentage changes between each year.

Prepare vertical analysis.
(SO 2) AP

E18–2 Operating data for Fleetwood Corporation follow:

	2008	2007
Sales	$800,000	$600,000
Cost of goods sold	500,000	390,000
Gross profit	300,000	210,000
Operating expenses	200,000	156,000
Income before income tax	100,000	54,000
Income tax expense	25,000	13,500
Net income	$ 75,000	$ 40,500

Instructions

Prepare a vertical analysis for each year.

Prepare horizontal and vertical analyses of income statement.
(SO 1, 2) AP

E18–3 Here are the comparative income statements of Olympic Corporation:

OLYMPIC CORPORATION
Income Statement
Year Ended December 31

	2008	2007
Net sales	$600,000	$550,000
Cost of goods sold	460,000	400,000
Gross profit	140,000	150,000
Operating expenses	55,000	50,000
Income before income tax	85,000	100,000
Income tax	34,000	40,000
Net income	$ 51,000	$ 60,000

Instructions

(a) Prepare a horizontal analysis.
(b) Prepare a vertical analysis for each year.

Prepare horizontal and vertical analyses of balance sheet and comment.
(SO 1, 2) AP

E18–4 The condensed comparative balance sheet of **Mountain Equipment Co-operative**, an outdoor equipment supplier, is presented here:

MOUNTAIN EQUIPMENT CO-OPERATIVE
Balance Sheet
December 31
(in thousands)

	2005	2004
Assets		
Current assets	$ 69,237	$58,150
Property, plant, and equipment	37,587	39,225
Deferred store opening costs		296
Total assets	$106,824	$97,671
Liabilities and Members' Equity		
Current liabilities	$ 21,271	$18,873
Long-term liabilities	641	4,113
Total liabilities	21,912	22,986
Members' equity	84,912	74,685
Total liabilities and members' equity	$106,824	$97,671

Instructions

(a) Prepare a horizontal analysis.
(b) Prepare a vertical analysis for each year.
(c) Identify any significant changes from 2004 to 2005.

E18–5 The following is a list of the ratios we have calculated in this text:

___ Asset turnover	___ Interest coverage
___ Collection period	___ Inventory turnover
___ Current ratio	___ Payout ratio
___ Days sales in inventory	___ Price-earnings ratio
___ Debt to total assets	___ Profit margin
___ Earnings per share	___ Receivables turnover
___ Free cash flow	___ Return on assets
___ Gross profit margin	___ Return on equity

Instructions

Classify each of the ratios as a liquidity (L), solvency (S), or profitability (P) ratio.

E18–6 Nordstar, Inc. operates hardware stores in several provinces. Selected financial statement data for a recent year are as follows:

NORDSTAR, INC.
Balance Sheet (partial)
December 31
(in millions)

	2005	2004
Cash and cash equivalents	$ 30	$ 91
Accounts receivable	676	586
Inventory	628	586
Prepaid expenses	61	52
Total current assets	$1,395	$1,315
Total current liabilities	$ 710	$ 627

For the year ended December 31, 2005, net credit sales were $3,894 million and the cost of goods sold was $2,600 million.

Instructions

(a) Calculate the liquidity ratios for 2005.
(b) Using the data in the chapter, compare Nordstar's liquidity to the liquidity of (1) Canadian Tire Corporation, Limited, and (2) the industry averages for the retail-department store industry.

E18–7 The following selected ratios are available for Pampered Pets Inc. for the most recent three years:

	2008	2007	2006
Current ratio	2.6:1	1.4:1	2.1:1
Receivables turnover	6.7 times	7.4 times	8.2 times
Inventory turnover	7.5 times	8.7 times	9.9 times

Instructions

(a) Has the company's collection of its receivables improved or weakened over the last three years?
(b) Is the company selling its inventory faster or slower than in past years?
(c) Overall, has the company's liquidity improved or weakened over the last three years? Explain.

E18–8 The following selected ratios are available for Ice-T Inc. for the three most recent years:

	2008	2007	2006
Debt to total assets	50%	45%	40%
Interest coverage	2.0 times	1.5 times	1.0 times

Instructions

(a) Has the debt to assets improved or weakened over the last three years?
(b) Has the interest coverage improved or weakened over the last three years?
(c) Overall, has the company's solvency improved or weakened over the last three years?

Evaluate profitability.
(SO 3) AN

E18–9   **Imperial Oil** and **Petro-Canada** reported the following investor-related information recently:

	Imperial Oil	Petro-Canada
Earnings per share	$2.54	$3.45
Payout ratio	12.0%	10.0%
Price-earnings ratio	13.4 times	12.4 times
Profit margin	9.4%	9.6%

Instructions

(a) Based on the above information, which company is more profitable?
(b) Which company do investors favour?
(c) Would investors purchase shares in these companies mainly for growth or for dividend income?

Calculate ratios.
(SO 3) AP

E18–10   Selected comparative financial data (in thousands, except for share price) of Canada's #1 bookseller, **Indigo Books & Music Inc.**, are presented here for two years ended March 31:

	2006	2005
Revenue	$849,616	$787,527
Interest expense	3,917	5,809
Income tax expense	360	612
Net income	25,337	11,702
Total assets	391,103	393,085
Total liabilities	275,447	304,217
Total shareholders' equity	115,656	88,868
Cash provided by operating activities	67,106	38,453
Cash used by investing activities	17,407	13,758
Market price per share	$14.10	$6.00
Weighted average number of common shares	24,134	24,067

Instructions

Calculate the following ratios for 2006 and indicate whether each one is a measure of liquidity, profitability, or solvency:

(a) Asset turnover
(b) Debt to total assets
(c) Earnings per share
(d) Free cash flow
(e) Interest coverage

(f) Price-earnings ratio
(g) Profit margin
(h) Return on assets
(i) Return on equity

Analyze ratios.
(SO 3) AN

E18–11   The following selected ratios are available for a recent year for **Suncor Energy Inc.** and **Husky Energy Inc.**:

	Suncor	Husky	Industry Average
Liquidity			
Current ratio	1.0:1	0.6:1	1.4:1
Receivables turnover	11.3 times	15.7 times	7.3 times
Solvency			
Debt to total assets	60.1%	52.4%	32.0%
Interest coverage	13.4 times	19.2 times	27.5 times

	Suncor	Husky	Industry Average
Profitability			
Profit margin	12.5%	19.6%	15.6%
Return on assets	9.3%	13.9%	8.8%
Price-earnings ratio	26.9 times	12.5 times	n/a

Instructions

(a) Which company is more liquid? Explain.
(b) Which company is more solvent? Explain.
(c) Which company is more profitable? Explain.
(d) Which company do investors favour? Is this consistent with your findings in (a) to (c)? Explain.

E18–12   Davis Ltd. has income from continuing operations of $270,000 for the year ended December 31, 2008. It also has the following items (before considering income taxes): (1) a net gain of $40,000 from the discontinuance of an identifiable business segment, which includes a $110,000 gain from the operation of the segment and a $70,000 loss on its disposal, and (2) a change in accounting principle that resulted in a $30,000 increase in the prior years' amortization. Assume that the income tax rate on all items is 30%.

Prepare discontinued operations section.
(SO 4) AP

Instructions

(a) Prepare a partial income statement, beginning with "Income from continuing operations."
(b) Indicate the statement presentation of any items not included in (a).

E18–13   Petrie Ltd. reported the following information for the year ended May 31, 2008:

Prepare income statement.
(SO 4) AP

Cost of goods sold	$ 400,000
Gain on disposal of discontinued electronics division	100,000
Interest expense	50,000
Investment revenue	20,000
Loss on sale of available-for-sale securities	10,000
Loss on operations of discontinued electronics division	40,000
Operating expenses	300,000
Sales	1,000,000

Additional information: The company's income tax rate is 25%.

Instructions

Prepare the income statement.

Problems: Set A

Prepare horizontal analysis
and comment.
(SO 1) AP

P18–1A The following condensed financial information (in thousands) for the most recent five-year period is available for **WestJet Airlines Ltd.**:

	2005	2004	2003	2002	2001
Operating revenues	$1,388,716	$1,052,739	$859,596	$679,996	$478,393
Operating expenses	1,287,553	1,029,857	741,289	593,192	418,355
Interest expense	49,188	38,858	20,912	3,960	2,249
Income tax expense	27,974	1,192	36,856	31,064	21,079
Net income (loss)	$ 24,001	$ (17,168)	$ 60,539	$ 51,780	$ 36,710

	2005	2004	2003	2002	2001
Current assets	$ 319,576	$ 195,075	$ 276,857	$143,015	$ 85,730
Total assets	2,213,092	1,877,354	1,476,858	784,205	393,413
Current liabilities	376,897	304,449	238,077	175,064	95,095
Total liabilities	1,542,939	1,287,462	896,046	428,449	171,733
Share capital	486,706	412,446	376,081	211,564	129,268
Retained earnings	201,447	177,446	204,731	144,192	92,412

Instructions

(a) Prepare a horizontal analysis.

(b) What components in WestJet's balance sheet and income statement are mainly responsible for the change in the company's financial position and performance over the five-year period?

(c) How has WestJet mostly been financing its operations?

Prepare vertical analysis,
calculate profitability ratios,
and comment.
(SO 2, 3) AN

P18–2A Comparative income statement data for Manitou Ltd. and Muskoka Ltd., two competitors, follow for the year ended December 31, 2008:

	Manitou	Muskoka
Net sales	$350,000	$1,400,000
Cost of goods sold	200,000	720,000
Gross profit	150,000	680,000
Operating expenses	50,000	272,000
Income from operations	100,000	408,000
Interest expense	3,000	10,000
Income before income taxes	97,000	398,000
Income tax expense	23,000	100,000
Net income	$ 74,000	$ 298,000

Additional information:

	Manitou		Muskoka	
	2008	2007	2008	2007
Total assets	$535,000	$380,000	$1,700,000	$1,550,000
Total shareholders' equity	425,000	360,000	1,250,000	975,000

Instructions

(a) Prepare a vertical analysis of the income statement for each company.

(b) Calculate the gross profit margin, profit margin, return on assets, asset turnover, and return on equity ratios for both companies.

(c) Comment on how profitable each company is.

P18–3A   The comparative financial statements of Rosen Inc. are presented here:

Calculate ratios.
(SO 3) AP

ROSEN INC.
Income Statement
Year Ended December 31

	2008	2007
Net sales	$780,000	$624,000
Cost of goods sold	540,000	405,600
Gross profit	240,000	218,400
Operating expenses	143,880	149,760
Income from operations	96,120	68,640
Interest expense	9,920	7,200
Income before income tax	86,200	61,440
Income tax expense	26,550	18,500
Net income	$ 59,650	$ 42,940

ROSEN INC.
Balance Sheet
December 31

Assets	2008	2007
Current assets		
Cash	$ 23,100	$ 21,600
Available-for-sale securities	24,800	33,000
Accounts receivable	116,200	93,800
Inventory	86,400	64,000
Total current assets	250,500	212,400
Property, plant, and equipment	465,300	459,600
Total assets	$715,800	$672,000
Liabilities and Shareholders' Equity		
Current liabilities		
Accounts payable	$174,850	$132,000
Income tax payable	2,500	2,000
Other payables and accruals	12,800	22,000
Total current liabilities	190,150	156,000
Bonds payable	80,000	120,000
Total liabilities	270,150	276,000
Shareholders' equity		
Common shares (15,000 issued)	150,000	150,000
Retained earnings	303,850	246,000
Accumulated other comprehensive loss	(8,200)	0
Total shareholders' equity	445,650	396,000
Total liabilities and shareholders' equity	$715,800	$672,000

Additional information:

1. All sales were on account.
2. The allowance to adjust available-for-sale securities to market was $8,200 (credit) in 2008 and nil in 2007.
3. The allowance for doubtful accounts was $5,500 in 2008 and $4,500 in 2007.
4. In 2008, $1,800 of dividends were paid to the common shareholders.
5. Cash provided by operating activities was $89,000.
6. Cash used by investing activities was $53,500.

Instructions

Calculate all possible liquidity, solvency, and profitability ratios for 2008.

P18–4A Financial information for Star Track Ltd. is presented here:

STAR TRACK LTD.
Balance Sheet
December 31

	2008	2007
Assets		
Cash	$ 50,000	$ 42,000
Accounts receivable	100,000	87,000
Inventories	340,000	300,000
Prepaid expenses	25,000	31,000
Held-to-maturity securities	180,000	100,000
Land	75,000	75,000
Building and equipment	570,000	600,000
Total assets	$1,340,000	$1,235,000
Liabilities and Shareholders' Equity		
Notes payable	$ 125,000	$ 125,000
Accounts payable	160,750	140,000
Accrued liabilities	52,000	50,000
Bonds payable, due 2011	200,000	200,000
Common shares (100,000 issued)	500,000	500,000
Retained earnings	302,250	220,000
Total liabilities and shareholders' equity	$1,340,000	$1,235,000

STAR TRACK LTD.
Income Statement
Year Ended December 31

	2008	2007
Sales	$1,000,000	$940,000
Cost of goods sold	650,000	635,000
Gross profit	350,000	305,000
Operating expenses	205,000	185,000
Income from operations	145,000	120,000
Interest expense	30,000	30,000
Income before income taxes	115,000	90,000
Income tax expense	28,750	22,500
Net income	$ 86,250	$ 67,500

Additional information:

1. The allowance for doubtful accounts was $5,000 in 2008 and $4,000 in 2007.
2. Accounts receivable at the beginning of 2007 were $80,000, net of an allowance for doubtful accounts of $3,000.
3. Inventories at the beginning of 2007 were $350,000.
4. Total assets at the beginning of 2007 were $1,175,000.
5. Total shareholders' equity at the beginning of 2007 was $656,600.
6. All sales were on account.
7. In each of 2007 and 2008, $4,000 of dividends were paid to the common shareholders.
8. Cash provided by operating activities was $92,000 in 2008 and $65,000 in 2007.
9. Cash used by investing activities was $80,000 in 2008 and $50,000 in 2007.

Instructions

(a) Calculate all possible liquidity, solvency, and profitability ratios for 2008 and 2007.
(b) Discuss the changes in liquidity, profitability, and solvency by referring to the relevant ratios calculated in (a).

P18–5A **The Brick Group Income Fund** and **Leon's Furniture Limited** are two of Canada's retailers of household furniture. Selected financial data (in thousands) of these two close competitors are presented here for a recent year:

Calculate and evaluate ratios for two companies. (SO 3) AN

	The Brick	Leon's
Income Statement		
Net sales	$1,214,405	$547,744
Cost of sales	739,505	323,629
Gross profit	474,900	224,115
Operating expenses	440,203	170,048
Income from operations	34,697	54,067
Other income	1,087	20,658
Interest expense	(5,233)	
Income before income tax	30,551	74,725
Income tax expense (recovery)	(1,453)	25,761
Net income	$ 32,004	$ 48,964
Balance Sheet		
Current assets		
Cash and cash equivalents	$ 29,201	$ 20,592
Accounts receivable	54,192	20,705
Inventories	193,670	72,644
Other current assets	7,310	75,749
Total current assets	284,373	189,690
Property, plant, and equipment	602,241	182,023
Other assets	37,286	9,989
Total assets	$923,900	$381,702
Current liabilities	$278,213	$ 99,579
Long-term liabilities	167,298	21,685
Total liabilities	445,511	121,264
Shareholders' equity[1]	478,389	260,438
Total liabilities and shareholders' equity	$923,900	$381,702
Additional Information		
Average accounts receivable	$ 45,862	$ 19,234
Average inventories	181,266	71,962
Average total assets	892,200	376,316
Average total shareholders' equity	494,890	255,152

[1] The Brick calls its shareholders' equity "unitholders' equity."

Instructions

(a) For each company, calculate the following ratios. Industry averages are given in parentheses after each ratio, where available.

1. Current ratio (1.2:1)
2. Receivables turnover (8.3 times)
3. Inventory turnover (4.9 times)
4. Debt to total assets (40.1%)
5. Interest coverage (2.0 times)
6. Profit margin (1.6%)
7. Asset turnover (0.6 times)
8. Return on assets (0.8%)
9. Return on equity (2.3%)

(b) Compare the liquidity, solvency, and profitability of the two companies to each other and their industry.

P18–6A Selected ratios for two companies operating in the beverage industry follow. Industry ratios, where available, have also been included.

Ratio	Refresh Corp.	Flavour Inc.	Industry
Asset turnover	1.0 times	1.0 times	0.9 times
Current ratio	0.6:1.0	1.1:1.0	0.8:1.0
Debt to total assets	56%	72%	n/a
Earnings per share	$0.98	$1.37	$1.08
Gross profit margin	73.8%	60.0%	57.7%
Interest coverage	15.3 times	7.9 times	5.3 times
Inventory turnover	5.8 times	9.9 times	8.3 times
Price-earnings	50.3 times	24.3 times	32.2 times
Profit margin	12.3%	11.2%	8.1%
Receivables turnover	11.4 times	9.8 times	9.3 times
Return on assets	11.2%	9.3%	7.2%
Return on equity	25.7%	29.8%	26.4%

Instructions

(a) Both companies offer their customers credit terms of net 30 days. Indicate which ratio(s) should be used to assess how well the accounts receivable are managed. Comment on how successful each company appears to be at managing its accounts receivable.

(b) How well does each company appear to be managing its inventory? Indicate the ratio(s) that should be used to assess inventory management.

(c) Which company, Refresh or Flavour, is more solvent? Identify the ratio(s) that should be used to determine this and defend your choice.

(d) To your surprise, you notice that Refresh's gross profit margin is much higher than both Flavour's and the industry average. Identify two possible reasons for this.

(e) What is mostly responsible for Refresh's higher return on assets: its profit margin or its asset turnover? Explain.

(f) What is the market price per share of each company's common shares?

(g) Which company do investors appear to believe has greater prospects for growing its income and dividends? Indicate the ratio(s) that you used to reach this conclusion and explain your reasoning.

P18–7A The following ratios are available for toolmakers **The Black & Decker Corporation** and **Snap-on Incorporated** for a recent year:

	Black & Decker	Snap-on	Industry
Liquidity			
Current ratio	1.5:1	2.0:1	1.8:1
Receivables turnover	5.6 times	4.6 times	5.7 times
Inventory turnover	3.7 times	4.0 times	4.6 times
Solvency			
Debt to total assets	73.8%	52.0%	47.9%
Interest coverage	8.8 times	8.6 times	7.2 times
Profitability			
Gross profit margin	35.6%	45.6%	30.7%
Profit margin	7.8%	4.1%	4.1%
Asset turnover	1.2 times	1.1 times	1.2 times
Return on assets	9.1%	4.6%	4.8%
Return on equity	32.7%	9.5%	18.5%
Price-earnings ratio	14.1 times	24.9 times	18.1 times
Payout ratio	18.8%	60.8%	25.8%

Instructions

(a) Which company is more liquid? Explain.

(b) Which company is more solvent? Explain.

(c) Which company is more profitable? Explain.

(d) Which company do investors favour? Is your answer consistent with your findings in (a) to (c)? Explain.

P18–8A The following ratios and measures are available for Hubei Corporation:

Receivables turnover	10 times
Profit margin	10%
Earnings per share	$2
Debt to total assets	40%
Free cash flow	$25,000

Determine impact of transactions on ratios.

(SO 3) AN

Instructions

(a) Indicate whether each of the above would increase, decrease, or remain unchanged by each of the following independent transactions:

1. Hubei issues common shares.
2. Hubei collects an account receivable.
3. Hubei issues a mortgage note payable.
4. Hubei sells equipment at a loss.
5. Hubei's share price increases from $10 per share to $12 per share.

(b) Would your answers to any of the above change if the profit margin were negative and the earnings per share were a loss per share?

P18–9A Nexen Inc. reported the following selected information for the last four years (in millions, except for per share amounts):

Calculate and evaluate profitability ratios with discontinued operations.

(SO 3, 4) AP

	2005	2004	2003	2002
Net sales	$ 3,932	$2,944	$2,632	$2,142
Average shareholders' equity	3,438	2,471	1,832	1,362
Average total assets	13,486	10,050	7,191	6,048
Income from continuing operations	$ 700	$710	$507	$356
Discontinued operations	452	83	71	53
Net income	$1,152	$793	$578	$409
Earnings per share from continuing operations	$2.69	$2.76	$2.05	$1.45
Earnings per share	4.43	3.08	2.33	1.67

Instructions

(a) Calculate Nexen's profit margin, asset turnover, return on assets, and return on equity ratios before and after discontinued operations for 2005, 2004, and 2003.

(b) Evaluate Nexen's profitability over the last three years before and after discontinued operations.

(c) Which analysis is more relevant to investors? Explain.

P18–10A The ledger of Zurich Corporation at December 31, 2008, contains the following summary data:

Prepare income statement and statement of retained earnings, with irregular items.

(SO 4) AP

Net sales	$1,700,000
Cost of goods sold	1,100,000
Operating expenses	260,000
Other revenues	20,000
Other expenses	8,000
Retained earnings, January 1	940,000
Dividends	25,000

Your analysis reveals the following additional information that is not included in the above data:

1. The Communication Devices division was discontinued during the year. The gain from operations for the division before income taxes was $20,000. The division was sold at a loss of $70,000 before income tax.
2. During the year, Zurich changed its amortization method from double declining-balance to straight-line. The cumulative effect of the change on prior years' net income was an increase of $60,000 before tax. Amortization under the new method is correctly included in the ledger for the current year.
3. The income tax rate is 25%.
4. There were 100,000 common shares.

Instructions

(a) Prepare an income statement, including earnings per share.
(b) Prepare a statement of retained earnings.

Problems: Set B

Prepare horizontal analysis and comment.
(SO 1) AP

P18–1B   The following condensed financial information is available for **Big Rock Brewery Income Trust**. The company, previously a corporation, reorganized as an income trust in 2003.

	2005 (12 months)	2004 (12 months)	2003 (9 months)
BIG ROCK BREWERY INCOME TRUST			
Income Statement			
Year Ended December 31			
Revenues	$40,563,180	$38,789,564	$28,503,840
Cost of sales	15,255,008	13,696,549	10,298,575
Gross profit	25,308,172	25,093,015	18,205,265
Operating expenses	17,561,260	17,397,249	12,757,866
Income before income taxes	7,746,912	7,695,766	5,447,399
Income tax expense	1,127,036	928,858	891,543
Net income	$ 6,619,876	$ 6,766,908	$ 4,555,856

	2005	2004	2003
BIG ROCK BREWERY INCOME TRUST			
Balance Sheet			
December 31			
Assets			
Current assets	$12,770,157	$ 9,947,060	$10,006,747
Noncurrent assets	29,016,020	30,981,408	30,804,429
Total assets	$41,786,177	$40,928,468	$40,811,176
Liabilities and Unitholders' Equity			
Current liabilities	$ 3,895,903	$ 4,014,186	$ 4,958,338
Noncurrent liabilities	8,060,167	7,394,131	9,166,319
Total liabilities	11,956,070	11,408,317	14,124,657
Unitholders' equity	29,830,107	29,520,151	26,686,519
Total liabilities and unitholders' equity	$41,786,177	$40,928,468	$40,811,176

Instructions

(a) Prepare a horizontal analysis.
(b) What components in Big Rock's balance sheet and income statement are mainly responsible for the change in the company's financial position and performance over the three-year period?
(c) Is it meaningful to compare the results for 2003, 2004, and 2005 using a horizontal analysis when 2003 covers only a 9-month period but 2004 and 2005 cover 12-month periods? Explain.

P18–2B Comparative income statement data for Chen Inc. and Chuan Ltd., two competitors, follow for the year ended December 31, 2008:

Prepare vertical analysis, calculate profitability ratios, and comment.
(SO 2, 3) AN

	Chen	Chuan
Net sales	$1,849,035	$539,038
Cost of goods sold	1,080,490	338,006
Gross profit	768,545	201,032
Operating expenses	502,275	79,000
Income from operations	266,270	122,032
Interest expense	6,800	1,252
Income before income tax	259,470	120,780
Income tax expense	103,800	48,300
Net income	$ 155,670	$ 72,480

Additional information:

	Chen		Chuan	
	2008	2007	2008	2007
Total assets	$977,090	$812,410	$297,346	$205,279
Total shareholders' equity	802,265	646,595	222,478	149,998

Instructions

(a) Prepare a vertical analysis of the income statement for each company.
(b) Calculate the gross profit margin, profit margin, asset turnover, return on assets, and return on equity ratios for both companies.
(c) Comment on how profitable each company is.

P18–3B The comparative financial statements of Johnson Cables Ltd. follow:

Calculate ratios.
(SO 3) AP

JOHNSON CABLES LTD.
Income Statement
Year Ended December 31

	2008	2007
Net sales	$1,918,500	$1,750,500
Cost of goods sold	1,005,500	996,000
Gross profit	913,000	754,500
Operating expenses	506,000	479,000
Income from operations	407,000	275,500
Interest expense	28,000	19,000
Income before income tax	379,000	256,500
Income tax expense	113,700	77,000
Net income	$ 265,300	$ 179,500

JOHNSON CABLES LTD.
Balance Sheet
December 31

Assets	2008	2007
Current assets		
Cash	$ 60,100	$ 64,200
Accounts receivable	107,800	102,800
Inventory	143,000	115,500
Total current assets	310,900	282,500
Held-to-maturity securities	54,000	50,000
Property, plant, and equipment	625,300	520,300
Total assets	$990,200	$852,800
Liabilities and Shareholders' Equity		
Current liabilities		
Accounts payable	$165,000	$145,400
Income tax payable	43,500	42,000
Total current liabilities	208,500	187,400
Bonds payable	86,000	200,000
Total liabilities	294,500	387,400
Shareholders' equity		
Common shares (56,000 issued in 2008; 60,000 in 2007)	280,000	300,000
Retained earnings	415,700	165,400
Total shareholders' equity	695,700	465,400
Total liabilities and shareholders' equity	$990,200	$852,800

Additional information:

1. All sales were on account.
2. The allowance for doubtful accounts was $5,400 in 2008 and $5,100 in 2007.
3. On July 1, 2008, 4,000 shares were reacquired and cancelled.
4. In 2008, $15,000 of dividends were paid to the common shareholders.
5. Cash provided by operating activities was $313,900.
6. Cash used by investing activities was $161,000.

Instructions

Calculate all possible liquidity, solvency, and profitability ratios for 2008.

Calculate and evaluate ratios for two years.
(SO 3) AN

P18–4B Financial information for Click and Clack Ltd. follows:

CLICK AND CLACK LTD.
Income Statement
Year Ended December 31

	2008	2007
Sales	$900,000	$840,000
Cost of goods sold	620,000	575,000
Gross profit	280,000	265,000
Operating expenses	164,000	160,000
Income before income tax	116,000	105,000
Interest expense	30,000	20,000
Income before income tax	86,000	85,000
Income tax expense	30,000	30,000
Net income	$ 56,000	$ 55,000

CLICK AND CLACK LTD.
Balance Sheet
December 31

	2008	2007
Assets		
Cash	$ 70,000	$ 65,000
Available-for-sale securities	45,000	40,000
Accounts receivable	94,000	90,000
Inventories	130,000	125,000
Prepaid expenses	25,000	23,000
Land, buildings, and equipment	390,000	305,000
Total assets	$754,000	$648,000
Liabilities and Shareholders' Equity		
Notes payable	$110,000	$100,000
Accounts payable	45,000	42,000
Accrued liabilities	30,000	40,000
Bonds payable, due 2015	200,000	150,000
Common shares, 20,000 issued	200,000	200,000
Retained earnings	164,000	116,000
Accumulated other comprehensive income	5,000	0
Total liabilities and shareholders' equity	$754,000	$648,000

Additional information:

1. The allowance to adjust available-for-sale securities to market value was $5,000 (debit) in 2008 and nil in 2007.
2. The allowance for doubtful accounts was $5,000 in 2008 and $4,000 in 2007.
3. Accounts receivable at the beginning of 2007 were $88,000, net of an allowance for doubtful accounts of $3,000.
4. Inventories at the beginning of 2007 were $115,000.
5. Total assets at the beginning of 2007 were $630,000.
6. Total shareholders' equity at the beginning of 2007 was $269,000.
7. Of the sales amount, 75% was on account.
8. In each of 2007 and 2008, $8,000 of dividends were paid to the common shareholders.
9. Cash provided by operating activities was $68,000 in 2008 and $60,000 in 2007.
10. Cash used by investing activities was $120,000 in 2008 and $50,000 in 2007.

Instructions

(a) Calculate all possible liquidity, solvency, and profitability ratios for 2008 and 2007.
(b) Discuss the changes in liquidity, profitability, and solvency by referring to the relevant ratios calculated in (a).

P18–5B **Cascades Inc.** and **Domtar Inc.** are Canadian paper products companies. Selected financial data (in millions) of these two close competitors are presented here for 2005, before Domtar merged with Weyerhaeuser Company:

Calculate and evaluate ratios for two companies.
(SO 3) AN

	Domtar	Cascades
Income Statement		
Sales	$4,966	$3,460
Cost of sales	4,333	2,890
Gross profit	633	570
Operating expenses	1,096	634
Loss from operations	(463)	(64)
Other expense	(150)	(74)
Loss before income tax	(613)	(138)
Income tax recovery	(225)	(41)
Net loss	$ (388)	$ (97)

	Domtar	Cascades
Balance Sheet		
Current assets	$1,157	$1,125
Noncurrent assets	4,035	1,921
Total assets	$5,192	$3,046
Current liabilities	$ 703	$ 595
Noncurrent liabilities	2,880	1,554
Total liabilities	3,583	2,149
Shareholders' equity	1,609	897
Total liabilities and shareholders' equity	$5,192	$3,046
Additional information:		
Average accounts receivable	$ 260	$ 536
Average inventories	719	548
Average total assets	5,436	3,095
Average total shareholders' equity	1,828	978

Instructions

(a) For each company, calculate the following ratios. Industry averages are given in parentheses after each ratio, where available.

1. Current ratio (1.5:1)
2. Receivables turnover (7.9 times)
3. Collection period (46 days)
4. Inventory turnover (5.7 times)
5. Days sales in inventory (64 days)
6. Debt to total assets (88.0%)
7. Gross profit margin (24.7%)
8. Profit margin (−1.3%)
9. Asset turnover (0.9 times)
10. Return on assets (−1.0%)
11. Return on equity (−19.6%)

(b) Compare the liquidity, solvency, and profitability of the two companies to each other and their industry.

(c) Both Domtar and Cascades experienced losses for their most recent fiscal year, as did the industry. Because of these losses, are the company's profitability ratios still meaningful?

Analyze ratios.
(SO 3) AN

P18–6B Selected ratios for two companies operating in the office supply industry follow. Industry ratios, where available, have also been included.

Ratio	Paperclip	Stapler	Industry Average
Asset turnover	3 times	2 times	3 times
Current ratio	2:1	3:1	2:1
Debt to total assets	50%	33%	50%
Earnings per share	$3.50	$0.40	n/a
Gross profit margin	23%	40%	27%
Interest coverage	4 times	8 times	7 times
Inventory turnover	7 times	3 times	5 times
Payout ratio	8%	22%	10%
Price-earnings ratio	29 times	45 times	38 times
Profit margin	5%	4%	4%
Receivables turnover	11.8 times	9.1 times	10.2 times
Return on equity	25%	13%	16%

Instructions

(a) Paperclip offers its customers credit terms of net 30 days. Indicate the ratio(s) that should be used to assess Paperclip's accounts receivable management. Comment on how well Paperclip appears to be managing its accounts receivable.

(b) How well does Paperclip appear to be managing its inventory? Indicate the ratio(s) that should be used to assess the company's inventory management. How well is Paperclip managing its inventory compared to Stapler and the industry average?

(c) Which company, Paperclip or Stapler, is more solvent? Identify the ratio(s) that should be used to determine this and explain the significance of Paperclip's result. Is Paperclip more or less solvent than the industry?

(d) To your surprise, you notice that Paperclip's gross profit margin is less than both Stapler's and the industry average. Identify two possible reasons for this.

(e) Paperclip's payout ratio is lower than Stapler's and the industry average. Indicate one possible reason for this.

(f) What is the market price per share of each company's common shares?

(g) Which company do investors appear to believe has greater prospects for growing its income and dividends? Indicate the ratio(s) you used to reach this conclusion and explain your reasoning.

P18–7B The following ratios are available for agricultural chemicals competitors **Potash Corpo-ration of Saskatchewan Inc. (PotashCorp)** and **Agrium Inc.** for fiscal 2005:

Analyze ratios.
(SO 3) AN

	PotashCorp	Agrium	Industry
Liquidity			
Current ratio	1.0:1	2.2:1	1.8:1
Receivables turnover	8.6 times	7.9 times	7.5 times
Inventory turnover	5.1 times	4.6 times	4.8 times
Solvency			
Debt to total assets	60.2%	75.6%	57.0%
Interest coverage	10.8 times	10.2 times	10.2 times
Profitability			
Gross profit margin	32.3%	31.8%	28.4%
Profit margin	15.6%	8.6%	7.2%
Asset turnover	0.7 times	1.2 times	1.0 times
Return on assets	10.4%	10.4%	7.6%
Return on equity	24.0%	26.6%	13.5%
Earnings per share	$5.00	$2.14	n/a
Price-earnings ratio	18.6 times	12.0 times	24.4 times
Payout ratio	12.0%	4.9%	26.5%

Instructions

(a) Which company is more liquid? Explain.

(b) Which company is more solvent? Explain.

(c) Which company is more profitable? Explain.

(d) Which company do investors favour? Is your answer consistent with your findings in (a) to (c)?

P18–8B The following ratios are available for Yami Corporation:

Determine impact of transactions on ratios.
(SO 3) AN

Current ratio	1.5:1
Inventory turnover	10 times
Debt to total assets	40%
Asset turnover	2 times
Profit margin	10%

Instructions

(a) Indicate whether each of the above ratios would increase, decrease, or remain unchanged as a result of each of the following independent transactions:
  1. Yami pays an account payable.
  2. Yami collects an account receivable.
  3. Yami purchases a held-to-maturity investment.
  4. Yami sells merchandise for cash at a profit.
  5. Yami buys equipment for cash.

(b) Would your answers to any of the above change if the current ratio were 0.5:1 instead of 1.5:1?

Calculate and evaluate
profitability ratios with
discontinued operations.
(SO 3, 4) AP

P18–9B Alcan Inc. reported the following selected information for the last four years (in U.S. millions, except for per share amounts):

	2005	2004	2003	2002
Sales and operating revenues	$20,320	$24,948	$13,850	$12,483
Average shareholders' equity	10,025	10,342	9,124	8,271
Average total assets	29,990	32,644	24,854	17,656
Income from continuing operations	$155	$243	$262	$421
Discontinued operations	(26)	15	(159)	(21)
Net income	$129	$258	$103	$400
Earnings per share from continuing operations	$0.40	$0.64	$0.79	$1.29
Earnings per share	0.33	0.69	0.30	1.22

Instructions

(a) Calculate Alcan's profit margin, asset turnover, return on assets, and return on equity ratios before and after discontinued operations for 2005, 2004, and 2003.
(b) Evaluate Alcan's profitability over the last three years before and after discontinued operations.
(c) Which analysis is more relevant to investors? Explain.

Prepare income statement
and statement of retained
earnings, with irregular items.
(SO 4) AP

P18–10B The ledger of Hyperchip Corporation at November 30, 2008, contains the following summary data:

Net sales	$1,500,000
Cost of goods sold	800,000
Operating expenses	240,000
Other revenues	40,000
Other expenses	30,000
Retained earnings, December 1, 2007	1,225,000
Dividends	30,000

Your analysis reveals the following additional information that is not included in the above data:

1. The ceramics division was discontinued during the year. The loss from operations for this division before income tax was $150,000. The ceramics division was sold at a loss of $70,000 before income tax.
2. During the year, Hyperchip changed its amortization method from straight-line to declining-balance. The cumulative effect of the change on prior years' net income was a decrease of $30,000 before income tax. Amortization under the new method is correctly included in the ledger for the current year.
3. The income tax rate is 30%.
4. There were 235,000 common shares.

Instructions

(a) Prepare an income statement, including earnings per share.
(b) Prepare a statement of retained earnings.

Continuing Cookie Chronicle

(*Note:* This is a continuation of the Cookie Chronicle from Chapters 1 through 17.)

The balance sheet and income statement of Cookie & Coffee Creations Ltd. for its first year of operations, the year ended October 31, 2009, follows:

COOKIE & COFFEE CREATIONS LTD.
Balance Sheet
October 31, 2009

Assets

Current assets			
Cash		$29,294	
Accounts receivable		3,250	
Inventory		17,897	
Prepaid expenses		6,300	$ 56,741
Property, plant, and equipment			
Furniture and fixtures	$12,500		
Accumulated amortization—furniture and fixtures	(1,250)	$11,250	
Computer equipment	$ 4,200		
Accumulated amortization—computer equipment	(600)	3,600	
Kitchen equipment	$80,000		
Accumulated amortization—kitchen equipment	(8,000)	72,000	86,850
Total assets			$143,591

Liabilities and Shareholders' Equity

Current liabilities			
Accounts payable		$ 5,848	
Income tax payable		18,500	
Dividends payable		625	
Salaries payable		2,250	
Interest payable		188	
Note payable—current portion		3,000	$ 30,411
Long-term liabilities			
Note payable—long-term portion			4,500
Total liabilities			34,911
Shareholders' equity			
Contributed capital			
Preferred shares, 2,500 shares issued	$12,500		
Common shares, 23,180 shares issued	23,180		
Contributed capital—reacquisition of shares	250	$35,930	
Retained earnings		72,750	108,680
Total liabilities and shareholders' equity			$143,591

COOKIE & COFFEE CREATIONS LTD.
Income Statement
Year Ended October 31, 2009

Sales		$462,500
Cost of goods sold		231,250
Gross profit		231,250
Operating expenses		
Amortization expense	$ 9,850	
Salaries and wages expense	92,500	
Other operating expenses	35,987	138,337
Income from operations		92,913
Other expenses		
Interest expense		413
Income before income tax		92,500
Income tax expense		18,500
Net income		$ 74,000

Additional information:

Natalie and Curtis are thinking about borrowing an additional $20,000 to buy more kitchen equipment. The loan would be repaid over a four-year period. The terms of the loan provide for equal semi-annual instalment payments of $2,500 on May 1 and November 1 of each year, plus interest of 5% on the outstanding balance.

Instructions:

(a) Calculate the following ratios, using ending balances where appropriate rather than average balances:

1. Current ratio	6. Gross profit margin
2. Receivables turnover	7. Profit margin
3. Inventory turnover	8. Asset turnover
4. Debt to total assets	9. Return on assets
5. Interest coverage	10. Return on equity

(b) Comment on your findings from part (a).

(c) Based on your analysis in parts (a) and (b), do you think a bank would lend Cookie & Coffee Creations Ltd. $20,000 to buy the additional equipment? Explain your reasoning.

(d) What alternatives could Cookie & Coffee Creations consider instead of bank financing?

BROADENING YOUR PERSPECTIVE

Financial Reporting and Analysis

Financial Reporting Problem

BYP18–1 Refer to the consolidated financial statements and notes of **The Forzani Group Ltd.** in Appendix A.

Instructions

(a) Prepare a horizontal analysis for 2006 and 2005.
(b) Prepare a vertical analysis for 2006 and 2005.
(c) Comment on the significance of any trends you observe from your calculations in (a) and (b).

Interpreting Financial Statements

BYP18–2 Selected financial ratios for the **Canadian National Railway Company (CN)** and the **Canadian Pacific Railway Limited (CP)** are presented here for a recent year:

	CN	CP	Industry
Liquidity			
Current ratio	0.6:1	0.8:1	1.6:1
Receivables turnover	10.2 times	9.2 times	26.6 times
Inventory turnover	52.1 times	n/a	59.5 times
Solvency			
Debt to total assets	35.5%	40.5%	36.7%
Interest coverage	8.8 times	4.8 times	26.4 times
Free cash flow	$1,630 million	$181.5 million	n/a

	CN	CP	Industry
Profitability			
Profit margin	21.5%	12.4%	7.5%
Asset turnover	0.3 times	0.4 times	1.3 times
Return on assets	8.5%	6.4%	7.6%
Return on equity	18.8%	13.0%	13.2%
Price-earnings ratio	14.4 times	13.3 times	18.4 times
Payout ratio	18%	17%	n/a

Instructions

(a) Comment on the relative liquidity of the two companies.
(b) Comment on the relative solvency of the two companies.
(c) Comment on the relative profitability of the two companies.

Critical Thinking

Collaborative Learning Activity

Note to instructor: Additional instructions and material for this group activity can be found on the Instructor Resource Site.

BYP18-3   In this group activity, you will apply your knowledge of financial analysis to two public companies.

Instructions

(a) Your instructor will divide the class into groups and distribute selected financial and ratio information of two large companies. Your group will split into two smaller groups, with each taking the information for one company and answering the following questions:
  1. Is the company able to pay its maturing obligations and meet unexpected needs in cash?
  2. Will the company survive over a long period of time?
  3. How profitable is the company in comparison to other companies in its industry?
  4. Based on the answers to the first three questions, respond to this statement: The company is extremely healthy. Do you strongly agree, agree, disagree, or strongly disagree?
(b) When the smaller groups are finished, each should explain its answers to the other members of the larger group and support its opinion regarding which company is in better financial condition.

Study Aids:
Working in Groups

Communication Activity

BYP18–4   You are a new member of the board of directors and audit committee of Shifty Inc. You are preparing for your first meeting of the audit committee and want to review the limitations of financial statements with management and the auditors.

Instructions

Write a list of questions that you should raise at the audit committee meeting in order to satisfy any concerns you may have about the limitations of financial statements.

Study Aids:
Writing Handbook

BYP18–5   Sabra Surkis, president of Surkis Industries, wants to issue a press release to improve her company's image and share price, which has been gradually falling. As controller, you have been asked to provide a list of financial ratios along with some other operating statistics from Surkis Industries' first quarter operations.

Study Aids:
Ethics in Accounting

Two days after you provide the ratios and data requested, Carol Dunn, the public relations director of Surkis, asks you to review the financial and operating data contained in the press release written by the president and edited by Carol. In the news release, the president highlights the sales increase of 25% over last year's first quarter and the positive change in the current ratio from 1.5:1 last year to 3:1 this year. She also emphasizes that production was up 50% over the prior year's first quarter.

You note that the release contains only positive or improved ratios, and none of the negative or weakened ratios. For instance, there is no mention that the debt to total assets ratio has increased from 35% to 55%. Nor was it mentioned that inventories are up 89%. There was also no indication that the reported income for the quarter would have been a loss if the estimated lives of Surkis' machinery not been increased by 30%.

Instructions

(a) Who are the stakeholders in this situation?
(b) Is there anything unethical in president Surkis' actions?
(c) Should you as controller remain silent? Does Carol have any responsibility?

ANSWERS TO CHAPTER QUESTIONS

Answers to Accounting in Action Insight Questions

Business Insight, p. 930

Q: Are the percentage changes for Laperrière based on horizontal or vertical analysis?
A: The growth percentages reported in the press release are an example of horizontal analysis, which calculates percentage changes across years. Vertical analysis reports percentages within the same year.

Business Insight, p. 932

Q: What could management do to influence a company's current ratio?
A: Management can affect the current ratio by speeding up or withholding payments on accounts payable just before the balance sheet date. Management can change the cash balance by increasing or decreasing long-term assets or long-term debt, or by issuing or repurchasing common shares.

Ethics Insight, p. 936

Q: The Rosens warn analysts to watch for "too-good-to-be-true" situations and accounting games. Can you give an example of what they might be referring to?
A: There are many examples that could be mentioned here. Examples of "too-good-to-be-true" situations could include inexplicable changes in trends and percentages from period to period. If the reason for the changing results does not seem intuitive or even obvious, it could be a sign that questionable accounting is occurring. Examples of accounting games could include overstated revenues, delayed write-downs of goodwill and long-lived assets, or delayed expenditures.

Situations such as these raise questions about the quality of earnings. If analysts cannot rely on the information they are analyzing to be accurate and complete, then the results of the analysis may be misleading.

Answer to Forzani Review It Question 5, p. 937

Forzani did not report any changes in accounting principle or discontinued operations in fiscal 2006.

Answers to Self-Study Questions

1. d   2. c   3. a   4. c   5. b   6. b   7. b   8. b   9. b   10. d

 Remember to go back to the Navigator Box at the beginning of the chapter to check off your completed work.

appendix A
Specimen Financial Statements:

The Forzani Group Ltd.

In this appendix we illustrate current financial reporting with a comprehensive set of corporate financial statements that are prepared in accordance with generally accepted accounting principles. We are grateful for permission to use the actual financial statements of The Forzani Group Ltd.—Canada's largest sporting goods retailer.

Forzani's financial statement package features a balance sheet, combined statement of operations (or income statement as we know it) and retained earnings, cash flow statement, and notes to the financial statements. The financial statements are preceded by two reports: a statement of management's responsibilities for financial reporting and the auditors' report.

We encourage students to use these financial statements in conjunction with relevant material in the textbook. As well, these statements can be used to solve the Review It questions in the Before You Go On section within the chapter and the Financial Reporting Problem in the Broadening Your Perspective section of the end-of-chapter material.

Annual reports, including the financial statements, are reviewed in detail on the companion website to this textbook.

www.wiley.com/canada/weygandt

Annual Report Walkthrough

THE FORZANI GROUP LTD.

MANAGEMENT'S RESPONSIBILITIES FOR FINANCIAL REPORTING

The Annual Report, including the consolidated financial statements, is the responsibility of the management of the Company. The consolidated financial statements were prepared by management in accordance with generally accepted accounting principles. The significant accounting policies used are described in Note 2 to the consolidated financial statements. The integrity of the information presented in the financial statements, including estimates and judgments relating to matters not concluded by year-end, is the responsibility of management. Financial information presented elsewhere in this Annual Report has been prepared by management and is consistent with the information in the consolidated financial statements.

Management is responsible for the development and maintenance of systems of internal accounting and administrative controls. Such systems are designed to provide reasonable assurance that the financial information is accurate, relevant and reliable, and that the Company's assets are appropriately accounted for and adequately safeguarded. The Board of Directors is responsible for ensuring that management fulfills its responsibilities for final approval of the annual consolidated financial statements. The Board appoints an Audit Committee consisting of three directors, none of whom is an officer or employee of the Company or its subsidiaries. The Audit Committee meets at least four times each year to discharge its responsibilities under a written mandate from the Board of Directors. The Audit Committee meets with management and with the independent auditors to satisfy itself that they are properly discharging their responsibilities, reviews the consolidated financial statements and the Auditors' Report, and examines other auditing, accounting and financial reporting matters. The consolidated financial statements have been reviewed by the Audit Committee and approved by the Board of Directors of The Forzani Group Ltd. The consolidated financial statements have been examined by the shareholders' auditors, Ernst & Young, LLP, Chartered Accountants. The Auditors' Report outlines the nature of their examination and their opinion on the consolidated financial statements of the Company. The independent auditors have full and unrestricted access to the Audit Committee, with and without management present.

Bob Sartor
Chief Executive Officer

Richard Burnet, CA
Vice-President & Chief Financial Officer

AUDITORS' REPORT

To the Shareholders of
The Forzani Group Ltd.

We have audited the consolidated balance sheet of The Forzani Group Ltd. as at January 29, 2006 and the consolidated statements of operations and retained earnings and cash flows for the 52 weeks then ended. These financial statements are the responsibility of the Company's management. Our responsibility is to express an opinion on these financial statements based on our audit.

We conducted our audit in accordance with Canadian generally accepted auditing standards. Those standards require that we plan and perform an audit to obtain reasonable assurance whether the financial statements are free of material misstatement. An audit includes examining, on a test basis, evidence supporting the amounts and disclosures in the financial statements. An audit also includes assessing the accounting principles used and significant estimates made by management, as well as evaluating the overall financial statement presentation.

In our opinion, these consolidated financial statements present fairly, in all material respects, the financial position of the Company as at January 29, 2006 and the results of its operations and its cash flows for the 52 weeks then ended in accordance with Canadian generally accepted accounting principles.

The consolidated balance sheet as at January 30, 2005 and the consolidated statements of operations and retained earnings and cash flows for the 52 weeks then ended were audited by other auditors who expressed an opinion without reservation on those statements in their report dated March 21, 2005.

Calgary, Canada
March 23, 2006

Ernst & Young LLP

Ernst & Young LLP
Chartered Accountants

THE FORZANI GROUP LTD.

THE FORZANI GROUP LTD.
Consolidated Balance Sheets
(in thousands)

As at	January 29, 2006	January 30,2005
ASSETS (note 6)		
Current		
Cash	$ 19,266	$ 26,018
Accounts receivable	68,927	58,576
Inventory	278,002	278,631
Prepaid expenses	2,647	3,022
	368,842	366,247
Capital assets (note 3)	193,594	179,702
Goodwill and other intangibles (note 4)	75,805	52,790
Other assets (note 5)	10,080	9,415
Future income tax asset (note 9)	4,885	-
	$ 653,206	$ 608,154
LIABILITIES		
Current		
Accounts payable and accrued liabilities	$ 244,293	$ 238,239
Current portion of long-term debt (note 6)	5,135	1,580
	249,428	239,819
Long-term debt (note 6)	58,805	40,278
Deferred lease inducements	62,883	62,613
Deferred rent liability	3,810	2,213
Future income tax liability (note 9)	-	384
	374,926	345,307
SHAREHOLDERS' EQUITY		
Share capital (note 8)	138,131	137,811
Contributed surplus	4,271	2,915
Retained earnings	135,878	122,121
	278,280	262,847
	$ 653,206	$ 608,154

See accompanying notes to the consolidated financial statements.

Approved on behalf of the Board:

Roman Doroniuk, CA   John M. Forzani

THE FORZANI GROUP LTD.
Consolidated Statements of Operations and Retained Earnings
(in thousands, except share data)

	For the 52 weeks ended January 29, 2006	For the 52 weeks ended January 30, 2005
Revenue		
Retail	$ 856,149	$718,820
Wholesale	273,255	266,234
	1,129,404	985,054
Cost of sales	746,313	651,158
Gross margin	383,091	333,896
Operating and administrative expenses		
Store operating	225,218	190,891
General and administrative	88,720	66,536
	313,938	257,427
Operating earnings before undernoted items	69,153	76,469
Amortization	41,343	35,885
Interest	6,145	4,447
Loss on write-down of investment (note 14)	-	2,208
	47,488	42,540
Earnings before income taxes	21,665	33,929
Provision for income taxes (note 9)		
Current	8,784	10,207
Future	(876)	2,177
	7,908	12,384
Net earnings	13,757	21,545
Retained earnings, opening	122,121	101,528
Adjustment arising from normal course issuer bid (note 8(b))	-	(952)
Retained earnings, closing	$ 135,878	$ 122,121
Earnings per share (note 8(c))	$ 0.42	$ 0.66
Diluted earnings per share (note 8(c))	$ 0.42	$ 0.66

See accompanying notes to the consolidated financial statements.

THE FORZANI GROUP LTD.

THE FORZANI GROUP LTD.
Consolidated Statements of Cash Flows
(in thousands)

	For the 52 weeks ended January 29, 2006	For the 52 weeks ended January 30, 2005
Cash provided by (used in) operating activities		
Net earnings	$ 13,757	$ 21,545
Items not involving cash		
Amortization	41,343	35,885
Amortization of deferred finance charges	637	828
Amortization of deferred lease inducements	(10,661)	(10,459)
Rent expense (note 7)	2,281	4,565
Stock-based compensation (note 8(d))	1,356	27
Write-down of investment and other assets	-	2,213
Future income tax expense	(876)	2,177
	47,837	56,781
Changes in non-cash elements of working capital (note 7)	(1,979)	(6,545)
	45,858	50,236
Cash provided by (used in) financing activities		
Net proceeds from issuance of share capital	320	967
Increase in long-term debt	23,573	3,563
Decrease in revolving credit facility	-	-
Debt assumed on acquisition (note 15(c))	(17,922)	-
Proceeds from deferred lease inducements	9,368	13,402
	15,339	17,932
Changes in non-cash elements of financing activities (note 7)	(2,450)	(4,375)
	12,889	13,557
Cash provided by (used in) investing activities		
Net addition of capital assets	(50,837)	(45,726)
Net addition of other assets	(3,751)	(7,112)
Acquisition of wholly-owned subsidiary (note 15)	(12,428)	(9,589)
	(67,016)	(62,427)
Changes in non-cash elements of investing activities (note 7)	1,517	1,337
	(65,499)	(61,090)
Increase (decrease) in cash	(6,752)	2,703
Net cash position, opening	26,018	23,315
Net cash position, closing	$ 19,266	$ 26,018

See accompanying notes to the consolidated financial statements.

F2006 ANNUAL REPORT

The Forzani Group Ltd.
Notes to Consolidated Financial Statements
(Tabular amounts in thousands)

1.   Nature of Operations

The Forzani Group Ltd. "FGL" or "the Company" is Canada's largest sporting goods retailer. FGL currently operates 260 corporate stores under the banners: Sport Chek, Sport Mart, Coast Mountain Sports and National Sports. The Company is also the franchisor/licensor of 204 stores under the banners: Sports Experts, Intersport, RnR, Econosports, Atmosphere, Tech Shop/Pegasus, Nevada Bob's Golf, and Hockey Experts. FGL operates four websites, dedicated to the Canadian online sporting goods market, www.sportchek.ca, www.sportmart.ca, www.sportsexperts.ca and www.nationalsports.com.

2.   Significant Accounting Policies

The consolidated financial statements have been prepared by management in accordance with Canadian generally accepted accounting principles ("GAAP"). The financial statements have, in management's opinion, been prepared within reasonable limits of materiality and within the framework of the accounting policies summarized below:

(a)   Organization

The consolidated financial statements include the accounts of The Forzani Group Ltd. and its subsidiaries, all of which are wholly owned.

(b)   Inventory

Inventory is valued at the lower of laid-down cost and net realizable value. Laid-down cost is determined using the weighted average cost method and includes invoice cost, duties, freight, and distribution costs. Net realizable value is defined as the expected selling price.

Volume rebates and other supplier discounts are included in income when earned. Volume rebates are accounted for as a reduction of the cost of the related inventory and are "earned" when the inventory is sold. All other rebates and discounts are "earned" when the related expense is incurred.

(c)   Capital assets

Capital assets are recorded at cost and are amortized using the following methods and rates:

Building	- 4% declining-balance basis
Building on leased land	- straight-line basis over the lesser of the length of the lease and estimated useful life of the building, not exceeding 20 years
Furniture, fixtures, equipment and automotive	- straight-line basis over 3-5 years
Leasehold improvements	- straight-line basis over the lesser of the length of the lease and estimated useful life of the improvements, not exceeding 10 years

The carrying value of long-lived assets are reviewed at least annually or whenever events indicate a potential impairment has occurred. An impairment loss is recorded when a long-lived asset's carrying value exceeds the sum of the undiscounted cash flows expected from its use and eventual disposition. The impairment loss is measured as the amount by which the carrying value exceeds its fair value.

(d)   Variable Interest Entities

Variable interest entities ("VIE") are consolidated by the Company if and when the Company is the primary beneficiary of the VIE, as described in CICA Accounting Guideline 15 "Consolidation of Variable Interest Entities".

(e)   Goodwill and other intangibles

Goodwill represents the excess of the purchase price of entities acquired over the fair market value of the identifiable net assets acquired.

Goodwill and other intangible assets with indefinite lives are not amortized, but tested for impairment at year end and, if required, asset values reduced accordingly. The method used to assess impairment is a review of the fair value of the asset based on its earnings and a market earnings multiple.

Non-competition agreement costs are amortized, on a straight-line basis, over the life of the agreements, not exceeding five years.

THE FORZANI GROUP LTD.

(f)   Other assets

Other assets include deferred financing charges, system and interactive development costs, long-term receivables and a long-term investment in a trademark licensing company.

Financing charges represent fees incurred in establishing and renegotiating the Company's credit facilities. These costs are being amortized over the term of the facilities.

System development costs relate to the implementation of computer software. Upon activation, costs are amortized over the estimated useful lives of the systems (3 – 8 years).

Interactive development costs relate to the development of the sportchek.ca interactive web site, designed as a part of the Company's multi-channel retailing and branding strategy. These costs are being amortized over five years following the commencement of the web site's operations in June, 2001.

Long-term receivables are carried at cost less a valuation allowance, if applicable.

Long-term investments are carried at cost and periodically reviewed for impairment based on the market value of the shares.

(g)   Deferred lease inducements and property leases

Deferred lease inducements represent cash and non-cash benefits that the Company has received from landlords pursuant to store lease agreements. These lease inducements are amortized against rent expense over the term of the lease.

The Company capitalizes any rent expense during the fixturing period as a cost of leasehold improvements. Such expense is recognized on a straight-line basis over the life of the lease.

(h)   Revenue recognition

Revenue includes sales to customers through corporate stores operated by the Company and sales to, and service fees from, franchise stores and others. Sales to customers through corporate stores operated by the Company are recognized at the point of sale, net of an estimated allowance for sales returns. Sales of merchandise to franchise stores and others are recognized at the time of shipment. Royalties and administration fees are recognized when earned, in accordance with the terms of the franchise/license agreements.

(i)   Store opening expenses

Operating costs incurred prior to the opening of new stores, other than rent incurred during the fixturing period, are expensed as incurred.

(j)   Fiscal year

The Company's fiscal year follows a retail calendar. The fiscal years for the consolidated financial statements presented are the 52-week periods ended January 29, 2006 and January 30, 2005.

(k)   Foreign currency translation

Foreign currency accounts are translated to Canadian dollars. At the transaction date, each asset, liability, revenue or expense is translated into Canadian dollars using the exchange rate in effect at that date. At the year-end date, monetary assets and liabilities are translated into Canadian dollars using the exchange rate in effect at that date, or by rates fixed by forward exchange contracts, and the resulting foreign exchange gains and losses are included in income in the current period, to the extent that the amount is not hedged.

(l)   Financial instruments

Accounts receivable, accounts payable and accrued liabilities, long-term debt and derivative transactions, constitute financial instruments. In the normal course of business the Company also enters into leases in respect of real estate and certain point-of-sale equipment.

The Company enters into forward foreign currency contracts and options, with financial institutions, as hedges of other financial transactions and not for speculative purposes. The Company's policies do not allow leveraged transactions and are designed to minimize foreign currency risk. The Company's policies require that all hedges be linked with specific liabilities on the balance sheet and be formally assessed, both at inception, and on an ongoing basis, as to their effectiveness in offsetting changes in the fair values of the hedged liabilities.

(m)   Measurement uncertainty

The preparation of the financial statements, in conformity with GAAP, requires management to make estimates and assumptions that affect the reported amounts of assets and liabilities and disclosures of contingent assets and liabilities at the date of the consolidated financial statements and the reported amounts of revenue and expenses during the reporting period. Actual results could differ from these estimates. Estimates are used when accounting for items such as product warranties, inventory provisions, amortization, uncollectible receivables and the liability for the Company's loyalty program.

The Forzani Group Ltd.
Notes to Consolidated Financial Statements
(Tabular amounts in thousands)

(n) Stock-based compensation

The Company accounts for stock-based compensation using the fair value method. The fair value of the options granted are estimated at the date of grant using the Black-Scholes valuation model and recognized as an expense over the option-vesting period.

(o) Income taxes

The Company follows the liability method under which future income tax assets and obligations are determined based on differences between the financial reporting and tax basis of assets and liabilities, measured using tax rates substantively enacted at the balance sheet date.

Changes in tax rates are reflected in the consolidated statement of operations in the period in which they are substantively enacted.

(p) Asset retirement obligations

The Company recognizes asset retirement obligations in the period in which a reasonable estimate of the fair value can be determined. The liability is measured at fair value and is adjusted to its present value in subsequent periods through accretion expense. The associated asset retirement costs are capitalized as part of the carrying value of the related asset and amortized over its useful life.

(q) Comparative figures

Certain 2005 comparative figures have been reclassified to conform with the presentation adopted for the current year ending January 29, 2006.

3.   Capital Assets

| | | 2006 | | | 2005 | |
	Cost	Accumulated Amortization	Net Book Value	Cost	Accumulated Amortization	Net Book Value
Land	$ 3,173	$ -	$ 3,173	$ 3,173	$ -	$ 3,173
Buildings	20,007	3,197	16,810	17,637	2,498	15,139
Building on leased land	4,564	2,330	2,234	3,159	1,898	1,261
Furniture, fixtures, equipment and automotive	176,670	104,254	72,416	145,838	84,042	61,796
Leasehold improvements	205,519	106,595	98,924	187,141	89,177	97,964
Construction in progress	37	-	37	369	-	369
	$ 409,970	$ 216,376	$193,594	$357,317	$177,615	$179,702

4.   Goodwill and Other Intangibles

| | | 2006 | | | 2005 | |
	Cost	Accumulated Amortization	Net Book Value	Cost	Accumulated Amortization	Net Book Value
Goodwill	$ 47,818	$ 1,187	$ 46,631	$ 25,243	$ 1,187	$ 24,056
Trademarks/Tradenames	28,693	626	28,067	25,715	561	25,154
Non-competition agreements	4,000	2,893	1,107	5,680	2,100	3,580
	$ 80,511	$ 4,706	$ 75,805	$ 56,638	$ 3,848	$ 52,790

THE FORZANI GROUP LTD.

The Forzani Group Ltd.
Notes to Consolidated Financial Statements
(Tabular amounts in thousands)

5.   Other Assets

| | | 2006 | | | 2005 | |
	Cost	Accumulated Amortization	Net Book Value	Cost	Accumulated Amortization	Net Book Value
Interactive development	$2,649	$2,649	$ -	$2,649	$2,133	$ 516
Deferred financing charges	1,660	286	1,374	3,598	2,284	1,314
System development	1,569	1,407	162	1,569	1,277	292
Other deferred charges	3,030	853	2,177	1,808	704	1,104
	$8,908	$5,195	$3,713	$9,624	$6,398	$3,226

	2006	2005
Depreciable other assets net book value (see above)	$ 3,713	$ 3,226
Long-term receivables (at interest rates of prime plus 1% and expiring between September 2009 and July 2010)	3,279	2,973
Investment in a trademark licensing company	3,088	3,088
Other	-	128
	$10,080	$ 9,415

6.   Long-term Debt

	2006	2005
G.E. term loan	$ 50,000	$ 25,000
Vendor take-back, unsecured with interest rate of prime plus 1% due August 1, 2006	4,606	4,428
Mortgages, with monthly blended payments of $79,625, including interest at rates from approximately 4.9% to 6.2%, compounded semi-annually, secured by land and buildings, expiring between September 2006 and October 2009 (each with a fifteen year amortization).	9,078	9,658
Amounts due under non-competition agreements, (payment negotiated and retired in 2006)	-	2,680
Asset retirement obligation	97	92
Other	159	-
	63,940	41,858
Less current portion	5,135	1,580
	$ 58,805	$40,278

Principal payments on the above, due in the next five years, are as follows:

2007	$ 3,810
2008	$ 523
2009	$50,519
2010	$ 529
2011	$ 557

Effective June 30, 2005, the Company extended its existing credit agreement to June 30, 2008. The amended and restated agreement with GE Canada Finance Holding Company, National Bank of Canada and Royal Bank of Canada increased the $175 million credit facility to $235 million, comprised of a $185 million revolving loan (2005 - $150 million), and a $50 million term loan (2005 - $25 million) repayable at maturity. Under the terms of the credit agreement, the interest rate payable on both the revolving and term loans is based on the Company's financial performance as determined by its interest coverage ratio. As at January 29, 2006, the average interest rate paid was 4.80% (January 30, 2005 - 4.05%). The facility is collateralized by general security agreements against all existing and future acquired assets of the Company. As at January 29, 2006, the Company is in compliance with all covenants.

The Forzani Group Ltd.
Notes to Consolidated Financial Statements
(Tabular amounts in thousands)

Based on estimated interest rates currently available to the Company for mortgages with similar terms and maturities, the fair value of the mortgages at January 29, 2006 amounted to approximately $8,553,000 (2005 - $9,658,000). Interest costs incurred for the 52-week period ended January 29, 2006 on long-term debt amounted to $2,318,000 (2005 - $1,358,000). The fair value of the other long-term debt components above approximates book value given their short terms to maturity and floating interest rates.

7. Supplementary Cash Flow Information

	2006	2005
Rent expense		
Straight-line rent expense	$ 1,484	$ 2,213
Non-cash free rent	797	2,352
	$ 2,281	$ 4,565
Changes in non-cash elements of working capital		
Accounts receivable	$ (10,038)	$ (22,257)
Inventory	24,544	(13,607)
Prepaid and other expenses	1,140	8,270
Accounts payable and accrued liabilities	(17,761)	20,363
Non-cash free rent	136	686
	$ (1,979)	$ (6,545)
Changes in non-cash elements of financing activities		
Non-cash lease inducements	$ (2,450)	$ (4,375)
Changes in non-cash elements of investing activities		
Non-cash capital asset additions	$ 1,517	$ 1,337
Cash interest paid	$ 6,183	$ 4,685
Cash taxes paid	$ 7,285	$ 20,613

8. Share Capital

(a) Authorized

An unlimited number of Class A shares (no par value)
An unlimited number of Preferred shares, issuable in series

(b) Issued

Class A shares

	Number	Consideration
Balance, February 1, 2004	31,791	$ 128,880
Shares issued upon employees exercising stock options	634	2,477
Shares issued to acquire businesses (note 15)	585	7,012
Shares redeemed pursuant to normal course issuer bid	(135)	(558)
Balance, January 30, 2005	**32,875**	**$ 137,811**
Shares issued upon employees exercising stock options	**47**	**320**
Balance, January 29, 2006	**32,922**	**$ 138,131**

During 2005, 135,100 Class A shares were purchased pursuant to the Company's Normal Course Issuer Bid for a total expenditure of $1,510,000. The price in excess of carrying value was charged to retained earnings.

THE FORZANI GROUP LTD.

The Forzani Group Ltd.
Notes to Consolidated Financial Statements
(Tabular amounts in thousands)

(c) Earnings Per Share

	2006	2005
Basic	$ 0.42	$ 0.66
Diluted	$ 0.42	$ 0.66

The Company uses the treasury stock method to calculate diluted earnings per share. Under the treasury stock method, the numerator remains unchanged from the basic earnings per share calculation, as the assumed exercise of the Company's stock options does not result in an adjustment to earnings. Diluted calculations assume that options under the stock option plan have been exercised at the later of the beginning of the year or date of issuance, and that the funds derived therefrom would have been used to repurchase shares at the average market value of the Company's stock, 2006 - $12.41 (2005 - $12.83). Anti-dilutive options, 2006 - 749,000 (2005 – 1,740,000) are excluded from the effect of dilutive securities. The reconciliation of the denominator in calculating diluted earnings per share is as follows:

	2006	2005
Weighted average number of class A shares outstanding (basic)	32,899	32,572
Effect of dilutive options	248	155
Weighted average number of common shares outstanding (diluted)	33,147	32,727

(d) Stock Option Plan

The Company has granted stock options to directors, officers and employees to purchase Class A shares at prices between $9.39 and $19.19 per share. These options expire on dates between August 22, 2006 and December 2, 2010.

The Company has two stock option plans. The first plan has the following general terms: options vest over a period ranging from 2 to 5 years and the maximum term of the options granted is 5 years. During the year, 250,000 options (2005 – 205,000 options) were issued under this plan. The related stock based compensation was $1,356,000 (2005 - $27,000). The second plan has the following general terms: options vest over a period ranging from 3 to 5 years dependent on the Company achieving certain performance targets, and the maximum term of the options granted is 5 years. During the year, 525,000 options (2005 – 950,000 options) were issued under this plan. There was no related stock based compensation in either 2006 or 2005 as the Company has deemed the targets may not be met. The total number of shares authorized for option grants under both option plans is 3,262,833.

During the 52-weeks ended January 29, 2006, the following options were granted:

Options issued	Weighted average fair value per option	Weighted average risk-free rate	Weighted average expected option life	Weighted average expected volatility	Weighted average expected dividend yield
775,000	$5.52	3.64%	4.08 years	46.55%	0.00%

A summary of the status of the Company's stock option plans as of January 29, 2006 and January 30, 2005, and any changes during the year ending on those dates is presented below:

Stock Options	2006		2005	
	Options	Weighted Average Exercise Price	Options	Weighted Average Exercise Price
Outstanding, beginning of year	2,159	$ 12.13	2,809	$ 13.34
Granted	775	$ 12.15	1,156	$ 10.71
Exercised	47	$ 6.85	634	$ 3.91
Forfeited	100	$ 19.19	1,172	$ 18.12
Outstanding, end of year	2,787	$ 11.88	2,159	$ 12.13
Options exercisable at year end	755		742	

The Forzani Group Ltd.
Notes to Consolidated Financial Statements
(Tabular amounts in thousands)

The following table summarizes information about stock options outstanding at January 29, 2006:

Range of Exercise Prices	Number Outstanding	Options Outstanding Weighted Average Remaining Contractual Life	Weighted Average Exercise Price	Options Exercisable Number of Shares Exercisable	Weighted Average Exercise Price
$9.39 - $10.25	1,160	3.91	$10.24	20	$ 9.39
$11.36 - $12.66	982	2.58	$11.78	497	$11.36
$13.05 - $19.19	645	2.69	$15.01	238	$16.68
	2,787	3.16	$11.88	755	$12.99

9. Income Taxes

The components of the future income tax liability (asset) amounts as at January 29, 2006 and January 30, 2005, are as follows:

	2006	2005
Current assets	$ 3,353	$ 4,342
Capital and other assets	15,842	19,141
Tax benefit of share issuance and financing costs	(166)	(314)
Deferred lease inducements	(22,122)	(22,785)
Non-capital loss carry forward	(1,792)	-
Future income tax liability (asset)	$ (4,885)	$ 384

A reconciliation of income taxes, at the combined statutory federal and provincial tax rate to the actual income tax rate, is as follows:

	2006		2005	
Federal and provincial income taxes	$8,044	37.1%	$11,743	34.6%
Increase (decrease) resulting from:				
Effect of substantively enacted tax rate changes	(68)	(0.3%)	663	2.0%
Other, net	(68)	(0.3%)	(22)	(0.1%)
Provision for income taxes	$7,908	36.5%	$12,384	36.5%

Federal Part I.3 tax and provincial capital tax expense in the amount of $952,000 (2005 - $1,053,000) is included in operating expenses.

The Company has non-capital losses being carried forward of $1,489,000 which expire in 2011 and $2,551,000 which expire in 2015.

10. Commitments

(a)   The Company is committed, at January 29, 2006 to minimum payments under long-term real property and data processing hardware and software equipment leases, for the next five years, as follows:

	Gross
2007	$ 75,904
2008	$ 73,146
2009	$ 70,366
2010	$ 63,921
2011	$ 54,517

In addition, the Company may be obligated to pay percentage rent under certain of the leases.

(b)   As at January 29, 2006, the Company has open letters of credit for purchases of inventory of approximately $4,579,000 (2005 - $3,108,000).

THE FORZANI GROUP LTD.

The Forzani Group Ltd.
Notes to Consolidated Financial Statements
(Tabular amounts in thousands)

11. Employee Benefit Plans

The Company has a defined contribution plan and a deferred profit sharing plan. Deferred profit sharing contributions are paid to a Trustee for the purchase of shares of the Company and are distributed to participating employees on a predetermined basis, upon retirement from the Company. Contributions are subject to board approval and recognized as an expense when incurred. Defined contributions are paid to employee retirement savings plans and are expensed when incurred.

The Company has accrued $100,000 (2005 - $36,000) to the employee deferred profit sharing plan and $807,000 (2005 - $666,000) to the defined contribution plan.

12. Contingencies and Guarantees

In the normal course of business, the Company enters into numerous agreements that may contain features that meet the Accounting Guideline ("AG")14 definition of a guarantee. AG-14 defines a guarantee to be a contract (including an indemnity) that contingently requires the Company to make payments to the guaranteed party based on (i) changes in an underlying interest rate, foreign exchange rate, equity or commodity instrument, index or other variable, that is related to an asset, a liability or an equity security of the counterparty, (ii) failure of another party to perform under an obligating agreement or (iii) failure of a third party to pay its indebtedness when due.

The Company has provided the following guarantees to third parties:

(a) The Company has provided guarantees to certain franchisees' banks pursuant to which it has agreed to buy back inventory from the franchisee in the event that the bank realizes on the related security. The Company has provided securitization guarantees for certain franchisees to repay equity loans in the event of franchisee default. The terms of the guarantees range from less than a year to the lifetime of the particular underlying franchise agreement, with an average guarantee term of 5 years. Should a franchisee default on its bank loan, the Company would be required to purchase between 50% – 100%, with a weighted average of 65%, of the franchisee's inventory up to the value of the franchisee's bank indebtedness. As at January 29, 2006, the Company's maximum exposure is $32,034,000 (2005 - $31,506,000). Should the Company be required to purchase the inventory, it is expected that the full value of the inventory would be recovered. Historically, the Company has not had to repurchase significant inventory from franchisees pursuant to these guarantees. The Company has not recognized the guarantee in its financial statements.

(b) In the ordinary course of business, the Company has agreed to indemnify its lenders under its credit facilities against certain costs or losses resulting from changes in laws and regulations and from any legal action brought against the lenders related to the use, by the Company, of the loan proceeds, or to the lenders having extended credit thereunder. These indemnifications extend for the term of the credit facilities and do not provide any limit on the maximum potential liability. Historically, the Company has not made any indemnification payments under such agreements and no amount has been accrued in the financial statements with respect to these indemnification agreements.

(c) In the ordinary course of business, the Company has provided indemnification commitments to certain counterparties in matters such as real estate leasing transactions, securitization agreements, director and officer indemnification agreements and certain purchases of assets (not inventory in the normal course). These indemnification agreements generally require the Company to compensate the counterparties for costs or losses resulting from any legal action brought against the counterparties related to the actions of the Company or any of the obligors under any of the aforementioned matters or failure of the obligors under any of the aforementioned matters to fulfill contractual obligations thereunder. The terms of these indemnification agreements will vary based on the contract and generally do not provide any limit on the maximum potential liability. Historically, the Company has not made any payments under such indemnifications and no amount has been accrued in the financial statements with respect to these indemnification commitments.

(d) Claims and suits have been brought against the Company in the ordinary course of business. In the opinion of management, all such claims and suits are adequately covered by insurance, or if not so covered, the results are not expected to materially affect the Company's financial position.

13. Financial Instruments

The Company is exposed to credit risk on its accounts receivable from franchisees. The accounts receivable are net of applicable allowance for doubtful accounts, which are established based on the specific credit risks associated with individual franchisees and other relevant information. Concentration of credit risk with respect to receivables is limited, due to the large number of franchisees.

F2006 ANNUAL REPORT

The Forzani Group Ltd.
Notes to Consolidated Financial Statements
(Tabular amounts in thousands)

The Company purchases a portion of its inventory from foreign vendors with payment terms in foreign currencies. To manage the foreign exchange risk associated with these purchases, the Company hedges its exposure to foreign currency by purchasing foreign exchange options and forward contracts to fix exchange rates and protect planned margins. The Company has the following derivative instruments outstanding at January 29, 2006 and January 30, 2005:

| | Notional amounts maturing in | | 2006 | 2005 |
	Less than 1 year	Over 1 year	Total	Total
Foreign exchange contracts ($CAD)				
United States dollar contracts	$2,386	-	$2,386	$2,751
EURO contracts	-	-	-	507
Total	$2,386	-	$2,386	$3,258

The Company has included $359,000 (2005 - $320,000) of exchange losses in general and administrative expenses. No other amounts have been recognized in the consolidated financial statements. As at January 29, 2006, these instruments had $37,000 of unrealized losses (2005 - $38,000 unrealized gains).

The Company is exposed to interest rate risk on its credit facility and the term loan. Interest rate risk reflects the sensitivity of the Company's financial condition to movements in interest rates. For fiscal year 2006, a 1% change in interest rates would change interest expense by $1,449,000 (2005 - $1,108,000).

14. Write-down of Investment

During the year ended January 30, 2005, the Company reviewed the carrying value of its investment in a wholesale distribution company. As a result of this review, the Company determined that a decline in the value of this investment that was other than temporary had occurred and recorded a write-down in the amount of $2,207,952 to bring the carrying value of the investment to $26,000, this investment was subsequently disposed of in 2006.

15. Acquisitions

(a) Effective March 19, 2004, the Company acquired 100% of the outstanding shares of Gen-X Sports Inc. The acquisition was accounted for using the purchase method and accordingly the consolidated financial statements include the results of operations since the date of the acquisition.

The consideration for the transaction was $13,513,000 for all the outstanding Class A and Class B common shares. The purchase consideration consisted of $9,589,000 cash and the remainder in the form of a vendor take-back loan, payable over four years. The loan payments are in the form of 300,000 escrowed Company Class A shares distributed over the four-year period.

The assigned fair values of the underlying assets and liabilities acquired by the Company as at March 19, 2004, are summarized as follows:

Inventory	$ 6,208
Trademarks	3,280
Fixed assets	200
Goodwill	3,924
Total assets acquired	**13,612**
Current liabilities	(99)
Total liabilities acquired	**(99)**
Consideration	**$13,513**

(b) Effective December 17, 2004, the Company acquired a 14.29% interest in a trademark licensing company in exchange for 285,160 Class A shares of the Company, with a fair market value of $3,088,283. This acquisition was accounted for using the cost method and the investment is recorded in Other assets.

(c) Effective January 31, 2005, the Company acquired 100% of the outstanding shares of National Gym Clothing Ltd. The acquisition was accounted for using the purchase method and accordingly the consolidated financial statements include the results of operations since the date of the acquisition.

THE FORZANI GROUP LTD.

The consideration for the transaction was $13,026,000 in cash for all the outstanding common shares.

The assigned fair values of the underlying assets and liabilities acquired by the Company as at January 31, 2005, are summarized as follows:

Cash	$ 598
Accounts receivable	313
Inventory	23,915
Prepaid expenses	765
Trademarks	2,535
Fixed assets	2,261
Goodwill	21,848
Future income tax asset	4,393
Total assets acquired	**56,628**
Secured indebtedness	17,922
Accounts payable	23,815
Long-term debt	189
Deferred rent liability	113
Deferred lease inducements	1,563
Total liabilities acquired	**43,602**
Cash consideration	**$13,026**

16. Segmented Financial Information

The Company operates principally in two business segments: corporately-owned and operated retail stores and as a wholesale business selling to franchisees and others. Identifiable assets, depreciation and amortization and interest expense are not disclosed by segment as they are substantially retail in nature, with the exception of accounts receivable of $58.9 million (2005 - $48.1 million), capital assets of $16.8 million (2005 – $13.4 million) and goodwill/other assets of $8.1 million (2005 - $6.9 million) which are wholesale in nature.

In determining the reportable segments, the Company considered the distinct business models of the Retail and Wholesale operations, the division of responsibilities, and the reporting to the Board of Directors.

	2006	2005
Revenues:		
Retail	$ 856,149	$718,820
Wholesale	273,255	266,234
	1,129,404	985,054
Operating Profit:		
Retail	78,236	68,433
Wholesale	23,547	27,583
	101,783	96,016
Non-segment specific administrative expenses	32,630	19,547
Operating activities before under-noted items	69,153	76,469
Amortization	41,343	35,885
Interest expense	6,145	4,447
Loss on write-down of investments	-	2,208
	47,488	42,540
Earnings before income taxes	21,665	33,929
Income tax expense	7,908	12,384
Net earnings	$ 13,757	$ 21,545

The Forzani Group Ltd.
Notes to Consolidated Financial Statements
(Tabular amounts in thousands)

17. Related Party Transactions

(a) An officer of the Company holds an interest in a franchise store operation. During the year, that franchise operation transacted business, in the normal course and at fair market value, with the Company, purchasing product in the amount of $5,608,000 (2005 - $5,492,000). At the end of the year, accounts receivable from the franchise operation were $888,000 (2005 – $993,000). During the year, that franchise operation opened a prototype store in Kirkland Quebec in which, in the normal course of opening prototype stores, the Company owns equipment and fixtures in the amount of $330,000.

(b) The Company has an interest in a trademark licensing company in which an employee, employed by a subsidiary, holds a partial interest. During the year, the Company, in the normal course of operations on similar terms and conditions to transactions entered into with unrelated parties, paid royalties of $346,000 (2005 – $303,000).

(c) During the year the company purchased real estate valued at $215,000 from an officer of the company in the normal course of operations and on similar terms and conditions to transactions entered into with unrelated parties.

(d) During the year the Company entered into a contract to obtain services and paid $44,000 (2005 - $nil) to a company owned by a director of the Company in the normal course of operations and on similar terms and conditions to transactions entered into with unrelated parties.

18. Variable Interest Entities

At January 29, 2006, the Company had a long-term receivable due from an entity which is considered a variable interest entity (VIE) under CICA Accounting Guideline 15. The entity operates several franchise stores. The long-term receivable has been outstanding since July 2003 and the Company has received guarantees for the full amount of the receivable from the shareholders of the entity. The Company has concluded that it is not the primary beneficiary of the VIE and that it is not required to consolidate this VIE in its consolidated financial statements. The Company has no exposure to loss related to the long-term receivable.

19. Subsequent Event

Effective January 31, 2006 the Company has acquired 100% of the outstanding common shares of Fitness Source Inc. for $6.5 million.

Photo Credits

Logos are registered trademarks of the respective companies and are reprinted with permission.

Chapter 1

Opener: Courtesy The Forzani Group Ltd. Page 5: Courtesy 1-800-GOT-JUNK? Page 8: PhotoDisc, Inc.

Chapter 2

Opener: Courtesy Prestige Dance Academy. Page 57: CP(Jonathan Hayward) Page 63: Courtesy Goodyear Tire and Rubber Company. Page 71: PhotoDisc/Getty Images.

Chapter 3

Opener: Courtesy Seneca College of Applied Arts and Technology. Page 106: PhotoDisc/Getty Images. Page 119: Corbis Digital Stock. Page 123: PhotoDisc/Getty Images.

Chapter 4

Opener: Courtesy Moulé. Page 169: PhotoDisc, Inc. Page 174: CP(Adrian Wyld).

Chapter 5

Opener: Courtesy College of the North Atlantic. Page 232: Courtesy Liquidation World. Page 234: PhotoDisc, Inc.

Chapter 6

Opener: Courtesy Petro-Canada. Page 286: Courtesy Liaison Can./U.S. Page 301: PhotoDisc, Inc. Page 303: PhotoDisc, Inc.

Chapter 7

Opener: Barrett & MacKay Photography. Page 345: PhotoDisc/Getty Images. Page 350: PhotoDisc, Inc. Page 366: PhotoDisc, Inc.

Chapter 8

Opener: Courtesy Whitehill Technologies, Inc. Page 411: PhotoDisc/Getty Images. Page 424: Corbis Digital Stock. Page 429: Courtesy Sears Canada Inc.

Chapter 9

Opener: Courtesy Dawson College. Page 485: CP/AP(Douglas C. Pizac)

Chapter 10

Opener: Courtesy West Edmonton Mall. Page 529: Courtesy Canadian Tire Corporation, Limited. Page 531: CP(Marcos Townsend).

Chapter 11

Opener: Courtesy Voisey's Bay Nickel Company Limited. Page 573: Courtesy Air Canada. Page 584: PhotoDisc, Inc.

Chapter 12

Opener: Courtesy Heagy Bailey Altrogge Matchett LLP. Page 615: Pam Francis/Getty Images Entertainment. Page 619: PhotoDisc, Inc. Page 640: PhotoDisc/Getty Images

Chapter 13

Opener: Courtesy The TDL Group Corp. Page 676: PhotoDisc, Inc.

Chapter 14

Opener: CP(Adrian Wyld). Page 713: CP(Paul Chiasson). Page 718: CP/AP(Paul Sakuma). Page 729: Courtesy Sears Canada Inc.

Chapter 15

Opener: Courtesy Concordia University. Page 776: Courtesy Virgin Mobile.

Chapter 16

Opener: Courtesy Western Forest Products Inc. Page 811: Artville/Getty Images. Page 831: Courtesy Imperial Oil Limited.

Chapter 17

Opener: Courtesy TD Bank Financial Group. Page 879: PhotoDisc, Inc. Page 891: CP/AP(Elaine Thompson)

Chapter 18

Opener: Courtesy the Canadian Institute of Chartered Accountants. Page 936: IT Stock

Company Index

Subject Index